D1251917

Dictionary of Literary Biography

Documentary Series

1 *Sherwood Anderson, Willa Cather, John Dos Passos, Theodore Dreiser, F. Scott Fitzgerald, Ernest Hemingway, Sinclair Lewis*, edited by Margaret A. Van Antwerp (1982)

2 *James Gould Cozzens, James T. Farrell, William Faulkner, John O'Hara, John Steinbeck, Thomas Wolfe, Richard Wright*, edited by Margaret A. Van Antwerp (1982)

3 *Saul Bellow, Jack Kerouac, Norman Mailer, Vladimir Nabokov, John Updike, Kurt Vonnegut*, edited by Mary Bruccoli (1983)

4 *Tennessee Williams*, edited by Margaret A. Van Antwerp and Sally Johns (1984)

5 *American Transcendentalists*, edited by Joel Myerson (1988)

6 *Hardboiled Mystery Writers: Raymond Chandler, Dashiell Hammett, Ross Macdonald*, edited by Matthew J. Bruccoli and Richard Layman (1989)

7 *Modern American Poets: James Dickey, Robert Frost, Marianne Moore*, edited by Karen L. Rood (1989)

8 *The Black Aesthetic Movement*, edited by Jeffrey Louis Decker (1991)

9 *American Writers of the Vietnam War: W. D. Ehrhart, Larry Heinemann, Tim O'Brien, Walter McDonald, John M. Del Vecchio*, edited by Ronald Baughman (1991)

10 *The Bloomsbury Group*, edited by Edward L. Bishop (1992)

11 *American Proletarian Culture: The Twenties and The Thirties*, edited by Jon Christian Suggs (1993)

12 *Southern Women Writers: Flannery O'Connor, Katherine Anne Porter, Eudora Welty*, edited by Mary Ann Wimsatt and Karen L. Rood (1994)

13 *The House of Scribner, 1846-1904*, edited by John Delaney (1996)

14 *Four Women Writers for Children, 1868-1918*, edited by Caroline C. Hunt (1996)

15 *American Expatriate Writers: Paris in the Twenties*, edited by Matthew J. Bruccoli and Robert W. Trogdon (1997)

16 *The House of Scribner, 1905-1930*, edited by John Delaney (1997)

17 *The House of Scribner, 1931-1984*, edited by John Delaney (1998)

18 *British Poets of The Great War: Sassoon, Graves, Owen*, edited by Patrick Quinn (1999)

19 *James Dickey*, edited by Judith S. Baughman (1999)

See also DLB 210, 216, 219, 222, 224, 229

Yearbooks

1980 edited by Karen L. Rood, Jean W. Ross, and Richard Ziegfeld (1981)

1981 edited by Karen L. Rood, Jean W. Ross, and Richard Ziegfeld (1982)

1982 edited by Richard Ziegfeld; associate editors: Jean W. Ross and Lynne C. Zeigler (1983)

1983 edited by Mary Bruccoli and Jean W. Ross; associate editor Richard Ziegfeld (1984)

1984 edited by Jean W. Ross (1985)

1985 edited by Jean W. Ross (1986)

1986 edited by J. M. Brook (1987)

1987 edited by J. M. Brook (1988)

1988 edited by J. M. Brook (1989)

1989 edited by J. M. Brook (1990)

1990 edited by James W. Hipp (1991)

1991 edited by James W. Hipp (1992)

1992 edited by James W. Hipp (1993)

1993 edited by James W. Hipp, contributing editor George Garrett (1994)

1994 edited by James W. Hipp, contributing editor George Garrett (1995)

1995 edited by James W. Hipp, contributing editor George Garrett (1996)

1996 edited by Samuel W. Bruce and L. Kay Webster, contributing editor George Garrett (1997)

1997 edited by Matthew J. Bruccoli and George Garrett, with the assistance of L. Kay Webster (1998)

1998 edited by Matthew J. Bruccoli, contributing editor George Garrett, with the assistance of D. W. Thomas (1999)

1999 edited by Matthew J. Bruccoli, contributing editor George Garrett, with the assistance of D. W. Thomas (2000)

Concise Series

Concise Dictionary of American Literary Biography, 7 volumes (1988-1999): *The New Consciousness, 1941-1968; Colonization to the American Renaissance, 1640-1865; Realism, Naturalism, and Local Color, 1865-1917; The Twenties, 1917-1929; The Age of Maturity, 1929-1941; Broadening Views, 1968-1988; Supplement: Modern Writers, 1900-1998.*

Concise Dictionary of British Literary Biography, 8 volumes (1991-1992): *Writers of the Middle Ages and Renaissance Before 1660; Writers of the Restoration and Eighteenth Century, 1660-1789; Writers of the Romantic Period, 1789-1832; Victorian Writers, 1832-1890; Late-Victorian and Edwardian Writers, 1890-1914; Modern Writers, 1914-1945; Writers After World War II, 1945-1960; Contemporary Writers, 1960 to Present.*

Concise Dictionary of World Literary Biography, 20 volumes projected (1999-): *Ancient Greek and Roman Writers; German Writers; African, Carribbean, and Latin American Writers; South Slavic and Eastern European Writers.*

British Rhetoricians
and Logicians,
1500–1660
First Series

P
301.3
.G7
B75
2000

Dictionary of Literary Biography® • Volume Two Hundred Thirty-Six

British Rhetoricians and Logicians, 1500–1660
First Series

Edited by
Edward A. Malone
Missouri Western State College

ST. JOSEPH'S UNIVERSITY

3 9353 00329 3840

A Bruccoli Clark Layman Book
The Gale Group
Detroit • San Francisco • London • Boston • Woodbridge, Conn.

Advisory Board for
DICTIONARY OF LITERARY BIOGRAPHY

John Baker
William Cagle
Patrick O'Connor
George Garrett
Trudier Harris
Alvin Kernan
Kenny J. Williams

Matthew J. Bruccoli and Richard Layman, Editorial Directors
C. E. Frazer Clark Jr., Managing Editor
Karen L. Rood, Senior Editor

Printed in the United States of America

The paper used in this publication meets the minimum requirements
of American National Standard for Information Sciences–Permanence
Paper for Printed Library Materials, ANSI Z39.48-1984. ∞™

This publication is a creative work fully protected by all applicable copyright laws,
as well as by misappropriation, trade secret, unfair competition, and other applicable laws. The authors and editors of this work have added value to the underlying
factual material herein through one or more of the following: unique and original
selection, coordination, expression, arrangement, and classification of the information.

All rights to this publication will be vigorously defended.

Copyright © 2001 by The Gale Group
27500 Drake Road
Farmington Hills, MI 48331

All rights reserved including the right of reproduction in
whole or in part in any form.

Library of Congress Cataloging-in-Publication Data

British rhetoricians and logicians, 1500–1660. First series / edited by Edward A. Malone.
    p. cm.–(Dictionary of literary biography: v. 236)
"A Bruccoli Clark Layman book."
Includes bibliographical references and index.
ISBN 0-7876-4653-9 (alk. paper)
1. Rhetoric–Great Britain–Bio-bibliography. 2. Logic–Great Britain–Bio-bibliography. I. Malone,
Edward A. II. Series.

Z7004.R5 B75 2000
[P301.3.G7]
808'.0092'241–dc21   00-048423
[B]   CIP

10 9 8 7 6 5 4 3 2 1

Hayatımın ışıkları
Havva, Ayşen, ve Adem 'e.

Contents

Plan of the Series

. . . Almost the most prodigious asset of a country, and perhaps its most precious possession, is its native literary product—when that product is fine and noble and enduring.

Mark Twain*

The advisory board, the editors, and the publisher of the *Dictionary of Literary Biography* are joined in endorsing Mark Twain's declaration. The literature of a nation provides an inexhaustible resource of permanent worth. Our purpose is to make literature and its creators better understood and more accessible to students and the reading public, while satisfying the needs of teachers and researchers.

To meet these requirements, *literary biography* has been construed in terms of the author's achievement. The most important thing about a writer is his writing. Accordingly, the entries in *DLB* are career biographies, tracing the development of the author's canon and the evolution of his reputation.

The purpose of *DLB* is not only to provide reliable information in a usable format but also to place the figures in the larger perspective of literary history and to offer appraisals of their accomplishments by qualified scholars.

The publication plan for *DLB* resulted from two years of preparation. The project was proposed to Bruccoli Clark by Frederick G. Ruffner, president of the Gale Research Company, in November 1975. After specimen entries were prepared and typeset, an advisory board was formed to refine the entry format and develop the series rationale. In meetings held during 1976, the publisher, series editors, and advisory board approved the scheme for a comprehensive biographical dictionary of persons who contributed to literature. Editorial work on the first volume began in January 1977, and it was published in 1978. In order to make *DLB* more than a dictionary and to compile volumes that individually have claim to status as literary history, it was decided to organize volumes by topic, period, or

*From an unpublished section of Mark Twain's autobiography, copyright by the Mark Twain Company

genre. Each of these freestanding volumes provides a biographical-bibliographical guide and overview for a particular area of literature. We are convinced that this organization—as opposed to a single alphabet method—constitutes a valuable innovation in the presentation of reference material. The volume plan necessarily requires many decisions for the placement and treatment of authors. Certain figures will be included in separate volumes, but with different entries emphasizing the aspect of his career appropriate to each volume. Ernest Hemingway, for example, is represented in *American Writers in Paris, 1920–1939* by an entry focusing on his expatriate apprenticeship; he is also in *American Novelists, 1910–1945* with an entry surveying his entire career, as well as in *American Short-Story Writers, 1910–1945, Second Series* with an entry concentrating on his short fiction. Each volume includes a cumulative index of the subject authors and articles.

Since 1981 the series has been further augmented by the *DLB Yearbooks,* which update published entries, add new entries to keep the *DLB* current with contemporary activity, and provide articles on literary history. There have also been nineteen *DLB Documentary Series* volumes which provide illustrations, facsimiles, and biographical and critical source materials for figures works, or groups judged to have particular interest for students. In 1999 the *Documentary Series* was incorporated into the *DLB* volume numbering system beginning with *DLB 210, Ernest Hemingway.*

We define literature as the *intellectual commerce of a nation:* not merely as belles lettres but as that ample and complex process by which ideas are generated, shaped, and transmitted. *DLB* entries are not limited to "creative writers" but extend to other figures who in their time and in their way influenced the mind of a people. Thus the series encompasses historians, journalists, publishers, book collectors, and screenwriters. By this means readers of *DLB* may be aided to perceive literature not as cult scripture in the keeping of intellectual high priests but firmly positioned at the center of a nation's life.

DLB includes the major writers appropriate to each volume and those standing in the ranks behind them. Scholarly and critical counsel has been sought in deciding which minor figures to include and how full their entries should be. Wherever possible, useful references are made to figures who do not warrant separate entries.

Each *DLB* volume has an expert volume editor responsible for planning the volume, selecting the figures for inclusion, and assigning the entries. Volume editors are also responsible for preparing, where appropriate, appendices surveying the major periodicals and literary and intellectual movements for their volumes, as well as lists of further readings. Work on the series as a whole is coordinated at the Bruccoli Clark Layman editorial center in Columbia, South Carolina, where the editorial staff is responsible for accuracy and utility of the published volumes.

One feature that distinguishes *DLB* is the illustration policy—its concern with the iconography of literature. Just as an author is influenced by his surroundings, so is the reader's understanding of the author enhanced by a knowledge of his environment. Therefore *DLB* volumes include not only drawings, paintings, and photographs of authors, often depicting them at various stages in their careers, but also illustrations of their families and places where they lived. Title pages are regularly reproduced in facsimile along with dust jackets for modern authors. The dust jackets are a special feature of *DLB* because they often document better than anything else the way in which an author's work was perceived in its own time. Specimens of the writers' manuscripts and letters are included when feasible.

Samuel Johnson rightly decreed that "The chief glory of every people arises from its authors." The purpose of the *Dictionary of Literary Biography* is to compile literary history in the surest way available to us—by accurate and comprehensive treatment of the lives and work of those who contributed to it.

The *DLB* Advisory Board

Introduction

For students of British literature the study of Renaissance rhetoric and logic begins with Wilbur S. Howell's *Logic and Rhetoric in England, 1500–1700* (1956). Although often criticized for exaggerating the impact of Ramism on English intellectual life, for focusing on obscure texts, and for misunderstanding the history of logic (E. J. Ashworth, for example, says that "no attention should be paid" to his "bizarre" account of scholasticism), Howell's book practically stands alone as an introduction to many of the rhetorical and logical texts of this period in England. It focuses on the connection between the complementary disciplines of logic and rhetoric: in both cases, Howell suggests a pattern of development that involves first an accepted tradition, then a reform, then a counterreform, and finally a new tradition. In logic or dialectic (the two terms were often used synonymously during the Renaissance), the accepted tradition at the beginning of the sixteenth century was scholastic or Aristotelian logic, which was based on Aristotle's works as filtered through ancient and medieval commentators. Howell treats both Thomas Wilson's *The Rule of Reason* (1551) and Ralph Lever's *The Arte of Reason* (1573) as scholastic logic manuals. A virulent challenge to the scholastic tradition came from French educational reformer Pierre de La Ramée (known as Petrus Ramus), who simplified and reorganized the university arts curriculum, including especially rhetoric and dialectic. Abraham Fraunce's *The Lawiers Logike* (1588) and William Chappell's *Methodus concionandi* (Method of Preaching, 1648) are among the examples that Howell provides of Ramist dialectical works. The Ramist reform was followed by a counterreform that combined parts of the scholastic and Ramist traditions. Howell refers to these logicians as Systematics and discusses Robert Sanderson's *Logicæ artis compendium* (Compendium of the Art of Logic, 1618) and John Prideaux's *Heptades Logicae* (The Seven Divisions of Logic, 1639) as examples. Finally, a new tradition emerged from a reaction against both the Ramists and the Systematics. Howell associates this new tradition with the *Port-Royal Logic* (1685), the English version of an influential French logic manual.

Similarly, in rhetoric, the pattern begins with traditional rhetoric, which follows Cicero and Quintilian in acknowledging five parts, or operations, of rhetoric: invention, arrangement, style, memory, and delivery. Howell identifies three subgroups of this tradition: Ciceronian, treating all or most of the five parts, as Wilson's *The Arte of Rhetorique* (1553); stylistic, emphasizing the third part, as Richard Sherry's *A Treatise of Schemes & Tropes* (1550); and formulary, emphasizing imitation and exercise rather than precept, as Richard Rainolde's *The Foundacion of Rhetorike* (1563). This tradition was challenged starting in the 1570s by Ramist rhetoric, which restricted rhetoric to style and delivery. Abraham Fraunce's *The Arcadian Rhetorike* (1588) and John Barton's *The Art of Rhetorick* (1634) are English adaptations of the *Rhetorica* (Rhetoric, 1548) of Ramus's collaborator, Omer Talon (known as Audemarus Talaeus). To the counterreformers, who reacted against Ramist rhetoric, Howell gives the name Neo-Ciceronians. Like their "mixed" counterparts in logic, they attempted to reconstruct traditional rhetoric, usually on a Ramist foundation. Again, Howell identifies three subgroups: works that treat all or most of the five parts, such as Thomas Vicars's Χειραγωγία: *Manuductio Ad Artem Rhetoricam* (Manuduction: A Handbook to the Rhetorical Art, 1621); works that emphasize style, such as Prideaux's *Sacred Eloquence* (1659); and works that emphasize imitation and formula, such as Thomas Blount's *The Academie of Eloquence* (1654). Finally, in *The Tvvoo Bookes of Francis Bacon. Of the proficience and aduancement of Learning, diuine and humane* (1605), better known as *The Advancement of Learning,* Howell sees the seeds of a new tradition reacting against (and to some extent appropriating) Ciceronian and Ramist rhetorics. As one would expect, Howell's model and terminology, though somewhat dated, are invoked repeatedly throughout the entries in this volume.

Rhetoric and dialectic have been associated since antiquity, even before Aristotle defined rhetoric as the counterpart of dialectic. The *septem artes liberales,* or seven liberal arts, originating in late antiquity, promoted the association between the two arts by grouping them with grammar at the beginning of a student's course of study. As is well known, the medieval arts curriculum consisted of a trivium (grammar, logic, rhetoric), a quadrivium (arithmetic, astronomy, geometry, music), and three advanced subjects (natural philosophy, moral philosophy, metaphysics). The trivium focused on language arts; the quadrivium, on mathematics and science; and the advanced subjects, on philosophy. The subjects of the trivium were fundamental to the attainment of higher learning and thus played a central role in the educational process. Throughout much of the Middle Ages, grammar and rhetoric occupied an inferior position to logic; over time, however, they improved their standing in the academy considerably. In English universities, the curricular paradigm of the seven liberal arts proved remarkably adaptable to Renaissance humanism. The trivium became stronger as logic became less technical and subtle and more practically associated with communication. Whereas an undergraduate at Cambridge University before 1558 was required to study mathematics during his first year, dialectic during his second, and philosophy during his third and fourth, an undergraduate after that date was expected to study rhetoric during his first year, logic during his next two, and philosophy during his fourth. The official statutes in this case seem to indicate what was happening in practice: students were studying more rhetoric, and they were studying rhetoric in closer relation to dialectic.

The time-worn tradition of representing the liberal sciences, or arts, as sisters continued to promote the association among the language arts throughout the Renaissance. A representative poem from the sixteenth century prefaces Ulpian Fulwell's *The First Part of the Eight[h] Liberall Science* (1576), a series of humorous dialogues about the art of flattery. The opening stanzas, spoken by the first three of the "Sisters seauen," illustrate the special connection between rhetoric and logic:

Grammer.

If learning may delight thy youthfull brest
If tender years to skilfull lore be bent
Approch to me, voutchsafe to be my guest:
My entertainement shall thy mynd content.
My key in hand shall ope the gate of skill,
My booke on brest shall teache thy tong and quill.

Logike.

From Grammers schoole approch to me with speed,
Where thou maist learne the rule to reasone right,
I geue the fruit though Grammer sow the seede:
In me thou maist deserne the darke from light.
My fastened fist much matter doth import,
Coucht in few wordes fit for the learned sort.

Rethorike.

When Grammers grace, and Logicks learned lore,

Hath deckt thy mynde, and mended nature well,
My golden study shall yelde thee suche store,
Of flowing wordes and phrases that excell.
Lo here with open hande I do display,
The flowing flood of eloquence alway.

This poem, like the one in Thomas Wilson's *The Rule of Reason* (1551), to which it perhaps alludes, implies a pedagogical as well as a compositional sequence. After mastering grammar, the student progresses to the study of logic. A visit to the "golden study" of rhetoric is then necessary for the attainment of eloquence.

Fulwell's poem also invokes the conventional image of rhetoric as an open hand, or palm, and logic as a closed hand, or fist, suggesting that rhetoric and logic consist of the same substance but take different forms. The comparison, which originated with Zeno the Stoic in ancient times and was repeated by Cicero, Quintilian, and others, was used throughout the British Renaissance, from Wilson to William Thorne to Prideaux, to illustrate the difference between rhetoric and logic, or dialectic. Some of the most important figures of the period analyzed, explained, and eventually accepted or rejected it. Sir Thomas More, for example, exploited it argumentatively in a 1515 letter to Maarten van Dorp, which has been translated by Daniel Kinney:

If you grant this [that Erasmus is a skillful rhetorician], then I fail to see how you can deny him any dialectical skill whatsoever. After all, not the least of philosophers had reason to think dialectic and rhetoric as closely akin as a fist and a palm, since dialectic infers more concisely what rhetoric sets out more elaborately, and where dialectic strikes home with its daggerlike point rhetoric throws down and overwhelms the opponent with its very weight.

More implies some proficiency in the other art. Ramus, in his *Scholae in Liberales Artes* (Lectures in the Liberal Arts, 1569), argues that logic should be the palm in Zeno's comparison because it is the more encompassing art. In *The Advancement of Learning,* Francis Bacon accepts the basic comparison, but he expands it considerably: "It appeareth also that Logic differeth from Rhetoric, not only as the fist from the palm, the one close the other at large; but much more in this, that Logic handleth reason exact and in truth, and Rhetoric handleth it as it is planted in popular opinions and manners."

As critic Peter Mack has noted, Continental humanists also employed a nautical metaphor to illustrate the difference between rhetoric and logic. In *Repastinatio dialecticæ et philosophiæ* (The Replowing of Dialectic and Philosophy, 1439), Italian humanist Lorenzo Valla uses a nautical metaphor to suggest that rhetoric is more difficult to master than logic, as seen in Mack's translation of Valla's Latin:

For it rejoices in sailing on the open sea and among the waves and in flying with full and sounding sails, nor does it give way to the waves, but rules them. I am speaking of the highest and most perfect eloquence. Dialectic, on the other hand, is the friend of security, the fellow of the shores, looking at the lands rather than the seas, it rows near the shore and the rocks.

In *De rhetorica libri tres* (Three Books on Rhetoric, 1519), a work that had a more immediate impact on British writers, the German theologian and rhetorician Philipp Melanchthon seems to superimpose Zeno's analogy over Valla's metaphor; for him, rhetoric and dialectic become sailboats, with the sail either open or closed, respectively, again in Mack's translation: "The latter travels within the confines of the matter proposed with its sails reefed, the former spreads itself more freely." Although Valla implies a greater difference between rhetoric and logic and betrays his preference for rhetoric, both writers emphasize that the two arts use the same medium of "travel." Melanchthon, following the emphasis of Roelef Huysman, or rather Rodolphus Agricola, insisted that the two subjects had to be taught together. He writes in the 1542 edition of *Elementorum rhetorices libri duo* (Two Books of the Elements of Rhetoric) that "Ita admixta dialectica rhetoricae, non potest ab eas prorsus divelli. . . ." (Because dialectic is so intimately related to the rhetoric, it is not possible for them to be separated completely. . . .)

As writers of the period say over and over, rhetoric and logic must go together in practice, for they are essential to successful oratory and critical reading. In one of his letters to Roger Ascham, Johann Sturm writes that "without the resource of eloquence, the profession of the dialectician is unintelligible and base. This same eloquence without the art of disputation is puffed up and swollen, wanders aimlessly, and accomplishes nothing by method or reason and nothing skillfully." In his *Ciceronianvs* (The Ciceronian, 1577) Gabriel Harvey emphasizes the need for combining the two arts to achieve "wise eloquence" in both speaking and writing and something similar in textual analysis. The marginalia in his copy of Quintilian's *De Institute Oratoria* (On an Oratorical Education) further indicate that he viewed both logic and rhetoric as the complementary tools of the perfect orator. Richard Holdsworth, in his *Directions for a Student in the Universitie,* not published until 1961, proclaims that "Logick without Oratory is drye & unpleasing and Oratory without Logick is but empty babling." To John Selden, in his section on preaching in *Table-Talk* (1689), "Rhetoric without logic is like a tree with leaves and blossoms, but no root."

This volume is the first in the *Dictionary of Literary Biography* series to focus on Renaissance British writers who produced texts (1500–1660) concerned with rheto-

ric or logic. Most studies of the history of rhetoric and logic have omitted women because they did not produce texts on discourse of interest to men; only since the 1980s have they become the focus of serious scholarship in this area. Thus, a future volume of the *DLB* will include an entry on Margaret Cavendish as a rhetorical theorist. Welsh, Irish, and Scottish writers have often been neglected or omitted from these studies. This volume includes an entry on Henri Perri, who wrote about rhetoric in Welsh, and a future volume will include other Welsh, Scottish, and Irish rhetoricians and logicians, such as William Salesbury and John Mair. Ranging from the obscure to the luminous, the twenty-six writers whose biographies are included here wrote mainly in vernacular languages, though sometimes in Latin, about rhetoric or logic. Writers such as Wilson, Fraunce, Dudley Fenner, Bacon, and Prideaux made contributions to both fields. Viewed in roughly chronological order, their works tell part of the story of the related development of rhetoric and logic in early modern Britain.

The first rhetoric textbook in English was written by a Welshman, Leonard Cox, whose biography has been moved to the second series. Although other writers, such as Stephen Hawes, had discussed rhetoric in English earlier, they did so in the context of larger works. In his *Passetyme of Pleasure* (1509), for example, Hawes discusses logic and rhetoric as part of his poet-protagonist's training in the seven liberal arts. Cox's *The Arte or Crafte of Rhetorike* (1530?), however, is an extended treatment of rhetorical invention, based on Melanchthon's *Institutiones rhetoricæ* (Institutes of Rhetoric, 1521). Cox identifies four rather than five parts of rhetoric: invention (involving the discovering of matter), judgment (involving discernment or selection of matter), disposition (involving the arrangement of matter), and elocution (involving the expression of matter in speech). The second part, judgment, more properly belongs to dialectic and is usually regarded as the counterpart of arrangement in rhetoric. Almost all of *The Arte or Crafte of Rhetorike,* however, is concerned with invention. The discussion is organized by four kinds of themes or orations: logical (also called "disputacion"), demonstrative, deliberative, and judicial. Under each type Cox identifies its parts and the relevant "places" that one can go to for content. It is apparent that Cox shared Melanchthon's conviction in the close relationship between rhetoric and dialectic.

Writing in the following decade, Richard Taverner was one of the earliest and most prolific English translators of the Dutchman Desiderius Erasmus, and his significance lies mainly in his dissemination of Erasmian texts. Joan Marie Lechner in *Renaissance Concepts of the Commonplaces* (1962) sandwiches Taverner between

Wilson and Ascham as "other Elizabethan rhetoricians who provided directions and 'copy' (copia)" for instruction. Although not a rhetorician in the same sense as Wilson, Taverner did produce several books, such as *The garden of wysdom* (1539), that were probably used by students in grammar schools for rhetorical imitation. Perhaps better than any other writer discussed in this volume, his works illustrate the commonplace tradition in rhetoric. His corpus consists mainly of collections of material for imitation and memorization. He offers *A Catechisme or institution of the Christen Religion* (1539), for example, as "an agrume[n]t and mater for sklender shepherdes whervpon to instructe theyr cure," and his *Epistles and Gospelles* (1540) was intended as a homiletic resource for "Prestes and Curates." He also translated Erasmus Sarcerius's *Loci aliquot communes et theologici* (1538?) as *Com[m]onplaces of Scripture* (1538).

Ascham, lecturer at Cambridge University and humanist of international reputation, was a lifelong advocate of rhetorical imitation. He was one of the most sought after tutors in his day. As Princess Elizabeth's private tutor, he implemented his pedagogical strategy of "double translation" in which the student first translates a passage or text into English and then back into Latin. The syllabus for the future queen included Cicero, Isocrates, Demosthenes, and other classical authors, as well as Melanchthon's *Loci communes rerum theologicarum* (Commonplaces of Theological Matters, 1521), a book of both religious and rhetorical significance. Although he did not write a manual or textbook on rhetoric, his works reveal his devotion to the subject, whether he is writing about archery in *Toxophilus. The schole of shootinge conteyned in two bookes* (1545) or education in *The Scholemaster* (1570). Ascham's correspondence with Sturm includes many references to rhetoric and dialectic, including discussions of Ramus's views on both subjects. In a 1551 letter Sturm praises Ascham's abilities, showing appropriate humility, as translated from Latin by Lewis W. Spitz and Barbara Sher Tinsley: "Both of us wish to be dialecticians and rhetoricians. You are indeed, but I struggle and strive to be." Both men were conscious of the fact that they were fashioning and maintaining international reputations, and they were particularly interested in being regarded as rhetoricians and dialecticians.

Sometime between 1544 and 1552, a young reader in humanities and rhetoric at Corpus Christi College, Oxford, delivered an ironical oration against rhetoric, in which he pretends to renounce the study of eloquence and encourages his students to do the same. The reader, John Jewel, later Bishop Jewel, was parodying the most adamant detractors of rhetoric, no doubt a growing lot in his day. Many of the objections have a sobering ring of truth to them. For example, Jewel

laments the neglect of soul, mind, and heart at the preferment of the tongue, and he alludes to the countless hours that young people waste in pursuit of eloquence, perhaps memorizing tropes and schemes. Jewel's speech seems to simultaneously denounce those who would deny the efficacy of rhetoric and those who would reduce rhetoric to mere style without substance. Nurtured by the practices of zealous schoolteachers, stylistic rhetoric had grown gradually into an imposing ogre that must have chased schoolboys even in their sleep. Petrus Mosellanus's *Tabulæ de schematibus et tropis* (Tables of Schemes and Tropes, 1516), a work covering almost 100 figures of speech, was used in British schools from the 1520s onward, and Melanchthon's books on rhetoric were well known. Johann Susenbrotus's *Epitome troporum ac schematum* (Epitome of Tropes and Schemes, 1535?), covering more than 130 figures, had probably made its English debut as a Continental import in the early 1540s. It was printed in England at least a dozen times between 1562 and 1635.

Published in 1550, Sherry's *A treatise of Schemes & Tropes,* the next major work of rhetoric in England, belongs to the "stylistic" tradition, but Sherry takes a definite stand against the droll practices of "common scholemasters," insisting they go beyond mere mimicry and memorization. Although he repeatedly asserts the primacy of style over the other parts of rhetoric, and devotes the bulk of his treatise to a catalogue of tropes and schemes, he nevertheless defends the virtue of plain speaking and denounces extraneous ornamentation: "the proper vse of speach is to vtter the meaning of our mynd with as playne wordes as maye be," but it "so chaunceth som tyme either of necessitie, or to set out the matter more plai[n]ly we be compelled to speake otherwyse" and then "we muste nedes runne to the helpe of schemes & fygures." He offers his book as a better-organized collection of tropes and schemes, accusing previous writers of obscuring the line between grammar and rhetoric. The 1555 revision of his work represents a major reorganization of essentially the same material. The new title, *A Treatise of the Figures of Grammer and Rhetorike,* shifts the emphasis from tropes and schemes to the relationship between grammar and rhetoric. Sherry attempts to further clarify the nature of the figures by carefully dividing them between grammar and rhetoric, with "tropes" positioned transitionally between the two. His new arrangement underscores his continued frustration with the overlapping areas of these two "trivial" arts.

Between the first and second editions of Sherry's book, Wilson, Cambridge graduate and later secretary of state under Queen Elizabeth, published both the first textbook on logic in English and the first full-course Ciceronian rhetoric in English. *The rule of*

Reason, conteinyng the Arte of Logique (1551) is an example of a traditional logic manual in that it discusses first judgment ("the maner of makyng an argumente"), then invention ("the maner of findying of an Argumente"), and finally sophistry ("the capcious and deceiptfull Argumentes"). In his treatment of judgment, Wilson covers the predicables, the categories, method, and the syllogism. His discussion of invention, which shows signs of Agricola's influence, focuses on twenty-three places ("couertes or boroughes, wherin if any one searches diligently, he maie finde game at pleasure"). The discussion proper is prefaced by a sixteen-line poem about the seven liberal arts, offering a context for understanding logic. A section titled "The difference betwene Logique and Rhetorique" invokes Zeno's familiar hand analogy. Wilson's book went through three revised editions in rapid succession, followed by a gap of several years, while Wilson was in exile on the Continent. Upon his return to England his book was printed three more times. Its only vernacular competition during the 1570s was *The Arte of Reason, rightly termed, Witcraft, teaching a perfect way to Argue and Dispute* (1573) by Ralph Lever, Wilson's longtime nemesis. Lever's book was printed only once, apparently unable to compete with Wilson's popular textbook.

After publishing his logic, Wilson went to work on a companion volume. *The Arte of Rhetorique* (1553) is an example of a Ciceronian rhetoric in that it identifies and discusses five parts of rhetoric–invention, disposition, elocution, memory, and delivery. Under invention, which constitutes the bulk of his discussion, Wilson includes the types of oration (demonstrative, deliberative, judicial), the parts of an oration (entrance, narration, proposition, division, confirmation, confutation, conclusion), and various strategies for amplification, including emotional appeals. Disposition, or arrangement, receives only cursory attention, as do memory and delivery (voice and gesture). Elocution, however, is discussed at some length, under the headings of "Plainnesse," "Aptnesse," "Composition," and "Exornation" (tropes and schemes). Wilson gives unusual descriptive labels, such as "Stomach Grief" and "Outcrying," to the various figures of speech. Influenced by Cicero, Quintilian, and Melanchthon, as well as the anonymous *Rhetorica ad Herennium* (Rhetoric to Herennius, circa 85 B.C.), Wilson's *Arte of Rhetorique* was very popular during the Elizabethan period. Even a Ramist "rhetorician" such as Harvey owned a copy and praised it in his marginalia. After Wilson's return from exile, *The Arte of Rhetorique* was printed seven more times, with two posthumous editions in 1584 and 1585. For students of literature Wilson's name has become almost synonymous with the study of sixteenth-century English rhetoric and logic.

Published in 1563, Rainolde's *A booke called the Foundacion of Rhetoric,* the next book on rhetoric in English, cites Wilson as an authority: "one, who floweth in all excellencie of arte." Rainolde is credited with introducing the *progymnasmata* (preliminary exercises) to English (though not England). The *progymnasmata* are composition exercises, arranged in a progressive sequence, in which a student reworks a famous story, engages in an extended comparison, composes a speech from an historical or fictional point of view, and so on. The most famous compilation of these exercises, which included both instructions and examples, was Aphthonius of Antioch's *Progymnasmata* (fourth century A.D.), a text consisting of fourteen exercises in Greek. The work was translated many times into Latin and used widely during the Middle Ages. A Latin translation of the *Progymnasmata* was printed in England as early as 1520, but apparently it went into only one edition. A more popular Renaissance version was edited by Reinhard Lorich from translations done by Agricola and Joannes Cataneo and was used in Britain as early as the 1540s, but it was not printed in England until 1572. Thus, Rainolde's English adaptation, printed only once, precedes Lorich's Latin one in a British edition by almost a decade.

Henry Peacham the Elder's *The Garden of Eloquence Conteyning the Figures of Grammer and Rhetorick* (1577), the second important stylistic rhetoric in English, shows no signs of Ramus's influence, though Ramism was being championed in England during this period, particularly at Cambridge. Influenced by Sherry's *A treatise of Schemes & Tropes* and Susenbrotus's *Epitome troporum ac schematum,* Peacham's book provides definitions and examples of almost two hundred figures of speech. The typical entry in the 1577 edition begins with a definition (for instance, "Lyptote, when more is understoode then is sayd"), followed by several examples, each explained carefully. Peacham uses biblical passages, as well as classical authors, to illustrate most of his terms. For the second edition in 1593, he expanded the entries considerably and made substantive changes in the definitions and examples: "Leptotes is when the speaker by a negatio[n] equipollent doth seeme to extenuate the which he expresseth." His examples of litotes are different, his explanations longer. He added a note on the use of this figure: "This form of speech tendeth most usually to praise or dispraise, and that in a modest forme and manner." He also added a caution: "It is meete to foresee some good cause and fit occasion to use this forme of speaking, lest a man should either praise himselfe with out desart, or dispraise another without cause, the one is token of arrogance, the other of malice, be the forme of speech neuer so modest." Examples from Peacham's treatise found their way into several subsequent manuals, including Perri's *Eglvryn Phraethineb* (The Elucidator of Eloquence, 1595) and John Smith's *The Mysterie of Rhetorique Vnuail'd* (1657), two works owing some debt to English Ramism.

Although British intellectuals were apparently reading and discussing Ramus's works at least as early as 1550, when Ascham and Sturm discussed Ramus in their correspondence, Ramist dialectic probably made its official debut in England in the lectures of Lawrence Chaderton, reader in logic at Cambridge University. Chaderton was the first in a long line of Ramus's advocates at Christ's Church College, Cambridge, and his pupils included Harvey and Fraunce, on whom he exerted some influence. In "The Sheapheardes Logike," an early version of *The Lawiers Logike* (1588), Fraunce refers several times to the authority of "master Chaterton": "so I here name him for the reverence I owe to his lyfe and learninge."

In Scotland Ramus's works were also being discussed. Andrew Melville, who had met Ramus in France, became his disciple and implemented some of his curricular reforms at the University of Glasgow. In 1574 Roland MacIlmaine, a graduate of St. Andrews University in Scotland, produced a Latin edition and the first English translation of Ramus's *Dialectica*, or more accurately the *Dialectica A. Talaei praelectionibus illustrata* (Dialectic Illustrated with Explanations by O. Talon, 1569). These two books, printed in London, were the first of many editions and translations of Ramus's logic in Britain.

Gabriel Harvey, well known for his correspondence with the poet Edmund Spenser, was one of the earliest and most important advocates and disseminators of Ramist rhetoric in England. As praelector in rhetoric at Cambridge University, he lectured on rhetoric while Chaderton was still lecturing on logic. In his *Ciceronianvs,* a Latin oration delivered in 1575 and printed two years later, Harvey revels in his conversion from false to true Ciceronianism: "You perceive, kind listener, how I escaped from the turbulent waves of my folly and at length was borne into the tranquil harbor of eloquent wisdom or at any rate of wise eloquence." He advises his audience, Cambridge students and faculty, to imitate not merely Cicero's style, but also his substance, and he encourages them to read other writers as well. His devotion to Ramus is evident not only in the title of his lecture, which alludes to a similar work by Ramus, but also in his reference to Ramus and recommendation of Talaeus's *Rhetorica*.

Based on two lectures delivered in early 1575 at Cambridge, Harvey's *Rhetor* (1577) instructs its audience in the nature, art, and practice of eloquence. Roughly half of the first lecture deals with nature, or the innate ability to speak eloquently. The second half focuses on art, or the artificial ways of attaining eloquence. Concerned mainly with circumscribing the boundaries of rhetoric, Harvey personifies Eloquence as an unhappy sister, who rebukes Tully (Cicero) for forcing her to wear her sisters' clothing. The sister most offended, of course, is Dialectic. The second lecture is spoken almost entirely by Practice personified.

Gabriel's brother, Richard Harvey, wrote a Latin poem in praise of Ramist logic: *Ephemeron, sive Pæan, in gratiam perpurgatæ reformatæ[que] Dialecticæ* (Ephemeron, or Paean, in Appreciation of the Purification and Reformation of Dialectic, 1583). Robert Batt, an undergraduate at Oxford, criticizes the "Paean Harveij de restituta logica," Harvey's hymn on a restored logic, in a 1583 letter to his cousin. Batt's letter is printed in G. C. Moore Smith's introduction to *Gabriel Harvey's Marginalia* (1913). It was a misreading of the manuscript letter that may have prompted Charles Schmitt, and later James McConica, to attribute *"De restitutione logica* (1583)" to Gabriel Harvey. As far as is known, Gabriel Harvey did not write a work solely on Ramist dialectic. (There will be an entry on Harvey in the second series.)

Despite the publication of his lectures, Harvey failed to win the coveted position of public orator of Cambridge in 1581. While Harvey was retooling for a career in law, Fenner, Puritan preacher and controversialist, produced the first English adaptation of Talaeus's rhetoric and the second English adaptation of Ramus's logic, printed as companion pieces in *The Artes of Logike and Rethorike* (1584). Both adaptations represent severe abridgments of the original material. In the first half on logic Fenner follows Ramus exactly in dividing dialectic into two parts: invention ("the spring of reason") and judgment. Invention is further divided into first reasons and subsequent ones, while judgment or arrangement is divided into those of single or multiple sentences. In the second treatise Fenner follows Ramus and Talaeus in restricting rhetoric to *elocutio* (style), which includes tropes and figures, and *pronuntiatio* (delivery), which includes voice and gesture. In Fenner's book, as in his source, memory is removed entirely from the province of rhetoric. As is well known, Ramist method is characterized by division into progressively more specific units, a practice illustrated by Fenner's (and Ramus's) serial bifurcation of his subjects. This arrangement is often represented visually as a tree diagram, one of the most distinctive features of Ramist works. Fenner's book, however, does not contain elaborate diagrams, but rather uses simple braces to mark individual dichotomies. To his text on rhetoric, Fenner appends a discussion of sophistry, somewhat blurring the Ramist distinction between rhetoric and logic.

Fraunce's involvement with Ramism began while he was a student at Cambridge. Influenced by Chaderton's lectures and encouraged by his friend Sidney's interest in Ramus, Fraunce produced a series of Ramist documents that survive in manuscript: "Tractatus de usu dialectices" (Treatise on the Use of Dialectic), "Of the Nature and Use of Logike," "A Bryef and General Comparison of Ramus His Logike w[i]th That of Aristotle," and "The Shepheardes Logike" (the last three bound together). The most interesting of these is the "Bryef and General Comparison," which takes the form of a debate between "too Cambridge sophisters," "an obstinate Aristotelian," and "a methodical Ramyst." Though both sides are satirized with equal skill, Fraunce seems to give the upper hand to the Ramist, who is allowed to respond point by point to the Aristotelian's argument. Fraunce, the "playne interpreter," refers the dispute to Sidney, asking him to judge the merits of the arguments. These early documents, composed probably between 1581 and 1583, were later reworked and printed in 1588 as *The Lawiers Logike,* a manual for lawyers that includes quotations from poetry and legal writing, as well as a famous dialectical analysis of Virgil's second Eclogue. Fraunce's *The Arcadian Rhetorike,* a companion work, was printed in the same year. This adaptation of Talaeus's rhetoric, the second in English, includes copious illustrations from English as well as Latin and Greek poetry. As the title suggests, the work is concerned with promoting Sidney as well as rhetoric. Fraunce's *The Arcadian Rhetorike* was the last English adaptation of Talaeus's rhetoric until John Barton's *The Arte of Rhetorick* in 1634.

Two years before Fraunce's books on rhetoric and logic were printed, Angel Day produced the first epistolary rhetoric in English with any claim to originality: *The English Secretorie* (1586). He claims to have started the project in 1579 or 1580 but says he was forced to set it aside. Six years later, prompted by friends to complete the project, he decided to start from scratch. There were precedents in England for Day's vernacular manual. William Fullwood's *The Enimie of Idlenesse* (1568), the first letter-writing manual in English, had already introduced the British middle class to the art of letter writing. More or less a straight translation of its French source, *The Enimie of Idlenesse* was extremely popular with readers, going through ten editions by 1621, one more edition than Day's manual. Abraham Fleming's *A Panoplie of Epistles* (1576), the second epistolary rhetoric in English, was a compilation of material translated from various Latin sources and was published in only one edition. Day's manual is by far the best early example of a letter-writing manual in English. As Day explains, it provides "a platforme or Methode, for the inditing and framing of all manner of Epistles and Letters." The book consists of general instructions for all letters and examples of letters organized by type. Unlike Fullwood and Fleming, Day uses his own letters as illustrations, and each letter is accompanied by marginal annotations identifying its parts and the figures of speech being used. In a prefatory epistle Day promises to add a second book to his manual that will "explane to the Learners view and for his readier vse" the figures, schemes, and tropes that were identified in the annotations. He indeed kept his promise in a second edition of 1592.

Perri's *Eglvryn Phraethineb* is a book on stylistic rhetoric for poets; published in 1595, it is also the first printed treatise on rhetoric in Welsh. The Renaissance Welsh interest in rhetoric was sparked by the efforts of Salesbury, Siôn Davydd Rhys, and other Welsh humanists to elevate the quality and prestige of vernacular poetry. Toward this end Salesbury adapted Mosellanus's *Tabulæ de schematibus et tropis* for Welsh poets, coining some Welsh terms for the Latin ones. His "Llyfr Rhetoreg" (Book of Rhetoric, 1552) was never printed, though it apparently circulated widely in manuscript, if the large number of extant copies is any indication. Much of Salesbury's treatise was later incorporated into Perri's book, and an abridgment of Perri's book was published twice under Salesbury's name in the nineteenth century. Perri's *Eglvryn Phraethineb* belongs to the stylistic tradition in rhetoric, dividing rhetoric into *elocutio* and *pronuntiatio* and emphasizing tropes and figures. Welsh scholar Ceri Lewis notes that Perri borrowed material from the 1593 edition of Peacham's *The Garden of Eloquence*. Still, the work is obviously marked by the influence of English Ramism, prompting another Welsh scholar, M. Wynn Thomas, to describe Perri as "a disciple of Ramus."

Perri was not the last Welshman during the Renaissance to try his hand at a rhetorical manual. The Welsh poet Tomos Prys wrote a rhetorical manual, never printed and no longer extant, and Siôn ap Hywel ab Owain is said to have made at least a partial Welsh translation of the *Rhetorica ad Herennium*. Two Renaissance Welsh humanists, Robert Vaughan and Thomas Wiliems, made transcripts of *Yr Areithiau Pros,* a collection of rhetorical exercises and orations, which served as rhetorical aids for Welsh writers. Throughout this period, brief discussions of rhetoric were included in Welsh grammar books.

Before the close of the century, Charles Butler, a former music teacher at Magdalen School, Oxford, produced a popular Latin edition of Talaeus's rhetoric. His *Rameæ Rhetoricæ Libri dvo* (Two Books of Ramist Rhetoric, 1597), later expanded as *Rhetoricæ*

Libri dvo (1598), follows the *Rhetorica* of Talaeus closely, treating style in the first book and delivery in the second. Butler's discussion of delivery, however, is much longer than Talaeus's. Butler wrote books about bees, grammar, and music in English, but about rhetoric in Latin, perhaps to fill a need for such homespun material in the Latin-based curriculum of the grammar schools. Although not well received initially, as Butler tells the reader in the preface to his *The Feminine Monarchie or A Treatise Concerning Bees* (1609), the textbook eventually found a market in the grammar schools and even among university students. Some version of Butler's textbook was being used by Cambridge students when John Milton was a student there (1624–1632). There are entries for "Butlers Rhetoric" in the account books of Joseph Mead, a Cambridge tutor, who may have been selling copies to his students.

Butler later wrote a companion volume, *Oratoriæ Libri Dvo* (Two Books of Oratory, 1629), in which he acknowledges the five parts of traditional rhetoric. This book was attached to some editions of *Rhetoricæ Libri Dvo*, perhaps to compete with Thomas Farnaby's more traditional *Index Rhetoricvs* (Rhetorical Index, 1625). The *Oratoriæ Libri Dvo* discusses such topics as the parts of an oration, the types of speeches, and pathetic appeals in book 1, and invention, arrangement, and memory in book 2, barely mentioning style and delivery, since they had been covered in the earlier work. He ends in a manner similar to that of Farnaby's *Index Rhetoricvs* (Rhetorical Index, 1625)—that is, with a discussion of the processes of rhetoric. The dedication to the 1633 edition of *Oratoriæ libri duo* reveals that it was being used in some of the most important schools in England.

Thomas Blundeville's *The Art of Logike* (1599), printed after the rise of Ramism in England, has more in common with Wilson's logic than with contemporary Continental works, though Blundeville mentions Ramus by name, and the title explains that his book was written "as well according to the docrine of Aristotle, as of all other moderne and best accounted Authors thefeof." Divided into six books, *The Art of Logike* consists of 170 pages in question-and-answer format, with chapters on predicables, predicaments, method, propositions, places, syllogisms, and fallacies. The detailed table of contents and the catechismal format certainly contributed to the reputation of the book as an accessible manual for nonacademic readers. The second edition, printed more than ten years after Blundeville's death, includes an address to the reader and a postscript not found in the first edition. Ostensibly written by Blundeville himself, the address to the reader identifies the intended readership of the book as those who cannot afford to send themselves or their children to a university; thus *The Art of Logike* is designedly a poor

man's logic. The postscript is even more specific: "a most necessary Booke for such Ministers as had not beene brought vp in any Vniuersitie." At least one seventeenth-century author felt that Blundeville's book might be useful in an academic setting. In his *Ideas of Education,* a manuscript not published until 1972, John Aubrey included Blundeville's logic among the recommended books for his model school library: "Blunderville [*sic*] has in print a logic in English in 4o, which is very plain and full of examples. I do fancy it is a useful book, though it is not taken notice of by any universities."

The seventeenth century was ushered in portentously by Bacon's *The Advancement of Learning,* a work published in 1605, which rearranged and reconceived the many branches of learning, including logic and rhetoric. Bacon grew up in an environment that nurtured his intellectual development. His father, Nicholas Bacon, Lord Chancellor under Queen Elizabeth I, was well known for his devotion to learning. John Nicols, in his *Progresses and Public Procession of Queen Elizabeth* (1823), reports that Nicholas Bacon had commissioned artists to decorate the walls of his banqueting house at Gorhambury with murals of the seven liberal arts. Over rhetoric were placed pictures of Cicero, Isocrates, Demosthenes, and Quintilian, with these words: "By me the force of wisdom is display'd, / And sense shines most when in my robes array'd." Over logic were placed pictures of Aristotle, Rodolph, Porphyry, and John Seton: "I sep'rate things perplex'd, all clouds remove, / Truth I search out, shew error, all things prove." His son Francis eventually took possession of the estate, but not the old allegiances.

In *The Advancement of Learning,* enlarged and translated into Latin as *De Dignitate & Augmentis Scientiarum* (Of the Advancement and Proficiency of Learning, 1623) and later translated back into English by Gilbert Wats, Bacon divides learning into three disciplines in relation to three faculties: history to memory, poetry to imagination, and philosophy to reason. Logic, the natural philosophy of man as a spiritual being, involves invention (finding), judgment (assessing), memory (storing), and tradition (conveying). These activities comprise the four logical arts. The art of tradition, in turn, has three parts: the organ of speech (mainly grammar), the method of speech (judgment or arrangement), and the illustration of speech (ornament or rhetoric). Most important is Bacon's appropriation and redistribution of the traditional parts of rhetoric and logic, as well as the subjects of the trivium. In his scheme of learning rhetoric becomes a part of logic, its purpose being to lead someone to appropriate action by making imagination an ally to reason rather than the myopic affections.

In *Novum Organum* (New Organon, 1620), a title that alludes to Aristotle's logical works, Bacon presents his plan for a new logic that would enable people to comprehend nature through a proper method of inquiry and interpretation. Divided into two books of aphorisms, Bacon's treatise first explains why a new logic is necessary and then proposes an investigatory method based on induction. The investigator, ever wary of mental impediments or biases, must first gather as much information about a subject as possible through observation and experimentation, then organize it according to three tables, and then systematically eliminate as much variety as possible. The goal is to find the subject's true form. This method had a profound effect on future philosophers and scientists, including members of the Royal Society.

After 1620 English writers produced a series of rhetoric textbooks, some quite popular, that had a considerable influence on subsequent generations of students. The authors of these textbooks are usually glossed over or ignored in the histories of rhetoric because their contributions were more practical than original or visionary. One neglected writer, obscured by the luminosity of Bacon and Thomas Hobbes, is the clergyman Thomas Vicars, who wrote the 1621 work Χειραγωγία: sive *Manuductio Ad Artem Rhetoricam*. Recommended by both John Brinsley and Richard Holdsworth as a useful textbook for students, Vicars's Χειραγωγία (*Cheiragogia*) treats all five parts of traditional rhetoric and devotes more than half of that discussion to invention. The material is presented as a series of questions and answers, which was not an uncommon format for rhetoric and logic textbooks of this period. Contemporaneous books with a catechismal format include Robert Fage's *Peter Ramus . . . his Dialectica in two bookes* (1632), a translation-adaptation of Ramus's *Dialectica,* and William Dugard's *Rhetorices Elementa* (The Rudiments of Rhetoric, 1648), an adaptation of Charles Butler's Ramist *Rhetoricæ Libri Dvo.* Although the Χειραγωγία (*Cheiragogia*) shows some signs of Ramus's influence, it owes a far greater debt to the German Bartholomaeus Keckermann. While Vicars acknowledges his predecessor William Thorne, author of *Ducente deo Willelmi Thorni Tullius* (God Guiding, William Thorne's Tully, 1592), as a native authority on rhetoric, Thomas Horne, author of Χειραγωγία, *sive Manuductio in Aedem Palladis* (Manuduction: Handbook in the Temple of Pallis, 1641), acknowledges Vicars as a native expert: the lineage is obscure and underscores the need for more studies of minor figures, particularly those who wrote in Latin.

Another neglected writer is Farnaby, one of the greatest schoolmasters of his day, who produced a "rhetorical index" for grammar school students. Written entirely in Latin, as Vicars's book was, the *Index Rhetoricvs* (1625) treats four of the five traditional parts of rhetoric, omitting only memory. Just as Susenbrotus had begun his *Epitome troporum ac schematum* with a disclaimer "Collector, non Autor, ergo sum" (I am a collector, not an author), so does Farnaby preface his books with a quotation from Seneca that disallows the possibility of creating anything new, except through the application and organization of old ideas. Farnaby's book is an index because it points to the works of other writers on the subject, with copious lists, making the material easy for students to digest. According to Farnaby's modern editor Raymond Nadeau, the treatise borrows heavily from the *Commentariorum rhetoricorum . . . libri sex* (Six Books of Rhetorical Commentaries, 1609) and the *Rhetorices contractæ . . . libri quinque* (Five Books of Rhetoric Abridged, 1621) of Gerardus Vossius (Gerrit Vos, 1577–1649), whose definition of rhetoric Farnaby borrows verbatim, and the *Systema rhetoricæ* (System of Rhetoric, 1606) of Keckermann. The only English Renaissance rhetorician that Farnaby cites (in a marginal note on page 58) is William Thorne.

Although English works on rhetoric during this period did not have a significant influence on Continental Europe, some of them were actually printed on the Continent. Fenner's *The Artes of Logike and Rethorike,* for example, was never printed in England, though it was certainly not intended for a large Continental audience, since it was written in English. British works on logic were more popular abroad, even if one discounts the important works of early-sixteenth-century logicians such as Mair and Maurice O'Fihely. John Case's *Summa veterum interpretum in universam dialecticam Aristotelis* (A Summary of the Ancient Interpreters into Aristotle's Complete Dialectic, 1584) was reprinted more often on the Continent than in England. The Ramist works of William Temple, George Downham, and others apparently circulated widely throughout Europe. There must have been a Continental audience for such texts as Nathaniel Baxter's *In Petri Rami dialecticam quæstiones et responsiones* (Questions and Responses in the Dialectic of Peter Ramus) published in Frankfurt in 1588; John Sanderson's *Institutiones dialecticarum libri quator* (Four Books of Dialectic Principles) published in Antwerp in 1589; Butler's *Rhetoricæ Libri Dvo,* published in Leiden in 1642; and Farnaby's *Index Rhetoricvs,* published in Amsterdam in 1648, 1659, and 1672. Farnaby dedicated his book to a Venetian senator.

During this period, John Prideaux, a professor and administrator at Oxford University, produced several textbooks in the liberal arts that attempted to effect a compromise between Ramism and Renaissance Aristotelianism. The first of these textbooks, published in 1607, was a work on grammar: *Tabvlæ ad*

Grammatica Græca Introductoriæ (Introductory Tables to Greek Grammar). More than two decades later, the *Tabulae ad grammatica Graeca introductoriæ* was republished with Prideaux's first work on logic, a twelve-page discussion titled *Tyrocinivm ad Syllogismvm Legitimum contexendum, & captiosum dissuendum, expeditissimum* (The Easiest Apprenticeship to the Weaving of Proper Syllogisms and the Unstitching of Sophisms, 1629). Both works were printed again in 1639 in a single volume with his second work on logic, a fourteen-page discussion titled *Heptades logicæ.* His crowning achievement, though, was a work titled *Hypomnemata Logica, Rhetorica, Physica, Metaphysica, Pneumatica, Ethica, Politica, Oeconomica* (Notes on Logic, Rhetoric, Physics, Metaphysics, Pneumatics, Ethics, Politics, Economics, 1650?). Reminiscent of Ramus's *Scholæ in liberales artes* (Lectures in the Liberal Arts, 1569), at least in scope, the *Hypomnemata* includes recognizable versions of the *Tyrocinium* and *Heptades,* which comprise only a small part of the 102-page opening section on logic of this book.

As had Wilson, Fenner, and Fraunce of the previous century, Prideaux wrote not only on logic, but also on rhetoric. His *Hypomnemata* includes a brief discussion in Latin of stylistic rhetoric, treating seven tropes, seven figures, and seven schemes in only nine pages, with rhetoric being defined according to both Ramus's and Aristotle's definitions. Both Ramus and Aristotle are cited in the text. His *Sacred Eloquence,* a full-length treatise in English on stylistic rhetoric, was published posthumously in 1659. In it Prideaux defines preaching as a "Logicall kind of rhetorick." Originating probably from lecture notes, all of these works betray Prideaux's obsession with the number seven. In his *Heptades,* he even divides the contemporary study of logic into seven schools. Prideaux is said to have been quite popular with students, and there is some evidence that his logic notes were admired by undergraduates. In his *Idea of Education,* a manuscript not published until 1972, John Aubrey recalls using Prideaux's logic notes when he was a student at Oxford: "The logic notes of Trinity College, Oxford, are as good perhaps as any are (by Bishop Prideaux). They are short and clear: we learned them by heart."

The first English work entirely about rhetorical gesture was printed in 1644. John Bulwer's *Chironomia: or, The Art of Manvall Rhetoricke* was bound with his *Chirologia: or The Natvrall Langvuage of The Hand* in all editions. *Chirologia* is essentially descriptive, focusing on the natural expression of the hands, while *Chironomia* is prescriptive, dealing with the art of gesture in oratory. The latter is divided into six parts: a prelude, the history of rhetorical gesture, rules governing the hand, rules governing the fingers, vices of gesture, and cau-

tionary notes. Both works were apparently inspired by a passage in Bacon's *The Advancement of Learning* in which Bacon criticizes Aristotle for not recognizing the power of gesture. Bulwer was familiar with Talaeus's *Rhetorica,* for he alludes to the work twice in his history of gesture, but his chief sources would seem to be Quintilian, Cicero, and the Italian rhetorician Ludovic Cresollius, author of *Theatrum veterum rhetorum, oratorum, et declamatorum quos in Gracia nominabant sofistas, expositum libris quinque* (The Theater of Ancient Rhetors, Orators, and Declaimers, Whom in Greece the Called Sophists, Set Forth in Five Books, 1620). One would expect Bulwer to invoke Zeno's metaphor of the fist and the palm, since the image seems to imply that all of rhetoric and logic are subsumed by the language of the hands. Not only do the fist and palm adorn the frontispiece of the *Chironomia,* but also Bulwer offers this summary and interpretation: "And the first inventor of the art of logic, to note the moods and brevity of argumentation, exhibited logic by a hand compressed into a fist, and rhetoric by an open and dilated hand, which is but *pugnus expansus* [an open fist]."

John Wilkins, Bishop of Chester and cofounder of the Royal Society, wrote at least two books important to the history of rhetoric. The first, the popular *Ecclesiastes* (1646), is a treatise on preaching, an art requiring both "a right understanding of sound doctrine" and "an ability to propound, confirm, and apply it unto the edification of others." This statement prefaces a series of implicit and explicit comparisons: understanding is to communication what a lawyer is to a pleader, what a divine is to a preacher, what a logician is to an orator. One can be a divine without being a preacher, but presumably not vice versa. Wilkins's concept of sacred oratory involves invention, disposition, and style, which he calls matter, method, and expression, respectively. Expression is divided into phrase and elocution (meaning delivery); Wilkins writes that the phrase must be "plain, full, wholesome, affectionate." In *Sacred Rhetoric: The Christian Grand Style in the English Renaissance* (1988) Debora Shuger credits Wilkins with introducing the passionate plain style into Anglican homiletics.

Wilkins's *Discourse Concerning the Gift of Prayer* (1651), frequently bound with the *Ecclesiastes, or, A discourse concerning the Gift of Preaching* is in essence a rhetoric of prayer, in which Wilkins explains the rules of matter, method, and expression for praying. Less concerned with persuading a deity than with expressing emotions, the art of praying requires some theory and practice, though Wilkins is quick to acknowledge that two-thirds of this "gift" is not taught or learned but given from above. A third part, however, is subject to the same kinds of rules that govern any other "ability," such as pleading or disputing. Wilkins explains how the devout Christian, bound by duty to pray, can find something meaningful to say, can organize his material effectively (always from general to specific), and can use appropriate language (usually "plain English"). Wilkins does allow for some ornamentation, such as "ingemination" (that is, the use of repetition to express intense emotion), but one should avoid "affectation," as well as "negligence" (that is, vulgar phrasing). One achieves proper expression, of course, by imitating the style of Scripture.

The rhetorical works of Blount and Smith serve as an appropriate terminus for Renaissance British rhetoric. Both works borrow heavily from earlier treatises by English authors and thus offer an odd mixture of rhetorical traditions. Blount's *The Academie of Eloquence* combines a stylistic rhetoric with an epistolary rhetoric and oratorical *formulæ* in one volume. Inspired by Bacon, who recommends the collecting of commonplaces in *The Advancement of Learning,* Blount's *formulæ* serve as ready-made rhetorical aids to wisdom and invention. The sections on tropes and schemes and letter writing are taken largely from John Hoskyns's "Direccōns for Speech and Style" (circa 1599). Published in 1657, Smith's *The Mysteries of Rhetorique Vnvail'd,* a catalogue of figures of speech, synthesizes several sources, Ramist and non-Ramist: Fenner's *The Artes of Logike and Rethorike,* Farnaby's *Index Rhetoricvs,* Blount's (or rather Hoskyns's) treatise, and Peacham's *The Garden of Eloquence.* It represents, perhaps more than any other work in English, a culmination of the Renaissance fascination with figures of speech. The significance of Blount's and Smith's works lies mainly in their popularity: they were frequently reprinted and probably used widely in the grammar schools. Smith's book, in particular, offers a careful selection of definitions and examples in an accessible format. It is for this reason, partly, that critic Charles Standford recommends it as "A good starting point for the study of primary materials."

British rhetoricians and logicians were deeply influenced by Continental sources, as this introduction has indicated. Matthew De Coursey discusses the Continental European rhetoricians and the rhetorical heritage at more length in an appendix. Since many of the terms used in this volume may be unfamiliar to the reader, a selected glossary of important rhetorical and logical terms has been provided. Many of the rhetorical works by the subjects of entries in this volume are available to the general reader only on microfilm; a finding list of the primary works discussed in the entries has also been provided. The checklist at the end of this volume includes approximately 150 secondary sources for further study. This checklist will be continued in the next volume, *British Rhetoricians and Logicians, 1500–1660, Second Series.*

Many corrections, changes, and additions (such as courtesy translations of titles) were made to the entries during the final editing stage of production. These were supervised by the in-house editor, Jan Peter F. van Rosevelt, who also wrote captions for the illustrations and edited the appendices. Both the outside editor and the in-house editor agreed that old spellings would be used in titles and quotations whenever possible. No attempt has been made to expand contractions, separate ligatures, correct substitutions of *v* for *u, i* for *j,* double *v* for *w,* and so forth, in the primary bibliographies. These typographical and orthographical features have been retained in many parts of the volume as artifacts in the history of early modern printing and the English language. Most titles were checked by Bruccoli Clark Layman staff against title pages of books on microfilm, as well as standard printed bibliographies and many on-line catalogues, such as the English Short-Title Catalogue. Most of the subjects in this volume have entries in *The Dictionary of National Biography,* produced in the late nineteenth and early twentieth centuries. *The New Dictionary of National Biography,* scheduled for publication in 2004, will probably add a great deal to our knowledge of the subjects in this volume. Several of the contributors to this volume, including the outside editor, have also written entries for the *New DNB.*

–Edward A. Malone

Acknowledgments

This book was produced by Bruccoli Clark Layman, Inc. Karen L. Rood is senior editor. Jan Peter F. van Rosevelt was the in-house editor.

Production manager is Philip B. Dematteis.

Administrative support was provided by Ann M. Cheschi, Dawnca T. Williams, and Mary A. Womble.

Accounting supervisor is Ann-Marie Holland. Accounting assistant is Amber L. Coker.

Copyediting supervisor is Phyllis A. Avant. The copyediting staff includes Brenda Carol Blanton, Allen E. Friend Jr., Melissa D. Hinton, William Tobias Mathes, Nancy E. Smith, and Elizabeth Jo Ann Sumner. Freelance copyeditor is Rebecca Mayo.

Editorial associates are Andrew Choate and Michael S. Martin.

Layout and graphics supervisor is Janet E. Hill. The graphics staff includes Karla Corley Brown and Zoe R. Cook.

Office manager is Kathy Lawler Merlette.

Photography supervisor is Paul Talbot. Photography editors are Charles Mims and Scott Nemzek.

Permissions editor is Jeff Miller.

Digital photographic copy work was performed by Joseph M. Bruccoli.

SGML supervisor is Cory McNair. The SGML staff includes Frank Graham, Linda Dalton Mullinax, Jason Paddock, and Alex Snead.

Systems manager is Marie L. Parker.

Typesetting supervisor is Kathleen M. Flanagan. The typesetting staff includes Mark J. McEwan, Patricia Flanagan Salisbury, and Alison Smith. Freelance typesetters are Wanda Adams and Vicki Grivetti.

Walter W. Ross did library research. He was assisted by Steven Gross and the following librarians at the Thomas Cooper Library of the University of South Carolina: circulation department head Tucker Taylor; reference department head Virginia W. Weathers; Brette Barclay, Marilee Birchfield, Paul Cammarata, Gary Geer, Michael Macan, Tom Marcil, Rose Marshall, and Sharon Verba; interlibrary loan department head John Brunswick; and interlibrary loan staff Robert Arndt, Hayden Battle, Barry Bull, Jo Cottingham, Marna Hostetler, Marieum McClary, Erika Peake, and Nelson Rivera.

Professor Malone wishes to thank Carolyn Cassady; Jerome Poynton; Peter Hale; Robert Cowley; John Bennett of the Ohio State University Rare Books Library; Jeff Ritchie; Carol Moore of the Arizona State University Library; John Skarstad of the Special Collections Library at the University of California at Davis; Bernard Crystal of Rare Books and Manuscripts Library, Butler Library, Columbia University; Rodney Phillips of the Berg Collection, New York Public Library; and Mike Simpson. Special thanks to his hardworking student assistant, Kelly King, and his colleagues in the English Department at Gardner-Webb University, especially Gayle Price.

Many people volunteered their time and expertise to this project; their contributions deserve to be acknowledged. The following people served as voluntary readers in the vetting of some entries: Elizabeth Skerpan Wheeler, Theo Bongaerts, Tamara Goeglein, Judith Rice Henderson, Jeffrey Wollock, Timothy Wengert, Jerome Dees, Lawrence D. Green, Thomas O. Sloane, Thomas Conley, and Andrew Breeze. The following people made suggestions that influenced the list of writers included in this volume: Thomas O. Sloane, Elizabeth Skerpan Wheeler, the late Jeremy Maule, Brent Nelson, Andrew Breeze, Kim Fedderson, and Richard Serjeantson. The following people suggested contributors for certain entries and offered useful advice: Tita French Baumlin, Judith Rice Henderson, Richard Serjeantson, Jeremy Maule, Andrew Breeze, Jacqueline Glomski, and David Stacey. Special thanks must go to Judith Rice Henderson, Tita Baumlin, Richard Serjeantson, and Lawrence D. Green for their generous assistance. These people are responsible for some of the strengths of this volume, but none of its weaknesses.

Thanks also to the Department of English, Journalism, and Foreign Languages at Missouri Western State College for supporting Professor Malone during this project from August 1996 to November 2000 and to the many librarians and archivists at Missouri Western State College, at the University of Kansas, and in various locations in England.

Dictionary of Literary Biography® • Volume Two Hundred Thirty-Six

British Rhetoricians and Logicians, 1500–1660
First Series

Dictionary of Literary Biography

Roger Ascham

(1515 or 1516 – 30 December 1568)

Brent L. Nelson
University of Toronto

BOOKS: *Toxophilus, The schole of shootinge conteyned in tvvo bookes. To all Gentlemen and yomen of Englande, pleasaunte for theyr pastyme to rede, and profitable for theyr use to folow, both in war and peace* (London: Edward Whytchurch, 1545);

A Report and Discourse written by Roger Ascham, of the affaires and state of Germany and the Emperour Charles his court, duryng certaine yeares while the sayd Roger was there (London: Printed by John Daye, 1570?);

The Scholemaster Or plaine and perfite way of teachyng children, to vnderstand, write, and speake, the Latin tong, but specially purposed for the priuate brynging vp of youth in Ientlemen and Noble mens houses, and commodious also for all such, as haue forgot the Latin tonge, and would, by themselues, with out à Scholemaster, in short tyme, and with small paines, recouer à sufficient habilitie, to vnderstand, write, and speake Latin, edited by Margaret Ascham (London: Printed by John Daye, 1570);

Disertissimi viri Rogeri Aschami, Angli, Regiae maiestati non ita pridem a Latinis epistolis, familiarium epistolarum libri tres, magna orationis elegantia conscripti. Quorum primo præfigitur elegantisima epistola de Imitatione Oratoria. Huc accesserunt eiusdem pauca quædam poëmata. Omnia in studiosorum gratiam collecta, & nunc primum ædita studio & labore Eduardi Grantæ, Scholæ Westmon. moderatoris. Addita est in fine eiusdem Ed. Gr. oratio, de vita & obitu Rogeri Aschami, ac eius dictionis elegantia, cum abhortatione ad adolescentulos, edited by Edward Grant (London: Printed by Henry Middleton for Francis Coldock, [1576]; revised, 1578);

Apologia Doctissimi Viri Rogeri Aschami, Angli, pro cæna Dominica, contra Missam & eius prestigias: in Academia olim Cantabrigiensi exercitationis gratia inchoata. Cui accesserunt themata quædam Theologica, debita disputandi ratione in Collegio D. Ioan. pronunciata. Exposi- *tiones item antiquę, in epistolas Diui Pauli ad Titum & Philemonem, ex diuersis sanctorum Patrum Gręcè scriptis commentarijs ab Oecumenio collectę, & à R. A. Latinè versę,* edited by Grant (London: Printed by Henry Middleton for Francis Coldock, 1577).

Editions: *The Scholemaster,* edited, with notes, by John E. B. Mayor (London: Bell & Daldy, 1863; New York: AMS Press, 1967);

The Whole Works of Roger Ascham, Now First Collected and Revised, With a Life of the Author, 3 volumes in 4, edited by J. A. Giles (London: John Russell Smith, 1864–1865; New York: AMS Press, 1965);

Toxophilus. 1545, edited by Edward Arber (London: A. Murray, 1868; New York: AMS Press, 1966);

The Scholemaster: Roger Ascham; First Edition, 1570, Collated with the Second Edition, 1571, edited by Edward Arber (London: Edward Arber, 1870);

English Works: Toxophilus, Report of the Affaires and State of Germany, The Scholemaster, edited by William Aldis Wright (Cambridge: Cambridge University Press, 1904);

The Scholemaster, edited by R. J. Schoeck (Don Mills, Ont.: Dent, 1966);

The Scholemaster, 1570, English Linguistics 1500–1800: A Collection of Facsimile Reprints, no. 20, edited by R. C. Alston (Menston, U.K.: Scolar, 1967);

The Schoolmaster (1570), edited by Lawrence V. Ryan (Ithaca, N.Y.: Published for the Folger Shakespeare Library by Cornell University Press, 1967);

The Scholemaster. London 1570, The English Experience: Its Record in Early Printed Books Published in Facsimile, no. 15 (Amsterdam: Theatrum Orbis Terrarum / New York: Da Capo Press, 1968);

Toxophilvs, The Schole of Shootinge. London 1545, The English Experience: Its Record in Early Printed Books Published in Facsimile, no. 79 (Amsterdam: Theatrum Orbis Terrarum / New York: Da Capo Press, 1969);

Toxophilus, 1545 (Menston, U.K.: Scolar, 1971);

Roger Ascham, Toxophilus, the Schole of Shootinge, London 1545, edited by Harald Schröter (Sankt Augustin, Germany: Richarz, 1983).

Roger Ascham has earned a place in the history of English rhetoric on several accounts: he was a strong advocate of the central importance of rhetoric not only to the arts curriculum but also to culture as a whole; his letters were widely recognized by his contemporaries as models of epistolary style; and he was the first Englishman from the traditional school to record his critical response to Ramist reform of the arts curriculum, most notably his removal of invention and arrangement from the province of rhetoric. But of chief importance is Ascham's summation, in the vernacular, of the methods for rhetorical instruction espoused by Continental educators, especially Johann Sturm. These methods include "double translation" (from Latin to English and back again) and imitation of the best models, chiefly Cicero. In the years following Ascham's death, such prominent Elizabethan and Jacobean grammar-school educators as William Kempe, John Brinsley, and Charles Hoole followed Ascham in advocating double translation as both a means of mastering Latin grammar and of fostering rhetorical style.

In 1605 Francis Bacon still deemed Ascham's brand of Ciceronianism significant enough to earn the notorious distinction in his *The Tvvoo Bookes of Francis Bacon. Of the Proficience and Aduancement of Learning* of exemplifying the "first distemper of learning, when men study words and not matter." Bacon charges Ascham with almost deifying Cicero and Demosthenes for their eloquence; however, he objects not so much to a Ciceronian emphasis on style as to an emphasis on style that precedes and sometimes precludes the study of matter (that is, intellectual content) to which one can apply eloquence. It is "vain," suggests Bacon, to learn eloquence before one has something substantial to say. Indeed, as a teacher of rhetoric, Ascham was not so much interested in subject matter as in teaching his students to fit appropriate words with whatever matter was at hand. Yet, it is a mistake to characterize Ascham as a mere stylist. His most consistent concern in his major works is to ensure a proper relationship between matter and manner through the cultivation of judgment and *decorum* (appropriateness).

Paradoxically, the work for which Ascham is most famous, his teaching on translation and imitation, is the very cause of his exclusion from so many discussions of Renaissance rhetoric. Although Wilbur Samuel Howell mentions Ascham in his *Logic and Rhetoric in England, 1500–1700* (1956) it is not for his ideas on rhetoric, but solely for his response to Pierre de La Ramée (known as Petrus Ramus). James J. Murphy's standard *Renaissance Rhetoric: A Short-title Catalogue of Works on Rhetorical Theory from the Beginning of Printing to A. D. 1700* (1981) includes only treatises on rhetorical precepts, and so excludes Ascham altogether. Yet, for Ascham and many of his contemporaries, the practice of imitating the best models, not a mastery of textbook rules, is what best teaches eloquence. Another cause of scholars overlooking Ascham's contribution to rhetoric is his thorough humanism. Ascham viewed his whole life and work as inextricable from his learning, in which rhetoric held first place. So thoroughly does the art of eloquence characterize his life, that discussions of rhetoric turn up in such unexpected places as his personal letters, translated from the Latin by Maurice Hatch and Alvin Vos as *Letters of Roger Ascham* (1989), and his discourse on archery in *Toxophilvs, The schole of shootinge conteyned in two bookes. To all Gentlemen and yomen of Englande, pleasaunte for theyr pastyme to rede, and profitable for theyr use to folow, both in war and peace* (1545), as well as in his treatise on grammar-school education, *The Scholemaster Or plaine and perfite way of teachyng children, to vnderstand, write, and speake, the Latin tong* (1570).

Roger Ascham was born at Kirby Wiske, Yorkshire, in 1515 or 1516. Although his father, John Ascham, steward to Henry, seventh Baron Scrope of Bolton, left his son no material legacy, he did provide him an education. He placed Roger in the household of Sir Humphrey Wingfield, a lawyer and later speaker of the House of Commons, where he spent his youth and was well prepared to enter Cambridge University. In 1530 Wingfield sent Ascham to St. John's College, Cambridge, from which he graduated with a bachelor of arts degree on 18 February 1534, at age eighteen. Ascham was soon thereafter elected fellow of the college before receiving his master of arts degree on 3 July 1537. At Cambridge he was strongly influenced by his teachers John Redman, Robert Pember, and John Cheke and included among his acquaintances the logician John Seton and logician and rhetorician Thomas Wilson. As a fellow at St. John's, Ascham lectured on dialectic, mathematics, and Greek, no doubt focusing on the rhetoricians and orators, his favorite authors.

In 1546 Ascham was elected to succeed Cheke as public orator, an office he held until 1554. As public orator, among his responsibilities was writing official letters on behalf of the university. His early success was disrupted by collegiate politics, failed bids at patronage, and prolonged absence owing to recurring illness.

Ascham's Protestantism also brought him into a certain amount of conflict with the predominantly Catholic administration of the university. In 1547 a controversy erupted at St. John's College over the nature of the Eucharist. In response to the prevailing Catholic party at the college, Ascham wrote a Protestant defense of the Lord's Supper, which he wisely did not publish. It finally appeared posthumously in 1577 as *Apologia Doctissimi Viri Rogeri Aschami, Angli, pro caena Dominica, contra Missam & eius prestigias: in Academia olim Cantabrigiensi exercitationis gratia inchoata,* together with two other of his early religious works, his *Themata Theologica* (Theological Themes), comprising commentaries on various Bible verses and theological themes, and a translation of Oecumenius's anthology of commentary on the Bible books of Titus and Philemon. Being overlooked for the Greek professorship vacated by Cheke in 1547, however, was perhaps Ascham's chief disappointment in an often frustrating tenure at Cambridge.

In 1545, while at St. John's College, Ascham published *Toxophilvs, The schole of shootinge,* a work that he thought to be of some rhetorical importance. In 1544, when it first became apparent that Cheke would be resigning his professorship, Ascham wrote a letter to Sir William Paget, secretary of state and counselor to King Henry VIII, asking that Paget recommend him for the vacant post. In this letter–translated by Hatch and Vos–he expressed his ironically worded hope that his book, which was in press at the time, would not be "an insignificant testimony of my inconsiderable learning." In a letter to Bishop Stephen Gardiner, which accompanied a gift copy of *Toxophilus,* Ascham makes it clear that he wrote the treatise as a model of English vernacular prose for the benefit of those "unlearned and thoughtless men" whose writing betrays a deficiency in all the offices of rhetoric. As is typical of Ascham, he describes the problem in terms of decorum: "they forsake appropriate and plain words, and are ignorant of metaphor and of words suited to the true splendor of the subject. And then they are unskilled and ignorant of how to organize it correctly. Dialectic for reasoning and rhetoric for adornment have not even touched their lips, and so in our vernacular they study to be not native and appropriate, but rather outlandish and bizarre." In *Toxophilus,* then, Ascham is going about instruction in rhetoric according to his own humanist principles as later set out in *The Scholemaster.* In Ascham's mind, what is needed is not another treatise on rhetoric, but a good model for imitation that demonstrates sound judgment and decorum.

In his preface Ascham puts forward two other purposes for writing this celebration of shooting: first, out of his own love for archery and a conviction of its benefit to the realm, he promotes a revival of the long-

Published by W Smith. 23 Lisle Street, Leicester Square.

ROGER ASCHAM,

Roger Ascham reading a letter to his pupil Queen Elizabeth I (frontispiece to William Elstob's 1703 edition of Ascham's letters; Hulton Getty/Archive Photo)

bow in England; and second, he decides to write in English, both in consideration of his audience and to try his hand at English prose with a view to applying the medium to "better game" in the future. The patriotism that moves Ascham to promote the weapon that enabled Henry V to win the battle of Agincourt similarly provides his impulse to improve the state of English letters. He laments that "as for ye Latin or greke tonge, euery thyng is so excellently done in them, that none can do better: In the Englysh tonge contrary, euery thinge in a maner so meanly, bothe for the matter and handelynge, that no man can do worse." Ascham inveighs against those English writers who obscure their prose with strange and borrowed words from Latin, French, and Italian, and notes the need for decorum and good judgment. "He that wyll wryte well in any tongue," says Ascham, "muste folowe thys councel of Aristotle, to speake as the cōmon people do, to thinke as wise men do: and so shoulde euery man vnderstande hym, and the iudgement of wyse men alowe hym."

Here Ascham also establishes an analogy between shooting, ethics, and eloquence, noting that "In our tyme nowe, when euery manne is gyuen to knowe muche rather than to liue wel, very many do write, but after suche a fashion, as very many do shoote. Some shooters take in hande stronger bowes, than they be able to mayntayne. This thyng maketh them sūmtyme, to outshoote the marke, sūmtyme to shote far wyde, and perchaunce hurte sūme that looke on." He continues to catalogue various common faults in shooting, leaving the reader to continue making the analogical connections. Ascham concludes, "Yf any man wyll applye these thynges togyther, [he] shal not se the one farre differ from the other," thus inviting the reader to anticipate that much of what he will have to say about shooting might also apply to rhetoric and virtuous living. In the next paragraph Ascham compares his decision to apply English prose to the subject of archery with that of novice archers who "bothe wyll begyn to shoote, for a lytle moneye, and also wyll vse to shote ones or twise about the marke for nought, afore they beginne a good."

The book itself is written as a dialogue between a rhetorician, Philologus, and an archer, Toxophilus, both of whom make analogical connections between rhetoric and archery. In the first part of the book, Toxophilus remarks about a certain affinity between shooting and virtue, citing a common discipline of mind that, the preface implies, can as readily apply to rhetoric: "By shoting also is the mynde honestly exercised where a mā alwaies desireth to be best (which is a worde of honestie) and that by the same waye, that vertue it selfe doeth, coueting to come nighest a moost perfite ende or meane standing betwixte .ii. extremes, eschewinge shorte, or gone, or eithersyde wide, for the which causes Aristotle him selfe sayth that shoting and vertue be very like." The connection between accuracy in shooting and judgment in rhetoric is made explicit in Toxophilus's discussion of the technicalities of shooting in the second half of the book, where he notes that one important factor in hitting the mark is a good and true arrow. The judgment involved in selecting an arrow, says Toxophilus, is comparable to that of a rhetorician. He explains: "Now howe big, how small, how heuye, how lyght, how longe, how short, a shafte shoulde be particularlye for euerye man . . . can not be toulde no more than you Rhethoricians can appoynt any one kynde of wordes, of sentences, of fygures fyt for euery matter, but euen as the man and the matter requyreth so the fyttest to be vsed." Far from disregarding matter, then, the good rhetorician studies words in relation to matter.

Good judgment in archery and rhetoric alike comes by practice and imitation of the best models,

with the aim of bringing the art to perfection. Ascham arrives at this method dialectically through the dialogue of the text, where Philologus urges the need to aim at ideal perfection while Toxophilus insists on the practical necessity of imitating the best models. In the second part of the book, taking Cicero's criterion of "cumlynesse" as the proper objective in all endeavors, Philologus asks Toxophilus to "teatche me to shoote as fayre, and welfauouredly as you can imagen." For Ascham, comeliness is equivalent to *decorum;* indeed, it was one of the English words commonly used in translating the Latin term, in the sense defined by the *Oxford Encyclopedic Dictionary* as "suitableness, becomingness, seemliness, decency, propriety." In a later digression on the poor judgment of fathers who select careers for their children that are inappropriate to their aptitudes, Philologus makes it clear that comeliness derives from a match that is "moste apte & fit." On Cicero's authority, Toxophilus agrees that "cumlinesse is the chefe poynt, & most to be sought for in all thynges," but objects that it "may be perceyued well when it is done, not described wel how it should be done." In other words, he can only instruct by example and imitation, not by precept.

This exchange continues a discussion that began at the conclusion of the first part of the book, where Philologus first requests that Toxophilus teach him perfection in shooting, citing a rhetorical precedent in Cicero who "doeth playnlye saye, that yf he teached any maner of crafte as he dyd Rhetorike he would labor to bringe a man to the knowlege of the moost perfitnesse of it." Toxophilus insists that while one may conceive of perfection, no man can attain it in practice. A combination of these two views, the ideal and the practical, represents Ascham's doctrine of the arts. In the end, both positions are incorporated into a model of imitation of the best models aiming at perfection. Philologus's desire for perfect "cumlynesse" is somewhat satisfied by Toxophilus's proposal of taking a handful of the best archers in the country and imitating the best in each of them so that a composite exemplar of shooting might be derived from the choice elements of each. But lacking the presence of such models at the moment, Toxophilus concedes to laying out the precepts of shooting in the remainder of the book. In the process, Ascham has achieved his intention of presenting a model of English prose.

The balance of Ascham's writing on rhetoric derived not from the environs of the university but from his life at court. Having been handpicked by the adolescent Princess Elizabeth to be her tutor, Ascham somewhat reluctantly left the university in 1548 to begin a twenty-year association with the future queen that outlasted the two-year tenure of his official tutorship. During this tutorship he tested the methods he later described in *The Scholemaster*. In the summer of 1550, after a brief return to Cambridge, Ascham embarked to the Continent as Sir Richard Morison's secretary on a three-year embassy to the Holy Roman Emperor Charles V. During this time he established relationships with various Continental humanists, including an epistolary friendship with the prominent Strasbourg scholar Sturm, whom he never met in person.

Rhetoric is a recurring interest in Ascham's letters, but nowhere more prominently than in his correspondence with Sturm. Ascham's first letter, dated 4 April 1550, sets the tone for the remaining twelve letters, all translated from the Latin by Hatch and Vos. Ascham meets Sturm on the common ground of humanist doctrine as he begins, "No art for the guidance of life nor any science for the cultivation of the intellect . . . has ever been discovered which can compare with the excellence of that faculty by whose aid reason is trained for thinking carefully and language for speaking clearly, and by whose aid the rest of man's life seems to be far removed from monstrous and savage custom and to come very near to the divine nature." It becomes clear in the next paragraph that Ascham is eulogizing the arts of rhetoric and logic that so distinguished ancient Greek and Roman culture. Eloquence, for Ascham, is essential to the civilized man, infusing his whole life. He continues this theme in complimenting his correspondent, praising Sturm for possessing both the eloquence and the humanity of Cicero. When Ascham subsequently turns to commend an acquaintance of his to Sturm (whether Cardinal Reginald Pole, Redman, or Lady Jane Grey) he invariably cites their learning and eloquence among their points of character. In this letter, for example, he praises Princess Elizabeth for her judgment both in dress and literature: "In every kind of writing she readily notices any dubious or far-fetched word. She cannot endure those foolish imitators of Erasmus who have tied Latin in knots with proverbs."

In this first letter, and in almost every subsequent letter, Ascham also mentions his desire to see Sturm's commentaries on Aristotle's works published—especially that on his *Rhetoric*. In his final and longest letter to Sturm, written shortly before his death (and probably never sent), Ascham expresses his interest in seeing another of Sturm's works-in-progress, his *De Imitatione Oratoria* (1574). After a brief outline of his own current work, *The Scholemaster*, Ascham summarizes a proposed section on Ciceronian imitation, which never made it into the finished treatise. In this letter Ascham emphasizes that by imitating Cicero he means not simply emulating Cicero's style (although that is part of it), but imitating the way in which Cicero went about imitating

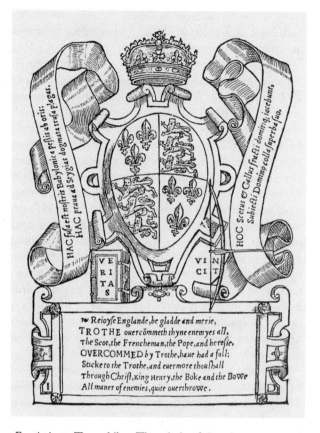

Frontispiece to Toxophilvs, The schole of shootinge conteyned in tvvo bookes *(1545), a work in which Ascham drew an analogy between archery and rhetorical eloquence*

Demosthenes or Plato, for example. "I must have Cicero the imitator as my model," he says, "not the imitator of Cicero." Ascham acknowledges throughout the letter that much of his thinking on imitation is derived from Sturm himself.

Perhaps the most noted feature of Ascham's letters to Sturm is his response to Ramus's reforms to the arts curriculum. Ramus, a French academic who was just becoming known in England, sought to clarify the respective properties of grammar, logic, and rhetoric and to thereby eliminate the considerable overlap between these arts-of-discourse as inherited from Aristotle and Cicero. Foremost in Ascham's mind was Ramus's removal of invention and arrangement from the purview of rhetoric, and his almost complete neglect of delivery. In this first letter, Ascham censures Ramus—that "big-mouth" as he calls him—for impudently attacking the authority of Aristotle and Cicero (a criticism he repeats in *The Scholemaster*) and also for implicitly undermining the principle of imitation that was so important to both him and Sturm. This censure does not prevent Ascham from adding his own complaint that Aristotle remains inaccessible because his commentators have not adequately illustrated his precepts (thus his interest in Sturm's commentary); for both logic and rhetoric, Ascham likes to see principles matched with examples.

Ramus seems to have been a common topic in Ascham and Sturm's correspondence. In a letter dated 29 January 1552, Ascham responds to rumors (which proved to be false) that Ramus had spoken negatively of a volume of their epistles that Sturm had recently published in Strasbourg. In his own defense, Ascham asks his friend to recall how much credit he had actually given Ramus in previous letters. While he refuses to retract his comments about Ramus's impudent tongue, Ascham does commend his intellect and learning, adding that his own criticism of Aristotelian commentaries was in fact a tacit approval of Ramus's intentions in reforming Aristotle's logic. Ascham does, however, take a clear stand in opposition to Ramus's redrawing of the boundaries of rhetoric, affirming with Sturm that invention belongs in "the foremost ranks of the art of speaking" and that delivery, which is all but neglected in Ramus's scheme, must be retained within the practice of rhetoric.

At the end of his time on the Continent, Ascham began writing an account of German politics drawn from his experience with the embassy. What remains of this unfinished work was published posthumously as *A Report and Discourse written by Roger Ascham, of the affaires and state of Germany and the Emperour Charles his court, duryng certaine yeares while the sayd Roger was there* (1570?). Shortly after news reached them of the death of Edward VI on 6 July 1553, Morison's embassy returned to England. Although a Protestant, Ascham managed to survive the reign of the fervently Catholic queen Mary, who granted him the Latin secretaryship in 1553, although his patent for the office was not sealed until 7 May 1554. As Latin secretary to Mary, Ascham composed official state letters and other documents in polished Latin prose, producing elegant handwritten copies for presentation. Many of Ascham's official letters survive, providing samples of his celebrated italic hand. He subsequently resigned his positions at Cambridge and married Margaret Howe on 1 June 1554. The couple had two sons, Sturm and Dudley, the former named after Ascham's friend and the latter named after Robert Dudley, first Earl of Leicester. He continued as secretary to Queen Elizabeth I after her accession in 1558, and resumed—in an unofficial capacity—his role as her private tutor, which he continued for the rest of his life.

In Ascham's later years an event occurred that, as he states in his preface to *The Scholemaster,* occasioned his writing of that work. During dinner one December evening in 1563 while in retreat from plague-ravaged London, Ascham and other learned and prominent men at court were informed by Sir William Cecil that "diuerse Scholers of Eaton, be runne awaie from the Schole, for feare of beating." Ascham alone spoke decisively against such severe disciplinary practice, suggesting instead that "yong children, were soner allured by loue, than driuen by beating, to atteyne good learning." Later that evening, in private, Sir Richard Sackville offered that if Ascham could recommend a like-minded tutor for his grandson, he would pay for the education of Ascham's son, Giles, under the same tutor. After continued discussion on the topic, Sackville requested that Ascham set down the main points they had covered in their talk on the ideal schoolmaster. *The Scholemaster* was written in answer to this request, although Sackville died before Ascham could complete the work.

Although *The Scholemaster* is commonly not recognized by scholars as a work on rhetoric, a fellow Cantabrigian of the next generation, Gabriel Harvey, suggested (in a somewhat backhanded way) that this is indeed its true genus. In a Latin lecture published as *Ciceronianus, Oratio post reditum, habita Cantabrigiae.* (1577), and translated in 1945 by Clarence A. Forbes, Harvey criticizes both those who place too much stock in commonplaces (as opposed to Ramus's topics of invention) and those who neglect them entirely. It is apparently as an example of the former that Harvey introduces Ascham into his lecture, even as he praises Ascham for his eloquence and learning. Harvey has no problem with *The Scholemaster,* as far as it goes; in his opinion, however, it simply does not go far enough to present the full rhetoric of Cicero. Specifically, Ciceronians of Ascham's stripe give short shrift to matters of invention and arrangement, faults that Harvey suggests would be rectified by recourse to Ramus's topics and method, that is, dialectic.

In Harvey's opinion Ascham's schoolmaster is "eminently refined, elegant, and even, if he be compared with the schoolmasters of others, truly most excellent and polished." He requires only that Ascham's schoolmaster be supplemented with the fruit of Ramus's reforms in the arts. But in an apparent contradiction, Harvey faults Ascham both for including not enough in his treatment of rhetoric and for including too much. He reserves his sharpest criticism for Ascham's crossing of the lines between grammar, rhetoric, and logic:

Were I minded to cast aspersions, however, (will the shade of that excellent man forgive me for saying this?) I am afraid you could not find excuses for him. If he intended to delineate a schoolmaster of grammar and not of rhetoric or dialectic, as someone will perhaps say by way of defending him—and in fact this has long since become the standard excuse—I should like to know what concern he has with metaphors and well-weighed synonyms, which are matters of rhetoric. What business has he with *diverse* and *contrary,* which are matters of dialectic, or with the types of oratorical exercises and particularly with the exquisite and artistic imitation of Cicero? If this is not making a foray into other people's possessions and preserves, and straying out of bounds, and trespassing across the boundaries, then what is?

Whatever the merits of Harvey's Ramus-inspired criticism, he clearly thought that *The Scholemaster* should be judged as a work of rhetoric and implies that others thought so as well.

Indeed, for Ascham rhetoric is the proper end of grammar-school education. In teaching Latin grammar, the schoolmaster aims to fit his students for further study in logic and rhetoric at university by giving special attention to training their judgment and memory. For this purpose Ascham proposes his method of double translation, which he briefly describes at the beginning of book 1 before turning to matters of academic discipline. In double translation, as in all matters rhetorical, Ascham defers to Cicero as both the ultimate source of his doctrine and as the best subject for translation (beginning with his epistles), although Ascham's friend Sturm and others bore considerable influence on his methods as well. Far from being a rote exercise, double translation is presented as a means of seeing grammatical rules and rhetorical principles applied and exemplified. The master first teaches the sense and occasion of Cicero's letter, repeatedly translating it into English until the student understands it, and then he parses it. The student repeats this process back to the master. In a paper notebook the student then translates the passage into English, and after a pause, back into Latin in a second notebook. Then the master compares the pupil's work with Cicero, taking the opportunity to teach his student where he fell short of the style of the original. In a third notebook the student collects from his reading exemplary samples of Latin expressions under six heads: *Propria* (literal); *Translata* (metaphorical); *Synonyma* (synonymous); *Diversa* (slightly differing); *Contraria* (opposite); and *Phrases* (expressions). By this method the schoolmaster aims to teach the student good judgment (the second aspect of invention) and to begin instilling principles of decorum exemplified in the assigned models. Not only does the method of double translation cultivate a judicious style, but (as he says later, in book 2) it facilitates invention and arrangement as well, instilling in the student "all right cōgruitie: proprietie of wordes: order in sentences: the right imitation, to inuent good matter, to dispose it in good order, to confirme it with good reason, to expresse any purpose fitlie and orderlie."

In book 2 Ascham turns his full attention to the methods suggested by learned men for "the learning of

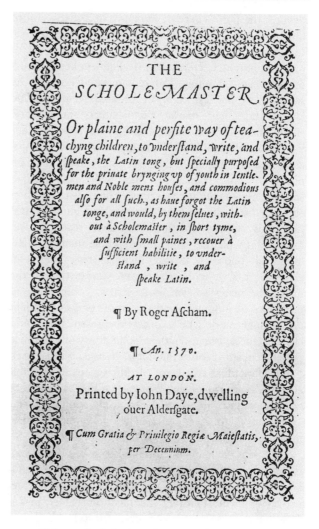

Title page for Ascham's response to Sir Richard Sackville's request that he describe the ideal tutor

tonges, and encrease of eloquence." Ascham names and describes *Translatio linguarum* (translation from one language to another), *Paraphrasis* (paraphrase), *Metaphrasis* (translation from verse to prose or prose to verse), *Epitome* (abridgement), and *Imitatio* (imitation). He includes *Declamatio* (oral delivery) in his list but does not discuss it. Only the first method is recommended for use in grammar schools. Ascham reiterates his approbation of double translation, making clear that it is profitable not only for learning "the hard congruities of Grammer" but for "that which is greater also"–rhetoric. Ascham claims that "in marking dayly, and following diligentlie thus, the steppes of the best Autors, like inuention of Argumentes, like order in disposition [arrangement], like vtterance in Elocution [style], is easelie gathered vp." In other words, translation is a preparatory exercise for the later study of imitation.

Maturity in the full exercise of imitation, however, is beyond a schoolboy's capacity. Nonetheless, Ascham devotes the lion's share of the book to a discussion of imitation and the models appropriate for this exercise. In rhetorical imitation, as in all study, decorum is of prime importance. Here again Ascham evokes the analogy between shooting and eloquence. Decorum, he says, "is the hardest point, in all learning, so is it the fairest and onelie marke, that scholers, in all their studie, must alwayes shote at, if they purpose an other day to be, either sounde in Religion, or wise and discrete in any vocation of the common wealth." Ascham notes, by way of example, that while the German scholar and religious reformer Philip Melanchthon employed a "caulme kinde of speaking and writing" that was appropriate for "teaching, reading, and expounding plainlie and aptlie schole matters," his uncritical followers, lacking their master's judgment, also use "a style, cold, leane, and weake, though the matter be neuer so warme & earnest." According to principles of judgment and decorum, one must adapt and change models to accord with present needs and circumstances. Imitation, then, is the study of difference rather than apish conformity: it is "*dissimilis materiei similis tractatio* [a similar treatment of different material]: and also, *similis materiei dissimilis tractatio* [a different treatment of similar material]," says Ascham. He continues with an extensive treatment of the literature on rhetorical imitation.

While Ascham's methods of translation and imitation involve the whole province of rhetoric (invention, arrangement, style, memory, and, to a lesser degree, delivery), his most famous statement on rhetoric in *The Scholemaster* does reveal an emphasis on style: "Ye know not, what hurt ye do to learning, that care not for wordes, but for matter, and so make a deuorse betwixt the tong and the hart." Yet, for Ascham, a proper care of words always entails a fit match with the matter at hand. When he goes on to praise *De Oratore* as Cicero's best work, for example, it is for two equally important qualities: "good matter, and good handling of the matter."

Roger Ascham died in humble circumstances on 30 December 1568. His widow published his most famous work, the unfinished *Scholemaster,* in 1570. By 1589 it had gone through at least four more editions. Ascham's familiar epistles were published in 1576 as *Disertissimi viri Rogeri Aschami, Angli, Regiae maiestati non ita pridem a Latinis epistolis, familiarium epistolarum libri tres, magna orationis elegantia conscripti* and went into four editions in England and three abroad. In the same year Abraham Fleming published English translations of selected letters by Ascham in his *A Panoplie of Epistles, Or a looking Glasse for the vnlearned* (1576) as "presidents" for imitation, along with epistles by classical and Continental authors. The popularity of Ascham's epistles as

models for imitation testifies that, by his own standards, he succeeded as a rhetorician.

Letters:
Letters of Roger Ascham, translated by Maurice Hatch and Alvin Vos and edited by Vos (New York: Peter Lang, 1989).

Bibliographies:
Samuel A. Tannenbaum and Dorothy R. Tannenbaum, *Roger Ascham: A Concise Bibliography* (New York, 1946); republished in their *Elizabethan Bibliographies,* volume 1 (Port Washington, N.Y.: Kennikat Press, 1967), pp. 1–20;

Robert Carl Johnson, *Minor Elizabethans: Roger Ascham: 1946–1966; George Gascoigne: 1941–1966; John Heywood: 1944–1966; Thomas Kyd: 1940–1966; Anthony Munday: 1941–1966,* Elizabethan Bibliographies Supplements, no. 9 (London: Nether Press, 1968);

Jerome S. Dees, "Recent Studies in Ascham," *English Literary Renaissance,* 10, no. 2 (1980): 300–310;

Dees, *Sir Thomas Elyot and Roger Ascham: A Reference Guide* (Boston: G. K. Hall, 1981).

Biographies:
Lawrence V. Ryan, *Roger Ascham* (Stanford: Stanford University Press / Oxford: Oxford University Press, 1963);

John Hazel Smith, "Roger Ascham's Troubled Years," *Journal of English and Germanic Philology,* 65, no.1 (1966): 36–46.

References:
J. W. H. Atkins, "The Rhetoric of Tradition: Jewel, Wilson, Ascham," in his *English Literary Criticism: The Renascence* (London: Methuen: 1947), pp. 66–101;

Francis Bacon, *The Advancement of Learning,* in *The Works of Francis Bacon, Baron of Verulam, Viscount St. Alban, and Lord High Chancellor of England,* volume 3, edited by James Spedding, Robert Leslie Ellis, and Douglas Denon Heath (London: Longman/ Simpkin/Hamilton/Whittaker/J. Bain/E. Hodgson/ Washbourne/Richardson Brothers/Houlston/Bickers & Bush/Willis & Sotheran/J. Cornish/L. Booth/J. Snow/Aylott, 1859; Stuttgart: Friedrich Frommann Verlag Gunther Holzboog, 1963), pp. 253–491;

Thomas M. Greene, "Roger Ascham: The Perfect End of Shooting," *English Literary History,* 36, no. 4 (1969): 609–625;

Gabriel Harvey, *Ciceronianus,* translated by Clarence A. Forbes, introduction and notes by Harold S. Wilson, Studies in the Humanities, no. 4 (Lincoln: University of Nebraska, 1945);

Judith Rice Henderson, "'Vain Affectations': Bacon on Ciceronianism in *The Advancement of Learning*," *English Literary Renaissance*, 25, no. 2 (1995): 209–234;

Wilbur Samuel Howell, *Logic and Rhetoric in England, 1500–1700* (Princeton: Princeton University Press, 1956);

Anthony LaBranche, "Imitation: Getting in Touch," *Modern Language Quarterly*, 31, no. 3 (1970): 308–329;

William E. Miller, "Double Translation in English Humanistic Education," *Studies in the Renaissance*, 10 (1963): 163–174;

Linda Bradley Salamon, "*The Courtier* and *The Scholemaster*," *Comparative Literature*, 25, no. 1 (1973): 17–36;

Thomas O. Sloane, *On the Contrary: The Protocol of Traditional Rhetoric* (Washington, D.C.: Catholic University of America Press, 1997), pp. 152–162;

Marion Trousdale, "Recurrence and Renaissance: Rhetorical Imitation in Ascham and Sturm," *English Literary Renaissance*, 6, no. 2 (1976): 156–179;

Alvin Vos, "'Good Matter and Good Utterance': The Character of English Ciceronianism," *Studies in English Literature*, 19, no. 1 (1979): 3–18;

Vos, "Humanistic Standards of Diction in the Inkhorn Controversy," *Studies in Philology*, 73, no. 4 (1976): 376–396;

Foster Watson, *The English Grammar Schools to 1660: Their Curriculum and Practice* (Cambridge: Cambridge University Press, 1908), pp. 362–367, 407;

Harold Ogden White, *Plagiarism and Imitation During the English Renaissance: A Study in Critical Distinctions* (Cambridge, Mass.: Harvard University Press, 1935);

K. J. Wilson, "Ascham's *Toxophilus* and the Rules of Art," *Renaissance Quarterly*, 29, no. 1 (1976): 30–51;

Wilson, "Roger Ascham: Ciceronian Archery," *Incomplete Fictions: The Formation of English Renaissance Dialogue* (Washington, D.C.: Catholic University of America Press, 1985), pp. 109–135.

Papers:

There is a scribal preliminary draft of part of *The Scholemaster* in the British Library, as well as several of Roger Ascham's personal letters (including his letter books) and letters he wrote as royal secretary. The Folger Shakespeare Library, Washington, D.C., holds diplomatic letters by Queen Elizabeth I written in Ascham's hand, as well as a copy of *Toxophilus* that includes a presentation epistle addressed to Sir William Parr. Other such gift copies are at the Pierpont Morgan Library, New York, and at Cambridge University Library. Fair copies of Ascham's Latin translations of Oecumenius's anthology of commentary on Titus and Philemon, in his best italic hand, are at the Bodleian Library, Oxford University, and St. John's College Library, Cambridge, respectively (both works were published as appendices to *Apologia Doctissimi*). The majority of Ascham's remaining letters are in the Public Records Office, London; Cambridge University Library; Corpus Christi College and St. John's College, Cambridge; the Carl H. Pforzheimer Library, and the Harry Ransom Humanities Research Center, University of Texas at Austin.

Francis Bacon

(22 January 1561 – 9 April 1626)

Elizabeth Skerpan-Wheeler
Southwest Texas State University

See also the Bacon entry in *DLB 151: British Prose Writers of the Early Sixteenth Century.*

BOOKS: *Essayes. Religious Meditations. Places of perswasion and disswasion. Seene and allowed.* (London: Printed by John Windet for Humfrey Hooper, 1597); revised and enlarged as *The Essaies Of S͡t. Francis Bacon Knight, the Kings Solliciter Generall* (London: Printed by John Beale, 1612); revised and enlarged as *The Essayes Or Covnsels, Civill And Morall, Of Francis Lo. Vervlam, Viscovnt S͡t. Alban. Newly Enlarged* (London: Printed by John Haviland for Hanna Barret & Richard Whitaker, 1625);

A Letter written out of England to an English Gentleman remaining at Padua, containing a true Report of a strange Conspiracie, contriued betweene Edward Squire, lately executed for the same treason as Actor, and Richard Wallpoole a Iesuite, as Deuiser and Suborner against the person of the Queenes Maiestie, anonymous (London: Printed by the Deputies of Christopher Barker, 1599);

A Declaration of the Practises & Treasons attempted and committed by Robert late Earle of Essex and his Complices, against her Maiestie and her Kingdoms, and of the proceedings as well at the Arraignments & Conuictions of the said late Earle, and his adherents, as after: Together with the very Confessions and other parts of the Euidences themselues, word for word taken out of the Originals, anonymous (London: Printed by Robert Barker, 1601);

A Briefe Discovrse, Touching The Happie Vnion Of The Kingdomes Of England, And Scotland. Dedicated In Private To His Maiestie, anonymous (London: Printed by Richard Read for Faelix Norton & sold by William Aspley, 1603); republished as *The Union Of The Two Kingdoms Of Scotland And England: Or, The elaborate Papers of Sir Francis Bacon, Lord Verulam, Viscount of St. Alban, sometime High Chancellor of England; The greatest Sates-man* [sic] *of his Nation, and Scollar of his Age, concerning that Affair. Published in this form, for the publick satisfaction,* edited by Christopher Irvin (Edinburgh, 1670);

National Portrait Gallery, London

Sir Francis Bacon His Apologie, In Certaine imputations concerning the late Earle of Essex. Written to the right Honorable his very good Lord, the Earle of Deuonshire, Lord Lieutenant of Ireland (London: Printed by Richard Field for Felix Norton, 1604);

Certaine Considerations touching the better pacification and Edification of the Church of England: Dedicated to his most Excellent Maiestie, anonymous (London: Printed by Thomas Purfoot for Henriè Tomes, 1604);

The Tvvoo Bookes of Francis Bacon. Of the proficience and aduancement of Learning, diuine and humane. To the King (London: Printed by Thomas Purfoot & Thomas Creede for Henrie Tomes, 1605); translated and enlarged as *Opera Francisci Baronis De Vervlamio, Vice-Comitis Sancti Albani; Tomvs Primvs: Qui continet De Dignitate & Augmentis Scientiarum Libros IX. Ad Regem Svvm* (London: Printed by John Haviland, 1623); translated by Gilbert Wats as *Of The Advancement And Proficience Of Learning or the Partitions of Sciences. IX Bookes. Written in Latin by the Most Eminent, Illustrious & Famous Lord Francis Bacon Baron of Verulam Vicont S.ᵗ Alban Counsilour of Estate and Lord Chancellor of England. Interpreted by Gilbert Wats* (Oxford: Printed by Leonard Lichfield for Robert Young & Edward Forrest, 1640);

Francisci Baconi Eqvitis Avrati, Procvratoris Secvndi, Iacobi Regis Magnæ Britanniæ, De Sapientia Vetervm Liber, Ad Inclytam Academiam Cantabrigiensem (London: Printed by Robert Barker, 1609); translated by Arthur Gorges as *The Wisedome Of The Ancients, Written In Latine By the right Honourable Sir Francis Bacon Knight, Baron of Verulam, and Lord Chancelor of England. Done into English by Sir Arthur Gorges Knight* (London: Printed by John Bill, 1619);

The Charge of Sir Francis Bacon Knight, His Maiesties Attourney generall, touching Duells, vpon an information in the Star-chamber against Priest and Wright. With The Decree of the Star-chamber in the same cause (London: Printed by George Eld for Robert Wilson & sold by Robert Wilson & William Bladen, 1614);

Francisci De Verulamio Summi Angliae Cancelsaris Instauratio Magna. Multi pertransibunt & augebitur scienta (London: Printed by Bonham Norton & John Bill, 1620)—includes *Novum Organum* and *Parasceve ad Historiam Naturalem et Experimentalem*);

The Historie Of The Raigne of King Henry the Seuenth. Written By the Right Honourable, Francis, Lord Verulam, Viscount St. Alban (London: Printed by William Stansby for Matthew Lownes & William Barret, 1622);

Francisci Baronis De Vervlamio, Vice-Comitis Sancti Albani, Historia Natvralis Et Experimentalis Ad Condendam Philosophiam: Sive, Phænomena Vniversi: Quæ est Instau- *rationis Magnæ Pars Tertia* (London: Printed by John Haviland for Matthew Lownes & William Barret, 1622); translated by R. G. [Robert Gentili?] as *The Naturall And Experimental History of Winds, &c. Written in Latine by the Right Honorable Franics Lo: Verulam, Viscount St. Alban* (London: Printed for Humphrey Moseley & Thomas Dring, 1653);

Francisci Baronis De Vervlamio, Vice-Comitis Sancti Albani, Historia Vitae & Mortis. Sive, Titvlvs Secvndvs in Historia Naturali & Experimentali ad condendam Philosophiam: Quae est Instavrationis Magnae Pars Tertia Historia Vitae et Mortis (London: Printed by John Haviland for Matthew Lownes, 1623); translated anonymously as *The Historie of Life and Death. With Observations Naturall and Experimentall for the Prolonging of Life. Written by the Right Honorable Francis Lord Verulam, Viscount S. Alban* (London: Printed by John Okes for Humphrey Mosley, 1638);

Apophthegmes New And Old. Collected By The Right Honovrable, Francis Lo. Vervlam, Viscount St. Alban (London: Printed by John Haviland for Hanna Barret & Richard Whittaker, 1625);

Sylva Sylvarvm Or A Naturall Historie. In Ten Centuries. Written By The Right Honourable Francis Lo. Verulam Viscount St. Alban. Published after the Authors death, By William Rawley Doctor of Diuinitie, late his Lordships Chaplaine, edited by Rawley (London: Printed by John Haviland & Augustine Mathewes for William Lee, 1626)—includes *New Atlantis, Magnalia Naturae,* and *Praecipue Quoad Usus Humanos;*

Considerations Tovching A Warre with Spaine. Written by the Right Honourable Francis Lo. Verulam, Vi. S.ᵗ Alban (London, 1629);

Certaine Miscellany Works Of The Right Honovrable, Francis Lo. Verulam, Viscount S. Alban. Pvblished By William Rawley, Doctor of Diuinity, one of his Maiesties Chaplaines (London: Printed by John Haviland for Humphrey Robinson, 1629)—comprises *Considerations touching a vvarre with Spaine, An advertisement touching an holy vvarre,* and *An offer to our late soveraigne King Iames, of a digest to be made of the lawes of England;*

The Elements Of The Common Lawes of England, Branched into a double Tract: The One Contayning a Collection of some principall Rules and Maximes of the Common Law, with their Latitude and Extent. Explicated for the more facile Introduction of such as are studiously addicted to that noble Profession. The Other The Vse of the Common Law, for preseruation of our Persons, Goods, and good Names. According to the Lawes and Customes of this Land. By the late Sir Francis Bacon Knight, Lo: Verulam and Viscount S. Alban (London: Printed by Robert Young for the Assignes of John More, 1630);

Three Speeches of The Right Honorable, Sir Francis Bacon Knight, then his Majesties Sollicitor Generall, after Lord Verulam, Viscount Saint Alban. Concerning the Post-Nati, Naturalization of the Scotch in England, Vnion of the Lawes of the Kingdomes of England and Scotland. Published by the Authors Copy, and Licensed by Authority (London: Printed by Richard Badger for Samuel Broun, 1641);

Cases Of Treason. Written By Sir Francis Bacon, Knight, His Maiesties Solicitor Generall (London: Printed by the Assignes of John More & sold by Matthew Walbancke & William Coke, 1641); reprinted in part as *The Office of Constables. Written by Francis Bacon Knight, His Majesties Atturney Generall in the yeare of our Lord 1610. Being an Answer to the Questions proposed by Sir Alexander Hay, touching the Office of Constables. Declaring what power they have, and how they ought to be cherished in their Office* (London: Printed for Francis Coules, 1641);

A Wise and Moderate Discourse, Concerning Church-Affaires. As it was written, long since, by the famous Authour of those Considerations, which seem to have some reference to this. Now published for the common good (London, 1641); republished as *True Peace: Or A Moderate Discourse To Compose the unsettled Consciences, and Greatest Differences In Ecclesiastical Affaires. Written long since by the no less famous then Learned Sir Francis Bacon, Lord Verulam, Viscount St. Alban* (London: Printed for A. C., 1663);

A Confession Of Faith. Penned By an Orthodox man of the reformed Religion: Dedicated to some eminent Persons, now assembled in Parliament (London: Printed for William Hope, 1641);

A Speech Delivered By Sir Francis Bacon, In the lower House of Parliament quinto Iacobi, concerning the Article of Naturalization of the Scottish Nation (London, 1641);

The Learned Reading Of Sir Francis Bacon, One of the Maiesties learned Counsell at Law, upon the Statute of Uses: Being his double Reading to the Honourable Society of Grayes Inne. Published for the Common good (London: Printed for Matthew Walbancke & Lawrence Chapman, 1642);

Ordinances made By The Right Honourable Sir Francis Bacon Knight, Lord Verulam and Viscount of Saint Albans, being then Lord Chancellor. For the better and more regular Administration of Iustice in the Chancery, to be daily observed saving the Prerogative of this Covrt (London: Printed for Matthew Walbanke & Lawrence Chapman, 1642);

The Remaines Of The Right Honorable Francis Lord Verulam Viscount of St. Albanes, sometimes Lord Chancellor of England. Being Essayes and severall Letters to severall great Personages, and other pieces of various and high concernment not heretofore published. A Table whereof for the

Readers more ease is adjoyned (London: Printed by Bernard Alsop for Lawrence Chapman, 1648); republished as *The Mirrour of State and Eloqvence. Represented In the Incomparable Letters of the Famous St. Francis Bacon, Lord Verulam, St. Albans, to Queene Elizabeth, King James, and other Personages of the highest trust and honour in the three Nations of England, Scotland, and Ireland. Concerning the better and more sure Establishment of those Nations in the affaires of Peace and Warre. With an ample and admirable accompt of his Faith, written by the express Command of King Iames: Together with the Character of a true Christian, and some other adjuncts of rare Devotion* (London: Printed for Lawrence Chapman, 1656);

The Felicity Of Queen Elizabeth: And Her Times, With other Things; By the Right Honorable Francis Ld. Bacon Viscount St Alban (London: Printed by Thomas Newcomb for George Latham, 1651);

Resuscitatio, Or, Bringing into Publick Light Severall Pieces, Of The Works, Civil, Historical, Philosophical, & Theological, Hitherto Sleeping; Of the Right Honourable Francis Bacon Baron of Verulam, Viscount Saint Alban. According to the best Corrected Coppies. Together, With his Lordships Life. By William Rawley, Doctor of Divinity, His Lordships First, and Last, Chapleine. Afterwards, Chapleine, to His late Maiesty, edited by William Rawley (London: Printed by Sarah Griffin for William Lee, 1657); republished in part as *Several Letters Written By This Honourable Author, To Queen Elizabeth, King James, Divers Lords, and Others* (London: Printed by T. R. for William Lee, 1671);

Opuscula Varia Posthuma, Philosophica, Civilia, Et Theologia, Francisci Baconi, Baronis de Verulamio Vice-Comitis Sancti Albani, Nunc primum Edita. Cura & Fide Guilielmi Rawley, Sacrae Theologiae Doctoris, primo Dominationi suae, postea Serenissimae Majestati Regiae, a Sacris. Vna cum Nobilissimi Auctoris Vita, edited by William Rawley (London: Printed by Roger Daniel, 1658)—comprises "Historia densi & rari," "Opuscula sex philosophica simul collecta," "Opus illustre in felicem memoriam Elizabethae Angliae Reginae," and "Confessio fidei";

New Atlantis. A Work unfinished. Written by the Right Honorable Francis, Lord Verulam, Viscount St. Albans (London: Printed by Thomas Newcomb, 1659);

A Letter Of Advice Written by Sr. Francis Bacon To the Duke of Buckingham, When he became Favourite to King James, Never before Printed (London: Printed for R. H. & H. B., 1661);

A Charge Given by the most Eminent and Learned Sr. Francis Bacon Kt. Late Lord Chancellor of England, at a Sessions holden for the Verge, in the Reign of the Late King James. Declaring The Latitude of the Jurisdiction thereof, and the Offences therein inquireable, as well by the Com-

mon-Law, as by several Statutes herein particularly mentioned (London: Printed for Robert Pawley, 1662);

The Second Part Of The Resuscitatio Or A Collection Of several pieces of the Works Of the Right Honourable Francis Bacon, Baron of Verulam, and Viscount of St. Albans. Some of them formerly Printed in smaller Volumes, and being almost lost, are now Collected and put into Folio, with some of his other Pieces, which never yet was published. Collected By William Rawley Doctor of Divinity, his Lordships first and last Chaplain, and lately Chaplain in Ordinary to his Majesty, edited by William Rawley (London: Printed by S. G. & B. G. for William Lee, 1670); republished in part as *A Preparatory To The History Natural & Experimental. Written Originally in Latine, by the Right Honourable Francis Lord Verulam, Lord High Chancellour of England, and now faithfully rendred into Enlgish. By a Well-wisher to his Lordships Writings* (London: Printed by Sarah Griffing & Benjamin Griffing for William Lee, 1670);

Baconiana. Or Certain Genuine Remains of Sr. Francis Bacon, Baron of Verulam, and Viscount of St. Albans; In Arguments Civil and Moral, Natural, Medical, Theological, and Bibliographical; Now the First time faithfully Published. An Account of these Remains, and of all his Lordship's other Works, is given by the Publisher, in a Discourse by way of Introduction, edited by Thomas Tenison (London: Printed by J. D. for Richard Chiswell, 1679);

The Works of Francis Bacon, Baron of Verulam, Viscount St. Alban, Lord High Chancellor of England. In Four Volumes. With Several Additional Pieces, Never Before Printed in Any Edition of His Works. To Which Is Prefixed, a New Life of the Author, 4 volumes, edited by David Mallet (London: Printed for A. Millar, 1740);

The Works of Francis Bacon, Baron of Verulam, Viscount St. Alban, and Lord High Chancellor of England, 7 volumes, edited by James Spedding, Robert Leslie Ellis, and Douglas Denon Heath (London: Longman/ Simpkin/Hamilton/Whittaker/J. Bain/E. Hodgson/ Washbourne/ Richardson Brothers/ Houlston/ Bickers & Bush/Willis & Sotheran/J. Cornish/L. Booth/ J. Snow/Aylott, 1858–1861; 15 volumes, Boston: Brown & Taggard, 1860–1864);

The Promus of Formularies and Elegancies (Being Private Notes, Circ. 1594, Hitherto Unpublished), edited by Mrs. Henry Pott (London: Longmans, Green, 1883; Boston: Houghton, Mifflin, 1883);

Collotype Facsimile & Type Transcript of an Elizabethan Manuscript Preserved at Alnwick Castle, Northumberland, by Bacon, Thomas Radcliffe, Philip Sidney, and Robert Dudley, edited by Frank James Burgoyne (London, New York & Bombay: Longmans, Green, 1904)–includes "Of Tribute, or Giving

What Is Due," "Of Magnaminitie," "Advertisement Touching Private Censure," "Advertisement Touching the Controversies of the Church," and "Letter to a French Gentleman Touching the Proceedings in England in Ecclesiastical Causes";

Francis Bacon's Natural Philosophy: A New Source: A Transcription of Manuscript Hardwick 72A, with Translation and Commentary, BSHS Monograph Series, no. 5, edited by Graham Rees and Christopher Upton (Chalfont St. Giles, U.K.: British Society for the History of Science, 1984)–comprises *De viis mortis.*

Editions: *Francisci Baconi Baronis De Vervlamio, Vice-Comitis Sancti Albani, Operum Moralivm Et Civilivm Tomus. Qui continet: Historiam Regni Henrici Septimi, Regis Angliae. Sermones Fideles, sive Interiora Rerum. Tractatum de Sapientia Veterum. Dialogum de Bello Sacro. Et Novam Atlantidem. Ab ipso Honoratissimo Auctore, praeterquam in paucis, Latinitate donatus. Cura & Fide Guilielmi Rawley, Sacrae Theologiae Doctoris, olim Dominationi suae, nunc Serenissimae Majestati Regiae, a Sacris. In hoc volumine, iterum excusi, includuntur: Tractatus de Augmentis Scientiarum. Historia Ventorum. Historia Vitae & Mortis* (London: Printed by Edward Griffin & John Haviland & sold by Richard Whitaker & Joyce Norton, 1638);

History Naturall And Experimentall, Of Life and Death, Or Of the Prolongation of Life. Written in Latine by the Right Honorable Francis Lo. Verulam, Vis-Count S^t. Alban, translated and edited by William Rawley (London: Printed by John Haviland for William Lee & Humphrey Mosley, 1638);

Francisci Baconi De Verulamio Scripta In Naturali Et Vniversali Philosophia, edited by Isaac Gruterus (Amsterdam: Elzevir, 1653);

Francisci Baconi . . . opera omnia, quae extant, philosophica, moralia, politica, historica . . . in quibus complures alii tractatus, quos brevitatis causa praetermittere visum est, comprehensi sunt, hactenus nunquam conjunctim edita, jam vero summo studio collecta, uno volumine comprehensa, & ab innumeris mendis repurgata: cum indice rerum ac verborum universali absolutissimo. His praefixa est auctoris vita, edited by Johann Baptist Schonwetter (Frankfort am Main: Printed by Mathias Kempffer for Johann Baptist Schonwetter, 1665);

Francisci Baconi Baronis de Verulamio . . . Opera omnia, quatuor voluminibus comprehensa: hactenus edita, ad autographorum maxime fidem, emendantur; nonnulla etiam, ex MSS. codicibus deprompta, nunc primum prodeunt, 4 volumes, edited by John Blackbourne (London: R. Gosling, 1730);

The Philosophical Works of Francis Bacon, Baron of Verulam, Viscount St. Albans, and Lord High Chancellor of England; Methodized and Made English, from the Originals, with Occasional Notes, to Explain What Is Obscure, and Shew How Far the Several Plans of the Author, for

the Advancement of All Parts of Knowledge, Have Been Executed to the Present Time, 3 volumes, edited by Peter Shaw (London: J. J. & P. Knapton/D. Midwinter & A. Ward/A. Bettesworth & C. Hitch/ J. Pemberton/ Osborn & Longman/C. Rivington/F. Clay/J. Batley/R. Hett/T. Hatchett, 1733);

The Works of Francis Bacon: Baron of Verulam, Viscount St. Alban, and Lord High Chancellor of England, 5 volumes, edited by Thomas Birch (London: Printed for A. Millar, 1765);

The Works of Francis Bacon, Lord Chancellor of England: A New Edition, 16 volumes in 17, edited by Basil Montagu (London: William Pickering, 1825–1834);

The New Organon, and Related Writings, edited, with an introduction, by Fulton H. Anderson (New York: Liberal Arts Press, 1960);

"Cogitata et Visa de Interpretatione Naturae, sive de Scientia Operativa," "Tempus Partus Masculus, sive Instauratio Magna Inperii Humani in Argumentum," and "Redargutio Philosophiarum," translated by Benjamin Farrington in his *The Philosophy of Francis Bacon: An Essay on its Development from 1603 to 1609, with New Translation of Fundamental Texts* (Liverpool: University of Liverpool Press, 1964), pp. 59–72, 73–102, 103–133;

The History of the Reign of King Henry the Seventh, edited by F. J. Levy (New York: Bobbs-Merrill, 1972);

The Advancement of Learning, edited by G. W. Kitchin (London: Dent, 1973);

The Advancement of Learning, and New Atlantis, edited by Arthur Johnson (Oxford: Clarendon Press, 1974);

Gli 'Essayes' di Francis Bacon: Studio introduttivo, testo critico e commento, edited by Mario Melchionda (Florence: L. S. Olschki, 1979);

The Great Instauration; and, New Atlantis, edited by Jerry Weinberger (Arlington Heights, Ill.: AHM Publishing, 1980);

The Essayes or Counsels, Civill and Morall, edited by Michael Kiernan (Oxford: Clarendon Press, 1985; Cambridge, Mass.: Harvard University Press, 1985);

Novum Organum with Other Parts of the Great Instauration, translated and edited by Peter Urbach and John Gibson (Chicago: Open Court, 1994);

Francis Bacon, edited by Brian Vickers (Oxford & New York: Oxford University Press, 1996);

The Advancement of Learning, edited, with an introduction, by Kiernan (Oxford: Clarendon Press, 2000);

The New Organon, edited by Lisa Jardine and Michael Silverthorne (Cambridge & New York: Cambridge University Press, 2000).

OTHER: Descriptions of dumb-shows, in *Certaine Devises and shewes presented to her Maiestie by the Gentlemen of Grayes-Inne at her Highnesse Court in Greenewich, the twenty eighth day of Februarie in the thirtieth yeare of her Maiesties most happy Raigne,* by Thomas Hughes and others (London: Printed by Robert Robinson, 1587), pp. 11–12, 22, 33, 40–41;

The Translation Of Certaine Psalmes Into English Verse: By The Right Honovrable, Francis Lo. Vervlam, Viscount St. Alban, translated by Bacon (London: Printed by John Haviland for Hanna Barret & Richard Whittaker, 1625);

"The Vse Of The Law. Provided for Preservation of Our Persons. Goods, and Good Names. According to the Practise of The Lawes and Customes of this Land," attributed to Bacon, in *The Lawyers Light: Or, A due direction for the study of the Law,* by John Doddridge (London: Benjamin Fisher, 1629);

"Speeches of the Counsellors," in *Gesta Grayorum: Or, The History Of the High and mighty Prince, Henry Prince of Purpoole, Arch-Duke of Stapulia and Bernardia, Duke of High and Nether Holborn, Marquis of St. Giles and Tottenham, Count Palatine of Bloomsbury and Clerkenwell, Great Lord of the Cantons of Islington, Kentish-Town, Paddington and Knights-bridge, Knight of the most Heroical Order of Helmet, and Sovereign of the Same; Who Reigned and Died, A. D. 1594. Together With A Masque, as it was presented (by His Highness's Command) for the Entertainment of Q. Elizabeth; who, with the Nobles of both Courts, was present threat* (London: Printed for W. Canning, 1688), pp. 32–41;

Argument in Slade's Case, in "New Light on Slade's Case," in *The Legal Profession and the Common Law: Historical Essays,* by J. H. Baker (London: Hambledon, 1986), pp. 401–408;

"Aphorismi de jure gentium," edited and translated by Mark S. Neustadt in his "The Making of the Instauration: Science, Politics, and Law in the Career of Francis Bacon," dissertation, Johns Hopkins University, 1987;

"A Direccon for the Readinge of Histories with Profitt," in "Francis Bacon: An Unpublished Manuscript," by David Bergeron, *Papers of the Bibliographical Society of America,* 84 (1990): 397–404.

"The mind is the man, and the knowledge is the mind. A man is but what he knoweth. The mind itself is but an accident to knowledge, for knowledge is a double of that which is. The truth of being and the truth of knowing is all one." Thus has Brian Vickers rendered, in his critical edition of the major English works in the Oxford Authors Series, *Francis Bacon* (1996), the words that Sir Francis Bacon wrote in one of his earliest works, the device "Of Tribute; Or, Giving That Which is Due" (written 1595; published 1734). From his own time to the present, there has been much debate over exactly what is due to Bacon. In his *History of the Royal Society* (1667) Thomas Sprat hailed him as the father of modern science; late-nineteenth-century scholars derided his work as derivative and amateurish. More recent research, however, has restored his place as one of the most significant thinkers of the seventeenth century, one whose ideas signal the change from a Renaissance to a modern worldview. Bacon's grand vision of restructuring the whole of philosophy inspired such seventeenth-century educational reformers, scientists, and linguists as Jan Amos Comenius, Samuel Hartlib, John Webster, William Petty, and John Wilkins. His perceptions of the operation of the human mind continue to be cited by historians of science and literary critics alike. Although often believed to have been hostile to rhetoric, and certainly not a rhetorician in any formal sense in that he wrote no textbooks or treatises devoted strictly to the subject, Bacon nevertheless has come to be recognized as a significant theorist, whose works reveal striking and often highly original insights into the process of thought as it relates to language and persuasion. A prolific writer and chronic reviser, many of whose papers remain unpublished, Bacon wrote about rhetoric throughout his career. Philosopher, poet, prose stylist, theologian, jurist, and politician, Bacon combined theoretical knowledge with the practical experience of a man who made his living through speaking and writing well, and one who fully understood that equally important as the pursuit of knowledge was its communication.

For all his later prominence, relatively little is known about Bacon's early life. He was born on 22 January 1561 at York House in the Strand, London, the youngest child of Sir Nicholas Bacon, counselor to Queen Elizabeth I and lord keeper of the Great Seal, and the second surviving child of Anne Bacon, Sir Nicholas's second wife. She was one of the five daughters of Sir Anthony Cooke, the militantly Protestant humanist given the task of educating the future Edward VI. Highly educated in Greek and Latin, Lady Anne Bacon translated Bishop John Jewel's *Apologia Ecclesiae Anglicanae* (Apology for the Church of England, 1562); in terms of its influence, her work is regarded as one of the most important Tudor translations. Her sisters also married prominent men. Francis Bacon's uncles included Sir Thomas Hoby, author of a brilliant 1561

The eighteen-year-old Bacon in a miniature by Nicholas Hilliard. The Latin motto translates as "If I could only paint his mind" (Collection of the Duke of Rutland, Belvoir Castle).

translation of Baldassare Castiglione's *Il Libro del Cortegiano* (The Book of the Courtier, 1528), and Sir William Cecil, who was created Baron Burghley in 1571 and served as lord high treasurer to Elizabeth I from 1572 to 1598. Nicholas Bacon had six surviving children from his first marriage, to Jane Farley: Elizabeth, Edwarde, Nicholas, Nathaniell, Anne, and Henry Nevell. Francis and his older brother, Anthony, were educated at home, tutored from 1566 to 1569 by John Walsall, who also served as chaplain to Sir Nicholas. In April 1573 Francis matriculated at Trinity College, Cambridge, where he was tutored by John Whitgift, later archbishop of Canterbury. According to Whitgift's accounts, among the classical authors and works Bacon studied were Cicero, Demosthenes, Hermogenes, Aristotle's *Rhetoric,* and the *Rhetorica ad Herennium* (Rhetoric to Herennias)—most of the significant classical rhetoricians and texts known to the Renaissance. At Christmas 1575 Bacon went down from Cambridge, and on 27 June 1576 he entered Gray's Inn. He did not remain there long, however. In September 1576 he went to Paris to serve with Sir Amyas Paulet, the English ambassador, returning to England after his father's death on 20 February 1579. Sir Nicholas's death was sudden: he had not yet completed a financial settlement for his youngest son. Hence, Francis, at the age of eighteen, returned to Gray's Inn to enter law as a profession. His legal career progressed rapidly: he became an *utter barrister* (a full member of the profession) in 1582; a *bencher* (senior member of the Inn) in 1586; *reader* (lecturer at the Inn) in 1587; and a double reader in 1600. His political career began at the same time, with his election as member of Parliament for Bossiney (Cornwall) in 1581, and for Weymouth and Melcombe Regis (Dorsetshire) in 1584. By 1591 he was associated with Robert Devereaux, second Earl of Essex. At the age of thirty, Bacon was at the center of late Elizabethan political life.

This same period marked the beginning of Bacon's literary life. From around 1589 to 1605 Bacon wrote occasional pieces, both entertainments and works of counsel, that circulated in manuscript, such as the three letters that comprise "Advice to the Earl of Rutland on His Travels" (circa 1596), first collected in volume two of James Spedding's *The Letters and the Life of Francis Bacon Including All His Occasional Works* (1861), and "Advice to Fulke Greville on His Studies" (circa 1599), first published by Vernon F. Snow in *The Huntington Library Quarterly* (1960), and re-edited by Vickers in his 1996 edition. These manuscript works formed the basis of his later, published books. Ideas, words, and phrases from "Advice to the Earl of Rutland on His Travels" and "Advice to Fulke Greville on His Studies," for example, reappear in *The Tvvoo Bookes of Francis Bacon. Of the proficience and aduancement of Learning, diuine and humane. To the King* (1605), better known as *The Advancement of Learning,* and its later, Latin revision, *Opera Francisci Baronis De Vervlamio, Vice-Comitis Sancti Albani; Tomvs Primvs: Qui continet De Dignitate & Augmentis Scientiarum Libros IX* (Works of Francis Baron of Verulam, Viscount St. Alban: Volume One: Which Contains The Worthiness & Advancement of Learning in Nine Books, 1623), better known as *De Dignitate & Augmentis Scientiarum.* In his early manuscript works, Bacon reveals a preference for the set speech as a method for organizing his ideas, a practice that extends to *The Advancement of Learning,* itself organized as a formal, if long, oration. For Bacon, then, the discipline of rhetoric was fundamental to his approach to composition and communication; whatever his subsequent critiques of rhetoric, readers should remember that he wrote from inside its traditions.

Nowhere is his traditional training clearer than in "Promus of Formularies and Elegancies," a manuscript notebook Bacon prepared for his own use beginning in December 1594. Running about forty quarto pages, it is a collection of sayings drawn from such varied places as the Bible; Latin poets; Desiderius Erasmus's *Adagiorum collectanea* (Collection of Adages, 1500); proverbs in English, French, Spanish, and Italian; and some sentences apparently of Bacon's own composition. The manuscript is now in the British Library. Excerpts were published in volume seven (1861) of *The Works of Francis Bacon, Baron of Verulam, Viscount St. Alban, and Lord High Chancellor of England* (1858–1861), the standard edition of Bacon's works, edited by Spedding, Robert Leslie Ellis, and Douglas Denon Heath. The full text of "Promus of Formularies and Elegancies" was first published in 1883, edited by Mrs. Henry Pott, who attempted to use the text to prove Bacon's authorship of the works of William Shakespeare. In his preface to the excerpts, Spedding characterized the notebook as an "exercise in the art of expression," and the collection certainly provides evidence of the way Bacon's mind operated. Moreover, some of the material definitely found its way into his later published works, notably *De Dignitate & Augmentis Scientiarum.* One such group, included in Spedding's edition, is a series of "lesser forms of oratory," phrases to be used in introductions, conclusions, and other parts of a formal speech. Another is a list of *antitheses*—positive and negative arguments on a series of topics—and *formulae,* defined by Bacon as "decent and apt passages and conveyances of speech, which may serve indifferently for differing subjects." His subsequent published work shows that Bacon used this notebook as other Renaissance and seventeenth-century writers used theirs: as a storehouse of useful quotations and ready phrases for future compositions.

Bacon's first published remarks on language and rhetoric appear in 1597. Printed to forestall unauthorized publication, *Essayes. Religious Meditations. Places of perswasion and disswasion. Seene and allowed,* the first edition of Bacon's essays was, according to the seventeenth-century biographer John Aubrey in his *Lives of Eminent Men* (1813), "a little booke no bigger than a primer." It was published with two other short works: *Religious Meditations* and *Places of Perswasion and Disswasion,* the latter better known by its subtitle as *Of the Colours of Good and Evil.* Both the *Essayes* and *Religious Meditations* are collections of short pieces, pithy and aphoristic, designed to present received wisdom in such a way as to encourage reflection, as readers consider the connections and contradictions among the aphorisms. Unlike the modern essay, the Baconian essay of 1597 presents no formal conclusion or single, reasoned argument. It is an open-ended form.

Two of the ten essays of 1597 concern language and rhetoric: "Of Studies" and "Of Discourse." In "Of Studies," Bacon collects insights into the value of reading, revealing a theme that was a constant in his thought: the need for practical application of learning in a public world. As Bacon characterizes them, in Vickers's 1996 critical edition, "Studies serve for pastimes, for ornaments, and for abilities. Their chief use for pas-

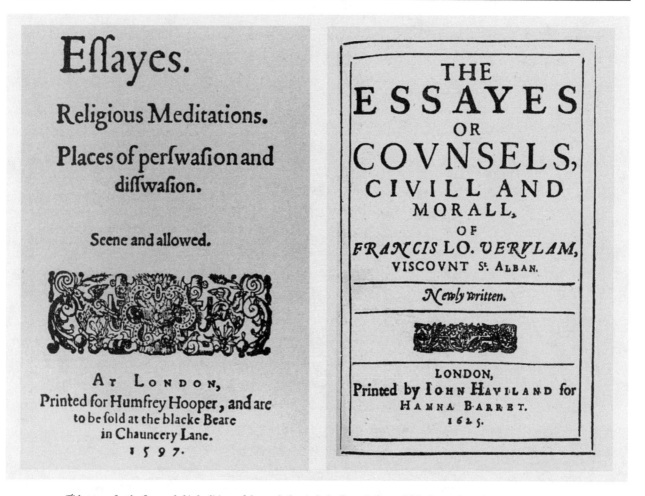

Title pages for the first and third editions of the work that includes Bacon's first published remarks on language and rhetoric

time is in privateness and retiring; for ornament is in discourse, and for ability is in judgment." In this explanation logic strengthens the judgment, while rhetoric concerns ornamentation. Further, "History makes men wise, poets witty; . . . logic and rhetoric able to contend." Bacon thus assigns argumentation to both logic and rhetoric, revealing his earliest assumptions about both disciplines. A similar division of labor occurs in "Of Discourse." There, readers are reminded that "Discretion of speech is more than eloquence, and to speak agreeably to him with whom we deal is more than to speak in good words or in good order." Bacon thus equates eloquence with ornamentation, while he leaves to "discretion" such important considerations as knowing the decorum of the situation; the ability of one's audience; when to be silent; how to blend argument, questions, anecdotes, and jokes; and how many examples to use.

Similar assumptions govern *Of the Colours of Good and Evil,* a so-called *promptuary* (storehouse or commonplace book) of the figures of speech of deliberative rhet-

oric. Also appearing in Vickers's 1996 edition, this fragmentary treatise, overtly declaring its debt to Aristotle's *Rhetoric,* explains "colours" as the shapes a rhetorician gives his arguments, not the arguments themselves–the shapes that make an argument appear good or bad to "a weak man, or . . . a wise man not fully and considerately attending and pondering the matter." In reading the promptuary, one may learn to recognize the colors and know their truths and fallacies in order to separate them from the matter of what is being argued. This practice ultimately "cleareth man's judgment" to protect him from error.

These early treatises illustrate Bacon's divergence from the classical practice of dividing rhetoric into five parts: invention, arrangement, elocution or style, memory, and delivery. For Bacon, invention and arrangement of arguments definitely belong to logic, while the articulation of arguments, their artful expression, is the sphere of rhetoric. In this practice Bacon follows the educational reformers of the Renaissance, notably the fifteenth-century Dutch humanist Roelof Huysman

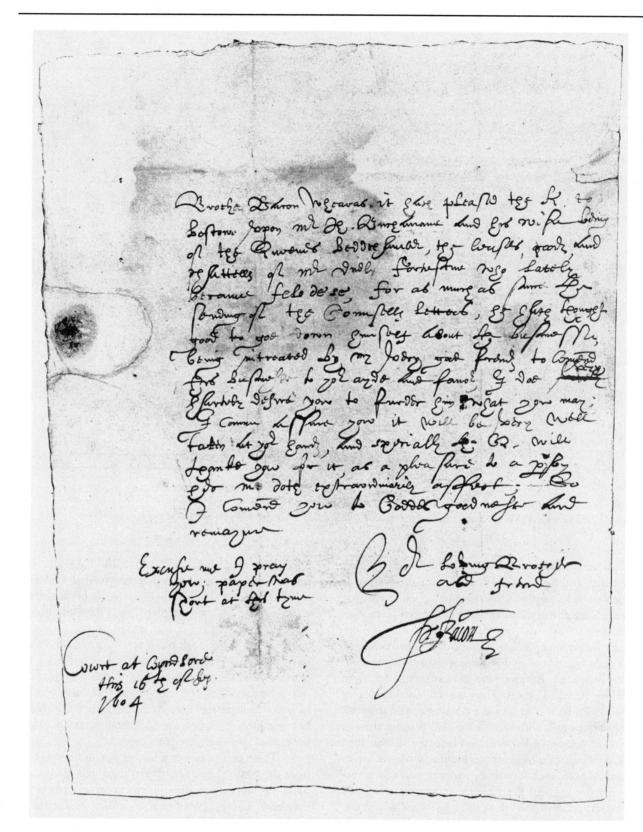

Letter from Bacon to his half brother Sir Nicholas Bacon (Pierpont Morgan Library)

(Rodolphus Agricola) and especially the French philosopher and logician Pierre de La Ramée (Petrus Ramus), Bacon's near contemporary, who saw the most important function of discourse as the clear communication of information in the service of truth. To these writers, therefore, any intellectual inquiry must be governed by logic; persuasion, the province of rhetoric, was a secondary concern.

Bacon's concern with rhetoric and public argument during the 1590s corresponded to the demands of his public life. In 1593 his eloquent opposition in Parliament to the Triple Subsidy Bill, a sharp increase in taxes demanded by the queen, severely alienated Elizabeth I and threatened to end his career of public service. Some scholars see the year as a watershed in Bacon's intellectual development: from this period onward, his writings show a bifurcation in thought, one group concerning itself with the practicalities of the public world, the other increasingly interested in a vision of a reformed, improved future world. Certainly, his practical writings of the 1590s address the needs of a public servant on the outs with a royal patron. From 1595 to 1600 he joined his brother, Anthony, in the informal service of the earl of Essex, in return for patronage. His letters reveal attempts to counsel Essex, urging prudent action. Essex's failure as lord lieutenant and governor general of Ireland to quell the uprising led by Hugh O'Neill, third Earl of Tyrone, however, caused Bacon to distance himself from the earl's political ambitions. Disgraced, Essex attempted to seize the queen and force her to dismiss his rivals in February of 1601, a coup that failed miserably. At the queen's request, in the winter of 1601 Bacon joined in the prosecution of the earl for treason. Seen by some contemporaries and biographers as evidence of double-dealing, Bacon's counsels may also be understood as sincere efforts to help a friend, by a man who knew the distinction between loyalty and folly. Certainly Bacon felt the need to explain his actions, publishing *Sir Francis Bacon His Apologie, In Certaine imputations concerning the late Earle of Essex. Written to the right Honorable his very good Lord, the Earle of Deuonshire, Lord Lieutenant of Ireland* in 1604. In any case, his fortunes were shortly to improve. Anthony Bacon died several months after Essex's execution, leaving his brother his property, and on 24 March 1603 Elizabeth I died, thereby clearing the way for Bacon's subsequent rise in power.

The decade following the Essex trial was marked by a notable increase in Bacon's literary output. Three works from this period extend his inquiries into logic and rhetoric: the manuscript work "Valerius Terminus: Of the Interpretation of Nature with the Annotations of Hermes Stella" (circa 1603), first published in 1734 and included in volume three (1859) of Spedding's edition

of the *Works; The Advancement of Learning,* published in 1605; and *De Sapientia Veterum* (1609; translated as *The Wisedome Of The Ancients,* 1619). Presented as the work of a fictitious philosopher and a fictitious annotator, "Valerius Terminus" is the fragmentary exploration of ideas that find their full expression in *The Advancement of Learning* and *Novum Organum,* the latter work first published in *Francisci De Verulamio Summi Angliae Cancelsaris Instauratio Magna. Multi pertransibunt & augebitur scientia* (Francis of Verulam Lord Chancellor of England's Great Instauration, in Which Many Things Are Inquired into and the Number of Things that Are Known, Increased, 1620). Influenced by Aristotle—as interpreted by Ramus—in "Valerius Terminus," Bacon declares the practical end of science as helping human life, its goal to expand the scope of human knowledge, and outlines the foundations of a new method of inquiry. To learn properly, one must become aware of the processes of thought, the ways by which the mind knows. To this end, Bacon sets forth his earliest, somewhat sketchy examination of the four idols of thought, what he defines as the "inward elenches [logical fallacies] of the mind."

His analyses of these idols, or mental impediments, lead Bacon to a critique of rhetoric as a way of knowing, since it is unsuitable as a means of inquiry. When misapplied, rhetoric contributes to "the great error of inquiring knowledge in Anticipations." Anticipations are:

> the voluntary collections that the mind maketh of knowledge; which is every man's reason. That though this be a solemn thing, and serves the turn to negotiate between man and man (because of the conformity and participation of men's minds in the like errors), yet towards inquiry of the truth of things and works it is of no value. . . . Of the nature of words and their facility and aptness to cover and grace the defects of Anticipations. That it is no marvel if these Anticipations have brought forth such diversity and repugnance in opinions, theories, or philosophies, as so many fables of several arguments.

Rhetoric deals in commonplaces drawn from widely held beliefs and is one of the necessities of public life and communication. As does music, it can bring listeners into direct contact with sensations and ideas without the mediation of "allusions." However, because it deals with probability and contingency, received wisdom and custom, rhetoric cannot serve as the ground upon which to build any method of invention. Following the medieval nominalists, Bacon assumes that true knowledge must then arise from direct intuition, without the mediation of words.

Scientific, true language should strive to be non-metaphorical. In common use, however, language must resort to metaphor to communicate meaning. In *De Sapientia Veterum,* dedicated to the University of Cambridge and its chancellor, his cousin Robert Cecil, Earl of Salisbury, Bacon analyzes Greek myths as metaphorical explanations of wisdom. As hieroglyphics prefigure letters, so parables prefigure arguments. They may disguise meaning, but they may also aid the grasp of the subject. Hence, the story of Cassandra becomes an object lesson in the need for care in giving advice and knowing when to speak. The Sphinx stands for science, monstrous to the ignorant but comprehensible and conquerable by those with the patience to examine it. The dual character of Orpheus's singing represents the dual nature of philosophy. In its ability to overcome the king of the underworld, the song embodies natural philosophy in its ability to restore human knowledge. In its ability to draw the beasts together, the song corresponds to moral and civil philosophy that teaches human beings to live and work together. Persuasion and the search for knowledge are thus separate functions.

The ideas in these two works reach their first full articulation in *The Advancement of Learning.* Dedicated to King James I, *The Advancement of Learning* marks a crucial step in Bacon's grand program for the reformation of knowledge, the project he pursued for the rest of his life. As its entry in the Stationers' Company Register suggests, he intended to publish the work in both English and Latin, the international language of scholarship. This Latin version, greatly expanded, did not appear until 1623. The English version betrays a certain unfinished quality, as does much of Bacon's work, which he constantly revised and imported into new works. In his note on the text, Vicars calls it "the most chaotically printed of Bacon's works," and his 1996 edition lists some variant readings and emends Speddings's standard text somewhat. *The Advancement of Learning* is divided into two books. The first is a formal defense and praise of knowledge, the *res,* or matter of the treatise; the second is a survey of the state of knowledge at the present time, noting areas of deficiency with an eye toward their eventual improvement—the *verba,* or illustration and amplification of the argument. In the dedication Bacon invokes Plato to defend his project: "all knowledge is but remembrance, and that the mind of man by nature knoweth all things, and hath but her own native and original notions (which by the strangeness and darkness of this tabernacle of the body are sequestered) again revived and restored. . . ." The intent of his project, then, is "to clear the way" for learning by identifying errors and misunderstandings so that they may be dispelled.

Book 1 is organized as an *epideictic* oration: a formal praise of learning, supported in true humanistic fashion by testimony, illustrations, and examples drawn from ancient and modern authors. Its first part defends knowledge from the prejudices against it deriving from religion, politics, and learning itself. The attack from religion essentially charges that desire for knowledge was the cause of the Fall, that continued pursuit of knowledge leads one to heresy, and that studies distract one from the contemplation and worship of God. Conceding that "superficial" knowledge may indeed give rise to these ills, Bacon argues that true, deep inquiry into nature will lead to God: "for in the entrance of philosophy, when the second causes, which are next unto the senses, do offer themselves to the mind of man, if it dwell and stay there, it may induce some oblivion of the highest cause; but when a man passeth on farther, and seeth the dependence of causes and the works of Providence; then, according to the allegory of the poets, he will easily believe that the highest link of nature's chain must needs be tied to the foot of Jupiter's chair." The attack from the world of politics—that study makes one soft and weak, unready for the discipline of war and public debate—Bacon answers with extensive examples of the compatibility of arms and letters, showing how learning makes subjects more governable, leaders more apt to lead in civilized ways. The criticism arising from learning itself needs more extensive examination and careful refutation. Easily dismissing objections based on learned men's relative poverty and frequently harsh manners, arguing that the first is "not in their power" and the second "accidental," or extraneous, Bacon turns his attention to the "errors and vanities" arising from studies themselves. These are the most serious charges, for they impede the search for truth. They must be recognized in order to be purged.

Bacon identifies three "vanities in studies": "fantastical learning; . . . contentious learning; and . . . delicate learning; vain imaginations, vain altercations, and vain affectations." Fantastical learning involves direct deception, both the act of deceiving and the willingness to be deceived. Under this category Bacon discusses the dangers of the pseudosciences: astrology, alchemy, and natural magic. This kind of learning is the most dangerous of the three "vanities" because it undermines "the essential form of knowledge, which is nothing but a representation of truth." Contentious learning is the pursuit of "vain matter," the mind working on itself, like a spider spinning a web, rather than the matter of the world. It becomes entirely self-referential. "Delicate learning" is ultimately an indictment of misdirected rhetoric, originating in the study of ancient authors and churchmen more for their elegance of expression than for their substance. The result was "an affectionate study of eloquence and copie of speech, which . . . grew speedily to an excess; for men began to hunt more after words than matter; and more after the choiceness of the phrase, and the round and clean composition of the sentence, and the sweet falling of the clauses, and the varying and illustration of their works with tropes and figures, than after the weight of matter, worth of subject, soundness of argument, life of invention, or depth of judgment." In sum, delicate learning occurs "when men study words and not matter." These statements, however, do not indicate an overall contempt for words or rhetoric. Truth presented unadorned may actually hinder intellectual inquiry by giving too quick satisfaction to the mind; truth as adorned by eloquence appears in such a way that it is accessible for use in public service, counsel, and persuasion. Rhetoric may be subordinate to logic in Bacon's view, but it is nevertheless essential in civic life. Book 1 concludes with an extensive praise of learning as Bacon describes its value, both to the general public and to the individual.

In book 2, Bacon undertakes a complete anatomy of the state of knowledge, identifying its parts and discussing the relationships among the parts. His explanation of the function and value of rhetoric is to be found here, within Bacon's discussion of human learning. The parts of human learning correspond to the three parts of understanding: history, which concerns memory; poetry, which engages the imagination; and philosophy, which addresses the reason. In its turn, philosophy itself divides into three subjects: God, nature, and man himself. "Man" may be understood in the "congregate, or in society," or in the "segregate" (as an individual). The individual consists of body and mind. Mind itself may be separated into substance and faculties. Substance involves inquiries into the nature of the soul and is best governed by religion. The faculties are the functions of the mind; the knowledge of the faculties is of two kinds. The first concerns understanding and reason, which produce general laws and principles; the second "Will, Appetite, and Affection," which produce action. Both kinds are also affected by imagination: "Sense sendeth over to Imagination before Reason have judged: and Reason sendeth over to Imagination before the Decree can be acted: for Imagination ever precedeth Voluntary Motion." Imaginative reason is the province of rhetoric; because it is reason influenced by imagination, rather than imagination informed by reason, Bacon therefore assigns rhetoric to reason and logic rather than to poetry.

The faculties of the mind are rational and moral. The moral faculties belong to the sphere of ethics and moral knowledge. The rational faculties are governed by four arts: "Art of Inquiry or Invention; Art of Examination or Judgment; Art of Custody or Memory; and

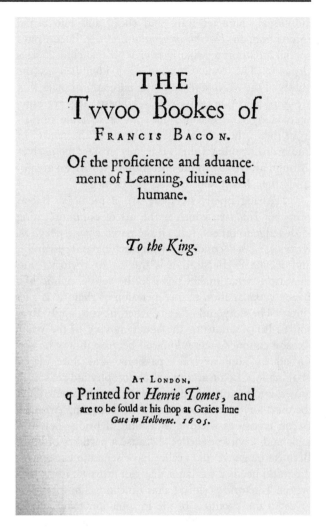

THE
Tvvoo Bookes of
FRANCIS BACON.

Of the proficience and aduancement of Learning, diuine and
humane.

To the King.

AT LONDON,
¶ Printed for *Henrie Tomes*, and
are to be fould at his fhop at Graies Inne
Gate in Holborne. 1 6 0 5.

Title page for the work that includes the first part of Bacon's projected "Great Instauration" of knowledge

Art of Elocution or Tradition." While these arts may look like four of the traditional five parts of rhetoric, Bacon's explanations clearly show that they are not. True invention, he says, is the discovery of new knowledge; invention as the rhetoricians understand it merely means recalling what one already knows by means of preparation, or collection of knowledge, and suggestion, or prompting by means of commonplaces or topics. Such invention is properly considered ornament, and thus truly rhetoric.

Judgment similarly belongs to logic, not rhetoric. It concerns proofs, and here Bacon discusses logical fallacies, the *elenches,* and the fallacies produced by the operation of the mind. This discussion becomes the second version of Bacon's idols of the mind. These *elenchi magni* (great fallacies) arise because the mind is not truly a mirror held up to nature but "an enchanted glass, full of superstition and imposture." The idols develop from individual character traits and social and intellectual convention. In *The Advancement of Learning,* Bacon pays special attention to what in later works, such as *Novum Organum* (The New Organon), are identified as the "Idols of the Market-place": "the false appearances that are imposed upon us by words." These idols are especially dangerous because one cannot separate oneself from them: they are an essential part of the nature of human beings. Individuals can only protect themselves through awareness of the operation of words, an area of study that Bacon finds notably deficient.

Passing briefly over the art of memory, Bacon turns to *Tradition,* which is the art of communicating knowledge to others. It has three parts: *organ* (speech or writing), *method* (concerned with teaching and research), and *illustration.* Illustration is the art of rhetoric, and rhetoric is what makes possible the active, public life. Bacon's explanation of the operation of rhetoric is succinct: "The duty and office of Rhetoric is to apply Reason to Imagination for the better moving of the will." Reason cannot function by itself because it may be disturbed by sophistry, the passions, and unregulated imagination. Logic and moral philosophy aid reason in governing the first two disruptive forces; for controlling the third force, reason needs rhetoric. Following Aristotle, Bacon envisions rhetoric as a kind of bridge between logic and "civil knowledge" because it partakes of both. Because language and reality have separate existences, the mind needs a mediator that can translate ideas into action. Rhetoric performs that function. The shapes it gives to the products of the imagination makes them more attractive to the will, which may then be prompted to action.

The Advancement of Learning makes a significant contribution to contemporary understanding of rhetoric. In its systematic presentation of the fields of knowledge, it locates rhetoric firmly in the domain of reason, subordinate to logic but essential to it. Although rhetoric is ornamentation, Bacon condemns the judgment of Plato and others that such ornamentation belongs with the arts of cookery and cosmetics. Such arts may be pleasant, but they are inessential. Rhetoric, however, is an essential component of civil life. It bridges the gulf between knowledge and action. Bacon's sense of decorum separates rhetoric from the discovery or transmission of the knowledge gained by science, which is not or should not be concerned with persuasion or action, and Bacon's foremost concern is with science. Still, rhetoric plays a crucial role in human psychology, and Bacon's is one of the clearest, postclassical explanations of the way rhetoric works.

Following the publication of *The Advancement of Learning,* Bacon became a prominent public figure. He continued to improve his financial situation; in 1606, at the age of forty-five, he married fourteen-year-old Alice Barnham, daughter and heiress of Benedict Barnham, a former alderman of London. The marriage produced no children. Although it was common knowledge among his contemporaries that Bacon was homosexual, the marriage was generally regarded as successful; in a biographical essay first published in 1657 and republished in volume one (1858) of Spedding's edition of the *Works,* his secretary, editor, and early biographer William Rawley reports "his good usage of his consort . . . whom he prosecuted with much conjugal love and respect, with many rich gifts and endowments." He virtually disinherited her shortly before his death, however, probably because she had begun an affair with her gentleman-usher (gentleman performing ceremonial functions in the household of a person of rank), Sir John Underhill, whom she subsequently married, and whom, Aubrey remarked, "she made deafe and blinde with too much of Venus." During the early years of his marriage, Bacon put his improved finances to use, in 1607 becoming a founder of the Newfoundland Company, and in 1609 a founder of the Virginia Company.

During this time Bacon's political fortunes improved as well. A vigorous defender of the king's prerogative, Bacon was named attorney general in 1613. Subsequently, in 1616 he was chief prosecutor in one of the most sensational trials of the day, the trial of Robert Carr, Earl of Somerset, the fallen favorite of James I, for the murder of Sir Thomas Overbury. Attracting the attention and influence of the king's new favorite, George Villiers, first Earl of Buckingham, Bacon was made privy councillor and, in 1617, lord keeper of the seal, his father's old office. On 4 January 1618 he became lord chancellor, enforcing the law and suppressing prominent dissidents, including Sir Walter Ralegh and Thomas Howard, Earl of Suffolk. Finally, on 12 July 1618 he was created Baron of Verulam and entered the House of Lords.

Despite his public activities, Bacon managed to progress further in his great project. In 1620 he published the first parts of his *Instauratio Magna,* including a preface, plan for the work, *Novum Organum,* and *Parasceve ad Historiam Naturalem et Experimentalem* (Preparative to a Natural and Experimental History). Published in Latin, and translated in volume one of Spedding's edition of the *Works,* these works mark Bacon's effort to contribute to the world scientific community, and include continued discussion of language and rhetoric. In his dedication of the work to King James, Bacon repeats his long-established goal of reconstructing the whole of philosophy from its foundations so that it may be purged of all mistakes and falsity for the benefit of the entire human race. As he explains in the plan of the work, the Great Instauration is to have six parts. The first, "The

Divisions of the Sciences," will be a summary description of all learning, both what it is and what it ought to be. It is not included in this volume; instead, Bacon refers readers to book 2 of *The Advancement of Learning* for a general idea of what the part is intended to be. Part 2 is "The New Organon; or Directions concerning the Interpretation of Nature," included in its entirety in the volume. Its role is to design a better use for human reason, grounded in a new kind of logic, differing from ordinary logic in its end, order of demonstrations, and starting point. The end is the actual invention of new arts, discovery of new first principles, and outlining of new directions in study. The order of demonstrations introduces Bacon's principle of induction. The old method of demonstration through syllogisms is unsuitable to the new sciences, Bacon argues, in Spedding's translation, because it is grounded ultimately in words, "the tokens and signs of notions," which may well be faulty. Induction, on the other hand, is grounded in the direct experience of the senses, progressing from simple to general axioms. The starting point of the new logic will be the examination of every assumption, as all assumptions derive ultimately from the senses, which may both deceive and inform. Assumptions are to be tested by experimentation and examined for the influence of the idols of the mind. The third part was to be "The Phenomena of the Universe; or a Natural and Experimental History for the Foundation of Philosophy," a compendium of natural histories designed to provide the solid base of observations necessary to the new philosophy. Never completed, it is represented in the volume by the *Parasceve ad Historiam Naturalem et Experimentalem,* which comprises preliminary remarks, a collection of axioms, and an outline of the histories to be included.

Three other proposed parts exist only in the descriptions of the plan. The fourth part, to be called "The Ladder of the Intellect," was to provide examples of invention and inquiry, as Bacon observes that learning of abstract concepts progresses rapidly when coupled with examples. The fifth part, "The Forerunners; or Anticipations of the New Philosophy," was to be only temporary, to serve until the great project was completed. It was to include Bacon's personal discoveries, designed to help the understanding. The sixth and most important part would have been the culmination of all the rest: "The New Philosophy; or Active Science." Considering its scope, Bacon expresses his belief that such an endeavor cannot be completed in his lifetime. It will be the continuing project of future ages.

The volume thus practically begins with the *Novum Organum.* In form, the work is a compendium of aphorisms, arranged in two books. The second book focuses specifically upon observations of and experi-

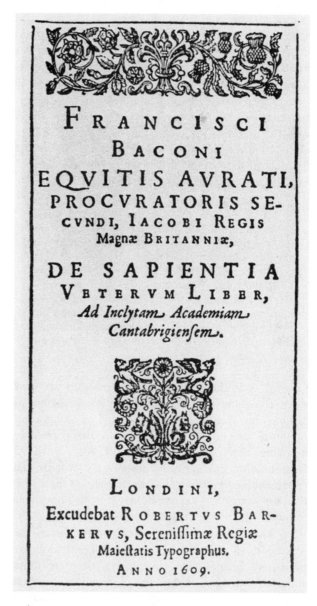

Title page for Bacon's work on logic and rhetoric that was translated in 1619 as The Wisedome Of The Ancients

ments with the natural world. The first book explores human understanding. Here occur the famous explanations of the four "Idols of the Mind," now fully defined and explored. An understanding of the idols is crucial to any development of a new science; otherwise, one may simply be building upon error. The first two may be considered innate, arising from the nature of the human mind. "Idols of the Tribe" derive from the operation of the mind, with its tendency to seek out abstractions. The "Idols of the Cave" derive from the nature of the individual, especially that individual's own prejudices. Human beings become attached to their own thoughts and knowledge, often becoming unwilling to question them and blind to their operations. The weapon against these idols is skepticism: "let every student of nature take this as a rule,–that whatever his mind seizes and dwells upon with peculiar satisfaction is to be held in suspicion."

The remaining two idols are external to the person but may interfere more severely than the others with the perception of truth. The most problematic of all four are the "Idols of the Market-place," those that develop "through the alliances of words and names." Words have a peculiar effect on reason:

> For men believe that their reason governs words; but it is also true that words react on the understanding; and this it is that has rendered philosophy and the sciences sophistical and inactive. Now words, being commonly framed and applied according to the capacity of the vulgar, follow those lines of division which are most obvious to the vulgar understanding. And whenever an understanding of greater acuteness or a more diligent observation would alter those lines to suit the true divisions of nature, words stand in the way and resist the change.

Careful definitions are really no solution, as they themselves consist of words. Words are the names of notions, but if they are not grounded in observation they may take on a life of their own so that there may be names of things that do not exist. Also, words of long-standing but imprecise usage may obscure the true meaning of a thing. The more abstract the word, the more likely it is to have deviated from a notion as intuited.

The "Idols of the Theater" derive "from the play-books of philosophical systems." These idols are persuasive because, like stage plays, they are more coherent and polished than any observations a person may make of the natural world. There are three classes of errors in philosophical systems. The first Bacon terms "Sophistical," which is represented by Aristotle's categorizing the natural world according to logic rather than experience. The result was a practice of conforming experience to preconceived ideas. "Empirical" errors are based on too few observations and experiments; a prime example is the system of alchemy. The most common and most dangerous kind of error is the intrusion of superstition and theology into science. This process flatters the understanding, "being fanciful and tumid and half poetical." It works on the imagination, creating the illusion of rationality and a false sense of understanding. The only way to defeat such error is to adhere to decorum, clearly separating the work of science from that of religion.

The volume concludes with the *Parasceve ad Historiam Naturalem et Experimentalem* (Preparative to a Natural and Experimental History). Its introduction declares that the envisioned completed work will be extremely long and will require the collaboration of many. Its purpose is to provide a comprehensive "Primary," or "Mother History"–the practical knowledge upon which the new philosophy will be based. The work as presented consists of a series of aphorisms and a catalogue of the histories to be included in the project. Aphorism 3 sums up briefly the arguments of the first book of *Novum Organum:* that all rhetoric and testimonies be banished from scientific inquiry. Words in science should be a means to an end, not a pleasurable end in themselves. All action on the imagination is inappropriate. The catalogue includes histories of physical properties, "Greater Masses," "Species," "Man," and "Pure Mathematics." Number 78 (out of 128), included under "Histories of Man," is "History of the Intellectual Faculties; Reflexion, Imagination, Discourse, Memory, &c." The study of language and rhetoric thus has its place in a comprehensive philosophy.

This volume of the *Instauratio Magna* marks a truly original contribution to the history of philosophy. With his identification of the idols of the mind, Bacon develops a new understanding of error. As Michael McCanles has argued, while the classical world equated it with faulty logic and Christians traditionally saw it as arising from will, Bacon associated error with desire: "Bacon discusses the idols of the mind as mental constructions of a world that conforms to human desires, as distinct from the natural world 'as it is.'" Bacon thus identifies the role of the perceiver in the construction of understanding, a role that he strives to minimize through induction. The role of desire also highlights the reason why scientific language must be purged of rhetoric. If, as *The Advancement of Learning* has it, the duty of rhetoric is "to apply Reason to Imagination for the better moving of the will," then rhetoric must concern itself with those parts of imagination that construct images from desire. Rhetoric thus cannot be free from desire; it can never be a neutral transmitter of information.

Bacon's public career reached its climax not long after the publication of the *Instauratio Magna*. His home at York House was the scene of elaborate celebrations for his sixtieth birthday, commemorated in an ode by the poet Ben Jonson. A few days later, on 27 January 1621, Bacon was created Viscount St. Albans and thereby elevated into the upper peerage. Clearly, this promotion was a reward for his faithful service to King James; it was just this close association that led to his fall from public life. Growing opposition to Stuart policy, notably royal monopolies, solidified into attacks on the king's closest advisors. So it was that on 20 March 1621 Bacon was officially charged with receiving bribes in cases he was judging. Modern legal scholars have proclaimed, in the words of William A. Sessions, in his *Francis Bacon Revisited* (1996), Bacon's "relative innocence," according to the standards of the day, but the political climate was such that he knew his public career could not be saved. So, in the last days of March, he submitted a carefully worded statement to the House of Lords, admitting to neglect. Subsequently, on 16 April, Bacon explained to the king that, of three kinds of bribery, he could be guilty of the second—"a neglect in the Judge to inform himself whether the cause to be fully at an end or no, what time he receives the gift; but takes it upon the credit of the party, that all is done; or otherwise omits to enquire." On 3 May his fall was complete: Bacon was sentenced to imprisonment, heavy fines, and banishment from all public life. The first part of the sentence was brief, the second mitigated, but the third remained in effect for the rest of Bacon's life.

After this reversal of fortune came another. Bacon's exile from public service inaugurated five years of extensive thought and writing, so productive that the nineteenth-century editor Spedding named it Bacon's *quinquennium* (special period of five years). During this period he composed twenty-two works, six of which were published before his death, the remainder edited and published by William Rawley beginning in 1626. Further, Bacon extended his intellectual contacts, including correspondence with Antoine Coeffier-Ruzé, Marquis d'Effiat, who was instrumental in the French translation and publication of *The Advancement of Learning.* In his will Bacon bequeathed to the marquis a copy of *The Essayes Or Covnsels, Civill And Morall, Of Francis Lo. Vervlam, Viscovnt St. Alban. Newly Enlarged* (1625), the last edition of the essays published in Bacon's lifetime. In addition to the *Essayes,* his final writings included such scientific works as *Francisci Baronis De Vervlamio, Vice-Comitis Sancti Albani, Historia Natvralis Et Experimentalis Ad Condendam Philosophiam: Sive, Phænomena Vniversi: Quæ est Instaurationis Magnæ Pars Tertia* (1622; translated as *The Naturall And Experimental History of Winds, &c.,* 1653), better known as *The History of Winds,* and *Francisci Baronis De Vervlamio, Vice-Comitis Sancti Albani, Historia Vitae & Mortis. Sive, Titvlvs Secvndvs in Historia Naturali & Experimentali ad condendam Philosophiam: Quae est Instavrationis Magnae Pars Tertia Historia Vitae et Mortis* (1623; translated as *The Historie of Life and Death. With Observations Naturall and Experimentall for the Prolonging of Life,* 1638); translations of psalms; *The Historie Of The Raigne of King Henry the Seuenth* (1622); the utopian treatise *New Atlantis,* left unfinished at his death and posthumously published in *Sylva Sylvarvm Or A Naturall Historie. In Ten Centuries* (1626); and *De Dignitate & Augmentis Scientiarum,* the long-planned revision of *The Advancement of Learning.*

The first work completed after his public disgrace, Bacon's account of the reign of Henry VII, gives

Engraved title page for the work in which Bacon's Novum Organum *(New Organon) was first published*

ample proof of his regard for rhetoric. Dedicated to Charles, Prince of Wales, the work is exemplary in the humanistic sense of the word: the life of the king is intended to provide both illustration and model for students of public life, as Bacon shows how his character contributed to the particular development of policy. While it develops chronologically, the narrative is periodically interrupted by set speeches—formal orations Bacon composes to represent what individual public figures may have said. The speeches follow the best models of Ciceronian style, full of embellishment, *copia* or variety of words, and vivid imagery. These are, above all, political speeches, not scientific discourses. They are meant to be persuasive. Bacon's use of the techniques of persuasion gives a practical illustration of his belief in their necessity in appropriate circumstances.

Bacon completed *The Historie of the Raigne of King Henry the Seuenth* in October 1621. By June 1622 he had finished the final draft of *De Dignitate & Augmentis Scientiarum.* While in many places it duplicates the insights of *The Advancement of Learning, De Dignitate & Augmentis Sci-*

entiarum is not simply a revised translation. It is a thorough expansion, developing and extending the ideas of the earlier work. Conceptually, it definitely belongs to the *Instauratio Magna,* as the intended preparative to the entire project, and Spedding includes his English translation in volume one of the *Works,* following *Parasceve ad Historiam Naturalem et Experimentalem.* The first of the nine books of the work consists of a hortatory oration on the worth of studies, a reworking of book 1 of *The Advancement of Learning.* The substance of the work commences with book 2, surveying all human knowledge to identify strengths and deficiencies. Book 2 opens with the division of human understanding into history, poetry, and philosophy; continues through twelve chapters with the examination of history, both natural and civil; and closes with a single chapter devoted to poetry. Book 3 concerns the sciences—theology and philosophy—and includes discussion of both magic and mathematics. The three chapters of book 4 examine the divisions of the study of man, closing with a brief description of the faculties of the soul. Discussion of the uses of the faculties continues in book 5, which devotes its five chapters to the arts of invention of arguments, judgment, and memory. The art of transmitting receives its own, extensive discussion in book 5 and includes an extensive essay on rhetoric, complete with three appendices. The final three books treat the subjects of moral knowledge, civil knowledge, and divinity.

Several chapters important to an understanding of Bacon's rhetorical theory appear before his formal discussion of eloquence. In book 2, chapter 12, Bacon closes his discussion of history with "*Appendices to History,*" in which he stresses the importance of preserving words as well as actions. While these words are often "inserted" into narrative history (as are the set speeches in Bacon's history of Henry VII), they are best "preserved" in collections of speeches, letters, and apothegms. The value of speeches is their eloquence; of letters, their solid, unaffected advice. Bacon's understanding of apothegms runs parallel to his subsequent explication of rhetoric. Quoting from Ecclesiastes, he observes that apothegms are both ornamental and useful because they are "(as was said) 'words which are as goads.'" There is something in them that may convert thought into action.

The discussion of the function of the faculties in book 5, chapter 1, begins to show how words may become goads. The two principal divisions of the human soul are Intellect and Will. They arose together, like twins, and were corrupted together at the Fall. Imperfect as they now are, they still retain a distorted form of their original tendencies: Intellect toward Truth, Will toward Goodness. The art governing will is ethics, that governing intellect is logic. And yet these are not two entirely separate provinces. They are linked by imagination:

> Logic discourses of the Understanding and Reason; Ethic of the Will, Appetite [or desire], and Affections: the one produces determinations, the other actions. It is true indeed that the imagination performs the office of an agent or messenger or proctor in both provinces, both the judicial and the ministerial. For sense sends all kinds of images over to imagination for reason to judge of; and reason again when it has made its judgment and selection, sends them over to imagination before the decree be put in execution. For voluntary motion is ever preceded and incited by imagination; so that imagination is as a common instrument to both,—both reason and will.

Moreover, the imagination is something of a free agent, governed but not wholly ruled by reason. Because of imagination, persuasion works. Eloquence chiefly affects the imagination, acting upon it and stimulating it until it may influence or even overpower reason.

Bacon extends his discussion of imagination in book 6, which is devoted to the art of transmission. As he did in *The Advancement of Learning,* Bacon divides transmission into three parts: *organ,* method, and illustration, or rhetoric. All three address the process by which the mind communicates images. Transmission— "all the arts which relate to words and discourse"—is the partner of reason, but a subordinate one. As the soul is to the body so reason is to discourse, and all must be studied separately. *Organ,* or grammar, concerns speech and writing—the study of language on the level of words. Quoting Aristotle, Bacon explains that "words are the images of thoughts and letters are the images of words." The imagination works upon images, which ultimately come from sense. Sense itself Bacon distinguishes from perception. As he explains in book 4, chapter 3, all natural bodies have perception, which may be likened to reflexes, but only sentient creatures have sense, which may be regarded as awareness. Sense forms images, upon which the imagination acts. The word Bacon uses for images is *idola,* a word that, as Marc Cogan points out in his article "Rhetoric and Action in Francis Bacon" (1981), emphasizes its kinship with the idols of the mind. Images thus are not always reliable, being as they are one step beyond the thing itself. For this reason Bacon expresses some interest in "real characters," such as Chinese ideograms: such characters represent "things and notions" rather than words. This concern for grounding words in things extends to Bacon's advocacy of a "philosophical grammar" that investigates the "analogy between words and things, or reason." He distinguishes between his envisioned system and any Platonic study of the origins of names. Instead, Bacon advocates a kind of comparative linguistics as a way of enhancing all languages so that they may better express what the mind conceives.

Chapter 2 is devoted to a full exposition of method, or the "Wisdom of Transmission." Method must be sharply distinguished from rhetoric as a form of communication because it has separate ends. One of these ends is magisterial or teaching, designed to convey to the general population of students the state of current wisdom. This end Bacon finds rather sterile—developed as far as it needs to go. The other is initiative, designed for scientists to aid their inquiry into the foundations of science. As Bacon defines it, "there belongs to architecture not only the frame of the whole building, but also the formation and shape of the several beams and columns thereof; and Method is as it were the architecture of the sciences." The goal of method, then, is to create a system of inquiry as independent as possible from the imagination and the deforming properties of images. As Michel Malherbe observes in his essay "Bacon's Critique of Logic" (1990), "the originality of the Baconian definition of method lies in the recognition that the ruler and the compass excuse the hand from all talent and all ability." Method thus is designed to use sensory information without being influenced by the illusions of the senses: to enable the senses to penetrate to the real nature of things.

This definition of method shows clearly why Bacon makes such a sharp distinction between it and rhetoric. Method provides a discourse that approximates pure reason to achieve wisdom. While it is inferior to wisdom, rhetoric is nevertheless essential to the public world—the world concerned with action rather than inquiry. Action requires imagination, and rhetoric serves the imagination in the same way as logic serves the understanding. Here Bacon refines the definition offered in *The Advancement of Learning*: the purpose of rhetoric is "to apply and recommend the dictates of reason to imagination, in order to excite the appetite and will." Thus he makes explicit what was implied in *The Advancement of Learning*. There are four faculties concerned with rhetoric—reason, imagination, will, and appetite. The will is concerned with rational desire and voluntary acts. The appetite, in contrast, governs natural desires and involuntary acts; more directly engaged with sensory experience, it is also more attuned to the perception of good and evil.

Rhetoric would not be necessary in a world of pure, unfallen reason. However, in the real world reason is assaulted by sophistry, misused words, and the passions. Logic aids the reason by enabling it to detect sophistry; moral philosophy restrains the passions. Rhetoric serves as a check to sensory impressions; and

yet, sensory impressions are the materials of the imagination, which transmits images to the intellect. Properly, what moves the intellect should be virtue and goodness, but these are abstractions, which must be made tangible, and this tangibility is rendered through words: "it is the business of rhetoric to make pictures of virtue and goodness, so that they may be seen. For since they cannot be showed to the sense in corporeal shape, the next degree is to show them to the imagination in as lively representation as possible, by ornament of words." Through words, the imagination creates images that it then conveys to the reason, producing rational thought.

When the imagination works on sense, it shapes the appetite and will. Again, if these were governable by reason, rhetoric would be irrelevant. These "affections," however, frequently dominate the reason, and, in concert with the imagination, can produce a wide range of errors. Rhetoric can overcome the affections by allying reason and imagination. It may do so because of the fundamental nature of the affections. The appetite, like reason, is drawn toward what it perceives as good. The reason can take the long view, but the appetite sees chiefly the present. What is present is more tangible to the imagination than the future, as the senses are more powerful than abstractions. Thus, appetite allied to the imagination may easily overcome reason. Rhetoric wins the imagination to reason by using eloquence to make what is remote appear present. The more artful the words (the images of thought), the more tangible the images to the imagination, which in its turn motivates the will to action. Bacon thus endorses the view of Aristotle that rhetoric participates in both logic and civil knowledge. Rhetoric has the advantage over logic in dealing with ordinary language and affairs because it is adaptable to circumstances and audiences. And here Bacon finds the art somewhat deficient. He recommends the development of what he names "*The Wisdom of Private Discourse*" to increase the adaptability of eloquence.

Bacon concludes his discussion of rhetoric with three appendices to remedy deficiencies in the "promptuary" dimension of the art. The first is a finished version of *Colours of Good and Evil*, first also published in 1597. It not only identifies and supplements the sophisms of rhetoric identified by Aristotle, but also provides answers to them and explains their use in moving the will. The second is a collection of *antitheses* on forty-seven topics to enrich the store of commonplaces for use in all three kinds of rhetoric—demonstrative, deliberative, and judicial. The final appendix concerns "lesser forms," such as prefaces, conclusions, and digressions, and includes examples drawn from the orations of Cicero.

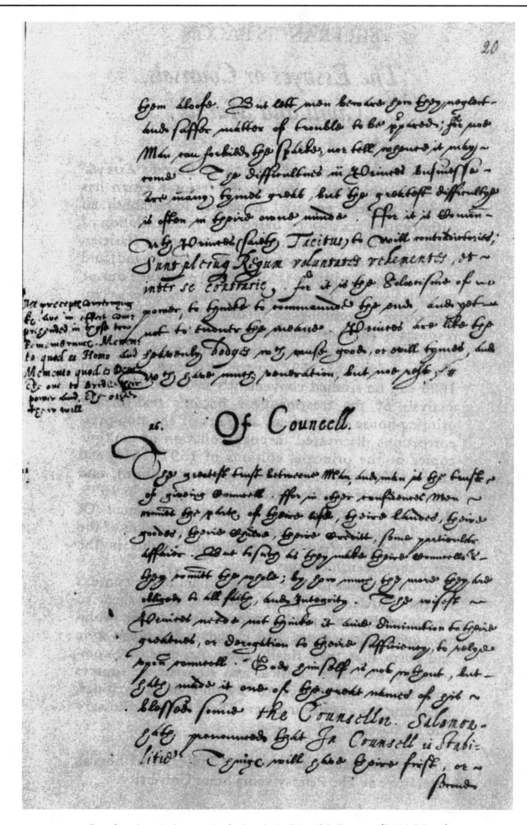

Page from the revised manuscript for the 1625 edition of the Essayes *(British Library)*

The "Wisdom of Private Discourse" taken together with the appendices offers a glimpse of a Baconian rhetoric that departs completely from conventional practice. In his 1987 article on Bacon's rhetoric, Cogan characterizes it as a systematic study of *elocutio* (oratorical delivery)—a "rational art of words," and "a grammar of the affective possibilities of language." It would seek, not to invent arguments, but to discover the variety of shapes those arguments could take. It would therefore branch into psychology and linguistics. The first branch would study the imagination to discover the kinds of images most likely to occur as present. The second would attempt to identify means by which "the images of symbolic forms may be given properties equivalent to those possessed by the images of material objects," and to investigate the ways in which language may provide those properties. Rhetoric would therefore be grounded firmly in science, something that could be applied systematically to the benefit of society as a whole.

De Dignitate & Augmentis Scientiarum is Bacon's major statement of the value of language and rhetoric. Although the idea was not original to him, his interest in real character found expression in a generation of language projectors who attempted to develop a system of writing for transmitting pure thought. With ideas similar to those of Ramus, Bacon also developed a method that, as Craig Walton argues in his 1971 article, emphasized "motion and act as operative principles in place of form as pure definition and contemplative object." Unlike Ramus, Bacon designed his method as a tool that all may use in any inquiry. It was as such that Sprat praised it as a forerunner of scientific method.

Although there never did evolve a Baconian rhetoric, Bacon offers an analysis of the art that systematically revises previous theory. Without expanding its province—and, in fact, contracting it severely—Bacon makes the strongest case possible for its necessity to human social and political life. As Cogan has shown, Bacon departs from tradition in analyzing rhetoric not from issues but from the operations of the mind, thereby locating it in psychology rather than politics. It works both inwardly and outwardly, for the audience of eloquence is the imagination, both that of the speaker and that of the listeners. Contrary to the practice of meditation, Bacon's rhetorical occasions are essentially generated from within, and they have as their object action, not contemplation. So closely linked are rhetoric and action that action itself must partake of rhetoric. Ultimately, one cannot act morally without rhetoric because without rhetoric one cannot translate thought into action.

While *De Dignitate & Augmentis Scientiarum* proved to be his final systematic examination of rhetoric,

Bacon continued its practical application and his inquiry into its theory in several of his last works, including *New Atlantis, Apophthegms New and Old* (1625), the final version of the *Essayes,* and *Sylva Sylvarum.* As Vickers has demonstrated, *New Atlantis* was Bacon's most popular and influential book. It was composed in 1624, published with *Sylva Sylvarum* in 1626, and republished in 1659, bound with *Mr Bushell's Abridgment of the Lord Chancellor Bacon's Philosophical Theory In Mineral Prosecutions.* The book is presented as a travel narrative that frames the presentation of a model of a community of intellectual inquiry: Salomon's House, or the College of the Six Days Works. Presented as the source of all moral and physical well-being in its imaginary country, Salomon's House encourages collaborative work and the sharing of information for the public good. Despite its fragmentary nature, the work inspired the educational and scientific projects of Samuel Hartlib, and Samuel Platt's utopian work *Macaria* (1641), which attempted to introduce Hartlib's ideas to the Long Parliament. Finally, *New Atlantis* was widely credited with providing the inspiration for the Royal Society. As the philosopher Joseph Glanville wrote in dedicating his *Scepsis Scientifica* (1665) to the Society in 1665, "The success of those your *great* and *Catholick Endeavours* will promote the *Empire* of *Man* over *Nature,* and bring plentiful accession of Glory to your Nation . . . For *You really* are what former Ages could contrive but in *wish* and *Romances;* and *Solomons House* in the NEW ATLANTIS, was a Prophetick Scheam of the ROYAL SOCIETY." As an imaginative work, *New Atlantis* takes full advantage of formal rhetoric. The bulk of the book is presented not as narrative but as a series of speeches, the climactic one delivered by the Father of Salomon's House, widely understood to be a persona for Bacon himself. Vickers shows that Bacon uses formal rhetorical division as the transition to the specific descriptions of scientific projects, and his syntax follows Cicero in its balanced clauses.

The *Apophthegmes New and Old,* published in the fall of 1625, were one of Bacon's efforts to remedy the deficiencies he discerned in the promptuary of rhetoric. As he explains in his preface, these short anecdotes with pointed insights may stand on their own or they may be incorporated into speeches to illustrate ideas. In the first edition Bacon collected two hundred and eighty apothegms from classical to modern times, including a few of his own, such as this witty play on words, as published in volume seven of Spedding's edition of the *Works:*

The book of deposing Richard the second, and the coming in of Henry the fourth, supposed to be written by Dr. Hayward, who was committed to the Tower for it, had much incensed queen Elizabeth. And she asked Mr. Bacon, being then of her learned counsel; *Whether there were no treason contained in it?* Mr. Bacon intending to do him a pleasure, and to take off the Queen's bitterness with a jest, answered; *No, madam, for treason I cannot deliver opinion that there is any, but very much felony.* The Queen, apprehending it gladly, asked; *How, and wherein?* Mr. Bacon answered; *Because he had stolen many of his sentences and conceits out of Cornelius Tacitus.*

The stories succinctly illustrate the ideas, thus rendering the ideas present to the imagination, as Bacon explains in *De Dignitate & Augmentis Scientiarum.* They are delightful as well, humor being a traditional embellishment of rhetoric.

The third edition of the *Essayes–The Essayes Or Covnsels, Civill And Morall*–appeared in 1625. This work represented the culmination of the thought of a lifetime, and Bacon acknowledged it as one of his most popular books. Each edition reveals Bacon expanding his ideas, reflecting the growing seriousness of his project. As Vickers shows, while the first edition comprised ten essays averaging a length of 325 words, the edition of 1612 expanded to thirty-eight, including twenty-nine new ones, averaging 490 words. The third edition added twenty new essays and extensively revised many of the old ones; the new essays averaged 950 words. A comparison of the editions of 1612 and 1625 with *The Advancement of Learning* and *De Dignitate & Augmentis Scientiarum,* first performed by Ronald S. Crane, reveals that the essays were designed to address deficiencies in learning identified in the two long works and thus formed an integral part of Bacon's great project. Further, in style the new essays capitalized on the linguistic and rhetorical insights of *De Dignitate & Augmentis Scientiarum.* Much less gnomic than those of 1597, these expanded essays make far greater use of the oratorical devices of partition and division. Their syntax is also far more balanced and symmetrical. The development of the essays is still nonlinear, but these expansions make more use of commonplaces, refined–as *De Dignitate & Augmentis Scientiarum* recommends–into sharp, pithy sentences so that the nonlinearity is much more recognizable as *antithesis*: the contrasting of ideas through use of parallel arrangements of words, clauses, or sentences. The essays of 1625 are thus far more ornamental than those of 1597, more highly rhetorical, and, perhaps, more imaginatively pleasing.

Several of the essays of 1625 have some direct bearing on language and rhetoric. Two of these are revised and refined versions of essays of 1597–"Of Studies" and "Of Discourse." Appearing first and second in 1597, the two are moved to fiftieth and thirty-second position in 1625. "Of Discourse" loses much of its aphoristic character but gains ornamenta-

tion, becoming far more eloquent than the earlier version. Bacon combines several of the earlier, separate aphorisms into paragraphs and expands his explanations and examples. These expansions derive from remarks made in the long works about the nature of eloquence, as may be seen in how Bacon's point about the value of questioning is treated in the two versions, both published in Vickers's 1996 Oxford Authors volume. The version of 1597 is succinct: "He that questioneth much shall learn much, and content much, specially if he apply his questions to the skill of the person of whom he asketh, for he shall give them occasion to please themselves in speaking, and himself shall continually gather knowledge." The version of 1625 is more concerned with effect on the audience:

> He that questioneth much, shall learn much, and content much; but especially if he apply his questions to the skill of the persons whom he asketh; for he shall give them occasion to please themselves in speaking, and himself shall continually gather knowledge. But let his questions not be troublesome; for that is fit for a poser. And let him be sure to leave other men their turns to speak. Nay, if there be any that would reign and take up all the time, let him find means to take them off, and to bring others on; as musicians use to do with those that dance too long galliards.

Bacon's revision emphasizes the *decorum* of speech and underscores the point that the purpose of discourse is public, social communication. The addition of the comparison to music echoes similar ideas going back to "Valerius Terminus" and expressed fully in *De Dignitate & Augmentis Scientiarum,* namely, that a speaker should adapt his discourse to his hearers, "like a musician accommodating his skill to different ears." Speech, Bacon reminds the reader, may like music be pleasing to the senses; the more fully it affects the senses, the more and fuller images they may transmit to the imagination.

The revised version of "Of Studies," included in Vickers's edition, clearly ties it to Bacon's *Instaurationis Magnæ.* Following the same methods as he did in the revision of "Of Discourse," Bacon combines aphorisms into paragraphs and expands the number of examples. In these revisions he puts greater emphasis on the need for studies to remedy deficiencies in the mind. The new essay combines the last two paragraphs of the original, which end just before the quotation from Ovid, with explanation of the way studies work:

> Reading maketh a full man; conference a ready man; and writing an exact man. And therefore, if a man write little, he had need have a great memory; if he confer little, he had need have a present wit; and if he read little, he had need have much cunning, to seem

to know that he doth not. Histories make men wise; poets witty; the mathematics subtile; natural philosophy deep; moral grave; logic and rhetoric able to contend. "Abeunt studie in mores" [Studies affect our behavior]. Nay there is no stond or impediment in the wit, but may be wrought out by fit studies: like as diseases of the body may have appropriate exercises. Bowling is good for the stone and reins; shooting for the lungs and breast; gentle walking for the stomach; riding for the head; and the like. So if a man's wit be wandering, let him study the mathematics; for in demonstrations, if his wit be called away never so little, he must begin again. If his wit be not apt to distinguish or find differences, let him study the schoolmen; . . . If he be not apt to beat over matters, and to call up one thing to prove and illustrate another, let him study the lawyers' cases. So every defect of the mind may have a special receipt.

In this quotation Bacon's use of concrete examples and comparisons illustrates well his arguments about making images present to the imagination. The physical exercises are easy to imagine, and the comparison follows neatly. Just as he surveyed all of learning with an eye to remedying deficiencies, so Bacon recommends surveying one's own mind to identify areas of weakness, to be strengthened by study. His program of reformation may occur on the level of macrocosm or microcosm.

Two new essays—both included in Vickers's edition—extend Bacon's ideas on the role of the imagination in the growth and transmission of knowledge. "Of Superstition," the seventeenth essay in the *Essayes* of 1625, attacks false beliefs as being more dangerous to the public welfare than atheism. Lack of a spiritual dimension limits human nature, leaving it to "sense, to philosophy, to natural piety, to laws, to reputation." Superstition, however, "dismounts all these, and erecteth an absolute monarchy in the minds of men." It is most popular among the people, who then invent systems of belief to accommodate their notions. The root causes of superstition are an imagination overstimulated by practices that are pleasing to the senses and a mind that possesses too high a regard for tradition. Thus, the combination of credulity and pleasure may overcome the reason, especially in those whose reason is weak.

Nowhere is his respect for the power of the imagination more evident than in Bacon's inaugural essay, "Of Truth." As Kenneth Alan Hovey has argued, this essay, new to the volume of 1625, is an extended response to the extreme skepticism of Michel de Montaigne, whom Hovey identifies as the model for Pontius Pilate in the famous opening lines: "'What is Truth?' said jesting Pilate; and would not stay for an answer." Bacon insists that truth can be known, but that human beings must recognize their penchant for falsehood. Lies are attractive because they please, often adding attractiveness to limited lives: "Doth any man doubt, that if there were taken out of men's minds vain opinions, flattering hopes, false valuations, imaginations . . . it would leave the minds of a number of men poor shrunken things, full of melancholy and indisposition, and unpleasing to themselves?" The senses were created before reason; thus the senses tend to have primacy. Still, the inquiry into, knowledge of, and contemplation of truth offer the chief good of human nature. Therefore, the skepticism of philosophers such as Montaigne not only hinders scientific progress, but also blocks the fulfillment of the human spirit.

In the last work he wrote, *Sylva Sylvarvm,* Bacon continued his quest to pursue truth by detaching it from imagination. Corresponding to the projected fifth part of the Great Instauration, "The Forerunners; or Anticipations of the New Philosophy," *Sylva Sylvarvm* presents ten "centuries," or groups of one hundred experiments conducted by Bacon in efforts to discover the foundations of a variety of features of the natural world. The tenth century concerns the powers of the imagination, including the question of whether the imagination can actually alter matter. It contains Bacon's last definition of imagination.

While rejecting the Pythagorean belief in a world-soul, Bacon nevertheless recognizes that "we, that hold firm to the works of God, and to the sense, which is God's lamp," need to inquire seriously into traditional beliefs in the influence of imagination to see whether any of them actually have any merit. He acknowledges the power of suggestion, remarking that "impressions" produced by the imagination can indeed travel, like infection, from mind to mind and influence especially those whose minds and spirits are weak. He further reminds readers that imagination can extend strong influence over the mind of the "imaginant." There are three kinds of imagination. The first associates with belief in what lies in the future, the second with memory of the past, and the third with "things present, or as if they were present." The art of memory teaches that visual images work best—the more detailed the image the stronger staying power it has. Experience shows that imagination has the greatest influence on "lightest and easiest motions," that is, "spirits," and probably none on inanimate objects. The problem with studying the imagination scientifically, Bacon conceded, is that it is virtually impossible even to conceive of any experiments that would demonstrate any material action of imagination on the mind of another who was unaware of the experiment. While willing to

Frontispiece, with portrait of Bacon by William Marshall, and engraved title page for the translation of Bacon's
De Dignitate & Augmentis Scientiarum *(1623)*

entertain the future possibility of such experiments, Bacon makes a strong case for excluding imagination from the realm of scientific inquiry. As his editor Rawley comments in his preface to the work, published in volume two of the *Works,* Bacon always strives to show us "the world as God made it, and not as men have made it; for that it hath nothing of the imagination."

Productive to the last and undaunted by his public disgrace, Bacon left volumes of work unpublished. His spirit of inquiry contributed to his death, making it an *exemplum* of his entire life. According to his early biographer Aubrey,

Mr. [Thomas] Hobb[e]s told me that the cause of his Lordship's death was trying an Experiment; viz. as he was taking the aire in a Coach with Dr Witherbourne . . . towards High-gate, snow lay on the ground, and it cam into my Lord's thoughts, why flesh might not be preserved in snow, as in Salt. They were

resolved they would try the Experiment presently. They alighted out of the Coach and went into a poore woman's house at the bottom of Highgate hill, and bought a Hen, and made the woman exenterate it, and then stuffed the body with Snow, and my Lord did help to doe it himselfe. The Snow so chilled him that he immediately fell so extremely ill, that he could not returne to his Lodging . . . but went to the Earle of Arundel's house at Highgate, where they putt him into a good bed warmed with a Panne, but it was a damp bed that had not been layn-in in about a yeare before, which gave him such a colde that in 2 or 3 dayes . . . he dyed of Suffocation.

Whatever his disgrace as a politician, Bacon's literary reputation only continued to grow after his death, especially in matters of his style. In his *Francis Bacon and Renaissance Prose* (1988), Vickers quotes Jonson as saying of Bacon, in words deriving from Seneca, "No man ever spake more neatly, more presly, more weightily, or suffer'd lesse emptiness, lesse idlenesse, in what hee utter'd." Editions of Bacon's works reached a peak in the 1650s and early 1660s, as the Hartlib circle pressed its arguments for scientific cooperation and the Royal Society was formed. Some works that were commonly attributed to Bacon, such as *An Essay of a King* (1642) and *A True and Historical Relation Of the Poysoning of Sir Thomas Overbury* (1651), were in fact probably not written by him.

Although interest in Bacon began a steady decline after 1660, reaching a low around 1780, his importance as a figure of learning continued into the Restoration and early eighteenth century. The playwright and poet John Dryden wrote admiringly of him, and in his 1950 bibliography R. W. Gibson lists 423 entries of Baconiana up to 1750, including citations by John Milton, Joseph Addison, Thomas Hobbes, Athanasius Kircher, René Descartes, Pierre Gassendi, Giambattista Vico, and Gottfried Wilhelm Leibniz. Bacon's reputation rose somewhat in the late eighteenth and early nineteenth centuries, as the English Romantics admired his estimate of the imagination. After a scathing attack on his character by Thomas Babington Macaulay in an 1837 essay, interest in Bacon plummeted, with the one notable exception of Spedding's monumental edition of his works, still the standard edition used in Bacon studies. Twentieth-century scholarship focused chiefly on his scientific and political works, although his rhetoric has received sporadic attention since the 1940s.

Since the 1980s, scholarship on both his rhetoric and his scientific thought has confirmed Bacon's pivotal position in the history of ideas. There is much in his work that anchors him to the sixteenth century. His method of reading, derived from Renaissance humanistic practice, his use of testimony in argument, the high value he places on ornamentation, and his own often highly ornamental style link him to his rhetorical predecessors, as his belief that intuition precedes concepts associates him with the medieval nominalists. On the other hand, his opposition to Hermeticism, his critique of the syllogism, and his belief in progress all look forward to the seventeenth century. Most estimations of the impact of his thought concentrate on his contribution to science. As Antonio Pérez-Ramos has argued in "Bacon's Legacy" (1996), these amount to four: his idea of restructuring knowledge from its foundations, the value he placed on experimentation, his separation of science and religion, and, most important, his belief in the betterment of humanity through science. Thanks to Bacon more than to any other early thinker, the general public typically sees science as a public, collaborative undertaking, prop-

erly funded by government rather than private patrons. So also Bacon's style has affected the development of plain, concise, modern, scientific writing.

Bacon's contribution to rhetoric has been more difficult to assess. In *Francis Bacon on Communication & Rhetoric* (1943), Karl R. Wallace has shown how he had very little effect on contemporary theorists. Wallace found only one seventeenth-century writer who acknowledged any debt to Bacon–Thomas Blount, whose *Academy of Eloquence* (1654) makes explicit use of Bacon's ideas about commonplaces, *formulae,* and lesser forms. William P. Sandford was first to point out that John Bulwer's two treatises on delivery, *Chirologia: Or The Natvrall Langvage Of The Hand* (1644) and *Chironomia: Or, The Art of Manuall Rhetorique. With The Canons, Lawes, Rites, Ordinances, and Institutes of Rhetoricians, both Ancient and Moderne* (1644), took inspiration from Bacon's comments on posture and facial expression. Sandford also argues for the possibility of Bacon's influence on such works as Thomas Vicars's Χειραγωγία: *Manvductio Ad Artem Rhetoricam* (*Handbook: Handbook of the Art of Rhetoric,* 1621), Thomas Farnaby's *Index Rhetoricus* (Rhetorical Index, 1625), Charles Butler's *Oratoriae Libri Duo* (Two Books of Oratory, 1629), and William Pemble's *Enchiridion Oratorium* (Handbook of Oratory, 1633), although none directly mentions Bacon and their understanding of rhetoric may be more directly informed by the study of classical authors. In the eighteenth century, John Lawson's *Lectures Concerning Oratory* (1752) endorsed the use of commonplaces and Bacon's belief in the public ends of rhetoric. George Campbell's *Philosophy of Rhetoric* (1776) acknowledges *De Dignitate & Augmentis Scientiarum* as the foundation of his discussion of the imagination, while Joseph Priestly's *Lectures of Oratory and Criticism* (1777) echoes Bacon in its treatment of the process of recollection in the formation of ideas. In the early nineteenth century, Richard Whately was the last rhetorician to claim a debt to Bacon; Whately's *Elements of Rhetoric* (1828) makes use of Bacon's work on the colors of rhetoric, sophisms, and *antitheta.*

Despite his relative lack of attention from contemporaries, Bacon's contribution to rhetorical theory is genuine. In *Francis Bacon on Communication & Rhetoric* Wallace notes Bacon's reorientation of the field to place more emphasis on content and reason than on style. Bacon's stress throughout his work is on practicality rather than ornament for its own sake, and the need for function to take precedence in composition. His treatment of the colors of rhetoric parallels his description of the Idols of logic: they cannot be eliminated because of the very nature of rhetoric, but one must become aware of them, and

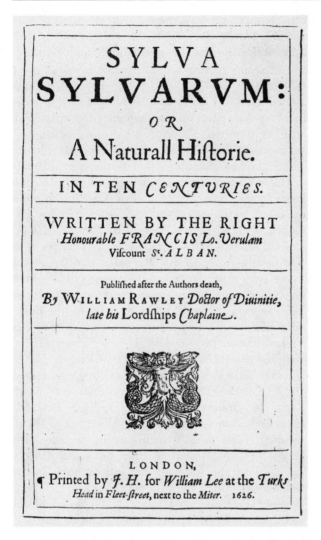

SYLVA
SYLVARVM:
OR
A Naturall Historie.

IN TEN *CENTURIES.*

WRITTEN BY THE RIGHT
Honourable FRANCIS Lo.Verulam
Viscount S*t*.*ALBAN.*

Published after the Authors death,
By WILLIAM RAWLEY *Doctor of Diuinitie,*
late his Lordships *Chaplaine.*

LONDON,
¶ Printed by *J. H.* for *William Lee* at the *Turks*
Head in *Fleet-street,* next to the *Miter.* 1626.

Title page for the posthumously published book that includes
The New Atlantis, *Bacon's utopian work that inspired*
the founding of the Royal Society

this awareness will protect the listener as well as the writer or speaker who wishes to ground speech in truth. Perhaps Bacon's most important contribution to theory, however, is his examination of the relationship between rhetoric and imagination. Of earlier thinkers, only Plato approximated Bacon's ideas when he compared rhetoric to poetry in its ability to captivate the spirit. For this reason, Plato distrusted both rhetoric and poetry. Bacon, however, took a much longer view. First, Bacon saw the public utility of rhetoric—its necessity in a fallen world that can never be governed by pure reason. Second, Bacon was concerned, unlike Plato, with seeking to know how rhetoric worked—exactly how it affected the imagination. In the course of his inquiry, Bacon goes a long way toward redeeming the imagination as a crucial faculty in moral and ethical life. Most impor-

tant, Bacon explains rhetoric by way of psychology—in the functioning of the mind rather than in the subjects under discussion. No other rhetorician before Bacon understood that the traditional offices of rhetoric could be summed up as the rational prompting of the imagination toward action.

Perhaps Bacon's greatest contribution to rhetoric and rhetorical theory is his approach to knowledge in general. Not content to be descriptive, Bacon strives to get to the core of a subject, to gain the most intimate kind of knowledge from it, not for its own sake but for useful ends. In *Francis Bacon's Idea of Science and the Maker's Knowledge Tradition* (1988) Pérez-Ramos has characterized this knowledge as "maker's knowledge"; that is, "knowledge which *determines* its object in the way in which a cobbler's knowledge of a shoe determines his activity in producing one" and "the unveiling of latent structures and processes which could enable man to (re)produce Nature's effects." For Bacon, the purpose of science is to be practical, and to achieve this end, Bacon must, among other projects, uncover the ways in which language impedes the discovery of truth. While believing in the possibility of a language of pure representation, Bacon nevertheless arrived at the important insight that language and reality are separate. His perception opened the way for a truly systematic study of language and its operations. While the classical language theorists following Bacon strove to cancel out language to find reality and postmodern theorists today debate the existence of any reality outside language, Bacon realized that one need not become paralyzed by the quest for truth, for Bacon knew that humans also inhabit the contingent world of daily life; and it is this life that a deep, maker's knowledge of rhetoric is best able to serve.

Letters:

Letters of Sr. Francis Bacon, Baron of Verulam, Viscount St. Alban, and Lord High Chancellor of England. Written During the Reign of King James the First. Now Collected, and Augmented with Several Letters and Memoires, Address'd by Him to the King and Duke of Buckingham, Which Were Never Before Published, edited by Robert Stephens (London: Printed for Benjamin Tooke, 1702);

Letters and Remains of the Lord Chancellor Bacon. Collected by Robert Stephens, Esq., edited by John Lockyer (London: Printed by W. Bowyer, 1734);

The Letters and the Life of Francis Bacon Including All His Occasional Works: Namely Letters, Speeches, Tracts, State Papers, Memorials, Devices and All Authentic Writings Not Already Printed among His Philosophical, Literary, or *Professional Works,* 7 volumes, edited by James Spedding (volumes 1–2, London: Longman, Green, Longman & Roberts, 1862; volumes 3–7, London: Longmans, Green, Reader & Roberts, 1868–1874)–comprises volume 1 (1862), volume 2 (1862); volume 3 (1868), volume 4 (1868); volume 5 (1869), volume 6 (1872), and volume 7 (1874);

Illustrations of Jack Cade's Rebellion: From Researches in the Guildhall Records; Together with Some Newly-found Letters of Lord Bacon, edited by B. Brogdon Orridge (London: John Camden Hotten, 1869);

E. R. Wood, "Francis Bacon's 'Couisin Sharpe,'" *Notes and Queries,* 196 (1951): 248–249;

Robert Johnson, "Francis Bacon and Lionel Cranfield," *Huntington Library Quarterly,* 23 (1960): 301–320;

Daniel R. Woolf, "John Seldon [sic], John Borough and Francis Bacon's *History of Henry VII* 1621," *Huntington Library Quarterly,* 47 (1984): 47–53.

Bibliographies:

R. W. Gibson, *Francis Bacon: A Bibliography of His Works and of Baconiana to the Year 1750* (Oxford: Scrivener Press, 1950);

Gibson, *Francis Bacon: A Bibliography of His Works and of Baconiana to the Year 1750: Supplement* (Oxford: Privately printed, 1959);

Brian Vickers, *Francis Bacon* (Harlow, U.K.: Published for the British Council by Longman, 1978), pp. 38–46;

Peter Beal, *Index of English Literary Manuscripts,* volume 1, *1450–1625* (London: Mansell / New York: Bowker, 1980), pp. 17–52;

William A. Sessions, "Recent Studies in Francis Bacon," *English Literary Renaissance,* 17 (1987): 351–371;

Sessions, "Bibliography," in *Francis Bacon's Legacy of Texts: "The art of discovery grows with discovery,"* edited by Sessions (New York: AMS Press, 1990), pp. 325–327.

Biographies:

John Aubrey, *Aubrey's Brief Lives,* edited by Oliver Lawson Dick (London: Martin Secker & Warburg, 1949; Ann Arbor: University of Michigan Press, 1962), pp. 8–16;

Fulton H. Anderson, *Francis Bacon: His Career and His Thought* (Los Angeles: University of Southern California Press, 1962);

Catherine Drinker Bowen, *Francis Bacon: The Temper of a Man* (London: Hamish Hamilton, 1963; Boston: Little, Brown, 1963);

Jonathan Marwil, *The Trials of Counsel—Francis Bacon in 1621* (Detroit: Wayne State University Press, 1976);

Joel J. Epstein, *Francis Bacon: A Political Biography* (Athens: Ohio University Press, 1977);

Nieves Mathews, *Francis Bacon: The History of a Character Assassination* (New Haven, Conn.: Yale University Press, 1996);

Perez Zagorin, *Francis Bacon* (Princeton: Princeton University Press, 1998);

Lisa Jardine and Alan Stewart, *Hostage to Fortune: The Troubled Life of Francis Bacon* (London: Victor Gollancz, 1998; New York: Hill & Wang, 1999).

References:

Vincent M. Bevilacqua, "Baconian Influence in the Development of Scottish Rhetorical Theory," *Proceedings of the American Philosophical Society,* 3 (1967): 212–218;

Marc Cogan, "Rhetoric and Action in Francis Bacon," *Philosophy and Rhetoric,* 14 (1981): 212–233;

Ronald S. Crane, "The Relation of Bacon's *Essays* to His Program for the Advancement of Learning," in *The Schelling Anniversary Papers by His Former Students* (New York: Century, 1923), pp. 87–105, republished in *Essential Articles for the Study of Francis Bacon,* edited by Brian Vickers (Hamden, Conn.: Archon, 1968; London: Sidgwick & Jackson, 1972), pp. 272–292;

Neal W. Gilbert, *Renaissance Concepts of Method* (New York: Columbia University Press, 1960);

Hanna H. Gray, "Renaissance Humanism: The Pursuit of Eloquence," *Journal of the History of Ideas,* 24 (1963): 497–514;

Paul E. J. Hammer, "The Earl of Essex, Fulke Greville, and the Employment of Scholars," *Studies in Philology,* 91 (1994): 167–180;

John L. Harrison, "Bacon's View of Rhetoric, Poetry, and the Imagination," *Huntington Library Quarterly,* 20 (1957): 107–125; republished in *Essential Articles for the Study of Francis Bacon,* edited by Vickers (Hamden, Conn.: Archon, 1968; London: Sidgwick & Jackson, 1972), pp. 253–271;

Virgil B. Heltzel, "Young Francis Bacon's Tutor," *Modern Language Notes,* 63 (1948): 483–485;

Judith Rice Henderson, "'Vain Affections': Bacon on Ciceronianism in *The Advancement of Learning,*" *English Literary Renaissance,* 25 (1995): 209–234;

Kenneth Alan Hovey, "'Mountaigny Saith Prettily': Bacon's French and the Essay," *Publications of the Modern Language Association of America,* 106 (1991): 71–82;

Wilbur Samuel Howell, *Logic and Rhetoric in England, 1500–1700* (Princeton: Princeton University Press, 1956);

Lisa Jardine, *Francis Bacon: Discovery and the Art of Discourse* (Cambridge & New York: Cambridge University Press, 1974);

Sachiko Kusukawa, "Bacon's Classification of Knowledge," in *The Cambridge Companion to Bacon*, edited by Markku Peltonen (Cambridge & New York: Cambridge University Press, 1996), pp. 47–74;

Thomas Babington Macaulay, "Lord Bacon," *Edinburgh Review*, 65 (July 1837): 1–104;

Maurice B. MacNamee, "Literary Decorum in Francis Bacon," *Saint Louis University Studies*, 1 (March 1950): 1–52;

Michel Malherbe, "Bacon's Critique of Logic," translated by Zenobia D. Sessions, in *Francis Bacon's Legacy of Texts: "The art of discovery grows with discovery,"* edited by William A. Sessions (New York: AMS Press, 1990), pp. 69–87;

Malherbe, "Bacon's Method of Science," in *The Cambridge Companion to Bacon*, edited by Peltonen (Cambridge & New York: Cambridge University Press, 1996), pp. 75–98;

Malherbe, "L'expérience et l'induction chez Bacon," in *Francis Bacon, science et méthode: Actes du colloque de Nantes*, edited by Malherbe and Jean-Marie Pousseur (Paris: Vrin, 1985), pp. 113–133;

Malherbe, "L'induction baconnienne: De l'échec metaphysique à l'échec logique," in *Francis Bacon, terminologia e fortuna nel XVII secolo: Seminario internazionale, Roma, 11–13 marzo 1984*, edited by Marta Fattori (Rome: Edizioni dell' Ateneo, 1984), pp. 179–200;

Malherbe, "L'induction des notions chez Francis Bacon," *Revue internationale de philosophie*, 40 (1986): 427–445;

Michael McCanles, "From Derrida to Bacon and Beyond," in *Francis Bacon's Legacy of Texts: "The art of discovery grows with discovery,"* edited by Sessions (New York: AMS Press, 1990), pp. 25–46;

J. R. Milton, "Bacon, Francis (1561–1626)," in *Routledge Encyclopedia of Philosophy*, 10 volumes, edited by Edward Craig (London & New York: Routledge, 1998), I: 624–632;

John Monfasani, "Humanism and Rhetoric," in *Renaissance Humanism: Foundations, Form and Legacy*, 3 volumes, edited by Albert Rabil, Jr. (Philadelphia: University of Pennsylvania Press, 1988), 3: 171–235;

Walter J. Ong, S.J., "Tudor Writings on Rhetoric," *Studies in the Renaissance*, 15 (1968): 39–69;

Sean Patrick O'Rourke, and others, "The Most Significant Passage on Rhetoric in the Works of Francis Bacon," *Rhetoric Society Quarterly*, 26, no. 3 (1996): 31–55;

Markku Peltonen, ed., *The Cambridge Companion to Bacon* (Cambridge & New York: Cambridge University Press, 1996);

Antonio Pérez-Ramos, "Bacon's Forms and the Maker's Knowledge," and "Bacon's Legacy," in *The Cambridge Companion to Bacon*, edited by Peltonen (Cambridge & New York: Cambridge University Press, 1996), pp. 99–120; 311–334;

Pérez-Ramos, *Francis Bacon's Idea of Science and the Maker's Knowledge Tradition* (Oxford: Clarendon Press / New York: Oxford University Press, 1988);

Graham Rees, "The Transmission of Bacon Texts: Some Unanswered Questions," in *Francis Bacon's Legacy of Texts: "The art of discovery grows with discovery,"* edited by Sessions (New York: AMS Press, 1990), pp. 311–323;

William P. Sandford, "English Rhetoric Reverts to Classicism, 1600–1650," *Quarterly Journal of Speech*, 15 (1929): 503–525;

William A. Sessions, "Francis Bacon and the Classics: The Discovery of Discovery," in *Francis Bacon's Legacy of Texts: "The art of discovery grows with discovery,"* edited by Sessions (New York: AMS Press, 1990), pp. 237–253;

Sessions, *Francis Bacon Revisited* (New York: Twayne / London: Prentice Hall International, 1996);

Thomas O. Sloane, "Rhetoric, 'Logic,' and Poetry: The Formal Cause," in *The Age of Milton: Backgrounds to Seventeenth-Century Literature*, edited by C. A. Patrides and Raymond B. Waddington (Manchester, U.K.: Manchester University Press / Totowa, N.J.: Barnes & Noble, 1980), pp. 307–337;

James Stephens, "Bacon's New English Rhetoric and the Debt to Aristotle," in *Speech Monographs*, 39 (1972): 248–259;

Stephens, *Francis Bacon and the Style of Science* (Chicago: University of Chicago Press, 1975);

Cesare Vasoli, *La dialectica e la retorica dell' Umanesmo: "Invenzione" e "Metodo" nella cultura del XV e XVI secolo* (Milan: Feltrinelli Editore, 1968);

Brian Vickers, "The Authenticity of Bacon's Earliest Writings," *Studies in Philology*, 94 (1997): 248–296;

Vickers, "Bacon and Rhetoric," in *The Cambridge Companion to Bacon*, edited by Peltonen (Cambridge: Cambridge University Press, 1996), pp. 200–231;

Vickers, *Francis Bacon* (Harlow, U. K: Longman, 1978);

Vickers, "Francis Bacon and the Progress of Knowledge," *Journal of the History of Ideas*, 53 (1992): 495–518;

Vickers, *Francis Bacon and Renaissance Prose* (Cambridge: Cambridge University Press, 1968);

Vickers, "The Myth of Francis Bacon's 'Anti-Humanism,'" in *Humanism and Early Modern Philosophy*, edited by Jill Kraye and M. W. F. Stone (London & New York: Routledge, 2000), pp. 135–158;

Vickers, "The Royal Society and English Prose Style: A Reassessment," in *Rhetoric and the Pursuit of Truth: Language Change in the Seventeenth and Eighteenth Centuries: Papers Read at a Clark Library Seminar, 8 March 1980,* edited by Vickers and Nancy S. Struever (Los Angeles: William Andrews Clark Memorial Library, University of California, Los Angeles, 1985), pp. 3–76;

Vickers, ed., *Essential Articles for the Study of Francis Bacon* (Hamden, Conn.: Archon, 1968; London: Sidgwick & Jackson, 1972);

Karl R. Wallace, *Francis Bacon on Communication & Rhetoric, Or: The Art of Applying Reason to Imagination for the Better Moving of the Will* (Chapel Hill: University of North Carolina Press, 1943);

Wallace, *Francis Bacon on the Nature of Man: The Faculties of Man's Soul: Understanding, Reason, Imagination, Memory, Will, and Appetite* (Urbana: University of Illinois Press, 1967);

Wallace, "Imagination and Francis Bacon's View of Rhetoric," in *Dimensions of Rhetorical Scholarship,* edited by Roger E. Nebergall (Norman: Department of Speech, University of Oklahoma, 1963), pp. 65–81;

Craig Walton, "Ramus and Bacon on Method," *Journal of the History of Philosophy,* 9 (1971): 298–302.

Papers:

The chief collections of Francis Bacon's official papers are housed at the British Library and the Public Record Office, London. Significant collections of manuscripts for the scientific, literary, and philosophical works are included in the Thomas Birch papers at the British Library (Add. MSS 4258–63), incorporating many materials from the papers of Bacon's earliest editor, William Rawley; the Basil Montagu collection at the Cambridge University Library (MSS Add. 4326–38); the University of London Library; the Francis Bacon Library, Claremont, California; and the private libraries of the duke of Northumberland, at Alnwick Castle, and the duke of Devonshire, at Chatsworth House. Additional manuscripts and letters are in the Bibliothèque Nationale, Paris; the Bodleian Library, Oxford; and at Aberdeen University, Scotland, and Manhattan College, New York City. Letters are also at the Folger Shakespeare Library, Washington D.C.; the Henry E. Huntington Library and Art Gallery, San Marino, California; the House of Lords Record Office, London; Hatfield House, Hertfordshire; and the Bibliotheca Bodmeriana, Cologny, Switzerland.

John Barton

(circa 1610 – July 1675)

K. R. Narveson
Luther College

BOOKS: *The Art of Rhetorick concisely and compleatly handled, exemplified out of holy Writ, and with a compendious and perspicuous Comment, fitted to the capacities of such as have had a smatch of learning, or are otherwise ingenious* (London: Printed for Nicholas Alsop, 1634);

The Latine Grammar Composed in the English Tongue; Wherein the Excrescencies of the ordinary Grammar are cut off, and the Deficiencies thereof (so generally complained against) supplied; for the more easie, speedy and certain direction of all those, that have a desire to attain unto the understanding of that usefull and necessary Language (London: Printed by A. Miller for Thomas Underhill, 1652).

John Barton's *The Art of Rhetorick concisely and compleatly handled, exemplified out of holy Writ, and with a compendious and perspicuous Comment, fitted to the capacities of such as have had a smatch of learning, or are otherwise ingenious* (1634), offers an example of what a religious schoolmaster of the early Stuart period felt useful both for colleagues and for the general reader insofar as that reader has had a "smatch of learning," as the title declares. Following the lead of the French philosopher and logician Pierre de La Ramée (known as Petrus Ramus) and his collaborator, the Irish-French rhetorician Omer Talon (known as Audomarus Talaeus), Barton covers only *elocutio* (ornamentaion or figures of speech) and *pronuntatio* (oratical delivery). His text provides an example of rhetorical preoccupations perhaps surprising to the modern eye; there is no attempt either to exalt or to analyze the power of figurative speech, or to provide guidance in the use of rhetoric for composition. Rather, Barton exhibits a keen interest in providing the basic tools, suited to nonscholarly capacities, for analysis of *figures* (intentional deviations from standard language, mainly in arrangement) and *tropes* (turns of speech in which words are used in a way that differs from the standard meaning) in a particular text, the Bible. While on the whole unoriginal in his rhetorical theory, Barton nonetheless gives the reader a telling glimpse of a godly schoolmaster's concern to make rhetoric useful to a correct reading of Scripture.

Master of the free school in Kinfare (now Kinver), Staffordshire, Barton was married on 17 October 1633 to Jane Mousley or Moseley, daughter of a prominent local family and niece to William Moseley of London, who when he died in 1617 had left a handsome endowment to the church and school, funds from which still provide part of the rector's salary in modern Kinver. Barton's date of birth is unknown; his wife was born in 1610, however, and it is reasonable to assume that he was about the same age. According to parish records (now in the Staffordshire Record Office), John and Jane had a son, Edward, who was baptized on 24 August 1634; Barton's first book, *The Art of Rhetorick,* was published in the same year. *A History of the County of Stafford* (1984) includes the information that the schoolmaster in 1635 received an income of £15 13s. 4d., as well as £6 13s. 4d. from leases and £3 6s. 8d. from William Moseley's 1617 endowment; thus, it seems that part of Barton's salary came from his wife's family.

Barton's reputation as an educator must have extended into neighboring Warwickshire. In 1639 he was hired to replace Richard Billingsley as chief master of King Edward's School, Birmingham. John Izon notes that his yearly salary in 1640 was £40, along with any income he might have had from leases. The parish register of St. Martin's Church records the baptism of Jane, daughter of John and Jane Barton, on 25 November 1641. Several other children were born to the Bartons after 1641. As head schoolmaster, Barton helped to found the Governor's Library in 1642; this library was the first in Birmingham and one of the earliest of its kind in England.

Barton was apparently living in Birmingham in 1643 when it was burned by men under the command of the Royalist leader Prince Rupert of the Rhine during the First English Civil War (1642–1646). Barton may be the author of an anonymous war tract titled *Prince Rvperts Burning love to England Discovered in Birminghams Flames* (1643), a graphic recounting of the destruction of the town. As Joseph Hill argues, the tract was "written in a scholarly manner" and published by Thomas Underhill, who later published a grammar book titled *The Latine Grammar composed in the English Tongue* (1652) by "J. B., Mr. of Arts, and not long since Master of the Free School of Birmingham in Warwickshire." There is nothing in the tract itself, however, to prove that Barton was the author.

On the other hand, the attribution in the British Library catalogue of the grammar book to "Barton (John) Master of the Free School of Kinfare" is supported by text. The six-page "Epistle to the Reader" is signed "John Barton" and uses the same style of enumeration ("Fifthly," "Sixthly," "Lastly") found in the prefatory address to *The Art of Rhetorick.* Moreover, in the earlier book, Barton had promised to "annex in future editions an Appendix of all grammaticall figures." There were no future editions of the rhetoric book, but the grammar book includes a chapter on figurative agreement (such as enallage, zeugma, and ellipsis), a section on figures of government (such as hendiadys, hypallage, and hysteron proteron), and a section on figures of word (such as prothesis, anthimeria, and tmesis).

According to Hill, Barton continued to teach at King Edward's School until about 1650, but documents edited by Izon in *The Records of King Edward's School, Birmingham* (1974) indicate that he left before 1645, when John Thompson became chief master of the school. Barton must have returned to Kinver at some point. The parish register records that a John Barton was buried in the chancel of the Kinver church on 16 July 1675. *A History of the County of Stafford* records that in 1715 an Edward Barton of London bequeathed £10 a year to the poor of Kinver, stipulating that part of that money be spent on clothing for needy children in the grammar school. He also left £20 a year to the Kinver schoolmaster, as long as he would act as reader in the church on Sundays. If this Edward Barton was John's son, which seems likely, then he may have been honoring his father's memory by endowing the Kinver school.

The Art of Rhetorick is Barton's main contribution to the history of rhetoric. It is a brief octavo volume, containing what Barton calls "these two-languaged twins": a thirty-five page English rhetoric followed by a Latin "Rhetorices Enchiridion" (Handbook of Rhetoric) of fourteen pages. Although the title page attributes the work simply to "J. B., Master of the free-school of Kinfare in Staffordshire," the two-page dedication to John, Lord Poulet, Baron of Hinton Saint George, is signed "John Barton." Barton prefaces his work with a ten-page epistle "To the Reader" in the form of instructions that serve "partly as apologies to the skilfull, for those additions, contractions, alterations herein made,"

First page of the dedicatory preface to John Barton's first book, The Art of Rhetorick concisely and compleatly handled *(1634)*

and "partly as directions to the studious." Barton uses the word *apologies* in the sense of *defenses,* and the instructions often strike a pugnacious note, as Barton justifies his idiosyncracies of terminology and categorization. Although some of Barton's qualifications and corrections of the tradition seem overly ingenious, his project has two primary aims: to pare rhetoric to its bare essentials; and to explain and illustrate the parts of rhetoric in terms a nonspecialist could understand.

The introduction insists on the importance of limiting rhetorical categories and terms to the most fundamental, preserving true distinctions and eliminating unnecessary ones, lest the reader be confused or buried in lists of figures. In Barton's view, too many rhetoric books invent a new name for every minute variation of standard figures, as if each of those variations is a figure in its own right. He will discuss only the main categories. As he explains, "It had been easie to have made my book confused and intricate with prolixitie. . . . if every phrase, whereunto I could have given a proper term to express the form thereof, should have been a Figure, I should have runne *in infinitum*." Rather, Barton claims to have "given generall terms whereto all kinde of pleasing speech may be reduced," so that any variation in figurative speech the reader encounters will fit into one of Barton's terms.

In keeping with this goal, Barton defines and illustrates only the most basic tropes and figures. His opening definition of rhetoric stresses the practical and psychological aim of the art: rhetoric is "the skill of using daintie words, and comely deliverie, whereby to work upon mens affections." Barton divides the art into two parts, "adornation" and "action," rejecting the more common "Elocution" and "Pronunciation" as a false distinction, since both words imply utterance and not gesture. Adornation covers both tropes and figures, which are defined as "an affecting kinde of speech," the former involving a semantic shift, "altering the native signification of a word," the latter a shift in wording or emphasis "without consideration of any borrowed sense."

Following other Ramist rhetorics, Barton distinguishes the tropes into four kinds, again coining his own terms as more evident than the traditional Greek; thus, *metonymy* (replacing the name of a thing with the name of something associated with it) becomes "substitution," *synecdoche* (using a part of something to signify the whole) becomes "comprehension," *metaphor* (when a word or phrase literally meaning one thing is applied to another to imply a likeness) becomes "comparation," and *irony* (in which the meaning intended differs from that which is ostensibly asserted) becomes "simulation." Substitution is further divided into two kinds, perfect and elliptic, one of Barton's innovations. Perfect substitution then falls into four categories which, as Wilbur Samuel Howell has noted, correspond to the first four of the ten Ramist places of logic: substitution of cause for effect, effect for cause, subject for adjunct, and adjunct for subject. The four-part division of comprehension likewise parallels Ramist places, in this case genus, species, whole, and part. Given these divisions, these two types of tropes take up the first fifteen pages; comparation and simulation take barely two pages apiece. Each definition is illustrated by verses from Scripture. Throughout the presentation, Barton's focus is on what he calls the "resolution" of a trope, that is, "the changing of it to a plain speech." Thus, the comments that follow the exposition of each kind of figure focus on explaining how to get from the figurative to the literal meaning of the scriptural illustrations.

Barton's interest in resolution appears also in the final section of the discussion of tropes, which details their "affections." Here "affection" has a technical sense distinct from the way in which he used "affecting" in his initial definition. Rhetoric is the affecting use of language in the sense that it touches the "affects" or emotions and passions as well as the intellect. Technically, though, "affection" applies to ways of further heightening tropes; Barton defines an affection as "the qualitie, whereby it [a trope] requires a second resolution." In cases requiring a second resolution, there is found in the trope "not onely the borrowing of the word, but that joyned with a further Rhetorical vertue," which must also be accounted for. By "borrowing of the word," Barton seems to mean the semantic shift whereby a word is "borrowed" for a figurative use. The affections are five: "abuse" (*catachresis,* "when a Trope is very farre fetcht"); "duplication" (*metalepsis,* "when there is a pluralitie of Tropes in one word"); "continuation" (*allegoryia,* "when a Comparation is continued"); "superlocution" (*hyperbole,* "when a Trope is stretcht beyond moderation"); and "sublocution" (*tapinosis,* "when a word speaks below the intention"). Thus one might have both metonymy and hyperbole in one locution, and the resolution of the locution would require recognizing both, as in the first part of Psalm 119:136: "Rivers of waters run down mine eyes, because they keep not thy law."

In the consideration of the figures that follows, Barton is if anything even more concise; unlike most followers of Ramist rhetorics, he gives less space to the figures than the tropes, for two reasons. First, he regards them as easier to grasp, apparently because they do not involve a borrowed sense that requires a knowledge of logical relations to identify. Second, he feels that in his brief definitions and examples he has "fully discovered" the basic theory, and while the theory may be learned "by art" the practice is largely "the gift of Nature" and cannot be learned by memorizing myriad small distinctions. Therefore, he holds that further rules for the composure of words would be a "hopelesse attempt" if the object were to teach the practice of rhetoric; such rules would only foster affected and forced composition. This explanation reveals Barton's sense that the greatest difficulty in explicating figurative speech lies in grasping the abstract logical relations that govern tropes; whereas the effect of the various figures of speech is direct and plain.

Barton's brief exposition of the figures divides them into the relative and the independent. In relative figures, the word or phrase derives its effect in relation to another word or phrase; thus the six relative figures—repetition, variation, gradation, correction, allusion, and composition—all relate to the preceding words.

Kinver Grammar School in Staffordshire, where Barton taught in the early 1630s

Independent figures, of course, stand alone; the seven independent figures are description, circumstance, diversion, reservation, exclamation, personation, and insinuation. Barton's interest in reducing rhetoric to the most general terms appears in his treatment of the figures; he contends that while perhaps "there may be some examples added to most of the Figures, that will be found somewhat after another manner," so that, for instance, "to Insinuation I might adde insinuation by concession, apologie, simulation, &c.," nonetheless all these variations are clearly subspecies of the terms that he has given, and "doubtlesse the distinguishing of them into so many species would rather obscure them, and puzzle the learner, then be any help to the understanding thereof."

Following this discussion, the English treatise concludes with one page on "action," asserting that of gesture nothing need be said, and of utterance singling out only emphasis. The Latin enchiridion that follows is a straightforward translation of the English exposition and examples, omitting the comments.

As part of his aim to make rhetoric accessible to those nonscholars of ingenious capacity, Barton claims

to have read through several rhetorics, and to have amended or refined where he found it necessary. Some of his attempted improvements, such as the coining of English terms, can still be viewed with sympathy; some, however, suggest the difficulty of fixing linguistic phenomena in categories, and the hazard of engaging in quibbles over definitions. In the introductory instructions, for instance, Barton points out that some examples of metaphor, such as *pronomination* (characterizing by means of a proper name of a person or place, such as "a Judas" or "an Eden"), have been seen instead by such earlier Renaissance rhetoricians as Bartholomew Keckermann or Charles Butler as metonymy or synecdoche, since one thing that conveys an idea is put for another. Thus, it could be an example of synecdoche to call a man a Judas, putting a particular word for a general, and similarly Christ's words to the thief on the cross, "to day thou shalt be with me in PARADISE," could be called synecdoche, "one place of felicitie being put for another." Impatient with this view, which he sees as a kind of loose terminology, Barton asks that his readers focus on crucial differences: "it would save much labour, and prevent a deal of errour, no more but to observe when the words bear the force of comparison; for all such are Metaphors," and thus his examples are clearly metaphors. To illustrate the difference between the comparative relation of metaphor and the real relation of metonymy and synecdoche, Barton gives the example of the phrase "they pricked up their ears." Whereas many would call this a metonymy of the adjunct, pricking of ears being a sign or quality adjoined to the subject "hearkening," Barton points out that it is a sign of hearkening "in beasts" and therefore to apply it to humans is to make a comparison, and speak metaphorically. Whatever the merit of qualifications and corrections of this sort, Barton's ingenuity expends itself almost exclusively on this level of fine-tuning rather than on the breakthroughs to the vital essence of rhetoric that he promises.

Barton is perhaps proudest of a distinction he claims to have discovered, that between perfect and elliptic metonomy. This distinction again signals his focus on resolution, on moving from the figurative to the literal meaning. The perfect metonymy is that where simple substitution of the literal word for the figurative resolves the meaning, or as Barton puts it, "the word wherein the Trope lies, is cast away in the Resolution." He gives as an example the phrase "the writing was in the Syrian tongue," in which language can simply be substituted for tongue. Elliptic metonymy is "when the Cause and Effect, or Subject and Adjunct do meet in the Resolution." In these cases, it is not enough to substitute the nonfigurative word. Thus, to resolve Gen. 25:23, "two nations are in thy womb" (metonymy placing effect for cause), one cannot simply substitute the cause ("two children are in thy womb") but must say "the fathers of two nations," with the "resolution" including both the cause and effect.

However, when Barton is not trying so hard to be ingenious, he can explain concepts quite clearly. For instance, in distinguishing substitution (metonymy) from comprehension (synecdoche), Barton explains that the relation between terms may be real or accidental. The latter, which characterizes metonymy, "continues only while they [the terms] are Tropes, or otherwise they are not necessarily considered together." The verse from Psalm 105, "he was laid in iron," is an example of metonymy because iron is put for fetters, and there may be "Iron, though no fetters." That is, "iron" does not necessarily have anything to do with fetters. But "in synecdoches there is a true Relation considered . . . the Genus must have his Species, and the whole his parts, and contrarily. These do subsist one in another." Thus when one uses Euphrates to mean rivers, the two terms have a necessary relation; the former is a subset of the latter. Summing up the distinction, Barton states, "In a word, Substitution [metonymy] is

from things that have but an affinitie; Comprehension [synecdoche] from things that have a consanguinitie."

While he thus attempts to discover and explain the logic behind rhetorical distinctions, Barton's concern for the nonscholar does lead him to recognize occasionally that absolute precision in terminology is a false goal. He observes, for instance, that "in some examples it skills not, which you call the Subject, which the Adjunct," and acknowledges at another point that "I think good here to note, that it will perhaps be difficult sometimes to hit upon a term whereby to resolve a Trope perfectly." Similarly, the unprecedented proportion of space that Barton gives to metonymy and synecdoche can be ascribed to his sensitivity to a nonscholarly audience, because he is well aware (as he notes in the introduction) that absolute mastery of rhetoric requires command of logic. Since resolution of metonymy and synecdoche depend on a knowledge of logical terms such as subject, adjunct, genus, and species, Barton allocates extra space to their treatment. He allows, though, that some relations "may perhaps be hard to conceive: for unlesse to scholars, it [the logical relation between terms] is not so readie to be apprehended"; nonscholars need not feel discouraged.

There are several characteristics and emphases in Barton's treatise that are worth placing in historical context, though none is striking in itself, and though the treatise apparently had no impact on rhetorical theory, practice, or teaching. The central context for understanding Barton should be that of early Stuart Protestantism. Two features are relevant: the eagerness to encourage and yet stabilize the interpretation of Scripture among laypeople; and the preacher's concern to define correctly the rhetorical nature of Scripture as an aid to exegesis.

During the last years of the sixteenth century there appeared the first of many guides to reading Scripture composed for laypeople. Writers of these guides stressed that this exercise was to be devotional, not critical, but they also acknowledged that lay readers needed some help in recognizing when a text was not to be read literally. As John Smith warns in *The Mysterie of Rhetorique Unvail'd* (1657), "ignorance of Rhetorique is one ground (yea, and a great one) of many dangerous Errors this day."

An even more relevant context in which to view Barton's book is the contemporary concern for accurate exegesis by ministers. Barton is consciously writing for nonscholars; nonetheless, the nature of early Stuart schooling entailed a focus on teaching skills useful to the learned professions, chief among them the ministry. Barton's work participates in an ongoing Protestant concern to come to grips with the figurative nature of Scripture so that preachers could correctly expound the text. As Barbara Kiefer Lewalski points out, Richard Bernard's influential treatise on preaching (*The Faithfull Shepheard*, 1607) places special emphasis on knowledge of rhetoric, because, as Bernard writes in the second edition (1621), "everie where a Divine shall meet with figurative speeches in holy Scripture, which without Retoricke hee cannot explain." Bernard's summary of the parts of rhetoric touches precisely the heads Barton covers, as does the fuller treatment in the German theologian Salomon Glass's *Rhetorica Sacræ* (Sacred Rhetoric), the fifth part of his *Philologia Sacræ* (Sacred Philology, 1623). Other authors compiled lists of figures found in Scripture, such as Robert Cawdrey's *A Treasvrie or Store-Hovse of Similies* (1600).

This interest by preachers in the figures of Scripture was, Lewalski notes, "not primarily directed to them as ornament, but was in the interest of the most precise apprehension of divine truth." Evidence that Barton shared this approach appears at the end of his introduction, when he laments, "That from the ignorance of Rhetorick (besides many other inconveniences) grosse misconstructions of Scripture have sprung, experience testifies." It is true that he begins the introduction with the assertion that the "beautifull varietie, majesticall style, and gracefull order" of Scripture "incomparably transcends the most pithie and pleasing strains of humane Eloquence." However, Barton devotes no space in his text to explaining this assertion. Rather, the emphasis on resolution of figures to their literal sense indicates the primary function of rhetoric for Barton's treatise, as does the single example he gives of how rhetoric may clarify Scripture. Barton explains that confronted with Dan. 4:27, "break off thy sinnes by righteousnesse, and thine iniquities by shewing mercy unto the poor," he was able to clear it "from seeming to confirm the Popish doctrine of making satisfactions for our sinnes by our works" by showing that "iniquities" was a synecdoche, "the generall word Iniquitie being put for Oppression, one kinde of iniquitie." The modern reader may not be satisfied that Barton is right to see a figure in the word, let alone that his resolution is self-evident. His example, however, indicates how rhetorical analysis was essential to Protestants who depended on Scripture alone to confirm their doctrine.

A final sign that Barton's approach was shaped by the early Stuart concern for preaching appears in his definitions of rhetoric and its two parts. Barton adds to the standard Ramist definition of rhetoric that it is the art of speaking well, the qualification "whereby to work upon mens affections." The comment on this definition adds that rhetoric uses words that are moving and pleasing. Likewise, the definitions of both tropes and figures describe them as "an affecting kinde of speech." As Deborah Shuger has shown, the affections (or feel-

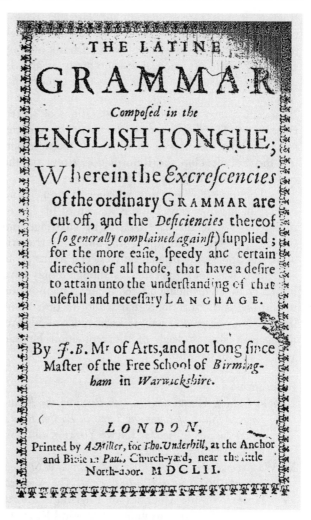

Title page for Barton's textbook, which includes a section on figurative language

ings, passions, and desires) were increasingly central to post-Reformation homiletic theory as it sought to define a Christian grand style that moved the emotions by a passionate intensity.

Viewing Barton's work within this context puts it in a more sympathetic light than has been shone on him by some critics of *The Art of Rhetorick*. Donald Lemen Clark found Barton's approach completely unsympathetic; in his *Rhetoric and Poetry in the Renaissance: A Study of Rhetorical Terms in English Renaissance Literary Criticism* (1922), Clark belittles Barton and others who focused on elocution for their "perversion" of rhetoric and their "jargon." However, Clark badly misrepresents Barton, presenting as a passage from the art what is in fact a pastiche of definitions taken from throughout Barton's work, and run together in such a way as to seem nonsensical. In his *Logic and Rhetoric in England, 1500–1700* (1961), Howell offers the only attempt to summarize Barton's work and his place in

English Renaissance rhetoric. For Howell, Barton offers little of interest; essentially, he "devotes himself to the Ramistic convention, and varies from it only by giving the topic of action almost no space at all." In her *Sacred Rhetoric: The Christian Grand Style in the English Renaissance* (1988), Shuger similarly finds Barton "innocent of any theoretical considerations of sacred rhetoric"; unlike those writers who wrote the magisterial preaching rhetorics upon which she focuses, Barton did not develop the Reformation stress on the relation between rhetoric and the affections.

The question remains whether Barton found success in his own day. Little is known of his life or career other than the bare facts of his marriage and that he was buried in July 1675. Since his rhetoric book was apparently printed only once, it seems probable that it was not a great success, though it may have been a factor in his being offered the teaching position in Birmingham. Izon notes that school records show that Barton was paid exactly twice as much as his predecessor—a sign, indeed, of the reputation he had acquired as an educator.

References:

Donald Lemen Clark, *Rhetoric and Poetry in the Renaissance: A Study of Rhetorical Terms in English Renaissance Literary Criticism* (New York: Columbia University Press, 1922);

M. W. Greenslade, ed., *A History of the County of Stafford*, volume 20, *Seisdon Hundred (Part)*, The Victoria History of the Counties of England (Oxford: Published for the Institute of Historical Research by the Oxford University Press, 1984), pp. 155–158;

Joseph Hill, *The Book Makers of Old Birmingham: Authors, Printers and Book Sellers* (Birmingham: Printed at the Shakespeare Press for Cornish Brothers, 1907);

Wilbur Samuel Howell, *Logic and Rhetoric in England, 1500–1700* (New York: Russell & Russell, 1961), pp. 258, 273–275;

T. W. Hutton, *King Edward's School, Birmingham: 1552–1952* (Oxford: Blackwell, 1952);

John Izon, ed., *The Records of King Edward's School, Birmingham,* volume 6: *A Supplementary Miscellany* (Oxford: Printed for the Dugdale Society at the University Press, 1974), pp. xiv, xviii, 34, 36, 40–41;

Barbara Kiefer Lewalski, *Protestant Poetics and the Seventeenth-Century English Religious Lyric* (Princeton: Princeton University Press, 1979);

James J. Murphy, "One Thousand Neglected Authors: The Scope and Importance of Renaissance Rhetoric," in *Renaissance Eloquence: Studies in the Theory and Practice of Renaissance Rhetoric,* edited by Murphy (Berkeley: University of California Press, 1983), pp. 20–36;

Walter J. Ong, *Ramus and Talon Inventory: A Short-title Inventory of the Published Works of Peter Ramus (1515–1572) and of Omer Talon (ca. 1510–1562) in Their Original and in Their Variously Altered Forms: with Related Material: 1. The Ramist Controversies: A Descriptive Catalogue. 2. Agricola Check List: A Short-title Inventory of Some Printed Editions and Printed Compendia of Rudolph Agricola's Dialectical Invention (De inventione dialectica)* (Cambridge, Mass.: Harvard University Press, 1958);

Deborah Shuger, *Sacred Rhetoric: The Christian Grand Style in the English Renaissance* (Princeton: Princeton University Press, 1988), pp. 96, 155.

Thomas Blount

(1618? – 26 December 1679)

Dana Aspinall
Assumption College

and

Douglas W. Hayes
University of Toronto

BOOKS: *The Academie of Eloquence. Containing a Compleat English Rhetorique, Exemplified, With Common-Places, and Formes, digested into an easie and Methodical way to speak and write fluently, according to the mode of the present times, Together with Letters, both Amorous and Moral, Upon emergent occasions* (London: Printed by Thomas Newcomb for Humphrey Moseley, 1654; enlarged edition, 1656; revised edition, London: Printed by Henry Lloyd for Anne Moseley, 1663; revised edition, London: Printed by Thomas Johnson for Peter Parker, 1670; revised editon, London: Printed for Chr. Wilkinson & Chae Harper, 1683);

Glossographia: Or A Dictionary, Interpreting all such Hard Words, Whether Hebrew, Greek, Latin, Italian, Spanish, French, Teutonick, Belgick, British or Saxon, as are now used in our refined English Tongue. Also the Terms of Divinity, Law, Physick, Mathematicks, Heraldry, Anatomy, War, Musick, Architecture; and of several other Arts and Sciences Explicated. With Etymologies, Definitions, and Historical Observations on the same. Very useful for all such as desire to understand what they read. By T. B. of the Inner-Temple, Barrester (London: Printed by Thomas Newcomb & sold by Humphrey Moseley & George Sawbridge, 1656; revised and enlarged edition, 1659; revised and enlarged edition, London: Printed by Thomas Newcomb & sold by John Martyn, 1670; revised and enlarged edition, London: Printed by Thomas Newcomb for Robert Boulter, 1674; London: Printed by Thomas Newcomb & sold by Thomas Flesher, 1681);

The Lamps of the Law, And Lights of the Gospel. Or The Titles of some late Spiritual, Polemical, Metaphysical new Books, diligently collected into a Volume. By Grass & Hay Wythers (London, 1658);

Boscobel: Or, The History Of His Sacred Majesties Most miraculous Preservation After the Battle of Worcester, 3. Sept. 1651 (London: Printed for Henry Seile, 1660); enlarged as *Boscobel: Or The Compleat History Of His Sacred Majesties Most Miraculous Preservation After the Battle of Worcester, 3 Sept. 1651. Introduc'd by an exact Relation of that Battle; and Illustrated with a Map of the City* (London: Printed for Ann Seile, 1662);

A catalogue of the lords, knights, and gentlemen (of the Catholick religion) that were slain in the Late Warr, in Defence of their King and Countrey. As also of those whose Estates were sold by the Rump for that Cause (London, 1660);

Calendarium Catholicum: Or, An Universall Almanack, 1661. The first after Leap-Year. With Memorable Observations, Never before Printed, anonymous (London, 1661); revised as *Calendarium Catholicum: Or An Universal Almanack, 1662. The Second after Leap-Year. With Memorable Observations, And An Exposition of all the Festival Dayes in the Year* (London, 1662); revised as *A New Almanack, after the Old Fashion; For 1663. The 3d after Leap-Year. With Memorable Observations: And An Exposition of all the Festival Dayes in the Year* (London, 1663); revised as *Calendarium Catholicum. Or, An Universal Almanack, 1664. Being Leap-Year. With Memorable Observations; And An Exposition of all the Feasts in the Year* (London, 1664);

Booker Rebuk'd For His Telescopivm Vranicvm, or Ephemeris: Wherein, from the Sun's Ingress into the Cardinal Points; the Eclipses of the two great Luminaries; the Conjunction & Configuration of the Planets, and other Celestial Appendices, 'tis more then probably conjectured, That John Bookers Almanack 1665. is very Erroneous, to say no more (London: Printed for Robert Crofts, 1665);

Νομο-λεξικον: A Law-Dictionary. Interpreting such difficult and obscure Words and Terms, As are found either in Our Common or Statute, Ancient or Modern Lawes. With Ref-

erences to the several Statutes, Records, Registers, Law-Books, Charters, Ancient Deeds, and Manuscripts, wherein the Words are used: and Etymologies, where they properly occur. . . . By Thomas Blount of the Inner Temple, Esq (London: Printed by Thomas Newcomb for John Martin & Henry Herringman, 1670);

The several Statutes Concerning Bankrupts, Methodically digested. Together with the resolutions of our learned Judges on them. As likewise the Statutes 13th. Eliz. and 27 Eliz. touching fraudulent Conveyences; with the like resolutions on them. By T. B. Esq (London: Printed for T. Twyford, 1670)–includes The Resolutions Of the Judges Upon the several Statutes Of Bankrupts: As also The like Resolutions upon 13 Eliz. And 27 Eliz. Touching Fraudulent Conveyances. By T. B. Esq; republished as The Judges Resolutions Upon the Several Statutes Concerning Bankrupts, With The like Resolutions on the Statutes of 13 Eliz. and 27 Eliz. touching fraudulent Conveyances. By George Billinghurst of Grays-Inne, Esq (London: Printed for Henry Twyford, 1676);

Animadversions Upon Sʳ Richard Baker's Chronicle, And It's Continuation. Wherein many Errors are discover'd and some Truths advanced. By T. B. Esq. (Oxford: Printed by H. H. for Richard Davis, 1672);

A World of Errors Discovered In The New World of Words. Or General English Dictionary. And In Nomothetes, Or The Interpreter of Law-Words and Terms. By Tho. Blount of the Inner Temple, Esquire (London: Printed by Thomas Newcomb for Abel Roper, John Martin & Henry Herringman, 1673);

Fragmenta Antiquitatis. Antient Tenures of Land, And Jocular Customs Of some Mannors. Made publick for the diversion of some and instruction of others. By T. B. of the Inner-Temple Esquire (London: Printed by the Assigns of Richard and Edward Atkins for Abel Roper, Thomas Basset & Christopher Wilkinson, 1679);

The 1675 Thomas Blount Manuscript History of Herefordshire, edited by Richard Botzum, Catherine Botzum, and Norman Reeves (Hereford, U.K.: Lapridge, 1997).

Editions: Boscobel, in The Boscobel Tracts: Relating to the Escape of Charles the Second after the Battle of Worcester, and His Subsequent Adventures, edited by John Hughes (London & Edinburgh: Blackwood / London: Cadell, 1830), pp. 165–263;

Boscobel, in Memoirs of the Court of Charles the Second by Count Grammont, with Numerous Additions and Illustrations, as Ed. By Sir Walter Scott. Also: The Personal History of Charles, Including the King's Own Account of His Escape and Preservation after the Battle of Worcester, as Dictated to Pepys. And The Boscobel Tracts, Or, Contemporary Narratives of His Majesty's Adventures, from the Murder of His Father to the Restoration (London: Bohn, 1846), pp. 477–536;

Tenures of Land & Customs of Manors Originally Collect by Thomas Blount and Republished with Large Additions and Improvements in 1784 and 1815. A New Edition Entirely Re-Arranged, Carefully Corrected and Considerably Enlarged, edited by William Carew Hazlitt (London: Reeves & Turner, 1874);

Boscobel, in Boscobel: Or, The History of the Most Miraculous Preservation of King Charles II. After the Battle of Worcester, September the Third, 1651 by Thomas Blount. To Which Is Added the King's Own Account of His Adventures, Dictated to Mr. Samuel Pepys, edited by Charles G. Thomas (London: Tylston & Edwards, 1894), pp. 3–119;

Boscobel, in After Worcester Fight: Being a Companion Volume to "The Flight of the King," edited by Allan Fea (London & New York: John Lane, 1904), pp. 45–153;

Glossographia, 1656, English Linguistics, 1500–1800, no. 153, edited by R. C. Alston (Menston, U.K.: Scolar Press, 1969);

Nomo-lexicon: A Law Dictionary (Los Angeles: Sherwin & Freutel, 1970);

The Academie of Eloquence, English Linguistics, 1500–1800, no. 296, edited by Alston (Menston, U.K.: Scolar Press, 1971);

Glossographia, Anglistica & Americana, no. 32 (Hildesheim, Germany: G. Olms Verlag, 1972);

Boscobel, or, The History of His Sacred Majesties Most Miraculous Preservation after the Battle of Worcester, 3 Sept. 1651 (Newtown, U.K.: Jacobas, 1996).

OTHER: Henry Estienne, The Art of making Devises: Treating Of Hieroglyphicks, Symboles, Emblemes, Ænigma's, Sentences, Parables, Reverses of Medalls, Armes, Blazons, Cimiers, Cyphres, and Rebus. First Written in French By Henry Estienne, Lord of Fossez, Interpreter to the French King for the Latine and Greek Tongues: And Translated into English by Tho: Blount of the Inner Temple, Gent., translated by Blount (London: Printed by William Ellis & John Grismond for Humphrey Moseley, 1646); revised and enlarged as The Art of making Devises: Treating of Hieroglyphicks, Symboles, Emblemes, Ænigma's, Sentences, Parables, Reverses of Medals, Armes, Blazons, Cimiers, Cyphers and Rebus. Written in French by Henry Estienne esquire, interpreter to the French King for the Latine and Greeke tongues: translated into English, and embelished with divers brasse figures by T. B. of the Inner Temple, Gent. Whereunto is added A Catalogue of Coronet-Devises both on the Kings, and the Parliaments side in the late Warre (London: Printed for Richard Royston, 1648);

"The Pedigree of the Blounts," in *The Compleat Gentleman: Fashioning Him absolute in the most Necessary and Commendable Qualities, concerning Mind, or Body, that may be required in a Person of Honor. To which is added the Gentlemans Exercise Or, An exquisite practice, as well for drawing all manner of Beasts, as for making Colours, to be used in Painting, Limming, &c,* third edition, by Henry Peacham the Younger, edited by Blount (London: Printed by Evan Tyler for Richard Thrale, 1661), pp. 230–234;

John Rastell, *Les Termes De La Ley: Or, Certain difficult and obscure Words and Terms of the Common Laws and Statutes of this Realm now in use expounded and explained. Newly corrected and enlarged. With an Addition of above one hundred Words,* edited and revised by Blount (London: Printed by John Streater, James Flesher & Henry Twyford, Assigns of Richard Atkyns & Edward Atkyns, 1667);

"The Several Forms Of Instruments Relating to the Affairs of Merchants, And Traders: Very useful for Scriveners in London, And other Maritim Towns, and Places of Trade. The Particulars of which will appear in the Table, next following. By T. B. Esq," in *Arcana Clericalia, Or, The Mysteries of Clarkship: Being A sure way of Settling Estates By Deeds, Fines, and Recoveries With the Forms of all manner of Charter-Parties in Maritime Cities, Towns and Corporations. With A Table of all the Principal matters therein contained,* by George Billinghurst (London: Printed for Henry Twyford, 1674), pp. 177–351.

Thomas Blount, Catholic, Royalist, lawyer, and antiquary, is known among scholars of rhetoric as the author of *The Academie of Eloquence* (1654). According to critic Wilbur Samuel Howell, Blount belongs to the so-called Neo-Ciceronian school of rhetoricians because his book combines the theories of both the Ramists (followers of French educational reformer Pierre de La Ramée) and the older Ciceronians (followers of the classical rhetorician Cicero). Blount's book is unusual, however, in that it combines three traditions in rhetoric: stylistic, formulary, and epistolary. Often criticized for his using, without acknowledgment, John Hoskyns's manuscript work "Direcōns for Speech and Style" (written circa 1599; not published until 1935), Blount deserves recognition not for the originality of his work but for the popularity it attained and the role it played in the rhetorical education of his society. He produced one of the most popular English rhetorics of the seventeenth century; he packaged Hoskyns for mass consumption; and he made minor but original contributions to epistolary and formulary rhetoric. He may have contributed indirectly to the rhetorical climate that encouraged the development of a plain style during the Restoration; more importantly, however, Blount broke new ground by addressing his book to a readership that included women as well as men.

Born at Bordesley Park, near Hewell, Worcestershire, probably in 1618, Thomas Blount was the eldest son of Myles Blount and Anne Bustard Blount. A descendant of Sir William Blount (or, le Blound) and Sir Robert Blount, both of whom came to England immediately following the Norman Conquest of 1066, Myles Blount was the only surviving son of Roger Blount of Grendon Warren; Myles Blount also owned property in Bircher and Yarpole, small villages in Herefordshire. Yet, for all his local influence and prestige, Myles Blount was devoutly Catholic and refused to accept the Anglican faith–even outwardly, as some contemporary recusants chose to do. Thomas Blount's mother's family also had some property and were the source of his later acquisitions in Essex and Warwickshire. Like the Blounts, the Bustards were stalwart Catholics, many of whom suffered for their faith during and after the war years.

Blount's early education remains something of a mystery, but in 1639 he became a student of the Inner Temple. His friend Anthony à Wood, in his *Athenæ Oxonienses* (1813), notes that Blount was "never advantaged in learning by the help of an university, only his own geny [natural bent] and industry, together with the helps of his scholastical acquaintance during his continuance in the Temple, before and after he was barrester." Blount was called to the Bar on 13 November 1648; however, as a Catholic, he was forbidden by statute to practice law in the courts. Although never a practitioner of law, he may have served as a conveyancer, or specialist in properties, an office that benefitted him greatly in the years to come.

After his departure from the Inner Temple, Blount produced *The Art of making Devises: Treating Of Hieroglyphicks, Symboles, Emblemes, Ænigma's, Sentences, Parables, Reverses of Medalls, Armes, Blazons, Cimiers, Cyphres, and Rebus* (1646), a translation of Henri Estienne's *L'Art De Fair Les Devises* (1645). Dedicated to "the Nobilitie and Gentry of England," *The Art of making Devises* also includes in Blount's rather long dedication both a useful history of the device tradition in England (starting with Henry III) and a detailed description of the preferred devices of the English kings, as well as a discussion of the evolution of emblem making in England. In addition, Blount makes reference to the ongoing First English Civil War (1642–1646), noting devices and mottoes used on cavalry pennants by supporters of Charles I and supporters of Parliament. In the 1648 edition Blount expanded on these descriptions of the Royalist and Parliamentarian devices, in catalogues added as addenda. Midway through the text Blount supplies

Engraved title page for the 1646 edition of Thomas Blount's translation and adaptation of Henri Estienne's L'Art De Fair Les Devises *(1645), with examples of impresas, devices used by noble families*

several original engravings of the reverses of medals. Alan R. Young's 1999 study of "the cultural aspirations underlying Estienne's work and their subsequent re-working by Blount" demonstrates the extent of Blount's shaping influence in this translation.

Blount's translation of *L'Art De Fair Les Devises* was sold by Humphrey Moseley, the acknowledged Royalist publisher throughout the English Civil Wars. Suffering an even worse plight than did other Royalists, Catholics loyal to Charles I generally were denied the right of compounding for (leasing back) their sequestered properties, lands that had been taken into custody by Parliament. Because of the severe sequestration ordinance of 27 March 1643, the Blount family temporarily lost two-thirds of the revenue from its estates in Herefordshire and Worcestershire.

During the worst of these times Thomas Blount married Anne Church, another Catholic recusant Royalist. Her father, Edmund Church, took up arms against Parliament and was taken prisoner at Shrewsbury. During his confinement, Church's lands in Essex

were seized and stayed in Parliamentary hands until his son-in-law, Thomas, regained control of the rents years later. Always foregrounding his own Catholicism, Blount mentioned these familial experiences in his *A New Almanack, after the Old Fashion* (1663), a revised edtion of the work first published in 1661 as *Calendarium Catholicum: Or An Universall Almanack, 1661,* an emotional description of the terrible treatment Catholics underwent during these years.

Following *The Art of making Devises,* Blount's next publication was *The Academie of Eloquence,* a popular English rhetoric published in 1654, with five further editions by 1683. The frontispiece, engraved by William Faithorne, a Royalist and probable acquaintance of Blount, depicts Mercury, messenger of the gods and eloquence personified, holding a cloth on which the title of the book and author's name are written. Mercury is surrounded by four labeled portraits of historical figures: Demosthenes, Cicero, Francis Bacon, and Philip Sidney. The engraving serves as an effective visual introduction to a book that includes a Ciceronian stylistic rhetoric, several quotations from Sidney's *Arcadia* (1590), two sections on formulae apparently inspired by Bacon, and a general assertion of the social and political value of eloquence, reminiscent of Demosthenes. The purpose of the book, as Blount states in his "Epistle dedicatory," was to "serve as an inducement to the youth of both Sexes" so that they might be "furnisht with all necessary materialls and helps in order to the acquiring so great a treasure [as eloquence]." The text of *The Academie of Eloquence* consists of four sections: "An English Rhetorique exemplified" (pages 1–48), "*Formulæ Majores,* or Common Places" (pages 49–118), "*Formulæ Minores,* or, Little Forms for Style or Speech" (pages 119–140), and a section on "Letters" (pages 149–232) prefaced by "Instructions for writing and addressing Letters" (pages 141–147).

The first section on stylistic rhetoric was apparently well known and respected. Not only was it recommended by Charles Hoole in *A New Discovery of the old Art of Teaching Schoole* (1660), but it served as a primary source for John Smith's *The Mysterie of Rhetorique Vnvail'd* (1657), which went through eleven editions before 1740. In a passage not found in Hoskyns's work, Blount defines *figures* and *tropes* as "the vertues of Speech and Stile" and then moves immediately to definitions and illustrations of rhetorical figures and tropes. He quotes passages from Sidney's *Arcadia,* as well as from Cicero, St. Augustine, Niccolò Machiavelli, and Desiderins Erasmus. As does Hoskins, Blount begins with *metaphor* and ends with *concessio.*

Hoyt H. Hudson has described Blount's first section as "nothing but a copy of the second, third, fourth, and fifth sections of Hoskins's *Directions,* with such omissions and changes as Blount's fancy, reason, or inadvertence dictated." Subsequent critics have faulted Blount for not identifying Hoskyns as his main source. They see a profession of originality in Blount's claim to have produced "a more exact English Rhetorique, then has been hitherto extant." In the "Epistle Dedicatory," however, Blount acknowledges his sources indirectly:

> The Formula's are but Analects, which like the Humble-bee I gather'd in Spring time out of the choisest Flowers of our English Garden; nor have I in the Rhetorick or Letters transplanted much from my own barren Seminary; I may say to some noble Correspondents, what the Poet did of old in a like Case, *sic vos non Vobis*—But, you will easily distinguish Tinsill from better mettal: what is mine will appear to be so, by the Bluntismes that frequently occur, the rest are of better allay; So that, if the defects of my own Essayes be but pardoned, the rest I am confident will abide the touch, and pass for Sterling.

Presumably, "Sterling" is Blount's reference to the material taken from Hoskyns's work, in contrast to his own "Tinsill."

Blount's second section, "*Formulæ Majores,* or Common Places," provides passages for readers to imitate in their speaking and writing. Blount quotes from a variety of contemporary authors, such as Henry Wotton and Thomas Browne, and arranges the passages under subject headings such as "Absence," "Beauty," and "Joy." Under "Absence," for example, he quotes this passage from an unidentified source: "In absence my grief grows, in finding my present estate so weak in fortune, and my deserts so slender in nature; that not knowing with Anthony how to requite his Cleopatra, I onely rest with Anthony, to dye for my Cleopatra." The "*Formulæ Minores,* or, Little Forms For Style or Speech" constitute a third section and function in much the same way as the commonplaces of the previous section. Readers have resources such as "He summon'd his wits together, and set them all on the Rack of Invention" to draw from in cultivating their own eloquence, and need only to scan the list to find what they require. Spaces are included in some of the *formulæ minores* so that the reader can insert the name of the person or thing being discussed or addressed: "Casting his eye (the Messenger of his heart) upon____." This format is yet another example of Blount's effort to make his book useful to his target audience, "the youth of both Sexes."

In his "Epistle Dedicatory," Blount suggests that Bacon inspired him to include the sections of formulae: "In the second part, you have formulae majores or Common-places, upon the most usual subjects for stile and speech; The use and advantage whereof is asserted by my Lord Bacon." He then quotes a passage from Bacon's *The Advancement of Learning* (1605), and mentions Bacon again in reference to the "Formulae minores (as my Lord calls them)." Karl R. Wallace has pointed out that Blount "appears not to have appreciated that Bacon's emphasis, both in his system as a whole and in the doctrine and use of commonplaces, was on invention and matter" rather than *elocutio* (style). According to Ray Nadeau, Blount's book was one of three collections—along with Thomas Earnaby's *Index Rhetoricus* (Rhetorical Index, 1626) and John Clarke's *Formulæ Oratriæ* (Oratical Formulas, 1630)—of oratorical formulae "holding the center of the formula stage" in seventeenth-century England and the only one in the vernacular. These collections all but disappeared in the eighteenth century because they relied almost exclusively on Latin examples and Latin was gradually becoming less and less important in the schools.

The last section of *The Academie of Eloquence* serves as a brief epistolary rhetoric. It is divided into three parts: "Instructions for writing and addressing letters,"

"Letters," and "Superscriptions for Letters." The first part (pages 141–148) is further divided into four parts: "the Invention; the Fashion, or inditing (as we call it); the Hand-writing, and the Orthography." Hudson has noted that Blount's instructions are derived almost entirely from Hoskins, "with the addition of some remarks on handwriting and orthography." George Williamson argues that Blount made "important but slight alterations" in Hoskins's discussions of brevity and perspecuity–that is, the first two of the four qualities of epistolary style that make up "the Fashion." The seventy-seven model letters (pages 149–226) that follow the "Instructions" have descriptive labels such as "A Letter to revive Freindship in the Son, by remembrance of the Fathers love" and "A facetious letter upon sending a Christmas Pye to a Friend." Each letter is numbered and signed with different initials, including "T. B." (probably Blount himself). These are followed by "Superscriptions for Letters, to be addressed to all sorts of persons, according to the usage of the present times." This section of *The Academie of Eloquence* seems to have served as a model for Henry Carey's *The Female Secretary* (1671), a letter-writing manual for women.

To modern critics, *The Academie of Eloquence* is especially important as an early edition of Hoskins's rhetoric. Both Hudson and Gary Grund have compared *The Academie of Eloquence* and *Directions for Speech and Style* with illuminating results, noting Blount's editorial work. Michael Bath, in a 1999 essay on Hoskins and Blount, points out that "the changes which Blount makes to Hoskins's text . . . may offer us some clues as to how at least one early reader construed its meaning" and thus contribute significantly to studies of Hoskins.

The *National Union Catalogue of Pre-1956 Imprints* lists a microfilm copy of a 1653 edition of Blount's *The Academie of Eloquence,* stating that the original is in the University of Michigan Library. Apparently on the authority of this *NUC* listing, the second edition of Donald Goddard Wing's *Short-title Catalogue of Books Printed in England, Scotland, Ireland, Wales, and British America, and of English Books Printed in Other Countries, 1641–1700* (1994) added the 1653 edition to its list of Blount's publications and assigned it a number. But Kathryn L. Beam, curator of the Humanities Collections in the Special Collections Library at the University of Michigan, confirms that the 1653 edition is a ghost, as Theo Bongaerts had suggested in his 1978 edition of Blount's correspondence.

Blount's first lexicographical work, *Glossographia: Or A Dictionary, Interpreting all such Hard Words, Whether Hebrew, Greek, Latin, Italian, Spanish, French, Teutonick, Belgick, British or Saxon, as are now used in our refined English Tongue,* was printed by Thomas Newcomb for Humphrey Moseley in 1656. It included a dedicatory poem by "J. S." (probably Blount's friend John Sergeant). With the infusion of so many new words into English during the seventeenth century and the absence of a worthy compendium for them since Henry Cockeram's *The English Dictionarie: or, An Interpreter of hard English words* (1623), Blount's *Glossographia* was an important work and met with immediate success.

In his prefatory "To the Reader," Blount claims the work took "up the vacancy" of more than twenty years to compile and that it originated from his own ignorance of recent evolutions in English idiom. From the start Blount asserts that this dictionary, only the fourth monolingual one in English, is much more comprehensive than any dictionary previous to it. He includes artisans' terms, commoners' slang, physicians' jargon, and illustrations, as well as a generous selection of legal terminology. *Glossographia* is also the first English dictionary to give credit to some sources and to attempt etymologies of selected words. According to M. M. Mathews, Blount cited the Bible and legal statutes most frequently, underlining his two most passionate intellectual occupations.

Glossographia also includes references to the current turmoil in England and opprobrious castigations of the Puritans, as well as equally laudatory commentary on those loyal to the monarchy. For instance, when defining "Populace," a word often employed by supporters of Parliament, Blount reveals his disdain by writing, "the Rascal people, base multitude, meaner sort of the vulgar." And when describing specific radical sects, Blount's rancor sharpens even more. Listing the "erroneous Tenets" of Anabaptists, for example, Blount scornfully records:

1 That Christ took not flesh from the Virgin Mary, but that he past through her, as the Sun beams do through glass, or rain through a spout.

2 That there is no original sin.

3 That children ought not to be baptized.

Blount's fervent adherence to Roman Catholicism and his concomitant loyalty to the Stuart monarchy blend frequently. Even comments such as, "When mens minds once begin to enure themselves to dislike, whatever is usual is disdained: They affect novelty in speech, they recal oreworn and uncouth words, they forge new phrases, and that which is newest is best liked," lose their seeming innocuousness after one reads Blount's complete work.

Glossographia went into a second edition in 1659, two more editions in 1661, and further editions in 1670, 1674, and 1681. Blount revised and expanded his *Glos-*

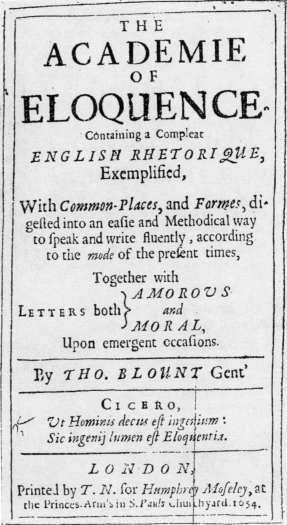

Frontispiece (engraved by William Faithorne) and title page for Blount's second book, one of the
most popular English rhetorics of the seventeenth century

sographia with each edition published in his lifetime. The
work also became either the inspiration or the direct
source of several other early dictionaries. These include
Edward Phillips's *The New World of English Words: Or, a
General Dictionary* (1658), and Phillips's subsequent revisions; John Dutton's *The Ladies Dictionary: Being a General
Entertainment For the Fair Sex* (1694); and the anonymous
Glossographia Anglicana Nova (1707).

In 1658 Blount's *The Lamps of the Law, And Lights of
the Gospel* was printed. In this pamphlet, which takes the
form of a mock catalogue of legal and religious works,
Blount mixes real titles and authors with imaginary
ones. Much in imitation of the Royalist John Berkenhead's satirical catalogues, Blount's *The Lamps of the Law*
betrays many of the same prejudices hidden in the definitions of his *Glossographia*.

When Charles II returned to England in 1660,
many Catholics led in cheering the Restoration. Much
of their celebratory rhetoric was echoed by Blount in
his *Boscobel: Or, The History Of His Sacred Majesties Most
miraculous Preservation After the Battle of Worcester, 3. Sept.
1651* (1660), the most popular contemporary account
of Charles II's escape after the Royalist defeat at
Worcester that effectively concluded the Second English
Civil War (1648–1651). A second edition was published in 1660; an enlarged edition was published in
1662 and again in 1680. The work was republished at
least six more times during the eighteenth century and
at least thirteen times in the nineteenth century.

Dedicated to the returning monarch, Blount's
work prides itself on its factual retelling of Charles's
movements from the defeat at Worcester on 3 Septem-

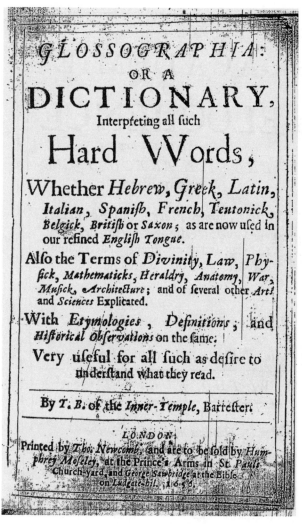

Title page for Blount's first lexicographical work, the first English dictionary to include etymologies

Necessary and Commendable Qualities, concerning Mind, or Body, that may be required in a Person of Honor in 1661 and attached to it "The Pedigree of the Blounts," a family tree that highlights the Blounts' Catholic lineage. By this time Blount had acquired the financial means to support his literary and legal pursuits. Thomas and Anne Blount's only child, Elizabeth, was born sometime before 24 September 1663, when she is mentioned in her grandfather's will. In 1669 he obtained all rights and titles to the Blount family property from his mother, who was buried on 8 May.

After *Booker Rebuk'd For His Telescopium Uranicum* (1665), a refutation of John Booker's *Telescopium Uranicum* (Urania's Telescope, 1665), a celestial diary that correlates astrological occurrences with Christian redemption, Blount returned to lexicography with a preface to a new edition of John Rastell's *Les Termes De La Ley: Or, Certain difficult and obscure Words and Terms of the Common Laws and Statutes of this Realm now in use expounded and explained* (The Terms of the Law, 1667; originally published in 1527 under the title *Expositiones Terminorum Legum Anglorum* [Expositions of the Terms of the Laws of England]). In his attached preface to this first-ever alphabetical dictionary of English law, Blount emphasizes the tremendous influence and value this book had within the law profession. Blount also briefly recounts the publication history of the book and its long-standing affiliation with Rastell's name. Blount then explains his reasons for undertaking the new edition: misspellings and factual errors in the older editions, their poor alphabetizing of the terms, and the many changes in law codes since their publications. Blount added about one hundred terms to his edition.

Alternating his time between his estate in Orleton and his rooms in Fig Tree Court, London, Blount had established acquaintances with leading antiquarians, Catholic apologists, and several prominent lawyers by the time his edition of *Les Termes De La Ley* was published. His passion for proper legal terminology, which paralleled his zeal for decorous formal rhetoric, became even more clear with Νομο-λεξικον: *A Law-Dictionary* (1670). Considered his most important legal work, the Νομο-λεξικον (*Nomo-lexicon*) was dedicated to Sir Orlando Bridgeman, Lord Keeper of the Great Seal of England; Sir John Kelyng, Lord Chief Justice of the King's Bench; and Sir John Vaughan, Lord Chief Justice of His Majesty's Court of Common Plea. As had Blount, these three men remained piously devoted to the Royalist cause during the English Civil Wars and equally committed to legal exactitude after the wars.

Blount's preface to the work is, predictably, another commitment to exactitude in legal language. His overall purpose with its publication is to stress "how necessary it is to know the signification of

ber 1651 until 9 September 1651, when he arrived at Bentley Hall, Staffordshire. According to Blount, Charles may have been aided in his escape by Catholics. His appreciation for the Catholic contribution to his cause informed his signing of the Declaration of Breda in April of 1660, which included a provision for liberty of conscience, that is, tolerance for any faith that did not threaten the crown. Upon his accession in May 1660, Charles II promised tolerance toward Catholics.

Despite their loyalties to the crown during the English Civil Wars and Charles II's initially favorable regard for them, Catholics enjoyed little tolerance or fiscal autonomy after the Restoration in 1660. By early 1663 the hostile stance of Parliament toward Catholics was clear; publications of Catholic books and treatises dwindled, including Blount's almanacs. However, he did edit a third edition of Henry Peacham the Younger's *The Compleat Gentleman: Fashioning Him absolute in the most*

Words." Blount's work springs from a thirty-year period wherein "I was hunting after the difficult and uncuth Terms of it [law], and got nothing, but my own satisfaction."

Blount begins his preface by anticipating any objections to a work of this sort and by pointing out the "Defects" in the three most prestigious prior legal lexicons: John Cowell's *The Interpreter, or, Booke containing the signification of words* (1607), Rastell's *Les Termes De La Ley,* and Edward Leighs's *Critica sacra or, Philologicall and Theologicall Observations, upon all the Greek words of the New Testament, in order alphabeticall* (1638). Blount believes that, in Cowell's work, the emphasis is on civil, not common, law. In addition, he berates Cowell for his prolixity and for incorrectly defining or confusing certain terms and phrases, including "Realty" and "Royalty" and "Commote" and "Comorth." These points, Blount assures his readers, have been corrected in the *Nomo-lexicon.* Regarding *Les Termes De La Ley,* Blount's primary concern is with the outdated language and style of the book; he also notes the paucity of actual terms defined in it and the scarcity of explications of cited cases. Many of the cases in both this work and Cowell's text also cover decisions now repealed or badly transmitted. Leigh's work receives little discussion beyond Blount's cursory estimation of the author as a "Commentator, not an Expositor."

Blount claims to have added "above a thousand Words" (including what he considers "Mechanick," or pedestrian, words) to his lexicon and to have used the legal writings of Sir Henry Spelman, Sir Edward Coke, and himself (particularly his *Glossographia* and his edition of *Les Termes De La Ley*) in his compilation. He also declares to have consulted legal archives and records for his information, and to have added etymologies of the terms—for "much illustration and delight."

Blount collected material for his dictionaries until the end of his life, always seeking a means of transmission that would secure and enhance his own reputation as a legal authority. In fact, his activities in 1670, the year his *Nomo-lexicon* was published, highlight Blount's obsessive work habits and desire for scholarly recognition. This same year he had published *The several Statutes Concerning Bankrupts, Methodically digested* was published, intended for "the generality of men," and the third edition (actually, the fifth printing) of *Glossographia,* replete with those additions and corrections that would gain him the same reputation as Coke, John Selden, William Dugdale, and Bridgeman—in spite of his exile from the courts.

In 1671, Blount turned his attentions to the English monarchy, another of his passions. Partially spurring these attentions may have been the recently published fifth edition of Richard Baker's *A Chronicle Of the Kings of England, From the time of the Romans Government Unto the Death of King James* (1670), a work first published in 1643. Blount managed to write, correct, and submit for publication his brief but pointed *Animadversions Upon Sʳ Richard Baker's Chronicle, And It's Continuation* (1672), a disputation not so much of the content of the book as it was a skeptical estimation of the continuator of the book, Phillips, the staunch Parliamentarian and the English poet John Milton's nephew. Also that year, Blount began to assemble materials for his potentially massive "Chronological History of England." Blount had asked his friend Wood to co-author the volume, but after Wood's refusal he selected John Belson. Much like his friend Blount, Belson was a staunch Catholic polemicist known for his erudition. The manuscript remained unfinished at Blount's death, and only parts of it are still in existence.

In early 1671, Blount caught wind of a new law dictionary in the works: Thomas Manley's edition of Cowell's *The Interpreter, or, Booke Containing The Signification of words.* Titled *Νομοθετησ the Interpreter: Containing the genuine Signification of such obscure Words and Terms Used either in the Common or Statute Lawes Of This Realm, First Compiled by the Learned Dr. Cowel, and now enlarged from the Collections of all others who have written in this kind* (1672). Manley's edition was based largely on Blount's *Nomo-lexicon,* but it altered Blount's wording in subtle ways, for example, substituting "little" for "small" or "matter concerning" for "Case of." Blount also knew of the third edition of his nemesis Phillips's dictionary, published in 1671 as *The New World of Words: Or, Universal English Dictionary.* In response to both *Νομοθετησ* (*Nomothētes*) and Phillips's tome, Blount wrote *A World of Errors Discovered In The New World of Words. Or General English Dictionary. And In Nomothetes, Or The Interpreter of Law-Words and Terms* (1673).

Split into two parts and attempting to correct the errors in both texts, *A World of Errors* includes two prefaces, violently peppering the author of *The New World of Words* and the editor of *Nomothētes,* respectively. Blount's first prefatory address takes on Phillips in no uncertain terms:

> Must this then be suffered? A Gentleman for his divertisement writes a Book, and this Book happens to be acceptable to the World, and sell; a Book-seller, not interested in the Copy, instantly employs some Mercenary to jumble up another like Book out of this, with some Alterations and Additions, and give it a new Title; and the first Author's out-done, and his Publisher half undone.

Speaking here of *Glossographia,* Blount then accuses Phillips of taking the work "almost wholly out of mine." He charges Phillips with erring in the few changes he

NOMO-ΛΕΞIKON:

A Law-Dictionary.

Interpreting such difficult and obscure

WORDS and TERMS,

As are found either in

Our *Common* or *Statute*, *Ancient* or *Modern*

LAWES.

WITH

References to the several Statutes, Records,
Registers, Law-Books, Charters, Ancient Deeds, and
Manuscripts, wherein the Words are used:

And *Etymologies*, where they properly occur.

Coke on Littl. fol.68. b.

Ad rectè docendum oportet primùm inquirere Nomina; *quia rerum
cognitio à* nominibus rerum *dependet.*

By *THOMAS BLOUNT*
of the *Inner Temple*, Esq;

In the *SAVOY*:

Printed by *Tho. Newcomb*, for *John Martin* and *Henry
Herringman*, at the Sign of the Bell in S. *Pauls*
Churchyard, and a little without *Temple-Bar*,
and in the *New Exchange*. 1670.

Title page for Blount's most important law book, the Nomo-lexicon,
which corrected and enlarged on earlier legal dictionaries

attempted, adding that the book has a "pompous Frontispiece," which only insults the men whose pictures are displayed on it: Geoffrey Chaucer, Spelman, Selden, and William Camden.

Concluding his attack on Phillips, the author self-righteously insists

All writers may modestly claim the benefit of Humanum est Errare [to err is human]; but certainly our Author has transgressed the bounds of that Indulgence. For, I did not read half his Book to pick up these, with many more Exceptions. What then would a more knowing Reader discover, that should seriously peruse the whole? Miserimam [sic] Authoris ignorantiam (the wretched ignorance of the author).

But that which chiefly incited me to this publication, was in some measure to redeem the *Terms of the Common Law* of the Land from the scandal of a most Barbarous

and Senceless Interpretation, which too too [sic] often occurs through his Book; though all other subjects have not scaped too without their share in his mistakes.

Many of Phillips's legal shortcomings, Blount alleges, stem from his fancying himself still "under a Commonwealth, and a Church without Bishops, as appears in Sequestration, Down, Court of Peculiars." In short, Blount's attack on Phillips is clearly personal, tied up in his own religious devotions and political convictions.

Blount's anger infuses even his corrections of Phillips's definitions. For example, Phillips had defined "gallon" as a measure consisting of two quarts. Blount writes, "Our Author had better omitted this word, since every Alewife can contradict him." At times Blount interrupts his corrections with parenthetical commentary aimed to malign Phillips's reputation:

In perusing this Dictionary, you may find some words twice explicated, and those too, with different Interpretations, where one must necessarily be false. Such are Dancet and Dansette; Dodkin and Dotkin; Jotacism and Herbert twice; Ockham and Okum; Rere-County and Rier-County; Varry and Verrey, with divers others. It seems our Authors memory also failed him, or he did not understand them to be the same.

While also harboring disgust for Manley, Blount's second letter to the reader never approaches the same vitriolic fervor of his attack on Phillips. Instead, Blount criticizes Manley's book in an almost cursory manner. He seems content merely to express his mild anger over the title of the book, which resembles the title of his own dictionary. He argues that the author has chosen the wrong Greek word for "Interpreter" and then has revealed an almost complete ineptitude for both the Greek language and English law. Blount also insists that many of the editor's word choices have little or nothing to do with law. Manley's most egregious slight, however, seems to be his total disregard for the plagiarism laws, which Blount excerpts partially to illustrate just how fully his work has been looted. Blount concludes his second preface by stating that he has corrected at least two hundred errors in Manley's book.

In 1674 Blount's "The Several Forms Of Instruments Relating to the Affairs of Merchants, And Traders: Very useful for Scriveners in London, And other Maritim Towns, and Places of Trade" was printed with George Billinghurst's *Arcana Clericalia, Or, The Mysteries of Clarkship.* As Bongaerts points out, Blount's work is a rhetorical resource for merchants, providing model contracts to fit various occasions, from hiring a ship to building a shop. The work was designed to empower ordinary men to draw up legal documents without professional assistance.

As an offshoot of his "Chronological History of England" activities, Blount spent much of 1677 and 1678 compiling notes for his proposed history of Herefordshire; part of this work was published for the first time in 1997. Blount's attentions during these years focused on the rising tide of anti-Catholic sentiment, which had crystallized in the withdrawal of the Declaration of Indulgence and the Test Act, both in early 1673. Many of Blount's letters to Wood voice his fear and uneasiness.

In 1676 Blount experienced his first direct conflict with the anti-Catholic authorities, when his London lodgings were searched for Catholic publications. Although nothing came of this clash (perhaps because of powerful friends and acquaintances in the legal profession), both he and his wife lived in constant fear of denunciation until his death. James Mew, in his entry on Blount for the *Dictionary of National Biography*, reports that the anti-Catholic agitation surrounding the Popish Plot of 1678–a widely believed but fictitious Jesuit conspiracy to assassinate the King–forced Blount to "fly in fear from his home and lead a wandering life"; however, Bongaerts asserts that the Blounts were apparently protected by powerful friends and neighbours.

On 5 January 1677, approximately two years before his death, Blount made his last will and testament, a transcript of which can be found in Bongaerts's book. To his daughter, Elizabeth, he gave Orleton Manor, including all stock and goods "except one Bed and furniture and such Plate and Lynnen as my Deare Wife shall choose." His wife, Anne, was also given his lease at Maldon, and as executrix of his will was charged with his burial. In a letter dated 28 April 1679, Blount informed Wood that he had "quitted all books, except those of devotion." Blount's last book, *Fragmenta Antiquitatis. Antient Tenures of Land, And Jocular Customs Of some Mannors. Made publick for the diversion of some and instruction of others,* was published in 1679. A collection of "tenures," or property histories, this book documents the entertaining customs of various English manors (the Latin in the title translates as Fragments of Antiquity).

In April 1680, Sir William Dugdale informed Wood that the sixty-one-year-old Blount had died at Orleton of "Apoplexie" on 26 December 1679. Blount is buried with his mother and father in the parish church of St. George.

Letters:

The Correspondence of Thomas Blount (1618–1679), A Recusant Antiquary: His Letters to Anthony Wood and Other Restoration Antiquaries, edited by Theo Bongaerts (Amsterdam: APA-Holland University Press, 1978).

Biographies:

Anthony à Wood, *Athenae Oxonienses. An Exact History of All the Writers and Bishops Who Have Had Their Education in the University of Oxford. To Which Are Added The Fasti, or Annals of the Said University,* volume 3, edited by Philip Bliss (London: F. C. & J. Rivington / Lackington, Hughes, Harding, Mavor & Jones / Payne & FOSS / Nichols, Son & Bentley / Longman, Hurst, Rees, Orme & Brown / Cadell & Davies / J. & A. Arch / Mawman / Black, Parbury / R. H. Evans / J. Booth / Baldwin, Cradock & Joy / Oxford: J. Parker, 1813; New York & London: Johnson Reprint Corporation, 1967); columns 149–151;

Joseph Gillow, "Blount, Thomas, Esq.," in *A Literary and Biographical History, or Bibliographical Dictionary of the English Catholics. From the Breach with Rome, in 1534, to the Present Time,* 5 volumes (New York: Burt Franklin, 1885), I: 239–242;

Theo Bongaerts, "Introduction: 1. Life and Family Background," in *The Correspondence of Thomas Blount (1618–1679), A Recusant Antiquary: His Letters to Anthony Wood and Other Restoration Antiquaries. With an Introductory Account of His Life and Writings* (Amsterdam: APA-Holland University Press, 1978), pp. 1–17.

References:

Michael Bath, "'Emblem' as Rhetorical Figure: John Hoskins and Thomas Blount," in *Aspects of Renaissance and Baroque Symbol Theory, 1500–1700,* edited by Peter M. Daly and John Manning (New York: AMS Press, 1999), pp. 51–61;

Theo Bongaerts, "Introduction: 2. The Writings," in *The Correspondence of Thomas Blount (1618–1679), A Recusant Antiquary: His Letters to Anthony Wood and Other Restoration Antiquaries. With an Introductory Account of His Life and Writings* (Amsterdam: APA-Holland University Press, 1978), pp. 17–82;

Gary R. Grund, "The Legacy of Arcadianism," in *John Hoskyns, Elizabethan Rhetoric & English Prose* (New York & London: Garland, 1987), pp. 147–174;

Katherine Gee Hornbeak, *The Complete Letter Writer in English: 1568–1800,* edited by Howard R. Patch, Margaret Rooke, Josef Wiehr, Caroline B. Bourland, and Elliott M. Grant, Smith College Studies in Modern Languages, vol. 15, nos. 3–4; April–July 1934 (Northampton, Mass.: Smith College, 1934), pp. 132–134, 146–148;

Wilbur Samuel Howell, *Logic and Rhetoric in England, 1500–1700* (New York: Russell & Russell, 1961), pp. 277, 331–333, 335;

Hoyt H. Hudson, "Introduction," in *Directions for Speech and Style,* by John Hoskyns, Princeton Studies in

English, no. 12, edited by G. H. Gerould (Princeton: Princeton University Press, 1935), pp. ix–xl;

Richard Foster Jones, *The Triumph of the English Language: A Survey of Opinions Concerning the Vernacular from the Introduction of Printing to the Restoration,* second edition (Stanford: Stanford University Press, 1966), pp. 260, 265, 273–276;

M. M. Mathews, *A Survey of English Dictionaries* (London: Oxford University Press, 1933), pp. 20–23, 30;

Ray Nadeau, "Oratorical Formulas in Seventeenth-Century England," *Quarterly Journal of Speech,* 38 (1952): 149–154;

J. Donald Ragsdale, "Invention in English 'Stylistic' Rhetorics: 1600–1800," *Quarterly Journal of Speech,* 51 (1965): 164–67;

James Rigney, "An Uncatalogued Item by Thomas Blount (1618–1679)," *Bodleian Library Record,* 16, no. 1 (1 April 1997): 110–113;

Jean Robertson, *The Art of Letter Writing: An Essay on the Handbooks Published in England During the Sixteenth and Seventeenth Centuries* (London: University Press of Liverpool, 1942), pp. 23–24, 68;

Jurgen Schafer, "The Working Methods of Thomas Blount," *English Studies,* 59 (1978): 405–408;

De Witt T. Starnes and Gertrude E. Noyes, "Thomas Blount's *Glossographia* (1956)," in their *The English Dictionary from Cawdrey to Johnson, 1604–1755* (Chapel Hill: University of North Carolina Press, 1946), pp. 37–47;

P. W. Thomas, *Sir John Berkenhead, 1617–1679: A Royalist Career in Politics and Polemics* (Oxford: Clarendon Press, 1969);

Karl R. Wallace, *Francis Bacon on Communication & Rhetoric; Or, The Art of Applying Reason to Imagination for the Better Moving of the Will* (Chapel Hill: University of North Carolina Press, 1943), pp. 217–220, 229, 241, 281, 369;

George Williamson, *The Senecan Amble: A Study in Prose Form from Bacon to Collier* (Chicago: University of Chicago Press, 1966), pp. 217–220, 229, 241, 281, 369;

Alan R. Young, "The Translation of Authority. Henri Estienne's *L'Art De Faire Les Devises* and Thomas Blount's *The Art of Making Devises,*" in *Aspects of Renaissance and Baroque Symbol Theory, 1500–1700,* edited by Daly and Manning (New York: AMS Press, 1999), pp. 201–228.

Papers:

Documents related to Thomas Blount's life and work are located in the Bodleian Library, Oxford (especially the MS Wood collection); the British Library, London; the library of the family of Clive in Whitfield; the Hereford City Library; the Essex Record Office, Chelmsford; the Berkshire Record Office, Reading; the Hereford County Record Office; the Public Record Office, London; the Orleton vicarage; and the Tardebigge vicarage.

Thomas Blundeville

(1522 – February 1606)

Daniel Bender
Pace University

BOOKS: *A newe booke containing the arte of ryding, and breakinge greate Horses, together with the shapes and Figures, of many and diuers kyndes of Byttes, mete to serue diuers mouthes. Very necessary for all Gentlemen, Souldyours, Seruingmen, and for any man that delighteth in a horse* (London: Printed by William Seres, 1560?);

The fower chiefyst offices belongyng to Horsemanshippe, That is to saye, The office of the Breeder, Of the Rider, of the Keper, and of the Ferrer. In the firste parte wherof is declared the order of breding of horses. In the seconde howe to breake them, and to make theym horses of seruyce, Conteyninge the whole arte of Ridyinge lately set forth, and nowe newly corrected and amended of manye faultes escaped in the fyste printynge, as well touchyng the bittes as otherwyse. Thirdely howe to dyet them, aswell when they reste as when they trauell by the way. Fourthly to what diseases they be subiecte, together with the causes of such diseases, the sygnes howe to knowe them, and finally howe to cure the same. Whyche bookes are not onely paynfully collected out of a number of authours, but also orderly dysposed and applyed to the vse of thys oure coutrey. By Tho. Blundeuill of Newton Flotman in Norff (London: Printed by William Seres, 1566?); part 4 republished as *The order of curing horses diseases* (London: Printed by William Seres, 1566);

The true order and Methode of wryting and reading Hystories, according to the precepts of Francisco Patricio, and Accontio Tridentino, two Italian writers, no lesse plainly than briefly, set forth in our vulgar speach, to the greate profite and commoditye of all those that delight in Hystories. By Thomas Blundeuill of Newton Flotman in Norfolke (London: Printed by William Seres, 1574);

A Briefe Description Of Vniversal Mappes and Cardes, And Of Their Vse: And Also The Vse Of Ptholemey his Tables. Necessarie for those that Delight In Reading Of Histories: and also for Traueilers by Land or Sea. Newly set foorth by Thomas Blvndeville, of Newton Flotman in the Countie of Norffolke. Gent. (London: Printed by Roger Ward for Thomas Cadman, 1589);

M. Blvndevile His Exercises, containing six Treatises, the titles whereof are set down in the next printed page: which

Thomas Blundeville (effigy at Newton Flotman Church, Norfolk)

Treatises are verie necessarie to be read and learned of all yoong Gentlemen that haue not bene exercised in such disciplines, and yet are desirous to haue knowledge as well in Cosmographie, Astronomie, and Geographie, as also in the Arte of Navigation, in which Arte it is impossible to profite without the helpe of these, or such like instructions. To the furtherance of which Arte of Navigation, the said M. Blundevile speciallie wrote the said Treatises and of meere good will doth dedicate the same to all the young Gentlemen of this Realme (London: Printed by John Windet, 1594); revised and enlarged as *M. Blvndevile His Exercises, containing eight Treatises, the titles whereof are set down in the next printed page: which Treatises are verie necessarie to be read and learned of all yoong Gentlemen that haue not bene exercised in such disciplines, and yet are desirous to haue knowledge as well in Cosmographie, Astronomie, and Geographie, as also in the Arte of Navigation, in which Arte it is impossible to profite without the helpe of these, or such like instructions. To the furtherance of which Arte of Navigation, the said M. Blundevile speciallie wrote the said Treatises and of meere good will doth dedicate the same to all the young Gentlemen of this Realme* (London: Printed by John Windet, 1597);

The Art Of Logike. Plainely taught in the English tongue, by M. Blundeuile of Newton Flotman in Norfolke, aswell according to the doctrine of Aristotle, as of all other moderne and best accounted Authors thereof. A very necessary Booke for all young students in any profession to find out thereby the truth in any doubtfull speech, but specially for such zealous Ministers as haue not beene brought vp in any Vniuersity, and yet are desirous to know how to defend by sound argumentes the true Christian doctrine, against all subtill Sophisters, and cauelling Schismatikes, & how to confute their false Sillogismes, & captious arguments (London: Printed by John Windet, 1599);

The Theoriques of the seuen Planets, shewing all their diuerse motions, and all other Accidents, called Passions, thereunto belonging. Now more plainly set forth in our mother tongue by M. Blundeuile, than euer they haue been heretofore in any other tongue whatsoeuer, and that with such pleasant demonstratiue figures, as euery man that hath any skill in Arithmeticke, may easily vnderstand the same. A Booke most necessarie for all Gentlemen that are desirous to be skilfull in Astronomie, and for all Pilots and Sea-men, or any others that loue to serue the Prince on the Sea, or by the Sea to trauell into forraine Countries. Whereunto is added by the said Master Blundeuile, a breefe Extract by him made, of Maginus his Theoriques, for the better vunderstanding of the Prutenicall Tables, to calculate thereby the diuerse motions of the seuen Planets. There is also hereto added, The making, description, and vse, of two most ingenious and necessarie Instruments for Sea-men, to find out thereby the latitude of any Place vpon the Sea or Land, in the darkest night that is, without the helpe of Sunne, Moone, or Starre. First inuented by M. Doctor Gilbert, a most excellent Philosopher, and one of the ordinarie Physicians to her Maiestie: and now here plainely set downe in our mother tongue by Master Blundeuile (London: Printed by Adam Islip, 1602).

Editions: "Thomas Blundeville's *True Order and Methode of Wryting and Reading Hystories* (1574)," edited by Hugh G. Dick, *Huntington Library Quarterly, 2* (January 1940): 149–170;

The Use of the Globe; the First Voyage of Sir Francis Drake by Sea unto the West and East Indies, Bound Outward and Homeward. Reprinted from a Tract of 1594 in the Plymouth Museum (Plymstock, U.K.: Printed by W. O. Reynolds at the Peacock Press, 1942);

Of Councils and Counselors (1570) by Thomas Blundeville: An English Reworking of El consejo i consejeros del principe (1559) by Federico Furió Ceriol, Introduction by Karl-Ludwig Selig (Gainesville, Fla.: Scholars' Facsimiles & Reprints, 1963);

The Arte of Logike, edited by R. C. Alston, English Linguistics, 1500–1800, no. 23 (Menston, U.K.: Scolar, 1967);

The Art of Logike, The English Experience, no. 102 (Amsterdam: Theatrum Orbis Terrarum / New York: Da Capo Press, 1969);

The Arte of Ryding and Breakinge Greate Horses, The English Experience, no. 118 (Amsterdam: Theatrum Orbis Terrarum / New York: Da Capo Press, 1969);

M. Blundevile, His Exercises Containing Six Treatises, The English Experience, no. 361 (Amsterdam: Theatrum Orbis Terrarum / New York: Da Capo Press, 1971);

A briefe description of vniversal mappes and cardes and of their vse, and also the vse of Ptholemey his tables, necessarie for those that delight in reading of histories and also for traueilers by land or sea, newly set foorth by Thomas Blvndeville. London, Printed by R. Ward for T. Cadman, 1589, The English Experience, no. 438 (Amsterdam: Theatrum Orbis Terrarum / New York: Da Capo Press, 1972);

A Brief Description of Universal Maps & Cards and of Their Use: Necessary for Those That Delight in Reading of Histories, and Also for Travellers by Land or Sea. Newly Set Forth by Thomas Blundeville; Transcribed from the Original Black Letter, edited by Harold M. Otness (Ashland, Ore.: Detu Press, 1977);

The True Order and Methode of Wryting and Reading Hystories: London 1574, The English Experience, no. 908 (Norwood, N.J.: W. J. Johnson / Amsterdam: Theatrum Orbis Terrarum, 1979);

The True Order and Methode of Wryting and Reading Hystories, edited by Hans Peter Heinrich, Bibliotheca Humanistica, volume 2 (Frankfurt am Main & New York: Peter Lang, 1986).

OTHER: *Three morall Treatises, no lesse pleasaunt than necessary for all men to reade, whereof the one is called the Learned Prince, the other the Fruites of Foes, the thyrde the Porte of rest, by Plutarch*, translated by Blundeville (London: Printed by William Seres, 1561);

"T. B. To the Reader," in *The Eyght Tragedie of Seneca Entituled Agamemnon. Translated out of Latin in to*

English, by Iohn Studley, Student in Trinitie Colledge in Cambridge, attributed to Blundeville (London: Printed by Thomas Colwell, 1566);

A very briefe and profitable Treatise declaring hovve many Counsells and vvhat maner of Counselers a Prince that will gouerne well ought to haue, by Frederico Furió Ceriol, translated by Blundeville (London: Printed by William Seres, 1570);

"T. B. In prayse of Gascoignes Posies," in *The Posies of George Gascoigne Esquire. Corrected, perfected, and augmented by the Author,* attributed to Blundeville (London: Printed by Henry Bynneman for Richard Smith, 1575).

Thomas Blundeville's writings are mentioned in passing in literary histories of the sixteenth century, in histories of astronomy and navigation, and in accounts of popularized arts of logic. In his own time, he received more specific notice and praise from his peers. Roger Ascham, for example, contributed prefatory verses to Blundeville's translation of Plutarch; Jasper Heywood, in the preface to his Latin translation *The seconde tragedie of Seneca entituled Thyestes faithfully Englished* (1560), refers to "the gentle Blundeville" who teaches "Plutarches lore / What frute by foes to fynde"; and Gabriel Harvey, in his *Pierces Supererogation Or A New Prayse Of The Old Asse* (1593), commends Blundeville's "painfull, and skillfull bookes on Horsemanship."

Aligning these various references, the reader forms a picture of a highly imaginative, self-educated man, whose interests centered on discerning the "logic" of various disciplines, from moral philosophy to the practical science of training and caring for horses, from persuading readers of what a true "counselour" should be to explaining a system of scholastic disputation in his *The Arte of Logike* (1599). By diversifying his studies, Blundeville taught himself and his readers a way of discerning a "logic" operating beneath the surface of subjects. In this sense, he quietly epitomizes the optimism and pedagogical fervor that fueled the "new" humanist learning. This resourcefulness and adaptability was not merely intellectual.

Patrons and politics exerted mixed influences on Blundeville, whose roles as scholar, translator, and writer evolved throughout his career. Initially, Blundeville seems to have regarded himself as a kind of ex-officio adviser to Elizabeth's government; later, his career reflected his own exploratory impulses and his desire to address "citizens" rather than high-ranking leaders.

Thomas Blundeville was born circa 1522; Arthur Campling, a twentieth-century relative of Blundeville, is alone among biographers of Blundeville in specifying the year–the Library of Congress catalogue merely states that Blundeville "flourished around 1561." His

A very briefe and profitable Treatise declaring hovve many counsells, and vvhat maner of Counselers a Prince that will gouerne well ought to haue.

The Booke speaketh.

All you that Honors woulde atcheeue,
And Counslers eke desire to bee,
Of selfe loue flee the false beleeue,
And learne my lore that you may see
What worthynesse in you doth reygne,
Such worthy state thereby tatteyne.

IMPRINTED
at London by William Seres.

Title page for Blundeville's translation and adaptation of Federico Furió Ceriol's El consejo i consejeros del principe (Of Councils and Councillors of the Prince, 1550)

parents, Elizabeth Godsalve and Edward Blomvill, had an estate in Norfolk, near the village of Newton-Flotman. The Blundeville name had an illustrious place in English history. Blundeville's namesake, Thomas Blunville, had been bishop of Norwich in the thirteenth century. Blundeville was apparently educated at Cambridge University and then went into law. According to Campling, he entered Gray's Inn in 1541. Blundeville then took his place as a learned resident of London and even a visitor to the court of Queen Elizabeth I. His situation at this time was that of a humanist whose "occupation" involved a fusion of reason and persuasion, of logic and rhetoric, into matters of the day. This conception of a rhetorical role seemed certain to place him in the track of "courtier," not as a cabinet member of Elizabeth's court but as one who fortifies national leadership through the timely provisions of his wisdom.

While living in London, Blundeville invested his intellectual energies in a widespread fascination with

Italy, the foreign culture that to English minds betokened sophistication and civility. Italian politics, architecture, historiography, and art all bespoke ways or "methods" that the studious scholar could relocate in British idiom. This fascination was not so much aesthetic as broadly political: the Italians' historic proximity to "virtu" or human capability, as enshrined in Roman oratory, government, and arts, stirred the English to patriotic envy and emulation. How could the English perceive themselves as sophisticated and dashing when they were so clearly overshadowed by their stylish counterparts on the Continent?

One of Blundeville's earliest works (published around 1560) was a carefully assembled translation and abridgement of Federico Grisone's *Gli ordini di cavalcare* (The Principles of Horsemanship, 1550), an Italian text on horse-breaking and training. Blundeville titled his translation *A newe booke containing the arte of ryding, and breakinge greate Horses*. If elegance and efficiency are related values, then Blundeville's translation fulfilled the national appetite for Italianate manners; however, it did more. As an island nation, England could be invaded and find no assistance from neighboring states. Rumors of an impending invasion had circulated periodically for more than thirty years before King Phillip II finally sent the Spanish Armada in May 1588 in an attempt to invade England. An effective British cavalry was more critical than whatever elegance might be had from advanced riding techniques; thus, the transference of Italian learning to England abetted Blundeville's nationalist and civic interests.

Before Blundeville's adaptations of these texts in English, British horse breeders and riders had worked by rough commonsense. Italian riding masters were solicited to instruct English nobility in the art of riding; English grooms and ferrers (veterinarians), too, had less than systematic knowledge of their own tasks. Now, by gathering and translating predominantly Italian texts on the subject, Blundeville provided his nation with a systematic approach to this essential means of transportation and military stratagem.

So successful was this first book that Blundeville went on to write several similar treatises. These were collected into one volume: *The fower chiefyst offices belongyng to Horsemanshippe, That is to saye, The office of the Breeder, Of the Rider, of the Keper, and of the Ferrer* (1566?). In the title Blundeville itemizes his subject with the self-conscious care of one who addresses each strata of citizenry, from the gentleman rider to the ferrer. The collection is made up of four treatises, three of which have separate title pages: *The Order of Breding* (no title page, undated), *The Arte of Rydynge* (undated), *The Order of Dietynge* (1565), and *The Order of Curing* (1566). Appended to *The Order of Curing* is a lengthy discussion of "paring and shooyng." The second treatise, *The Arte of Rydynge,* is a corrected version of Blundeville's 1560 translation of Grisone. The other three treatises, which may have been published separately before they were collected, are not merely translations, but compilations of various works.

Because the readership of these horse books is comprised of the different classes that cooperatively produce "horse power," Blundeville's rhetorical motive can be described in terms of leadership and innovation. In a sense, this choice of subject was traditional, reflecting humanist ambition to fuse scholastic acumen and practical benefit for the nation as a whole. Ascham, who tutored Princess Elizabeth, the future queen, in the liberal arts, wrote a well-received text on archery, *Toxophilvs, The schole of shootinge conteyned in two bookes* (1545), as well as a widely read text on education, *The Scholemaster* (1570). In his works, Blundeville thus followed a tradition of civic-oriented rhetoric. This tradition rejects the old association of scholasticism with theoretical knowledge in favor of practical wisdom, or prudence.

The expositions on horses are tinged with other rhetorical motives, ones that governed Blundeville's sense of purpose throughout his career. Untamed horses need to be "educated"—as Blundeville phrases it, to be of "servyce." So, too, the citizenry—though they should not be broken—should be provided with laws and literature that curb headstrong or misguided motives. This connection between Blundeville's texts on horses and government seems oblique until the reader considers some historical contexts surrounding Blundeville's texts.

First, he dedicated these works to Robert Dudley, first Earl of Leicester. In his various dedications, Blundeville takes care to note that Leicester is a valued counselor to Queen Elizabeth I, and therefore directly involved in the business of governing. As intermediaries between Leicester and the nation, Blundeville's books play the role of a "counselor," establishing new "policy" —in this case, a policy of animal husbandry and riding technique—for his nation.

Second, the books embody a related rhetorical motive, but this motive is present only by suggestion: Blundeville's self-advancement. In 1560—about the same time as the first treatise was published—the dashing and handsome Leicester had received considerable honors from Queen Elizabeth, who had ascended the throne in 1558. He had, for example, been granted a profitable license to export woolen clothes free of duty. More to the point, by April 1559, Leicester had also been named Master of the Queen's Horse. The brief interval between Leicester's appointment and Blundeville's publication may be coincidental; however, it is definite that Blundeville was living in London in the years preceding his father's death in 1568 and that he frequented the court of Elizabeth (after his death, an unpublished eulogy in Latin written to the queen was found). Blundeville had chosen his patron wisely. What better text to dedicate to the Master of Her Majesty's Horse than the first book in English on horsemanship? And, if Leicester were to recognize in Blundeville a keen student of national policy and the needs of the moment, would he not be asked to help in directing his countrymen? *The fower chiefyst offices belongyng to Horsemanshippe* seems to have met with success, with other editions appearing in circa 1570, 1580, 1593, 1597, and 1609. These treatises were used by many later writers, including Gervase Markham, Robert Barret, and Robert Almond. In *A New Method and Extraordinary Invention to Dress Horses And Work Them according to Nature* (1667), William Cavendish takes Blundeville to task for inaccuracies in his books, but also notes several later works on horses that are nothing "but Blundevil."

Blundeville's sense that his own talents should reach into the inner workings of government, and his conception of education as a national and civic benefit, are also apparent in a work that may have been printed, at least in part, as early as 1558. He unites education and politics in *Three morall Treatises, no lesse pleasaunt than necessary for all men to reade, whereof the one is called the Learned Prince, the other the Fruites of Foes, the thyrde the Porte of rest* (1561), a partial translation of Plutarch's *Moralia.* While the Learned Prince reprises a theme of wisdom and political authority as ancient as Socrates' notion of the "philosopher king," the dedication of the *Three morall Treatises* to Leicester again suggests Blundeville's wish to act as a kind of counselor-in-absentia, a rhetorical force who affects actual counselors.

This telescoping of rhetoric as a means of political enlightenment, however, may contain a far more specific motive when some historical circumstances surrounding Blundeville's patron are considered. The second treatise, *The Fruites of Foes,* has a separate title page announcing it as "newly corrected and cleansed of manye faultes escaped in the former printing." The suggestion is that the second treatise had been printed earlier as a separate publication. This suggestion is supported by Heywood's allusion in his 1560 work, and an entry in the Stationers' Register in 1558; however, though the work was republished in 1580, no copies of an edition earlier than 1561 appear to be extant. While this putative first edition would have appeared before Leicester's personal and political scandal, the showcased presentation of Blundeville's "cleansed" text occurs soon after a crisis in Leicester's career. The preface is dated 1561–a year in which Leicester was immersed in the scandalous claim that he had arranged his wife's death. Leicester's enemies were calling for investigations and his instant removal as Elizabeth's adviser.

Leicester had married Amy Robsart (a cousin to the Blundevilles and a native of Norfolk) in 1550. Ten years later, the marriage had perhaps become onerous to Leicester. Accepted by Queen Elizabeth as either her lover or the object of intense infatuation, Leicester realized that marriage to the queen of England was within reach–except that he was already married. According to rumors–and historical records are contradictory–machinations followed. In 1560 his youthful wife was found with a broken neck at the bottom of a staircase. An inquest that followed her death raised suspicions that were never allayed.

All of Leicester's servants were absent from the house, having taken that day to visit Abingdon Fair. A rumor circulated that Leicester had hired one Anthony Forster to throw Lady Amy downstairs. Such rumors persisted even when a jury returned a finding of mischance or accidental death. Suspicions were further fueled by the fact that Leicester did not attend his wife's funeral and–more brazenly still–that he had written a letter to the foreman of the jury during their deliberations. Blundeville's *The Fruites of Foes* may therefore have offered moral comfort and justification to the beleaguered Leicester, who, after his wife's purported accident, was in danger of being forced out of the government. The fact that this treatise is dedicated to Leicester in 1561–a year after his wife's death and at the height of public outcry against him–offers a particular motive for *The Fruites of Foes.* It suggests Blundeville's role as a fortifier of political authority who defends his "Learned Prince" against his enemies.

At this period, the family estate, deep in the farm country of Norfolk, in the village of Newton-Flotman, seems to have been far from Blundeville's interests. Only after the death of his father in 1568 did Blundeville return to Newton-Flotman. Now in his forties, he assumed the mantle of family history, a history made weighty by illustrious ancestors–not only the thirteenth-century bishop of Norwich, but also by one William de Blunvill "of Newton-Flotman and Essex." This ancestor epitomized order or the "rule of reason," since he had held the office of sheriff of Essex. While Blundeville is said to have prudently managed the estate he inherited, he felt the obligation–and allure–of his years at London and the Inns of Court, where his own logic and rhetoric might reach beyond the village of Newton-Flotman, into the reasoning and conduct of the nation.

This tradition of public leadership and governance informed Blundeville's life. Having left London, and with it whatever access to Elizabeth's court he had enjoyed, Blundeville continued in his joint role of cour-

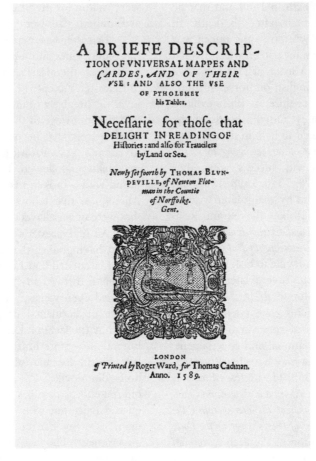

A BRIEFE DESCRIP-
TION OF VNIVERSAL MAPPES AND
CARDES, AND OF THEIR
VSE: AND ALSO THE VSE
OF PTHOLEMEY
his Tables,

Neceſſarie for thoſe that
DELIGHT IN READING OF
Hiſtories: and alſo for Trauelers
by Land or Sea.

Newly ſet foorth by THOMAS BLVN-
DEVILLE, of Newton Flot-
man in the Countie
of Norffolke.
Gent.

LONDON
¶ Printed by Roger Ward, for Thomas Cadman.
Anno. 1589.

Title page for Blundeville's book on mapmaking and world geography

tier/educator, noting in prefaces his hope that each work would benefit "God and country." By the end of his career, his works, whether on logic or cartography, were colored by a new focus and sentiment. There are those, Blundeville noted, who cannot afford a university education. They should not be deprived of study and learning. In Blundeville's transmutation from extramural courtier to advocate of those excluded from university life and gentility can be discerned the contradictory double movement of many Elizabethan intellectuals: first, their intention is to serve Elizabeth's court, to bring the "new learning" to the causes of civic contentment and national prosperity; second, once hopes of preferment are dampened and have to be re-imagined, they are forced to regroup psychologically and politically.

Whatever may have motivated him in publishing *The Fruites of Foes,* when Blundeville turned explicitly to the subject of political authority, as he did in *A very briefe and profitable Treatise declaring hovve many Counsells and vvhat maner of Counselers a Prince that will gouerne well ought to haue* (1570), there can be found a continuity of focus and interest: God and country as goals, translation from the Italian as means. Although *El consejo i consejeros del principe* (Of Councils and Councillors of the Prince, 1550) was written by the Spaniard Federico Furió Ceriol, it had been translated into Italian by Alfonso d'Ulloa, and Blundeville based his work on that translation. The choice of this text, at this juncture in Blundeville's career, is also revealing. It indicates the dual goal of the courtier-rhetorician, whose authority derives partly from the lively translation of political theory into English, and partly from the linkage in the text of civic service to legitimate political authority. This persuasive aim, mediated by the textual strategy of dramatizing both degenerate and attractive forms of political authority, suggests why Heinrich F. Plett describes *A very briefe and profitable Treatise* (commonly known as *Of Councils and Counselors*) as "a non-rhetorical work of rhetorical importance." Before, Blundeville's rhetoric of service and extramural "counsel" was only implicit. This text takes up two suasive ends: to set forth a picture of what government leaders should be and to chastise the conduct and intentions of people presently in office. The usual dedication to Leicester holds a new element of mirroring self-regard between author and patron, as Blundeville, a "counselor" from the republic of letters, writes to the queen's counselor. The preface to this translation expresses unusual warmth, suggesting intellectual familiarity between the two men: "I am bolde after my olde wonte, to present your Honor with Inke & paper, more to doe my bounde dutie in shewing my selfe thankfull towards you, for the great benefites bestowed on me: than for any profite or pleasure that I know your Honor can reape any way of my rude wryting."

The most notable continuity with the earlier works on horsemanship involves the issue of wild versus civil behavior, which was the founding issue of the books on horses. Blundeville, it might be argued, is drawn to this treatise for its language of misguided, as opposed to "wise," judgment. If the prince secures "wise, learned, and vertuous counselors," he writes, the Court would become "a schoole of vertue, and knowledge." Unfortunately, Blundeville says, many counselors are incapable of giving counsel. Instead, they "leawdely spende their tyme in idleness, vayne pastymes, and in wantonnesse of life." This passage sounds a note of reformist fervor and disapproval within an idiom of moral leadership. Furthermore, although the criticism is phrased in generic terms—"they," "counselors," "their tyme"—that very generality allows the writing to refer to any place or time, including the "present time" of Blundeville's readers. This access to the present occurs in another way. The passage speaks on behalf of wise counselors—a role that Blundeville, providing England with a meditation on leadership, himself seems to be filling. Finally, the work is highly rhetorical in form, its terms of contempt and praise unfolding according to the genre of epideictic rhetoric. Magisterially, Blundeville's translation delivers equal measures of praise and blame.

In 1574 Blundeville translated and combined two Italian works on the purposes of writing and reading history. *The true order and Methode of wryting and reading Hystories* is a free translation and adaptation of the last five dialogues of Francesco Patrizi's *Della Historia Diece Dialoghi* (Ten Dialogues on History, 1560) and most of the *Delle osseruationi, et auuertimenti che hauer si debbono nel legger delle historie* (Some Observations and Cautions in Reading History, circa 1564) of Giacomo Concio, also known as Jacobus Acontius. Here, too, can be found the moral fervor of Blundeville's other translations. History, Blundeville explains, provides examples of lives that the reader should follow "for their excellencie in vertue" or should avoid because of the historical subject's "excellencie in vice." In the absence of information that helps the reader to understand Blundeville's relation to his own writing—as disinterested service, as a

Title page for Blundeville's influential textbook on Aristotelian logic

bid for political inclusion—the reader might recall the Elizabethan view of history writing. Its presumed value is hortative: it directs readers toward "virtue" and national self-interest and leads them away from self-aggrandizement. Blundeville's missionary urge to have history edify—to "serve some good example"—represents his characteristic linkage of scholarly effort with national progress and education.

In Blundeville's later years, however, this urge to educate was increasingly less mediated by the "patron" of learning whose approval is sought. Blundeville apparently shifted sympathy away from the "learned" to those who cannot afford a university education. While he wrote to Leicester of governing well, of his gratitude in being able to "counsel" so great a counselor, this language seems to give way or be silently disowned as Blundeville approached old age. Instead, Blundeville seems concerned to offer the fruits of his own learning to all who might benefit—those of high estate, but even better, of low estate. This populist sentiment begins to be apparent in his work on mapmaking. *A Briefe Description Of Vniversal Mappes and Cardes, And Of Their Vse* (1589) is addressed "To the Reader" who, Blundeville says, will better appreciate the drama of history by knowing the distances traveled from one place to another. In addition to this direct relation to readers, the choice of subject is itself populist. Blundeville, like most of contemporary English society, seemed caught up in the fever for exploration. By 1589, the New World was beckoning; religious separatists as well as merchants in England were increasingly aware of America, which, Blundeville says, "men now call the West Indies." Navigation had progressed to the point that whole oceans could be crossed. It was time to equip the citizens of his country with lessons in world geography and measurements of its distances.

In 1594 Blundeville published a collection of six treatises under the title *M. Blvndevile His Exercises*. Each treatise, except the first one, on arithmetic, has a separate title page: *The Treatise of Arithmeticke, A Briefe Description of the tables of the three speciall right lines belonging to a Circle* (the first discussion of plane trigonometry in English), *A plain Treatise of the first principles of Cosmographie, A plaine description of Mercator his two Globes, A very brief and most plaine description of Master Blagraue his Astrolabe,* and *A new and necessarie Treatise of Nauigation.* The collection was enlarged in 1597 to include two more treatises: *A plaine and full description of Petrus Plancius his vniuersall Map* (a second edition of his 1589 book on this topic) and *The Trve Order of making Ptolomie his tables.* In his preface to both editions, Blundeville explains that he originally wrote the treatise on arithmetic for Elizabeth Bacon, daughter of Nicholas Bacon and half-sister of Francis Bacon, but she was unable to take full advantage of it. Now he is offering it as "a verie easie Arithmeticke so plainlie" written that "any man of a mean capacitie" can use it "without the helpe of any teacher," and pointedly he identifies his audience for the collection as "al young Gentlemen & seamen." There seems to have been an audience for the work: subsequent editions appeared in 1606, 1613, and 1622; an edition revised by Robert Hartwell was published in 1636; and a 1638 edition appeared in two separate issues.

The same populist sentiment expressed in the preface to *M. Blvndevile His Exercises* operates quietly but notably in Blundeville's *The Art Of Logike,* published in 1599. Although his book never rivaled the popularity of Thomas Wilson's *The Rule of Reason, conteinyng the Arte of Logique* (1551), Blundeville follows Wilson's pedagogical care in providing tables to illustrate the abstract logical structures he discusses. One point of difference, however, is that Blundeville concerns himself with those who are distinctly not of the court or any inner circle. "Everie man," he writes, "is not hable in these costly dayes to finde eyther himselfe or his childe at the Universitie" but might "by his owne industrie attaine unto right good knowledge & be made thereby the more able to glorify God & to profit his country." That does not mean that the book was only read by the self-educated. The *Calendar of State Papers* for 1623 indicates that Sir Edward Conway purchased Blundeville's *The Art Of Logike* (for 1 shilling) along with such prestigious works as William Perkins's theological studies and "the King's Workes" (for 13 shillings).

In the history of logic, Aristotle is the seminal figure, and Blundeville, ever concerned to provide England with the buried riches of history, wrote an Aristotelian book on logic. Aristotle's basic postulate, which initiates the terms of logic throughout the Renaissance, is that the mind produces "thoughts" by combining statements into some coherent succession. This process was schematically described in the concepts of "invention" and "arrangement."

Blundeville's own book is scholastic in that it follows this methodology for finding and organizing beliefs. More specifically, one discovers what one believes about a given issue in three broad areas of invention: the *judicial* (the guilt or innocence of a certain act and actor), the *deliberative* (choosing between two courses of action), and the *epideictic* (proving that something should be admired or disdained). Aristotle's second concept also inaugurates the vocabulary of method. No matter whether it was identified by the name "disposition," "judgment," or "organization," logic sought to advance the mind's reasoning to more and more particular foci. Thus the syllogism, by which Aristotelian logic will forever be identified, organizes a movement from genera to species as in the well-known schoolroom syllogism: "All men are mortal. Socrates is a man. Socrates is mortal." Accordingly, Wilbur Samuel Howell describes Blundeville's logic as Aristotelian.

Howell goes on to conjecture that the book, although published in 1599, was probably written around 1575, since Blundeville alludes in his preface to Ralph Lever's *The Arte of Reason* (1573), as recently published. This point is corroborated by Blundeville's own allusion to writing "this book many years past." Howell and other scholars have noticed that Blundeville's logic is colored by a native tradition. His book sustains the preoccupation with religious argument that characterized the turbulent period of the Renaissance when Protestantism gradually overcame the old faith, Catholicism. Wilson had been censured by the Catholic Church for his references to a "false" religion—as distinguished, logically—from a "true" religion of the spirit, which he of course identified with Protestantism. Blundeville is less acerbic in his references but presents his logic pointedly, as a means of theological self-preservation. As had Wilson, Blundeville writes that his concern is with "Ministers" who "had not beene brought up in any Universitie" and need "Logike to defende the truth of Gods worde." Blundeville's text thus reveals its indigenous origins, an extra-disciplinary strand of polemic woven into the scholastic tradition of Aristotelian logic.

The logical tradition in itself, however, produced native versions. Walter J. Ong has described Blundeville's logic as being closer to the medieval logician Boethius in that one can make a "judgment" or take a position based on some array of reasons and then look at ways to "invent" or conceptualize this argument. This reverses the sequence traditionally ascribed to logic: first, one determines what one believes (invention); then one sets about organizing an argument with sequentially arranged reasons that support that belief. In a culture, however, that was itself organized by traditional beliefs in the orderly cosmos, in the ascendancy of reason over desire, in the need for obedience, one did not have to "invent" as much as "arrange"–that is, to organize reasons already at hand into cogent progressions.

In addition to reversing the sequence of invention and organization, Blundeville reveals his desire to be a teacher rather than a complex theorist of logic. In this goal he was overshadowed–as everyone was–by the figure of Pierre de La Ramée (known as Petrus Ramus), whose reform of complex and labored Aristotelian logic was hailed as a victory for classroom instruction. Ramus, a professor at the University of Paris, wished to renovate the onerous categorizations of classical logic, to make logic something all students could use as a vital instrument of daily living rather than a system that could be mastered by only a few. In this sense Blundeville emerges as something of a Ramus-like figure. His book of logic is written with an underrepresented group in mind: those who have not been to university.

In the classical method of invention, one comes to a knowledge of a given issue or object by conducting a rigorous inventory of its general and specific traits. One schema meant to guide logicians was known as the *predicamentes* (categories), which allow closer and closer formulations of an issue's "place" in a network of contexts, associations, and manifestations. There are ten such "places" of invention. One begins by identifying the "substance" of a thing, that is, its essential, or "proper," being. So, for example, the United States is a nation unified by a Constitution. The United States also exhibits regional differences–as in "southern cooking" or "the Rocky Mountains"–and these are considered accidents, events that happen to inhabit the "substance." Each category is therefore an occasion to open up fur-

Effigies of Blundeville's father, grandfather, and great-grandfather, with commemorative verses written by Blundeville (Newton Flotman Church, Norfolk)

ther channels of meaning. This expandability is true of quantity, quality, relation, action or means of doing, passion or what is done to a given subject, when, where, the seat or relation of a subject to its surroundings, and its habit or customary mode of being. For Ramus such proliferating considerations represented bad pedagogy. He preferred to simplify the process of finding a belief, or working thesis, by offering two procedures: identifying the general class, or "genus," of an issue or object, and then dividing this generalization into its "special," or specific, form within the confines of its local manifestation. Thus, the United States is, by genus, a nation, but can then be known more fully by division or differentiation into species. For example, the United States was founded as a democracy in opposition to a government based on monarchy.

Blundeville's book on logic does preserve the old categories of scholastic logic. He includes the classical predicaments, as well as the *predicables* (assertions that can be made about a subject, in terms of genus, species, differences, property, and accident). He discusses simple and compound words and statements, and syllogism. Alongside this recapitulation of an old scholastic logic, however, the reader finds the simplifying and congenial vocabulary of a teacher who wishes to make logic intelligible to ordinary readers. Thus, a Ramus-like simplicity of defining something and then identifying its specific traits as a means of argument is present in Blundeville's introduction: ". . . Logike is chiefly occupied

. . . in discussing of questions, which is done by Definition, Division, & Argumentation." The intelligibility and relative simplicity of the text earned its author success. *The Art Of Logike* was republished and sold in London in 1617, eighteen years after its original publication, and again in 1619.

In *The Art Of Logike,* Blundeville turns away from the assumption behind his earlier works; in them, the nobleman patron-writer relation forms an apex from which knowledge diffuses downward. In this system, Leicester's approval initiates and legitimates a process of learning for others. In *The Art Of Logike* can be discerned the new trajectory of Blundeville's career, as a language of encouragement directed to "everie man" has gradually eclipsed a language of privileged advisement. Now, learning is something to which every person is naturally inclined. What is needed is education in the arts of logical discourse for those outside the charmed circle of entitlement. Thus, the "art of logike" is not the special preserve of those who negotiate law courts or political counsels, rather. It is a means of navigating changing seas of motive, discourse, and situation that the citizen-reader faces each day. The ability to deal with "subtill Sophisters, and cauelling Schismatikes," as the subtitle declares to be one of the purposes for logic, is a generic and open-ended capacity; the benefits of studying logic are also open-ended. Because logic guides one in learning the principles of "any Art or Science," it may therefore be said to be "the Art of arts." As a result, the "invention and judgment" that Blundeville defines as the two parts of logic are now incumbent upon the reader of the book. Blundeville has, finally, assumed his place as a counselor to his nation. His last book, *The Theoriques of the seuen Planets shewing all their diuerse motions, and all other Accidents, called Passions, therunto belonging,* an astronomical treatise, was published in 1602, four years before his death.

Blundeville's family life forms a painful counterpoint to this flowering of talent and service. Rose Puttenham, his first wife, died; a son from their marriage, Antony, is reported to have died in a battle in the Low Countries. In his early sixties, married to his second wife, Margaret Johnson, Blundeville fathered first Elizabeth and then Patience. But the author of *The Art Of Logike* found his family life upset by the impulsiveness of the patriotically named Elizabeth. Perhaps bored or rebellious, she turned against her prospective marriage to Robert King to run off with one Rowland Meyrick, esq. Despite her parents' demands and pleas, she did not return, except after her mother's death, when Elizabeth carried off possessions that she valued.

Meanwhile, King had returned from a trip to Europe to learn that his marriage prospects had disappeared. King was apparently solaced by Blundeville's solution: the younger daughter could substitute for the older. He suggested–with or without her assent is unknown–that Patience take King as her husband. Blundeville also asked that King change his name to Blundeville, thereby perpetuating the name, estate, and library that, Blundeville's will indicates, should be preserved intact for his progeny.

The arrangement seemed tolerable for all concerned, but Blundeville's hopes for posterity were never realized. There were no children from the marriage of Patience and her husband, who, some years after the death of Patience in 1638 and long after Blundeville's own death, sold the estate. According to Sir Frederick Smith, whose source was the old Register of Newton-Flotman Church, Blundeville died in February 1605. This date is probably old style, however, since other sources give 1606 as Blundeville's death date.

What endures of Thomas Blundeville are material and cultural artifacts. There are effigies of his great-grandfather, grandfather, and father that Blundeville had commissioned to be erected in his local church; his own effigy keeps them company. Above his grave is a statue of Blundeville in armor, kneeling bareheaded, with a book and a sword before him. A legacy of public service through the arts of logic and rhetoric also survives intact: the mind gains admission to the complexities of history, literature, astronomy, logic, or horsemanship through enthusiastic discipline and study. Blundeville is thus a paradigmatic figure of late-sixteenth-century literary culture, an individual whose confidence in finding the logic beneath a subject's multiplex appearance led others to partake of his learning.

Bibliography:

Heinrich F. Plett, *English Renaissance Rhetoric and Poetics: A Systematic Bibliography of Primary and Secondary Sources* (Leiden & New York: E. J. Brill, 1995), pp. 179, 312.

Biographies:

Charles Henry Cooper and Thompson Cooper, "Thomas Blundeville," in *Athenae Cantabrigienses,* 3 volumes (Cambridge: Deighton, Bell/Macmillan/London: Bell & Daldy, 1861), II: 342–344;

Arthur Campling, "Thomas Blundeville, of Newton Flotman, co. Norfolk (1522–1606). Author and Poet, tempo. Elizabeth," *Norfolk Archaeology; or, Miscellaneous Tracts Relating to the Antiquities of the County of Norfolk,* volume 21 (Norwich: Norfolk &

Norwich Archaeological Society, 1923), pp. 337–360.

References:

Calendar of State Papers of Elizabeth and James I, Addenda, 1580–1625, edited by Mary Anne Everett Green (Nendeln, Liechtenstein: Kraus Reprint, 1967);

Carey Herbert Conley, *The First English Translations of the Classics* (New Haven: Yale University Press / London: Printed by Humphrey Milford for Oxford University Press, 1927), pp. 24, 26, 28–29, 44, 91, 131, 140;

Jane Donawerth, *Shakespeare and the Sixteenth-Century Study of Language* (Urbana: University of Illinois Press, 1984), pp. 111, 137–138;

Mordechai Feingold, *The Mathematicians' Apprenticeship: Science, Universities and Society in England, 1560–1640* (Cambridge & New York: Cambridge University Press, 1984), pp. 50, 78, 97, 100, 102, 180, 215;

Wilbur Samuel Howell, *Logic and Rhetoric in England, 1500–1700* (Princeton: Princeton University Press, 1956), pp. 29–30, 216, 285–291, 297–301, 307, 315, 354;

Kenneth Muir, "Blundeville, Wyatt and Shakespeare," *Notes and Queries,* new series, 8 (1961): 293–294;

Walter J. Ong, *Ramus, Method and the Decay of Dialogue* (Cambridge, Mass.: Harvard University Press, 1958), pp. 112–113, 334;

Eleanor Rosenberg, *Leicester: Patron of Letters* (New York: Columbia University Press, 1955), pp. 46–53, 56, 58, 62, 64, 79, 156, 179, 180;

Frederick Smith, *The Early History of Veterinary Literature and Its British Development,* volume 1, *From the Earliest Period to A. D. 1700* (London: J. A. Allen, 1976), pp. 138–140, 150–177;

Virginia F. Stern, *Gabriel Harvey: His Life, Marginalia and Library* (Oxford: Clarendon Press, 1979), pp. 141, 143, 148–149, 159, 168, 201–202, 247, 265;

Louis B. Wright, *Middle-Class Culture in Elizabethan England* (Chapel Hill: University of North Carolina Press, 1935), pp. 134, 156, 288–299.

Papers:

The biographical article by Arthur Campling mentions that Thomas Blundeville wrote a treatise on fortifications, which is "amongst Lord Leconfield's MSS. at Petworth"; the Petworth House Archives are available through the West Sussex Record Office, Chichester. Charles Henry Cooper and Thompson Cooper's *Athenae Cantabrigienses* refers to a manuscript copy of the first part of *Three morall Treatises* "among the Royal MSS. 18.A.43."

John Bulwer

(May 1606 – October 1656)

Katherine Rowe
Bryn Mawr College

BOOKS: *Chirologia: Or The Natvrall Langvage Of The Hand. Composed of the Speaking Motions, and Discoursing Gestures thereof. Whereunto is added Chironomia: Or, the Art of Manvall Rhetoricke. Consisting of the Naturall Expressions, digested by Art in the Hand, as the chiefest Instrument of Eloquence, By Historicall Manifesto's, Exemplified Out of the Authentique Registers of Common Life, and Civill Conversation. With Types, or Chyrograms: A long-wish'd for illustration of this Argument. By J. B. Gent. Philochirosophus* (London: Printed by Thomas Harper, to be sold by Henry Twyford, 1644);

Chironomia: Or, The Art of Manuall Rhetorique. With The Canons, Lawes, Rites, Ordinances, and Institutes of Rhetoricians, both Ancient and Moderne, Touching the artificiall managing of the Hand in Speaking. Whereby the Naturall Gestures of the Hand, are made the Regulated Accessories or faire-spoken Adjuncts of Rhetoricall Utterance. With Types, or Chirograms: A new illustration of this Argument. By J. B. Philochirosophus (London: Printed by Thomas Harper, to be sold by Henry Twyford, 1644);

Philocophus: Or, The Deafe and Dumbe Mans Friend. Exhibiting The Philosophicall verity of that subtile Art, which may inable one with an observant Eie, to Heare what any man speaks by the moving of his lips. Upon The Same Ground, with the advantage of an Historicall Exemplification, apparently proving, That a Man borne Deafe and Dumbe, may be taught to Heare the sound of words with his Eie, & thence learne to speake with his Tongue. By I. B. sirnamed the Chirosopher (London: Printed for Humphrey Moseley, 1648);

Pathomyotomia Or A Dissection of the significative Muscles of the Affections of the Minde. Being an Essay to a new Method of observing the most Important movings of the Muscles of the Head, as they are the neerest and Immediate Organs of the Voluntarie or Impetuous motions of the Mind. With the Proposall of a new Nomenclature of the Muscles. By J. B. Sirnamed the Chirosopher (London: Printed by William Wilson for Humphrey Moseley, 1649);

John Bulwer (engraved by William Faithorne, for the 1653 edition of Anthropometamorphosis; *courtesy of The Lilly Library, Indiana University)*

Anthropometamorphosis: Man Transform'd; Or, The Artificial Changeling. Historically Presented, In the mad and cruel

Gallantry, Foolish Bravery, ridiculous Beauty, Filthy Finenesse, and loathsome Lovelinesse of most Nations, Fashioning & altering their Bodies from the Mould intended by Nature. With a Vindication of the Regular Beauty and Honesty of Nature. And An Appendix of the Pedigree of the English Gallant. By J. B. Sirnamed, The Chirosopher (London: Printed for John Hardesty, 1650); republished as *A View Of The People Of The Whole World: Or, A short Survey of their Policies, Dispositions, Naturall Deportments, Complexions, Ancient and Moderne Customes, Manners, Habits & Fashions. A Worke every where adorned with Philosophicall, Morall and Historicall Observations on the Occasions of their Mutations & Changes throughout all Ages. For the Readers greater delight Figures are annexed to most of the Relations. Scripsit J. B. Cognomento Chirosophus, M. D.* (London: Printed by William Hunt, 1654).

Editions: *Chirologia: or the Natural Language of the Hand and Chironomia: or the Art of Manual Rhetoric,* edited by James W. Cleary (Carbondale & Edwardsville: Southern Illinois University Press / London & Amsterdam: Feffer & Simons, 1974);

Chirologia: or, The naturall language of the hand, composed of the speaking motions, and discoursing gestures thereof, whereunto is added Chironomia: or, The art of manual rhetoricke, introduction by H. R. Gillis (New York: AMS Press, 1975).

OTHER: "Somnium Dramaticum Synesii Iunioris, Cognomento Chirosophi," in *Hvgo Grotivs His Sophompaneas, Or Ioseph A Tragedy. With Annotations. By Francis Goldsmith, Esq* (London: Printed by W. H., 1652).

The mid-seventeenth-century physician John Bulwer wrote prolifically and sometimes flamboyantly on subjects as diverse as rhetorical gesture, the passions, sign language for the deaf and dumb, and the cosmetic fashions of different nations. His work on gesture has always held interest for historians of rhetoric, both for its innovations and for its transitional nature: anticipating developments in eighteenth-century rhetorical theory, looking back to the preoccupations of the sixteenth century, and shaped by the profound changes taking place in medical science and psychology during the first half of the seventeenth century. Even for the period of Francis Bacon, William Harvey, and René Descartes, Bulwer's interests in natural philosophy were wide-ranging. In addition to his work on gesture, he published the first theoretical treatise in English on language training for the deaf and dumb; he planned what would have been the first practical academy for such training; and he did extensive (now lost) work on speech pathologies. Outside of the field of rhetoric, Bulwer's corpus has

been of increasing importance to historians of psychology, anthropology, and linguistics, as well as to literary scholars interested in ethnography, cosmetics, and the history of performance. In and of themselves, his works remain compelling for their peculiar combination of an intense, sometimes censorious morality and a remarkably curious, erudite, and wide-ranging intellect.

Until recently, what little was known about Bulwer's life came from two sources: his prolific writings and his will, entered into probate in London on 3 March 1657. Jeffrey Wollock's thorough detective work, represented in his "John Bulwer's (1606–1656) Place in the History of the Deaf" (1996), has substantially filled out the biographical picture and added a poem, the 1652 "Somnium Dramaticum Synesii Iunioris, Cognomento Chirosophi," to Bulwer's oeuvre. John Bulwer was born in London in May 1606 to Thomas Bulwer, an apothecary, and Marie Evanes of St. Albans, Hertfordshire; the family lived in London and later St. Albans, where his parents were buried. The nineteenth-century novelist, Sir Edward Bulwer-Lytton, Lord Dalling, later sprang from a branch of this family, the Bulwers of Wood Dalling. Where John Bulwer was educated is not known. His name is not on the alumni rolls of Oxford or Cambridge. Nor does he show up in the published records of English physicians educated at Leyden or in Scotland. In "John Bulwer's (1606–1656) Place in the History of the Deaf," Wollock suggests that he spent some time at Oxford in the late 1620s without matriculating (not an unusual practice for gentlemen's sons), and in his essay "John Bulwer and His Italian Sources" (1996) he dates Bulwer's long connection to Royalist and High Church circles from this period.

Bulwer was not a member of the Royal College of Physicians—though he claims to have been friendly with at least one fellow of the college, Robert Wright Jr. (himself trained in London and Leyden and a protégé of two prominent members of the college). Wright was one of the patrons Bulwer hoped to enlist in his projected academy for the deaf and dumb, but he died before Bulwer could present his studies to the Royal College. Toward the end of his life, after a long period of living as a gentleman writer, Bulwer apparently turned or returned to active medical practice. In the 1653 edition of *Anthropometamorphosis: Man Transform'd; Or, The Artificial Changeling* (first published in 1650) he uses the title "M.D." for the first time. Further, as Wollock points out in "John Bulwer's (1606–1656) Place in the History of the Deaf," the last lines of this edition renounce the study of natural philosophy and letters; instead, Bulwer plans to retire to the less public work of a physician.

Bulwer's interests and habits of mind are vividly present in all his writings. He was a classicist, drawing

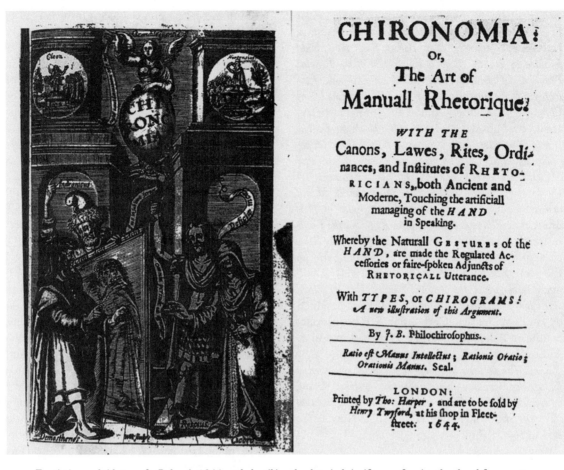

Frontispiece and title page for Bulwer's 1644 work describing the rhetorical significance of various hand and finger gestures

heavily on Quintilian and Cresollius for his basic theory and principles of rhetorical action. His prose style tends toward the Baroque rather than the Neo-Ciceronian, however. Bacon's influence is central, underwriting Bulwer's larger aim to advance learning in the neglected field of manual gesture, his encyclopedic sweep, and his ongoing interest in practical application. Methodologically, Bulwer's descriptions of gesture and expression reflect the pervasiveness of Ramist thought in this period–proceeding from general principles to specific aspects of performance within each essay. Finally, he was well read in sixteenth- and seventeenth-century anatomy, as many direct borrowings in *Chirologia: Or The Natvrall Langvage Of The Hand* (1644) attest. Anatomical method provides a governing organizational principle in all his published works. Thus, his writings are both compendious and intensive: copious in their use of biblical and scholastic sources but also committed to methodical anatomization of ideas and the world.

Bulwer's political and religious affiliations are less obvious and more difficult to trace. Wollock finds predominantly Royalist and High Anglican connections among the friends and patrons who turn up in his dedications and commendatory verses. These tributes show a long association with Gray's Inn circles in London, particularly with Edward and Francis Goldsmith; Bulwer wrote his one extant poem, "Somnium Dramaticum Synesii Iunioris Cognomento Chirosophi," for the latter's translation of Hugo Grotius's *Sophompaneas* (1652). Bulwer himself is surprisingly reticent about his politics for a writer in this turbulent period. What he does say is often oblique or coded–in keeping with the picture of a Royalist writing on the eve of revolution and during the Interregnum. Vividly monarchist language occasionally breaks through, however. For example, the first section of *Chirologia* ends with a long discussion of benediction and laying on of hands; the passage includes an encomium to the "inaugered monarchs of this land" and particularly Charles I. As Bulwer relates, "His sacred Majesty that now is hath practiced with as good success as any of His Royall Progenitors." Elsewhere, Bulwer's writing suggests he supported a consensual monarchy. The liberal bent of his political theory comes through vividly, for example, when he invokes the allegory of the body politic at the beginning of *Chirologia*. Reminding his readers of the profound social significance of manual gestures, he calls the hand "*another tongue,* which we may justly call the *Spokesman* of the *Body,* it *speakes* for all the members therof, denoting their *Suffrages,* and including their *Votes.*" Earlier versions of this famous metaphor imagine the hand differently, as the officer or soldier of the kingly head. As John of Salisbury puts it in *Policraticus* (1159), "the use of the hand testifies to the qualities of the head itself because, as Wisdom asserts, the iniquitous king has entirely impious ministers."

Bulwer's social connections to Laudian circles and his deep appreciation for manual ritual suggest High Anglican leanings. Passages of the *Chirologia* reinforce this supposition, as when Bulwer appreciatively describes the Roman Catholic Mass or quotes St. Paul to assert that "no man can lay the *Hand* upon himselfe and be as Basil tearmes *autocheirotonitos,* his own ordeiner." Several scholars have noted the way *Chironomia: Or, The Art of Manuall Rhetorique* (1644) offers guidance to those who might compete with the powerful Puritan preachers. Bulwer also frequently quotes Calvin on idolatry and discusses at length the efficacy of the "*Manuall* of Prayer," or joining hands in prayer, "to our private devotions." Together with these passages, his hostility to elaborate costume and the passionate, sometimes rabid morality expressed in *Anthropometamorphosis* can sound extraordinarily Puritan. And at first glance, the spare lines of the portrait that appears in the 1653 edition of *Anthropometamorphosis* seem to have Puritan overtones. The message the portrait conveys is particular to the satirical aims of the work, however, and not a statement of religious affiliation. In this engraving, by William Faithorne, Bulwer wears the long wavy hair of a natural man: it falls to his shoulders above an elegant white collar and dark coat, as if to admonish the exotic fashions and cosmetic "metamorphoses" that the author goes on to censure.

The fact that Bulwer could afford to commission a portrait for his first published treatise—by an engraver particularly fashionable among the Royalists—suggests that he was reasonably well-off. The information gained from his will substantiates this assumption. Together with books, goods, and chattels, Bulwer left three tenements in the borough of St. Albans (generating an annual rent of twenty-three pounds) to the use of his executrix and "lovinge friend," Mary Ashenden, who nursed him through a long period of illness. The family picture the will develops is an interesting one. Bulwer had married some time in the early 1630s, but by 1656, it appears, his wife and biological children, if any, had long since passed away. The relationship with

Ashenden was clearly a strong one, for Bulwer appoints her guardian of his adopted minor daughter, "Chirothea Johnson als. Bulwer (whome I bred up from a child as my owne)." He writes with real affection for both: "I commit the care and education of said Chirothea unto my said Executrix to dispose of her accordinge to her love and discretion. . . ." Chirothea stood to inherit the property after Ashenden's death and to pass it on to her heirs if she married with Ashenden's consent. After providing for his caregiver and ward, Bulwer left small amounts of money to a sister and brother-in-law, their children, and a close circle of friends—several of whom contributed dedicatory material to his books. He was buried at St.-Giles-in-the-Fields, Westminster, on 14 October 1656.

Among the most striking things Bulwer's will confirms is the early emergence of his passion for all things related to hands, exemplified by his daughter's remarkable name. He styled himself "philochirosophus" in his first two treatises on the rhetoric of manual gesture and, after their modest success, used the epithet "Chirosopher" on later title pages. The term presumably had advertising value, but it is also a serious act of self-definition. As one reads the dedicatory verses in which his friends reprise and pun on the name, it becomes clear that it epitomizes Bulwer's sense of self and purpose. Just as the hand integrates corporeal and spiritual motions (following Aristotle's influential definition), so it symbolizes both physical and literary activities. To synthesize physical and intellectual labor in this way is the proper work of an avid Baconian thinker, who systematically integrates detailed observation of the material world with classical and biblical authority. Thus, Bulwer's favorite epithet captures both the material and intellectual components of this encyclopedic philosophy.

Bulwer's first publications, the two studies of hand gesture *Chirologia* and *Chironomia,* were printed twice in 1644 under one cover. They were reprinted again in 1648, suggesting that they sold moderately well but without the real success of his later treatise *Anthropometamorphosis.* They have remained the best known of his works, available in James W. Cleary's useful modern edition and in facsimile reprint. As their titles suggest, *Chirologia* and *Chironomia* divide the field of manual gesture into two categories: natural and rhetorical movements of the hand. In each treatise Bulwer systematically surveys the motions of the hands and fingers, reducing every gesture to its basic semantic unit (a natural *gestus* or a rhetorical *canon*) and keying these alphabetically to illustrations, or "chirograms," appended at the back. He expounds upon each gestus and canon in a short essay, drawing on classical and biblical authority, contemporary medical writings, and, according to the full title, "the Authentique Registers of Common Life, and Civill Conversation." The result is a series of short "Historical manifestos" such as the essays of Michel Eyquem de Montaigne or Bacon. Bulwer's focus is narrower than these better-known writers, but his essays remain a rich and lively version of this Renaissance genre.

In *Chirologia* Bulwer describes and analyzes sixty-four different gestures of the hand, with twenty-five examples of the "Dactylogia or the Dialects of the Fingers" appended at the end. As Cleary notes in his editor's introduction, Bulwer differentiates between the motions of the hands and fingers in two curious ways. First, grosser hand gestures tend to signify emotional states, while finer motions of the fingers tend to express intellectual and argumentative ideas. Hand gestures such as clapping "THE RIGHT FIST OFTEN ON THE LEFT PALME" (*Gestus VII: Explodo*—"I explode in anger") and appearing "with FAINTING AND DEJECTED HANDS" (*Gestus VIII: Despero*—"I despair") contrast to finger gestures such as "THE FINGER IN THE MOUTH GNAWN AND SUCKED" (*Gestus I: Inventione laboro*—"I labor to discover") and holding up the thumb to give "voice or sufferage" (*Gestus III: Approbo*—"I approve"). Second, Bulwer devotes most of his analytical energy to gestures that have strongly moral or ethical components: gestures of suffrage, praying, pledging faith, blessing, and honoring. The more complex the intentions expressed by each motion, the more challenging the task of demonstrating a clear and essential connection between physical expression and internal states. Thus, a gestus such as *Oro* ("I Pray") warrants a longer discussion and fuller evidence than *Indignor* ("I am indignant").

From the simplest to the most complex cases, however, the same basic principle sustains Bulwer's analysis: the conviction that motions of the hand demonstrate the natural correspondence between passions of the mind and bodily performance. The striking use of the first-person address in the title of each gestus implies this principle throughout *Chirologia*, but Bulwer makes the claim explicit in his introduction: the hand is *mens corporis,* "another mouth or fountaine of discourse."

> And all these motions and habits of the hand are purely natural, not positive; nor in their senses remote from the true nature of the things that are implied. The naturall resemblance and congruity of which expressions, result from the habits of the minde, by the effort of an impetuous affection wrought in the invaded *Hand,* which is made very plyant for such impressions. . . . for when the fancy hath once wrought upon the *Hand,* our conceptions are display'd and utter'd in the very moment of a thought.

Chironomia deepens and complicates these claims. Bulwer begins with the famous Aristotelian analogy between the hand and reason, in regards to which "Man may well be called *Chirosophus,* id est, *Manu sapiens,* Hand-wise." Yet, for rhetorical purposes, "the actions of the *Hand* are not perfect by Nature." So Bulwer aims to provide seventeenth-century orators at "Churches, Courts of Common pleas, and the Councell-Table" a judicious compilation of ancient authority on gesture and a guide for its decorous employment. Bacon himself points out the absence of a comprehensive study of human gesture, and this comment ratifies Bulwer's project, as he says in his first preface. The signal effectiveness of the hand gives self-evident motivation for such a study, however. Indeed,

> . . . the ingenious are forced to confess that all things are more expressive in the *Hand,* as that which doth garnish the sense of words, and gives the shape, figure, and winning glory into eloquence. This strengthens *Speech* with nerves, and the sinewed cords of twisted Reason. SPEECH divided from the *Hand* is unsound, and brought into a poore and low condition, flags and creeps upon the ground. The babling tongue (indeed) may have a long and spacious walke, and the full mouth may prate and run ore with large and loud impertinencies, but without the concurrence of the *Hand,* the mouth is but a running sore and hollow fistula of the minde, and all such ayery trash but the cracks of an unprofitable lip that wants the assistance of those native Orators which were designed to attend the perfect issue of a well delivered cogitation.

Chironomia is arranged in four sections that lay out the principles and practice of such a well-delivered cogitation. The first section establishes forty-nine canons for hand gestures, which are particularly interesting for the vivid theatrical sensibility they display. Canon 1 offers a good example of Bulwer's ability to evoke dramatic action:

> The *Hand* lightly opened, timorously displayed before the breast, and let fall by short turnes under the heaving shoulders, is an *humble* and neat action becomming those who, *daunted* and *dismaied,* begin to speak as if their tongue were *afraid* to encounter with the publicke eare; and such who shunning a profuse excesse of words, would *sparingly* express their Mindes, or *asswage* and *mitigate* the censorious expectation of their Auditors, by an ingenious insinuation of a *diminutive* Action.

The second section of *Chironomia* continues with thirty-one canons for finger gestures, described with similar precision, as in Canon 25: "The *Middle Finger* put forth, and brandish'd in extent, is an action fit to *brand* and *upbraide men with sloth, effeminacie, and notorious vices.*" More general questions of decorum take up the third section, "The Apocrypha of Action: Or, certaine Prevarications against the Rule of Rhetoricall Decorum, noted in the *Hands* of the Ancient and Modern *Oratours*." Here Bulwer deals with secret sign alphabets, mimicry, "uncomely" and "irrational" gestures such as snapping the fingers, and "effeminate" gestures such as turning up the hand. Finally, the fourth section, "Certain Cavtionary Notions, Extracted out of the Ancient and Moderne Rhetoricians, for the compleating of this Art of *Manuall* Rhetorique, and the better regulating the important gestures of the *Hands & Fingers*," addresses broader performance issues: balance and timing, suiting the hand to the voice, practice and exercise.

As Cleary's introduction to the 1974 edition of *Chirologia* and *Chironomia* details, Bulwer's importance as a rhetorician and his influence on later rhetorical theory is considerable. Bulwer's study was the first "systematic and thorough treatise in English devoted exclusively to the art of gesturing in public speaking," and it seems also to be the first to illustrate most of its gestures graphically. *Chirologia* and *Chironomia* use what Bulwer calls "chirograms"–five plates illustrating 120 of the 169 hand and finger gestures in all–keyed alphabetically to the gestus and canons of each essay. With these illustrations Bulwer makes this ancient art readily accessible to a contemporary audience of professional speakers–for reference, for interpretation, and especially for practice. This interest in popular application is also evident in his treatment of the five Ciceronian procedures (invention, arrangement, style, memory, and delivery), which provide strong conceptual underpinnings to his canons of rhetorical gesture, rather than formal organization. As his title page promises, each discussion integrates scholastic authority with examples taken from "the authentique registers" of contemporary civil life.

Bulwer's influence on later studies of rhetorical gesture is evident but usually unacknowledged. Cleary offers a long, side-by-side analysis of passages from Obadiah Walker's *Some Instrvctions Concerning The Art Of Oratory* (1659) and *Chironomia* that makes a compelling case for Walker's unspoken debt to Bulwer. He finds significant similarities with Gilbert Austin's *Chironomia* (1806), as well. More importantly, Cleary finds in Bulwer's work several key conceptual antecedents of eighteenth-century rhetorical theory: specifically, an emphasis on regulating natural gestures with art and a consistent use of the term *elocution* to mean delivery and physical expression rather than style.

While Bulwer's studies of manual gesture seem poised at the beginning of eighteenth-century developments such as the elocutionary movement, they also illustrate the complex transformation of an earlier rhetorical tradition: universal language theory. In *Chirologia* and *Chironomia* Bulwer takes every opportu-

nity to repeat the point that the language of gesture is a universal one, based on common human passions and expressions:

> Nor doth the *Hand* in one speech or kinde of language serve to intimate and expresse our minde: It speakes all languages, and as an *universall character of Reason,* is generally understood and knowne by all Nations, among the formall differences of their Tongue. And being the onely speech that is naturall to Man, it may well be called the *Tongue and generall language of Humane Nature,* which, without teaching, men in all regions of the habitable world doe at the first sight most easily understand. This is evident by that trade and commerce with those salvage Nations who have long injoy'd the late discovered principalities of the West, with whom (although their Language be strange and unknowne) our Merchants barter and exchange their Wares, driving a rich and silent Trade by signes, whereby many a dumb bargaine without the crafty Brocage of the Tongue, is advantageously made.

Furthermore, Bulwer goes on to assure readers, gesture speaks without "the curse at the confusion of Babel" or the dissimulation of the "crafty" tongue. As Dilwyn Knox has shown, these are stock claims, which emerge in sixteenth-century theories of gesture and become central to universal language schemes in the seventeenth century. Knox attributes the increasing interest in the practical use of gesture to a variety of influences, including "contemporary needs to restore order to a world increasingly divided by linguistic barriers." Indeed, universal language schemes gain influence and popularity during the same period in which travel literature becomes a widespread and fashionable genre and climate and humoral theory evolve into modern theories of nation and race (as Mary Floyd-Wilson showed in her 1966 dissertation "Clime, Complexion, and Degree: Racialism in Early Modern England"). A theory of common human expressions based on gesture provides a powerful bridge across cultural differences illuminated by the rapidly expanding borders of the world.

Alongside a larger theory of gesture as a universal communicator, however, rhetoricians and travel writers regularly described the idiosyncratic habits specific to each region or race. Drawing on this literature, Bulwer records, for example, that "in France, he is not *a la mode,* and a compleat *monsieur,* who is not nimble in the discoursing garbe of his *Hand,* which proportionable to that language is very briske and full of quicke and lightsome expressions." While "The Spaniards have another Standert of moderation and gravity accorded to the lofty Genius of Spaine, where the *Hands* are as often principalls, as accessories to their proud expressions." Bulwer concludes *Chironomia* with these observations,

One of the "chirogram" plates used by Bulwer to illustrate his descriptions of hand gestures in his 1644 Chirologia: Or The Natvrall Langvage Of The Hand

shifting his attention directly to the problem of linguistic borders. Borrowing a metaphor from climate theory, he re-centers English as a powerful, "meridional" language "growne now so rich by the indenization of words of all Nations, and so altered from the old Teutonique, if the rule of *moderation,* be calculated according to the Meridionall propertie of our refined speech, we may with decorum and gravitie enough (as I suppose) meet the *Hand* of any of these warmer Nations halfe way, with the *Manual* adjuncts of our expressions."

These closing words point to Bulwer's increasing interest in national and ethnic character and suggest a writer remarkably open to the prospect of controlled "indenization." They also point to a developing tension in his larger body of work, however: for to draw detailed distinctions between the gestural habits of different nations or races is to destabilize the universalist theory that frames them. As Knox suggests, the promise of universal language theories became increasingly fraught in the seventeenth century, as expanding trade

and travel made communication across cultural barriers more complex and more intractable. Indeed, for Bulwer the "indenization" of foreign practices into England becomes the source of real national anxiety in *Anthropometamorphosis*. Thus, Bulwer's turn at the end of *Chironomia* to a discussion of national gestures anticipates the later unraveling of universalist theory. He planned but never wrote a third volume in the series, "Chirethnicalogia: the national expressions of the Hand," the title of which suggests the difficulties of retaining such a theory at a time when racial and national difference was newly emerging as an object of anxious study. The phrase *national expressions of the hand* describes two, implicitly contradictory projects: either the kind of early anthropological descriptions of different nations that Bulwer went on to pursue in *Anthropometamorphosis,* or a return to the theory of "international" gesture—the lingua franca of the hand—reducing gesture to universals that transcend its diverse national expressions.

Instead of writing "Chirethnicalogia," Bulwer pursued his interest in hand gestures in what became the earliest English study of deaf sign language and lip reading, *Philocophus: Or, The Deafe and Dumbe Mans Friend* (1648). His claim to priority in this field is complicated. There is no conclusive evidence that he put his theory into practice, as John Wallis and William Holder did a decade later. There is ample evidence to suggest his investigations were at least as thoroughgoing as theirs, however. Wollock, in "John Bulwer's (1606–1656) Place in the History of the Deaf," argues persuasively that Bulwer may have renamed his adopted daughter Chirothea—"goddess of the hand"—because she was deaf, in which case he must have spent her early years teaching her. Whatever its origins, Bulwer's interest in teaching the hearing impaired was both scholarly and personal. The dedication to *Philocophus* describes an intimate, valued relationship with two deaf adults, Sir Edward Gostwicke and his younger brother, William, who sought out Bulwer through a mutual friend after seeing the gestural alphabets in *Chirologia.* Dedicating his study to them, and to "other intelligent and ingenious Gentlemen, who as yet can neither heare nor speake," Bulwer goes on in the introduction to correct general misconceptions about the deaf and to express his esteem of the "pure" language they do speak: "although some who understand not the mystery of your condition, look upon you as misprisions in nature; yet to me who have studied your perfections, and well observed the strange recompenses Nature affords you, I behold nothing in you but what may be a just object of admiration!"

Following the pattern of his treatises on rhetoric, Bulwer's work on language for the hearing impaired evolved in two parts: the first theoretical and the second practical; the first published, and the second never completed but still extant in manuscript. (Two additional studies of language pathology, *Glossiatrus* and *Otiatrus,* are listed in the colophon to the 1653 edition of *Anthropometamorphosis,* but neither are extant.) The published *Philocophus* offers a theory of lipreading and describes the other skills that can be taught to the hearing impaired. It includes a long, line-by-line commentary on the earlier work of Sir Kenelm Digby, interlaced with anecdotes of Bulwer's own gleaning and experience. As he readily acknowledges, his ideas in *Philocophus* are largely based on Digby's belated memories of a Spanish teacher, Juan Pablo Bonet, whose pioneering work on the teaching of the deaf, *Reduction de las letras, y arte para enseñar a ablar los mudos,* was published in 1620 (translated as *Simplification of the Letters of the Alphabet and Method of Teaching Deaf-Mutes to Speak,* 1890). Bulwer clearly admits his debt to Digby, but does not explicitly credit Digby's own sources; in failing to do so, he has often drawn the charge of plagiarism. This charge arises in part from anachronistic notions of intellectual property, applied to a period in which medical writings were continually borrowed, translated, and anthologized. The charge also overstates Bonet's claims to a method he lifted in turn from Manuel Ramírez de Carrión. Furthermore, Digby's own sense of his sources was confused and vague, as Wollock has documented.

The charge also reflects the often overlooked evidence of a second manuscript, "Philocophus: the dumb man's academie: wherein is taught a new and admired Art instructing them who are borne Deafe and Dumbe to heare the sound of words with their Eie and thence learne to Speake with theire Tongue." This sequel to *Philocophus* appears to have been prepared for manuscript publication—as suggested by its neat hand, precise page layout, and careful planning for inserted illustrations. At fifty-one manuscript pages, it is only partially finished, however, with incomplete illustrations pasted in from another source. These illustrations are exceptionally good and quite technical, including a foldout anatomy of the vocal system. "Philocophus: the dumb man's academie" sets out to teach reading and writing to the deaf, as a kind of primer and instructional guide in one. It thus demonstrates Bulwer's ongoing interest in a plan for a real academy, first raised in *Philocophus: Or, The Deafe and Dumbe Mans Friend.* The manuscript consists largely of Bulwer's translation of Bonet's discussion of articulatory phonetics, beginning with "an ABC or demonstrative Alphabet for the Dumbe" and getting partly through a sign grammar of noun, verb, and conjunction that reduces "Speech to less diversitie than ordinaire Gramarians have done." As to the question of influence, Bulwer covers the murky territory as far as he is able. He offers a full chapter on the history

"of the first inventors and practitioners of this subtile and wonderfull Art," including Digby, Bonet, and the earlier Pedro Ponce de Leon. With characteristic self-assurance, he goes on to add that even had he received Bonet's book before publishing *Philocophus: Or, The Deafe and Dumbe Mans Friend,* it "would have but little advanced the Philosophie or Grounde worke of this Art which I there adventured to handle."

The underlying assumption of both *Philocophus: Or, The Deafe and Dumbe Mans Friend* and "Philocophus: the dumb man's academie" is again a universalist theory of language. Bulwer explores the new territory of deaf communications with the same confidence in the universal efficacy of deaf signing that he has in the gestures that facilitate New World encounters and trade conducted "without the crafty brocage of the tongue." Describing the ideas he first encountered in *Chirologia* and now returns to in *Philocophus,* he expands on the geographical theme:

> When coasting along the borders of gesture and voluntary motion, I discovered a community among the Senses, and that there was in the continent of humanity, a terra incognita of Ocular Audition, a treasure reserved for these times, which had escaped their privy search, who guided by the illumination of their owne endeavours had in *sudore vultus* ransackt the bosome of nature, wherein wisdome had hid it among other Arts and Sciences which have their foundation in nature. . . .

In the context of his frequent references to a growing market economy and to westering trade, the conceit of a terra incognita carries a real rather than a passing charge. It suggests a wide frame for early studies of language training such as Bulwer's—the larger pressures on communications theory that gave rise to universalist linguistic projects.

It is important to note, however, that Bulwer's absolute belief in "the foundation in nature" that frees manual gesture from the deceptions and artifice of speech is atypical of early educational schemes for the deaf. As James Knowlson shows in his *Universal Language Schemes in England and France, 1600–1800* (1975), "to the majority of seventeenth-century teachers and writers on the teaching of the deaf, gesture (except in its most rudimentary form)" required formal training and convention to be understood, "just as much as spoken languages did." Although theorists such as Francis Bacon and John Wilkins divided gesture into the same categories that Bulwer used (positive and natural gestures), they "regarded only those spontaneous and expressive gestures that convey emotions of joy, anger, and fear as signifying without artifice, training and convention." "Philocophus: the dumb man's academie"—with its emphasis on practical methods for

Frontispiece for the 1653 edition of Bulwer's Anthropometamorphosis
*(originally published in 1650), a Puritan denunciation of international
fashions of dress and decoration (Houghton Library,
Harvard University)*

training, the structure of a sign grammar, a hand alphabet, and so on—would seem to complicate the sweeping claims of the first treatise and follow the modulations Knowlson describes in Bacon and Wilkins. Here too, however, Bulwer seems to feel no contradiction between the practical requirements of training and craft and a theory of universal, natural signification. So, while he does not treat deafness as a separate kind of subjectivity, as current disability theory might advocate—indeed, such a position would be antithetical to the basic principle of universal language—he claims the same privilege and superiority for sign language as for manual gesture in general.

It is important to point out that Bulwer's theoretical framework shifts somewhat, from semiotics and rhetoric in *Chirologia* and *Chironomia* to semiotics and psychophysiology in the two treatises on deafness. The connections between these works show the fruitful crossings between seventeenth-century rhetoric and contemporary developments in physiology and psychology. Thus, for example, *Philocophus: Or, The Deafe and Dumbe Mans Friend* renovates claims in *Chirologia* and *Chironomia*. Where the hand is "another tongue" in the earlier treatise, the principles of lipreading demon-

strated in *Philocophus* show that speech is really a form of gesture. For the deaf, the faculties of the eye substitute for the faculties of the ear, perceiving speech as a system of visual rather than aural signs. Thus, lipreading produces a "metempsychosis or transmigration" of the senses. To illustrate this idea, the frontispiece of *Philocophus* borrows a set of visual devices from the frontispiece of *Chirologia,* where the pediment is graced with illustrated hands bearing an eye, mouth, ear, or tongue in their palms. In the later treatise, Bulwer's metempsychosis appears in the form of remarkable engravings of faces that have transposed features: a man who cannot speak has a tongue in his nose and another has an ear for his eye; a blind man with sealed eyelids has eyes in his ears. Though it sounds irrecoverably fanciful, the conceit of metempsychosis has a serious basis in contemporary physiology: the principle of a common or shared primary sense that informs all other sensory faculties. Bulwer plays on precisely this notion of a common perceptual faculty in his introduction to *Philocophus* when he describes his newly discovered "community among the senses."

Bulwer's interest in the physiology of perception intensifies in his later work, which details the connections between spiritual motions and corporeal expressions—what actually happens when the body communicates. As he puts it in the introduction to *Philocophus,* he aims to find out the "Radicall Derivations and Muscular Etymologies" of discoursing gestures. He planned to continue his study of corporeal rhetoric in a third pair of treatises, "Cephalelogia, or the naturall language of the head, being an extract of the most noble and practicall notions of Physiognomy" and "Cephalenomia, or the art of cephalicall rhetorick," but these were either lost or never completed. Instead, Bulwer pursued his muscular etymologies in a fascinating treatise on physiognomy and the passions, *Pathomyotomia Or A Dissection of the significative Muscles of the Affections of the Minde* (1649). He chose the muscles of the face, he explains, because they are closest to the seat of passions in the brain, and "in the semblances of those motions wrought in the parts by the endeavour of the Muscles, we may not only see, but as it were feel and touch the very inward motions of the Mind."

As its subtitle announces, *Pathomyotomia* is much less indebted to popular physiognomies than it is to contemporary medical anatomies, which share this preoccupation and its Aristotelian and Galenic principles. Bulwer's chief sources are wide-ranging, from the contemporary English anatomist Helkiah Crooke to Continental writers such as J. C. Scaliger, Girolamo Fabrizi d'Acquapendente, and Curzio Marinelli, noted for their work on muscular and animate motion. The order of dissection gives this treatise its methodical organization as well. Proceeding feature by feature, first describing muscular function and then describing affect, Bulwer discusses facial expressions as diverse as pursing the lips, yawning, kissing, narrowing the eyes, and creasing the nose. Bulwer's analysis is distinctly pre-Cartesian, shaped by the international Aristotelianism of early-seventeenth-century science that also influenced William Harvey. Thus, *Pathomyotomia* offers biomechanical but resolutely organicist explanations of the passionate, expressive self–moved "not with our minde onely, but with our mind and body both." Despite the sea change in natural philosophy inaugurated by René Descartes, this work was more influential–and more sophisticated–than its critical obscurity would suggest. Indeed, in his survey of early modern psychology, *Mental Machinery: The Origins and Consequences of Psychological Ideas, 1600–1850* (1992), Graham Richards argues that Bulwer's explanation of the biological basis of universal character "anticipates modern Psychology far more closely than that of Descartes' work"; and he notes that *Pathomyotomia* is the "very first work to receive a (respectful) footnote citation in Charles Darwin's *Expression of the Emotions in Man and Animals* (1872)."

Bulwer's last work turns from investigations of the physiological mechanics of human expression to a passionate, moral excoriation of practices that alter the body so perfectly crafted by God. *Anthropometamorphosis: Man Transform'd; Or, The Artificial Changeling* was reprinted four times in two editions between 1650 and 1658; a second edition in 1653 greatly expands the work, and a reprint in 1654 gives it a new title, *A View Of The People Of The Whole World: Or, A short Survey of their Policies, Dispositions, Naturall Deportments, Complexions, Ancient and Moderne Customes, Manners, Habits & Fashions*. The strong reception of these volumes can be explained in part by the way *Anthropometamorphosis* synthesizes several popular genres, including medical anatomy, moral sermons on fashion, and travel writing. It must also have owed part of its appeal, as it does now, to the rough woodcuts that graphically illustrate the "corporall fashions" by which every nation mutates and changes "the organicall parts of their bodies into diverse depraved Figures": from fantastical tonsures to dyed hair and skin, tattoos, body piercing, scarification, and circumcision. These bodily abuses from around the world lead into a long "Pedigree of the English Gallant," an appendix describing extravagancies that breed too close to home. Here, with striking juxtapositions of foreign and familiar, Bulwer demonstrates that barbarous scarification is cognate with the perversions of contemporary English fashion. For "the flashing, pinking, and cutting of our Doublets is but the same phansie and affectation with those barbarous Gallants who slash and carbonado their bodies, and who pinke and raze their Sattin, Damaske, and Duretto skins."

As its several titles suggest, *Anthropometamorphosis* surveys such "blasphemous fancies" of cosmetic alteration across the nations of the world. It proceeds part by part, however, as would a dissection or anatomy, rather than region by region, as would a travelogue. Indeed, the first authorities Bulwer cites are anatomists: Galen, from his seminal work *On the Usefulness of the Parts of the Body* (second century A.D.), and Crooke, who popularized medical texts by publishing them in English. The effects of Bulwer's anatomical method are interestingly contradictory. *Anthropometamorphosis* stands among the earliest attempts at detailed ethnographic description. Both Richards and Mary Baine Campbell, in "Anthropometamorphosis: John Bulwer's Monsters of Cosmetology and the Science of Culture," describe the work as a kind of proto-anthropology. The cumulative "body" that emerges in this anatomy of national "mutations" comes together as a normative, universal, and singular ideal. In this way, Bulwer evokes medieval microcosmic studies of the world that use the human body as a standard point of reference to unify and model all other cosmic systems. That standard appears independent of qualities like nationality or race. But the cosmetic practices Bulwer surveys and describes so carefully–vivid cultural expressions of nation and race–dominate the imagination of this work, pulling it toward anthropological description of difference and away from microcosmic correspondences.

The aim and tone of the work pull in two directions as well. What begins in Bulwer's familiar style of encyclopedic anatomy devolves, by the point of the "Pedigree of the English Gallant," into writing so frothing and censorious as to be satirical, in the mode of many contemporary treatises against cosmetics and fashion. Bulwer's style is always hyperbolic, but the appendix runs over the top. For example, after drawing the analogy between slashed doublets and carbonadoed bodies Bulwer denounces the current fashion for decorated codpieces and tight, revealing hose: "Now our hose are made so close to our Breeches, that, like Irish Trowses, they too manifestly discover the dimensions of every part. What would Turkes say to an English man thus strictly cloathed, who detest our little and streight breeches as dishonest, because they too much express our shamefull parts." The object of satire is of course fops and dandies, passionately concerned for their appearance and elaborately ridiculous (in Bulwer's moral assessment). The sharpness of such correspondences, and its satiric *imitatio* in invoking the opinion of the Turks, might explain the popularity of *Anthropometamorphosis*—otherwise a generic oddity of travel writing, surveying the world without offering any first-hand accounts of travel.

Remarkably forward-looking and remarkably belated—and full of such internal contradictions—Bulwer's work as a whole remains difficult to summarize. But his ability to cross and mix many generic forms—and the intellectual and literary dissonance such mixing produces—makes it particularly rich and compelling. For these dissonances illuminate the changing relationship between rhetorical theory and the larger cultural developments that make it communications theory: changing disciplinary boundaries, an expanding market economy, increasingly complex relations with the New World, and developing sciences of the body and mind. Remarkably little has been written about this complicated and intelligent scholar, and a great deal more remains to be done.

References:

Jean-Christophe Agnew, *Worlds Apart: The Market and the Theater in Anglo-American Thought, 1550–1750* (Cambridge & New York: Cambridge University Press, 1986);

William E. Burns, "The King's two monstrous bodies: John Bulwer and the English revolution," in *Wonders, Marvels, and Monsters in Early Modern Culture* (Newark, London, & Cranbury, N.J.: University of Delaware Press, Associated University Presses, 1999);

Mary Baine Campbell, "Anthropometamorphosis: John Bulwer's Monsters of Cosmetology and the Science of Culture," in *Monster Theory: Reading Culture,* edited by Jeffrey Jerome Cohen (Minneapolis & London: University of Minnesota Press, 1996), pp. 202–222;

James W. Cleary, "Editor's Introduction," in *Chirologia: or the Natural Language of the Hand and Chironomia: or the Art of Manual Rhetoric, by John Bulwer* (Carbondale & Edwardsville: Southern Illinois University, 1974), pp. xiii–xxxix;

Cleary, "John Bulwer: Renaissance Communicationist," *Quarterly Journal of Speech,* 45 (1959): 391–398;

Mary Floyd-Wilson, "Clime, Complexion, and Degree: Racialism in Early Modern England," dissertation, University of North Carolina, 1996;

Stephen Greenblatt, "Toward a Universal Language of Motion: Reflections on a Seventeenth-Century Muscle Man," in *Choreographing History,* edited by Susan Leigh Foster (Bloomington: Indiana University Press, 1995), pp. 25–31;

Christopher Hoolihan, "Too Little Too Soon: The Literature of Deaf Education in 17th-century Britain (Part 1)," *Volta Review,* 86, no. 7 (December 1984): 349–353;

James Knowlson, *Universal Language Schemes in England and France, 1600–1800* (Toronto & Buffalo: University of Toronto Press, 1975), pp. 212–214, 216–217, 225;

Dilwyn Knox, "Ideas on Gesture and Universal Languages c. 1550–1650," in *New Perspectives on Renaissance Thought: Essays in the History of Science, Education and Philosophy: In Memory of Charles B. Schmitt,* edited by John Henry and Sarah Hutton (London: Duckworth, 1990), pp. 101–136;

Palmer Morrel-Samuels, "John Bulwer's 1644 Treatise on Gesture," *Semiotica,* 79 (1990): 341–353;

H. J. Norman, "John Bulwer (f.1654) The 'Chirosopher,' Pioneer in the Treatment of the Deaf and Dumb in Psychology," *Proceedings of the Royal Society of Medicine,* 36 (1943): 589–602;

Graham Richards, *Mental Machinery: The Origins and Consequences of Psychological Ideas, 1600–1850* (London: Athlone, 1992; Baltimore: Johns Hopkins University Press, 1992), pp. 18, 70–73, 90, 168;

Joseph R. Roach, *The Player's Passion: Studies in the Science of Acting* (Newark: University of Delaware Press / London: Associated University Presses, 1985), pp. 33–38, 40, 42–44, 50, 53, 55, 64, 72–73;

Jeffrey Wollock, "John Bulwer and His Italian Sources," in *Italia ed Europa nella Linguistica de Rinascimento: Confronti e Relazioni: Atti del Convegno Internazionale: Ferrara, Palazzo Paradiso, 20–24 Marzo 1991,* 2 volumes, edited by Mirko Tavoni and Pietro U. Dini (Modena: F. C. Panini, 1996), II: 417–433;

Wollock, "John Bulwer's (1606–1656) Place in the History of the Deaf," *Historiographia Linguistica,* 23 (1996): 1–46.

Papers:

The British Library holds manuscripts of three works by John Bulwer in the Sloan manuscript collection: "Vultispex criticus, seu physiognomia medici" (17th c., BL Sl. ms. 805); "Philocophus: Or the Dumbe mans Academie" (17th c., BL Sl. ms. 1788); and extracts from his "Anthropometamorphosis," by Dr. C. L. Morley (17th c., BL Sl. ms. 1281).

Charles Butler

(circa 1560 – 29 March 1647)

Victor William Cook

BOOKS: *Rameæ Rhetoricæ Libri Dvo. In Vsvm Scholarvm* (Oxford: Printed by Joseph Barnes, 1597); enlarged as *Rhetoricæ Libri Dvo. Qvorvm Prior de Tropis & Figuris, Posterior de Voce & Gestu Præcipit. In Vsum Scholarum accuratiùs editi* (Oxford: Printed by Joseph Barnes, 1598);

The Feminine Monarchie Or A Treatise Concerning Bees, And The Dve Ordering of Them: Wherein The truth found out by experience and diligent observation, discovereth the idle and fond conceipts, which many haue written anent this subiect (Oxford: Printed by Joseph Barnes, 1609); revised and enlarged as *The Feminine Monarchie: Or The Historie of Bees. Shewing Their Admirable Nature, and Properties, Their Generation, and Colonies, Their Government, Loyaltie, Art, Industrie, Enemies, Warres, Magnanimitie, &c. Together With the right ordering of them from time to time: And the sweet profit arising thereof. Written out of Experience* (London: Printed by John Haviland for Roger Jackson, 1623); revised as *The Feminine Monarchi, Or The Histori Of Bee's. Shewing Their admirable Natur, and Propertis; Their Generation and Colonis; Their Government, Loyalti, Art, Industri; Enimi's, VVars, Magnanimiti, &c. Together With the right Ordering of them from tim to tim: and the sweet Profit arising ther of. Written out of Experienc* (Oxford: Printed for the author by William Turner, 1634);

Συγγε'νεια. De Propinqvitate Matrimonium impediente, Regvla. Quæ vna omnes quæstionis huius difficultates facilè expedias (Oxford: Printed by John Lichfield & William Turner, 1625);

Oratoriæ Libri Dvo. Qvorum Alter ejus Definitionem, Alter Partitionem Explicat: Jn Vsvm Scholarvm recèns editi (Oxford: Printed for the author by William Turner, 1629);

The English Grammar, Or The Institution of Letters, Syllables, and Words, in the English tongue. Whereunto is annexed An Index of Words Like and Unlike (Oxford: Printed for the author by William Turner, 1633); republished as *The English Grammar, or, The Institution of Letters, Syllables, and Words, in the English tung.*

Whereunto is annexed An Index of Woords Lik and Unlik (Oxford: Printed for the author by William Turner, 1634);

The Principles Of Musik, In Singing and Setting: With The twofold Use therof, (Ecclesiasticall and Civil) (London: Printed for the author by John Haviland, 1636).

Editions: *Charles Butler's English Grammar (1634),* edited by Albert Eichler, Neudrucke Fruhneuenglischer Grammatiken, no. 4 (Halle, Germany: M. Niemeyer, 1910);

"Charles Butler on Memory," translated by L. S. Hultzén, *Speech Monographs,* 6 (1939): 44–65;

The English Grammar, with Explanatory Remarks by Shoichi Watanabe. Grammatica Linguae Anglicanae, by Christopher Cooper, with Explanatory Remarks by Shozo Shibata, Reprint Series of Books Relating to the English Language, no. 4 (Tokyo: Nan'un do, 1967);

The Feminine Monarchie, The English Experience, no. 81 (Amsterdam: Theatrum Orbis Terrarum / New York: Da Capo Press, 1969);

The Principles of Musik, The English Experience, no. 284 (Amsterdam: Theatrum Orbis Terrarum / New York: Da Capo Press, 1970);

The Principles of Musik in Singing and Setting, Introduction by Gilbert Reaney, Music Reprint Series (New York: Da Capo Press, 1970);

"Charles Butler's *The Principles of Music in Singing and Setting, with the Twofold Use Thereof Ecclesiastical and Civil* (1636): A Computer Assisted Transliteration of Book I and the First Chapter of Book II, with Introduction, Supplementary Notes, Commentary, and Appendices," edited by Arthur Timothy Smith, dissertation, Ohio State University, 1974;

The Feminine Monarchie, or, The Historie of Bees (Hebden Bridge, U.K.: Northern Bee Books, 1985).

Charles Butler, a country parson of a small village in Hampshire, wrote introductory textbooks for pupils at grammar school or university. His most famous textbook was the *Rhetoricæ Libri Dvo* (Two

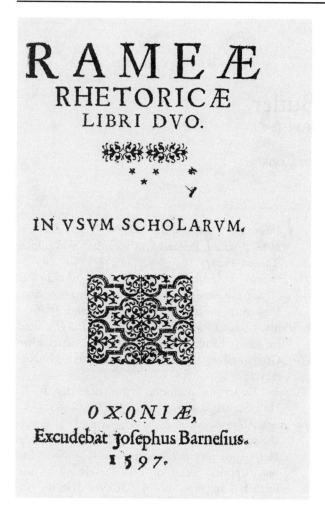

Title page for Charles Butler's influential adaptation of Audomarus Talaeus's Rhetorica *(Rhetoric, 1548)*

highly instrumental in spreading the ideas of Pierre de La Ramée (known as Petrus Ramus) and Ramus's collaborator, Talaeus, in Britain by means of his preparatory textbooks.

Although they respected his work, Butler's contemporaries must have been just as puzzled as later readers are by the diversity of his subjects. If there was a guiding principle to his life and work, it seems to have been a love of ordered systems both in nature and in conceptual frameworks, which enable topics to be treated clearly and concisely. As an avid Royalist, such an affection for well-structured hierarchies would have been natural for Butler.

Charles Butler was born, according to Anthony à Wood, in Great (that is, High) Wycombe, Buckinghamshire. His date of birth is uncertain, but the year is generally thought to be close to 1560. He was educated at Oxford University. A chorister from 1579 to 1585, he matriculated on 24 November 1581 at the age of twenty, according to Joseph Foster, as a student at Oxford's Magdalen College, where he later became one of the Bible Clerks. He graduated with a B.A. on 6 February 1584 and proceeded to attain an M.A. in 1587, on either 28 June, as Wood has it, or 1 July, as Foster has it. In 1593 he was appointed rector to the church at Nately Scures, a small village four miles east of Basingstoke. Two years later he became master of the Holy Ghost School in Basingstoke, where he received a stipend of £12 per year. At some time around 1600, he resigned his rectory and schoolmastership to become vicar of the nearby church at Wooton St. Lawrence, "a poor preferment, God wot, for such a worthy scholar," as Wood puts it. His wife died in 1628; Butler lived on for another twenty years until he too died, on 29 March 1647, at the age of eighty-eight or so. He is buried in the chancel at Wooton in an unmarked grave.

For more than forty years he kept the parish records and churchwarden's accounts, and these, according to the Reverend Frank R. Money, reveal him to have been conscientious and hardworking, both with regard to his parishioners and to the maintenance of the church. The parish records show that he had three sons, William, Edmund, and Richard, and two daughters. The first of his daughters, Briget, died in 1605 at the age of nine months; his daughter Elizabeth, baptized in 1612, was married on St. Valentine's Day 1633 to the Reverend Richard White, curate of Eastrop. Gilbert White, the author of *The Natural History and Antiquities of Selbourne* (1789), was the great-grandson of Elizabeth and Richard White.

Butler began his literary career with his 1597 edition of the *Rameæ Rhetoricæ Libri Dvo*. This book is a pared-down version of the *Rhetorica* of Talaeus, who was a colleague of and collaborator with Ramus, who

Books of Rhetoric, 1598), an annotated edition of *Rhetorica* (Rhetoric, 1548), the famous work of Omer Talon (known as Audomarus Talaeus), but he also wrote schoolbooks on grammar and music, as well as treatises for adult readers. Modern critics have not always been kind to Butler, finding his works intellectually and aesthetically unsatisfying. He is often criticized as being a dilettante or a gifted amateur. For example, Walter J. Ong says, in his *Ramus: Method, and the Decay of Dialogue; from the Art of Discourse to the Art of Reason* (1958), that Butler "was famed not as a seriously scientific logician or philosopher but as an author of preparatory-school textbooks in rhetoric." Occasionally, he is ridiculed for his idiosyncratic system of reformed spelling, which makes some of his later books, such as the one on English grammar, unpleasant to read; for his baroque literary style of writing, which has been described by at least one critic as "laughable"; and for his so-called bees's madrigal, or bee-swarming song, found in his book on bees. Even so, it cannot be denied that he was

was famous for introducing a reformation of teaching methods in schools and universities, both with regard to the general syllabus and in the methods employed in the individual subjects of grammar, logic, rhetoric, arithmetic, and so on. Butler, a keen teacher himself, sees in the Ramistic methods a clearness and perspicacity that he considers indispensable to the teaching of youth. The Ramistic methods were more popular on the Continent than in England, where interest in them was centered at Cambridge, and they eventually became the foundation of undergraduate studies. The more conservative Oxford, on the other hand, preferred the teaching of dialectic and rhetoric to be along the more traditional, Aristotelian lines. Indeed, J. M. Fletcher notes that in 1586–a year before Butler obtained his M.A. degree–the Oxford authorities had enacted a statute that "noted the use of different authors in the schools produced conflict," and therefore banned all views except those of Aristotle and his supporters as subjects "to be debated by the bachelors in their determination exercises." Ramus, however, may have been popular at Oxford's Magdalen College, with its large (and occasionally unruly) undergraduate population.

Butler probably became interested in Ramism while in this milieu, but he did not publish his version of Talaeus's work until 1597, when he was in his mid-thirties. However, it would appear from the dedication, which is dated 5 May 1593, that some version of the book may have existed earlier. The origins of the book may date back to Butler's student days, since as an M.A. he might have been expected to lecture at the college, in which case he could have used some version of it as a textbook. Like Dudley Fenner's *The Artes of Logike and Rethorike* (1584) and Abraham Fraunce's *The Arcadian Rhetorike* (1588), which were English adaptations of Talaeus, Butler's Latin book includes only part of Talaeus's original text. Butler uses only those parts pertinent to the essential, nonpolemical elements of Talaeus, those elements peculiar to the basic definitions of technical terms and their interrelationships.

In 1598 Butler published an annotated edition, the *Rhetoricæ Libri Dvo*. Earlier commentaries had been written by Claudius Minos, Gulielmus Adolphus Scribonius, Johann Piscator, Johannes Bilsten, and Snellius (Rudolph Snel van Roijen), but Butler's edition was the first in England. Although the adjective "Rameæ" (meaning "Ramist") has been removed from the title, both Ramus and Talaeus are eulogized in the preface: Ramus with respect to the truth of his precepts, the brevity of his method, and the perspicacity of his examples, and Talaeus for being the skilled artificer who extended into rhetoric the methods employed by Ramus in his book on dialectic. Although highly influ-

ential in spreading Ramism in Britain (at least to the young), Butler's *Rhetoricæ Libri Dvo* was apparently at first ignored; in *The Feminine Monarchie Or A Treatise Concerning Bees, And The Dve Ordering of Them: Wherein The truth found out by experience and diligent observation, discovereth the idle and fond conceipts, which many haue written anent this subiect* (1609), Butler comments that this book too may "lie hidden in obscurity, as the book of *tropes* and *figures* did for a while go unregarded, without friends or acquaintance" until "by litle & litle" it insinuated itself "into the loue & liking of many schooles, yea of the Vniuersity it selfe."

Butler's actual contribution consists in annotations of specific words in the whittled-down text of Talaeus. Sometimes he adds things not in Talaeus, sometimes he expands upon an idea or goes further in Talaeus's purpose of applying Ramus's dialectical notions to rhetoric, sometimes he refers the reader to a similar idea in the works of a (usually) classical rhetorician (notably Cicero and Quintilian), but primarily he supplies, for didactic purposes, a set of examples to be studied and applied to the definitions of tropes and figures. These annotated examples are all from about thirty Latin classical authors–in particular, Virgil, Martial, Lucan, Ovid, Lucretius, Terence, Pliny, Plautus, Salust, and Juvenal–and their didactic usefulness is witnessed in contemporary accounts of the way Butler's books were taught in schools. Indeed, Charles Hoole in *A New Discovery of the Old Art of Teaching Schoole* (1660) gives an actual case of how Butler was used: he says that Mr. Bonner of Rotherham School had his fifth form spend their forenoons studying the *Rhetoricæ Libri Dvo*, "which they said *memoriter* [from memory], and then construed, and applyed the example to the definition." The student was presumably expected to express the exact manner in which the example was an instance of the general definition.

The interest in the book is shown by the number of editions that it went through in subsequent years. It was republished eight times in Butler's lifetime, and five times after his death. The 1642 Leiden edition indicates that interest in the *Rhetoricæ Libri Dvo* extended as far as the Continent. The 1642 Cambridge edition was the first one to directly attribute authorship to Butler; previously, Butler's name appeared only in the prefatory letters. The first edition to appear after his death was the 1649 London edition; the last edition was printed in 1684 in London. In addition, there were several works based upon Butler's book: the simplified *Rhetoricæ Libri Dvo* of William Dugard's *Rhetorices Elementa* (The Rudiments of Rhetoric, 1648), which went into at least fifteen editions up to 1721, and the even more simplified version of John Newton's *An Introduction to the Art of Rhetorick* (1671), which embodies a treatment of *inventio*

THE
Feminine Monarchie:
OR
THE HISTORIE OF BEES.

SHEWING

Their admirable Nature, and Properties,
Their Generation, and Colonies,
Their Gouernment, Loyaltie, Art, Induſtrie,
Enemies, Warres, Magnanimitie, &c.

TOGETHER

With the right ordering of them from time to
time : And the ſweet profit ariſing thereof.

Written out of Experience
By
CHARLES BVTLER. *Magd:*

Plaut: in Trucul: Act: 2. Sc. 6.
Pluris eſt oculatus teſtis unus, quam auriti decem.

LONDON,
Printed by IOHN HAVILAND for *Roger Iackſon*,
and are to be ſold at his Shop in Fleetſtreet, ouer
againſt the Conduit. 1 6 2 3.

Title page for the revised edition of Butler's pioneering book on beekeeping, the first work to refer to the chief bee as a queen, rather than a king

(invention) and *disposito* (arrangement) following Michael Radau's *Orator Extemporaneus* (Extemporaneous Orator, 1657), and a partial paraphrase of Butler's *elocutio* (style) section only.

The earliest known reference to Butler's *Rhetoricæ Libri Dvo* is in John Brinsley's *Ludus Literarius: or, The Grammar Schoole* (1612). The first reference is in a marginal note on page 162 where "for most exquisite observation of placing and measuring sentences, Rhetorically, in prose by schollars of riper iudgement, in their Theames, Declamations, Orations or the like," one is advised to read either the relevant chapters in Talaeus, or (in the margin): "Butlers Rhetor. Chap. 15." Then, on page 197, "for the Figures belonging to Poetry," Butler's chapter 14 ("on meter") is recommended. There is another specific recommendation, on page 214, to read book 2, which concerns *pronuntiatio*, or "delivery"–that is, the more physical aspects (including posture and gesture) of rhetoric. It is perhaps interesting that the first two of these references are to parts

of the book that have little to do with Talaeus, since they contain all that Butler has to say of metrical matters for both prose and poetry, while the last one concerns book 2, which everyone from Talaeus (judging from the amount of space he devotes to it) to Newton (who does not include it) considers of less importance to the science of rhetoric. However, a more general, and important, commendation is found on page 204 where Brinsley says that "in stead of Talaeus, you may vse Master Butlars Rhetoricke . . . which I mentioned before: being a notable abbridgement of Talaeus, making it most plaine, and farre more easie to be learned of Schollars, and also supplying very many things wanting in Talaeus." He goes on to say that though it is a book "which (as I take it) is yet very little knowne in Schooles, though it haue beene forth sundry yeares," yet "the vse and benefit will be found to be farre aboue all that euer hath beene written of the same," that is, rhetoric.

Later, in his *A Consolation for Our Grammar Schooles* (1622), Brinsley suggests where Butler might fit into the school curriculum: first, he recommends the reading of Thomas Farnaby's work, and second, "for a more full vnderstanding of that little booke, and of all other matters belonging to Rhetoricke, as for a methodicall handling, and short comprizing of the whole Art," he suggests "M. Butlers Rhetorick . . . now for the 4. time printed." Finally, for "the vse of Rhetoricke, viz. for the practise thereef in Theames, Declamations, Orations &c," he recommends the work of Thomas Vicars. Butler's book hereby occupies an intermediate position between a book for beginners (Farnaby's *Figvrae, Tropi et Schemata; Figures, Tropes, and Schemes,* 1616) and a book for the more advanced practitioner of the art (Vicars's *Ceiragwgia: Manuductio ad Artem Rhetoricam;* Handbook: A Handbook to the Rhetorical Art, 1621).

Hoole, in his *A New Discovery of the Old Art of Teaching Schoole,* also recommends the reading of Butler, or rather, Dugard's version of him, when he tells teachers that in "the Art of fine speaking," they may use the book "lately printed by Mr. Dugard, and out of it learn the Tropes and Figures, according to the definitions given by Talaeus, and afterwards more illustrated by Mr. Butler." "Out of either of which books," Hoole continues, "they may be helped with store of examples, to explain the Definitions, so as they may know any Trope or Figure that they meet with in their own authours. When they have thoroughly learnt that little book, they may make a Synopsis of it, whereby to see its order, and how every thing hangs together, and then write the Commonplace heads in a Paperbook . . . unto which they may referre." The result will be that they will come to "the perfect understanding of them [Tropes and Figures] in a quarter of a yeares time, and with more ease commit it all to memory by constant parts, saying a whole Chapter together at once; which afterwards they may keep by constant Repetitions, as they do their Grammar."

The earliest criticism of the book is in the preface to John Barton's *The Art of Rhetorick* (1634). After several general criticisms of earlier rhetorics, Barton specifically points out a problem in Butler's treatment of synecdoche. For Butler, the word *build* in the sentence *"they build an horse"* (from Virgil, in the sense of building the Trojan horse) is an example of "synecdoche of the species," in which a word for a species is applied to the genus. In Butler's opinion, the normal sense of *build* is specifically "to build a *house,*" whereas here the sense is the more generic "build anything" (in this case, a wooden horse). For Barton, however, it is perfectly normal to use the word *build* when speaking of building a house or a wooden horse. The point of this criticism is that an overly general definition of synecdoche (and metonymy) could lead to a situation in which the concept of a metaphor would be irrelevant.

It would seem that Butler eventually came to think that the *Rhetoricæ Libri Dvo* was inadequate as a textbook in the sense that it restricted its subject matter to elocutio and pronuntiatio, at a time when students were also expected to know something about the rest of the classical rhetorical syllabus. The *Oratoriæ Libri Dvo* (Two Books of Oratory), first published in 1629, was intended to cover the remainder of the subject. It does so in a Classical (and non-Ramist) manner, but without abrogating any of the contents of the *Rhetoricæ Libri Dvo.* In other words, his chapter on elocutio and pronuntiatio merely refers the reader to the earlier book. The close relationship between the two books is also shown by the fact that the 1629 and 1635 editions of the *Rhetoricæ Libri Dvo* were originally intended to comprise both books, as their title pages indicate, although only the 1629 edition actually includes the two books. Butler explains in the preface to this edition that he wrote the book, not because he thought that he had to improve upon any of the books currently available, but because certain well-wishing schoolmasters, impressed with the success of the earlier book, had asked him to cover the whole of the subject of oratory in a similarly brief and perspicacious manner. The admission that his book will have to compete against a large number of other good ones might help to explain why *Oratoriæ Libri Dvo* was out of print by the mid 1640s, after only a few editions. The *Rhetoricæ Libri Dvo,* however, went through a total of fifteen editions up to the year 1684.

In the book, *oratoria* (oratory) is defined as "Facultas formandi Orationem de qualibet Qvæstione" (the faculty of forming an oration on any question). An *oratio* (oration), in turn, is defined as "Dictionū & Sententiarū structura ad persuadendū accomodata" (a structure of words and sentences appropriate to what is to be persuaded). An oration is used for *conciliando* (gaining favor), *concitando* (inciting), and *docendo* (teaching). In addition, this first half of the book deals with style, the parts of an oration (the *exordium,* and so on), types of "causes" (demonstrative, deliberative, and judicial), as well as types of questions and answers. The ideas found in the works of Ramus (as related to inventio and dispositio) are discussed in the second book—in particular, with regard to the treatment of *argumenta* (arguments). *Memoria* (memory), which for Ramus (and Butler) was a natural faculty and consequently not a matter of art, is also covered; L. S. Hultzén published a translation of this section in 1939.

In spite of the non-Ramistic elements in the book, Butler still retains his earlier ideas on the subject. The precepts on *loci* (types of arguments), Butler tells the reader, are taken entirely from Ramus, whose singular skills in rebuilding the arts he cannot admire enough. On the other hand, Butler's deep admiration for Ramism never degenerates into the polemical fervor well noted in the chief originators. For example, often Butler simply restates an idea in Ramus in terms of Aristotle, without any of the adverse remarks that one might have expected from either Ramus or Talaeus.

The rest of Butler's publications were on other topics. Perhaps the most important of all is his beekeeping book, *The Feminine Monarchie,* first published in 1609. It is important because it is the first book to be printed on the subject in England. Indeed, it was on the basis of his bee book that Money, then vicar of Wooton, sought to solicit funds, by means of his pamphlet *Charles Butler, Vicar of Wooton 1600–1647 Father of English Bee-Keeping and Celebrated Philologist* (1953), for the memorial window that was unveiled in Butler's honor in the north aisle of the Wooton St. Lawrence Church on 14 November 1954. The inscription reads, "To the Glory of God. In memory of Charles Butler, Vicar of this Parish from 1600–1647. Author of a notable Book on Bees 'De Feminin^c Monarki^c [using Butler's system of spelling]. This Window was placed here to mark the Coronation of Queen Elizabeth II in 1953." The reference to the queen's coronation was added "somewhat belatedly," Frank Vernon reports, by the main financial backers of the project, the British Beekeepers' Association, as a concession to the local parishioners, who would have liked to see the coronation commemorated and who probably did not know much about Butler. No doubt Butler would have approved of this addition, given his Royalist sympathies.

Butler tells the reader on the title page that he wrote the book "from experience," in the hope of rectifying the errors of earlier writers, such as Aristotle,

ORATORIÆ
LIBRI DVO.

QVORVM
Alter ejus Definitionem,
Alter Partitionem
EXPLICAT:

IN VSVM SCHOLARVM
recèns editi.

Authore CAROLO BVTLERO, Magd.

OXONIÆ
Excudebat GVILIELMVS TVRNER,
impensis Authoris. 1629.

Title page for Butler's continuation of Ramæ Rhetoricæ Libri Dvo
(Two Books of Ramist Rhetoric), which includes discussion
of oratory omitted from the earlier work

Pliny, Columella, Varro, Palladius, and Averroës. He writes of how he admires bees because they express "a perfect Monarchie, The Most Natvral And Absolute Forme Of Gouernment," in which there are "subordinate Gouernours and Leaders, not vnfitly resembling Captaines and Coronels of Souldiers." Here Butler reveals both his love of hierarchical orderliness and his monarchical politics. Indeed, the third edition of 1634 is dedicated to Queen Henrietta Maria, who married Charles I in 1625, and who was a vociferous exponent of the divine right of kings. This dedication set a precedent with subsequent writers on bees to dedicate their books to queens. In the book, Butler shows an early interest in the subject of bee "language," a topic not developed until the twentieth century. He is also aware that swarms consist of bees of all ages, that they work upon one kind of flower at a time, that the drones are male and the workers female. But his most important contribution to the understanding of bees was the notion, first found in Butler, that the chief bee is female. Before Butler, this bee was called a "King"; Butler is the first apiarist to call her a "Queen," an idea so astonishing that it took about a hundred years for it to be generally accepted.

One of the well-known oddities of the book is the so-called *melissomelos* (Mellissa's song) or "bees' madrigal," which is a song the bees supposedly sing when they are about to swarm. It is written in triple time in the musical notation current at the time; in the third edition, the song was expanded into a lyrical composition for four voices. The music historian Nan Cooke Carpenter writes of the piece that "Butler's gifts of musical invention—like his poetical gifts—were apparently far from overwhelming, judged by his composition with its rather monotonous rhythm reminiscent of metrical psalm setting, his ofttimes awkward voice leading, distorted word accent, general heavyhandedness, and lack of humour." The piece was nevertheless sung at the 1954 memorial service at Wooton by students of Worcester and Somerville Colleges.

The book ends with what may be the only one of Butler's sermons to survive, one that deals with the subject of paying tithes, and that reveals Butler's exigency: "what with the newfound lay parsonages, what with pretended immunitie, what with hard lawes and harder constructions, what with vnwilling and false tithers, what with the subtil practises of Patrons, & what with the vnkind dealing of many neighbours," the priest's portion is so meager, that the country has "made Priests of the lowest of the people." It is possible, therefore, that Butler kept bees in order to supplement his slender income. The sermon is not included in the 1634 edition, perhaps because, by this time, he had (one way or another) sorted out his pecuniary worries.

That the bee book was popular is shown by the fact that the second edition of 1623 is reprinted as the last part of Gervase Markham's *A Way to get Wealth, by approued rules of practice in good husbandry and huswifrie* (1625). Markham, who was probably one of the most important writers on husbandry at the time, introduces *The Feminine Monarchie* by means of a short footnote (at the end of the preceding *The Country Housewifes Garden*): *The Booke of Bees . . . written heretofore by Mr Charles Butler, and now so much desired, shall shortly be set forth againe, corrected and augmented by the Authors further experience.*" The third edition of Butler's book appeared nine years later, in 1634, rewritten following Butler's spelling system. Furthermore, the 1623 edition was translated into Latin by Richard Richardson in 1673 (with another edition in 1682), which was then translated back into English by "W. S." in 1704, this date being the latest publication of any of Butler's books (exclusive of the modern editions and reprints).

His book Συγγε΄νεια (Syngenia, Same Family), published in 1625, may have been partially in response to his son William's upcoming marriage to his cousin Mary (which took place in 1627), but more likely it seeks to justify the right of kingship of Charles I, who was crowned king in the same year as the book appeared. Antimonarchist elements may have sought to characterize the succession as illegitimate, on the grounds that Charles was the ancestor of an incestuous relationship, namely that between the two cousins Mary Stuart, Queen of Scots, and Henry Stuart, Duke of Albany, the parents of his father, James I.

After listing the biblical injunctions against incest found in Leviticus and various other illicit marriages based on certain commonsense generalities, he then formulates a single general rule to cover all the cases: basically, two people may marry if there are at least two degrees (levels in a family tree) of distance between the two to be married and their closest common ancestor. As the closest common ancestor of two cousins is a grandparent, two degrees distant, it is thereby admissible for two cousins to marry. This section of the book is remarkable for the modern sounding (that is, mathematical) way it discusses the problem largely in terms of properties of tree structures. (The treatment is reminiscent of the fascination with diagrams Ramus exhibits in his works). The remainder of the book corroborates the rule by means of canon and civil law, and refutes objections. Butler's text was republished in Frankfurt in 1643, bound with a treatise on consanguinity by Francis Florens.

Butler returned to the instruction of youth in 1633 with the publication of *The English Grammar, Or The Institution of Letters, Syllables, and Words, in the English tongue. Whereunto is annexed An Index of Words Like and Unlike.* The 1634 edition of the book (once again in a Royalist fashion) is dedicated to "the Most^c Noble Yvng Princ^c Charls Stweeward." Apart from the added dedication, reset preliminaries, and a new title page, the 1634 book is a reissue of the 1633 first edition. Its intended audience are those "whose Bodi's ar weaned from the tender brests of their indulgent Nurses" but who are not yet "fit to receiv the strong meat of a riper knowledg [Humane and Divine]." Grammar is described, baroquely, as "a second Milk for Bab's: which . . . their Mind's must suk from the learned brests of their diligent Tutors." The book is, according to Emma Vorlat, in her *The Development of English Grammar* (1975), among the first English grammars written in the vernacular, preceded only by those of William Bullokar, Paul Greaves, Alexander Hume, and Alexander Gill. In writing such a grammar, Butler is essentially faithful to his mentor Ramus, in the sense that he tries (with occasional lapses) to write the grammar

in purely formal terms without any mixture of philosophical or psychological factors.

The book does not appear to have been extensively used, possibly on account of its having to compete not only with the four earlier vernacular grammars, but also with William Lily's Latin grammar for English, which was immensely popular at the time. Moreover, the book suffers from several flaws. In her 1975 book Vorlat says of Butler's work that "patriotic feelings find a feeding soil in pseudoscientific, if not flatly ridiculous arguments." She refers specifically to Butler's ideas about the origin of the English language, which according to Butler is nearly as ancient as Hebrew, since it goes back almost unchanged to the confusion at Babel; it is as elegant in its literature as any of ancient Rome or Greece, and in terms of its "generality" exceeds all other languages, because it has spread over a greater area than was achieved even by Latin. The logic behind this assertion seems to be based upon another overapplication of synecdoche of the species, similar to the flaw in Butler's *Rhetoricæ Libri Dvo* that Barton points out, for by "English" Butler here means any "Teutonic" language.

In her *Progress in English Grammar 1585–1735: A Study in the Development of English Grammar and of the Interdependence among the Early English Grammarians* (1963) Vorlat remarks of the grammatical content of Butler's book that "The work does not compare favorably with Gill's: it lacks a syntax, the etymological part is restricted to a minimum, and it is inferior . . . both in the theoretical and the practical field." In *The Development of English Grammar* Vorlat asserts that Butler's "theory of word classes is sketchy and at times self-contradictory." The book went into only two contemporary editions, though modern editions were published in Germany in 1910 and Japan in 1967.

Many grammatical issues that are still relevant make what are possibly their first appearances in this book. For example, Butler is the first grammarian in Vorlat's study to differentiate nouns from verbs on the basis of "time," to classify pronouns as being neither substantives nor adjectives, but rather a sort of "imperfect noun," and to partition verbs into "absolute" and "suppletive." As Vivian Salmon has demonstrated, Butler is also important in that he is probably the first person to remark upon the two sorts of intonation contour in English questions: a rising contour for questions in statement form or where the subject and verb are inverted, and a falling contour in the case of questions introduced by an interrogative.

This book is also the first one that Butler wrote in his own system of orthography, and in which he attempted to explain his spelling reform. Butler was

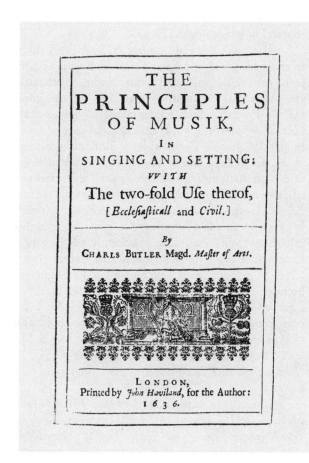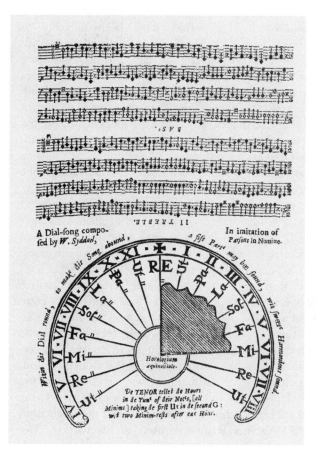

Title page and interior page for Butler's music textbook, in which he argued that music and oratory can be used to persuade

not the first person to try to reform English spelling, but his system was probably one of the least well received. He wrote all of his subsequent books according to this system; the consensus in the biographical literature is that the books written in Butler's system are difficult and unpleasant to read. Samuel Johnson, in the grammatical section of *A Dictionary of the English Language* (1755), describes Butler as "a man who did not want an understanding, which might have qualified him for better employment." The system largely consists in introducing an orthographical distinction between the voiced and voiceless aspirates; for example, a horizontal line is drawn through the unaspirated sequence *th* to give the corresponding aspirate.

Butler's final book was *The Principles Of Musik, In Singing and Setting: With The twofold Use therof, (Ecclesiasticall and Civil),* which appeared in 1636, nine years before his death. In the history of musical primers, it is to be found between Thomas Morley's *Plaine and Easie Introduction to Practicall Musicke* (1597) and John Playford's *Introduction to the Skill of Musik* (1655). Butler, in his epilogue, advises readers to study Morley's book if

they wish to advance their studies. For his part, Playford says in his preface that "books of instruction to Musick . . . printed in this Nation worthy of perusal are only two, *viz.* Mr. Morley's *Introduction,* and Mr. Butler's *Principles Of Musick,* both of which are very rare and scarce to be had, the Impressions of them being long since sold off." In *A General History of Music from the Earliest Ages to the Present Period* (1789), Charles Burney says that Butler's book "is a work of a person of considerable musical acumen and wit." The book is in some respects conservative, and, in certain others, innovative. Butler's conservatism is shown, for example, in his preference for vocal music as opposed to the increasingly more popular instrumental. He is innovative, for example, in being probably the first author to discuss the omission of *ut* and *re* in solmization.

Like many of Butler's other books, this one too is intended for the instruction of the young. He says in the dedication to Prince Charles that nothing more "conduceth to the prosperiti and happines of a Kingdom, than the good education of yuthe and children." He points out the connection of music to grammar as found in the writings of Quintilian, where it is said that grammar cannot be made "perfect" without music, and how it was often the case that grammarians taught both subjects, as they were so intimately connected. That music also has a connection to oratory is also found in Quintilian–in particular, "from the efficacy it hath, in mooving affections and vertues," which is similar to how oratio is defined in the *Rhetoricæ Libri Dvo.* Both music and oratory can be used to persuade, and such persuasion can be toward either virtue or vice. For this reason, the second half of *The Principles Of Musik* is devoted to the uses of music. In this section, Butler endeavors to persuade the reader of the value of music (mainly church music) against Puritan views that music was dangerous to religion and morality, or "effeminate" in some sort of derogatory way, views that Linda Phyllis Austern discusses. He concludes his book with an exhortation: "Yea let us, in our wolᶜ conversation, escew evil and dooᶜ good: let us bee zealous in đe servicᶜ of God, abhorring Sacrilegᶜ and Superstitions: let us be faithful in đe loov of our neighbour, abhorring Robberi and Oppression: and let us so usᶜ đe transitori Pleasurᶜs of đis lif, that we losᶜ not đe permanent joys of đe lifᶜ to coom."

The outbreak of the First English Civil War in 1642 must have distressed Butler, a staunch Royalist. Parliamentary forces occupied his home region soon after the outbreak of hostilities. The forces loyal to the king (whose headquarters were at Oxford) held the town of Newbury about fifteen miles to the west of Basingstoke; while to the east, at nearby Basing, John Paulet, the fifth Marquis of Winchester, lay besieged for four years at Basing House, which was finally taken by Oliver Cromwell's men–and burned to the ground–in 1645. In 1643 Wooton was visited by the Parliamentary general Sir William Waller, who in March of the following year defeated the western army of Charles at the battle of Cheriton fifteen miles to the south. During this period Butler ceased to write the parish records, yet, according to Money, he was not removed from his position by the authorities. Because of his age, he evidently was not felt to pose any threat to the Parliamentary cause. It is interesting to note, however, that the 1642 Leiden edition of Butler's *Rhetoricæ Libri Dvo* came out at a time when Queen Henrietta Maria was living in the Netherlands and trying to raise funds for the king. Furthermore, the only other book by Butler to be published during the war was the 1643 Frankfurt edition of the *Syngenia,* which was the only one of his books especially devoted to defending the Stuart lineage. Butler died on 29 March 1647, soon after Charles I was handed over to Parliamentary forces by the Scottish army.

Bibliographies:

Falconer Madan, *Oxford Books: A Bibliography of Printed Works Relating to the University and City of Oxford or Printed or Published There with Appendixes and Illustrations,* volume 1: *The Early Oxford Press, 1468–1640* (Oxford: Clarendon Press, 1895), pp. 48, 73–74, 109, 122, 143–144, 165–166, 172, 176–177, 230, 233;

Heinrich F. Plett, *English Renaissance Rhetoric and Poetics: A Systematic Bibliography of Primary and Secondary Sources* (Leiden & New York: E. J. Brill, 1995), pp. 30, 141.

Biography:

Anthony à Wood, "Charles Butler," in *Athenae Oxonienses, an Exact History of All the Writers and Bishops who Have Had Their Education in the University of Oxford: To Which Are Added the Fasti, or Annals of the Said University,* edited by Philip Bliss, 5 volumes (London: J. Rivington, 1813–1820), III: columns 209–210;

Frank Reginald Money, *Charles Butler, Vicar of Wooton, 1600–1647 Father of English Bee-Keeping and Celebrated Philologist* (Basingstoke, U.K.: Aldworth Printing Works, 1953).

References:

Linda Phyllis Austern, "'Alluring the Auditorie to Effeminacie': Music and the Idea of the Feminine in Early Modern England," *Music & Letters,* 74, no. 3 (1993): 343–354;

David Michael Baker and Jennifer Elizabeth Baker, "A 17th Century Dial-Song," *Musical Times,* 119 (1978): 590–593;

Ron Brown, "The Rev. Dr Charles Butler 1559–1647," in his *Great Masters of Beekeeping* (Burrowbridge, U.K.: Bee Books New & Old, 1994), pp. 11–17;

Charles Burney, *A General History of Music from the Earliest Ages to the Present Period (1789),* with historical and critical notes by Frank Mercer, 2 volumes (London: G. T. Foulis, 1935; New York: Dover, 1957), II: 317–318;

Nan Cooke Carpenter, "A Reference to Marlowe in Charles Butler's *Principles of Musik* (1636)," *Notes & Queries,* new series, 198 (1953): 16–18;

Carpenter, "Charles Butler and Du Bartas," *Notes & Queries,* new series, 199 (1954): 2–7;

Carpenter, "Charles Butler and the Bees's Madrigal," *Notes & Queries,* new series, 200 (1955): 103–106;

J. M. Fletcher, "The Faculty of Arts," in Joseph Foster, *Alumni Oxonienses: The Members of the University of Oxford: Their Parentage, Birthplace, and Year of Birth, with a Record of Their Degrees: Being the Matriculation

Register of the University, Alphabetically Arranged, Revised, and Annotated (Oxford: Parker, 1891);

John Hawkins, *A General History of the Science and Practice of Music,* 5 volumes (London: Printed for T. Payne, 1776–1789);

Gerald R. Hayes, "Charles Butler and the Music of Bees," *Musical Times,* 46 (1925): 512–515;

Wilbur Samuel Howell, *Logic and Rhetoric in England 1500–1700* (Princeton: Princeton University Press, 1956), pp. 193, 258, 262–274, 280, 319, 340;

L. S. Hultzén, "Seventeenth Century Intonation," *American Speech,* 14 (1939): 39–43;

Christopher Lewis, "Incipient Tonal Thought in Seventeenth Century English Theory," *Studies in Music from the University of Western Ontario,* no. 6 (1981): 24–47;

James McConica, ed., *The History of the University of Oxford,* volume 3: *The Collegiate University* (Oxford: Clarendon Press, 1986);

Daphne More, *The Bee Book: The History and Natural History of the Honeybee* (Newton Abbot, U.K.: David & Charles, 1976 / New York: Universe Books, 1976), pp. 51, 77, 87–93, 119, 121;

Walter J. Ong, *Ramus: Method, and the Decay of Dialogue; from the Art of Discourse to the Art of Reason* (Cambridge, Mass.: Harvard University Press, 1958), pp. 9, 303;

G. A. Padley, *Grammatical Theory in Western Europe, 1500–1700: Trends in Vernacular Grammar I* (Cambridge: Cambridge University Press, 1985), pp. 54, 57, 62, 68, 70–72, 75–80, 171, 202–204;

James W. Pruett, "Butler, Charles," in *The New Grove Dictionary of Music and Musicians,* edited by Stanley Sadie, volume 3 (London: Macmillan, 1980), pp. 517–518;

Pruett, "Charles Butler–Musician, Grammarian, Apiarist," *Musical Quarterly,* 49 (1963): 498–509;

Vivian Salmon, "Wh- and Yes/No Questions: Charles Butler's *Grammar* (1633) and the History of a Linguistic Concept," in *Language Form and Linguistic Variation: Papers Dedicated to Angus McIntosh,* edited by John Anderson (Amsterdam: Benjamin, 1982), pp. 401–426;

William Phillips Sandford, "English Rhetoric Reverts to Classicism 1600–1650," *Quarterly Journal of Speech,* 15 (1929): 503–525;

Sandford, *English Theories of Public Address, 1530–1828* (Columbus, Ohio: H. L. Hedrick, 1931), pp. 60–62, 104–107;

Charles Sarton, "The Feminine Monarchie of Charles Butler, 1609," *Isis,* 34 (1943): 469–472;

Betty Showler and Frank Showler, "Charles Butler," *Bee Culture,* 43 (1 September 1999): 43;

Nicholas Tyacke, ed., *The History of the University of Oxford,* volume 4: *Seventeenth Century Oxford* (Oxford: Clarendon Press, 1997), pp. 20, 21, 636, 638;

Frank Vernon, *Hogs at the Honeypot: The Story of Hampshire Beekeepers* (Burrowbridge, Somerset, U.K.: Bee Books New & Old, 1981);

Emma Vorlat, *Progress in English Grammar 1585–1735: A Study of the Development of English Grammar and of the Interdependence among the Early English Grammarians,* 4 volumes (Louvain, Belgium: Catholic University of Louvain, 1963);

Vorlat, *The Development of English Grammatical Theory, 1586–1737, With Special Reference to the theory of Parts of Speech* (Louvain, Belgium: University Press, 1975).

William Chappell

(10 December 1582 – 14 May 1649)

Mary Morrissey
University of Aberdeen

BOOKS: *Methodus concionandi,* anonymous (London: Printed by M.F. for Timoth Garthwaite, 1648); translated as *The Preacher, Or The Art and Method Of Preaching: Shewing the most ample Directions and Rules for Invention, Method, Expression, and Books whereby a Minister may be furnished with such helps as may make him a Useful Laborer in the Lords Vineyard. By William Chappell Bishop of Cork, sometime Fellow of Christs College in Cambridge,* edited by Phil. Christianus (William Brough) (London: Printed for Edward Farnham, 1656);

The Use Of Holy Scripture Gravely and Methodically Discoursed: By William Chappell Bishop of Corke, sometimes Fellow of Christs Colledg in Cambridge. A Work of singular benefit to Divines, and all men, to establish themselves, and others in the Perfection, Perspicuity, and Efficacie of Gods Word, against Atheists, Heathens, Romanists, Enthusiasts, and all other Unbeleevers and Misbeleevers, &c. To Which is prefixed a Preface, by a friend to the Author, as an Introduction to the Treatise, edited by "Philo-biblius" (London: Printed by Ellen Coles for Andrew Crook, 1653).

Edition: *The Preacher, 1656,* English Linguistics, 1500–1800, no. 295, edited by R. C. Alston (Menston, U.K.: Scolar Press, 1971).

OTHER: *Vita Guilielmi Chappel Episcopi Corcagiensis & Rossensis, A seipso conscripta,* in *Desiderata curiosa; or, A Collection of Divers Scarce and Curious Pieces (Relating Chiefly to Matters of English History) in Six Books,* by Francis Peck (London, 1732), pp. 414–422; another version published in *De Rebus Britannicis Collectanea,* by John Leland, edited by Thomas Hearne (London, 1770), V: 259–268.

It is often assumed that Renaissance preachers considered their art a form of rhetoric. Certainly, by modern definitions of preaching, the use of the arts of speech to influence a listener's opinions is rhetorical. Yet, this assumption misses the complexities of Renaissance views of preaching, and in particular it ignores the preacher's stated aims, to interpret scripture and teach its doctrines. William Chappell's Ramist approach to preaching is instructive in this respect. Chappell presents the arts of grammar and dialectic as tools essential to the preacher's task, to the exclusion of almost all treatment of rhetorical matters. His preaching manuals are, therefore, primarily methods of exegesis and exposition, not of persuasion. This emphasis suggests that for Chappell, and perhaps for other early-modern instructors in the art of preaching, the preacher's primary tasks are interpretation and instruction. Persuasion, therefore, becomes merely the consequence, not the aim, of the preacher's oration, challenging the classification of preaching as a branch of rhetoric.

The son of Robert Chappell, William Chappell was born in Laxton, Nottinghamshire, on 10 December 1582, and was educated in Mansfield Grammar School until the age of seventeen, when he went to Cambridge. He was an undergraduate at Christ's College and was elected a fellow of the college in 1607, a position he retained until 1634. He was also one of the most-respected tutors in the college and served as dean in 1610–1611 and Hebrew lecturer from 1614 to 1633.

Chappell was commended by his contemporaries as a man "precise" in his lifestyle and "painful" in his teaching duties. In *The History of the Worthies of England* (1662) Thomas Fuller described him among the "worthies" of Nottinghamshire as a tutor who "bred more and better *Pupils*" than any other he can remember, "so exact his care in their Education," and as "a most subtile Disputant, equally excellent with the Sword and the Shield, to reply or answer." This praise is borne out by the records of Christ's College, Cambridge, which show that Chappell consistently taught more undergraduates than most Cambridge fellows at the time. Chappell's best-known student at Christ's College was John Milton, who is reported by John Aubrey in *Brief Lives* (1681) to have received an "unkindnesse" at Chappell's hand. This "unkindnesse" has been taken as the cause of Milton's supposed rustication in 1626, as recorded in *Elegy 1* (written in 1626), and his supposed

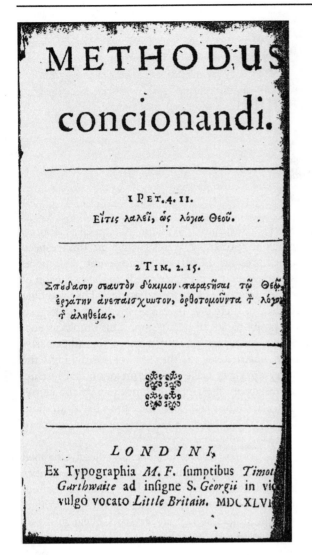

Title pages for the two published versions of the observations on sermon writing that Chappell probably prepared for circulation in manuscript among his students

transfer of tutor to Nathaniel Tovey. As taken up by others, notably Samuel Johnson in *The Lives of the Most Eminent English Poets* (1779), the report is that Milton was "whip'd" by Chappell, although such treatment was unlikely, as Milton was close to eighteen, the age at which corporal punishment was forbidden. Scholars now argue that the whipping, rustication, and transfer of tutors did not happen, and that the dispute with Chappell was at most a private disagreement caused by an able student's resentment at being asked to repeat lessons performed at school. It is apparent, however, that Milton was assigned to Chappell because he was known to be a rigorous and effective tutor.

Chappell's connections with Trinity College, Dublin, date from 1613, when he acted as divinity professor and catechist. In 1634 Chappell became provost there, a position he retained until 20 July 1640. Chap-

pell also received other preferments in the Irish Church: in 1633 he was appointed dean of Cashel; in 1636 he was made treasurer of St. Patrick's Cathedral in Dublin; and in 1638 he was installed as bishop of Cork and Ross. Chappell gained these positions through the patronage of Archbishop William Laud and William Wentworth, Earl of Stratford and Lord Deputy of Ireland. Chappell does not seem to have welcomed these appointments, and in his Latin verse autobiography, *Vita Guilielmi Chappel Episcopi Corcagiensis & Rossensis, A seipso conscripta* (The Life of William Chappell, Bishop of Cork and Ross, Written by Himself, written after 1641), he claimed that he had not sought the offices or the move to Ireland. Because he proved a useful agent for Laud and Wentworth's party, Chappell was unwelcome to many in Ireland, including Archbishop James Ussher. During his time as provost, Chappell was instrumental in ensuring that Laud's revised statutes of the college of 1637 were enforced. These statutes were unpopular because they imposed Church of England ecclesiastical ceremonies on the rigorously Puritan college, because they abandoned the stipulation that holders of the Irish scholarships learn Irish, and because they restricted the number of College Visitors from seven to two–the vice chancellor (who was Laud) and the archbishop of Dublin–and so deprived powerful interests, particularly the lord mayor of Dublin, of any say in the college.

Chappell's observance of ecclesiastical ceremonies in the college chapel and his association with Laud and Wentworth gained him enemies in both Ireland and England. Chappell was taken into custody by the Irish Parliament in May 1641, and, according to the *Journal of the House of Commons of Ireland* (1796), on 9 June 1641 the House of Commons declared "all and every of his proceedings" as provost of Trinity College, Dublin, to be "great grievances, and fit to receive redress." Chappell was released in December 1641, and he set sail for England, but his troubles were not over. He arrived at Milford and traveled to Tenby, in Pembrokeshire, where he was again imprisoned, this time by the authority of the mayor, until 16 March 1642. On his release he traveled to Bristol to recover his belongings, only to find that the ship carrying his books from Ireland had been wrecked off Minehead. He returned to his native Nottinghamshire, where he died on 14 May 1649.

Chappell's works were all published in unauthorized editions, many of them posthumously. It is impossible to ascribe them to periods of his life. There is no evidence that Chappell prepared any of his works for the press, and there is good evidence that he did not wish his works to be published. Two different versions of Chappell's preaching rhetoric appeared in the seventeenth century, and neither of them appears to have been prepared for publication by the author. The first of these printed versions was anonymously published in Latin as *Methodus concionandi* (Method of Preaching, 1648). An English translation of this Latin edition was printed in 1656, seven years after Chappell's death, as *The Preacher, Or The Art and Method of Preaching*. Neither version has an authorial preface, and there is no prefatory material at all in the Latin version. The title page to the English translation attributes the work to "William Chappell Bishop of *Cork,* sometime Fellow of Christs College in *Cambridge*." The epistle to the reader is signed "Phil. Christianus," who appears to be the editor and publisher of the work. His epistle describes "this elaborate peece" as "coming to" his hands, and he explains that he decided to "expose it to publick view" because of "the great advantage the church of God might reap by it." Chappell may have been the translator, but it is unlikely that he intended it for publication.

In the preface to *The Use of Holy Scripture Gravely and Methodically Discoursed* (1653), a similar publication history is described, throwing light on how Chappell may have viewed his *Methodus concionandi* and how it found its way into print. *The Use of Holy Scripture* is Chappell's notes for a sermon on 2 Timothy 3:16 ("All scripture is given by inspiration of God, and is profitable for doctrine, for reproof, for correction, for instruction in righteousness"). Most seventeenth-century preachers, including Chappell, did not write out their sermons in full before delivery. They made notes on the structure of the sermon and spoke from these outlines, often writing up the sermon in full at a later date. *The Use of Holy Scripture* is attributed to Chappell on the title page, and the long preface is signed "Philo-biblius," who is identified on the title page as "a friend to the Author." In his preface this editor states that Chappell gave him the work "neare Twenty yeares since . . . to be privately used by mee, as by some other of his friends." He describes Chappell as "So exemplarily modest, and yet so discreetly exact," that "hee liked not to be much in sight of a censorious world." This attitude is not surprising, as the so-called stigma of print that was current at the time clung as much to the publisher of "godly" works as it did to those who presented more-secular writings to the public. Justifications for publication were frequently included in the prefaces to religious works. Yet, the publisher of *The Use of Holy Scripture* claimed that he had not treacherously ignored its author's wishes because he published the work only to defend Chappell's reputation by hindering those who threatened to produce pirated editions of his work: "And I have the rather been so rude with my once very reverend friend, lest some other should (for I hear that his papers are enquired for abroad, to benefit the publick, as they are) put this scorn upon me, that any man should be readyer than myself, to bear blame for so deserving a friend."

The owner of the manuscript for *The Use of Holy Scripture* also saw an opportunity to benefit from the prior publication of Chappell's *Methodus concionandi*. The interior title page that follows Philo-biblius's preface reads:

> Of the Holy Scripture: or Sermon-Notes on II *Timothie* III. 16. Being the Theologicall Ground of another Treatise of the Author extant under the title of METHODUS CONCIONANDI, Containing a learned and brief exemplification of the same Method. Translated (a great part) out of his Latine Copie.

It seems probable that Chappell intended his *Methodus concionandi* to circulate in manuscript for the

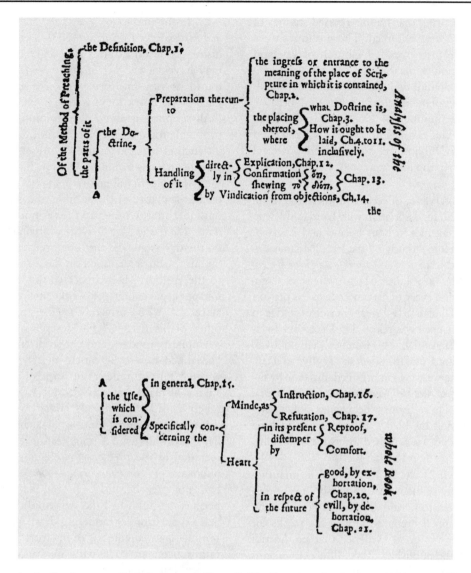

Diagram showing Ramist commonplaces of argument in Chappell's The Preacher, Or the Art and Method of Preaching

benefit of his close circle of friends and students. The existence of Manuscript 333 in the library of Trinity College, Dublin, adds weight to this suggestion. This manuscript is described in the catalogue only as "a treatise on preaching," but it has since been identified as another translation of Chappell's *Methodus conciona-ndi*. The manuscript was the gift of one William Barry, probably the William Barry (died 1745) who graduated from the college in 1700 and was curate of St. Bride's in Dublin.

Chappell's work has been criticized for its difficult phraseology and vocabulary. It is certainly the most difficult of sixteenth- or seventeenth-century manuals of preaching for the modern reader. This difficulty may be caused partly by the unfinished form in which it was printed, but it is mostly owing, however,

to the dialectical, and specifically Ramist, approach Chappell takes to his subject. Ramists reorganized the spheres of dialectic (or logic, as the terms were used interchangeably) and rhetoric, so that the part of rhetoric traditionally described as "invention" (the formulation of the argument or theme) and "disposition" (the organization or structuring of the argument) pertained to dialectic rather than to rhetoric. Rhetoric was confined to matters of style—the tropes and figures to be used in an oration—and the gestures and voice the orator should adopt. Chappell's preaching manual is exclusively concerned with the "invention" and "disposition" of a sermon and approaches these tasks according to Ramist principles.

Chappell's treatise presents the reader with a complete method for constructing sermons using dialectic techniques and describes this method in the terms of dialectic. The preacher was to prepare his sermon by resolving his biblical text into axioms or syllogisms. When preaching, he was to explain these axioms to his hearers, and, using arguments derived from the "topics" of dialectic, persuade them to accept the argument and act accordingly. These "topics," or "commonplaces" of argument, were headings for the types of argument that the speaker could apply to a particular issue. Pierre de La Ramée (known as Petrus Ramus) had simplified the classification of these commonplaces, finally reducing them to ten: six primary arguments (from causes, effects, subjects, adjuncts, opposites, and comparatives), three derived (reasoning from name, reasoning by division, and reasoning by definition), and testimony, an "inartificial" proof because it proves a point by citing a "witness" or authority instead of by reasoning. Chappell was clearly indebted to Ramus for the "commonplaces" he used. In the diagram laying out ways of inventing arguments on the "aggravations of sin," Chappell listed appropriate arguments from the topics of cause, effect, subjects, adjuncts, opposites, comparatives, and testimony—seven of the ten commonplaces recommended by Ramus—and combines two others, name and definition, under a single heading. According to Chappell's method, the preacher would use these "places" to discover arguments forceful enough to persuade his hearers to avoid the "aggravations of sin." Argument, rather than eloquence, is the persuasive center of Chappell's method of preaching.

Chappell barely addressed issues pertaining to rhetoric (by Ramus's definition of that art) such as the style, figures of speech, or gestures to be used in the pulpit. Almost the only references to rhetoric in Chappell's treatise occur when it describes how the preacher should interpret a scriptural passage by examining the rhetorical figures it uses, as these often obscure the meaning of the text. This subject was an important topic in most sixteenth- and seventeenth-century handbooks on preaching. Most notably, William Perkins's *Prophetica, Sive, De Sacra Et vnica ratione Concionandi Tractatvs* (1592; translated as *The Arte of Prophecying; or, A Treatise Concerning the Sacred and Onely True Manner and Methode of Preaching,* 1607), probably the first English preaching manual influenced by Ramism, has a large section devoted to the interpretation of the figures of speech used in scripture. Chappell's treatment of rhetoric in scripture, however, is summary indeed, stressing only how the different constructions can be resolved into axioms. So, for example, the phrase "Thus saith the Lord" is an additional proof for the axioms in the statement to which it is connected, and "Ecce" lends emphasis to a statement. In this lack of attention to rhetoric Chappell's treatise is unlike most other seventeenth-century

handbooks on preaching, which often give detailed rules for the interpretation of scripture and describe the grammatical constructions and rhetorical figures commonly used in the Bible before they proceed to discuss the construction of a sermon. In all versions of his preaching manual, Chappell summarily refers to the grammatical and rhetorical aspects of the scriptural text as something appended to the logical meaning of the words that must be stripped away in order to find the "axioms" hidden beneath.

Chappell integrated his logical approach to scripture with the form of sermon most popular in the seventeenth century: the method of describing "Doctrine *and* Use." The "doctrines" were the abstract precepts derived by analysis of the scriptural text on which the preacher spoke. In the "uses" the preacher showed how these precepts applied to his hearers and sought to persuade them to reform their actions in accordance with these precepts. "Uses" often described, for example, how the scriptural text of the sermon demanded that the hearers discontinue sinful actions (the "use of reprehension") or consoled them in times of doubt or grief (the "use of consolation"). Chappell conflated Ramist dialectic with this method of sermon composition by describing a doctrine as "a divine axiom." In all versions of his preaching manual Chappell admitted that this definition is unusual and provided an explanation. As he wrote in *The Preacher:*

> I call Doctrine a divine axiome comprehended in the text. Of which definition (because it seems to mean some novelty) I must give some reason for each particular part.
> 1. *Axiome* for I lay this as a ground and foundation, That there is nothing true or false, unlesse it be an Axiome. And therefore whatsoever is revealed to us of Divine Truth (for there can be no falsehood in the Word of God) is contained in the Axiomes of holy Scripture.

As the words of God in scripture were necessarily true, the "invention" of the preacher's theme meant resolving these statements into axioms, and his explication of the doctrines meant "laying out" or explaining how these axioms were found in the scriptural text. Chappell went on to describe the different sort of axioms that are found in scripture and how the preacher should approach each in "laying out" his doctrines. In the "crypsis" that ends almost every chapter, he explained the "method" by which the axioms were to be ordered and presented in the sermon and how this "method" might be hidden from the hearer. This emphasis on the "method" used in constructing an oration and the "crypsis," or "hiding," of that structure from the auditors, shows the importance of Ramist dialectic to Chappell's theory of preaching.

Having described how the preacher arrives at and expounds the "axioms" or "doctrines" in his text, Chappell moved on to discuss the "uses," and again his logical approach to his subject is apparent. Unlike other English writers on preaching, Chappell did not present the "uses" as the part of the sermon in which rhetorical techniques for rousing the affections of the hearers might be employed. As the "uses" related the sermon theme to the hearers' actions, it was imperative for the success of the sermon that the hearers be persuaded to adopt the advice offered, rather than merely give their intellectual assent to the precepts presented. Most other English writers on preaching saw the role of rhetoric as particularly pertinent to this persuasive function of preaching. This viewpoint is clearly seen in Richard Bernard's *The faithfull shepheard* (1607):

> Exhort heereupon, summarily repeating the reasons; enforce and enlarge some one of the waightiest and stir vp to the meanes: that affection may take hold, and endeauour be vsed to the thing, as well as to know the duty. This is the most speciall point: and heerein this place comes in the vse of Rhetoricke, and to set abroach all the engins of that Arte and grace in speaking, to moue to the feruent study of any thing.

In his 1646 preaching handbook, *Ecclesiastes, or, A Discourse concerning the Gift of Preaching, as it fals under the rules of Art,* John Wilkins suggested that the preacher add to his arguments for rousing the affections some "affectionate conjurements and obsecrations, like those of the blessed Apostle, *Ephes.* 4.1." Chappell did not assign a persuasive function to the art of rhetoric in his discussion of the "uses" of a sermon. In Chappell's scheme the persuasion of the hearers, by gaining the assent of both mind and affections, should be achieved through the employment of arguments derived from dialectic. He divided those "uses" that work primarily on the hearers' understanding from those that act mainly on the will or the affections. He admitted that "uses" working on the understanding may also touch the will, but he advised caution:

> The first head of use is, in the applying of the Doctrine to the mind or understanding And here, because the heart of will hath a great influx into the mind (according to that, *Those things which we will, we easily believe*) therefore it is lawful (though it is possible and customary to falter exceedingly in this thing). It is lawfull (I say) in a good cause, to insinuate something either hiddenly or openly, whereby we may possesse the hearers affections, and by them, as by setting scaling ladders, invade the fort of the mind.

For each type of "use" Chappell described the "commonplaces of argument" that should be employed to impress these arguments on the hearers. There is only one sentence in which Chappell allowed the use of rhetorical techniques for appealing to the hearers' affection, and even this statement is qualified: "Now follow the uses, which have respect to the heart, or will, and affections. But these especially doe vindicate to themselves all manner of Rhetorical preparation; but not to be undertaken without the salt of wisdom and gravity, as is befitting a sacred person and businesse."

In relation to none of the "uses" did Chappell describe the figures of speech to be used in presenting arguments so that they would be made more persuasive to the hearers. There is a single reference to the argumentative uses of rhetoric, when Chappell allowed that prosopopoeia (allowing an imaginary or absent person, or an inanimate object, to speak or act like a living, present person) and apostrophe (interrupting one's speech to address a present or absent person or thing directly), might be used in reprehending sinfulness.

It is clear, therefore, that rhetoric, defined by Ramists as the art of ornamenting and delivering an oration, is almost entirely neglected in this method of preaching. Two inferences are possible from this omission. First, it might be that Chappell's method—as printed and as found in the Trinity College manuscript—is incomplete and that the rhetorical aspect of preaching was to be dealt with elsewhere. Although this possibility exists, a more probable explanation is that Chappell considered the art of rhetoric less important for the preacher than the art of dialectic. Chappell's works suggest that he considered the persuasive function of the sermon best effected by the use of argument rather than by rhetorical language. It is for this reason that he presented methods of argumentation as the key aspect of preaching, the "method" by which it should be conducted.

This hypothesis is corroborated by Chappell's *The Use of Holy Scripture,* in which he employs his own method. In this work, Chappell's notes for a sermon on 2 Timothy 3:16, the axioms in each part of the text are first uncovered, and the various uses of these axioms for instruction, refutation, reprehension, and consolation are then given. In keeping with his advice in *The Preacher* Chappell briefly explicated the text where the "influx of latter arts" (grammar or rhetoric) impinge on its logical propositions. For example, on the word *doctrine* in his text, he showed how it is "synecdochically . . . taken for *information* of the minde with holy doctrine." In his first exhortation, that ministers take care to instruct the people from scripture only, he detailed the rules for interpreting the grammar and rhetoric of scripture that had been passed over in his handbook of preaching. He wrote that the preacher must examine his text to see whether it is a literal or figurative statement and what its context in the Bible is (when, to whom, and by whom it was spoken) and that he must then compare it with other texts in scripture. These instructions are the same rules for interpreting the grammar of scripture that are described in detail by Perkins in *The Arte of Prophecying* and only summarily referred to by Chappell in his preaching manual. Chappell did not, however, show what figures of speech he would have used when preaching this sermon, either by giving their names or by using expressions that suggest their use. The substance of the exhortations are stated and the means to persuade the hearers are given, but exhortation as a figure, rather than a structural division of the sermon, is not evident. The persuasive function of the sermon is carried out by the arguments showing the means to and the motives for putting the "uses" in practice. His advice that ministers make frequent use of scripture to exhort their hearers is baldly stated as follows: "To those to whom God hath in speciall committed his word, that they would, seeing it is profitable for Exhortation, use it in this kinde, and be frequent in exhortation by it."

Occasionally in *The Use of Holy Scripture,* Chappell integrated quotations from scripture with his own words in a way that suggests he may have employed them as metaphors or similes when the sermon was preached. In the exhortation to the "use of Gods word" in reprehending sinners, he wrote that the minister should do it "so far, as his pearls be not trampled, and he rent by swine, for whom he hath the keys to shut them out, or the dust of his feet to shake off against them, and so leave them," clearly using Matthew 7:6 ("Give not that which is holy unto the dogs, neither cast ye your pearls before swine, lest they trample them under their feet, and turn again and rend you") and Matthew 10:14 ("And whosoever shall not receive you, nor hear your words, when ye depart out of that house or city, shake off the dust of your feet"). In all Chappell's works this reference is the only one found to his style of preaching or his use of rhetoric in the pulpit. In *The Use of Holy Scripture,* as in his preaching manual, dialectic is advanced as the art essential to preaching to the almost total exclusion of rhetoric. In both works, rhetoric is treated mainly as a tool of exegesis, and even this role is quickly passed over in the preaching manual.

Chappell's exclusion of rhetoric from the preacher's art is certainly more extreme than other English writers on the subject; yet, his reliance on dialectic rather than rhetoric as the persuasive force in preaching is echoed by other English writers on the subject. In his *Arte of Prophecying* Perkins paid considerable attention to the analysis of the tropes and figures

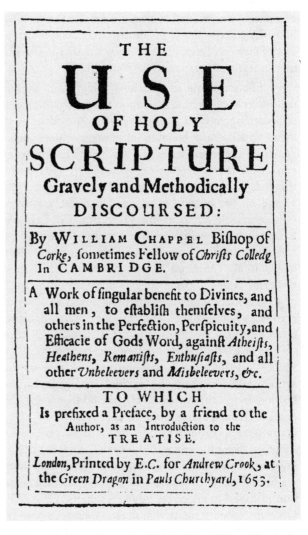

Title page for the posthumously published edition of Chappell's notes for a sermon on 2 Timothy 3:16

found in scripture, but his advice on the delivery of a sermon is pointedly antirhetorical. According to Perkins, the "demonstration (or shewing) of the spirit" is the persuasive force in the sermon. For this demonstration of the spirit, the speech must be "simple and perspicuous" so that it communicates the doctrine and the preacher's personal conviction of the truth of that doctrine. Wilkins, who did allow for rhetorical figures in exhortations, was nonetheless close to Perkins in his demands that the style of a sermon be "plain, full, wholsome, affectionate." Like Perkins, he used 1 Corinthians 2:4 ("And my speech and my preaching was not with enticing word of man's wisdom, but in demonstration of the Spirit, and of power") to place the persuasive force of the sermon in the preacher's ability to communicate personal belief. Although Bernard gave rhetoric a role in persuading the hearers of a sermon, he granted dialectic a far greater role in both the interpretation of the text and its application to the hearers. Logic, rather than rhetoric, is the primary means of persuasion for Bernard.

The emphasis in preaching rhetoric on gaining the hearer's intellectual assent, on the didactic function of preaching, and on a simple prose style evident in all these writers runs counter to development in other genres of rhetorical writing at this time. The primary reason for this difference between sacred and secular rhetoric lies in the status accorded to the scriptural source of the preacher's oration. The Bible was an unimpeachable authority for Protestant preachers. As Chappell states in his opening definition of an axiom, "all divine truths" revealed to humankind are "contained in the Axiomes of holy Scripture." The most powerful means of persuading an audience of the truth of an argument was, therefore, to demonstrate that this argument was included, expressly or "by good consequence," in the words of scripture. Chappell defended the use of dialectic in the analysis and composition of a sermon on the grounds that this method anchors the sermon in the words of the text and thereby makes the sermon more authoritative. His method prevents the preacher from straying from his text, which would lead his hearers to dismiss his arguments as unverified by scripture. By adhering to the sense of the text, as it is uncovered by logical analysis, the preacher can more readily persuade his hearers to endorse his interpretation of it and to adopt the advice he offers. Chappell's method of preaching, is, therefore, a defensive one. By it the preacher composes a sermon whose proof in the "divine axioms" of scripture is evident to the hearers. Otherwise, Chappell suggested, these hearers would be all too ready to say "(as they commonly doe, especially in Reproofs) *he strayed far from his Text.*" In the dry technicalities of Chappell's treatise is clearly seen the belief of seventeenth-century preachers, Puritan and anti-Puritan, in scripture as the unimpeachable authority on doctrine and morals. Chappell suggested, however, that the preacher shares this authority only when he can show that his oration is based on scripture. The preacher needs unassailable proofs for his arguments because a recalcitrant public will otherwise dismiss his teachings. Although it is tempting to call Chappell's *Methodus concionandi* a rhetoric for preachers, its insistence on the importance of dialectic in the analysis of scripture and the composition of sermons challenges this description. Indeed, Chappell's book bespeaks a profound uncertainty in the power of rhetoric, the "art of persuasive speech," to teach and persuade.

References:

Donald Leman Clark, "John Milton and William Chappell," *Huntington Library Quarterly,* 18 (1955): 329–350;

Harris Francis Fletcher, *The Intellectual Development of John Milton,* 2 volumes (Urbana: University of Illinois Press, 1961);

Wilbur S. Howell, *Logic and Rhetoric in England, 1500–1700* (Princeton: Princeton University Press, 1956);

Jameela Lares, "Milton and the 'Office of a Pulpit,'" *Ben Jonson Journal,* 3 (1996): 109–126;

John Pentland Mahaffy, *An Epoch in Irish History: Trinity College, Dublin, Its Foundation and Early Fortunes, 1591–1660* (London: Unwin, 1903), pp. 228–263;

Leo Miller, "Milton's Clash with Chappell: A Suggested Reconstruction," *Milton Quarterly,* 14, no. 3 (1980): 77–87;

Perry Miller, *The New England Mind: The Seventeenth Century* (New York: Macmillan, 1939);

W. Fraser Mitchell, *English Pulpit Oratory from Andrewes to Tillotson: A Study of its Literary Aspects* (London: Macmillan, 1932);

Harold Lawson Murphy, *A History of Trinity College Dublin from its foundation to 1702* (Dublin: Hodges, Figgis, 1951), pp. 88–99;

Fitzroy Pyle, "'And Old *Damaetas* Lov'd to hear our Song,'" *Hermathena,* 71 (1948): 83–92.

Papers:

William Barry's manuscript copy of "A Method of Preaching" (written before 1641) is Manuscript 333 in the library of Trinity College, Dublin, which also has William Bedell's college statutes with corrections by Chappell (MS 760). Chappell's autobiography in Latin iambics (written after 1641) is at the British Library (MS 34, 729, f. 106), which also has letters from Chappell to T. Whitehead, 1616 (33,935 ff. 14, 16), W. Moreton, 1623–1647 (33,935 ff. 46, 106; 33,936 f. 21; 33,937 ff. 15–17, 19, 21, 23, 25), and P. Moreton, 1627 (33,935 f. 189).

Angel Day

(fl. 1583 – 1599)

Judith Rice Henderson
University of Saskatchewan

See also the Day entry in *DLB 167: Sixteenth-Century British Nondramatic Writers, Third Series.*

BOOKS: *The English Secretorie. VVherein is contayned, A Perfect Method, for the inditing of all manner of Epistles and familiar Letters, together with their diuersities, enlarged by examples vnder their seuerall Tytles. In which is layd forth a Path-waye, so apt, plaine and easie, to any learners capacity, as the like wherof hath not at any time heretofore beene deliuered. Nowe first deuized, and newly published by Angel Day* (London: Printed by Robert Waldegrave & sold by Richard Jones, 1586); revised and enlarged as *The English Secretorie: Or, plaine and direct Method, for the enditing of all manner of Epistles or Letters, as well Familliar as others: destinguished by their diuersities vnder their seuerall titles, The like whereof hath neuer hitherto beene published. Studiouslie, now corrected, refined & amended, in far more apt & better sort then before: according to the Authors true meaning, deliuered in his former edition: Togeather (also) with the second part then left out, and long since promised to be performed. Also, a declaration of all such Tropes, Figures or Schemes, as either usually, or for ornament sake, are in this Method required. Finally, the partes and office of a secretorie, in like maner, amplie discoursed. All which to the best and easiest direction that may be, for young learners and practizers: are now, newlie, wholelie and ioyntly published. By Angel Day* (London: Printed by Richard Jones, 1592 [i.e., 1593]; revised again, London: Printed by Richard Jones for Cuthbert Burby, 1595); revised again as *The English Secretary, or Methode of writing of Epistles and Letters: with A declaration of such Tropes, Figures, and Schemes, as either vsually or for ornament sake are therin required. Also the parts and office of a Secretarie, Deuided into two bookes. Now newly reuised and in many parts corrected and amended: by Angel Day* (London: Printed by Peter Short for Cuthbert Burby, 1599);
Vpon the life and death of the most worthy, and thrise renowmed knight, Sir Phillip Sidney: A Commemoration of his worthines, Contayning a briefe recapitulation, of his valiant vsage and death taken, in her Maiesties seruices of the warres in the Low-countries of Flaunders (London: Printed by Robert Waldegrave, 1587);
Daphnis and Chloe excellently describing the weight of affection, the simplicitie of loue, the purport of honest meaning, the resolution of men, and disposition of Fate, finished in a Pastorall, and interlaced with the praises of a most peerlesse Princesse, wonderfull in Maiestie, and rare in perfection, celebrated within the same Pastorall, and therefore termed by the name of The Shepheards holidaie. by Angell Daye (London: Printed by Robert Waldegrave, 1587).

Editions: *Daphnis and Chloe: The Elizabethan Version from Amyot's Translation by Angel Day,* edited by Joseph Jacobs, The Tudor Library, volume 2 (London: David Nutt, 1890);
The English Secretorie 1586, English Linguistics 1500–1800: A Collection of Facsimile Reprints, no. 29, edited by R. C. Alston (Menston, U.K.: Scolar, 1967);
The English Secretary Or Methods of Writing Epistles and Letters with A Declaration of such Tropes, Figures, and Schemes, as either usually or for ornament sake are therein required. (1599). Two Volumes in One, Introduction by Robert O. Evans (Gainesville, Fla.: Scholars' Facsimiles and Reprints, 1967);
Vpon the life and death of the most worthy, and thrise renowmed knight, Sir Phillip Sidney, in *Elegies for Sir Philip Sidney (1587): Facsimile Reproductions,* Introduction by A. J. Colaianne and W. L. Godshalk (Delmar, N.Y.: Scholars' Facsimiles and Reprints, 1980).

OTHER: "A. D. In commendation of the Author and his Book," in *The Anatomie of Abuses: Contayning a Discouerie, or Briefe Summarie of such Notable Vices and Imperfections, as now raigne in many Christian Countreyes of the Worlde: but (especiallie) in a verie famous Ilande called Ailgna: Together, with most fearefull Examples of Gods Iudgementes, executed vpon the wicked for the same, as well in Ailgna of late, as in other places, elsewhere. Verie Godly, to be read of all true Christians, euerie*

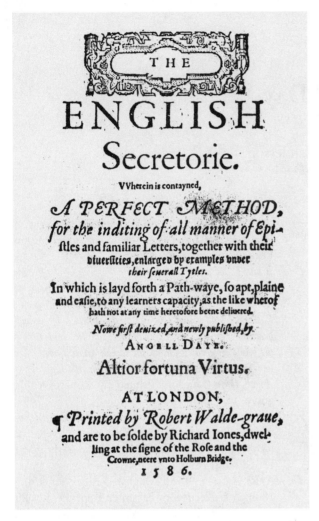

THE ENGLISH Secretorie.

VVherein is contayned,

A PERFECT METHOD,
for the inditing of all manner of Epistles and familiar Letters, together with their
diuersities, enlarged by examples vnder
their seuerall Tytles.

In which is layd forth a Path-waye, so apt, plaine
and easie, to any learners capacity, as the like whereof
hath not at any time heretofore beene deliuered.

Nowe first deuized, and newly published, by
ANGELL DAYE.

Altior fortuna Virtus.

AT LONDON,

¶ Printed by Robert Walde-graue,
and are to be solde by Richard Iones, dwelling at the signe of the Rose and the
Crowne, neere vnto Holburn Bridge.
1586.

Title page for the first edition of Angel Day's influential letter-writing manual, popular among members of the emerging Elizabethan middle class

where: but most needefull, to be regarded in Englande. Made dialogue-wise, by Phillip Stubbes (London: Printed by Richard Jones, 1583);

Giovanni Battista Nenna, *Nennio, Or A Treatise of Nobility: Wherein is discoursed what true Nobilitie is, with such qualities as are required in a perfect Gentleman. Written in Italian by that famous Doctor and worthy knight Sir John Baptista Nenna of Bari. Done into English by William Iones Gent.,* includes commendatory verses by Day, Edmund Spenser, Samuel Daniel, and George Chapman (London: Printed by Peter Short for Paul Linley and John Flasket, 1595).

Editions: *Nennio or A Treatise of Nobility by Giovanni Battista Nenna, Translated by William Jones, 1595,* introduction by Alice Shalvi, Renaissance Library Facsimile Edition (Jerusalem: Israel Universities Press / London: H. A. Humphrey, 1967);

Phillip Stubbes, *The Anatomie of Abuses,* preface by Arthur Freeman, The English Stage: Attack and Defense 1577–1730, edited by Freeman (New York: Garland, 1973).

Although he also wrote prose fiction and occasional verse in English, Angel Day has been remembered primarily for *The English Secretorie,* a manual of instruction in letter writing first published hastily in 1586. Thoroughly revised by 1593—when it was enlarged with a second part and appended treatises on rhetorical figures and the duties of a secretary—the manual was carefully polished for subsequent editions in 1595 and 1599. At least five more editions had appeared by 1635. Twentieth-century scholars have duly noted Day's place in the development of English epistolary rhetoric. Jonathan Goldberg and Richard Rambuss have observed Day's emphasis on the obligation of the Elizabethan secretary to secrecy in conducting the affairs of his employer. Yet, scholars have not shown enough interest in Day's life to penetrate its mysteries. Clues in his works suggest that he used his rhetorical skills not only to instruct others in the duties of a secretary but also to serve the Elizabethan regime.

The Stationers' Register records that "Angell Daye, the sonne of THOMAS DAYE of LONDON parysshe clerke hath put hym self apprentice to Thomas Duxsell Cytizen and Stacioner of London" for twelve years from Christmas 1563. Since apprenticeship ended in the twenty-fifth year of age, Day was probably born about 1550 and apprenticed at age thirteen. Several clerks named "Thomas Day" appear in records for the middle of the Tudor period, including two clerks or priests in the diocese of Bath and Wells, who in 1555 were deprived of "churches and dignities" for having married. A document published in John Strype's *Ecclesiastical Memorials* (1721) orders that they be separated from their wives and that both men and women be punished with "penances." Thomas Day of London and his family might have experienced similar troubles from the pendulum swings in religion during the reigns of the Protestant Edward VI (1547–1553) and the Catholic Mary I (1553–1558). Angel Day's master, the bookseller Thomas Duxsell (or Duxwell), was active in the Stationers' Company from its charter in 1557 until 1566, but his name does not appear in the register thereafter, and the register for 1575, when Day should have completed his apprenticeship, is missing.

The verses "A. D. In commendation of the Author and his Booke" appeared in *The Anatomie of Abuses* (published on 1 May 1583), an attack on what its author Phillip Stubbes considered vices, including the theaters. The poem, concerned with selling the book as much as with denouncing sin, suggests that Day had already established an association with Richard Jones, who later published *The English Secretorie:*

If Mortall-man may challenge prayse,
   For any thing done in this lyfe:
Than may our *Stubbes,* at all assayes,
   Inioy the same withouten stryfe.
Not onely for his Godly zeale,
   And Christian life accordinglie:
But also for this booke in sale,
   Heare present, now before thine eye:
Herein the Abuses of these dayes,
   As in a glasse thou mayest behold:
Oh buy it than, hear what he sayes,
   And giue him thankes an hundred fold.

Day's previous biographers have not noticed this poem, but following W. Carew Hazlitt's *Handbook to the Popular, Poetical, and Dramatic Literature of Great Britain* (1867), they have erroneously attributed to Angel Day an undated, apocalyptic warning in two parts (prose and verse) published by Robert Waldegrave: *Wonderfull straunge sightes seene in the Element, ouer the Citie of London and other places, on Munday being the seconde day of September: beginning betweene eight and nine of the clocke at night, Increasing and continuing till after midnight: most strange and fearefull to the beholders.* The author of this work may be Angel Day's father. The prose section, signed Thomas Day, describes what seems a spectacular display of the aurora borealis in the night sky of London on 2 September 1583, interpreting it as one of the last of God's warnings to repent before the Day of Judgment. The witness of these wonders would have been capable of naming his son "Angel Day" (an apocalpytic name) and perhaps enlisting him to contribute the unsigned ballad that follows the prose work, if he did not write it himself. However, Hazlitt's attribution is untrustworthy; he ignores the signature of Thomas Day and misdates the work 1585. In the accompanying ballad, God himself seems to speak about the event:

Ful twenty yeares and foure thou hast
   at large, heard out my cry,
And stil by word, I say repent
   by waters, earth, and skie.
     Repent england, &c.

Although the ballad ends with a prayer for Elizabeth I, it implies Puritan dissatisfaction with the Elizabethan Settlement of 1559.

Angel Day called *The English Secretorie* "the first worke in shew that euer I deliuered." By "first worke" he may have meant the initial draft of the treatise made at the request of friends "now six yeeres passed," in 1580. Perhaps he served as a secretary soon after completing his apprenticeship. In his 1593 appendix *Of the parts, places and Office of a Secretorie* Day modestly declined to claim the perfection he demanded in this role, "yet haue I not beene in some time of the yeares I haue spent, altogither excluded from any sauour or tast thereof." By 5 November 1586, the date of the preface to *The English Secretorie,* he was working in the legal milieu of London. During the long summer vacation, about a month before Michaelmas (29 September), he had rediscovered his manuscript on letter writing and, urged by the printer, had begun revising it "to finish some part thereof to bee published in this instant terme." He also expressed the hope to publish an enlarged second edition "in the next terme." Day may have gone on to write at least *The second part of the English Secretory* during the Christmas holiday, for Waldegrave licensed it on 10 January 1587. As he explained in his 1593 preface, however, the demands of his "present profession" and the publisher's desire to sell out the first edition had delayed publication of the enlarged edition. At the end of *The second part* Day excused errors by explaining that he could not concentrate on this project, "For my profession wil not suffer it, being otherwise occupied in my place and calling, and that very diuersely." He was employed by "the Right worshipfull, Francis Gawdey Esquier, one of the Iudges of her Maiesties Court of Kings bench, and his especiall good master," to whom, with "the right worshipfull Sir William Hatton knight, and Thomas Beddingfield, Esquier," he dedicated all the material "newlie published by A. D."

The first edition of *The English Secretorie,* prepared in great haste, was entered in the Stationers' Register on 7 November 1586 to Jones, with the consent of Waldegrave. Day complained that the printer accidentally misplaced the marginal notations to many rhetorical figures and described being "forced as fast as I could to scrible out the coppy, and to deliuer it to presse, least therby he should be compelled to stay and hinder his worke." In contrast to the authors of previous English manuals, Day wrote most of the sample letters himself, as he noted at the end of the table of contents. In the preface of 24 January 1593, he also recorded his effort in 1586 "presently to deuise examples wherewith to answere euery title." One exception in 1586, a letter purportedly written by Robert Bowes to Henry Carey, Lord Hunsdon, on affairs in Scotland of 1582, was dropped in later editions.

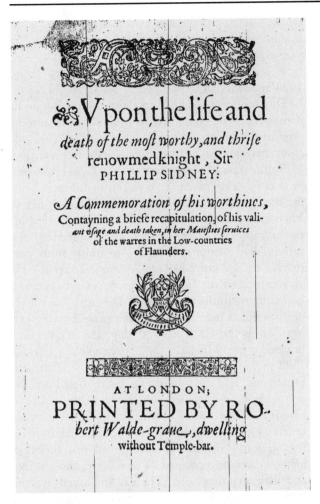

Vpon the life and

death of the moſt worthy, and thriſe
renowmed knight , Sir
PHILLIP SIDNEY:

A Commemoration of his worthines,
Contayning a briefe recapitulation, of his valiant vſage and death taken, in her Maieſties ſeruices
of the warres in the Low-countries
of Flaunders.

AT LONDON;
PRINTED BY RO-
bert Walde-graue, dwelling
without Temple-bar.

*Title page for Day's contribution to the outpouring of elegies on the
poet and courtier considered by many Elizabethans to embody
all the character traits they most admired*

As Day polished and expanded his manual in 1593, he redefined his audience. Waldegrave and Jones probably hoped to rival the handbooks published for the middle class by other London printers: *The Enimie of Idlenesse* by William Fullwood (1568) and *A Panoplie of Epistles* by Abraham Fleming (1576). In 1586 Day called the letter "a faythfull and secrete Ambassadour" and hoped to assist with art the natural rhetoric of "the vnlearned," because they find it "greeuous . . . to participate their moste secreat causes to an other, and to laye vp their chiefest trust in the affiaunce of anothers credite," that is, to hire a professional to write a letter for them. A few pages later, though, Day thought of training professional secretaries, and on the whole his model letters are more appropriate to gentlemen than to merchants and craftsmen. In *The second part* of 1593, Day praised a publication that he had just seen, *The Marchants Auizo* (1589) by John Browne, and declined to com-

pete with it by offering additional examples of commercial letters. Instead, Day concentrated his attention on the would-be secretary. The implied reader is no longer "ignorant and studious," as in 1586, but rather "the Scholler or any other that is vnfurnished of the knowledge" of letter writing, as Day explained almost apologetically in the new preface "To the learned and curteous Readers." He supplemented the reader's education in Latin with specific advice on correspondence in English, a language that has quite different formulas of epistolary etiquette. This version of his manual is more scholarly than the first. For instance, the revised opening chapter follows the pattern of schoolbooks by defining the word *epistle* instead of claiming, as in 1586, that "no other definition needeth therof, then that which vse and common experience hath induced vnto vs."

Day's 1593 preface records complaints that his first edition was wordy and disordered. These charges were serious, for the subtitle had promised his readers a "a perfect method" of letter writing "In which is layd forth a Path-waye . . . apt, plaine and easie, to any learners capacity." *Methodus* was the usual term for an efficient, graded course of instruction. In 1593 Day ruthlessly cut and rearranged material, eliminating much of his repetitious 1586 commentary on particular examples and substituting general directions for the major types of letters. He kept his promise to complete the manual and to append "descriptions of the FIGURES, SCHEMES and TROPES . . . and . . . a Discours of the partes and office of a SECRETORIE." The 1586 manual discusses and illustrates only demonstrative and deliberative letters. *The second part* added in 1593 discusses and illustrates judicial and familiar letters. These categories are adapted from the textbooks by which English schoolboys were taught Latin composition through letter writing: Desiderius Erasmus's *Opus de conscribendis epistolis* (Work on Letter Writing, 1522) and its imitators, especially the *Methodus conscribendi epistolas* (Method of Writing Letters, 1526) by Christoph Hegendorff (Christophorus Hegendorphinus) and the *Methodus de conscribendis epistolis* (Method of Letter Writing)—originally *Epistolica* (Epistolary Matters, 1543) of Georgius Macropedius. In 1586 Day recommended as models the "Epistles of *Cicero, Lucian, Politian* and others," all writers admired by Erasmus, as well as the epistolary textbooks of Erasmus, Hegendorphinus, Macropedius, and Joannes Ludovicus Vives, the Spanish humanist who had tutored the English Queen Mary I. Vives' *De conscribendis epistolis, libellus vere aureus* (Truly Golden Little Book on Letter Writing, 1533) had appeared with textbooks of Erasmus and Hegendorphinus in Continental editions, as well as in a 1573 London collection that also included Macropedius and others. Hegendorphinus and Macropedius were published together in twelve London editions from 1576 to 1649, and Fleming translated Hegendorphinus as "An epitome of precepts" in *A Panoplie of Epistles*.

Day's address to a more educated audience may help to explain why in 1593 he removed much of the humorous and satiric material in the first edition. He retained an amusing example of purple prose to "Egregious Doctors, and maysters of the eximious & Archane Science of Phisick," as well as two ironic letters: a recommendation of a worthless servant and a consolation for the death of a troublesome wife. However, he omitted a story about that favorite jestbook character, "learned *Skelton*" and soberly revised almost the entire section on love letters. Day's 1586 "Epistles Amatorie" tell a story of the unsuccessful courtship of Mistress Mawdlin by B.L. Perhaps Day was imitating *The Image of Idlenesse* (1555), which Michael Flachmann has called the first English epistolary novel. With four editions by 1581, that fictional correspondence between "Walter Wedlocke and Bawdin Bachelor" may have suggested to Fullwood the alternative title, *The Enimie of Idlenesse*. Fullwood translated love letters from his French source and added several poems. By 1593 Day's love letters had become, even more than Fullwood's, serious general models of marital courtship. T. W. Baldwin, examining a 1599 edition in the University of Illinois Library, complained that Day's "Epistles Amatorie" are "impeccably correct, arid, academic, and uninteresting"; yet, Baldwin added, this section seems to have been well thumbed and annotated by "one 'ffrancis Harding.'" Day's successive revisions of *The English Secretorie* tended toward the general situation and character type: he omitted more and more concrete detail with each new edition from 1593 to 1599. Yet, contemporary readers clearly found his models useful in negotiating the affairs of their daily lives. In its revised versions, *The English Secretorie* became not only a self-study manual for middle-class youths who aspired to be secretaries but also a courtesy book for the gentlemen and ladies they hoped to serve. More than its predecessors, it must have guided the late Tudor and Stuart aristocrats who were developing the English familiar letter into a literary genre.

As many rhetoricians before him had done, Day instructed in the margins of his treatise, sometimes noting the divisions of a model—exordium (beginning), narratio (narration), and so on—sometimes stating the topics of invention, and almost always pointing out the rhetorical figures. The "col-

ors of rhetoric" had been part of medieval manuals on letter writing, and Macropedius had appended rhetorical figures to his manual of letter writing, so in 1593 Day added a glossary of the figures noted: *A Declaration of all such Tropes, Figures or Schemes, as for excellencie and ornament in writing, are specially vsed in this Methode: Collected and explaned togethers, according to their applications, vsages, and properties.* Several such handbooks were already available in English: Richard Sherry's *A treatise of Schemes & Tropes very profitable for the better vnderstanding of good authors* (1550), his Latin and English edition, *A Treatise of the Figures of Grammer and Rhetorike* (1555), and Henry Peacham the Elder's *The Garden of Eloquence* (1577; revised, 1593), Thomas Wilson's *The Arte of Rhetorique* (1553; revised, 1560), and George Puttenham's *The Arte of English Poesie* (1589) had also discussed the figures. Day paraphrased an epigram to Puttenham but did not follow him in devising English equivalents for the Greek and Latin names. Rather, in revising the *Declaration*, principally in 1599, he became more scholarly, sometimes replacing a Latin term by a more erudite Greek one (thus *communicatio* became *epitropis*) and refining distinctions (for instance, between *epanodis* and *prolepsis*). Both *communicatio* and *epitropis* invite the audience to contribute. *Prolepsis*, like *epanodis*, expands a generalization by dividing it into its parts, but it also repeats or elaborates the terms of the division. Like his predecessors, Day relied on the Continental textbooks used in English schools. Baldwin describes Day's *Declaration* as "an abbreviated and adapted translation or paraphrase" of Joannes Susenbrotus's *Epitome Troporum ac Schematum* (Epitome of Tropes and Schemes, 1541), published in twelve London editions between 1562 and 1635.

The other appendix that Day added in 1593 is *Of the parts, places and Office of a Secretorie*, partly drawn from Francesco Sansovino's *Del Secretario* (1565). It defines an ideal servant who not only writes letters in his master's name but also screens suitors to him and otherwise assists him in public and personal affairs. The qualifications for this office include a respectable family, pleasant appearance and personality, good judgment, the ability to keep a confidence, commitment to the needs of the poor, appropriate associates and friends, education in classical and foreign languages, facility in composition, penmanship, intelligence, understanding, memory, administrative skill, and industry. The secretary must maintain the honorable reputation of a gentleman, even though he may not have been born into the gentry. He should be not only a faithful servant but also a friend who, even at the risk of losing his position, will anticipate difficulties and honestly counsel his master rather

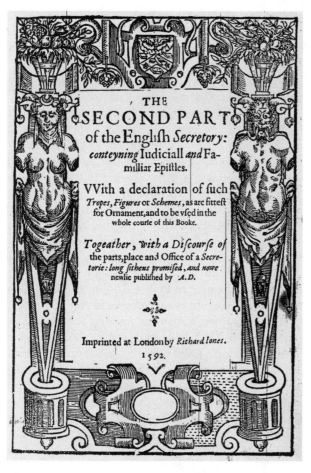

Title page for the selection of judicial and familiar letters that Day added to the second, revised and enlarged edition of his manual

than pursuing his own advantage with flattery. Day struggled with certain issues. If the secretary is not the equal of his master in social status, how can he be a friend? Is physical deformity a sure sign of viciousness? How far should self-denial go? Day wrote with admiration of an Irish boy who died trying to protect his English master, Captain Henry Davells, from assassination by the rebel Sir John of Desmond, but he considered this sacrifice a child's irrationality, for it did not save Davells. On the other hand, a servant to the Turkish ruler, who had assisted the Christian traitor Scanderbeg out of fear, at last made the honorable choice to die for his fault rather than wade farther into treason. Day did not face all issues quite so squarely. He offered in 1593 (but in 1599 omitted) a story of a secretary who successfully dissuaded his master from treason. What if the master had not been dissuaded? Day derived the word *secretary* from *secret,* but should all confidences be kept? When is it appropriate to lie for the sake of loyalty? The potential conflicts implied by Day's description of the sec-

retary's role were real ones in a society that barely conceived a distinction between the personal and the professional. They were the stuff of contemporary fiction and drama. Perhaps they were also a source of tension in Day's life as he reconciled what seem to have been militant Protestant and even Puritan convictions with loyalty to the more conservative Elizabethan regime he served.

The 1593 preface to *The English Secretorie* excused the inadequacies of the first edition by an enigmatic reference to "some hard stormes then casually betyding." Day's publication of three works in quick succession in 1586–1587 implies that he needed patronage. They are dedicated to Queen Elizabeth's courtiers: *The English Secretorie* to Edward De Vere, Earl of Oxford; an elegy on Sir Philip Sidney to Sir Francis Walsingham, the queen's principal secretary; and an English adaptation of the Greek romance *Daphnis and Chloe* to Sir William Newport, alias Hatton, nephew and adopted heir of Sir Christopher Hatton, the longtime favorite that Elizabeth appointed lord chancellor on 25 April 1587. None of these dedications acknowledges a special relationship or previous support. To Oxford in 1586, Day implied his desire to share in "the exceeding bountie wherewith your good L.[ordship] hath euer wonted to entertaine the desertes of all men." The aristocratic Oxford was renowned as both a poet and patron, and although generally out of favor with Elizabeth after 1581, he continued to hold the hereditary office of lord great chamberlain. In 1593 Day acknowledged Oxford's "so great bounty" when he presented the first edition to him "fiue yeares passed," and the earl may have continued to reward subsequent revisions of *The English Secretorie,* for the dedication to him is changed slightly through each edition up to 1599.

Waldegrave licensed elegies for the funeral of Sir Philip Sidney on 22 February 1587, among which he published *Vpon the life and death of the most worthy, and thrise renowmed knight, Sir Phillip Sidney: A Commemoration of his worthines, Contayning a briefe recapitulation, of his valiant vsage and death taken, in her Maiesties seruices of the warres in the Low-countries of Flaunders.* The dedication to Walsingham presents the poet "A. D." as "one, who in al humble duty and reuerence, gladly would bind himself to do your honor anie seruice." Sidney, wounded on 22 September 1586, while fighting Spanish troops on behalf of the Dutch Protestants at Zutphen, died on 17 October, and Walsingham, Sidney's father-in-law, bankrupted himself staging the funeral on 16 February 1587 as propaganda for militant Protestantism. Many contemporary poets wrote elegies. In his poem Day used rhyme-royal stanzas competently but the medieval *ubi sunt* motif (referring to *ubi sunt qui ante nos fuerunt,* or "where are those who went before us") awkwardly recalls Sidney's accomplishments. The speaker asks in vain for the nymphs of pastoral Ida and the Muses of comic, lyric, and heroic poetry, as well as for the Destinies, Fate, Chance, Casualties, and Mischance. They roam in confusion, "Griefs griping t' one, and shame for t' others dome." The poem alludes to Sidney as "rarest *Tipe* of courtly gentlenes" and as "stately noble knight" of the war goddess Bellona but emphasizes his poetic accomplishments. It mentions specifically the *Countess of Pembroke's Arcadia* (1590), then circulating in manuscript.

Sidney's *Arcadia* was one model for Day's 1587 adaptation of *Daphnis and Chloe,* a pastoral romance attributed to Longus, and Edmund Spenser's *The Shepheardes Calender* (1579) seems to have been another. The first printed edition of the original Greek story appeared in 1598, and a much-admired French translation by Jacques Amyot, tutor to the sons of Henri II and later Bishop of Auxerre, had been published anonymously in 1559. Day partially filled in the lacuna in the Greek manuscript that Amyot used: it lacked the description of the first awakenings of love as Chloe watches Daphnis bathe and as Daphnis wins a kiss from Chloe in a contest with the cowherd Dorcon. Amyot had expurgated Daphnis's education in intercourse by a married woman named Lycaenion. Day made many additional changes in the story, which have been carefully catalogued by Samuel Lee Wolff. Like Sidney and the Continental writers that Sidney imitated, Day interspersed songs in the prose narrative. As the pastoral work proceeds through spring, summer, harvest, vintage, winter, and once more through the cycle to an autumn marriage, the young goatherd Daphnis sings his love complaints and his praises of the shepherdess Chloe in a variety of verse forms, including poulter's measure (iambic couplets with the first line in hexameter and the second in heptameter), fourteeners (fourteen syllables arranged in iambs), and quatrains (four-line stanzas). The young lovers are harassed by pirates, foreign hunters, and jealous suitors and suffer other misadventures usual in late Greek romance, but the two foundlings are protected by the gods until they finally discover their aristocratic parentage and marry.

Day omitted part of book 3 to insert *The Shepheards Holidaie.* Just as Elizabethan courtiers honored the Queen's Accession Day each 17 November with tilts and other pageantry, so Day's pastoral characters sing the praises of their island's Virgin Queen, Eliza, in a winter celebration of her accession. Critics have disparaged Day's adaptation of *Daphnis and Chloe,* especially this poetic interpolation, but pastoral romance was a genre that the Elizabethans expected to be used for political ends, and *The Shepheards Holidaie* celebrated Elizabeth's reign at a critical moment for English Protestantism. Her rival Mary Queen of Scots was executed on 8 February 1587 for complicity in the Babington Plot, and England was anticipating the invasion that culminated in the defeat of the Spanish Armada in 1588. Meleboeus, enumerating the virtues of Eliza's reign, glances at the "deepe deceipt" of Mary and her supporters, celebrates English imperialism "in soile till then vnknowne," the New World, and claims that "lands subdued tofore by forraigne states" (the Spanish Netherlands) "sue and seeke and humblie make request, / To yeeld them-selues vnto thy hie behest." *The Shepheards Holidaie* seems a risky bid for attention in the highest court circles, made perhaps because of a crisis in Day's career. Day's dedication to Sir William Hatton begs his protection against "all kinde of biting serpents" and apologizes, "Herein if I presume on your VIRTUES, I vrge the necessity." The valediction, "Your worships in all to be commaunded," seems an appeal for employment. Sir William, having married the daughter and heir of Francis Gawdy in June 1589, perhaps obliged by recommending Day for the position he held in 1593.

When Day began serving Gawdy is uncertain, and given his obsession with secrecy, the reader may wonder whether his prefaces of 1586–1587 should be taken at face value. Joseph Jacobs, who edited Day's *Daphnis and Chloe* (1890), found only one extant copy of the poem and postulated Puritan suppression; yet, the romance was published by Waldegrave, who had been imprisoned for six weeks in 1584 and for twenty weeks in 1585 for printing Puritan tracts. It seems more likely that copies of *Daphnis and Chloe* were lost when the government raided Waldegrave's publishing house. On 16 April 1588 the authorities seized copies of *The State of the Church of Englande,* an anti-episcopal tract, but failed to capture Waldegrave, who escaped with some type. On 13 May his press was destroyed by order of the Stationers' Company. Waldegrave went underground. He became the first printer of the series of satirical attacks on the bishops of the Church of England published from October 1588 to September 1589 under the pseudonym "Martin Marprelate." The establishment fought back both with pamphlets and with interrogations and punishment of those who printed and distributed the works and those who harbored the presses. Waldegrave abandoned the project in April 1589, fled to

Scotland, and became an official printer to King James VI.

One of the investigators and judges of the Marprelate culprits in 1590–1591 was Day's employer in 1593, Justice Gawdy. He had been one of the Queen's serjeants (that is, lawyers) since 17 May 1582 and had participated with Oxford, Walsingham, and Sir Christopher Hatton in the trial of Mary Queen of Scots. On 25 November 1589 he was appointed a justice of the Court of Queen's Bench. After the death of Sir Christopher on 20 November 1591, he was one of a commission to hear causes in Chancery until a new lord chancellor could be appointed. On 29 June 1590, in connection with the examination of Humphrey Newman, a cobbler who distributed the Marprelate tracts, Justice Gawdy was listed as a member of a special commission appointed by the Privy Council to investigate Martin's anti-episcopal satire. Later that summer he was one of the justices of the court of assize in Warwick that decided to transfer the case of Job Throkmorton (perhaps the author of the tracts) to Westminster. In the winter of 1590 or spring of 1591, Justice Gawdy tried John Hodgskin, apprehended in August 1589 as the second printer of the tracts, following Waldegrave. Day must have been working in Waldegrave's shop to revise *The English Secretorie* in late 1586, and presumably he was at least a frequent visitor there through much of 1587 as he oversaw the printing of his other works. The preface of 1593 hints that he had been in his "present profession" for some years. Was Day sent to keep watch on Waldegrave's illicit activities, enlisted by the government because his Puritan connections would make him appear trustworthy? Or if his dedications of 1586–1587 were sincere, did he win by 1593 the court patronage he sought because his observations of those who frequented Waldegrave's shop proved useful to the subsequent investigation of the Marprelate conspiracy? Why was Day's 1593 dedication to Gawdy, Hatton, and Bedingfield omitted from later editions of *The English Secretorie?* Perhaps he had revealed too much for their comfort, or for his own.

The 1593 dedication of the new material in *The English Secretorie* thanks not only Gawdy and his son-in-law Hatton but also Thomas Bedingfield, Esquire, one of the gentlemen pensioners who guarded the Queen's Presence Chamber. As translator of three Italian treatises, Bedingfield shared Oxford's literary interests. In the New Year's gift exchange of 1572, he presented to Oxford a work of consolation by Girolamo Cardano. Subsequently *Cardanus Comforte . . . published by commaundement of the right honourable the Earle of Oxenforde* (1573 and 1576)

appeared with letters and verses by Oxford and Thomas Churchyard. A commendatory sonnet by George Gascoigne replaced Churchyard's letter in 1576. Bedingfield later translated part of a treatise by Claudio Corte as *The Art of Riding* (1584) and *The Florentine Historie . . . by Nicholo Macchiavelli. Citizen and Secretarie of Florence* (1595), which was dedicated to Sir Christopher Hatton from the Court on 8 April 1588. Perhaps Day, with his experience in the book trade, was employed to assist Bedingfield with one of these publications, and perhaps he considered *The English Secretorie* an especially appropriate presentation to the translator of a work by the Florentine secretary. Unfortunately, neither Day's works nor Bedingfield's clearly reveal the relationship between them.

In 1595, "Ang. Day," along with Spenser, Samuel Daniel, and George Chapman, contributed commendatory verses to *Nennio, Or A Treatise of Nobility: Wherein is discoursed what true Nobilitie is, with such qualities as are required in a perfect Gentleman. Written in Italian by that famous Doctor and worthy knight Sir John Baptista Nenna of Bari. Done into English by William Iones Gent.* Jones seems also to have translated works by Justus Lipsius and Francesco Guicciardini, published in 1594 and 1595 by William Ponsonby, publisher of Spenser's *The Faerie Queene* (1590, 1596). Jones complimented Robert Devereux, Earl of Essex, by dedicating this treatise on nobility to him on 1 November 1595. Day, with the other poets, now seemed to be seeking patronage from the new leader of the militant Protestant circle in Elizabeth's court.

In his commendatory sonnet to *Nennio*, Day perhaps justly assessed his "artlesse Muse (if any muse at all)" as "once . . . handmaid vnto skill." The only work for which Day was well known in his time was his letter-writing manual. Wolff found evidence that *Daphnis and Chloe* was used by Robert Greene in *Pandosto* (1588), but a romance that has survived in only one copy is unlikely to have been widely influential. Day's occasional verse is at best pedestrian. His career is nevertheless interesting, partly because he may have been useful to the investigation of "Martin Marprelate," but also because his works reflect the aspiration to gentility of a middle-class Elizabethan. The metrical irregularity of his commendatory verse to Stubbes's *The Anatomie of Abuses* and the humorous fictional elements of the first edition of *The English Secretorie* are in the popular literary tradition. Day seems gradually to have refined his skills even as he refined his manual of letter writing into a course of instruction for the would-be secretary and a courtesy book for the gentry. The commendatory sonnet of 1595 to *A Treatise of Nobility* seems a fitting coda to his works. The last traces of his life yet discovered are the careful revisions, apparently authorial, to the 1599 edition of *The English Secretorie.* The date of his death is unknown.

References:

T. W. Baldwin, *William Shakspere's Small Latine & Lesse Greeke,* 2 volumes (Urbana: University of Illinois Press, 1944), II: 138–175;

Leland H. Carlson, *Martin Marprelate, Gentleman: Master Job Throkmorton Laid Open in His Colors* (San Marino, Cal.: Huntington Library, 1981);

Sir Ernest Clarke, "The English Secretorie, 1586," *Secretary,* 8, no. 12 (1911): 401–406;

Michael Flachmann, ed. "The First English Epistolary Novel: *The Image of Idleness* (1555). Text, Introduction, and Notes," *Studies in Philology,* 87 (1990): 1–74;

Jonathan Goldberg, *Writing Matter: From the Hands of the English Renaissance* (Stanford: Stanford University Press, 1990), pp. 251–272;

Maude Bingham Hansche, "The Formative Period of English Familiar Letter-writers and Their Contribution to the English Essay," dissertation, University of Pennsylvania, 1902, pp. 23–27;

W. Carew Hazlitt, *Handbook to the Popular, Poetical, and Dramatic Literature of Great Britain, from the Invention of Printing to the Restoration* (London: John Russell Smith, 1867), p. 146;

Katherine Gee Hornbeak, *The Complete Letter-Writer in English, 1568–1800,* Smith College Studies in Modern Languages, 15, no. 3–4 (Northampton, Mass., April–July 1934), pp. 1–49, 128–145;

Richard Rambuss, *Spenser's Secret Career,* Cambridge Studies in Renaissance Literature and Culture, no. 3 (Cambridge: Cambridge University Press, 1993), pp. 30–48;

Jean Robertson, *The Art of Letter Writing: An Essay on the Handbooks Published in England during the Sixteenth and Seventeenth Centuries* (London: University Press of Liverpool, 1942), pp. 9–24;

Elbert N. S. Thompson, *Literary Bypaths of the Renaissance* (New Haven: Yale University Press, 1924), pp. 91–126;

Katherine S. Van Eerde, "Robert Waldegrave: The Printer as Agent and Link between Sixteenth-Century England and Scotland," *Renaissance Quarterly,* 34 (1981): 40–78;

Samuel Lee Wolff, *The Greek Romances in Elizabethan Prose Fiction* (New York: Columbia University Press, 1921);

Louis B. Wright, *Middle-Class Culture in Elizabethan England* (Chapel Hill: University of North Carolina Press, 1935), pp. 139–146.

Thomas Farnaby
(1575? – 12 June 1647)

R. W. Serjeantson
Trinity College, Cambridge

BOOKS: *Figuræ, Tropi Et Schemata,* by "T. F." (London, 1616);

Index Rhetoricus, Scholis & institutioni tenerioris æatis accommodatus (London: Printed by Felix Kyngston, 1625);

Phrases elegantiores ex optimis autoribus selectae, anonymous (London: Printed for Ralph Rounthwait, 1625?); enlarged as *Phrases Oratoriæ Elogantiores. Editio Sexta. Cui accesserunt Phrases aliquot Poëticæ* (London: Printed by Felix Kyngston, 1631);

Η τῆς ἀνθολογίας Ανθολογία. Florilegium epigrammatvm Græcorvm, eorvmque Latino versv à varijs redditorum (London: Printed by Felix Kyngston, 1629);

Index Poeticus Commonstrans Descriptiones, Comparationes, Allusiones, Ritus, Locos communes, Fabulas illustriores, &c. Quæ habentur apud Poetas veteres & recentiores majorum & minorum gentium, anonymous (London: Printed by Felix Kyngston, 1634);

Index Rhetoricvs Et Oratorivs, Scholis & institutioni tenerioris aetatis accommodatus, cui adjiciuntur Formvlae Oratoriae, Et Index Poeticus. Operâ & studio Thomae Farnabii. Editio Tertia, Avctior et Emendatior (London: Printed by John Legat for Philemon Stephens and Christophor Meredith, 1640);

Systema Grammaticvm Operâ & studio Tho. Farnabii (London: Printed by Thomas & Richard Cotes for Andrew Crooke, 1641);

Regulae de genere nominium, de nominibus heteroclitis, de praeteritis et supiuis, verborum, ex Vossio, Farnabio, aliisque collectae (London, 1661).

Editions: *Troposchematologia: Maximam Partem ex Indice Rhetorico Farnabii Deprompta, Additis insuper Anglicanis Exemplis. In usum Scholae Regiae Grammaticalis apud S'. Edmundi Burgum,* edited by Thomas Stephens (London: For Richard Royston, 1648);

Farnaby Illustrated: or, the Latin Text of Farnaby's Rhetoric Exemplified, by Various Passages, from the Sacred Scriptures; the Roman Classics; and the Most Distinguished British Authors. For the Use of Schools (York: Printed by A. Ward for Mr. Etherington, 1768);

"The *Index rhetoricus* of Thomas Farnaby," translated and edited by Raymond Nadeau, dissertation, University of Michigan Graduate School, 1951;

Systema Grammaticum, 1641, edited by R. C. Alston, English Linguistics 1500–1800, no. 160 (Menston, U.K.: Scolar, 1969);

Index rhetoricus, 1625, edited by Alston, English Linguistics 1500–1800, no. 240 (Menston, U.K.: Scolar Press, 1970).

OTHER: "Incipit Thomas Farnaby alias Bainrafe," in *Coryats Crudities Hastily gobled vp in five Moneths trauells in France, Sauoy, Italy, Rhetia comonly called the Grisons country, Heluetia aliàs Switzerland, some parts of high Germany, and the Netherlands; Newly digested in the hungry aire of Odcombe in the County of Somerset, & now dispersed to the nourishment of the trauelling Members of this Kingdome,* by Thomas Coryat (London: Printed by William Stansby, 1611), G4v–r;

Juvenal and Persius, *Ivnii Ivvenalis Et Avli Persii Flacci satyræ: Cum Annotationibus ad marginem, quæ obscurissima quaeque dilucidare possint,* annotated by Farnaby (London: Printed by Richard Field for William Welby, 1612);

Seneca, *L. & M. Annæi Senecae Atqve Aliorvm Tragoediae. Animadversionibvs Et Notis Marginalibus fideliter emendatæ atque illustratæ,* annotated by Farnaby (London: Printed by Felix Kyngston for William Welby, 1613);

Martial, *M. Val. Martialis epigrammatⱳn Libri. Animadversi, Emendati Et Commentariolis Lvculenter explicati,* annotated by Farnaby (London: Printed by Felix Kyngston for William Welby, 1615);

Lucan, *M. Annæi Lvcani Pharsalia, siue, De Bello Ciuili Cæsaris et Pompeii Libri X. Adiectis ad marginem Notis T. Farnabii, quae loca obscuriora illustrent,* annotated by Farnaby (London: Printed by Richard Field, 1618);

Untitled poem, in *Ecloge Sententiarvm Et Similitvdinvm Familiarivm Ex Divo Ioanne Chrysostomo desumpta: Sive Isagoge ad Linguam Graecam:quâ praelibatâ, via ad* reconditiora sternitur; Graece & Latine edita. Studio I. H. Art. Magist. Col. Magd. Oxon., by John Harmar (London: Printed by John Haviland for Thomas Pavier, 1622), A8r;

Untitled figure poem, in Tomvs Alter Annalivm Rervm Anglicarvm, Et Hibernicarvm, Regnante Elizabetha, Qui nunc demum prodit: Sive Pars Qvarta. Avtore Gvil. Camdeno (London: Printed by William Stansby for Simon Waterson, 1627), A4r;

John Clarke, Formulae oratoriae in usum scholarum concinnatae, privati olim Lincolniensis Scholæ, exercitijs, &c. accommodatae. Tertia editio, longe & auctior, & emendatior: cui accesserunt, T. Farnabij formulae, quas diverso a caeteris charactere distinguimus (London: Printed by Felix Kyngston for Robert Milbourne, 1630);

"Ad Clarissimvm Atqve Doctissimvm Virvm D. Gvlielmvm Alabastrvm S. T. D. super Tragoedia sua Roxana ex jure repetita, secundum vindicias asserta, & nunc ab ipso edita," in Roxana Tragaedia A plagiarij unguibus vindicata, aucta, & agnita ab Authore Gvlielmo Alabastro, by William Alabaster (London: Printed by William Jones, 1632);

Virgil, P. Virgilii Maronis Opera. Notis a Thomae Farnabii, annotated by Farnaby (London: Printed by Felix Kyngston for Robert Allot, 1634);

Ovid, Publii Ovidii Nasonis Metamorphoseωn libri xv. Ad fidem editionum optimarum & codicum manuscriptorum examinati. Opera & studio T. Farnabii (London: Printed by Anne Griffin for Joyce Norton and Richard Whitaker, 1636);

Thomas Horne, Χειραγωγία, sive, Manuductio in aedem Palladis qua Utilissima Methodus Authores bonos legendi indigitatur, includes formulae by Farnaby (London: Printed for Robert Young, 1641);

Terence, Pub. Terentii Comoediae Sex, Ex recensione Heinsianâ: Cum Annotationibus Thomae Farnabii, in Quatuor Priores: Et M.C. Is. F. in Duas Posteriores, annotated by Farnaby and Meric Casaubon (London: Printed by William Dugard for Lawrence Sadler, William Welles, and Thomas Williams, 1651).

Thomas Farnaby, according to Anthony à Wood's life of him in his Athenae Oxonienses (Bliss edition, 1813–1820), was "the chief grammarian, rhetorician, poet, Latinist, and Grecian of his time, and his school was so much frequented, that more churchmen and statesman issued thence, than from any school taught by one man in England." In contemporary references to him, "famous" competes with "learned" for preeminence. His Index Rhetoricvs, Scholis & institutioni tenerioris ætatis accomodatus (Rhetorical Index, Suited to the Schools and Training of Those of More Tender Years, 1625), a self-conscious synthesis of the classical and Continental riches of the Renaissance rhetorical tradi-

tion, went through thirteen English editions between its first publication in 1625 and 1700; it was thus one of the most popular rhetoric textbooks in seventeenth-century England in terms of the number of copies printed. Farnaby was a corresponding member of the European scholarly republic of letters, and his editions of Latin poets and dramatists were staples of English schools and were extensively pirated on the Continent. Throughout his life he manifested a close concern with maintaining his rights over the publication of his original works and editions of classical authors—with good cause, for his career also exemplifies the flexibility and capacity for appropriation of the early modern rhetoric textbook.

Thomas Farnaby was born in London around 1575. His father, also named Thomas, was a carpenter. His mother, Dorothy, was the daughter of Thomas Foxcroft of Batley in Yorkshire. His grandfather on the father's side had been a mayor of Truro in Cornwall; his great-grandfather was an Italian musician; and he was also related to the madrigal composer Giles Farnaby (fl. 1598). The details of Thomas Farnaby's schooling are unknown, but he matriculated at Merton College, Oxford, on 26 June 1590. His talents led to his becoming a postmaster (scholar) there under the patronage of a fellow of the college named Thomas French. These same talents then seem to have led him into intellectual and spiritual rebellion, for he escaped after some time in Oxford to a Jesuit college in Spain as a convert to Roman Catholicism. He clearly benefited from the rigorous education he got there but eventually tired of the discipline his teachers demanded of their charges and slipped away to return to England.

In 1595–1596, on the strength of a connection with Sir John Hawkins, he shipped with him and Sir Francis Drake on their belligerent and ill-fated last expedition to the Canary Islands and the Caribbean. On his return to Europe he turned from pirate to mercenary, fighting in the Low Countries in the Eighty Years' War against Spain. This employment, which he is reported to have relished, did not last, and at some point in the latter 1590s he landed in poverty in Cornwall. Calling himself Bainrafe (an anagram of his surname) to mask his shame, he took to teaching school. He began by teaching the rudiments of reading and writing as an "abecedarian," but after settling at Martock in Somerset he progressed to teaching higher forms. It was probably during these years that he married his first wife, Susan Pierce, a native of Cornwall. Together they had three children, John, Judith, and Margaret.

After a few years of teaching in the southwest of England, Farnaby took himself to London and set up his own school off Redcross Street in Cripplegate. This establishment was set among spacious gardens and

M. VAL.
MARTIALIS
EPIGRAMMA-
TΩN LIBRI.

ANIMADVERSI, E-
MENDATI

ET COMMENTARIOLIS LV-
culenter explicati.

LONDINI,
Excudebat *Felix Kingstonius* impenfis *Gulielmi Welby.*
1615.

Title page for one of Thomas Farnaby's annotated editions of
Latin works

large houses, the first perhaps to entice and the latter to accommodate the pupils he seems to have had little difficulty attracting. At its largest, the school had more than three hundred students, principally sons of the nobility and gentry. Farnaby employed a resident writing master, a rarity for the time. He was perhaps also the first English schoolmaster to separate the higher and lower forms into different classrooms. The success of the school, and Farnaby's reputation, reached such a height that on 24 April 1616 he was incorporated as a Master of Arts at Cambridge and then later in the same year at Oxford. Farnaby's school was a private institution, not a public grammar school, which may account for the wealth that it clearly brought him. By 1631 he had made enough money to buy an estate at Kippington and a country house at Otford, both near Sevenoaks in Kent; and in the preface to *Index Rhetoricus* he makes a pointed jibe against those who criticize schoolmasters for making money from their profession.

The autobiography of the lawyer Sir John Bramston, published in 1845, provides the only record of Farnaby's character as a schoolmaster:

> I came to Mr. Farnabie, whoe taught schoole in a garden house in Goldsmyths' allie, a fine airie place; he had ioyned two or three gardens and houses togeather, and had a great manie boarders and towne schollars; soe manie that he had 2, sometymes three, vshers besides himselfe. I boarded with him, tho' my father liued then in Phillip lane, very near the schoole. The first day I came he tooke me into his studie; and after he had inquired what bookes I learnt, he gaue me pen, ink, and paper, and bid me make a theame on "*Ex argillâ quidvis imitaberis udâ* [From soft clay you can mould whatever you please]." I sayd i vsed to haue a weekes tyme to make a theame. I doe not desire much, sayes he, but let me see what thou canst doe. I sett myselfe to it, and did as well as I could. He came at xj of the clock to see what I had done; and, reading it, cryed out, "Oh Heauens! where has thou binn bred?" Soe in the afternoone he placed me in a forme vnder those that read Virgil; which yet was too high for me, but I thinck he was vnwillinge to discourage me too much. With him I stayd more than two, nay full three yeares. At partinge, he shewed me my first and last theames, and sayd, "Thus you came, and thus you goe; God speed you!" From him I went vnto Wadham College, in Oxford.

Some of Farnaby's ushers, or assistants, went on to become teachers themselves, including William Burton, who subsequently set up his own school in Kingston-upon-Thames, and Alexander Gill the Younger, an usher between 1619 and 1621, who went on to succeed his father as high master of St. Paul's School in London. This connection of Farnaby with St. Paul's was used by Donald Lemen Clark in his *John Milton at St. Paul's School* (1948) to support the conjecture that Milton was taught the many figures and tropes he knew from an early copy, either printed or manuscript, of *Index Rhetoricus;* Milton certainly owned and annotated a copy of Farnaby's later *Systema Grammaticum* (Grammatical system, 1641). With at least one of his former pupils, the future Sir John Borough, Farnaby pursued a correspondence, some letters of which were printed during his lifetime. He remained friendly with Gill, too: in January 1624 his former employee sent him a New Year's verse and a skin of Canary wine from which he had already drawn a toast.

Other pupils of Farnaby's included Sir Richard Fanshawe, the diplomat, who may have owed his excellent latinity to his teacher; Thomas Henshaw, the courtier and member of the Royal Society; the Latin poet Henry Birkhead; the physician Assuerus Regimorterus; the Cavalier Edward Sherburne; and Henry Killigrew, the clergyman, occasional dramatist, and father of the poet Anne Killigrew. Roger King, the elder brother of the Edward King who is elegized by John Milton in "Lycidas" (1638), was also a student of Farnaby's: it is thus possible that Edward King may have been too.

Once he was established as a schoolmaster in London, Farnaby began his long and successful publishing career. The books he wrote and edited were all motivated by the same guiding principle: teaching the skills of reading and writing the Latin and Greek of classical antiquity. He published editions of Latin dramatists and poets, textbooks of grammar and rhetoric, and an index to and collections of epigrams and choice poetic phrases. He began as an editor of the kinds of Latin authors encountered in the middle and higher forms of the Renaissance grammar school. Between 1612 and 1618 he published annotated editions of the works of Juvenal and Persius (1612), Seneca (1613), Martial (1615), and Lucan (1618). A second bout of publication produced annotated editions of the works of Virgil (1634) and Ovid (1636), and his editorial labors were crowned by a posthumous edition of the plays of Terence (1651). The attention Farnaby gave to these Latin poets in his editions was not principally textual. He tended to use others' recensions, such as Daniel Heinsius's of Terence, *Pub. Terentii comoediae sex: ex recensione Heinsiana* (1618). Farnaby's talent lay in annotating these authors in order to help render them comprehensible to Renaissance schoolchildren, and it was for this reason that his works were widely printed. His annotations are sometimes, but not principally, rhetorical in nature.

Dates of first publication cannot adequately convey the significance of Farnaby's publications throughout the seventeenth century: all were reprinted at least once; the Juvenal and Persius went through eleven editions by 1689. Farnaby was modest about his scholarly capacities, as appears from a letter of 13 March 1618 to Barten Holyday that was printed in the posthumous 1673 publication of Holyday's English translation of Juvenal and Persius. Holyday's English translation of Persius alone had appeared in 1616, and Farnaby thanks him for the honor of having been mentioned among the other expositors who had shed light on the poems. He alludes to his early life and goes on to claim to have deserted the schoolroom for print only at the request of a stationer: "The unfortunate mispending of my younger and better years in Sea affairs, as one hoping and labouring never to be beholding to Scholarship, may not pretend any claim to learning." Holyday scarcely accepted these protestations, noting in his preface to the same work that "Mr. *Farnaby* (whose learned Industry speaks much for him in a little) procur'd me a fair Manuscript Copy from the famous Library at St. *James's*." Holyday is referring to the Royal Library, and

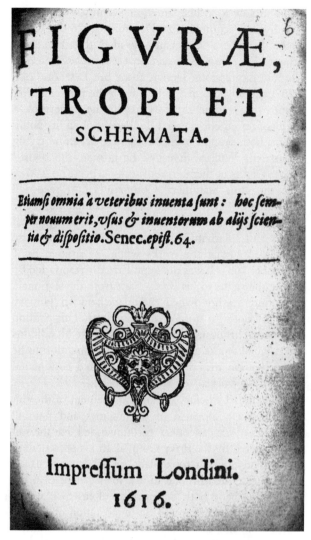

Title page for the only extant copy of the unauthorized edition of the work Farnaby published in 1625 as Index Rhetoricvs *(courtesy of The Trustees of the National Library of Scotland)*

Farnaby's access to it (probably through Patrick Young, the librarian) says something of the connections his school and his scholarship gave him. Farnaby's 1612 edition of Juvenal and Persius is dedicated to Prince Henry, the eldest son of James I, who died in the same year. His royal connections and sympathies continued throughout his life and were carried on through his eldest son, John, who was granted arms for his services to the royal family in 1664.

Farnaby's publishing success began to work against him, however. His school texts of classical authors, and latterly even his original publications, were extensively pirated on the Continent. Furthermore, these books were sufficiently cheap that it was economic for them to be imported back into England and sold there. This undercutting made Farnaby's printers unwilling to continue to bring out editions of his works in London. The situation eventually provoked Farnaby into action. On 26 December 1626 the Court of the Stationers' Company decided that Farnaby's rights to his *Phrases elegantiores ex optimis autoribus selectae* (Elegant Expressions Drawn from the Best Authors, 1625?) should be ceded to him from the printer Ralph Rounthwait; and in the early 1630s he undertook a more concerted effort to get the benefit of all his publications, both original and editorial. He began by trying to persuade William Stansby, the printer who owned the copyrights to them, to reprint his works: on 2 May 1631 the same Stationers' Company Court recorded that "This day Mr Farnaby came to complaine of Mr Stansbye for the not printing of Martiall and Juuenal and Persius." Farnaby's complaint produced a promise from Stansby that the works would be printed by 1 November 1631. It was not kept. Farnaby responded by buying the rights to his works back from the stationers and printers who owned them and, on 16 January 1632, presenting a suit to King Charles I. This petition emphasized his desire to amend and enlarge his editions and original works and pleaded for an inhibition to be imposed upon the importation of pirated continental copies of his works.

Charles I, "being," as an endorsement of the suit records, "well informed of the abilities and painfull endeavors of the peticõner," recommended that the suit be considered by the Privy Council. In his presentation to this body, which took place on 25 January 1632, Farnaby extended his suit to ask for a patent of privilege that forbade both the printing of his own works without his permission and the importation of printed copies from abroad. The lords of the Privy Council, "conceiuing a very good opinion of the peticõner, and of his sufficiencie in his profession," approved his suit and granted him these rights for the space of twenty-one years. In March of the same year the Signet Office docket books record payment of 6s. 8d. for the license signed by the king on the twenty-sixth of that month, which mandated forfeiture of stock as the punishment for anyone printing, importing, or selling Farnaby's works within the realms of England and Ireland without the author's permission. The patent that was the end-product of these procedures was enrolled on 16 April 1632. Farnaby would have received his own copy of the Letters Patent under the Great Seal to prove his legal right.

Farnaby immediately set about taking advantage of this right. Copies of his royal privilege are printed on the reverse of the title pages of the editions of *Index Rhetoricvs*, the Martial, and the Juvenal that were published in 1633. A year later he republished his edition of Seneca. The Privy Council submission had mentioned hitherto unpublished editions of Virgil and another work, *Index poeticus* (Poetical index); these were both published in 1634. The petition also referred to an edition of Petronius, a work described as "another booke of his owne entitled Orationes Ethicæ," and an edition of Aristotle's *Nicomachean Ethics,* none of which were ever published. There are suggestions, however, that Farnaby's legal endeavors were not entirely successful in preventing pirate editions: in the year of his death, 1647, the Cambridge University printer, Roger Daniel, was accused of printing an edition of *Index Rhetoricvs* with a false Lyon imprint.

It is likely that Farnaby initially composed *Index Rhetoricvs* for use by himself and his students in his London school. In the preface to the 1625 edition, Farnaby describes its genesis. Before his twentieth year, he says, he had produced a work on rhetorical schemes and tropes. This manuscript, however, was acquired by a "plagiarius quidam Bibliopola" (a certain plagiarist bookseller) and, Farnaby implies, printed without his permission. The pirate did not put Farnaby's name on the edition of *Figuræ, Tropi Et Schemata* (Figures, Tropes, and Schemes) that appeared in 1616, attributing the work to "T. F."; the edition is sufficiently rare that the *Short-Title Catalogue* lists only the copy in the National Library of Scotland. Two early references to Farnaby's rhetorical work attest to its circulation before the printing of the 1625 edition he eventually brought out in order to supersede this early illegitimate and uncorrected printing. In his *Logonomia Anglica* (The Science of the English Language, 1619), Alexander Gill the Elder, the high master of St. Paul's School in London, refers to Farnaby and quotes the definitions of the figures *polysyndeton* (frequent use of connectives such as *and*)and *synaeresis* (contraction of two vowels into one) that later appear in *Index Rhetoricvs.* A few years later, in his *A Consolation for Ovr Grammar Schooles* (1622), John Brinsley also mentions Farnaby's rules for the tropes and figures, "so shortly comprized in verse." These references, and the pirate printing, suggest that Farnaby's work was scribally published or at least circulated among fellow schoolmasters, a suggestion reinforced by the fact that Brinsley also cites the *Phrases elegantiores* before its first publication around 1625.

The *Index Rhetoricvs* is in form just that: an index to the art of rhetoric as treated by the classical and modern masters of the subject. In his preface, "Ad lectores" (To the readers), Farnaby describes the work as a "compendium" taken from the "greater and lesser fathers of this kind of art." Farnaby lists many of his sources in this preface and annotates the body of the work with extensive marginal references to these sources and to further reading. In its content the *Index Rhetoricvs,* like many rhetorical textbooks, is not particularly original. It is principally notable for its references to more than sixty Greek, Roman, late antique, medieval, and Renaissance sources and for its popularity. As Raymond Nadeau established in his 1950 doctoral dissertation, which remains the fullest study of the work, its main influences are the Dutch scholar Gerardus Joannes Vossius with respect to organization; the German philospher Bartholomew Keckermann in its treatment of tropes and figures; and Quintilian in the concluding section on practice. The prominence of an Aristotelian rather than a Ciceronian account of invention is also noteworthy.

In its first edition of 1625 the *Index Rhetoricvs* consists of a preface to its readers; synoptic tables outlining its organization and arguments; and sections on invention, on the three rhetorical *genera*–demonstrative, deliberative, and judicial–and on disposition. This last section is subdivided into discussions of the *exordium* (introduction), *narratio* (background information), *propositio* (position statement), *confirmatio* (supporting arguments), *amplificatio* (development), *confutatio* (refutation of opposing arguments), and *peroratio* (conclusion), which are followed by a separate section on *elocutio,* or style. The work proper ends with a short section on *pronunciatio* (delivery) and a rather more extended discussion of the importance of *exercitatio,* or practice, for attaining proficiency in the art. This final section of the slim octavo volume overran onto a fourth half-sheet, and in order that there should not be wasted empty pages at the end, Farnaby added four sides of commonplace headings suitable for constructing a memorandum book. These included such topics as *amicitia* (friendship), *brevitas* (brevity), and *novercae* (stepmothers). The second edition of 1629, a page-by-page reprint apart from the "Ad lectores," repeats the postscript and the excuse; but the enlarged and augmented third edition of 1633 makes a virtue of what had hitherto been a necessity and retains the commonplace heads despite the enlargement of the volume.

The third edition includes a new dedication to Dominic Molino, a Venetian senator; additional notes and textual corrections to the sections on *inventio* (discovery of matter) and *dispositio* (arrangement); further development of the section on tropes and figures, with added examples and references; and an extensive new second part, as long as the rest of the work itself, consisting of *formulae oratoriae* (oratorical formulas). These are set phrases intended to aid, much in the Erasmian way, in the development of copious discourse: topics covered include the handling of transitions, the citing of testimonies, excusing, and ridiculing. Some of them had first appeared in another collection of *formulae oratoriae* made by John Clarke in 1630; some again were to reappear in Thomas Horne's Χειραγωγία (Handbook, 1641). Editions of the *Index Rhetoricvs* from 1640 were

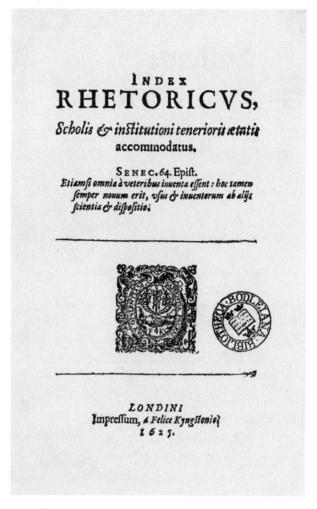

Title page for one of the most widely used seventeenth-century rhetorical textbooks (Bodleian Library, Oxford University)

also frequently printed with Farnaby's *Index poeticus*. Whereas the *Index Rhetoricvs* is a treatise in its own right, this little work literally is an index to words and phrases elegantly used by writers of Latin, and some neo-Latin, literature; it is notable for citing the poetry of Elizabeth Jane Weston among the latter.

Farnaby was a correspondent of some of the leading lights of Northern European scholarship and a friend of several well-known intellectuals of early Stuart England. He exchanged letters with Vossius, whose writings he often drew upon and praised; a typical letter finds them discussing difficulties in the interpretation of Martial. In none of this correspondence, however, do they discuss rhetoric. The Dutch scholar Daniel Heinsius, whose ideas on the nature of tragedy are so prominent in Ben Jonson's *Timber- or, Discoveries; Made Vpon Men and Matter* (1640), was also venerated by Farnaby: the preface to his edition of Seneca pays tribute to Heinsius, who in turn contributed a commendatory poem to the volume.

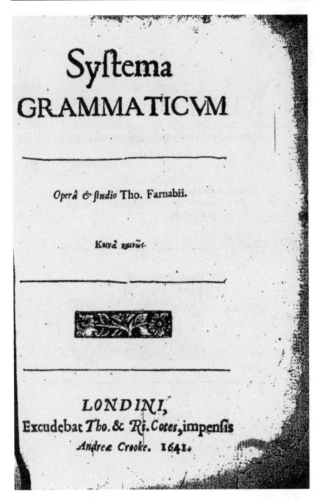

Systema
GRAMMATICVM

Operâ & studio Tho. Farnabii.

Κοινᾷ κριτῶς·

LONDINI,
Excudebat Tho. & Ri. Cotes, impensis
Andreæ Crooke. 1641.

Title page for the Latin grammar book that Farnaby prepared at the command of Charles I

Farnaby was an intimate, at least initially, of the historian and lawyer John Selden, with whom he corresponded about manuscript-hunting and who is highly praised in a note (subsequently excised) to the preface of the first two editions of the *Index Rhetoricus.* Farnaby acknowledges his debt in mastering the Greek Sophists and rhetoricians to Augustine Lindsell, the Greek scholar and later Bishop of Hereford. He was one of the sixty or so contributors of prefatory verses to Thomas Coryate's *Coryats Crudities Hastily gobled vp* (1611): in his English poem he indulges in a witty Hebrew pun about a monstrous wine barrel at Heidelberg described by Coryate. Prefatory verses by Farnaby encouraged the purchaser of John Harmar the Younger's *Ecloge Sententiarvm Et Similitvdinvm* (Selection of Sententine and Similitudes, 1622) to imitate the passages taken from Chrysostom, which, like Farnaby's own models in his Greek florilegium, *Η τῆς ἀνθολογίας Ανθολογία.* (1629), were intended as an aid to the learning of Greek. A figure poem in the shape of a column helped

prop up the 1627 portion of William Camden's *Annals.* He also contributed commendatory verses to William Alabaster's ranting neo-Latin tragedy *Roxana* (1632).

A longtime friend of Ben Jonson, he is described as "Farnabius meus" (my Farnaby) by Jonson in an inscription to a copy of Farnaby's edition of Martial that the playwright sent to Richard Brigges. Jonson contributed prefatory verses for both authors to Farnaby's edition of Juvenal and Persius and to his edition of Seneca, in which he praises Farnaby's talent for explicating his subjects. In turn, Farnaby acknowledges Jonson in the preface to his edition of Martial for having helped him with the volume and pays tribute to his deep learning in all poets, historians, manners, customs, and antiquities. This mutual regard appears ultimately to have led Farnaby into the indiscretion of lending Jonson money: a suit by Farnaby against Jonson on 4 December 1634 is recorded in a Petition Book from the Lord Chamberlain's department for the substantial sum of £120, which Jonson eventually paid.

In 1636 the machinations of his London landlord and the depredations of the plague combined to cause Farnaby to remove his school to his estate in Kent. He prospered there as previously and grew rich enough to buy another estate, near Horsham in Sussex. The date of Farnaby's first wife's death is not recorded, but by 1634 he was married for a second time, to Ann Howson, the daughter of John Howson, Bishop of Durham; they had two sons, Charles and Francis.

Farnaby's last original publication was the *Systema grammaticum* of 1641. He had received a special command from Charles I to compose a new Latin grammar that would be briefer and more useful than the aging but statutorily prescribed grammar by William Lily. Farnaby composed the work, and the king recommended it to the Privy Council, which in turn referred it to the masters of various public schools in and around London for trial and criticism. Farnaby incorporated these suggestions into his work, which was given its imprimatur on 28 July 1640 and published by June 1641; on 10 July 1641 Farnaby petitioned the House of Lords for legal permission for his grammar to be used by those who approved of it. While this grammar had the potential to be of some importance, political circumstances and a lukewarm reception by Farnaby's peers conspired against it, and it was never reprinted. With the epistle dedicatory, in which Farnaby commended the work to Vossius for his perusal and correction, he gave public form to a lifetime of admiration and emulation; like the *Index Rhetoricus,* the *Systema grammaticum* owes much to Vossius's publications.

When the English Civil Wars came, Farnaby's royal connections translated into active Royalist sympathies, and these made a ruin of his last years. When the

Protestation was urged in 1641 he apparently said that it was better to have one king than five hundred. Despite this position, he was appointed in 1643 by the House of Commons to be one of the licensees for their scheme of controlling book publication; his specific remit covered books of philosophy, history, poetry, morality, and arts. Later in the same year, however, there was a popular rising on behalf of the king around Tunbridge in Kent, and Farnaby was suspected by parliamentary forces of having favored it. He was imprisoned in Newgate Gaol and aboard a gaol ship. The same House of Commons that had appointed him now considered whether he should be transported to the American colonies, apparently encouraged in their deliberations by some of his neighboring Kentish landowners who were desirous of his estates, and even some of his former pupils in Parliament. This harsh punishment did not come to pass, however, and instead he was imprisoned in Ely House in Holborn, where he was kept until 1645. At the time of his release, Farnaby was working on a new set of annotations to the plays of Terence, until (as Meric Casaubon wrote of him) the thread of his writing and of his life were broken together. Left unfinished at his death, his notes were completed by Casaubon and published in 1651. Farnaby died on 12 June 1647 at the age of seventy-two and was buried in the chancel of the church at Sevenoaks.

Farnaby's works are extensively recommended by Charles Hoole in *A New Discovery of the Old Art of Teaching Schoole* (1660), a book that perhaps gives the fullest impression of what Farnaby's teaching methods may have been like. Hoole recommends Farnaby's *Systema grammaticum* for the fourth form, his epigrams and *Phrases elegantiores* for the fifth form, his annotated editions of the Latin poets for the sixth form, and several portions of the *Index Rhetoricus*: the tropes and figures, the commonplace headings, and the *formulae oratoriae*. The *Index Rhetoricus* is also recorded as being among the few books known to have been used in early New England grammar schools and slightly later at Harvard. In the year of Farnaby's death the noted royalist publisher Richard Royston brought out an edition of the figures and tropes from the *Index Rhetoricus* compiled by Thomas Stephens. Like that work and its companion, the *Index poeticus,* this unauthorized *Troposchematologia* was reprinted several times to the end of the century. It was itself copied by John Stirling for his *A System of Rhetoric, in a Method Entirely New: Containing All the Tropes and Figures* (1733), a shortened version of Stephens's work. The Latin definitions of schemes and tropes in John Smith's *The Mysterie of Rhetorique Unvail'd* (1657) are taken verbatim and seriatim from Farnaby. The last full working edition of the *Index Rhetoricus* was published in 1768, under the title *Farnaby Illustrated: or, the Latin Text of Farnaby's Rhetoric Exemplified, by Various Passages, from the Sacred Scriptures; the Roman Classics; and the Most Distinguished British Authors. For the Use of Schools.* Like the other versions and editions that escaped authorial control, this edition is an indication of the pervasive popularity and flexibility of Farnaby's rhetorical treatise in particular, and of the Renaissance rhetorical tradition in general.

Letters:

Gerardus Joannes Vossius, *Gerardi Joannis Vossii Et Clarorum Virorum Ad Eum Epistolae. Collectore Paulo Colomesio Ecclesiae Anglicanae Presbytero. Opus omnibus Philologiae & Ecclesiasticae Antiquitatis Studiosis utilissimum,* 2 parts (London: Printed by R. R. and M. C. for A. Mill, 1690), part 2, pp. 71–78, 85–86, 212–213, 302–303.

Bibliographies:

M. A. Shauber, *Check-List of Works of British Authors Printed Abroad, in Languages Other than English, to 1641* (New York: Bibliographic Society of America, 1975), p. 69;

Heinrich F. Plett, *English Renaissance Rhetoric and Poetics: A Systematic Bibliography of Primary and Secondary Sources* (Leiden & New York: E. J. Brill, 1995), pp. 33–35, 104–105, 133, 193.

Biography:

Anthony à Wood, "Thomas Farnabie," in *Athenae Oxonienses, an exact history of all the writers and bishops who have had their education in the University of Oxford,* edited by Philip Bliss, 4 volumes (London: J. Rivington, 1813–1820), III: columns 213–216.

References:

T. W. Baldwin, *William Shakspere's Small Latine and Lesse Greeke,* 2 volumes (Urbana: University of Illinois Press, 1944);

J. W. Binns, *Intellectual Culture in Elizabethan and Jacobean England: The Latin Writings of the Age* (Leeds: Francis Cairns, 1990);

Sir John Bramston, *The Autobiography of Sir John Bramston,* Camden Society Publications, no. 32 (London: Printed for the Camden Society by J. B. Nichols and Son, 1845);

Donald Lemen Clark, *John Milton at St. Paul's School: A Study of Ancient Rhetoric in English Renaissance Education* (New York: Columbia University Press, 1948);

Anne Fanshawe, *Memoirs of Lady Fanshawe, wife of Sir Richard Fanshawe, Bart. Ambassador from Charles the Second to the Courts of Portugal and Madrid. Written by Herself. With Extracts from the Correspondence of Sir*

Richard Fanshawe (London: Henry Colburn & Richard Bentley, 1829);

Harris F. Fletcher, *The Intellectual Development of John Milton, Volume 2: The Cambridge University Period, 1625–1632* (Urbana: University of Illinois Press, 1961);

Edward Hasted, *The History and Topographical Survey of the County of Kent. Containing the antient and present state of it, civil and ecclesiastical; collected from public records, and other authorities,* second edition, 12 volumes (Canterbury, U.K.: Printed by W. Bristow, 1797–1801);

Wilber Samuel Howell, *Logic and Rhetoric in England, 1500–1700* (Princeton: Princeton University Press, 1956);

Arnold Hunt, "Book Trade Patents, 1603–1640," in *The Book Trade and Its Customers, 1450–1900: Historical Essays for Robin Myers,* edited by Hunt, Giles Mandelbrote, and Alison Shell (Winchester, U.K.: St. Paul's Bibliographies / New Castle, Del.: Oak Knoll, 1997), pp. 27–54;

Raymond Nadeau, "The *Index Rhetoricus* of Thomas Farnaby," dissertation, University of Michigan, 1950;

Nadeau, "Oratorical Formulas in Seventeenth-Century England," *Quarterly Journal of Speech,* 38 (1952): 149–154;

Nadeau, "A Renaissance Schoolmaster on Practice," *Speech Monographs,* 17 (1950): 171–179;

Nadeau, "Talaeus Versus Farnaby on Style," *Speech Monographs,* 21 (1954): 59–63;

Nadeau, "Thomas Farnaby: Schoolmaster and Rhetorician of the English Renaissance," *Quarterly Journal of Speech,* 36 (1950): 340–344;

C. S. M. Rademaker, *Life and Work of Gerardus Joannes Vossius (1577–1649)* (Assen: Van Gorcum, 1981);

William P. Sandford, "English Rhetoric Reverts to Classicism, 1600–1650," *Quarterly Journal of Speech,* 15 (1929): 503–525;

Foster Watson, "A Great Private Schoolmaster," *Journal of Education* (January 1895): 63–65.

Papers:

Thomas Farnaby's complaints about Ralph Rounthwait and William Stansby are in the Stationers' Company, Court Book "C," fols 94r and 112v. The initial suit to the King of 16 January 1632 is in the Public Record Office, SP 16/210/35. The record of the referral of the suit to the Privy Council of 25 January 1632 is PRO, PC 2/41, pp. 362–363. The Signet Office docket book recording Farnaby's payment is PRO, SO 3/10, under March 1632. The Sign Manual of Charles I granting the license is PRO, SP 39/30/91. The enrolled patent is PRO, C 66/2596/17. Ben Jonson's debt to Farnaby is recorded in PRO, LC 5/183, fol. 151r. Farnaby's correspondence with Gerardus Joannes Vossius is in the Bodleian Library, Oxford, among MSS Rawlinson Letters 83 and 84.

Dudley Fenner
(1558? – 1587?)

Stephen Collins
Northwestern University

BOOKS: *An Ansvvere Vnto The Confvtation Of Iohn Nichols his Recantation, in all pointes of any weight conteyned in the same: Especially in the matters of Doctrine, of Purgatorie, Images, the Popes honor, and the question of the Church* (London: Printed by John Wolfe for John Harrison and Thomas Manne, 1583);

The Artes Of Logike And Rethorike, plainelie set foorth in the Englishe tounge, easie to be learned and practised: togeather with examples for the practise of the same, for Methode in the gouerment of the familie, prescribed in the word of God: And for the whole in the resolution or opening of certaine partes of Scripture, according to the same (N.p., 1584)—includes *The order of Housholde, described methodicallie out of the worde of God, with the contrarie abuses found in the worlde; The resolution and interpretation of the Lords prayer, out of Mat. 6.9 and Luke. 11.2;* and *The Epistle to Philemon;*

A Covnter-poyson, Modestly written for the time, to make aunswere to the obiections and reproches, wherewith the aunswerer to the Abstract, would disgrace the holy Discipline of Christ, attributed to Fenner (London: Printed by Robert Waldergraue, 1584);

A Booke of the forme of common prayers, administration of the sacraments: &c. agreeable to Gods worde, and the use of the reformed churches, attributed to Fenner (London, 1585?);

Sacra Theologia, Sive Veritas quæ est secundum Pietatem, Ad Vnicæ et veræ methodi leges descripta, & in decem libros per Dvdleivm Fennervm digesta (London: Printed by T. Dawson, 1585?);

A Defence Of the godlie Ministers, against the slaunders of D. Bridges, contayned in his answere to the Preface before the Discourse of Ecclesiasticall gouernement, with a Declaration of the Bishops proceeding against them. Wherein chieflie, 1 The lawfull authoritie of her Maiestie is defended by the Scriptures, her lawes, and authorised interpretation of them, to be the same which we haue affirmed, against his cauilles and slaunders to the contrarie. 2 The lawfull refusinge also of the Ministers to subscribe, is maintayned by euident groundes of Gods worde, and her Maiesties lawes, against his euident wresting of both. 3 Lastlie, the

forme of Church-gouernement, which we propounde, is according to his demaunde Sillogisticallie proued to be ordinarie, perpetuall, and the best, attributed to Fenner (Middelburg: Richard Schilders, 1587);

The Groundes of Religion necessarie to be knowen of euery one that may be admitted to the Supper of the Lord (Middelburg: Printed by Richard Schilders, 1587);

A Short and profitable Treatise, of lavvfull and vnlavvfull Recreations, and the right vse and abuse of those that are lawefull (Middelburg: Printed by Richard Schilders, 1587);

The Song of Songs, that is, the most excellent song which was Solomons, translated out of the Hebrue into Englishe meeter, VVith as little libertie in departing from the wordes, as any plaine translation in prose can vse: and interpreted by a short commentarie (Middelburg: Printed by Richard Schilders, 1587);

The VVhole doctrine of the Sacramentes, plainlie and fullie set dovvne and declared out of the word of God. Written by Maister Dvdley Fenner, and nowe published for the vse of the Church of God (Middelburg: Printed by Richard Schilders, 1588);

A brief Treatise vpon the first Table of the Lavve, orderly disposing the principles of Religion, whereby we may examine our selues. Written by Maister Dvdley Fenner, Minister of the Gospell (Middelburg: Printed by Richard Schilders, 1588?);

Certain Godly And Learned treatises Written by that worthie Minister of Christe, M. Dvdley Fenner; for the behoofe and edification of al those that desire to grovv and increase in true Godlines. The Titles Whereof, are set downe in the Page following (Edinburgh: Printed by Robert Waldegraue, 1592)—includes *The Order of Houshold gouernment, described out of the word of God, with the contrarie abuses found in the world; The Resolvtion and Interpretation of the Lordes praier, out of Math. 6. 9. And Luke 11. 2; An Interpretation vpon the Epistle to Philemon; A short and Plaine Table, orderly disposing and Principles of Religion, and first, of the first Table of the Law, wherby we may examine our selues; The Whole Doctrine of the Sacraments, plainlie and fullie set downe, and declared out of the word of God;* and *A Short and Profitable Treatise of lawful and vnlawfull recreations, and of the right vse and abuse of those that are lawfull;*

A parte of a register, contayninge sundrie memorable matters, written by diuers godly and learned in our time, which stande for, and desire the reformation of our Church, in Discipline and Ceremonies, according to the pure worde of God, and the Lawe of our Lande, attributed to Fenner (Middelburg: Richard Schilders, 1593?)–includes *A Covnter-Poyson, Modestly written for the time; Master Dudley Fenners Defence of the godlie Ministers against D. Bridge's slaunders;* and *A Defence of the reasons of the Covnter Poyson* [sometimes attributed to Fenner].

Editions: *The Art Of Rhetorick Plainly set forth: With Pertinent Examples for the more easie understanding, and Practice of the same. By a concealed Author,* in *A Compendium Of the Art of Logick And Rhetorick in the English Tongue. Containing All that Peter Ramus, Aristotle, and Others have writ thereon: With Plaine Directions for the more easie understanding and practice of the same* (London: Printed by Thomas Maxey, 1651), pp. 283–323;

The Art Of Rhetorick Plainly set forth; with Pertinent Examples For the more easie understanding and Practice of the same. By Tho. Hobbes, of Malmsbury, in *The Art Of Rhetoric, With A Discourse Of The Laws of England. By Thomas Hobbes of Malmesbury* (London: Printed for William Crooke, 1681), pp. 135–168;

"The Art of Rhetoric" and "The Art of Sophistry," in *The English Works of Thomas Hobbes of Malmesbury,* 11 volumes, edited by William Molesworth (London: John Bohn, 1839–1845), VI: 511–536;

"Solomon's Song. Chapter IV," excerpt from *The Song of Songs,* in *Select Poetry, Chiefly Devotional of The Reign of Queen Elizabeth,* 2 volumes, edited by Edward Farr (Cambridge: Cambridge University Press, 1845), II: 341–343;

The Epistle to Philemon, in *Shakespeare's Use of the Arts of Language,* by Sister Miriam Joseph (New York: Columbia University Press, 1947), pp. 349–353;

The Artes of Logike and Rethorike, in *Four Tudor Books on Education,* edited by Robert D. Pepper (Gainesville, Fla.: Scholars' Facsimiles & Reprints, 1966), pp. 143–180;

A Parte of a Register, contayninge sundrie memorable matters, The English Experience, no. 509 (Amsterdam: Theatrum Orbis Terrarum; New York: De Capo, 1973);

A Counter-poyson, The English Experience, no. 735 (Amsterdam: Theatrum Orbis Terrarum; Norwood, N.J.: W. J. Johnson, 1975);

Treatise of Lawfull and Unlawfull Recreations (1590), The English Experience, no. 870 (Amsterdam: Theatrum Orbis Terrarum; Norwood, N.J.: W. J. Johnson, 1977);

Thomas Martin Walsh, "A Sixteenth Century Translation of Ramus and of Talaeus: Dudley Fenner's 'The Artes of Logike and Rethorike': An Edition and Study," dissertation, Saint Louis University, 1978.

Dudley Fenner was a Cambridge-educated Puritan divine known for his vocal disagreement with the Anglican Church and its policies. He wrote *The Artes Of Logike And Rethorike* in 1584, and though Roland MacIlmaine's *The Logike of the Moste Excellent Philosopher P. Ramus, Martyr* (1574) precedes it by ten years, Fenner's work distinguishes itself as the first combined English translation and adaptation of both the logic of Pierre de La Ramée (known as Petrus Ramus) and the rhetoric of Omer Talon. Fenner's integrated treatment of both logic and rhetoric was the first Ramistic effort in England to compete against the earlier integrated Ciceronian treatment of logic and rhetoric in Thomas Wilson's *The Rule of Reason* (1551) and *The Arte of Rhetorique* (1553). The work has received little scholarly attention, even though it appeared in seven editions over almost one hundred years (four times anonymously in 1584, once in 1588 with attribution to Fenner, once in 1651 with attribution to "a concealed Author," and once in 1681 with a mistaken attribution to Thomas Hobbes). The rhetoric additionally comprised a significant portion of John Smith's *The Mysterie of Rhetorique Unveil'd,* which went through at least eleven editions from 1657 to 1739.

Dudley Fenner was born in Kent circa 1558 to unknown parents of some wealth and went on to matriculate as a fellow commoner of Peterhouse at Cambridge on 15 June 1575. He may have known and attended the lectures of the Ramists Gabriel Harvey or Laurence Chaderton while at Cambridge, a connection that would help explain his commitment to Ramistic pedagogy throughout his life. He also began an association with Thomas Cartwright during this time–though quite likely not at the university proper–and as a result of this fellowship with Cartwright, who had been forced to leave the university in 1570 because of a series of lectures he gave espousing presbyterian government, Fenner left Cambridge before receiving his degree. He became a minister at Cranbrook Church in Kent under Richard Fletcher, vicar of Cranbrook, although his episcopal ordination is not a matter of certainty. Soon dissatisfied with the episcopal order in England, he followed Cartwright to Antwerp, where he possibly renounced his former ordination and was ordained as a minister of the reformed churches in the Netherlands. He stayed in Antwerp for several years working with

Cartwright and while there married a woman whose name is unknown.

Fenner returned to Kent in the spring of 1583 after the death of John Stroud, curate of Cranbrook Church, possibly reassured by a recent degree of tolerance afforded Puritans under the purview of Edmund Grindal, Archbishop of Canterbury, and became a minister at Cranbrook in July of the same year. A record of baptism for the church in the same year reveals that he had a son by the name of "More Fruit Fenner." The tolerance for Puritans faded later that same year with the death of Grindal and the appointment of John Whitgift as the new archbishop. Whitgift soon insisted that all members of the clergy universally accept three articles of conformity, a subscription that was unacceptable to many dedicated Puritans. Fenner and sixteen of his fellow ministers from Kent petitioned the archbishop in January 1584, declaring that they could not in good conscience subscribe to the articles and seeking some form of favorable license. Whitgift's response was to suspend them. Fenner was arrested for his nonconformity soon afterward and spent about a year in jail. Upon subscription to the articles, he was granted his freedom and made his way back to the Netherlands with his family and a new daughter, named perhaps hopefully "Faint Not Fenner." He remained in Middleburg, ministering to the English Merchant Adventurers in the reformed church until his death.

Conjectures as to the year of Fenner's death range from 1587 to 1589, but the evidence supplied by his publications suggests 1587 as the most likely date. An edition recorded in *A parte of a register, contayninge sundrie memorable matters* (1593), for example, specifies the date in its subtitle: *Master Dudley Fenners Defence of the godlie Ministers against D. Bridge's slaunders; with a True Report of the ill-dealings of the Bishops against them, written a month before his Death, Anno. 1587.* The *Dictionary of National Biography* suggests that Fenner's apparently unfulfilled promise to complete a translation of the Lamentations of Jeremiah, made in the dedication "To the right worshipfull companie of the Marchant aduenturers" in his 1587 *The Song of Songs, that is, the most excellent song which was Solomons, translated out of the Hebrue into Englishe meeter,* supports a death date of that year. The 1592 printing of *Certain Godly And Learned treatises Written by that worthie Minister of Christe, M. Dvdley Fenner* recounts in the dedicatory epistle that "Dvdley Fenner was one, whome the Church of God in this age could haue hardliest spared: he ended his testimonie in this life, being vnder thirtie yeares of age," which would put the date of his death before 1588. Perhaps what speaks even more to his probable death in 1587 is the publishing record of *The Artes Of Logike And Rethorike,* which shows four editions printed anonymously in 1584 and then a fifth edition

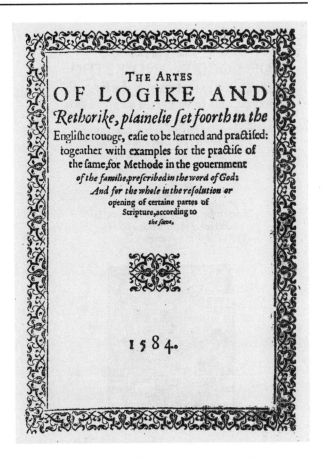

Title page for the work in which Dudley Fenner adapted Ramist logic and Talonist rhetoric for use in the Puritan cause

with Fenner's name affixed to the title page in 1588, suggesting that the author no longer needed to worry about his anonymity. Fenner's works published after 1587 are either reprints or indicate an earlier date of authorship, with a single exception; the new work, published in 1588, includes a cryptic note in its title that suggests Fenner may have been dead at the time of publication: *The VVhole doctrine of the Sacramentes, plainlie and fullie set dovvne and declared out of the word of God. Written by Maister Dvdley Fenner, and nowe published for the vse of the Church of God.*

Fenner's best-known work, *The Artes Of Logike And Rethorike, plainelie set foorth in the Englishe tounge, easie to be learned and practised: togeather with examples for the practise of the same, for Methode in the gouernment of the familie, prescribed in the word of God: And for the whole in the resolution or opening of certaine partes of Scripture, according to the same* (1584), is the only book he wrote not dealing explicitly with Puritan theology. The volume incorporating *The Artes Of Logike And Rethorike* actually comprises three additional works, including *The order of Housholde, described methodicallie out of the worde of God, with the contrarie abuses found in the worlde* as well as *The resolution and interpretation*

119

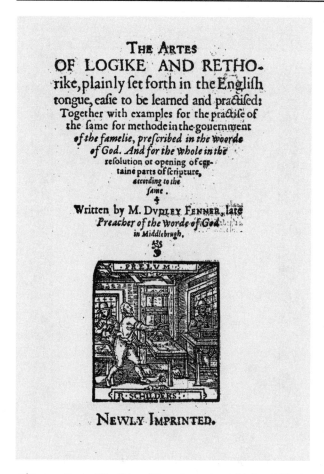

*Title page for the fifth edition of Fenner's popular and influential book,
the first edition to include his name on the title page*

make them more efficient in their functioning. This strict separation of the arts meant that logic and rhetoric could not deal with the same subjects but must instead complement each other. Whereas the classical tradition had treated rhetoric as a system of five canons—invention, arrangement (or judgment), elocution, memory, and delivery—Ramism separated invention, arrangement, and memory from rhetoric and brought them under the purview of logic, leaving rhetoric without any claim to the topical and syllogistic creation of persuasive appeals and their apt ordering; rhetoric, instead, became only an art of elocution and delivery, of decoration and embellishment.

Fenner's work on Ramistic logic, thus, is divided into one book on invention and a second on judgment. His discussion of invention illustrates well the Ramistic tendency toward bifurcation in the discussion of each art. Invention, for instance, is divided into two types of reason, the first and that which arises out of the first; the first type of reason is divided into uncompared arguments—"Men in earth"—and compared arguments—"Thy will be donen in earth, as it is in heauen." Compared arguments are further divided into agreeable—"Love suffereth long"—and disagreeable sorts—"Love enuieth not." The agreeable sort, in turn, is split into the more agreeable and the less agreeable, and the more agreeable are then broken into those arguments dealing with cause and those with effect. The arguments dealing with cause are divided into the making or efficient cause and others within the thing caused—its matter and form. Those reasons that "arise of the first," noted above, are divided into reasons more artificial and less artificial; the more artificial are divided into reasons of division and definition, with division further splitting into the more agreeable and less agreeable while definition breaks into the perfect and the imperfect.

Fenner's book on judgment breaks down the ordering of reasons into "one sentence, called an axiome," and more than one sentence or "moe axiomes." Under "moe axiomes," he identifies both the syllogism and the method. These three tools of the logician, the "axiome," the syllogism, and the method, all work as bifurcating aids in analyzing any matter: "For as we consider in an axiome truth or falshood, in a Sillogisme, necessary following or not following, so in Methode the best and perfectest, the worst and troublesomest way to handle a matter." Fenner describes this characteristic "methode" of Ramism as an ordering that continues until a whole matter is fully understood: "Methode is the iudgement of more axiomes, whereby many and diuers axiomes being framed according to the properties of an axiome perfectly or exactly iudged, are so ordered as that the easiest and most generall be set downe first, the harder and lesse

of the Lords prayer, out of Mat. 6.9 and Luke 11.2 and *The Epistle to Philemon.* As the full title indicates, the latter three works are "examples for the practise" of logic and rhetoric supplied by Fenner. The first two works in the volume, the logic and rhetoric, respectively, closely follow the format found in Ramus's *Dialecticae libri duo* (Dialectic in Two Books, 1572) and Talaeus's *Audomari Talaei Rhetorica e Petri Rami praelectionibus observata* (Audemorus Talaeus's Rhetoric Conformed to Petras Ramus's Explanations, 1572), as Thomas Martin Walsh pointed out in his unpublished dissertation, "A Sixteenth Century Translation of Ramus and of Talaeus: Dudley Fenner's 'The Artes of Logike and Rethorike': An Edition and Study" (1978). Unlike Ramus and Talaeus, Fenner did not embellish the logic and rhetoric with classical illustrations but rather with biblical quotations and Puritan sententiae.

The academic reform brought about by Ramus and, to a lesser degree, his associate Talaeus differed from the classical and scholastic views of academia popular at the time. Ramistic educational reform sought to compartmentalize the liberal arts in order to generall next, vntill the whole matter be so conueied, as all the partes may best agree with themselues, and be best kept in memorie."

Fenner's rhetoric is divided into two parts, the first dealing with the "garnishing of speech, called Eloquution," while the second, "the garnishing of the maner of vtterance, called Pronunciation," was not translated by Fenner, since he believed that the Ramistic treatment was still imperfect: "it is not yet perfect (for the preceptes for the most part pertaine to an Oratour) which when it shalbe perfect, it shall eyther only conteine common preceptes for the garnishing of vtterance in all, or also proper preceptes for the same in Magistrates, Ambassadours, Captaines, and Ministers, therefore vntill it be so perfected, we think it vnnecessarie to be translated into English." Fenner, then, only discussed the precepts of elocution, which consisted mainly of explicating many different tropes and figures and illustrating each with one or more biblical or moral examples: "The change of name or Metonymie, where the subiect or that which hath any thing adioined, is put for the thing adioined or adioynt. So *the place is put for those or that in the place. Set thine house in an order,* that is, thy household matters. . . ."

There are a few key distinctions in Fenner's logic and rhetoric that make it distinct from the work of Ramus and Talaeus and that of another Ramist in England, Abraham Fraunce, who published *A Lawier's Logike* and *The Arcadian Rhetorike* in 1588. Fenner's logic, for instance, instead of discussing arguments as artificial and nonartificial or artistic and inartistic, classifies them as "more artificiall" or "lesse artificiall." Additionally, Fenner simplifies the Ramistic presentation of the four causes—the final, the formal, the efficient, and the material—by collapsing the final and efficient causes into a single heading and the formal and material causes into another, in order to show that each pairing shared a privileged connection. As he notes, the formal and material causes are those that are "within the thing, are those causes whiche are always inseparablie remaining together for the being of the thing." The final and efficient causes are both inextricably linked, as God (an efficient cause) is to God's will (a final cause). Fenner offers a useful example emphasizing the role of faith in an individual's salvation in order to clarify the associations made between these several causes:

> The thing caused, is that which is by the whole force of all the causes. As *So GOD loued the worlde as hee gaue his only begotten sonne, that whosoeuer beleeueth in him shoulde not perishe, but haue eternal life.* Where our happinesse is the thing caused: the loue of GOD, and faith the efficient cause. Christ the materiall cause, and eternall life.

This sense of Christ as the material manipulated by faith in order to guarantee happiness in the form of eternal life illustrates the strong sense of Puritanism infused into Fenner's work.

Fenner's rhetoric makes its distinction as noted above by not addressing the canon of pronunciation or delivery that is typically included in the Ramistic system of rhetoric, a discussion that is found in Fraunce's *The Arcadian Rhetorike,* for instance. Fenner, additionally, does not cite classical authors in abundance, as Fraunce does, to illustrate his theory. Moreover, Fenner's rhetoric is distinct for its inclusion of a section dealing with deception or "sophistrie," "the feined art of Elenches, or coloured reasons" where a "colourable reason, or Elenche, is a shewe of reason to deceiue withall." As Walter J. Ong noted in "Hobbes and Talon's Ramist Rhetoric in English" (1951), such a section on sophistry was far from a Ramistic idea: it was "a non-Ramist business indeed, for good Ramism was itself proof against error and felt no need to stoop to study deceptions in order to conquer them. But even in this treatise Fenner courts consistency in a self-conscious explanatory note and a brave effort to expose sophistry in Ramist terminology."

The additional titles found in Fenner's *The Artes Of Logike And Rethorike,* which are not explicitly theories of logic or rhetoric, have received little attention from scholars even though they integrate well into the compilation as a whole. Robert D. Pepper, in the introduction to *Four Tudor Books on Education* (1966), has argued that although the five books were probably written at the same time, there is no reason to believe that Fenner intended them to be published in one volume; instead, it was possibly the act of an independently minded printer, Richard Schilders: "he seems to have left it up to the printer to publish them as he saw fit. During this period an author usually had nothing to do with the title-page of his book, and Schilders' decision to combine the five treatises was perhaps an afterthought." The inclusion, however, of one work dealing with Puritan precepts for a better life, *The order of Housholde,* and two Ramistic explications of Scripture, *The resolution and interpretation of the Lords prayer* and *The Epistle to Philemon,* suggests that Fenner offered them as extended examples of Ramist logic and rhetoric in practice.

The order of Housholde describes the proper duties and precepts for life in a Christian household, exhibiting in the discussion of each duty or instruction the typical two-fold structure. The tract opens with a discussion of order in the household:

> The order of an Housholde called Oiconomia, is an order for the gouernement of the matters of an housholde, according to the worde of God. . . .

Nowe the wisedome meant in this booke is that which is allowed of Gods word: especially when he ioyneth such blessing vnto it. The housholde order hath two partes, The first of these which concerne the gouernours of the famies. The seconde of those which are gouerned in the same.

1. Tim 5.8. *If one care not for his owne, especiallie those of his house:* whiche sheweth an especiall rule of mutual duetie betweene these two.

As the tract continues Fenner proceeds to bifurcate each precept: "Of the dueties of orderinge the houshold, by the chiefe of the same: There are 2. sortes, The first regardeth those in the houshold. The other, straungers or guestes comminge into the same. . . . Nowe both of these are in regarde of [1.] Christian holines. [2.] The things of this life." Further on in the tract Fenner delineates the two-fold duties of the wife: "The matters of this life are, her labour: [1.] In regard of her family. And [2.] her owne worke."

The resolution and interpretation of the Lords prayer, out of Mat. 6. 9. and Luke 11. 2 shows the same predictable two-fold division; Fenner uses this structure to teach his audience how to read texts. Fenner instructs readers, for instance, how to analyze the petitions made within the Lord's Prayer:

The petitions are of two sortes, The firste which beggeth concerning God only in the first place, as the place and end of euery request sheweth. The second which require concerning our selues. . . .

The first sorte also is double, First for the right vse of Gods name. The second for Christes kingdome, and the fruit of it, as the Apostle willeth to pray that the woorde haue passage, and be glorified. 2. Thes. 3.1.

The first is set downe in a simple axiome of the adioint *hallowed,* and the subiect *thy name,* coupled by the forme of praying or desiringe, vttered by vs in the word *bee:* where sanctified is a Metaphore or fines of speache noting a comparison taken from thinges dedicated to God or the Temple, & signifieth that Gods name, (one kind being put for the whole by a Sinechdoche, the titles, which is, his name & memorial wherby he is known for his works, word, Sacraments, and mysteries, &c.) be put apart from all prophane abuses, vnto the right vse prescribed in the third commaundement. . . .

The tract continues by looking at the second sort of petition as well as even further divisions and continues to analyze the text in a clear, Ramistic manner.

Similarly, *The Epistle to Philemon* advances the Ramistic reading technique from its opening line: "The entrance of this Epistle hath 2. parts, [1.] The inscription or title./ [2.] Prayers. The inscription setteth downe [1.] The persons which do writte. [2.] The persons to who it is written."

These two-fold classifications, as well as the discussion of "axiomes" and "adioynts," show Fenner integrating his theory of logic into his discussion of metaphor and "Sinechdoche"—both matters of rhetoric—in a manner designed to instruct readers in the use of these two arts. As Sister Miriam Joseph has observed in her landmark study, *Shakespeare's Use of the Arts of Language* (1947), quoting *The Epistle to Philemon* in its near entirety, "the complete Ramist technique of reading, which combines logic and rhetoric, is exemplified in the analysis of Saint Paul's Epistle to Philemon with which Dudley Fenner concludes his work on *The Artes of Logike and Rhetorike*. In this analysis Fenner appears in a three-fold role as a logician exemplifying his precepts; as a rhetorician illustrating the figures; as a Puritan minister of the Gospel elucidating Holy Scripture by the enthusiastic application of the arts of reading."

Indeed, separating Fenner's Ramism from his Puritanism in any of his other works is not only ill advised but also rather futile. From his beginnings as a writer, Fenner had closely connected the two. His *A brief Treatise vpon the first Table of the Lavve, orderly disposing the principles of Religion, whereby we may examine our selues*—printed posthumously in about 1588 but identified in the preface as his earliest work, written before he was twenty years of age—shows the ready integration of his religious beliefs with his Ramistic leanings:

To obtaine Christ 2 meanes are ordained. The Lawe & [the] Gospell preached. . . . By these two Instrumentes the holy Ghost worketh . . . two things necessarie to be in vs for the obtayning of Christ. . . . By the first, *a* a true knowledge and feeling of sinne, & the punishment due to the same, *b* whiche maketh vs seeke Christe. . . . By the second, *a* a true knowledge and feeling of grace, *b* with power by faith to receyue Christ.

Fenner's close intertwining of both his Puritanism and his Ramism not only illustrates how he used each to facilitate an understanding of the other, but also how his logic and rhetoric played an important part in his radicalism as a Puritan; *The Artes Of Logike And Rethorike* was published at a time of great controversy in Fenner's life, in which he wrote openly scathing tracts critical of the Anglican Church, published by printers known for their antagonism toward the established religion in England. In 1584 Fenner was embroiled in a critical attack against the church over Archbishop Whitgift's newly created articles of conformity designed to force Puritans to conform to precepts dictated by the established church. Although the authorship is not completely certain, he likely wrote *A Covnter-poyson, Modestly written for the time, to make aunswere to the obiections and reproches, wherewith the aunswerer to the Abstract, would disgrace the holy Discipline of Christ* (1584), a defense of William

Stoughton's *An abstract, of certaine acts of Parlement* (1583) and a response to Richard Cosin's *An answer to the two first and principall treatises of a certeine factious libell* (1584). Written in the same year that Fenner petitioned the archbishop not to enforce the articles of conformity and the same year in which Fenner was arrested for his nonconformity, this tract is likely the reason for his imprisonment; its preface, "A Faithfull Brother to the Christian Reader," clearly illustrates the acerbic nature of the work:

> . . . the common enemy to the state and Church of God among vs, hath very villanously and traiterously, vovved himselfe, to put out the happy light of this most peaceable kingdome, euen by desperate and slauishe bloud-suckers. . . . you ye reuerend fathers, which take vpon you to rule the sterne of God his ship, to your consciences be it appealed, whether you thrust not out of your brethren, faithful & skilful mariners, nourishing the idle & vnfit. . . . You after many molestations and vexations of your brethren, euen to the turning avvay of many good schollers, godly affected, from the study of diuinity, haue at the length contrary to al lavv of God and man, offered violence to the consciences of your brethren, by a forced subscription. . . .

Fenner had published a year earlier *An Ansvvere Vnto The Confutation Of Iohn Nichols his Recantation, in all pointes of any weight conteyned in the same: Especially in the matters of Doctrine, of Purgatorie, Images, the Popes honor, and the question of the Church,* which came out in support of John Nichols's published recantation, *A declaration of the recantation of J. Nichols, for the space of almost two yeeres, the popes scholar in the English seminarie at Rome,* and against *A discoverie of J. Nicols minister* (1581), an attack on Nichols by the Jesuit Robert Persons. He had proven himself to be a man willing to attack the Roman Catholic Church. With the publication of *A Covnter-poyson,* however, Fenner demonstrated to his fellow Englishmen that he was not just an anti-papist, but also a sharp critic of the prelates of the Anglican Church.

The choices of Robert Waldegrave in London as printer for *A Counter-poyson* and Richard Schilders in Middleburg, Zealand (the Netherlands), for *The Artes Of Logike And Rethorike* also testify to the radical environment of which Fenner's logic and rhetoric were a part. As J. Dover Wilson argued in "Richard Schilders and the English Puritans" (1910–1911), Fenner could not have associated himself with two more controversial printers; beginning in the 1580s, the Puritans turned to one of these two men whenever they had anything dangerous to print. The fact that both works were published anonymously by Fenner indicates that he was probably quite aware of the effect their Puritan agenda would have on the English establishment. His anonymity

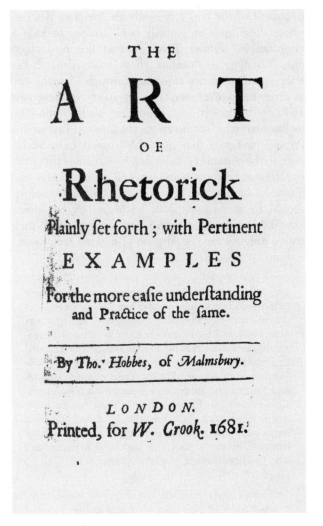

Title page for one of the editions in which Fenner's work is misattributed to the author of Leviathan

may have been a futile effort to avoid Anglican retribution, or in the case of *The Artes Of Logike And Rethorike,* it may have been the hesitancy of someone familiar with the inside of a prison cell. Pepper suggests that Fenner probably wrote his logic and rhetoric along with their accompanying three books while incarcerated. Prison conditions, according to Pepper, may even explain why the chapters of the second book of the logic are haphazardly misnumbered (1-2-4-5-5-7), though this may have been a simple printing error.

In light of this rich and subversive context, Fenner's preface to *The Artes Of Logike And Rethorike* takes on a new and radical significance. "To the Christian Reader" anticipates three possible objections to the logic and the rhetoric: that "they are made common too all which are wont to fit in the *Doctours* chayre"; that "they will seem newer than the newest"; and that any treatment of the two arts needs an adequate defense, since "these artes in generall" are "accused as vain & vnprofitable." Fenner flatly dismisses the third objection, deciding to "confute them with silence," but addresses the first two objections through a lengthy and at times interwoven response. In justifying these new and now "common" arts, Fenner signals his opposition to the hierarchy of the Anglican Church. Just as the Puritans believed that the Bible should be available even to the common man so that he too could judge the righteousness of his world as well as its secular and divine leaders, so too, Fenner argued, logic and rhetoric should be at their disposal; he begins by explaining how the Greeks and Romans kept the two arts in their native tongues for the purpose of making their works commonly available:

> . . . the ende why these artes haue been kept in these tounges doth not only propte, but also holde vp this our practise [of translation into English], seeing it was done because these tounges being most general by reason of the spread that the *Grecian* and *Romane* Empyre had made of them, they were the fittest to be made the storehouse of the worlde for these commodities. A storehouse I say, not to keepe them for the *Romanes* and *Grecians* alone, or for the expert in these toungs theyr free denizons: but at the least that by their trafficke, it might with their gaine of the prayse and glory, become common to euery particular nation, that euerie one who had neede, might buie of the same.

Fenner thus justified the English translation in analogous fashion, as a means to enable the commoner to understand and judge for himself the secular and divine matters of his world:

> Let them take heede also of open iniustice, for seeing the common vse and practise of all men in generall, both in reasoning to the purpose, and in speaking with some grace and elegancie, hath sowen the seede of these artes, why should not all reape where all haue sowen? . . . the simple plainesse of these treastises, which draw men to no curious or doubtfull discourses but onely put them in minde of that which they may easily seeke and know in most familiar examples with great fruite and delight, shall sufficiently answere for themselues in this behalfe: praying all men to vse them with some studie as their callings may suffer, to strengthen their iudgement, to discerne of the sayinges and writinges of other men, to keepe better that which they learne, and not beyonde their gifte and calling, to aduenture to a further vse then they can reach vnto.

Fenner's *The Artes of Logike and Rethorike*, thus, was an important attempt to aid the Puritan cause in England. It gave the common man the logical and rhetorical skills needed to read "so many Treatises as are written both to hurte and benefite the worlde," both civil and divine, as well as the power to judge his divine and secular leaders and condemn them if needed. It is no wonder that the four editions printed in 1584 were published anonymously in Middleburg. It was not until 1588, a year after his probable date of death, that his name was attached to the title page of the fifth edition. With the misattribution of Fenner's work to Thomas Hobbes in the late 1600s and the significant use of it by John Smith in eleven editions up until 1739, Fenner's importance went unacknowledged well into the eighteenth century. Christine W. Sizemore, in "The Authorship of *The Mystery of Rhetoric Unveiled*" (1975), supplies evidence that Fenner's influence even extended to one of the most renowned Puritans of the eighteenth century, Cotton Mather; Smith's *The Mysterie of Rhetorique Unveil'd*, with its heavy reliance on Fenner's work, was the only rhetorical work given any value by Mather, who recommends it to students of the ministry in his *Manuductio Ad Ministerium* (Directions for a Candidate of the Ministry, 1726). Fenner, thus, indirectly carried influence with respected Puritans well into the first half of the eighteenth century.

Fenner went on to write several other Puritan tracts, including *Sacra Theologia, Sive Veritas quæ est secundum Pietatem, Ad Vnicæ & veræ methodi leges descripta, & in decem libros per Dvdleivm Fennervm digesta* (1585?), a detailed exposition of Christian theology that avoids the controversy characteristic of his other work. The publication of the work twice in Geneva, in 1586 and 1589, and once in Amsterdam in 1632 attests to Fenner's influence on the Continent as a respected divine. Fenner also wrote *A Defence Of the godlie Ministers, against the slaunders of D. Bridges, contayned in his answere to the Preface before the Discourse of Ecclesiasticall gouernement, with a Declaration of the Bishops proceeding against them* (1587) and smaller, instructive tracts such as *The Groundes of Religion necessarie to be knowen of euery one that may be admitted to the Supper of the Lord* (1587) and *A Short and profitable Treatise, of lavvfull and vnlavvfull Recreations, and the right vse and abuse of those that are lawefull* (1587).

Other works have been attributed to Fenner, but his authorship has not been confirmed. *A Briefe and plaine declaration, concerning the desires of all those faithfull ministers* (1584) is arguably Fenner's work, but more probably the work of William Fulke. *A Booke of the forme of common prayers* (1585?) has been attributed to either Fenner or Robert Harrison. *A Defence Of The Reasons of the Counter-poyson* (1586) has been attributed to Fenner or Stoughton, but the author of this work is clearly not the author of *A Counter-poyson*, as the preface, "To the Christian Reader," indicates: "the trueth is, the author of the *Counterpoyson* neuer coulde gette the answeres in writing as nowe I haue got them. . . . The Author of the

Counter-poyson I am sure will take it in good part." The likelihood that Fenner wrote *A Counter-poyson* argues against his authorship of *A Defence of the reasons of the Counter-poyson.* The preface of *The Sacred Doctrine Of Divinitie, Gathered Out Of the worde of God. Togither with an explication of the Lordes Prayer* (1589), sometimes attributed to Fenner, indicates that the writer "hath brought Mr Fenners booke for helpe of memorie, into a great deale smaller rowme"; other comments also indicate that the work is not Fenner's. There is ample evidence to support the publication of a work titled *Dudley Fenner his Catechisme* (1592), but no copy of this work is extant. *An Antiqvodlibet, Or An Advertisement To Beware Of Secular Priests* (1602) has been attributed to Fenner, but it is clearly not his work since it is a response to William Watson's *A decacordon of ten quodlibeticall questions concerning religion and state* (1602), written after Fenner's death.

At no time in Fenner's career did he separate his Puritanism from his Ramism. The one volume devoted to the Talaeo-Ramistic logic and rhetoric in his corpus therefore becomes a key work, not only because it is the first combined treatment of these two arts in England, but because it is a critical work aiding the cause of a controversial divine who sought to increase the Puritan influence within the Anglican Church.

References:

John C. Adams, "Ramus, Illustrations, and the Puritan Movement," *Journal of Medieval and Renaissance Studies,* 17 (1987): 195–210;

Mary C. Dodd, "The Rhetorics in Molesworth's Edition of Hobbes," *Modern Philology,* 50 (1952): 36–42;

Donna B. Hamilton, *Shakespeare and the Politics of Protestant England* (Lexington: University Press of Kentucky, 1992);

Wilbur Samuel Howell, *Logic and Rhetoric in England, 1500–1700* (New York: Russell & Russell, 1961);

Howell, "Ramus and English Rhetoric: 1574–1681," *Quarterly Journal of Speech,* 37 (1951): 299–310;

Walter J. Ong, "Hobbes and Talon's Ramist Rhetoric in English," *Transactions of the Cambridge Bibliographical Society,* 1 (1951): 260–269;

Ong, *Ramus, Method, and the Decay of Dialogue: From the Art of Discourse to the Art of Reason* (Cambridge, Mass. & London: Harvard University Press, 1983);

Ong, *Ramus and Talon Inventory: A Short-tile Inventory of the Published Works of Peter Ramus (1515–1572) and of Omer Talon (ca. 1510–1562) in Their Original and in Their Various Altered Forms* (Cambridge, Mass.: Harvard University Press, 1958);

Robert D. Pepper, Introduction to *Four Tudor Books on Education,* edited by Pepper (Gainesville, Fla.: Scholars' Facsimiles & Reprints, 1966);

Eleanor Rosenberg, *Leicester: Patron of Letters* (New York: Columbia University Press, 1955);

Christine W. Sizemore, "The Authorship of *The Mystery of Rhetoric Unveiled,*" *Papers of the Bibliographical Society of America,* 69 (1975): 79–81;

Keith L. Sprunger, *Dutch Puritanism: A History of English and Scottish Churches of the Netherlands in the Sixteenth and Seventeenth Centuries,* Studies in the History of Christian Thought, volume 31 (Leiden: E. J. Brill, 1982);

William Tarbutt, *The Annals of Cranbrook Church: Its Monuments, Ministers, Officers, and People: in a Series of Lectures* (Cranbrook, U.K.: Mr. Dennett, Printed by G. Waters, 1875), pp. 10–16;

J. Dover Wilson, "Richard Schilders and the English Puritans," *Transactions of the Bibliographical Society,* 11 (1910–1911): 65–134.

Papers:

There are manuscript versions of Dudley Fenner's *Sacra Theologia* in the Harleian Collection of the British Library (MSS. 6879), Dr. Williams's Library (MSS 3.1), and the Lambeth Palace Library (MSS. 465).

Abraham Fleming

(1552? – 18 September 1607)

Patricia Brace
Laurentian University, Sudbury

BOOKS: *A Panoplie of Epistles, Or, a looking Glasse for the vnlearned. Conteyning a perfecte plattforme of inditing letters of all sorts, to persons of al estates and degrees, as well our superiours, as also our equalls and inferiours: vsed of the best and the eloquentest Rhetoricians that haue liued in all ages, and haue beene famous in that facultie. Gathered and translated out of Latine into English, by Abraham Flemming,* compiled and translated in parts by Fleming (London: Printed by Henry Middleton for Ralph Newberry, 1576);

A straunge, and terrible Wunder wrought very late in the parish church of Bongay, a Tovvn of no great distance from the citie of Norwich, namely the fourth of this August, in ye yeere of our Lord 1577. In a great tempest of violent raine, lightning, and thunder, the like wherof hath been seldome seene. With the appeerance of an horrible shaped thing, sensibly perceiued of the people then and there assembled. Drawen into a plaine method according to the written copye, by Abraham Fleming (London: Printed for Francis Godly, 1577?);

The Footepath of Faith, leading the Highwaie to Heauen. Whereunto is annexed the Bridge to blessednes. Compiled and made by Abraham Fleming, and by him newlie altered and augmented (London: Printed by William Hoskins, 1578?; first extant edition, London: Printed by Henry Middleton for Edward White, 1581);

The Conduit of Comfort. Containing sundrie comfortable Prayers, to the strengthening of the faith of a weak Christian (London: Printed by Henry Denham, 1579?);

A Memoriall of the famous monuments and charitable almes-deedes of the Right worshipfull Maister William Lambe Esquire, somtime Gentleman of the Chappell, in the reigne of the most renowned King Henrie the eight, &c. And late Citizen of London, and free of the Right worshipfull companie of Clothworkers: deceased the 21. Of April. An. 1580. Recorded in print, according to the tenour and trueth of his last will and Testament by Abraham Fleming (London: Printed by Henry Denham for Thomas Turner, 1580);

An Epitaph, or funerall inscription, vpon godlie life and death of the Right worshipfull Maister William Lambe Esquire, *Founder of the new Conduit of Holborne, &c. Deceased the one and twentith of April, and intumbed in S. Faiths Church vnder Povvles, the sixt of Maie next and immediatly follovving. Anno. 1580. Deuised by Abraham Fleming* [broadside] (London: Printed by Henry Denham for Thomas Turner, 1580);

The Diamond of deuotion, Cut and squared into six seuerall points: Namelie, 1. The Footpath to Felicitie. 2. A Guide to Godlines. 3. The Schoole of Skill. 4. A Swarme of Bees. 5. A Plant of Pleasure. 6. A Groue of Graces. Full of manie fruitfull lessons, auaileable to the leading of a godlie and reformed life. By Abraham Fleming (London: Printed by Henry Denham, 1581).

Editions: *A straunge and terrible Wunder, wrought very late in the parish church of Bongay* (London: Printed by J. Compton for T. & H. Rodd, 1820);

The Diamond of Deuotion [excerpts], in *Select Poetry Chiefly Devotional of the Reign of Queen Elizabeth,* edited by Edward Farr, 2 volumes (Cambridge: Parker Society, 1845), II: 546;

Some Account of William Lambe, Citizen and Clothworker, 1568; Master, 1569, Born 1495, Died 1580, transcribed for Charles Frederick Angell (London: Printed by J. E. Adlard, 1875);

"An Epitaph, or Funerall Inscription, Upon Godlie Life and Death of the Right Worshipfull Maister William Lambe Esquire," in *Ballads & Broadsides Chiefly of the Elizabethan Period and Printed in Black-Letter,* edited, with notes, by Herbert L. Collman (Oxford: Printed for the Roxburghe Club, 1912), pp. 136–138;

OTHER: Virgil, *The Bucolikes of Publius Virgilius Maro, with Alphabeticall annotations upon proper nams of Gods, Goddesses, men, women, hilles, floudes, cities, townes, and villages &c. orderly placed in the margent. Dravvne into plaine and familiar Englishe, verse for verse by Abraham Fleming. Student. The page following declareth the contentes of the Booke,* translated by Fleming (London: Printed by John Charlewood for Thomas Woodcock, 1575);

Claudius Aelianus, *A Registre Of Hystories conteining Martiall exploits of worthy warriours, Politique practises of Ciuil Magistrates, wise Sentences of famous Philosophers, And other matters manifolde and memorable. Written in Greeke by Aelianus a Romane: and deliuered in Englishe (as well, according to the truth of the Greeke text, as of the Latine) by Abraham Fleming,* translated by Fleming (London: Printed by Henry Middleton for Thomas Woodcock, 1576);

John Caius, *Of Englishe Dogges, the diuersities, the names, the natures, and the properties. A Short Treatise written in latine by Iohannes Caius of late memorie, Doctor of Phisicke in the Uniuersitie of Cambridge; And newly drawne into Englishe by Abraham Fleming Student,* translated by Fleming (London: Printed by John Charlewood for Richard Jones, 1576);

"Abraham Fleming vppon G. Whetstons worke," in *The Rocke of Regard, diuided into foure parts. The first, the Castle of delight: Wherin is reported, the wretched end of wanton and dissolute liuing. The second, the Garden of Vnthriftinesse: Wherein are many sweete flowers (or rather fancies) of honest loue. The thirde, the Arbour of Vertue: Wherein slaunder is highly punished, and vertuous Ladies and Gentlewomen, worthily commended. The fourth, the Ortchard of Repentance: Wherein are discoursed, the miseries that followe dicing, the miseries of quareling, the fall of prodigalitie: and the souden ouerthrowe of foure notable cousners, with diuers other morall, natural, & tragical discourses, documents and admonitions: being all the inuention, collection and translation of George Whetstone Gent,* collected and translated by George Whetstone (London: Printed for Robert Waley, 1576);

"Solertia: non Socordia," in *The Zodiake of Life, written by the excellent and Christian Poet, Marcellus Palingenius Stellatus. Wherein are contened twelue seuerall labours, painting out moste liuely, the whole compasse of the world, the reformation of manners, the miseries of mankinde, the pathway to vertue and vice, the eternitie of the Soule, the course of the Heauens, the mysteries of nature, and diuers other circūstances of great learning, and no lesse iudgement. Translated out of Latine into Englishe, By Barnabie Googe and by him newly recognised. Probitas laudatur & alget. Hereunto is annexed (for the Readers aduantage) a large Table, as well of wordes as of matters mentioned in this whole worke,* by Marcellus Palingenius, with an index possibly by Fleming (London: Printed for Ralph Newberry, 1576);

"Abraham Fleminge upon T. K. his translated Eipgrammes," in *Flovvers Of Epigrammes, Ovt of sundrie the moste singular authours selected, as well auncient as late writers. Pleasant and profitable to the expert readers of quicke capacitie: By Timothe Kendall, late of the Uniuersitie of Oxford: now a student of Staple Inne in London,* by Timothe Kendall (London: Printed by John Shepperd, 1577);

"A Rythme Decasyllabicall, upon this last luckie voyage of worthie Capteine Frobisher. 1577," in *A true reporte of the laste voyage into the West and Northwest regions, &c. 1577. Worthily atchieued by Capteine Frobisher of the sayde voyage the first finder and Generall. With a description of the people there inhabiting, and other circumstances notable. Written by Dionyse Settle, one of the companie in the sayde voyage, and seruant to the right honourable the Earle of Cumberland,* by Dionyse Settle (London: Printed by Henry Middleton, 1577);

Frederick Nausea, *Of all blasing starrs in generall, as well supernaturall as naturall, to what countrie or people for euer they appeare in the world vniuersall. The indgement of the right reuerend Frederick Nause, Bishop of Vienna. Written and dedicated to the most high and puisaunt Emperour Ferdinand. Translated out of Latine into English,* by Abraham Fleming, translated by Fleming (London: Printed for Thomas Woodcocke, 1577); republished as *A Treatise of Blazing Starres In Generall. As well supernaturall as naturall: To what countries or people soeuer they appeare in the spacious world* (London: Printed by Bernard Alsop for Henry Bell, 1618);

"A rythme decasyllabicall, comparatiue, and congratulatorie," in *A true report of the third and last voyage into Meta incognita: atchieued by the worthie Capteine, M. Martine Frobisher Esquire. Anno. 1578. Written by Thomas Ellis Salier and one of the companie,* by Thomas Ellis (London: Printed by Thomas Dawson, 1578?);

Girolamo Savonarola, *A Pithie Exposition vpon the. 51. Psalme intituled, Miserere mei Deus, &c. Also a godly meditation vpon the. 31. Psalme, intituled, In te Domine speraui. Written by Hierome of Ferrarie: And now newly augmented and amended,* by Abraham Fleming, edited by Fleming (London: Printed by Thomas Dawson, 1578);

Synesius, *A Paradoxe, Prouing by reason and example, that Baldnesse is much better than bushie haire, &c. Written by that excellent Philosopher Synesius, Bishop of Thebes, or (as some say) Cyren. A Prettie pamplet, to peruse, and replenished with recreation. Englished by Abraham Fleming. Hereunto is annexed the pleasant tale of Hemetes the Heremite, pronounced before the Queenes Maiestie. Newly recognised both in Latine and English, by the said A. F.,* translated, with an address to the reader, by Fleming (London: Printed by Henry Denham, 1579);

John Hooper, *Certeine comfortable Expositions of the constant Martyr of Christ, M. Iohn Hooper, Bishop of Glocester and Worcester, written in the time of his tribulation and imprisonment, vpon the XXIII. LXII. LXXIII. and LXXVII. Psalmes of the Prophet Dauid. Newly recog-*

nised, and neuer before published, edited, with an address to the reader, by Fleming (London: Printed by Henry Middleton, 1580);

John Knox, *A Fort for the afflicted. Wherin are ministred many notable & excellent remedies against the stormes of tribulation. Written chiefly for the comforte of Christes little flocke, which is the smal number of the Faithfull, by Iohn Knox*, edited, with an address to the reader, by Fleming (London: Printed by Thomas Dawson, 1580);

"In Barretti Aluearium repurgatum," in *An Alvearie Or Quardruple Dictionarie, containing foure sundrie tongues: namelie, English, Latine, Greeke, and French. Newlie enriched with varietie of Wordes, Phrases, Prouerbs, and diuers lightsome obseruations of Grammar. By the Tables you may contrariwise finde out the most necessarie wordes placed after the Alphabet, whatsoeuer are to be found in anie other Dictionarie: Which Tables also seruing for Lexicons, to lead the learner vnto the English of such hard wordes as are often read in Authors, being faithfullie examined, are truelie numbered. Verie profitable for such as be desirous of anie of those languages*, by John Baret, edited, with an index, by Fleming (London: Printed by Henry Denham, the assign of William Seres, 1580);

Thomas Cooper, *Certaine Sermons wherin is contained the Defense of the Gospell nowe preached, against such Cauils and false accusations, as are obiected both against the Doctrine it selfe, and the Preachers and Professors thereof, by the friendes and fauourers of the Church of Rome. Preached of late by Thomas by Gods sufferance Byshop of Lincolne*, edited, with an index, by Fleming (London: Printed by Ralph Newberry, 1580);

Michael Cope, *A Godly and learned Exposition vppon the Prouerbes of Solomon: Written in French by Maister Michael Cope, Minister of the woorde of God, at Geneua: And translated into English by M. O.*, translated into English by Marcelline Outred, edited, with an index, by Fleming (London: Printed by Thomas Dawson for George Bishop, 1580);

Philips van Marnix van sant Aldegonde (Isaac Rabbotenu), *The Bee hiue of the Romishe Churche. A worke of al good Catholikes too bee read and most necessary to bee vnderstood. Wherein both the Catholike Religion is substantially confirmed, and the Heretikes finely fetcht ouer the coales. Translated out of Dutch into English by George Gilpin the Elder. Newly Imprinted with a table thereunto annexed*, edited, with indexes, by Fleming and John Stell (London: Printed by Thomas Dawson for John Stell, 1580);

Niels Hemmingsen, *The Epistle Of The Blessed Apostle Saint Paule, which he, in the time of his trouble and imprisonment, sent in writing from Rome to the Ephesians. Faithfullie Expounded, Both For the benefite of the learned and vnlearned, by Nicholas Hemming, Professor of Diuini-*

tie in the Vniuersitie of Coppenhagen in Denmarke. Familiarlie Translated ovt of Laatine into English, by Abraham Fleming. Herein Are Handled The high mysteries of our saluation, as maie appeare by the Table of common places necessarilie annexed by the same A. F. Perused and authorised, edited and translated in parts, with an index, by Fleming (London: Printed by Thomas East, 1580);

Frederick Nausea, *A Bright Burning Beacon, forewarning all wise Virgins to trim their lampes against the coming of the Bridegroome. Conteining A generall doctrine of sundrie signes and wonders, specially Earthquakes both particular and generall: A discourse of the end of this world: A commemoration of our late Earthquake, the 6. of April, about 6. of the clocke in the euening 1580. And a praier for the appeasing of Gods wrath and indignation. Newly translated and collected by Abraham Fleming. The summe of the whole booke followeth in fit place orderly diuided into Chapters* (London: Printed by Henrie Denham, 1580);

Edward Hutchins, *Davids Sling against great Goliah: Conteining diuers notable Treatises, the names whereof follow next after the Epistle to the Reader: by E. H.*, edited by Fleming (London: Printed by Henrie Denham, 1581);

Jacobus Wittewronghelus, *De vera Christiani hominis fide, Dialogus elegantissimus et utilissimus Jacobe Wittewronghelo authore. Huc accessit, praeter annotationes marginales praecipuas doctrinas indicantes oratio pia et luculenta, quae ipsam totius operis hypothesin breviusculis quibusdam petitionibus complectiture per Abrahamum Flemingum Londinigenum*, edited and annotated by Fleming (London: Thomas Purfoot, 1581); translated by Fleming and Arthur Golding as *Concerning the true Beleefe of a Christian man, a most excellent and profitable Dialogue, By S. C. Herevnto, besides the Marginall Notes, declaring the chiefe points of Doctrines, there is added a godlye and lightsome prayer, which in certain breefe petitions, comprehendeth the very contents of the vvhole vvorke: vvritten in Latine, By Abraham Fleming Londoner borne. To the right Reuerend Father in Christ, Iohn Bishop of London. Translated out of Latine, by Arthur Golding*, translated by Fleming and Golding (London: Printed by Thomas Purfoot, 1582?);

Ambrosius Autpertus, *A Monomachie of Motives in the mind of man: Or a Battell betweene Vertues and Vices of contrarie qualitie. Wherein the imperfections and weaknesses of Nature appeare so naked, that anie reasonable soule may soone see by what spirit he is lead: Herevnto also, besides sundrie deuout praiers necessarilie interlaced, diuers golden sentences of S. Barnard are annexed: and also a briefe conclusion of his vpon this Theame, that Victorie is obtained by resisting temptation. Newlie englished by Abraham Fleming*, compiled and translated, with additions, by Fleming (London: Printed by Henry Denham, 1582?);

John Calvin, *The Sermons of M. Iohn Calvin Vpon The Fifth Booke of Moses called Deuteronomie: Faithfully gathered word for word as he preached them in open Pulpet; Together with a preface of the Minsters of the Church of Geneua, and an admonishment made by the Deacons there. Also there are annexed two profitable Tables, the one containing the chiefe matters; the other the places of Scripture herein alleged. Translated out of French by Arthur Golding,* translated by Golding, edited, with an index, by Fleming (London: Printed by Henry Middleton for George Bishop, 1583);

"In Vberrimos nec non vtilissimos Guilielmi Morelij verborum Commentatios Latinograecos, Anglica nomenclatura locupletatos; Abrahami Flemingi Londinigenae ad iuuentutem studiosam carmen encomiasticon & paraeneticon," in *Verborvm Latinorvm Cvm Graecis Anglicisque Conivnctorum, locupletissimi Commentarij: Ad Elaboratvm Gvilielmi Morelli Parisiensis, Regij in Graecis Typographi Archetypum accuratissimè excusi, Novaqve Vocvm Passim Insertarvm Accessione adaucti, vt stellulae, quae singulis lucent paginis, indicabunt. Consvltis, Praeter Ditissima Aliorvm Dictionaria, viuis etiam nonnullorum doctorum vocibus, quò Anglica versio perspicua magis sit, fructiosiorq. ad communem studiosorum usum emanet. Qvid Vtilitatis In His Commentariis Contineatvr, quaequa conscribendi eos ratio à primo authore inita sit, ex ipsius Morelii praefatione studiosi facillimè percipient,* by Guillaume Murel, edited by Fleming (London: Printed by Henry Bynneman for Richard Hutton, 1583);

Pietro Martire Vermigli, *The Common Places of the most famous and renowmed Diuine Doctor Peter Martyr, diuided into foure principall parts: with a large addition of manie theologicall and necessarie discourses, some neuer extant before. Translated and partlie gathered by Anthonie Marron, one of the Sewers of hir Maiesties most Honourable Chamber. Meliora spero. In the end of the booke are annexed two tables of all the notable matters therein conteined,* translated by Anthonie Marren, edited, with indexes, by Fleming (London: Printed by Henrie Denham, Thomas Chard, William Broome, and Andrew Maunsell, 1583);

Reginald Scot, *The discouerie of witchcraft, Wherein the lewde dealing of witches and witchmongers is notablie detected, the knauerie of coniurors, the impietie of inchantors, the follie of soothsaiers, the impudent falshood of cousenors, the infidelitie of atheists, the pestilent practises of Pythonists, the curiositie of figurecasters, the vanitie of dreamers, the beggerlie art of Alcumystrie, The abhomination of idolatrie, the horrible art of poisoning, the vertue and power of naturall magike, and all the conueiances of Legierdemaine and iuggling are deciphered: and many other things opened, which haue long lien hidden, howbeit verie necessarie to be knowne. Heerevnto is added a treatise vpon the nature and substance of spirits and diuels, &c: all latelie written by Reginald Scot Esquire,* includes Fleming's translations of verses by classical authors (London: Printed by William Broome, 1584);

John Withals, *A Shorte Dictionarie in Latine and English, verie profitable for yong beginners. Compiled at the first by Iohn Withals: afterwards reuised and increased with Phrases and necessarie additions by Lewis Euans. And nowe lastlie augmented with more than six hundred rythmical verses, wherof many be prouerbial, some heretofore found in old authours, and othersome neuer before this time seene or read in the Latine tongue, as hauing their originall grace in English: Newlie done by Abraham Fleming. What is added to this edtion which none of the former at any time had, these markes ¶ * may sufficiently shew,* edited, with additions, by Fleming (London: Printed by Thomas Purfoot, 1584); republished as *A Dictionarie in English and Latine for Children, and yong beginners: Compiled at the first by Iohn Withals, (with the phrases, and Rhythmicall, and prouerbiall verses &c. which haue bin added to the same, by Lewis Evans, and Abraham Fleming, successively.) And (newlie) now augmented, with great plentie of latine words, sentences, and phrases: with many proper Epigrams: Descriptions: Inscriptions: Histories: Poeticall fictions besides. Framed (all) to their yong vnderstandings which be learners in the Latin tongue, to leade them on to riper knowledge, with delight,* edited by William Clerk (London: Printed by Thomas Purfoot, 1602);

Jean Veron, *A Dictionarie in Latine and English, heretofore set forth by Master Iohn Veron, and now newlie corrected and enlarged, For the vtilitie and profit of all yoong students in the Latine toong, as by further search therein they shall find: By R. W.,* edited, with additions, by Fleming (London: Printed by Ralph Newberry and Henry Denham, 1584);

"Ad studiosos Abrahami Flemingi," in *The Nomenclator, or Remembrance of Adrianus Iunius Physician, diuided in two Tomes, conteining proper names and apt termes for all things vnder their conuenient Titles, which within a few leaues doe follow: Written by the said Ad. Iu. in Latine, Greeke, French and other forrein tongues: and now in English, by Iohn Higins: With a full supplie of all such vvords as the last inlarged edition affoorded; and a dictional Index, conteining aboue fourteene hundred principall words with their numbers directlly leading to their interpretations: Of special vse for all scholars and learners of the same languages,* by Adrian Junius, edited, with an index, by Fleming (London: Printed by Ralph Newberry and Henry Denham, 1585);

Raphael Holinshed and others, *The First and second volumes of Chronicles, comprising 1 The description and his-*

torie of England, 2 The description and historie of Ireland, 3 The description and historie of Scotland: First collected and published by Raphaell Holinshed, William Harrison, and others: Now newly augmented and continued (with manifold matters of singular note and worthie memorie) to the yeare 1586. by Iohn Hooker aliàs Vowell Gent. and others. With conuenient tables at the end of these volumes, edited, with indexes and additions, by Fleming and others (London: Printed by Henry Denham for John Harrison, George Bishop, Ralph Newberry, Henry Denham, and Thomas Woodcocke, 1587);

John Foxe, *Eicasmi Seu Meditationes, In Sacram Apocalypsin. Authore Io. Foxo Anglo.,* edited, with an index in Latin, by Fleming (London: Printed for George Bishop, 1587);

Virgil, *The Bvcoliks Of Pvblivs Virgilivs Maro, Prince Of All Latine Poets; otherwise called his Pastoralls, or shepeherds meetings. Together with his Georgiks or Ruralls, otherwise called his husbandrie, conteyning foure books. All newly translated into English verse by A. F.,* translated by Fleming (London: Printed by Thomas Orwin for Thomas Woodcock, 1589);

James Cancellar, *The Alphabet of Praiers, verie fruitfull to be exercised and vsed of euerie Christian. Newlie drawne, into no lesse direct an order than aptlie agreeth with the name: by A. Fleming,* edited by Fleming (London: Printed by Richard Yardley and Peter Short for the assigns of William Seres, 1591).

Editions: Raphael Holinshed, *The Scottish Chronicle or, a complete history and description of Scotland, etc,* 2 volumes (Arbroath, U.K.: J. Finlay, 1805);

Holinshed's Chronicles of England, Scotland, and Ireland, 6 volumes (London: Printed for J. Johnson and others, 1807–1808);

"A Rythme Decasyllabicall, upon this last luckie voyage of worthie Capteine Frobisher. 1577.," in *Restituta; or Titles, Extracts, and Characters of Old Books in English Literature Revived by Sir Egerton Brydges,* 4 volumes (London: Longman, Hurst, Rees, Orme & Brown, 1814–1816) II: 202;

"To the religious reader," in *The Works of John Knox,* edited by David Laing, 6 volumes (Edinburgh, 1846–1864), III: 117–118;

"Abraham Fleming vppon G. Whetstons worke," in *Illustrations of Early English Poetry,* edited by J. P. Collier, 5 volumes, 2 (London: Privately printed, 1866–1870), pp. xi–xii;

Dionyse Settle, *A true reporte of the laste voyage into the West and Northwest regions, &c. 1577* (Providence, R.I.: John Carter Brown, 1868);

"Abraham Fleminge upon T. K. his translated Eipgrammes," in *Flovvers Of Epigrammes by Timothe Kendall,* Publications of the Spenser Society, no. 15 (Manchester: Printed for the Spenser Society, 1874), pp. 13–14;

John Caius, *Of Englishe dogges, the diversities, the names, the natures, and the properties. A short treatise written in Latine,* in *An English Garner,* edited by Edward Arber, 8 volumes (London: Unwin, 1877–1897), III: 225–268; enlarged to 12 volumes (Westminster, U.K.: Constable, 1903–1904), IX: 1–44;

Caius, *Of Englishe dogges, the diversities, the names, the natures, and the properties. A short treatise written in Latine* (London: A. Bradley, 1880);

The Discoverie of Witchcraft by Reginald Scot, Esquire, Being a Reprint of the First Edition Published in 1584, edited by Brinsley Nicholson (London: E. Stock, 1886);

Of English dogges: tr. by Abraham Fleming (1576), in *The Works of John Caius, M.D., second founder of Gonville and Caius college and master of the college, 1559–1573. With a memoir of his life by John Venn . . .* (Cambridge: Cambridge University Press, 1912);

The Discoverie of Witchcraft by Reginald Scot, edited by Montague Summers (London: John Rodker, 1930);

Dionyse Settle, *A true reporte of the laste voyage into the West and Northwest regions, &c. 1577* and Thomas Ellis, *A True Report of the Third and Last Voyage into Meta Incognita,* in *The Three Voyages of Martin Frobisher,* edited by Vilhjalmur Stefansson, 2 volumes (London: Argonaut, 1938);

Marcellus Palingenius, *The Zodiake of Life,* edited, with an introduction, by Rosemond Tuve (New York: Scholars' Facsimiles & Reprints, 1947);

Caius, *Of Englishe dogges,* The English Experience, no. 110 (Amsterdam: Theatrum Orbis Terrarum / New York: Da Capo Press, 1969);

Caius, *Of English Dogs* (Alton, U.K.: Beech, 1993).

In accounting for the significance of Abraham Fleming, Sarah C. Dodson argues that "his unflagging industry, his fidelity to sources, and his zeal in promoting certain religious and intellectual principles give him a place of some importance among the writers of the Elizabethan period." Dodson's tribute emphasizes the chief feature of Fleming's literary life: he participated in a broad range of literary production, in which he "did much . . . to pass on a store of knowledge to his contemporaries and to posterity; and his research activities doubtless spurred on others in the same fields." As a servant to Richard Tottel, one of the most significant of the midcentury printers, Fleming appears to have worked as a "learned corrector," editor, and indexer. For later printers—especially Henry Denham, who is known for the high quality of his output—Fleming engaged in similar activities and produced a large number of translations. While he is probably best known as an editor of the 1587 edition of Raphael Holinshed's *Chronicles,* Fleming is of interest to students of rhetoric chiefly for *A Panoplie of Epistles, Or a looking Glasse for the vnlearned* (1576), the second English epistolary rhetoric. In this work, which includes models from Latin and Greek literature as well as examples from Continental and English humanist writers, Fleming combined features of humanist educational theory and those of self-education manuals for the literate merchant classes, which had surged in popularity with the rise of printing.

Abraham Fleming was born in London where, aside from the terms he spent as a student at Peterhouse College, Cambridge, he lived the greater part of his life as a translator and learned corrector and, later, as the rector of the parish of St. Pancras Soper Lane. There is some debate about the date of his birth. While it is generally accepted that Fleming was born in 1552, Dodson notes that a deposition witnessed by Fleming in 1591 gives his age as forty-seven, which places his birthdate at 1544. Given that Fleming entered Peterhouse College in Michaelmas term 1570, this earlier date would make him an unlikely twenty-seven at his matriculation. Furthermore, his epitaph states that Fleming was fifty-six years old at the time of his death. In the face of these dates, consensus is that the age given in the deposition is incorrect and that Fleming was likely born in 1552. While little is known of Fleming's parents, the family was not well-to-do, for Fleming entered Cambridge as a sizar, or poor scholar, and his university career is marked, as William C. Miller has discovered, by interruptions. Fleming was intermittently in residence through Lent term of 1575 but did not receive his B.A. until 1582. Where Fleming prepared for university is unknown. His elder brother attended Eton College for two years, possibly on a scholarship, but no such school records exist for Abraham. The family appears to have been Reformist in its religious leanings, for the three children were given Old Testament names, and Abraham Fleming's devotional works are strongly Protestant. The sermons he preached at Paul's Cross in London in the years 1589–1606 indicate that Fleming was solidly Reformist, although not so radical as to offend authorities.

Fleming's name began to appear on publications immediately following his last appearance in the Peterhouse records with the appearance of *The Bucolikes of Publius Virgilius Maro* (1575) in verse, the first of several translations Fleming produced between 1575 and 1581. The title pages for *The Bucolikes* and *Of Englishe Dogges* (1576), a translation of John Caius's *De Canibus Brittanicis* (1570), list Fleming as "student." His translations range from classical Greek and Latin texts such as Claudius Aelianus's *A Registre Of Hystories conteining Martiall exploits of worthy warriours* (1576) and Synesius's *A Paradoxe, Prou-*

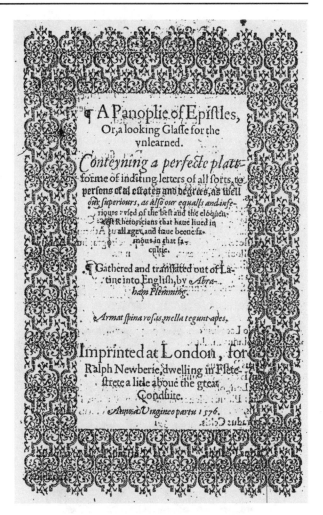

Title page for the second English book on the
rhetoric of letter writing

 ing by reason and example, that Baldnesse is much better than bushie haire (1579) through more contemporary material such as Girolamo Savonarola's *A Pithie Exposition vpon the. 51. Psalme* (1578), to devotional works including Frederick Nausea's *Of all blasing starrs in generall* (1577). In the same period, Fleming contributed commendatory verses to Marcellus Palingenius's *The Zodiake of Life* (1576), George Whetstone's *The Rocke of Regard* (1576), and Timothy Kendall's *Flovvers Of Epigrammes* (1577). His original writings during this time consisted of a sensational occasional work, *A straunge, and terrible Wunder wrought very late in the parish church of Bongay* (1577?) and a devotional treatise, *The Condvit of Comfort* (1579?).

As a scholar Fleming seems to have been regarded with some favor, for his name appears in the roll of English writers for the year 1576 in the first edition of Holinshed's *Chronicles* (1577), and material from his *Memoriall of the famous monuments and charitable almesdeedes of the Right worshipfull Maister William Lambe Esquire* (1580)

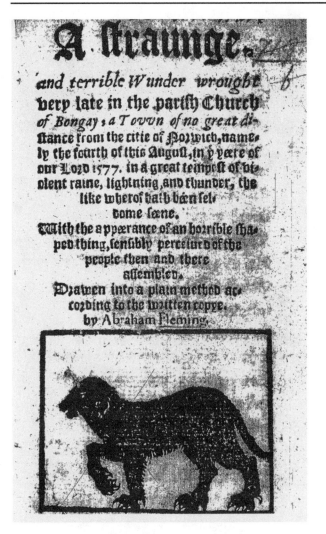

Title page for the book Fleming wrote to capitalize on widespread speculation about unexplained events in a rural church

was inserted into the 1587 revised edition of the *Chronicles,* which Fleming probably supervised through press. Both Dodson and Miller argue that because of Fleming's scholarly abilities he was likely put to use by printers and publishers as a "learned corrector." This contention is supported by Fleming's statement in *The Footepath of Faith* (1578?) that he was a "seruant" to Richard Tottel, the publisher renowned for the 1557 collection *Songes and Sonettes,* generally known as Tottel's Miscellany. However, according to the records of the Company of Stationers, Fleming was never presented to the company as an apprentice. While it is possible that he did serve a regular seven-year apprenticeship as a printer from 1576 to 1583 and that Tottel simply failed to register him, it is more likely that Tottel made use of Fleming's talents by having him correct manuscripts and proofread printed texts produced by his

shop. Other notable Protestant scholars, including Miles Coverdale and John Foxe, also performed such work. Fleming's later association with Henry Denham, a former apprentice of Tottel's, could then be explained by their meeting in this period.

Fleming's chief contribution to the history of rhetoric occurred immediately following his departure from Cambridge, while he still regarded himself as a student. Published in 1576, *A Panoplie of Epistles, Or a looking Glasse for the vnlearned* was the second English epistolary rhetoric. Such rhetorics are based on classical principles of oratory but focus their concerns with the use of language on the art of letter writing rather than on the production of speeches or treatises. Jean Robertson notes that the background of the English handbooks lies in the emergence throughout the middle ages of "treatises formulating hard and fast rules for writing every kind of letter." A series of Renaissance treatises derived from these Latin formularies, the earliest known of which is Alberic of Monte Casino's *Breviarum de dictamine* (circa 1075). In the sixteenth century Continental scholars such as Libanius, Ludovicus Vives, Simon Verepaeus, Justus Lipsius, and Lippus Brandolinus wrote Latin treatises on letter writing that were printed separately or included in anthologies published in England and exerted considerable influence over the English works that followed. For example, the 1573 London edition of Brandolinus's *De Ratione Scribendi* (On the Method of Writing, 1549) includes treatises by Desiderius Erasmus, Vives, Georgius Macropedius, Conradus Celt, and Christopher Hegendorff. The latter's work is adapted by Fleming in *A Panoplie of Epistles.*

Among the most influential works on letter writing was Erasmus's *Libellus de conscribendis epistolis* (Pamphlet on the Writing of Letters, 1521). Its form is characteristic of these Latin texts. Erasmus argued that letters may be divided into four broad categories: persuasive, encomiastic, judicial, and personal. As Robertson points out, regardless of category, Erasmus instructed readers that letters must observe the strict sequence of *exordium* (introduction), *narratio* (background information), *propositio* (position statement), *confirmatio* (supporting arguments), *confutatio* (refutation of opposing arguments), and *peroratio* (conclusion), providing examples from classical authors for each of these steps. As well as setting out the rules for formulating various types of letters, Erasmus specified a pedagogical function for letter writing on which Fleming drew in his work. As an exercise, he argues in the following translated passage, letter writing furthers the aims of humanist education by requiring the development of an ample style and offering the opportunity to imitate and manipulate the language of classical authors:

The poem Fleming wrote for Dionyse Settle's 1577 account of Captain Martin Frobisher's second voyage in search of a Northwest Passage to India

It is advisable that young men should have varied and thorough practice in this branch of study because, in addition to the stylistic advantages, they will unconsciously assimilate ancient tales worth remembering and fix them deep in their memory, and will become familiar with the names of persons and places. Above all, they will learn the meaning of decorum and the nature of moral integrity, which are important elements of rhetorical narration. Thus it will be the function of the teacher, before setting out the form of the letter to be written, to explain the story to the pupils. . . . then he will point out several passages where these topics are treated in the classical authors, so that the pupils may collect a store of words and maxims or may imitate them with similar expressions.

Because familiar letters allow more scope for invention than any of the other kinds, imitating models for them prepares the student for "original" speech. Robertson notes that the Latin formularies continued to be used in schools throughout the seventeenth century as the basis for instruction in the composition.

For the merchant familiar with neither classical texts nor the composition of letters, the epistolary rhetoric occupied a role similar to the Latin formulary for the student. The four English epistolary rhetorics that appeared in the sixteenth century exhibit a pedagogical bent similar to Erasmus's formulary. All, including Fleming's work, are indebted to the formulary tradition. For example, the immediate predecessor to *A Panoplie of Epistles* is William Fullwood's *The Enimie of Idlenesse: Teaching the maner and stile how to endite, compose and write all sorts of Epistles and Letters* (1568), which Katherine Gee Hornbeak has identified as a faithful translation of the French *Le Stile et maniere de composer, dicter, et escrire toute sort d'epistre, ou lettres missiues, tant part response, que autrement* (1566). Fullwood's popular book went though at least nine editions between 1568 and 1635. Fullwood's intended audience is mercantile, and the stance of his book is practical rather than intellectual. Hornbeak notes that Fullwood used the structure of the Latin formulary, but adapted it to the needs of a rising bourgeoisie. The same observation is also true of Fleming's text and certainly true of a later letter-writing book, John Browne's *The Merchants Auizo: Verie necessarie for their Sons and Seruants, when they first send them beyond the Seas, as to Spain and Portingale, or other Countries* (1589, with seven editions by 1640). As the subtitle suggests, Browne's work has an even stronger mercantile orientation than Fullwood's.

Other popular letter-writing guides that succeed Fleming's are Angel Day's *The English Secretorie* (1586), which went through at least nine editions between 1586 and 1635, and Nicholas Breton's extremely successful *A Poste VVith a madde Packet of Letters* (1602), with seven subsequent editions by 1630 and a further eight between 1634 and 1685. William G. Crane notes that Day followed the model of Erasmus "in an general Way" for his explanatory matter and his grouping of letters. Like Fullwood, Day includes a large number of amatory letters. A key difference, however, lies in the source for the samples, for Day appears to have composed his own. Hornbeak speculates that this move made Day's letters more appropriate to the needs of his audience and was responsible for its ongoing popularity. Breton moved away from the more utilitarian focus of the earlier guides and emphasized the sensational in his hugely popular "packet" of fictionalized amatory letters.

From its title alone Fleming's *A Panoplie of Epistles, Or, a looking Glasse for the vnlearned. Conteyning a perfecte plattforme of inditing letters of all sorts, to persons of al estates and degrees, as well our superiours, as also our equalls and inferiours: vsed of the best and the eloquentest Rhetoricians that haue liued in all ages, and haue beene famous in that facultie* projects a middle-class audience similar to Fullwood's. Like Fullwood, Day, and Browne, Fleming participated in the newly created market for autodidactic works that, Elizabeth Eisenstein argues, developed as a result of print technology and the concomitant increase in the availability of inexpensive books on a much broader range of topics than was previously possible. Enterprising printers parlayed the new potential for learning from books into a variety of pedagogical works designed to appeal to readers of "the middling sort," who had the means to acquire them and with an appreciation for the opportunity to acquire new skills without the expense of ongoing tuition.

However, Fleming positioned his book more as a teacher of rhetoric than as a provider of models for business or amatory writing. This lack of an immediate application for his epistolary rhetoric may have contributed to its lack of success in the marketplace, for only a single edition was published. The principle of the epistolary rhetoric is essentially humanist, for it emphasizes the use of sample letters as sources for imitation, through which the reader may achieve linguistic competence. Fleming's work adds the element of moral and political shaping that belongs to humanist pedagogical discourse as a central concern, which he expressed largely through the headnotes and marginal glosses to the sample letters.

This interest in humanist rhetorical theory is apparent immediately in the dedicatory epistle "To the Right Worshipful, Sir William Cordell knight, Maister of the Queene's Maiesties Rolles &c. health, wealth, and happinesse euerlasting." There, Fleming selected for his central metaphor the image of a garden in which he found himself lost and from which he gleaned his examples. He noted that

> Among many and sundrie sortes of flowres therefore, (the very woorst of all beeing of great vertue and value) such as in my fancie, bare the brauest hue and gallantest glosse, I gathered with a certaine greedinesse, esteeming highly of the opportunitie of the time, which was then presently ministred, and fearring least another should take my labour out of my hande: which caused me with so much the more speede . . . to finish that which I had begun.

This metaphor is one of a cluster typically used to describe the humanist process of gathering literary material. The purpose of such images is to point out both the importance of imitating a variety of linguistic models and the necessity of developing a store of verbal material to have at the ready for use in future verbal or written production. In Fleming's view, this need applied as fully to the writing of letters as to the production of learned treatises and he "that loueth orderly to indite, & plausibly to occupie his penne, in deuising and disposing as well both meete matter, as also fit wordes, in any kind of letter . . . must make meanes and prouision, for him selfe in this case, that those wantes and imperfections of Art & cunning may be supplied," here by the contents of Fleming's book. To such an end he provided "here ready to serue thy turne, many presidents and examples, not broched in the seller of myne owne braine, but drawne out of the most pure and cleare founteines of the finest and eloquentest Rhetoricians, that have liued and flourished in all ages." Thus, Fleming's work was designed to make available in a more contracted sphere the garden or storehouse of literary models to which he, the product of a classical education, had access.

The other key component that Fleming drew from humanist educational theory, specifically from Roger Ascham's *The Scholemaster Or plaine and perfite way of teachyng children, to vnderstand, write, and speake, the Latin tong* (1570), is the notion that learning should be pleasurable and its moral substance absorbed. In his choice

The Bee hiue
of the Romishe
Churche.

A worke of al good Catholikes
too bee read and most necessary
to bee vnderstood.

Wherin both the Catholick Religion is substantially confirmed, and the Heretikes finely
fetcht ouer the coales.

Translated out of Dutch into Englishe
by George Gilpin the Elder.

1. Thes.5.21.
Prooue all thinges, and keepe
that which is good.

Newly Imprinted with a table
thereunto annexed.
1580.

These bokes are to be solde in Paules
Churchyarde, at the signe of the
Parret.

Title page and illustration from a work edited and indexed by Fleming

of a title Fleming indicated that this dual aim is a key feature of the text; according to the *Oxford English Dictionary,* the term *panoply* means "complete armour for spiritual or mental warfare," with Fleming's being the initial usage of this sense of the word. He reinforced the idea of the book as a form of moral armor when he pointed out that it includes

sufficient furniture to arme and enable them against *ignoraunce, the aduersarie and sworne enimie of vnderstanding.* . . . As it is not for a naked and unarmed souldier, to encounter his enimie being harnessed at all pointes, and to the proofe prouided, except his intent be, wilfully to incurre daunger of violence: so it is not for any man, to tye the vse of his penne, to the vanities of his owne imagination, which commonly be preposterous & carelesse in keeping order, vnlesse his meaning be, of set purpose, to reape reprehension for his securitie and negligence. Hee therefore that is to play the part of a warriour, ought with his force and valliantnesse, to ioyne substantiall furniture, that the seruice of his natu-

rall abilities, and the vse of his instrumentall powers, may concurre and goe together, making him the more uenturous to withstand his enimies assault, and fuller of force also to giue him the discomfiture.

Fleming's interest in humanist pedagogy is further seen in his debt to well-known humanist educators within the work. In his "Epitome of Precepts," he adapted a dialogue between teacher and pupil that outlines the purposes and types of letters and the construction of different types of letters from examples chiefly drawn from Cicero and Pliny as they appear in Christopher Hegendorff's *Methodus de conscribendi epistolus* (1526). Within the dialogue, the student begins citing not only authors as sources for examples for different subtypes of letters, but also pages within *A Panoplie of Epistles* where such examples might be found. The dialogue closes with the master praising the student for his performance and giving him "a newe Panoplie of epistles, which thou vsing to read at thy leasure, shalt be in

Title page for the second edition (1587) of the first vernacular attempt to document the entire history of England in one book. This edition, which Fleming helped to edit, was the one William Shakespeare used for his history plays.

all points furnished to write letters of all sorts, and shall want nothing, that necessarily for such a purpose may be required." Fleming thus incorporated his book into the process of humanist education.

The selection and organization of the exemplary letters in *A Panoplie of Epistles* emphasizes Fleming's humanist focus, for not only are the letters organized by author, rather than by epistolary type, but they are drawn from both classical sources and contemporary advocates of humanism and humanist education. As in Ascham's *The Scholemaster,* the chief model is Cicero, with letters to and from him filling the first 153 of 448 pages, followed by Isocrates' "Epistles of Most Famous Philosphers, Prudent Princes, and Other Men of Great Wisedome" (a group that includes Solon, Aristotle, Socrates, Virgil, Pliny, and Hippocrates), and finally a collection of modern examples from Aldus Manutius, Desiderius Erasmus, Georgius Macropedius, Hegendorff, Walter Haddon, and Ascham. While the choice of classical letters matches closely the Latin formulary tradition, Fleming grouped the letters by author rather

than by type and provided a perfunctory index to the pages on which different types of letters may be found. This arrangement indicates that his interest lay more in exposing readers to classical authors than in giving them literary models for everyday use.

Within the main text of *A Panoplie of Epistles* the emphasis of the prefatory material is maintained through the headnotes and marginalia that Fleming appended to the letters. In both earlier and later epistolary rhetorics, notes that precede the letters indicate the type of letter being modelled and how it might be used. *The Merchants Auizo* is the most prescriptive in its approach, with statements such as "A letter to bee written to your Master presentlie vpon your arrivall at your Port." This same letter includes specific places for inserting personal news, with a note in the margin instructing the writer to "Note that you inquire & also write the prises of all other vendible wares." While Fullwood's *The Enimie of Idlenesse* uses some classical letters as examples, the headnotes give instructions for the construction of different types of letters. That is, they focus on the form of the letter and the use to which it might be put, rather than on its content. His models also include exchanges of letters representing personal and business relationships. Fleming's approach was similar in form, but the content of his headnotes (each headed "The Argument") and glosses differs dramatically. The vast majority of them explain the rhetorical construction or argument of the letter or the context within which it was produced without identifying the category that the letter represents. For example, writing about an epistle from Cicero to Curio, Fleming noted that

this epistle hath foure members, or portions. In the first, Cicero being accused of Curio for his seldome writing, excuseth him self by the commemmoration of his duetie. In the second, he discouereth the griefe of his mynde conceiued through the absence of Curio, and his ioy on the otherside, for Curio his worship. In the thirde is conteined an admonition to the deseruing of praise, and to the imbracing of vertue. In the fourth, hee commendeth to Curio the estate of his old age, being fiftie six yeares old when he wrote this letter.

The index lists this letter as "Excusatorie," a word that does appear in "The Argument," but without explanation of the structure or function of that particular form of letter. The marginal glosses indicate the sections of the argument, along with two moments at which Cicero uses excusatory strategies, but they also explain other rhetorical strategies and refer the reader to volumes of Cicero's letters for further study. For example: "He commendeth and exhorteth together, bycause exhortation should be tempered with commendation. Epi.12.Li.15." Fleming's concern lay with the use of Cicero as a rhetorical model in a more general sense, with the result that the exercise of the excusatory letter slips to the background. In other letters in the volume the marginalia fill in the historical events that surround the composition of the letters (for example: "He meaneth the Augurship wherein they were both Gerents at one time"), the strategy of argument in use ("An argument A Maiori ad Minus"), or the moral to be drawn from the letter ("Because the hart of euery true gentleman, ought to be much more moued with the miseries of the common wealth, then with the death of his children").

For the letters drawn from contemporary sources, Fleming's concern with the promotion of humanism as a system of moral, as well as rhetorical, instruction is pronounced. In the headnote to a letter of Ravisius Textor to N. L. Malverino, Fleming summarized the argument as follows:

> This letter, not being sent of Textor to any manner of person: but made and inuented for the behoofe of yong scholers, runneth altogether vpon the dispraise of idlenesse: the whole scope of the same may serue for Imitation, and may rather be called a Theame, then an Epistle (as many more may be of his making) although he giueth it that name and title. After he hathe shewed (to the supplanting of idlenesse and slouthe) howe all as well heauenly as earthly attend on theis calling, and do such seruice diligently and ordinarily, as is to them appointed, hee draweth toward an end, vsing reasons of persuasion to auoid such a vicious annoyaunce. Lastly, he writeth in that sort, as of one young scholer were incouraging another young scholer, to some scolerly exercise, & immagining that audience is present to heare what they haue to say, he feigneth to one of them a declamation, whereof he setteth down a methodicall and proper beginning.

Fleming's concern here was less with the epistle as a model of a specific type of letter, but with its subject ("theame" rather than "epistle") as a source for imitation. The function of the letter as a pedagogical exercise draws attention away from its practical application to the way in which the process of imitation teaches both rhetorical strategies and moral content. In a headnote to a letter by Hegendorff, Fleming made explicit his scholarly, as opposed to mercantile, interests by using as an example of a persuasive letter one in which Hegendorff worked "to winne his friends minde, from the trade of a merchant, and to frame himselfe to some facultie of learning." The question is not just of the framing of the letter—that the argument "goeth about by counsell and reason drawne from that which is dishonest, from that which is discommodious, from that which is hard and laborious, from that which is not necessarie,

from that which is wicked, from that which is daungerous, and from that which is vnpossible"—but also, and possibly more significantly, of the shaping of the recipient. "Framing" is not only a rhetorical, but a moral and social strategy. This position is noted, although not elaborated, by Louis B. Wright, who assumes Fleming's reference to the "vnlearned" to be tradespeople and argues that Fleming's goal was not only to teach businessmen to write, but to inculcate moral virtues.

Two translations that Fleming did toward the end of his literary career, just before his entry into orders, show his dual concerns with pedagogical method and self-education. The year of Fleming's greatest output was 1580, when his name was attached to ten publications, ranging from translations of tracts and sermons by John Hooper and Nicholas Hemming to the compilation and indexing of John Knox's *A Fort for the afflicted* and Philips van Marnix van sant Aldegonde's *The Bee hiue of the Romishe Churche* and the provision of commendatory verses for John Baret's *An Alvearie Or Quardruple Dictionarie*. In the early part of the decade Fleming's concerns lay largely with Reformist texts and included the compilation of a *Manuell of Christian priaers made by diuers deuout and godly men, as Caluin, Luther, Melangton, and others,* (1581; no known copy in existence), editorial work on Arthur Golding's translations of *The Sermons of M. Iohn Calvin Vpon The Fifth Booke of Moses called Deuteronomie* (1583) and Jacob Wittewronghal's *De vera Christiani hominis fide* (1581), and the compilation and translation of material by Ambrosius Autpertus and St. Bernard of Clairvaux in *A Monomachie of Motives in the mind of man: or A Battell betweene Vertues and Vices of contrarie qualitie* (1582). Other works from this period include original devotional works, *The Footepath of Faith, leading the Highwaie to Heauen* (1578?) and *The Diamond of deuotion, Cut and squared into six severall points* (1581), and poetical translations for Reginald Scot's *The discouerie of witchcraft* (1584). Miller notes that the publication of *The Diamond of Deuotion* led to proceedings against Fleming at the Court of the Stationers' Company because of his inclusion of material from *The Footepath of Faith,* which had been printed earlier in 1581 by Henry Middleton, not by Henry Denham, the printer of the later volume. The resulting order to leave out all of the material from *The Footepath of Faith* in further printings of *The Diamond of Deuotion* does not appear to have been complied with, but no further proceedings were taken. *The Diamond of Deuotion* also shows some of Fleming's literary connections, for it is dedicated to Henry Carey, Lord Hunsdon, and his daughter-in-law Lady Elizabeth Carey, a patron of poets and author of a play, *The tragedie of Mariam* (1613).

Fleming's pedagogical interest reappeared with a revision of Withals's *A Shorte Dictionarie in Latine and*

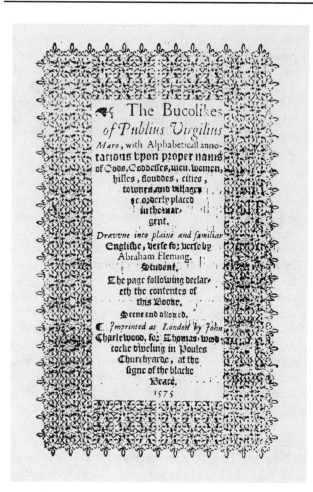

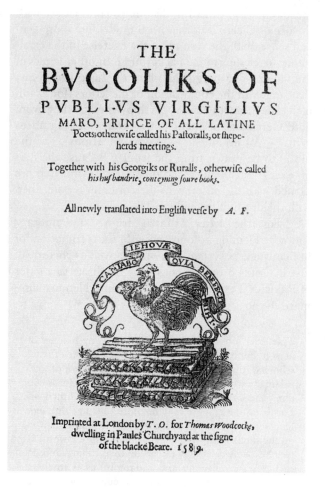

Title pages for two different translations of Virgil's panegyrics on rural life, the works with which Fleming began and ended his literary career

English, verie profitable for yong beginners (1584). Shortly after, between finishing his work on the second edition of Holinshed's *Chronicles* in January 1587 and taking orders in August 1588, Fleming translated Virgil's *Eclogues* and *Georgics*. These were published in 1589 and represent his final printed works. Miller argues that these translations were undertaken as what John Brinsley later called "grammatical translations" in his *Lvdvs Literarivs: or, The Grammar Schoole* (1612) to support the method of double translation promoted by Vives and adapted by Ascham as a means to teach Latin. For Fleming, these literal translations appear intended to serve as the basis for retranslating English into Latin. Miller points out that Fleming's notes "can be interpreted as helps to one stage or another of double translation," but that marginal notes giving examples of Virgil's Latin indicate that Fleming had the English-to-Latin step in mind. Early in the seventeenth century John Brinsley brought together Ascham and Fleming in his own series of translations designed for use in gram-

mar schools. As Miller notes, Brinsley's method was based on Ascham's double translation, but Miller also mentions Fleming's translations of Virgil favorably as tools to facilitate this process in a less instructor-intensive manner.

After his ordination in the diocese of Peterborough, Fleming largely ceased his literary activities, with only one more publication, a revised edition of James Cancellar's *The Alphabet of Praiers* (1591), appearing after that date. As a priest, Fleming served as chaplain to Catherine, Lady Howard, possibly as a result of connections through Peterhouse to John Whitgift, who had become Archbishop of Canterbury in 1583 and to whom Fleming dedicated the *Eclogues* and *Georgics*. Another connection that may have helped him to gain this post was his dedication of works such as *The Diamond of deuotion* to Lady Elizabeth Carey, who was Lady Howard's sister-in-law. After 1593 he became rector of St. Pancras Soper Lane, a small and poor parish in London. Little is known of his activities during this period beyond his preaching sermons at Paul's Cross on eight occasions between 1589 and 29 December 1606. He died during a visit to his brother, Samuel, on 18 September 1607, a date confirmed by the memorial brass in the Church of St. Mary the Virgin in Bottesford, Leicestershire. (Samuel appears as a fictional character in Hilda Lewis's 1956 novel *The Witch and the Priest.*) Fleming's manuscripts were catalogued by Francis Peck in *Desiderata Curiosa* (1735) and titles of many of them are listed in the entry for Fleming in Charles Henry Cooper and Thompson Cooper's *Athenae Cantabrigienses* (1858–1913), as well as in William C. Miller's biography and critical study of Fleming. The manuscript collection itself, however, cannot be traced.

Biographies:

Charles Henry Cooper and Thompson Cooper, "Abraham Fleming," in *Athenae Cantabrigienses,* 3 volumes (Cambridge: Deighton, Bell & Macmillan, 1858–1913), II: 459–464;

William C. Miller, "Life of Abraham Fleming," in his "Abraham Fleming, Elizabethan Man of Letters: A Biographical and Critical Study," dissertation, University of Pennsylvania, 1957, pp. 1–73.

Bibliographies:

Francis Peck, *Desiderata Curiosa* (London: James Bettenham, 1735), volume 1, book 6, pp. 49–56;

William C. Miller, "A Tentative Short-Title Bibliography of the Writings of Abraham Fleming," in his "Abraham Fleming, Elizabethan Man of Letters: A Biographical and Critical Study," dissertation, University of Pennsylvania, 1957, pp. xxxiii–xlii.

References:

T. W. Baldwin, *William Shakepere's Small Latine and Lesse Greeke,* 2 volumes (Urbana: University of Illinois Press, 1944);

Mary Thomas Crane, *Framing Authority: Sayings, Self, and Society in Sixteenth-Century England* (Princeton: Princeton University Press, 1993);

William G. Crane, *Wit and Rhetoric in the Renaissance: The Formal Basis of Elizabethan Prose Style* (New York: Columbia University Press, 1937);

Sarah C. Dodson, "Abraham Fleming, Writer and Editor," *Texas Studies in English,* 34 (1955): 51–66;

Elizabeth Eisenstein, *The Printing Press as an Agent of Change,* 2 volumes (Cambridge: Cambridge University Press, 1979);

Richard Halpern, *The Poetics of Primitive Accumulation: English Renaissance Culture and the Genealogy of Capital* (Ithaca, N.Y.: Cornell University Press, 1991);

Katherine Gee Hornbeak, *The Complete Letter Writer in English: 1568–1800,* Smith College Studies in Modern Languages, 15, nos. 3–4 (Northampton, Mass.: Smith College, 1934);

Jean Robertson, *The Art of Letter Writing: An Essay on the Handbooks Published in England During the Sixteenth and Seventeenth Centuries* (Liverpool: Liverpool University Press / London: Hodder & Stoughton, 1942);

De Witt T. Starnes, *Renaissance Dictionaries: English-Latin and Latin-English* (Austin: University of Texas Press, 1954);

Louis B. Wright, *Middle-Class Culture in Elizabethan England* (Chapel Hill: University of North Carolina Press, 1935).

Abraham Fraunce

(circa 1560 – 1592 or 1593)

William Barker
Memorial University of Newfoundland

BOOKS: *The Lamentations of Amyntas for the death of Phillis, paraphrastically translated out of Latine into English Hexameters by Abraham Fraunce* (London: Printed by John Wolfe for Thomas Newman & Thomas Gubbin, 1587; corrected edition, London: Printed by John Charlewood for Thomas Newman & Thomas Gubbin, 1588);

Abrahami Fransi, Insignium, Armorum, Emblematum, Hieroglyphicorum, Et Symbolorum, quæ ab Italis Imprese nominantur, explicatio: Quæ Symbolicæ philosophiæ postrema pars est (London: Printed by Thomas Orwin for Thomas Gubbin & Thomas Newman, 1588); third part revised as *Symbolicæ Philosophiæ Liber Quartus et Ultimus,* edited by John Manning and translated by Estelle Haan (New York: AMS Press, 1991);

The Arcadian Rhetorike: Or The Præcepts of Rhetorike made plaine by examples, Greeke, Latin, English, Italian, French, Spanish, out of Homers Ilias, and Odissea, Virgils Æglogs, Georgikes, and Æneis, Sir Philip Sydneis Arcadia, Songs and Sonets, Torquato Tassoes Goffredo, Aminta, Torrismondo, Salust his Iudith and Both his Semaines, Boscan and Garcilassoes Sonets and Æglogs. By Abraham Fraunce (London: Printed by Thomas Orwin, 1588);

The Lawiers Logike, exemplifying the præcepts of Logike by the practise of the common Lawe, by Abraham Fraunce (London: Printed by William How, 1588);

The Countesse of Pembrokes Emanuel. Conteining the Natiuity, Passion, Buriall, and Resurrection of Christ: togeather with certaine Psalmes of Dauid. All in English Hexameters. By Abraham Fravnce (London: Printed by Thomas Orwin for William Ponsonby, 1591);

The Countesse of Pembrokes Yvychurch. Conteining the affectionate life, and vnfortunate death of Phillis and Amyntas: That in a Pastorall; This in a Funerall: both in English Hexameters. By Abraham Fravnce (London: Printed by Thomas Orwin for William Ponsonby, 1591)—includes revised edition of *The Lamentations of Amyntas for the death of Phillis;*

The Third Part of the Countesse of Pembrokes Yvychurch. Entituled, Amintas Dale. Wherein are the most conceited tales of the Pagan Gods in English Hexameters, together with their auncient descriptions and Philosophicall explications. By Abraham Fravnce (London: Printed by Thomas Orwin for Thomas Woodcocke, 1592);

Victoria, A Latin Comedy, edited by G. C. Moore Smith, in Materialen zur Kunde des älteren Englischen dramas, volume 14, edited by W. Bang (Louvain, Belgium: A. Uystpruyst, 1906; New York: Kraus, 1963);

The Shepherd's Logic (ca. 1585?), English Linguistics, 1500–1800, no. 185 (Menston, U.K.: Scolar, 1969).

Editions: *The Countesse of Pembroke's Emanuell together with Certaine Psalmes (1591),* Miscellanies of the Fuller Worthies' Library, volume 3, edited by Alexander B. Grosart (Blackburn, U.K.: Privately printed, 1871);

The Arcadian Rhetorike, edited by Ethel Seaton (Oxford: Published by Blackwell for the Luttrell Society, 1950; Westport, Conn.: Hyperion Press, 1979);

Thomas Watson's Latin Amyntas (1585) Edited by Walter F. Staton, Jr. & Abraham Fraunce's Translation: The Lamentations of Amyntas (1587) Edited by Franklin M. Dickey, edited by Walter F. Staton Jr. and Franklin M. Dickey, Publications of the Renaissance English Text Society, volume 2 (Chicago: Published by University of Chicago Press for the Newberry Library, 1967);

"A Critical Edition of Abraham Fraunce's 'The Sheapheardes Logike' and 'Twooe General Discourses,'" edited by Mary M. McCormick, dissertation, Saint Louis University, 1968);

The Lawyer's Logic, 1588, English Linguistics, 1500–1800, no. 174 (Menston, U.K.: Scolar, 1969);

The Arcadian Rhetoric (1588), English Linguistics, 1500–1800, no. 176 (Menston, U.K.: Scolar, 1969);

The Third Part of the Countesse of Pembrokes Yuychurch, Entitled Amintas Dale, edited by Gerald Snare, Renaissance Editions, no. 8 (Northridge: California State University, 1975);

The Golden Booke of the Leaden Gods: London 1577, Stephen Batman; The Third Part of . . . Yvychurch: London 1592, Abraham Fraunce; The Fountaine of Ancient Fiction: London 1599, Richard Lynche, introduction by Stephen Orgel (New York & London: Garland, 1976);

Insignium, armorum: London, 1588, Abraham Fraunce. Traicté des devises: Paris, 1620, Adrian d'Amboise. The Art of Making Devises: London, 1650, Henri Estienne, introductory notes by Orgel (New York: Garland, 1979);

Victoria, in *Hymenaeus. Abraham Fraunce Victoria. Laelia,* introduction by Horst-Dieter Blume (Hildesheim, Germany & New York: Olms, 1991).

Abraham Fraunce belonged to an active circle of writers in the 1570s and 1580s who were associated with Philip Sidney, his brother Robert, and his sister Mary Herbert, Countess of Pembroke. Although he did write a play in Latin and was an experimenter in verse, Fraunce was not himself what would now be termed a creative writer. His most significant works in his short career of publication (from 1587 to 1592) were translations, textbooks in rhetoric and logic, and a work of mythological explication. These were important in the intellectual life of his time and are still of great interest to anyone who wishes to understand how the learning of the university was disseminated in the broader culture of the Elizabethan period. Fraunce was extremely learned and sharply attuned to literary fashion; his abilities made him a successful popularizer of Latin and Continental materials, and he contributed significantly to the growth of an increasingly sophisticated public culture in English. His works, ranging from a play and poetry to textbooks in rhetoric and logic, all fall under the general rubric of the arts of language.

Abraham Fraunce was born in Shrewsbury, in northern England, about the year 1560. His exact date of birth is not recorded and is derived by counting back from his matriculation at Cambridge (he probably started university at the normal age of sixteen or seventeen, and his name is first registered there in 1576). His family had a long history in the region and was secure and reasonably well off, and was principally associated with the Glovers' Company, a guild in Shrewsbury. Not a gentleman by birth, Fraunce attained this status later by virtue of his attendance at the university and the Inns of Court.

Fraunce is listed as a student at Shrewsbury School in the register of the school for 1571. Founded just a few years earlier in 1562, Shrewsbury grew quickly and was for a time the largest grammar school

in England (360 students by 1581). Fraunce's first master may have been the well-known Thomas Ashton, who left the school about 1571; Fraunce was later taught by Thomas Lawrence. At the school, according to its ordinances, as quoted in T. W. Baldwin's *William Shakspere's Small Latine and Lesse Greeke* (1944), the boys studied "for prose in latten Tullie [Cicero], Caesar his Comentaries, Salust and Livie, also two litle books of Dialogues, drawn out of Tulleys Offices and Lodovicus Vives by Mr Thomas Ashton sometyme cheife schoolemaster of the said schoole: for verse, Virgill, Horace, Ovid and Terence: for greke the greke grammer of Cleonarde, the greke testament, Isocrates ad Demonicum or Xenophon his Cyrus . . ."–in other words, a fairly standard but demanding humanist curriculum introducing the boys to some basic texts in Latin and Greek. In addition to the regular classroom curriculum, both masters trained the boys to present plays and public orations, apparently of high quality. Shrewsbury was an exceptionally good school, good enough for Philip Sidney and Fulke Greville, who attended just a few years before Fraunce. That such a well-placed young man as Sidney went to the school would have been unusual; at that time the well-to-do gentry and the nobility usually did not send their boys to public schools. Perhaps Fraunce met Sidney at Shrewsbury; certainly he knew him and his family well in later years.

In 1576 Fraunce began university at St. John's College, Cambridge. There is a record of his matriculation on 26 May of that year. St. John's was by then one of the most intellectually respectable of the colleges, with Roger Ascham and John Cheke as two of its most famous fellows in an earlier time. Thomas Ashton had also attended this college, and there seems to have been a close association between St. John's and Shrewsbury School. Although Fraunce began as a pensioner (a paying student), two years later, on 8 November 1578, he was registered as a scholar, meaning that he was now to be supported by a foundation in the college; perhaps he or his family had run into some financial difficulty. In the preface to *The Lawiers Logike, exemplifying the præcepts of Logike by the practise of the common Lawe* (1588) Fraunce suggests that he was supported in his studies by Sidney, and in 1592 his patron Henry Herbert, the second Earl of Pembroke, writing on behalf of Fraunce, says he was "bred up by my brother [that is, Pembroke's brother-in-law] Sʳ *Philip Sidney* longe in *Cambridge.*" In 1581 on completion of the B.A., he became a fellow of the college and stayed there until he completed the M.A. in 1583.

Fraunce's earliest known work was the Latin comedy *Victoria.* He must have written it prior to 1583, while he was still at St. John's, Cambridge (the play makes reference to Sidney before he was knighted,

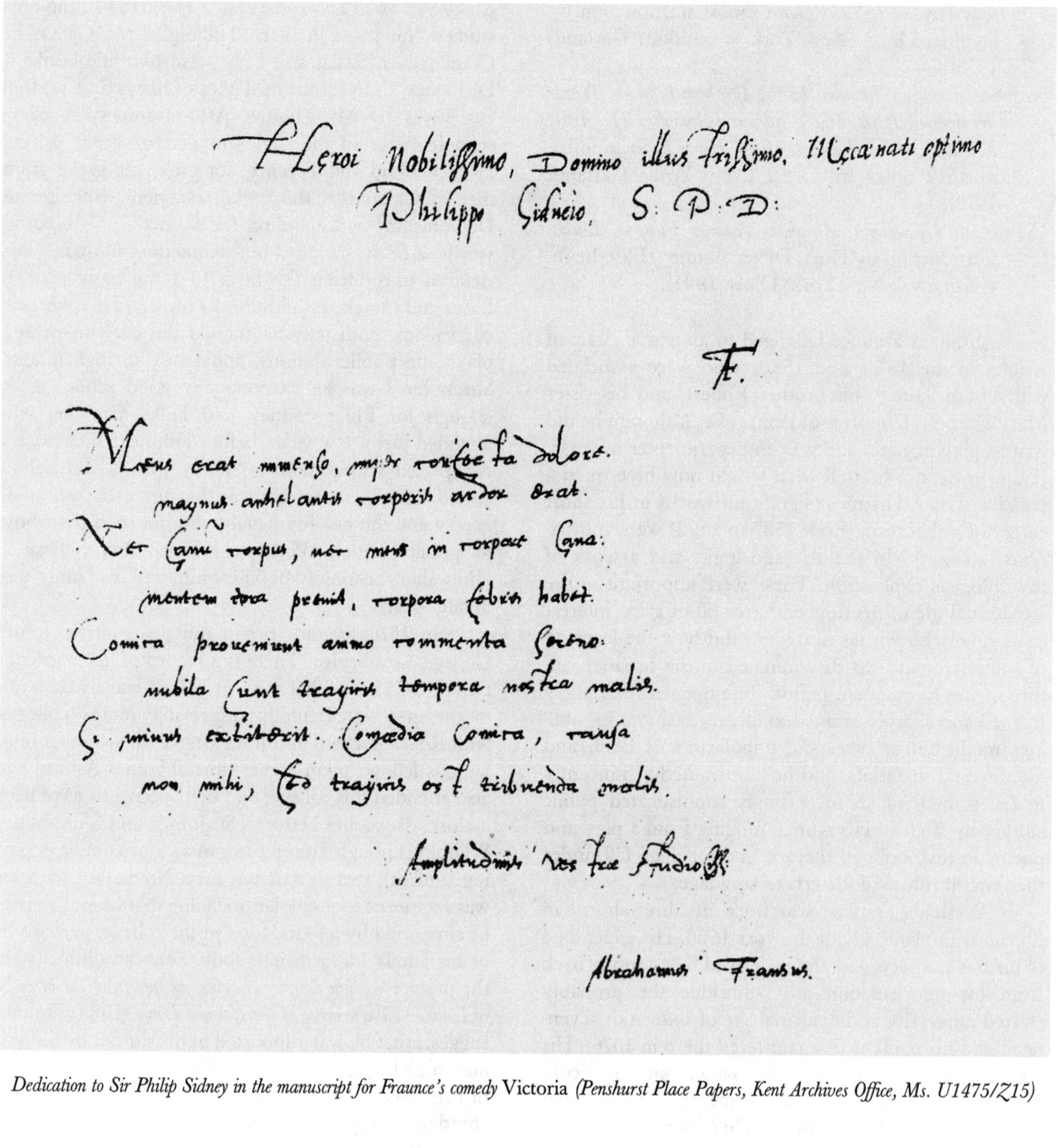
Heroi Nobilissimo, Domino illustrissimo, Mecænati optimo
Philippo Sidneio. S. P. D.

F.

Mæror erat immensus, mihi confecta dolore.
magnus anhelantis corporis ardor erat.
Nec sanum corpus, nec mens in corpore sana:
mentem cura premit, corpora febris habet.
Comica proveniunt animo commenta sereno:
nubila sunt tragicis tempora nostra malis.
Si minus exhibeat Comœdia comica, causa
non mihi, sed tragicis est tribuenda malis.

Amplitudinis tuæ studiosiss.

Abrahamus Fransus.

Dedication to Sir Philip Sidney in the manuscript for Fraunce's comedy Victoria *(Penshurst Place Papers, Kent Archives Office, Ms. U1475/Z15)* which was in January 1583). It remained in manuscript until G. C. Moore Smith edited and published it in 1906. Shrewsbury School was known for its theatrical productions, and it seems likely that Fraunce began his involvement in the drama there. He continued at Cambridge: as Moore Smith notes, in 1579 he acted in Thomas Legge's *Richardus Tertius* (or *Richard III*, as Civis Secundus, or Second Citizen) and in an anonymous *Hymenaeus* (as Ferdinandus, father of Erophilus). That he would turn to prepare his own play seems a natural consequence.

Although the debt is not announced, *Victoria* is an adaptation of Luigi Pasqualigo's *Il Fedele* (The Faithful One), an Italian play that appeared first in 1576 and in a revised edition in 1579. (It was also the basis for Anthony Munday's *Fidele and Fortunio, the Two Italian Gentlemen,* 1585.) Fraunce's version tells the story of a young woman, who, though married to Cornelius, is in love with Fidelis, then with Fortunius; and Victoria in turn is loved by Onophrius, the teacher of Fidelis. The play contains the usual tricky servants, a boasting soldier named Frangipetra ("Rock-breaker"), generational conflicts, a conclusion that seems practically miraculous in its tidiness, and other recognizable devices from the plays of Terence and Plautus and Greek New Comedy. Yet, the play has more characters than is usual for such imitations and several active subplots. Many of the individual lines are lifted directly from classical drama; there are also many passages reminiscent of the works of Ovid, Cicero, and Catullus; and there are other scraps of lore and learning, some of them absurd (for instance act 2, scene 7, in which Victoria's maid Attilia and the servant Narcissus argue over definitions of what kind of person she is, in part using the Aristotelian predicaments). All of the referentiality is typical of the university entertainment of the time; there was special enjoyment to be had in the recognition of a tag or classical sentence. The play is clever in this regard, but as a sustained piece of drama it is not a success, and the Italian original is much more successful as stageable drama than this highly academic experiment. Nevertheless, it is a fine display of learning and the manuscript was a suitable gift to the patron of his university years, Philip Sidney.

Another gift was his manuscript titled "The Sheapheardes Logike: Conteyning the præcepts of that art put downe by Ramus; Examples fet. owt of the Sheapheards Kalinder; Notes and expositions collected owt of Bourhusius, Piscator, Mr Chatterton; and diuers others. Together wth twooe general Discourses, the one touchinge the prayse and ryghte vse of Logike: the other concernynge the comparison of Ramus his Logike, wth that of Aristotle. To the Ryght worshypful Mr Edwarde Dyer." This work, not published until 1969, is actually in three parts: "The Sheapheardes Logike" (about 18,000 words long), "Of the Nature and Use of Logike" (2,300 words), and "A Brief and General Comparison of Ramus his Logike with that of Aristotle" (3,400 words). The manuscript is dedicated on the title page to Sir Edward Dyer, a member of the Sidney circle and himself a well-known poet, though the third treatise is dedicated separately to Philip Sidney. These works are a series of introductions to the writings of Pierre de La Ramée (known as Petrus Ramus), a sixteenth-century French teacher and philosopher whose writings were immensely influential throughout Europe. In "The Sheapheardes Logike" Fraunce summarizes the main points of Ramus's doctrines, and, following Ramus, uses as his examples of various logical devices passages from literature. What makes Fraunce's work especially interesting is that he uses in his first section Edmund Spenser's popular *The Shepheardes Calender Conteyning tvvelue Æglogues proportionable to the twelve monethes* (1579). By so doing, he is introducing the work of Ramus to Dyer and Sidney and at the same time accommodating Continental writing to English literary life. Much of this material is reused in his much longer work *The Lawiers Logike,* published a few years later.

Related to this work is another short treatise, written about the same time. The "Tractatus de usu dialectices" (Treatise on the Use of Dialectic) is the short opening section of a manuscript (Bodleian Rawlinson D.345), also dedicated to Philip Sidney. This beautifully prepared work of fifty-six leaves begins with the "Tractatus de usu dialectices" and concludes with forty leaves of emblematic poems, pictures, and some prose commentary written around the devices of celebrated rulers and religious figures on the Continent, most from the preceding one hundred years–for example, Lorenzo de' Medici, Alexander Farnese, Duke of Parma, Louis XII of France, Francis I of France, and Pope Alexander VI– each with a motto and a poem. These devices are based on Paolo Giovio's well-known *Dialogo dell'imprese* (Dialogue on Impresas, 1555). As Katherine Duncan-Jones has shown in a 1971 article, Fraunce follows the expanded edition prepared by Gabriele Simeoni, published by Rouillé in Lyons in 1574. The emblem pictures are attractively drawn, and the verses are elaborated expansions of shorter poems that appeared in the originating text. That Fraunce would combine a study on dialectic with a series of emblem poems may seem odd to a modern reader; however, in the Renaissance the two projects were seen to be related: dialectic is concerned with the way words may be used to signify, emblematics with the way meaning can be conveyed through nonverbal signs.

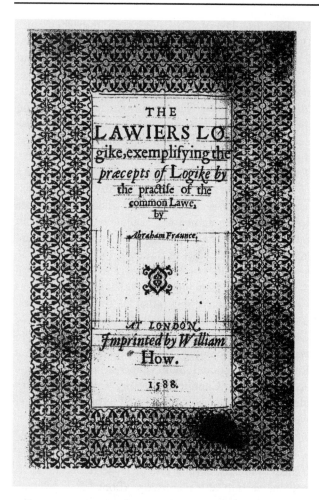

Title page for the work Fraunce wrote after realizing "the practice of Law to bee the use of Logike, and the methode of Logike to lighten the Lawe"

University graduates often opted for the church, but Fraunce took another common route upon completion of his M.A. degree. On 5 June 1583 he became a student of Gray's Inn in London, one of the Inns of Court where young men trained in a formal apprenticeship to the law. Fraunce studied the law for five years, and on 8 February 1588 he was called to the bar. Soon afterward he began to work in Wales, in the Court of Marches (a court that resolved pleas of debt or damages), as a lawyer. Yet, he continued to publish, following the themes already established in his manuscript writings. Despite the so-called stigma of print (according to which many authors of the time professed themselves to be embarrassed to find their work in print), one way to prove oneself to be an interesting young man was to publish literary works that demonstrated learning. The early writings of Christopher Marlowe (before he turned to the more disreputable stage), the poetry of Spenser, the Latin verses of Gabriel Harvey,

the writings of Dyer, Thomas Watson, Lodowick Bryskett, and many others are all bids for notice and patronage. The idea was to appear in public reluctantly, but with some deftness of style, and to demonstrate learning and intelligence in one's writings. The writings themselves paid the writer little or nothing, but the result of a well-written and well-dedicated piece of writing might be a position gained through court patronage. Fraunce's literary writing should be seen within this context. The early manuscripts were private manifestations of his allegiances to Philip and Robert Sidney and to Dyer. The printed works were public manifestations, the later ones above all to Philip's sister Mary Herbert, Countess of Pembroke. The manuscripts are often shorter, preparatory versions of longer printed works. If anything characterizes the overall literary output, it is the way Fraunce seeks to bring materials from new sources into English culture. His art consists of this mediation, and he is, in his writing, an extremely clever and entertaining teacher.

Fraunce's first published literary work was *The Lamentations of Amyntas for the death of Phillis, paraphrastically translated out of Latine into English Hexameters,* a translation of Watson's *Amyntas* (1585), a sequence of pastoral lamentations in Latin. Fraunce's translation came out in 1587, while he was still at Gray's Inn. Watson had a reputation as a sophisticated university wit (he had spent seven years in Italy and had close ties with Marlowe), and his English writing, above all his pioneering sonnet sequence *The Hekatompathia or passionate centurie of love* (1582), was greatly admired. Fraunce does not reveal that his work is a translation of Watson's poem, and Watson, in an introduction to his eclogue *Melibœus Thomæ Watsoni siuè, ecloga in Obitum Honoratissimi Viri, Domini Francisci Walsingham, Equitis auratæ divæ Elizabethæ a secretis, sanctioribus consiliis* (1590; translated as *An eglogue vpon the death of sir F. Walsingham,* 1590), complains about Fraunce's oversight. He had cause to complain—up to 1600 the text went through one edition in Latin and six editions in Fraunce's English, making the English version as widely circulated as Spenser's *The Shepheardes Calender.*

Fraunce gives a fair representation of Watson's reasonably skillful Latin text, but he pushes it in new directions. The English hexameters are strongly accented and favor heavy repetition of sound and even of words, as an example from the end of the second lamentation demonstrates:

Officiis ibi te vincam, tu me quoque vinces,
Florea serta tuo capiti mea dextera texet,
Florea serta meo capiti tua dextera texet,
Amboque sub viridi myrto repetemus amores,
Quos olim parili versu cantauimus ambo.

In Dana Sutton's modern prose translation, this passage reads:

> There I shall best you in dutifulness, or you will best me; my hand will weave garlands for your head, yours will weave them for mine. Beneath a green myrtle we shall regain our loves, of which we once sang in equal-shared song.

Fraunce renders this passage as:

> There shal Phillis againe, in curtesie striue with Amintas.
> There with Phillis againe, in curtesie striue shal Amintas,
> There shall Phillis againe make garlands gay for Amintas,
> There for Phillis againe, gay garlands make shal Amintas,
> There shal Phillis againe be repeating songs with Amintas,
> Which songs Phillis afore had made and song with Amintas.

Although such a passage is hardly delightful to the modern ear, it gives a good sense of the way Fraunce likes to play with variations. He picks up the two repeated lines in Watson and runs with them. Perhaps this poem is meant to be a display of the abundant style, in the tradition of Desiderius Erasmus's *De duplici copia rerum ac verborum commentarii duo* (Two Commentaries on the Abundance of Both Things and Words, 1512), with its famous two hundred variations in Latin of the greeting to his friend Thomas More: "Always, as long as I live, I shall remember you." But such a heavy hand may not be quite what Erasmus had in mind. Fraunce does it again and again in *The Lamentations of Amyntas for the death of Phillis*. In some instances it seems to work a bit better, as in a passage near the beginning of the ninth lamentation, in which repetition fits the psychology of the distracted lover:

> But whilst naked lims with roabs al ragged he cou'red,
> Oft did he call and crie for Phillis, for bon[n]y Phillis,
> With deepe sighs and grons still Phillis, Phillis he called . . .

The work may seem awkward, but the reader must remember that Fraunce is experimenting. He continued using the English hexameters in his later writings, up to his last work, *Amintas Dale*.

The use of hexameters for English verse was a fairly new phenomenon that had its encouragement from such talented writers as Philip Sidney and Spenser. It was given academic respectability by Gabriel Harvey and Thomas Drant, who encouraged this classicizing movement. Although ideally such verse, like the classical, sought to have its force in quantities (the length and shortness of the syllables), in English such verse could not avoid accentuation. The rhythms are boldly repetitive; Derek Attridge refers to Fraunce's verse as "jogtrot." The verse form has occasionally been revived in

English (for instance, by the nineteenth-century poet A. C. Swinburne, who understood the force of the accent in the line), but generally is regarded to be unsuccessful. Certainly the work of the Elizabethans, which arose out of a political project to strengthen ties between the classical language and an "impoverished" English, was undertaken with good intentions. But it was doomed. Despite the praise of George Peele, who in *The Honour of the Garter* (1593) calls Fraunce "a peerless sweet translator of our time," Fraunce was open to criticism and parody. Richard Barnfield's "Helens Rape, or a Light Lanthorne for Light Ladies" (the concluding part of his *The Affectionate Shepheard. Containing the complaint of Daphnis for the loue of Ganymede* of 1594) begins in mockery of the extreme Frauncian manner: "Lovely a Lasse, so loved a Lasse, and (alas) such a loving / Lasse, for a while (but a while) was none such a sweet bonny Love-Lasse / As *Helen*. . . ." Ben Jonson, who had as good an ear for the comparative merits of Latin and English as any writer of his age, said, in conversation with William Drummond of Hawthornden, "That Abram Francis in his English Hexameters was a Foole." Though verse experiments improved with the later poems, Jonson's assessment may be true.

In 1588, the year that Fraunce began work as a lawyer, he saw three of his most important books published. All three continue themes established in his manuscript writings, with the logic being the strongest thread in his writing and thinking. In the preface to *The Lawiers Logike* he describes how over the period of seven years (that is, from about 1580 or 1581 onward) he has been "a medler with these Logical meditations." In the beginning, he says, he wrote the treatises for "that right noble and most renowmed knight sir Philip Sydney," then afterward repeatedly revised the work until he came to Gray's Inn and his new profession of the law, when he undertook a further revision, this time perceiving that "the practice of Law to bee the use of Logike, and the methode of Logike to lighten the Lawe." In "The Sheapheardes Logike," for instance, Fraunce had used passages from Spenser's *The Shepheardes Calender* to exemplify the logical principles. Although the printed text is a considerable expansion of this earlier work, it retains the general structure and also the examples from *The Shepheardes Calender* (which come to a total of ninety-seven). The main difference is a slight modification of the principles examined, the addition of sometimes lengthy commentaries or "annotations" to the principles, and many new quotations, sometimes extremely lengthy, from Edmund Plowden's commentaries on cases in common law and other legal texts.

The Lawiers Logike is a strange, heterogeneous text, combining as it does the new Ramist dialectic, the older logic as it was taught in the university, the "new literature" of Spenser, and copious selections in law French and law Latin. Fraunce's preface is a vigorous defense of this enterprise, arguing that university learning and the law have much to teach one another, and that the study of each is equally plagued by obscurity:

> I know by experience, there is no word so out-worne, no speach so vast and gaping in Brytton, Bracton, Glanvyll, Lytleton, Parkins, and the rest of our Law autors and reporters of the law, as is in Bricot, Burley, Bonaventure, Duns, Durand, D'orbell, Aquinas, Andreas, Albertus, and a farre more infinite number of those Moonkish cloysterers devoured of Schollers, than bee of thease others perused by Lawyers. And yet, notwithstanding all their Perseities, Formalities, Quiddities, Haecceities, Albedinities, Animalities, Substantialities, and such like, hee that would not gather gould out of Aquinas dregs, as Virgill did out of Ennius, I shall thinke him as wise, as some seelly Pettyfogger, who rather than hee would trouble his conscience with Feetayl and Feesimple, will lyve like a simple foole, and never take fee.

Having established that the two types of learning have something to say to one another, Fraunce also tries to show that the common law can be treated as methodically as the civil, and that logic has a place in this methodizing. Finally, he attempts to resolve the debate then current in England between the old logic of Aristotle and the new dialectic of Ramus. One of the criticisms of Ramist logic is that it puts the tools of method in the hands of the ignorant: "Hereby it comes to passe that every Cobler can cogge a Syllogisme, every Carter crake of Propositions. Hereby is Logike prophaned, and lyeth prostitute, removed out of her Sanctuary, robbed of her honour, left of her lovers, ravyshed of straungers, and made common to all, which before was proper to Schoolemen, and only consecrated to Philosophers." Fraunce rejects this argument entirely. "Coblers bee men, why therefore not Logicians? and Carters have reason, why therefore not Logike?" So much for the argument against the making of logic available to all. And as for Ramus being an enemy of Aristotle, "where Aristotle deserveth prayse, who more commendeth him then Ramus?"

Fraunce's answer to the need for a synthetic logic for the practical rhetorician is a structured presentation of the basic principles of logic, but demonstrated by literary and legal examples. This potent exemplification of dialectic by examples traditionally related to these other areas of the arts of discourse was one of the most appealing aspects of the Ramist program. In his French *Dialectique De Pierre De La Ramee, A Charles De Lorraine Chardinal, son Mercene* (Dialectic, 1555) and the revised Latin translation *Dialecticæ libri duo, Audomari Talaei praelectionibus illustrati* (Two Books of Dialectic, Illus-

trated with Omer Talon's Annotations, 1556), Ramus used literary examples from Cicero, Ovid, Horace, and Virgil to exemplify his rules, many of the passages translated by such contemporary poets as Etienne Pasquier, Rémy Belleau, Pierre de Ronsard, and Jean Du Bellay. Fraunce's *The Lawiers Logike* follows Ramus in offering a simplified guide to the basic ideas of logic as reorganized by the new method, but it brings the material into the English context, with examples taken from the best known of contemporary literary experiments, *The Shepheardes Calender,* and from that most English of institutions, the common law. The simplification of the dialectic and the addition of the sophisticated literary and legal passages put him in the center of the Ramist tradition—not only had Ramus used literary examples, but his followers, such as Johannes Thomas Freigius (also known as Freig), used Ramist dialectic to analyze legal texts.

Ramism was of great interest in England at the time, in part because it greatly simplified the instruction of logic. Richard Hooker wrote in his *Of the Lavves of Ecclesiaticall Politie* (1593) about the speed by which people could learn logic, "as much almost in three dayes, as if it dwell threescore yeares with them." Ramus's dialectic certainly offered a swift outline of some of the basic divisions and principles of logic, and for that reason was a powerful textbook. But this was not the old logic of the scholastics, which was grounded on formal syllogistic reasoning. Instead Ramus, following the fifteenth-century Rodolphus Agricola (Roelof Huysman), a fifteenth-century scholar who spent most of his life traveling about universities in Germany and Italy, presented a single art of discourse, called "dialectic," which combined elements of both Aristolelian logic and dialectic, as well as rhetoric. The new emphasis was on the methods of finding and generating arguments (by a process called invention), to make what Agricola called an "art of influencing," which allowed a single method for the use of certainty (in the syllogism) and likelihood (found in the enthymeme). Thus, when Ramus and Fraunce find "logic" in literature (or even the law), they are merely pointing out that the arts of persuasion cannot be separated apart into scientific and nonscientific modes. Both syllogistic and nonsyllogistic reasoning find their sources in the unifying principles of dialectic, which are based on what Ramus referred to as "natural" mental operations.

The Ramist approach was quickly adopted across Europe. Not only did Ramism offer an interesting new theory of logic, but it supplanted the way of doing syllogistic logic with a set of simpler procedures (broader categories, more acceptance of the branching method, and so on). Indeed, many scholars have argued that this emphasis on simplification and accessibility of logic, more than any new theory of logic, was Ramus's great gift. Certainly Ramus was a brilliant writer of textbooks. His personal reputation also played a part in the spread of the doctrines: he was known to have defended a thesis opposing Aristotle (though daring, it was not a radical position); he was a known iconoclast and enemy of the status quo; and he became a staunch Protestant who was killed in Paris during the St. Bartholomew's Day Massacre of 1572. He was a philosopher, touched with the mysterious sanctity of the martyr and true believer. His ideas caught on among the young and sophisticated in many European countries.

Fraunce may have first encountered the Ramist theories at Cambridge, either in books of his own reading (the texts were becoming widely available, with Roland MacIlmaine's Latin edition and his English translation of *Dialecticæ libri duo* having been published as early as 1574), or in the lectures (never published) of Laurence Chadderton, fellow of Christ's College from 1568 to 1577, or in rhetoric lectures of Gabriel Harvey in 1575 and 1576, published in 1577 as his *Ciceronianus.* There were, of course, strong reactions against Ramist thought, some arguing that it oversimplified and that it claimed far too much as a philosophy. In 1580 Everard Digby wrote against the Ramist method (arguing that there were instead two methods of working scientifically, and that Ramus was incorrectly conflating logic and rhetoric); Digby was thought to be a papist and was expelled from St. John's, Cambridge. The strongest defense came from William Temple, fellow of King's College, Cambridge, who in 1581 argued strongly for Ramus, countering not only Digby but also Georgius Lieblerus and Johannes Piscator, two Continental anti-Ramists. Three years later, Temple published a Latin edition with commentary of the *Dialecticae libri duo,* dedicating his work to Philip Sidney, and later on wrote a Ramist commentary on the Psalms. At the same time, London printers produced commentaries on Ramus by two Germans, Friedrich Beurhaus, in 1581, 1582, 1589, and William Adolf Scribonius, 1583.

All this activity in the 1580s gives important background to Fraunce's work. It is clear that Fraunce was working within a well-defined field of controversy (he refers directly to the work of Beurhaus) and patronage (Philip Sidney had obviously been identified as a patron of the Ramist cause). One has the sense that Fraunce was asked on several occasions to explain the Ramist phenomenon to others, and the manuscripts for Sidney and Dyer are just two of these attempts. The printed work for lawyers is his fullest and most elaborate explication.

The Lawiers Logike follows the order of topics in Ramist dialectic, beginning with the definition of logic

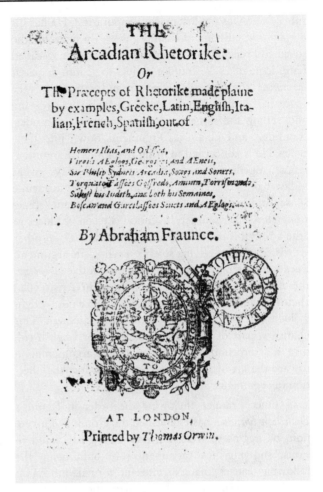

Title page for the work in which Fraunce quoted passages from manuscript versions of Sidney's The Countess of Pembrokes Arcadia *and Edmund Spenser's* The Faerie Queene, *neither of which had yet been published*

(it is an "art of reasoning" with rules and a method). But despite the familiar beginning from first principles, this work is not to be the same kind of logic studied by "those miserable *Sorbonists,* & dunsicall *Quidditaries.*" Rather, "Reade *Homer,* reade *Demosthenes,* reade *Virgill,* read *Cicero,* reade *Bartas,* reade *Torquato Tasso,* reade that most worthie ornament of our English tongue, the *Countesse of Penbrookes Arcadia,* and therein see the true effectes of natural Logike which is the ground of artificiall, farre different from this rude and barbarous kind of outworne sophistrie." Following Ramus, Fraunce is rewriting the "art" of logic to reflect its natural operations, and nowhere is that "natural" activity of logic more apparent than in literature, hence the large number of examples.

Fraunce follows the same branching method of Ramus (the relation between *ramus,* the Latin word for "branch," and Ramus's system of binary division and subdivision was not lost on contemporaries). He has his eye on two editions of Ramus's work on dialectic, the so-called French logic of 1555 and perhaps the so-called Latin logic of 1572. Fraunce divides logic into its parts: *exposition,* "the particular affection and nature of every severall argument," and *disposition,* which, "by ordering and setling the same, causeth judgement and understanding," and he breaks arguments down into their types. He is concerned to bring two kinds of argumentation together—arguments from infallibility (what today would be called logic in the strict, academic sense) and arguments that are more contingent (something closer to rhetoric). Invention is to move closer to "the severall force or affection of arguments"; in other words, instead of relying solely on syllogistic argument, the student is now going to rely more on the *enthymeme,* the nonsyllogistic proof so important in Aristotelian rhetoric. One learns to sway one's audience not by tight syllogistic reasoning, but by paralogical argument. This change is part of Ramus's significance for English culture, a redirection of logic from simple argumentation toward the art of speaking well, to allow for "the affection of arguments."

Once Fraunce (following the order in Ramus's *Dialectic æ libri duo*) has established the grounds of invention, he begins to work his way through its subdivisions, showing how arguments are built using the following: causes (material, efficient, formal, and final); the thing caused; the whole, the part, the general, and the special; the subject; the adjunct; the difference; the opposite; the contrary; secondary arguments; distribution (of causes, of effects, of arguments); definition, description; borrowed argument; compared argument; of the equal, the greater, the less.

In the second book Fraunce proceeds to disposition, also called judgment. He begins with axioms (negative and positive, true and false, simple and congregative, "connexive" and disjunctive and "discretive"). Then he moves to syllogisms, which are made up of more than one axiom. These are divided up into simple, contracted, explicative, connexive, and disjunctive. Each section begins with definitions (often from several sources), then examples from *The Shepheardes Calender.* Then follow annotations and further elaborations on the definitions and explication of the terms, usually presented with considerable law material, in law French or Latin or sometimes English.

The work concludes its main part with some observations on method. Ramus's *Dialectic æ libri duo* concludes similarly, and Fraunce follows his master in his technical definition of the subject, by relating it to disposition:

> Method is a disposition of divers coherent axiomes, whereby the most general is ever first placed: and of divers syllogismes whereby the best and principall is first put downe, in such sort that thereby all of them may bee the more easily perceaved and better remembred.

This kind of method is to be used in any art or teaching, that is, to begin with the universal axiom and lay out the arguments descending from the central claim, moving through more and more detailed arguments until one reaches the level of example. Historians, poets, orators, and the like also require the universal axiom to be present in the work, yet may have to change the pattern and sequence in order to please the readership. They often require a "concealed or hidden methode." The point is to "use art, without any suspition of art." Their disposition is perforce different from that used in the outline of an "art" which follows a highly regulated order.

Then follow two analyses based on the principles of this method. The first is a breakdown of the arguments in Virgil's Second Eclogue (following material from the Ramist writer Freigius). Fraunce supplies the Latin text and a translation into his beloved hexameters. Then follows the analysis in point form, using elaborate sets of printer's braces to show the way the meaning can be broken down sequentially, mostly in binaries. The eclogue is treated as an argument by Corydon directed both to the young shepherd Alexis and to Corydon himself. The second analysis is a long breakdown of the arguments in two legal documents of some moment, the transcript of the trial of Thomas Percy, seventh Earl of Northumberland, who led a rebellion against Queen Elizabeth I in 1569, and the *Plees del Coron* (or "Crown Pleas," extant editions from 1560 onward) of Sir William Stanford (1509–1558). The legal arguments are shown to consist of causes, adjuncts, and testimonies. Fraunce points out the syllogisms and enthymemes in the presentation of the case. Again, the whole is broken down with printer's braces into many divisions and subdivisions. As a method for finding one's way through testimonies and arguments in a long and complex case, the branching method may have been helpful as a system of analysis, but in the remarkably elaborate form displayed here, it is difficult to know whether the method helped or hindered the young lawyer in training. Of course, the technique of dichotomizing was already known to English readers from such pre-Ramist works as the second part of Roger Ascham's *Toxophilus, The schole of shootinge conteyned in two bookes* (1545), which methodizes the "art" of archery in a series of binary divisions, but Fraunce's work carries the technique to more elaborate lengths.

One of the strengths of Fraunce's work is its treatment of fallacies, as C. L. Hamblin and Ralph S. Pomeroy have both argued. Aristotle, in the *Sophistical Refutations,* had argued that a fallacy was a mistake in reasoning; Ramus, in his *Dialectic æ libri duo,* claimed that the fallacy was a dialectical vice resulting from a deliberate attempt to deceive; Fraunce, however, takes the fallacy as a kind of false argument that counterfeits a good argument. By discussing good arguments and false arguments together, Fraunce is able to establish a relationship between good and false argumentation that is still, argues Hamblin, of great interest to logicians. Pomeroy analyzes the way this understanding of fallacies is made integral to the structure of *The Lawiers Logike,* because the fallacies are analyzed within the general discussion of invention and disposition, and not, as had traditionally been the case, separated out.

Ultimately, for Fraunce the skill of the logician was to be discovered not in abstract mastery but in practice. Near the end of *The Lawiers Logike,* he says:

> Hee that hath a generall sight in Logike, hath but the shadowe. He that is acquainted with the particuler practise, is the only true and perfit logician. I will never call him a Musitian that never sang: a Carpenter that never builded house: a Souldier that never fought . . . no more will I thinke him worthie of the title and name of a Logician, that never put his generall contemplation of logicall precepts in particuler practise.

Fraunce's other work on language published in 1588 was his *The Arcadian Rhetorike: Or The Præcepts of Rhetorike made plaine by examples.* This work also follows a Ramist text, this time a rhetoric book first published in 1544 by Ramus's main collaborator, Omer Talon, known as Audemarus Talaeus. Fraunce is probably working from a later edition of this work; quite possibly a 1567 Paris text with the title *Rhetorica, Petri Rami praelectionibus illustrata* (Rhetoric, Illustrated by the Commentaries of Petrus Ramus), as Fraunce's editor Ethel Seaton argues. Parts of Talaeus's rhetoric were adapted into English by Dudley Fenner as *The Artes of Logicke and Rhetorike, plainelie set fourth in the Englishe tounge, easie to be learned and practised* (1584). Fraunce's version is not a translation as such, but an adaptation. It gives a remarkably compressed review of the subject. It begins with the requisite definition: "Rhetorike is an Art of speaking. It hath two parts, Eloquion and Pronuntiation." Those who knew the ancient tradition of rhetoric would have been astonished by this claim, for, after all, most ancient commentators would have said that rhetoric consisted of at least four and usually five parts: invention, disposition, style, memory, and delivery. Talaeus and Ramus—and Fraunce following them—carved out the first two areas of invention and disposi-

tion and assigned them to dialectic (and included in them many parts of the traditional curriculum in logic). Memory is also included implicitly in dialectic. The last two areas, *elocutio* and *pronuntiatio,* Fraunce's "Eloqution and Pronuntiation," what today might be called style and delivery, are all that now remain of rhetoric in the scheme of Talaeus and Ramus.

Fraunce marches quickly through his two main areas. In part one, on style, he begins with *tropes* ("a trope or turning is when a word is turned from his naturall signification, to some other . . . This was first invented of necessitie for want of words, but afterwards continued and frequented by the delight and pleasant grace thereof"). Tropes are broken down under only four categories: metonymy, irony, metaphor, and synecdoche. Then Fraunce, always following Talaeus, proceeds to *figures* ("A figure is a certeine decking of speech, whereby the usual and simple fashion thereof is altered and changed to that which is more elegant and conceipted"). Next he considers verse forms, then figures of repetition: epizeuxis ("a joyning of the same word or sound"), anadiplosis ("reduplication" of sound "in the ende of the sentence going before, and in the beginning of the sentence following after"), climax ("reduplication by diuers degrees and steps . . . of the same word or sound"), anaphora ("the same sound . . . iterated in the beginning of the sentence"), epistrophe ("turning to the same sound in the ende"), symploce ("the same sound . . . repeated both in beginnings and endings"), epanalepsis ("when the same sound is iterated at the beginning and ending"), epanodos ("when one and the same sound is repeated in the beginning and middle, or middle and end"), paranomasia ("when a word is changed in signification by changing of a letter or sillable"), and polyptoton ("when as words of one ofspring haue diuers fallings or terminations"). Then he moves through "figures in sentences": *exclamation* (protestation, grief, and so on), epanorthosis, aposiopesis, apostrophe, prosopopeia, *addubitation* (internal debate), *communication* (deliberation with others), *preoccupation* (objection and its answer), and *sufferance* (a mocking leave to do something). Each is dealt with briefly and succinctly, with the longer examples following. Throughout Fraunce favors a rich yet restrained style. He concludes: "Thus much of Eloqution in tropes and figures: in al which observe this one lesson, the more the better: yet with discretion, and without affectate curiositie."

The second part of the book is much shorter and deals with delivery, which is broken down into voice and gesture. This section may be one of the most interesting in all of Fraunce's works for the modern reader, because he sets out specific rules for the performance of text and offers ways to interpret text in the light of emo-

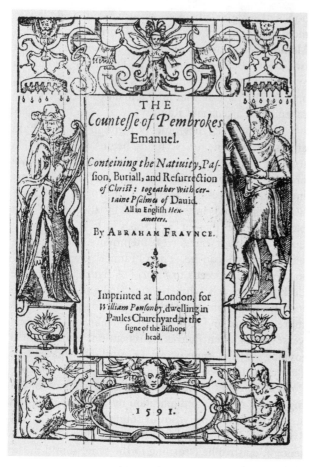

THE
Counteſſe of Pembrokes
Emanuel.

Conteining the Natiuity, Paſ-
ſion, Buriall, and Reſurrection
of Chriſt: togeather with certaine Pſalmes of Dauid.
All in Engliſh Hex-
ameters.

By ABRAHAM FRAVNCE.

Imprinted at London, for
William Ponſonby, dwelling in
Paules Churchyard, at the
ſigne of the Biſhops
head.

1 5 9 1 .

Title page for the volume in which Fraunce collected
his religious poems and translations

tional tone and gesture. Thus, in an analysis of a few lines from the second book of Virgil's *Aeneid,* he concludes, "in the last verses everie thing must be dilated and produced, the mouth opened, the vowells drawen out, that the *Troyan* calamitie may there especiallie appeare." He sees poetry as requiring the actual performance of emotional response, a performance in both voice and physical gesture, for example, "The casting out of the right arme is as it were an arming of the speach, and becommeth continued and flowing sentences, where the verie speach it selfe seemeth to powre forth it selfe with the stretching out of the arme."

Most of *The Arcadian Rhetorike* consists of exemplary quotations in Greek, Latin, Spanish, Italian, French, and English, principally from the works of Homer, Virgil, Juan Boscán, Tasso, Guillaume de Salluste du Bartas, and Sidney. Some of the passages are lengthy. The material quoted from Sidney seems to come from a manuscript version of *The Countesse of Pembrokes Arcadia,* his prose romance first published in 1590. Fraunce's editor Seaton suggests a text along the lines of Bodleian Ms e. Mus. 37, though there are dif-

ferences. Besides the principal authors, there are many other represented, including the late classical poet Ausonius, French near contemporaries Etienne Jodelle and Belleau, the Spanish Garcilaso de la Vega, and even a passage from Petrarch. Spenser is cited three times, once with a whole stanza from *The Faerie Queene,* showing that Fraunce had access to the manuscript two years before publication. Surprisingly, because it was not well known at this time (though it had been republished in 1550 and 1561), William Langland's fourteenth-century religious poem, *Piers Plowman,* is cited once. The overall use of the untranslated quotations suggests that Fraunce expected his readers to be able to follow his arguments as they are exemplified in the passages. The book gives a sophisticated and very poetical notion of "rhetoric" compared to other rhetoric books of the time, which were much more concerned with the structuring and minutiae of both oral and written orations. The poetry gives the book a courtly style. This manual is one that is both simple (the definitions and analyses are extremely brief) yet sophisticated (to understand the foreign languages the reader must have a good education, and the presence of the Sidney quotations aligns the work with the most fashionable literary circle of the time).

In 1588, his most active year of printed work, Fraunce also produced a Latin treatise, *Abrahami Fransi, Insignium, Armorum, Emblematum, Hieroglyphicorum, Et Symbolorum, quæ ab Italis Imprese nominantur, explicatio* (Abraham Fraunce's Explication of Insignia, Arms, Emblems, Hieroglyphics, and Symbols, Which are Called Imprese by Italians), dedicated to Robert Sidney. Shortly thereafter he produced a small manuscript book called "Symbolicæ Philosophiæ Liber Quartus et Ultimus" (The Fourth and Final Book of the Philosophy of Symbols), subtitled "De Symbolis Absolutis" (Concerning Symbols, Completed). According to John Manning, who edited the work for its first publication in 1991, this manuscript is a revision of the third part of the printed work, now corrected and slightly revised, again for presentation to Robert Sidney, who is named on the title page as the recipient. Its tantalizing title "liber quartus" or "fourth book" suggests that there are three preceding, but no others have been found; it may be that this "fourth" book is really to be seen as having a direct relation to the treatise already in print, which consists of three books.

Insignium, Armorum, Emblematum, Hieroglyphicorum, Et Symbolorum begins with book 1, "De Insignibus," an essay on insignia and marks and their origin in book 18 of Homer's *Iliad* and the description of Achilles' shield. Fraunce outlines various associated signs in antiquity and even up to modern times (the bow of the Persians, the lion and book of Venice), and he works through, usually briefly, many heraldic devices, generally conventional or institutional marks from England and the Continent. In his analysis he is following, as he says, Giambattista della Porta, Pierio Valeriano, Claude Mignault, and other scholars. In book 2, "De Armis" (On Arms), he outlines the coats of arms of nobility, in this case not adopted so much as hereditary. Such marks also trace their origin from antiquity, from patronymics and other signs of relation. He runs through the symbolic features of heraldic devices, including color, which seems of great interest to him, and at the end of the section he quotes in full Emblem 118 of Andrea Alciato, the poem "In Colores" (On Colors).

Book 3 is on symbols, emblems, and hieroglyphics. It is a general analysis, with examples at the end, and specifically names as sources the Italians Paolo Giovio, Girolamo Ruscelli, Alessandro Farra, Luca Contile, and Scipione Bargagli; he also relies on Claude Mignault's essay on symbols prefaced to many editions of Alciato's *Book of Emblems* from 1573 onward (Manning's edition of the manuscript provides a useful account of these sources). For Fraunce a symbol is "the means by which we infer and know something . . . it is a representation by which something is concealed." But it is clear early on that by "symbolum" he refers to the *impresa* (an Italian term sometimes translated as "device"), thus following the scheme of public symbolization (and not any modern sense of private metaphor) found throughout this work. He follows Giovio's five rules in the construction of the impresa: that there be, first, proportion (between concept and embodiment in the impresa); second, reasonable clarity; third, charm; fourth, no use of the human figure; and fifth, a motto (to foreground the concept, or soul, of the device). He goes on to discuss why mottoes were added to images, how many images can be allowed in the impresa, and why the human form is to be disallowed (though later, following Bargagli, he explains that one can have a hand holding a torch, if the symbolic emphasis is on the torch, not the hand or the act of holding). Following his sources, Fraunce differentiates the impresa and the emblem: in the latter "the words describe the image" and more images are permitted; emblems provide a more complex scene of interpretation; they are not personal in the way that the impresa can be ("the product of a single inventor"). This last point turns out to be quite important, because the expressive force of the impresa comes from "one mind" (there is to be no "plurality of mottos, images, and intentions") and has therefore a more intense meaning than other symbolic forms. There is a long section on hieroglyphics that largely replicates passages from the *Hieroglyphica siue de sacris aegyptiorum literis* (Hieroglyphics, or Concerning the Sacred Letters of the Egyptians, 1556) of Valeriano. The work concludes

with short analyses of imprese taken from Giovio and others, with the last section an addition of Fraunce's own, two imprese of Philip Sidney's: the first, an image of "a sheep marked with the star of Saturn," with the motto "Macular, modo noscar" (I am marked only that I may be recognized); the second image "a fly stuck in an eye already virtually closed," with the motto "Sic ultus peream" (Thus avenged I will die).

Fraunce's work on emblematics displays the abiding interest in the nature of language, representation, style, and dialectical forms of argument. After all, the problem of the impresa is one of compression, not (as in his rhetoric) one of expansion. But he is reliant on his sources to organize his theoretical claims and the *Explication* does not really carry the discussion of the impresa much beyond the sources. Yet, this subject was a sophisticated literary one and, like all his projects, must be seen as an expression of his commitment to the literary world that was forming around the Sidneys.

The commitment to the Sidneys was even more fully demonstrated in Fraunce's publications in 1592. At this time, he was still a lawyer in Wales, attempting to advance himself in his career. In the early 1590s the earl of Pembroke, his patron, twice wrote to Queen Elizabeth's principal adviser, William Cecil, first Baron Burghley, requesting that Fraunce be made solicitor-general (a position in which he would represent the interests of the crown in matters brought to the court), probably in recognition of the family relation and the many dedications made to Philip and Robert Sidney, to Mary Sidney (now Mary Herbert, Countess of Pembroke), and the earl of Pembroke himself. The suit was unsuccessful. Nevertheless, Fraunce, now in his mid thirties, was well launched on a career in the law and had a good prospect for some kind of role in public service. His writing, moreover, continues to be related to his career in public life.

In the later work, all published in 1591 and 1592, he moves away from the Ramist material to publication in verse. One of the books is religious: *The Countesse of Pembrokes Emanuel. Conteining the Natiuity, Passion, Buriall, and Resurrection of Christ: togeather with certaine Psalmes of Dauid. All in English Hexameters* (1591). The other is secular: *The Countess of Pembroke's Yuychurch* in three parts, the first two in *The Countesse of Pembrokes Yuychurch. Conteining the affectionate life, and vnfortunate death of Phillis and Amyntas: That in a Pastorall; This in a Funerall: both in English Hexameters* (1591), that is, bringing together in a first part the old translation of Watson's *Amyntas* and in a second part a new translation of Tasso's *Aminta*. The sequence concludes with *The Third Part of the Countesse of Pembrokes Yuychurch. Entituled, Amintas Dale. Wherein are the most conceited tales of the Pagan Gods in English Hexameters, together with their auncient descriptions and Philosophicall expli-*

cations (1592). "Yuychurch" (Ivychurch) is the name of a property in Kent owned by the Pembroke family.

The Countess of Pembrokes Emanuel includes a two-part sequence of the title poem "The Natiuity of Christ, in Ryming Hexameters" and "The Passion, Buryall, and Resurrection of Christe," followed by translations of Psalms 1, 6, 8, 29, 38, 50, 73, 104 (a compliment, no doubt, to Mary Sidney's own work as a translator of the Psalms). Here the verse seems much less formulaic than in the earlier work and shows that Fraunce has been able to take the hexameters past his first experimentations. The strong use of alliteration, the emphatic caesura, and fewer end-stopped lines sound more native to the English ear, despite the peculiar rhythms of the dactylic hexameter. Moreover, in the two parts of *The Countess of Pembrokes Emanuel,* the rapid hesitations of the verse and the repetitions give a kind of urgency to the narratives and enforce the tone of praise.

The Countesse of Pembrokes Yvychurch. Conteining the affectionate life, and vnfortunate death of Phillis and Amyntas consists, as the subtitle shows, of two parts, the first being *Amyntas Pastoral,* a version of Tasso's *Aminta,* and the second being the old translation of Watson's *Amyntas,* now revised. There are two additional exercises, a translation of Virgil's Eclogue 2 (also used at the end of *The Lawiers Logike*) and a verse translation of the opening chapter of Heliodorus's *Ethiopian History,* the popular Greek romance (and one of the models for Sidney's *The Countesse of Pembrokes Arcadia*).

The relation between *Aminta* and *Amyntas* are interesting, especially in the way that Fraunce has made changes to Tasso's poem. Most important, Tasso's Sylvia is renamed Phillis, to signal that the narrative of Tasso's *Aminta* is now to fit more closely with Watson's *Amyntas,* whose main female character is Phillis. There are other name changes. And as is customary with Fraunce, the matter is often expanded, so that a twelve-line speech by Aminta in Italian tetrameters at the beginning of act 1, scene 2, becomes twenty-one lines in English classical hexameters. The "brave Lady Regent of these woods, *Pembrokiana,*" is also introduced into the narrative. In one of the most elaborate changes, near the end of the play Pembrokiana kills a female bear; just before the bear dies, Pembrokiana offers to care for the bear's two newborn cubs. Mary Ellen Lamb considers the episode to be an elaborate compliment by Fraunce to the patronage of Mary Sidney. Fraunce's version of Tasso's pastoral comedy explains how Amintas and Phillis got together as lovers; his version of Watson presents the tragedy of Phillis's death and Amintas's lamentations for her.

Not only has Fraunce modified the text of Tasso to fit that of Watson, he also revised the text of Watson to fit that of Tasso. Formerly in eleven parts, Fraunce's new version of *Amyntas* has a lamentation added for the eleventh day, so that the cycle is rounded out to a pleasing twelve in number. Fraunce's new section is an apostrophe by Amintas to sheep, kids, dog, pipe, roses, hills, dales, handkerchief, wedding ring, and so on, and includes these lines: "Yuychurch farewell; farewel fayre *Pembrokianaes* / Parck and loved lawndes; and, if fayre *Pembrokiana* / Scorne not my farewel, farewell fayre *Pembrokiana*"—further incorporation of the Amintas and Phillis narrative into the scene of patronage which suffuses the whole.

Fraunce knew he was taking a chance with this work. In his dedicatory epistle to the countess of Pembroke, he offers a short defense "for such as generally mislike this reformed kinde of verse" (arguing in part, and perhaps not too effectively, that if one does not like this kind of writing, one is under no obligation to read it). An interesting moment between the third and fourth day of the lamentations shows how touchy Fraunce could be in relation to his own schemes of repetition: "Some litle men fynde great fault, that this word, *stil,* being twice used, is but an idle repetition to make up the verse. Where, if they could see, that in the first place it is an Adverb, and an Adjective in the second, they might aswel bee stil, and not speake any thing, as stil talk, and yet say noething." Clearly, certain of his contemporaries expressed dismay at the more excessive features of the Frauncian style.

The Third Part of the Countesse of Pembrokes Yuychurch (known by its subtitle as *Amintas Dale*) is the last part of the Ivychurch series and is viewed by many readers as Fraunce's best work. That it is meant to be part of the series is announced not just by the title but also by the design of the title page, which, despite the new printer, uses the same woodcut border as had *The Countesse of Pembrokes Yuychurch* and *The Countesse of Pembrokes Emanuel. Amintas Dale* is an unusual work that presents a series of verse hexameter narratives based on Ovid, all within a fictional prose explication. The mixed form would have been familiar to contemporaries from *The Shepheardes Calender* or the annotated volumes of verse by the French poet Pierre de Ronsard, though the model really carries forward from the medieval and early Renaissance editions of Ovid's *Metamorphoses,* with the difference that Fraunce's scholarly explication, which frames the tales, is set forth as a device of fiction. Derivative in many of its details, the overall idea is, however original in the English context, structurally combining the very qualities of pleasure and instruction that the work sets out to examine. It is the most extensive work of allegorical mythology published in sixteenth-century England. It seems to have been read carefully by some of his contemporaries: Anthony Brian Taylor suggests that Miranda's famous line in

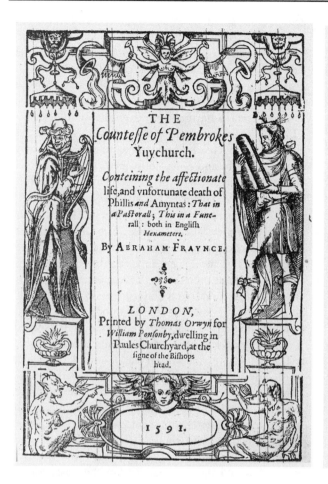

Title pages for the pastoral poem in which Fraunce adapted Torquato Tasso's Aminta, *Thomas Watson's* Amyntas, *and stories from Ovid's* Metamorphoses *to create an elaborate allegorical tribute to his patron, Mary Herbert, Countess of Pembroke*

William Shakespeare's *The Tempest* (1623), "O brave new world, / That hath such people in't," may come from Fraunce's "Thus was an ougly Chaos transformd at last to a brave worlde, / Soe brave, that t'was a world soe woorthy a world to be seeing. . . ." But subtle influences like this one aside, the work is of great interest to students of the history of Ovidian mythography and allegorical interpretation in England.

The arrangement of the frame narrative is simple: the shepherd Amintas has now died and the lady Pembrokiana has ordered her "nymphs and pastors" to remember Amintas by telling tales of "Some one God transformd." Thus follow tales told by the shepherds and the shepherdesses about transformations of the ancient gods, with the emphasis on love narratives: Thirsis on creation, Menalcas on Pan and Syrinx, Damaetas on Jupiter and Io, Fulvia on Echo and Narcissus, Philovevia on Acis and Galatea, Amaryllis on Pluto and the tale of Proserpina, Alphesibaeus on Apollo and Daphne, Damon on Mercury and Apollo, Corydon on Mars and Venus, Licoris on Vulcan, Aresia on Diana and Actaeon, Cassiopaea on Venus and Adonis, Ergastus on Venus and Hermaphroditus, Meliboeus on Bacchus and Venus, Sylvia on Vertumnus and Pomona, and Dieromena on Rhamnusian Nemesis. Between each of these tales are found lengthy explications of names and attributes of the mythological characters by Elpinus, a learned shepherd (the sage Elpino, borrowed from Tasso's *Aminta,* had already appeared as Elpinus in the first part of the Ivychurch series). The storytelling concludes with the merry prose allegory of the garden, an academic jeu d'esprit told by Daphne, and the work ends with a Latin poem purportedly written by Amintas for his beloved Phillis.

The poetic narratives follow Ovid fairly closely and are clearly grounded on the original Latin text; however, Taylor has demonstrated that occasionally, mainly in scenes of rustic dialogue, Fraunce shows he has been reading the *Metamorphoses* in the 1567 English translation by Arthur Golding. Most of the narratives are single episodes, broken up into sections in the same manner as is also found in the editions by Georgius

Sabinus (the German Georg Schuler), to whom Fraunce refers on several occasions in his own commentary. The main interest of the work lies in the interpretive essays, which are based on a three-part scheme of interpretation. Elpinus begins his analyses with the old notion, found most notably in Giovanni Boccaccio's sixteenth book of the *Genealogia deorum gentilium* (Genealogy of the Pagan Gods), that "both poetry, a speaking picture, and paynting, a dumbe poetry, were like in this, that the one and the other did under an amyable figure and delightsome veyle, as it were, cover the most sacred mysteries of auncient philosophie." There are three ways to absorb the tales, three types of interpreter, of whom only the last, the allegorical reader, is able ultimately to remove the veil:

> He that is but of a meane conceit, hath a pleasant and plausible narration, concerning the famous exploites of renowmed *Heroes,* set forth in most sweete and delightsome verse, to feede his rural humor. They, whose capacitie is such, as that they can reach somewhat further then the external discourse and history, shall finde a morall sence included therein, extolling vertue, condemning vice, every way profitable for the institution of a practicall and common wealth man. The rest, that are better borne and of a more noble spirit, shall meete with hidden mysteries of naturall, astrologicall, or divine and metaphysicall philosophie, to entertaine their heavenly speculation.

Elpinus is the character able to understand these "hidden mysteries." His method of explanation is typical of the standard commentary on Ovid for the sixteenth century, in the tradition of the medieval moralizing Ovids, the work of John Ridewall and Pierre Bersuire, and the Neo-Latin commentators such as Sabinus. Fraunce (or his character Elpinus) also follows the work of the mythographers, such as the *Genealogy of the Pagan Gods* of Boccaccio, the *Mythologies* (1567) of Natalis Comes (Natale Conti) and the *Images of the Gods* (1556, revised with pictures in 1571) of Vincenzo Cartari; and he makes reference to or quotes from the French poet Rémy Belleau, the emblem writer Barthélemy Aneau, the scholar Julius Caesar Scaliger, and Tasso, among others. The range of classical reference is enormous, but many of the references could have been picked up from the Neo-Latin intermediaries.

Elpinus's explication of the names and stories usually begins with etymology, some of which is quite playful and even fanciful, for instance, "Iris hath her name *apo tou eirhein,* of speaking, for she speaketh and telleth when rayne is towards," which is an absurd pun on the Ionic Greek *eirhein* (to speak) and the English *rain.* The character is then analyzed in his or her relation with other gods, by attribute, by place, and by action, always with a strong moral emphasis. Thus, the story of Phaeton, first told in the verse translation, is outlined again in prose, to be interpreted first historically, following Lucian, then ethically, following Ovid in his *Tristia,* so that "*Phaeton,* a youth, and therefore unable to governe, will needes be a magistrate: but alas, it is too great a burden for his weake shoulders. . . . This chariot is the glorious type of earthly honor and dignitie. . . . Phoebus his horses note the vulgar people . . . altogether fierce and outragious: the bridles are the stay of governement. . . ." and so on. Nothing is without meaning in this scheme of relentless interpretation.

The concluding section of *Amintas Dale* is a kind of in-joke for the academic reader. The tale tells of three gardeners who ascend to the gods to see if a flood is to take place. The three have foreseen this flood through their astrological predictions. The characters are given an interesting and likely interpretation by Harvey's biographer Virginia Stern: Hemlock (also named Damoetas) is John Harvey, "Pasnip" (or Parsnip) is Richard Harvey (who was small in stature), and "Thistle" is Gabriel Harvey (a bristling and difficult individual, "more auncient . . . wholly addicted to contemplation"). All three were celebrated academics in Cambridge, well known too for their interest in astrology. In the tale, the gods and goddesses become annoyed with these pretentious visitors and cast them back to earth. This small satire, if it is an attack on the Harveys, is one the earliest, and would have helped to lay the basis for the famous pamphlet war between Thomas Nashe and Gabriel Harvey that erupted in 1593. As a counterpoint to Elpinus's explanations, it seems to serve as a caution against too much academic learning, a gentle mocking of the overall direction of the work, which does in fact provide very learned and credible explications of many of the mythological figures. It is, however, unclear why Fraunce chose to attack the Harveys, for Gabriel Harvey thought highly of Fraunce.

Fraunce's accomplishment as a mythographer in *Amintas Dale* has long been recognized. Don Cameron Allen sees the work of George Sandys, who translated and wrote a commentary on Ovid in 1627, as a natural and more detailed extension of the kind of moralization carried into the English tradition through Fraunce's *Amintas Dale*. For many readers, *Amintas Dale* may be the culmination of Fraunce's work as teacher in print, as a writer who is concerned to bring university learning into the public sphere. For it is in his learned adaptations that Fraunce shows himself at his most entertaining, while remaining, as he does consistently elsewhere, a confirmed borrower and reshaper of the work of others. He was clearly drawn to some of the livelier experiments in Continental writing and thinking, and he imported them to the English scene with style and flourish. He was not a translator so much as a gifted adapter, constructing his works out of multiple sources. Yet, in his work of adaptation he has been called by Pomeroy "a far-seeing often innovative Elizabethan intellectual leader," and in his logical work he shows an ability to move beyond some of his sources. His works provide an important glimpse into the way metrics, logic, rhetoric, emblematics, and mythography could be seen to intersect in the 1580s and early 1590s, all participating to lay the basis for an educated literary style. He prepares readers for the excitement felt at that time by the writing of Sidney and Spenser. Lisa Jardine and Anthony Grafton refer to Gabriel Harvey as a "knowledge facilitator." This phrase could be applied equally well to Fraunce. He did his work both privately (in the manuscripts for the two Sidney brothers and for Edward Dyer) and publicly (through the medium of print). Although an interesting and possibly important literary figure in his own short life, he was not, however, well remembered, and his books did not begin to be reprinted until the late nineteenth century.

Fraunce's publications suddenly stopped in 1592. For a long time, it was thought that he had lost interest in literary publication, that he held some kind of legal position, and that he died in 1633. These beliefs were based on a prose epistle to "An Epithalamium, Presented to Sir Gervase Cutler . . . on his Marriage with Lady Magdalen Egerton the daughter of John, Earl of Bridgewater" dated 1633 and incorrectly believed by the antiquary Joseph Hunter, in his unpublished "Chorus Vatum" (The Choir of Prophets, 1838–1854), to have been written by Fraunce. Since Hunter's initial claim, many scholars have accepted this date. Although the Library of Congress catalogue still gives Fraunce's dates as "fl. 1587–1633," modern scholarship has corrected this claim. Harry Morris believed that Fraunce had died before 1595; Victor Skretkowicz showed that Hunter had mistakenly attributed the epithalamium to Fraunce (instead of Abraham Darcie); more recently, Michael G. Brennan has argued that Fraunce died in 1592 or 1593, probably in Wales, of unknown causes. Lines in Thomas Lodge's sonnet cycle *Phillis* (1593) refer to Fraunce and Watson as having been both recently deceased. In these lines Lodge suggests that the continued interest of his patroness, Mary, Countess of Shrewsbury, will save the two authors of *Amintas* from undeserved oblivion:

And tho the fore-bred brothers they haue had,

(Who in theyr Swan-like songes *Amintas* wept)

For all their sweet-thought sighes had fortune bad,

And twice obscur'd in *Cinthias* circle slept:

Yet these (*I* hope) under your kind aspect,

(Most worthy Lady) shall escape neglect.

Fraunce's short life and long attendance in university and the inns of court meant that he had an extremely brief career as a writer. His earliest writings are manuscripts formally prepared for members of the Sidney family, dating from the late 1570s or early 1580s. His printed works appeared between 1587 and 1592. Yet, it is clear that despite his fairly obscure origins, Fraunce made a mark among his literary contemporaries. He was known to Robert Greene, who mentions that he imitates Fraunce's *Yuychurch* in the title he gave to his *Philomela, the Lady Fitzwalter's Nightingale* (1592), and Nashe, who praises him as "sweete Master France," in the preface to Greene's *Menaphon* (1589); Fraunce had graduated with these men in 1583. Fraunce may be the figure Corydon in Spenser's *Colin Clouts Come Home Again* (1595); certainly he knew Spenser well, for in *The Arcadian Rhetorike* he gives the earliest known quotation from *The Faerie Queene*. In Gabriel Harvey's *Foure Letters* (1592), he is named, along with Spenser, Richard Stanyhurst, Watson, Samuel Daniel, and Nashe (in 1592, just before the great quarrel between Harvey and Nashe), as one of the men who were "commendably employed in enriching and polishing their native tongue." Indeed, in one of his marginal notes to George Gascoigne's *Certayne Notes of Instruction* (1575), Harvey puts Fraunce with Sidney and Spenser as "owr excellentest poets." In the roll call of writers in Francis Meres's *Palladis Tamia* (Wit's Treasury, 1598), he is listed after Sidney, along with Spenser, Richard Barnfield, and others, as "amongst . . . the best" in pastoral poetry. He was an active participant in a group of well-educated, highly literary, and ambitious young men who gathered around the Sidneys for mutual encouragement and patronage. His works remain fascinating hybrids of philosophy, rhetoric, emblematics, and experiments in English versification.

Bibliographies:

Walter J. Ong, *Ramus and Talon Inventory: A Short-Title Inventory of the Published Works of Peter Ramus (1515–1572) and of Omer Talon (ca. 1510–1562) in Their Original and in Their Variously Altered Forms* (Cambridge, Mass.: Harvard University Press, 1958), pp. 111–112, 218–220, 462–464, 518;

Heinrich F. Plett, *English Renaissance Rhetoric and Poetics: A Systematic Bibliography of Primary and Secondary Sources,* Symbola et Emblemata, volume 6 (Leiden, New York & Cologne: E. J. Brill, 1995), pp. 143–144, 177–178, 270, 285, 319–320.

References:

Don Cameron Allen, *Mysteriously Meant: The Rediscovery of Pagan Symbolism and Allegorical Interpretation in the*

Renaissance (Baltimore & London: Johns Hopkins Press, 1970), pp. 186–189;

Derek Attridge, *Well-weighed Syllables: Elizabethan Verse in Classical Metres* (London: Cambridge University Press, 1974), pp. 198–204;

T. W. Baldwin, *William Shakspere's Small Latine and Lesse Greeke,* 2 volumes (Urbana: University of Illinois Press, 1944), I: 392–393; III: 7, 14–16, 57–58, 67, 118, 236, 304, 431, 466–467, 596, 669;

Michael G. Brennan, "The Date of the Death of Abraham Fraunce," *Library,* sixth series 5 (1983): 391–392;

D. Coulman, "'Spotted to be Known,'" *Journal of the Warburg and Courtauld Institutes,* 20 (1957): 179–180;

Katherine Duncan-Jones, "Sidney's Personal Imprese," *Journal of the Warburg and Courtauld Institutes,* 33 (1970): 321–324;

Duncan-Jones, "Two Elizabethan Versions of Giovio's Treatise on Imprese," *English Studies,* 52 (1971): 118–123;

C. L. Hamblin, *Fallacies* (London: Methuen, 1970), pp. 139–142;

Margaret P. Hannay, *Philip's Phoenix: Mary Sidney, Countess of Pembroke* (New York: Oxford University Press, 1990);

Wilbur Samuel Howell, *Logic and Rhetoric in England, 1500–1700* (Princeton: Princeton University Press, 1956);

Lisa Jardine, "Humanistic Logic," in *The Cambridge History of Renaissance Philosophy,* edited by Charles B. Schmitt, and others (Cambridge & New York: Cambridge University Press, 1988), pp. 173–198;

Jardine and Anthony Grafton, "'Studied for Action': How Gabriel Harvey Read His Livy," *Past and Present,* 129 (November 1990): 30–78;

Christine Kenyon, "The Literary Career of Abraham Fraunce," B. Litt. thesis, Oxford University, 1973;

Katherine Koller, "Abraham Fraunce and Edmund Spenser," *English Literary History,* 7 (1940): 108–120;

Mary Ellen Lamb, *Gender and Authorship in the Sidney Circle* (Madison: University of Wisconsin Press, 1990), pp. 30–47;

Harry Morris, "Thomas Watson and Abraham Fraunce," *Publications of the Modern Language Association,* 76 (1961): 152–153;

Walter J. Ong, *Ramus, Method and the Decay of Dialogue: From the Art of Discourse to the Art of Reason* (Cambridge, Mass.: Harvard University Press, 1958);

Ralph S. Pomeroy, "The Ramist as Fallacy-Hunter: Abraham Fraunce and *The Lawiers Logike,*" *Renaissance Quarterly,* 40 (1987): 224–246;

R. J. Schoeck, "Rhetoric and Law in Sixteenth-Century England," *Studies in Philology,* 50 (1953): 110–127;

Victor Skretkowicz, "Abraham Fraunce and Abraham Darcie," *Library,* fifth series 31 (1976): 239–242;

Virginia Stern, *Gabriel Harvey: His Life, Marginalia and Library* (Oxford: Clarendon Press, 1979);

Anthony Brian Taylor, "Abraham Fraunce's Debts to Arthur Golding in *Amintas Dale,*" *Notes and Queries,* 231 (1986): 333–336;

Taylor, "'O Brave New World': Abraham Fraunce and *The Tempest,*'" *English Language Notes,* 23 (June 1986): 18–23;

Rosemond Tuve, *Elizabethan and Metaphysical Imagery: Renaissance Poetic Imagery and Twentieth-Century Critics* (Chicago: University of Chicago Press, 1947);

C. Marengo Vaglio, "Words for the English Nation: Torquato Tasso in Abraham Fraunce's *The Arcadian Rhetorike* (1588)," *Revue de Littérature Comparée,* 62 (1988): 529–532;

Alan Young, "Sir Philip Sidney's Tournament Impresas," *Sidney Newsletter,* 2 (1985): 6–24.

Papers:

The manuscript source for Abraham Fraunce's work first published in 1906 as *Victoria, A Latin Comedy* is "Comoedia Latina per Abrahamum Fransum ad Philippum Sydneium," at Penshurst Place, Penshurst, Kent, on deposit at the Kent Archives Office as Ms. U1475/Z15; "The Sheapheardes Logike Conteyning the præcepts of that art put downe by Ramus; Examples fet owt of the Sheapheards Kalinder; Notes and expositions collected owt of Bourhusius, Piscator, Mr Chatterton; and diuers others. Together wth twooe general Discourses, the one touchinge the prayse and ryghte vse of Logike: the other concernynge the comparison of Ramus his Logike, wth that of Aristotle. To the Ryght worshypful Mr Edwarde Dyer," is Additional Ms. 34361, British Library; "Tractatus de usu dialectices," with "Emblemata varia, ad principes Europæ et rem historicam spectantia, calamo bene depicta, et versibus latinis illustrata," comprises Ms. Rawlinson D 345, Bodleian Library, Oxford University; the manuscript for *Symbolicæ philosophiæ liber quartus et ultimus* is Ms. U1475.Z16, Kent County Archive Office.

William Fullwood

(fl. 1568)

Carl W. Glover
Mount Saint Mary's College

BOOKS: *A New Ballad against bnthrifts*, as W. F. [broadside] (London: Printed by John Allde, 1562);

The Shape of, ii, Mosters. M, D, Lxii, as W. F. [broadside] (London: Printed by John Allde, 1562);

A Supplication to Eldertonne, for Leaches vnlewdnes: Desiring him to pardone, his manifest vnrudenes [broadside] (London: Printed by John Allde, 1562?);

The Enimie of Idlenesse: Teaching the maner and stile how to endite, compose and write all sorts of Epistles and Letters: as well by answer, as otherwise. Deuided into foure Bokes, no lesse pleasaunt than profitable. Set forth in English by William Fulwood Marchant, &c. The Contentes hereof appere in the Table at the latter ende of the Booke. An Enimie to Idlenesse, A frend to Exercise: By practise of the prudent pen, Loe here before thine eyes (London: Printed by Henry Bynneman for Leonard Maylard, 1568); republished as *The Enimie of Idlenesse: teaching a perfect platform how to indite epistles and letters of all sortes* (London: Printed by Henrie Middleton, 1578);

A spectaclc fo_ pe_iu_e_s, Deus Videt. 27. Die Nouemb. 1589 [broadside] (London: Printed by Edward Allde, 1589).

Editions: *The Enimie of Idlenesse* [excerpts], in *William Fullwood: The Enimie of Idlenesse: Der alteste englische Briefsteller*, by Paul Wolter (Potsdam: A. W. Hayn's Erben, 1907), pp. 29–80;

A spectaclc fo_ pe_iu_e_s, in *Proof-Reading in the Sixteenth Seventeenth and Eighteenth Centuries*, by Percy Simpson (London: Printed by Humphrey Milford for Oxford University Press, 1935), pp. 68–69.

OTHER: *The Castel Of Memorie: Wherein is conteyned the restoring, augmenting, and conseruing of the Memorye and Remembraunce, with the safest remedies, and best preceptes thereunto in any wise apperteyning: Made by Gulielmus Gratarolus Bergomatis Doctor of Artes and Phisike. Englished by Willyam Fulwod. The Contentes whereof appeare in the Page next folowynge*, translated by Fullwood (London: Printed by Rowland Hall, 1562);

Ralph Lever, *The Most Noble auncient, and learned playe, called the Philosophers game, inuented for the honest recreation of students, and other sober persons, in passing the tediousnes of tyme, to the release of their labours, and the exercise of their wittes. Set forth with such playne precepts, rules, and tables, that all men with ease may vnderstande it, and most men with pleasure practise it. by Rafe Leuer and augmented by W. F.*, edited by Fullwood? (London: Printed by Rowland Hall for James Rowbotham, 1563?).

Editions: *The Castel Of Memorie* [excerpts], in *The New Art of Memory: upon the principles taught by M. Gregor von Feinaigle* (London: Sherwood, Neely & Jones, 1812), pp. 17–38;

The Castel Of Memorie, The English Experience, no. 382 (Amsterdam: Theatrum Orbis Terrarum / New York: Da Capo, 1971).

William Fullwood's primary contribution to the development of a practical rhetoric in Renaissance England is the production of the first known guide to letter writing in the English language. Published in 1568 and beginning a long tradition of such books, *The Enimie of Idlenesse* is significant because it was written not for scholars but for middle-class citizens, such as the members of the guild to whom the book is dedicated. The importance of this work is further evidenced by its many editions, strongly suggesting its role in meeting the letter-writing needs of an emergent middle class in Elizabethan England. Fullwood also introduced another rhetorical text, *The Castel Of Memorie* (1562).

Fullwood flourished during the second half of the sixteenth century, though the dates of his birth and death are not known. He is identified as a merchant on the title page of his letter-writing manual, which is dedicated to the Merchant Taylor's Company. In *William Fullwood: The Enimie of Idlenesse: Der alteste englische Briefsteller* (1907), Paul Wolter points out that the Merchant Taylor's Company in Fullwood's day consisted of tailors who maintained textile or fabric stores in addition to their workshops. The guild was one of the oldest of

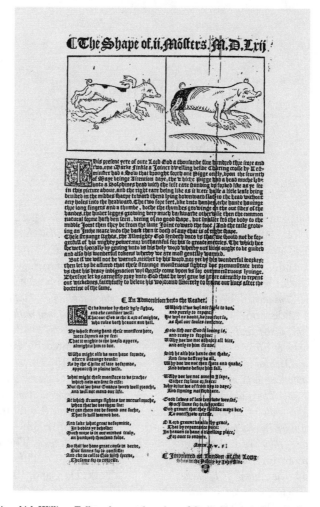

Broadside in which William Fullwood warned readers of God's "heavy indignacion" toward sinners

the country, founded in the early fourteenth century and chartered by King Edward III. Over the years, this guild earned a high reputation for learning. During the sixteenth century, as trade between England and new countries flourished, so did the wealth and worldly exposure of merchants, who were further motivated to master foreign languages. This study inevitably involved them in the production of grammar and rhetoric textbooks, as well as handbooks in the art of letter writing, often translated from Continental sources.

As a young merchant tailor, Fullwood may have had ties to the court of King Henry VIII. The *Calendar of Letters and Papers* for 1543 lists a "Wm. Fulwoode, merchant tailor," to be reimbursed "for necessaries bought for the lady Anne of Cleves." In 1545 a William Fullwood was listed in the household accounts as a gentleman pensioner of Henry VIII. That same year a sum of money was dispersed to a "Wm. Fullewoode" for "wages of divers captains, Italian," and a reward was

authorized to Richard Knevett and William Fullwood for "conducting certeyne strawngers northwarde." This same Fullwood is also mentioned in a letter, dated 9 June 1545, from Edward Seymour, Earl of Hertford, to Secretary of State William Paget (as summarized in the *Calendar of Letters and Papers*):

> The Council write for the despatch thither of such Pensioners as remain in the King's service here [Newcastle]. There are no more but Mr. Markham, who had the King's licence to serve in this voyage, and Mr. Fulwood "who for his language, with also Richard Knevet, were expressly commanded by his Highness to have the leading hither of the Italians." Has sent up Markham; but desires that, if he may be spared, he may return hither in post. Fulwood, because of his language, cannot be spared from the Italians, "lying so far off as they do at this present; and also if that place were otherwise furnished, forasmuch as he hath the Spanish tongue it were very necessary he should remain here with Seignior Gamboa when I shall depart hence."

This Fullwood, a translator in the service of the king, may well be the same person who translated texts during Elizabeth's reign.

Fullwood's first book, *The Castel Of Memorie,* is a translation of Guglielmo Grataroli's *De memoria reparanda, augenda, servandaque* (On Restoring, Increasing, and Preserving the Memory, 1553), a medical-rhetorical treatise in Latin. The translation is preceded by an eight-page dedicatory verse to Fullwood's contemporary Robert Dudley, first Earl of Leicester, a distinguished knight and patron of the Innes of Court. C. H. Conley, in *The First English Translators of the Classics* (1927), argues that Fullwood was probably a member of the Innes of Court, to which at least fifty-four translators belonged. Fullwood's dedication is followed by an "Address to the Reader" in prose, then a foreword in six short stanzas, called "the Books verdicte." Consisting of seven chapters, the text first discusses the nature of memory, citing the authority of Plato, Aristotle, and Cicero, then describes a method by which students may improve their memories through medicinal treatment and mental exercises. The artificial memory system discussed in chapter 7 is derived from the pseudo-Ciceronian *Rhetorica ad Herennium* (circa 84 B.C.). What is unusual about this translation, according to Wolter, is that Fullwood digresses often from the Latin text, seeking to explain abstract observations using popular speech.

During this same period Fullwood was apparently gaining recognition among his contemporaries as a writer of ballads. Special praise is bestowed upon him by Richard Robinson in *The rewarde of Wickednesse* (1574):

And sayde good Ladies call againe,
this charge if it maye bee.
Commit it to some other man,
that hath much better skill,
and better knowth an hundreth times,
to seale your learned Hill.
Your Honours haue in Th'innes of Court,
a sort of Gentlemen,
That fine would fit your whole intentes,
with stately stile to Pen.
Let Studley, Hake, or Fulwood take,
that William has to name,
This piece of worke in hande, that bee
more fitter for the same.

Robinson's praise of Fullwood's poetic gift would not have been justified if Fullwood had limited his poetry to the few verses scattered throughout his prose translations. Unfortunately, only three of his ballads survive from this early period of his life. *A New Ballad against bnthrifts,* a poem in thirteen stanzas, admonishes louts, drunkards, "roisters" (carousers), gamblers, loiterers,

and dolts to live better lives. *The Shape of, ii, Mosters,* a broadside published by "W. F." in 1562, features a woodcut of two hideously deformed pigs, one with two inverted bodies and double sets of fore and hind legs, and the second with humanlike hands. In prose and verse, Fullwood depicts these two monsters as reminders of "God's mighty power" and "greate mercies" and the importance of living according to "his holy word." The two monstrous pigs portend God's "heavy indignacion" toward those who fail to heed this warning. *A Supplication to Eldertonne, for Leaches vnlewdnes,* another broadside, rebukes a poet of questionable character, given to overindulgence in drink. The *Short-Title Catalogue* suggests 1562 as a possible date for this ballad.

Fullwood's name is also mentioned in connection with Ralph Lever's *The Most Noble auncient, and learned playe, called the Philosophers game* (1563?), a treatise about rythmomachy, a medieval numbers game. The basis for suspecting Fullwood's collaboration lies on the title page in the phrase "augmented by W. F." Scholars have been debating the true identity of "W. F." for some time. *The Dictionary of National Biography* identifies this person as William Fulke, and Wolter finds no reason in the text to suspect that Fullwood brought out this edition. In *Leicester: Patron of Letters* (1955), Eleanor Rosenberg offers a detailed discussion of this question and also concludes that Fulke was the true "W. F." She bases this conclusion mainly on a statement made by Fulke in the dedicatory epistle to his *Goodly Gallerye* (1563): "for that one Iames Rowbothum . . . hath not ben ashamed to dedicate vnto your Lordship [Leicester] of late a treatise of myne, which I gathered out of diuerse writers, concerning the Philosophers game." To the contrary, however, Wilbur Samuel Howell identifies "W. F." as William Fullwood, citing the "better authority of the Huntington Library Catalogue," which points out that the lines in "The bookes verdicte" form an acrostic that reads "W I L Y A M F V L V O D." William Carew Hazlitt had earlier noted the acrostic in his *Second Series of Bibliographical Collections and Notes of Early English Literature, 1474–1700* (1882). R. B. McKerrow observes that, even without the acrostic, a comparison of the prefatory verses with those of *The Castel Of Memorie* suggests Fullwood as the writer. While the true identity of "W. F." may never be known, this unauthorized version of *The Most Noble auncient, and learned playe, called the Philosophers game* riled Lever so much that he mentioned it in "The Forespeache" to his *The Arte of Reason* (1573): "For the booke, named the Philosophers game, is entituled to bee set forth by Raphe Leuer, and to be augmented by one W. F. But I assure thee (gentle reader) that, the pamphlet or worke neuer passed from mee, with so many and so grosse ouersightes, as in the booke nowe printed are so common to be sene."

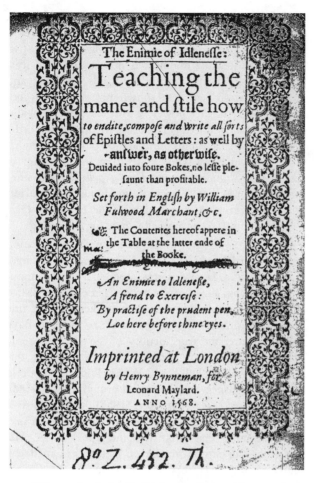

Title page for the first English-language letter-writing manual

Fullwood's next (and most famous) work was *The Enimie of Idlenesse* (1568), a vernacular letter-writing manual. Handbooks were not uncommon in the Western world. As the Greek culture in the late fifth and early fourth centuries B.C. began to move from orality to literacy, the need arose for an efficient way to educate mass populations. This shift marked the advent of the handbook in Western culture. The first handbooks were primarily rhetorical in nature, since the increasing demands of public life required citizens to be more effective readers, writers, and speakers. Though often criticized for their reductive nature (Isocrates railed at those handbook writers who attempted to apply hard and fast rules to a creative process), handbooks nonetheless proliferated. In Elizabethan England, with its burgeoning middle class, handbooks were needed to fill the cultural void that had developed amid the rapidly growing prosperity of that segment of the population. *The Enimie of Idlenesse* is the first handbook of the "complete letter-writer" variety in English. A great many more complete letter-writers followed.

Prior to the twentieth century, published accounts of *The Enimie of Idlenesse* in sources such as the *Dictionary of National Biography*, Samuel Egerton Brydges's *Censura Literaria* (A Literary Opinion, 1805–1809), and Thomas Corser's *Collectanea Anglo-Poetica* (English Poetry Collection, 1860–1883) credited Fullwood as the author of an original work. Shortly after the turn of the century, however, critics such as Wolter and Maude Bingham Hansche in *The Formative Period of English Familiar Letter-writers and Their Contribution to the English Essay* (1902) had either found or conjectured about the sources of some of the theoretical sections of the work and of the letters themselves. In 1906 McKerrow was the first scholar to identify the source for *The Enimie of Idlenesse*. The subject matter of the sample letters, along with the French names and places in many of them, suggested to McKerrow that the work was of French origin. In addition, McKerrow points to the words on the title page, "Set forth in English by William Fullwood Marchant," strongly suggesting that the work is a translation. McKerrow's suspicions were confirmed when he located the source: an anonymous book published in Lyon in 1555, with reprints in 1566 and 1579. Fullwood's book is an accurate translation of *Le Stile et maniere de composer, dicter, et escrire toute sorte d'epistre, ou lettres missiues, tant par response, que autrement* (The Style and Manner of Composing, Dictating and Writing All Sorts of Letters, Prepared to be sent, as much for Response, as for Other Uses). McKerrow's discovery went unnoticed by Katherine Gee Hornbeak, who in *The Complete Letter Writer in English: 1568–1800* (1934) claimed to be the first person to discover Fullwood's French source.

The Enimie of Idlenesse went through at least nine editions between its initial publication and 1621, which suggests that this first letter-writing formulary in English was of great interest to the reading public. For the most part, the editions were altered by slight modifications or the insertion of an additional letter or two. With the 1578 edition, however, the subtitle was changed from *Teaching the maner and stile how to endite, compose, and write all sorts of Epistles and Letters* to *Teaching a perfect platform howe to indite Epistles and Letters of all sortes*. It is quite possible the title was altered to imitate the subtitle of Abraham Fleming's 1576 treatise on letter writing: *A Panoplie of Epistles, Or, a looking Glasse for the unlearned. Conteyning a perfecte plattforme of inditing letters of all sorts, to persons of al estates and degrees, as well our superiours, as also our equalls and inferiours.* This work, though never popular, shared the same "vnlearned" audience and may have been perceived as a threat to Fullwood's manual.

Fullwood uses the prefatory pages to clarify the target audience and intent for the book. *The Enimie of*

Idlenesse is dedicated "To the right Worshipfull the Maister, Wardens, and Company of the Marchant Tayllors of London." The opening verses leave little doubt of Fullwood's audience:

> For know you sure, I meane not I
> the cunning clerkes to teach:
> But rather to the vnlearned sort
> a few precepts to preach.

His book is intended not for the educated population but for the commoner, who will use the book to learn the art of letter writing.

The first section offers a theoretical explanation of epistolary style. The letter is defined as an "Oration" that the "Orator" furnishes to one who is absent, which is, however, composed as if that person were present. The persistence of these rhetorical terms points to the vague distinction between oratory and prose style that extended throughout the sixteenth century in Europe. The letters are then divided into three groups according to recipient: one's superiors, such as "Emperors, kings, and princes"; one's equals, including "Marchants, Burgesses, and Citizens"; and one's inferiors, such as servants and laborers.

The letters are further classified according to rank in terms of three essential points: salutation, subscription, and superscription. In the salutations of letters to one's superiors, for example, the writer should employ the expressions "most high, most mighty, right honorable, most redoubted, etc.," always corresponding to the rank of the recipient. The manual advises, however, never to exceed three of these expressions in the address. In letters to one's equals, the writer should adopt a tone of familiarity and esteem, using terms such as "wise, sage, honorable, worshipful," but superlatives should be limited. Writing to an underling, one should observe a civil and polite tone. For instance, a merchant who has many servants will address the chief servant as "You," but those of lesser rank the merchant may address as "Thou." This address is also appropriate in a letter from a father to his son.

Also with regard to the subscription, or signature, at the end of a letter, the three groups must be differentiated. In a letter to one of higher rank, the signature must stand at the right bottom margin of the page, preceded by an expression such as "By your most humble and obedient sonne. &c." When writing to an equal, the signature must be placed in the middle of the page, following the words, "By your faithfull frend for ever, &c." Letters to subordinates should be signed on the left at the bottom margin of the sheet, with a brief phrase such as "By yours." *The Enimie of Idlenesse* also advises that the address, or superscription, follow a similar pattern of placement according to rank.

Next, the letter writer must consider such issues as whether one is writing to a public or a private person, a rich or a poor person, a friend or a stranger, or even an enemy. The writer must also consider whether the recipient likes to read letters or not, whether the letter is written to an educated or uneducated person, and whether the issue addressed is appropriate or not.

Of particular interest is Fullwood's insistence that the language of the letter should be "common and familiar speech"—in other words, colloquial. The language should be free of muddled speech ("rare and diffused phrases"), stilted expressions and bowdlerizations from Latin ("inckhorne termes, skummed from the Latine"), and vulgar and obscure expressions ("base termes and barbarous, or termes unknown except in certaine places"). Fullwood's use of "inckhorne terms," as McKerrow points out, may reflect Thomas Wilson's use of the term in his *Arte of Rhetorique* (1553), a work that Fullwood recommends for those who wish to improve their writing skills. Fullwood also speaks highly of Richard Rainolde's *A booke called the Foundacion of Rhetorike* (1563), a treatise Howell credits as the first English work to qualify as a true "formulary rhetoric."

Continuing this practice of triadic subdivision, the text distinguishes three groups of letters: those "of Doctrine, of Myrth, or of Grauitie." Letters of doctrine should deal with matters "of good and evill things to them that be absent" and instruct the readers in proper conduct and correct moral choice. Those of mirth must treat of cheerful subjects, "using joyfull and merry language, pleasant speech and jests." Letters of gravity must be "of Morall or Civill matters, tending to honour" and must adopt a tone of respect and sobriety.

In a discussion of the parts of a letter, *The Enimie of Idlenesse* and its original source reveal a penchant for Aristotle, Cicero, and the classical rhetorical tradition by drawing an analogy between letter writing and the logical syllogism. Accordingly, every letter is divided into three parts: the cause, the intent, and the consequence, like the syllogism, "which consisteth of the *Maior*, the *Minor*, and Conclusion." The text includes examples of how these three parts function in actual letters.

Next, the translation gives a "threefold consideration" that should apply to all letters: that the demand is just; that it is possible; and that the reward is appropriately given in accordance with the demands of the situation. If these considerations are not explicitly addressed in the letter, "then are they understood."

In a cautionary note, Fullwood translates four things that "hinder the demaund from being granted": proportion, time, place, and cause. The first hindrance, proportion, must be considered if one "is to demand a thing to great and more than a man ought . . . aske thy duetie and no more." In terms of time, one should not demand payment of rent or any other obligation prior to the agreed-upon due date. The letter writer is warned not to change the location at which a debt must be paid ("as if my debter should owe me tenne pound, to be payde in the Paules Church, & I should demaunde it of him in Westminster Hall"). As for the cause, the letter writer must consider any intervening circumstances before demanding that an original promise be kept.

The Enimie of Idlenesse follows this advice with a practical discussion of the length of letters. Letters that require several "partes and divisions" must adopt the language of "brevitie." By the same token, if the letter contains a "Narracio" (another term borrowed from classical rhetoric) concerned with timely issues such as court news or wars, "it must be dispatcht very briefly, & plainly, in using common termes, without long clauses or parentheses." The remainder of book 1 is devoted to several other types of letters for a variety of occasions.

Hornbeak observes that many of the letter categories are drawn from Desiderius Erasmus's *Brevissima Maximeque Compendiaria conficiendarum Epistolarum formula* (A Very Short, Extremely Concise Formulary for Composing Letters, 1521), as translated from *Le Stile et maniere.* They were clearly selected to illustrate the standard types in the Latin formularies. Many of these letters are by figures from the classical world, such as Cicero, Catiline, and Brutus.

Book 2 of *The Enimie of Idlenesse,* which includes "the copies of sundrie learned mens *Letters and Epistles,*" consists of twenty-three letters. The source for most of these letters is *Illustrium virorum Epistolae ab Angelo Politiano partim scriptae, partim collectae* (Letters of Illustrious Men, Partly Written and Partly Collected by Angelo Politan, 1526), as translated from *Le Stile et maniere.* Of the "sundrie learned men" whose letters appear in book 2, Politian is represented by sixteen letters. Others included in this second book are Pico della Mirandola, Marsilio Ficino, Merula, and Pope Innocent VIII.

The letters in the third book of *The Enimie of Idlenesse,* "conteyning the maner and forme how to write by answere," are a radical departure from book 2. All of the letters in the third book are drawn from practical issues of everyday life, from the foibles of family relationships to the challenges of daily existence in the business world. Excerpts from the first two letters in the third book address a situation that remains commonplace. A father writes his son who has left home to attend college:

It is alredy three months ago, and now at thys present going on the fourth, since we receiued any Letters from thee: me thinkes thou mightest haue coniectured with thy selfe (if thy heart had not ben altogether stony) in what troubles and calamities I with thy weeping and sorowfull mother doe lyue.

The son's predictable reply is a request for more money:

But bicause I wil not be long in writing, it may please you to understand, that in this Towne of *Paris,* we haue great scarcitie of victualles this yeare. Corne is at a high pryce: I say nothing vnto you of wyne, which at this day is risen vnto such a pryce that of many persons it is quite forsaken. I know well, my dere Father and Mother, that you would not haue me to endure scarcitie of victualles, for the which my garments alreadie foure months ago, are gauged to myne Host, which causeth me to be more importunate to demaund money of you, which through your goodnesse I attend for with earnest desire.

The fact that all the cities mentioned in book 3 (Paris, Lyons, Boulogne) are French, and that many of the names (Frances, Antoinette) are also French, is what led McKerrow and Hornbeak to seek a French source for *The Enimie of Idlenesse.*

The fourth book is a handbook of love letters, both in verse and in prose, in which lovers exchange favors and expressions of pining to be in each other's arms. The sentimental and flattering tone characteristic of all the letters in book 4 is evidenced by the letter under the heading "A certaine Louer writeth vnto his Lady":

My Deere, if the gentle Emperour of the Firmament, with all hys study (as it plainly appeareth) hath vouchsafed to adorne you with heavenly and Angelicall beautie, which vertue more than humaine, with apparant modesty and with royall customes who then douteth but that you are pleasaunt, pitifull, gentle, and gracious: certes none.

Bicause that in your faire forehead and shynyng eyes, love sheweth it selfe alwayes apparalled with Liberalitie, whiche thinges have boldened my half alive heart (nowe of long time linked unto you with ardent sighes) to saye with mazed minde, these fewe unadorned wordes which shall be the secrete messangers of me, your assured seruitour, humbly requesting you not to deny me your sweete love.

The Enimie of Idlenesse was the first in a long line of popular letter-writing manuals in English. Another formulary was Fleming's *A Panoplie of Epistles,* which draws heavily on Latin sources. In addition to providing instruction and models for improvement in letter-writ-

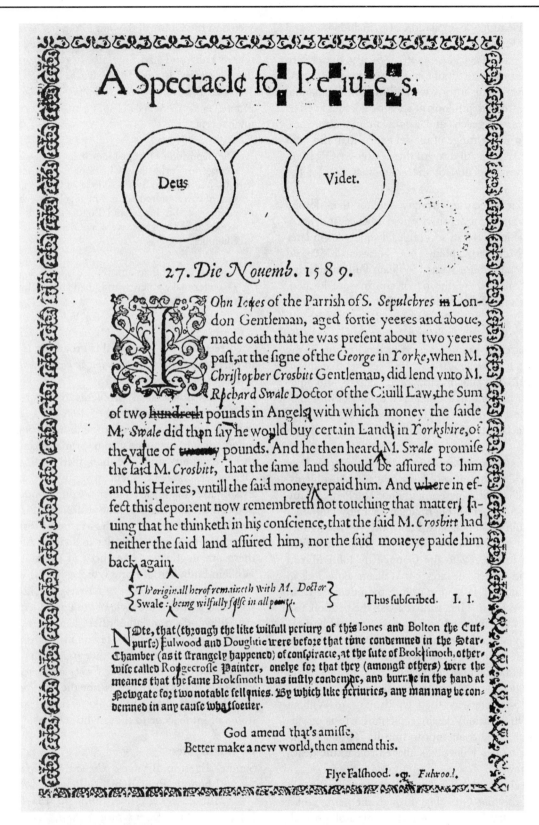

Corrected proof for the broadside in which Fullwood claimed he had been the victim of perjured testimony (from Percy Simpson,
Proof-reading in the Sixteenth Seventeenth and Eighteenth Centuries, *1935)*

ing skills, Fleming's compilation also included several suggestions for moral improvement. A third formulary, Angel Day's *The English Secretorie* (1586), also underwent several printings, no doubt a sign of its popularity. Strictly Ciceronian in its formalism, Day's manual offered a more in-depth look at rhetorical issues such as tone, figures of speech, and argumentative strategies, and an even wider range of model letters than did Fullwood's translation. All three of these letter-writing manuals were designed not for the aristocracy but for the unlearned.

Historical records strongly suggest that despite Fullwood's apparent sensitivity to audience and decorum, he was involved in several legal squabbles in later years. As McKerrow points out, between 1580 and 1592 a merchant tailor named William Fullwood living on Long Lane, where the pawn shops were located, engaged in one dispute after another with his neighbors, resulting in several petitions and counterpetitions to the Privy Council. Fullwood's connection with the pawnshop area of London seems to have begun in the 1570s, for the *Calendar of Patent Rolls* reports that on 20 January 1578 a William Fullwood, "citizen and merchant taylor of London . . . acquired from Thomas Castle of London" a property "at the North end of Longe Lane in the parish of St. Sepulchre in the suburbs of London."

The *Calendar of State Papers* and the *Acts of the Privy Council* provide a sampling of Fullwood's legal problems. In 1580 William Sherington petitioned the Privy Council to stay a judgment brought against him by Fullwood and to uphold his suit against Fullwood "for wrongfully withholding a statute staple of 300£." A petition filed possibly in June 1582 to the Council by John Martin reports "the unjust dealing of William Fulwood in defrauding him of 410£ due to him by indenture from Henry Francklande." In a bizarre twist, the petition also alleges that "W. Fulwood had brought the said Francklande to an obscure death" and had kept Martin in prison "most wrongfully" for five years. Annexed to the petition is a statement accusing Fullwood of "lewd and fraudulent dealing." An entry in the *Calendar of State Papers* for 1584 refers to "the lewd dealings of William Fulwoode, his usurious dealings, factious arrests of various persons, &c; his attempt to murder Thomas Walbut" and reiterates Fullwood's alleged role in the death of Francklande.

Several years later Fullwood was apparently condemned in the Star Chamber through the perjury of a witness. This legal proceeding is the subject of a broadside signed "Fulwood" and titled *A spectaclc fo_ pe_iu_e_s* [for perjurers]. Dated 27 November 1589, it refers to the deposition of John Jones and a thief named Bolton whose perjured testimony had two innocent men con-

victed in the Court of the Star Chamber. The complainant Jones in this case was from St. Sepulchre's parish, where Fullwood had purchased property more than a decade earlier. In his *Handbook to the Popular, Poetical, and Dramatic Literature of Great Britain, from the Invention of Printing to the Restoration* (1867) Hazlitt offers the following excerpt:

> The deposition of John Jones that, at the signe of the George in Yorke, Mr. Christopher Crosbitt did lend unto Mr. Richard Swale, Doctor of the Civill Law, the sum of two hundred pounds in angels. By which wilfull perjury of this Jones, and Bolton the Cutpurse, Fulwood and Doughtie were condemned in the Star Chamber.

> God, amend thats amisse:
> Better make a new world, then amend this.
> Flye Falshood.
> q. Fulwood.

A corrected proof sheet of this broadside is reproduced in Percy Simpson's *Proof-reading in the Sixteenth Seventeenth and Eighteenth Centuries* (1935).

Fullwood's legal problems did not stop there. McKerrow reports that the *Acts of the Privy Council* include several references to petitions brought by Fullwood's neighbors against him, primarily in response to the "vexatious suits" he had filed against them. In December 1591 he spent several days in the Fleet Prison and was released after posting bond. McKerrow points out that on 11 June 1592 the Privy Council handed the matter over to the Master of Rolls, who was instructed to bring the matter to a close. After this date there are no further references in the state papers to William Fullwood of Long Lane.

Prior to *The Enimie of Idlenesse*, English epistolary style had followed the style of the Latin formulary models. Fullwood's translation offered a departure from this norm by providing model letters in English and a new and popular direction for other translators and writers to follow. A lesson that *The Enimie of Idlenesse* helped to impart is that knowledge is not the sole possession of the elite, and that handbooks can at least open the doors of knowledge to those who seek it.

Bibliographies:

Samuel Egerton Brydges, *Censura Literaria,* volume 5 (London: Printed by T. Bensley for Longman, Hurst, Rees & Orme, 1807), pp. 134–135;

J. Payne Collier, *Extracts from the Registers of the Stationers' Company,* 2 volumes (London: The Shakespeare Society, 1848), I: 62–63, 157–158; II: 11;

William Carew Hazlitt, *Collections and Notes, 1867–1876* (London: Reeves & Turner, 1876), p. 175;

Hazlitt, *Second Series of Bibliographical Collections and Notes of Early English Literature, 1474–1700* (London: B. Quaritch, 1882), p. 347;

Heinrich F. Plett, *English Renaissance Rhetoric and Poetics* (New York: E. J. Brill, 1995), pp. 76–77, 150.

References:

Harold Cook Binkley, "Early English Formularies," in his "Letter Writing in English Literature," dissertation, Harvard University, 1925, pp. 40–59;

C. H. Conley, *The First English Translators of the Classics* (New Haven: Yale University Press, 1927), pp. 18, 26, 133, 148;

Thomas Corser, *Collectanea Anglo-Poetica* (Manchester: Chetham Society, 1878), III: 397–401;

Maude Bingham Hansche, *The Formative Period of English Familiar Letter-writers and Their Contribution to the English Essay* (Philadelphia, 1902), pp. 22–23;

William Carew Hazlitt, *Handbook to the Popular, Poetical, and Dramatic Literature of Great Britain, from the Invention of Printing to the Restoration* (London: John Russell Smith, 1867), pp. 215–216;

Katherine Gee Hornbeak, "Elizabethan Letter-Writers," in her *The Complete Letter Writer in English: 1568–1800,* Smith College Studies in Modern Languages, volume 15, nos. 3–4, April–July 1934 (Northampton, Mass.: Smith College, 1934), pp. 1–13;

Wilbur Samuel Howell, *Logic and Rhetoric in England, 1500–1700* (Princeton: Princeton University Press, 1956), pp. 59, 143–145;

R. B. McKerrow, "Retrospective Review: W. Fulwood's 'Enemy of Idleness,'" *Gentleman's Magazine* (May 1906): 390–403;

Jean Robertson, *The Art of Letter Writing: An Essay on the Handbooks Published in England during the Sixteenth and Seventeenth Centuries* (Liverpool: Liverpool University Press, 1942), pp. 13–17, 73;

Eleanor Rosenberg, *Leicester: Patron of Letters* (New York: Columbia University Press, 1955);

Foster Watson, ed., *English Writers on Education, 1480–1603* (Gainesville, Fla.: Scholars' Facsimiles & Reprints, 1967), pp. 68–69;

Louis B. Wright, "Handbook Learning of the Renaissance Middle Class," *Studies in Philology,* 28 (1931): 69–86;

Wright, *Middle-Class Culture in Elizabethan England* (Chapel Hill: University of North Carolina Press, 1935);

Wright, "The Renaissance Middle-Class Concern over Learning," *Philological Quarterly,* 9 (1930): 273–296;

Frances A. Yates, *The Art of Memory* (Chicago: University of Chicago Press, 1966), pp. 82–83, 260.

John Jewel

(24 May 1522 – 23 September 1571)

Kim Fedderson
Lakehead University

BOOKS: *The copie of a Sermon pronounced by the Byshop of Salisburie at Paules Crosse the second Sondaye before Ester in the yere of our Lord. 1560. wherupon D. Cole first sought occasion to encounter, shortly setforthe as nere as the authour could call it to remembraunce, without any alteration or addition* (London, 1560);

The Trve Copies Of The Letters betwene the reuerend father in God Iohn Bisshop of Sarum and D. Cole, vpon occasion of a Sermon that the said Bishop preached before the Quenes Maiestie, and hyr most honorable Cousayle. 1560. Set forthe and allowed, according to the order apointed in the Quenes Maiesties iniunctions (London: Printed by John Day, 1560);

Apologia Ecclesiæ Anglicanæ (London, 1562); translated as *An Apologie, or aunswer in defence of the Church of England, concerninge the state of Religion used in the same. Newly set forth in Latine, and nowe translated into Englishe* (London: Reginalde Wolfe, 1562);

An Apologie of priuate Masse sediciously spredde abroade in writyng without name of the authour: as it semeth, against the offer and protestacion made in certain sermons by the reuerende father Byshop of Salisburie. With an answere and confutacion of the same, set forth for the defence and maintenance of the trueth (London: Printed by Thomas Powell, 1562);

A Replie Vnto M. Hardinges Ansvveare: By perusinge whereof the discrete, and diligent Reader may easily see, the weake, and vnstable groundes of the Romaine Religion, whiche of late hath beene accompted Catholique. By John Jewel Bishoppe of Sarisburie (London: Printed by Henry Wykes, 1565);

A Defence of the Apologie of the Churche of Englande, Conteininge an Answeare to a certaine Booke lately set foorthe by M. Hardinge, and Entituled, A Confutation of &c. By John Jewel Bishoppe of Sarisburie (London: Printed by Henry Wykes, 1567; enlarged, 1570);

Iniunctions given by the reuerend father in Christ John by Gods prouidence, Bishop of Sarisburie, aswel to the Cleargie, as to the Churche wardens and enquirers of euerye seueral parish, aswel of his peculiar as general iurisdiction within and of the Diocese of Sarum to be obserued and kept of

John Jewel, circa 1560–1570 (portrait by an unknown artist; National Portrait Gallery, London)

euery of them in their offices and callings, as to them shal appertaine, for the aduauncement of Gods honor, thincrease of vertue, and good order to be continued within his sayd Diocese, and the same to be enquired of and put in vse by all the Archdeacons, Commissaries, and other officers exercising Ecclesiastical iurisdiction vnder the sayde Bishop according to the limittes of their seueral offices and iurisdictions, in their Synodes, visitations, inquiries, and Courts (London: Printed by Henry Denham for Richard Jackson, 1569);

A Sermon made in latine in Oxenforde, in the raigne of King Edwarde the sixt, by the learned and godly Father Iohn Iuel, late Bishop of Salisburie, and translated into Englishe, by R. V. Dedicated Vnto the Bishop of London, as appeareth in the Commentarie of Ma. Caluine, upon the Galathians, in Englishe (London: Printed by Thomas Purfoote, 1581?);

A Viewe Of A Seditiovs Bul sent into Englande, from Pius Quintus Bishop of Rome, Anno. 1569. Taken by the reuerende Father in God, Iohn Iewel, late Bishop of Salisbvrie. Wherevnto is added A short Treatise of the holie Scriptures. Both which hee deliuered in diuers Sermons in his Cathedral Church of Salisburie, Anno. 1570, edited by John Garbrand (London: Printed by Ralph Newberry, & Henry Bynneman, 1582);

An Exposition vpon the two Epistles of the Apostle Sainct Paule to the Theslalonians . . . By the reuerende Father Iohn Iewel late Byshop of Sarisbvrie, edited by Garbrand (London: Printed by Ralph Newberry, and Henry Bynneman, 1583);

Certaine Sermons preached before the Queenes Maiestie, and at Paules crosse, by the reuerend father Iohn Ievvel late Bishop of Salisbury. Whereunto is added a short Treatise of the Sacraments, gathered out of other his sermons, made vpon that matter, in his cathedrall Church at Salisburie, edited by Garbrand (London: Printed by Christopher Barker, 1583);

Seven Godly And Learned Sermons, preached by the Reuerend Father in God Iohn Ivel, late Bishop of Salisburie. Neuer before imprinted. Newly published to the glorie of God, and benefit of his Church, edited by I. K. (London: Printed for George Bishop, 1607);

The Works Of The Very Learned And Reuerend Father in God Iohn Ievvell, not long since Bishop of Salisbvrie. Newly set forth with some amendment of diuers quotations: And a briefe discourse of his life (London: Printed by Eliot's Court Press for Iohn Norton, 1609);

Certaine Frivolovs Obiections Against The Governement Of The Chvrch of England; Answeared By Iohn Iewel, sometimes Bishop of Sarisbury (London: Printed by Thomas Cotes, 1641);

A Sermon Preached Before Q. Elizabeth By That Learned And Reverend Man Iohn Iewel Bishop Of Sarisbury. Vpon these words, Psal. 69. 9. The zeale of thy house hath eaten me up. With An Answer Of The Same Authour To some frivolous objections against the government of the Church (London, 1641);

The Works of John Jewel, Bishop of Salisbury, 4 volumes, edited by John Ayre, Publications of the Parker Society, volumes 23–26 (Cambridge: Cambridge University Press, 1845–1850);

The Works of John Jewel, D. D. Bishop of Salisbury, 8 volumes, edited by Richard William Jelf (Oxford: Oxford University Press, 1848).

Editions: *An Apologie or answere in defence of the Churche of Englande, with a briefe and plaine declaration of the true Religion professed and vsed in the same,* translated by Lady Anne Bacon (London: Printed by Reginald Wolfe, 1564);

Hoyt H. Hudson, "Jewel's Oration Against Rhetoric: A Translation," *Quarterly Journal of Speech,* 14 (1928): 374–392;

An Apology of the Church of England, in *English Reformers,* edited by Thomas H. L. Parker (Philadelphia: Westminster Press, 1966), pp. 14–57;

An Apologie, or aunswer in defence of the Church of England, concerninge the state of Religion vsed in the same, The English Experience, no. 470 (Amsterdam: Theatrum Orbis Terrarum / New York: Da Capo, 1972);

"Oration against Rhetoric," in *Renaissance Debates on Rhetoric,* edited and translated by Wayne H. Rebhorn (Ithaca, N.Y.: Cornell University Press, 2000), pp. 162–172.

OTHER: *The Seconde Tome of homelyes, of such matters as were promysed and Intituled in the former part of homelyes, set out by the aucthoritie of the Quenes Maiestie: And to be read in euery paryshe Churche agreablye,* probably compiled by Jewel (London: Printed by Richard Jugge & John Cawood, 1563).

John Jewel is known to modern scholars as the first apologist of the Church of England, a reputation based on his *Apologia Ecclesiæ Anglicanæ* (1562), which established the basis for the Elizabethan settlement–the middle way between the competing demands of a Roman Catholic Church from which England sought to disentangle itself and an emerging Puritanism whose ecclesiastical and theological reforms England soon came to oppose. Jewel was better known to his contemporaries, and certainly to Queen Elizabeth I, as the most accomplished and distinguished Christian orator in England. His best-known works–the *Oratio contra Rhetoricam* (Oration against Rhetoric, delivered circa 1548), *The Challenge Sermon* (1560), and the *Apologia Ecclesiæ Anglicanæ* (1562)–and his life, specifically his involvement in establishing the doctrine of the Church of England, his preaching, and his public exchanges with Thomas Harding, provide a vivid and comprehensive portrait of a mid-sixteenth-century English theologian-rhetorician. Taken together, the life and work reveal the tensions between preceptive and imitative traditions of rhetoric, between oral and written rhetoric, between the literary and rhetorical motives for eloquence, between Catholic and Protestant conceptions of rhetoric and, most important, the tensions within humanism between classical and Christian rhetoric.

The first twelve years of Elizabeth's reign were a period of intense controversy in which the theological and ecclesiastical positions that came to define the *via media* (middle way) were haltingly revealed and hesitantly established. During this time, Jewel emerged as the most visible apologist for the new Church of England. Also, Jewel was charged with the responsibility of addressing the nation from Paul's Cross, the most important pulpit of that church, establishing himself as the most distinguished—and perhaps most popular, preacher of his era. According to his contemporary Gabriel Harvey, Jewel was one of the ornaments of English eloquence. Jewel's life was a public one and thus quite well documented. From his extensive correspondence with leading reformers such as Peter Martyr (Pietro Martire Vermigli), from his engagement in ongoing public controversy with leading recusant figures such as Henry Cole and Thomas Harding and leading reformers such as Laurence Humphrey and Thomas Sampson, from his appearances at Paul's Cross, from the records of the diocese of Salisbury, and from a biography written by his friend Humphrey immediately after Jewel's death, a fairly complete picture of the life and the man emerges.

John Jewel was born 24 May 1522 at Buden, in the parish of Berinber, Devonshire. He began his earliest training in Greek and Latin grammar, the first part of the trivium, with his maternal uncle, John Bellamy, the rector of Hampton. Jewel was next educated at Bampton, South Molton, and, finally, Barnstaple, where he was instructed by Walter Bowen. At the age of thirteen, Jewel entered Merton College, Oxford, and studied with Thomas Borow, a teacher known to be critical of the emerging reforms. When Borow assumed the vicarage of Croydon, he committed Jewel to the care of his colleague and sometimes disputant, John Parkhurst. Parkhurst, who later became bishop of Norwich, had become a committed reformer during his studies at Magdalen College, Oxford. Under Parkhurst, Jewel became increasingly familiar with, and dedicated to, theological and ecclesiastical reform. Parkhurst's teaching embodied that confluence of religious and rhetorical studies that defined Christian humanism, and his commitment to the "new learning"— which focused on grammar, rhetoric, and religious reform—is evident in his assigning Jewel to make a comparative study of the New Testament translations of William Tyndale and Miles Coverdale. Recognizing the considerable linguistic and theological talents of his student, Parkhurst is alleged to have predicted correctly that "surely Paul's Cross will, one day, ring of this boy."

After four years of study at Merton, including a period when his studies were interrupted by the plague and a subsequent sickness that left him lame, Jewel, at Parkhurst's suggestion, moved to Corpus Christi, the college most friendly to the spirit of reform, where he graduated with a B.A. in 1540. At Corpus Christi he distinguished himself as a student and is reputed to have aroused jealousy among his classmates because of his devotion to his studies. According to a nineteenth-century biographer, Charles Webb Le Bas, it was Jewel's "custom to rise at four in the morning, and to retire to rest at about ten at night. And nearly the whole of the interval, full eighteen hours, was employed by him in such intense study, that he seemed to require some one to remind him of his meals." His studies during this period focused on the Latin and Greek classics, collections of Desiderius Erasmus's adages and the works of the early Church Fathers—Jerome, Augustine, Ambrose, and Origen—were consonant with a Christian humanist curriculum. Given the religious instability of the times, a student's identification with this curriculum was not without its risks, but Jewel's personal integrity seems to have been sufficient to win over many of his antagonists. The persuasive force of his moral nature was attested to by John Moren, dean of Corpus Christi, who said, "I should love thee Jewel if thou wert not a Zuinglian. Thou art a heretic in thy faith; but, certainly an angel in life. Truly, thou art an honest man,—but thou art a Lutheran."

In 1542 Jewel was elected a fellow of Corpus Christi and was granted his M.A. in 1545. Immediately thereafter he gained a considerable reputation as a teacher and was appointed the college prelector of humanity and rhetoric. In this office he delivered a series of public lectures on the art of rhetoric that, according to Daniel Featley, one of Jewel's earliest biographers, were delivered with such "diligence and facilitie that many came from divers other colledges to behold Rhetorik so richlie set forth, with her own costlie apparel, and furniture, by the dexterite of his wit and learning." While these lectures have not survived, something of their character is likely reflected in the *Oratio contra Rhetoricam,* one of Jewel's earliest and most important writings, an oration delivered while he was prelector, perhaps circa 1548.

The *Oratio contra Rhetoricam* is Jewel's only contribution to the preceptive tradition of rhetoric, an evolving body of precepts or rules governing the rhetorical canons of invention, disposition, style, delivery, and memory that was committed to Latin in the writings of Cicero and Quintilian and made available in English to the Tudor world through such works as Thomas Wilson's *The Arte of Rhetorique* (1553). Unlike Wilson's work, the *Oratio contra Rhetoricam* is not a handbook designed to provide its audience with systematic instruction in the arts of rhetoric. What Jewel offers, under the guise of a critique, is an elaborate and delightful defense of rhetoric, which, in its paradoxical turns, captures much of the midcentury ambivalence about

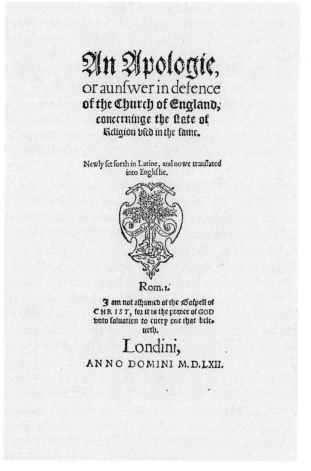

Title pages for the first edition and the first English translation of the seminal work in which Jewel described the doctrines and practices of the Church of England and defended their deviations from those of Roman Catholicism

the art on which the existence of the Elizabethan state and its church depended.

Jewel's initial target seems to be Ciceronianism, and in the late 1540s, when the *Oratio contra Rhetoricam* was composed and delivered at Corpus Christi, there was certainly a context for his apparently anti-Ciceronian sentiments. Erasmus had criticized extreme Ciceronians in his *Ciceronianus* (1528), and both William Caxton in *The Myrrour of the Worlde* (1481) and Sir Thomas Elyot in *The Boke Named the Gouernour* (1531) had condemned the superfluous expression and excessive amplification characteristic of Italian Ciceronians. Jewel rehearsed the familiar charges:

> so these fellows give their entire devotion to Cicero alone, so they imitate every tiny distinction, and stuff their sentences with rimes; and, as if they had no sense of their own, they know nothing unless Cicero knew it before them, ... in one Cicero they pitch their tents for life; and in him they seek out not learning, not the knowledge of things, not judgement, but letters,

accents, vowels, elegance of speech and supply of words.

(Quotations from the *Oratio contra Rhetoricam* are from the modern translation by Hoyt H. Hudson.)

Anticipating the debates over style that occupied English rhetoricians for the next century, Jewel argued that because truth is "clear and simple . . . perspicacious and plain," it has no need of the "flowers of artful speech" provided by a style that is, as he says, "feeble, enervate, Asiatic." This attack on Ciceronian excess, however, culminates in Jewel's recalling a time at Oxford when "Cicero, neglected and scorned, lay in mould and darkness." During this time, Jewel remarked in an apostrophe–"O then fortunate University! O happy time!"–not Cicero but "Scotus held the ports of the schools and the paths of literary study." What is puzzling in this passage is that Jewel, a rising humanist, advanced John Duns Scotus over Cicero to the audience of Oxford scholars that he refers to and represents in the oration. Jewel had left Merton, where "the old learning" and the traditions of scholasticism represented by Scotus had held their place as long as possible, for Corpus Christi, a college at the forefront of pedagogical and theological reform. During the Oxford visitation of 1535 John Tregonwell and Richard Layton, the examiners sent by Henry VIII, had set out to clear a space for the new learning. The zealous visitants had condemned old scholastic studies and "scattered the time honoured manuscripts of medieval philosophy to the winds." After they left, the works of Scotus served the scholars in their toilets.

Given this outright rejection of scholasticism, it is hard not to agree with Hudson's assessment that "when he glorifies the Scotists and laments the decay learning in his own age, surely Jewel is indulging in pure irony." In fact, there are clues within Jewel's oration. He concludes his barrage against Cicero by telling his audience that: "All these evils Cicero brought upon you, Cicero emptied our study-halls, Cicero gave the death blow, the mortal thrust, Cicero quenched the light and flame of Oxford." Following this climax, he continues his address to the audience, noting "I see that my time is up, and that you are judging my criticism of eloquence as frivolity and fruitlessness, itself to be fruitless and frivolous." Here the oration suggests that the audience doubts the orator's sincerity. Their incredulity is an oratorical effect, and it is clear from Jewel's use of "us" and "we" throughout the peroratio (conclusion) that he still identifies with his audience. His admission that they suspect his intentions then comes in the form of a shared joke, not chastisement. Further, the essence of that joke is present in the style Jewel uses to describe the audience's reaction to his critique of Cicero. Hudson's English translation preserves Jewel's artful use of chiasmus and polyptoton, schemes whose presence denies the claim against ornamental language the oration appears to make. Those inclined to conclude with Atkins that the *Oratio contra Rhetoricam* is "the most definite and outspoken attack by an Englishman against the Ciceronian heresy" can only do so by ignoring the extratextual context that surrounds the *Oratio contra Rhetoricam* and the intratextual context inscribed into its fabric.

It is fitting that the first classical allusion in the *Oratio contra Rhetoricam* is to Janus, the two-faced god of Roman mythology, for the oration looks in two different directions. As the plain sense of its title suggests, it is an oration against rhetoric; however, it can equally be regarded as jest, an eloquent case against rhetoric that is properly read ironically. Read as irony, Jewel's vituperation becomes an encomium in which the superiority of rhetoric is paradoxically demonstrated by its ability to make the case against itself.

There is, of course, considerable historical precedent for feigned epideictic oratory: Gorgias's praise of Helen, Isocrates' praise of Thersites, Synesius's praise of Baldness, and Lucian's praise of a fly are all orations made paradoxical by the speakers' choices of subjects generally considered unworthy of praise. Menander of Laodicia included the paradoxical encomium in his list of epideictic types in the *Peri Epideiktikon* (On Epideictic Rhetoric). During the Renaissance, this form became enormously popular: for example, Erasmus's *Moriae Encomium* (*Praise of Folly,* 1511) and Sir John Harington's *Metamorphosis of Ajax* (1596), a paradoxical encomium to a water closet. Strictly speaking Jewel's *Oratio contra Rhetoricam* is not, however, mock encomium, but, its obverse, mock vituperation—a paradoxical attack on a subject generally considered praiseworthy. Here too there are historical precedents, and, in particular, for feigned vituperation directed at rhetoric. Giovanni Pico Della Mirandola's letter to Ermolao Barbaro in 1485 appears to dispraise rhetoric while commending the barbarous style of the schoolmen, and notwithstanding Philipp Melanchthon's taking the attack seriously enough to respond to it, subsequent commentary has come to regard it as paradoxical. The same pattern of revision holds true for Henricus Cornelius Agrippa von Netlesheim's vituperation of rhetoric in *De incertitudine & vanitale scientiarum & artium* (1530; translated as *The Vanitie and Uncertaintie of Artes and Sciences,* 1569); the inconsistencies in that text are now read in such a way to suggest that Agrippa's tongue was firmly in his cheek when he sought to condemn eloquence.

Recognizing the importance of context in questions of interpretation, Quintilian argues that the presence of irony "is made evident to the understanding either by the delivery, the character of the speaker, or the nature of the subject, for if any one of these is out of keeping with the words it becomes clear that the intention of the speaker is other than what he says." The otherness of Jewel's intentions are amply demonstrated throughout the oration.

Most of the charges Jewel makes against rhetoric have been made before. As an accomplished orator, he recapitulates them all in his peroratio:

Accordingly, most learned youths, do not consent to spend so much time and effort on a thing which is absurd and idle . . . ; which nature herself has planted in the hearts and minds of all; which darkens a good cause, illuminates and adorns a bad one; which lays down rules for deceits, frauds and lies; . . . which avoids the judicious censure of the wise; which has overthrown great commonwealths; which the most ancient states rejected; which philosophers of times and countries have repudiated; which our own forefathers held in contempt; which dimmed the old and ancestral glory of this seat of learning; which, finally, rhetoricians themselves are ashamed, after they have learned it, to admit they know.

Of the eleven charges made here, only two are specifically concerned with Ciceronian excess, the rest are part of a generalized attack on the art of rhetoric itself. Jewel, while acknowledging the case against rhetoric, makes it difficult for his audience to take any of his arguments completely seriously.

At the outset he justifies his decision to abandon the study of rhetoric by citing Marcus Cato's decision to study "Greek letters, which previously he had ever hated." Yet, later in the oration, Jewel undermines Cato's authority by noting that "he . . . pitted Anthony against Augustus [and] straightway the might of Rome . . . the labours of a single orator, in a short time demolished." Jewel's tendency to allege an authority and then undermine it occurs with sufficient frequency in the *Oratio contra Rhetoricam* that phrases such as "that divine pair, Cicero and Demosthenes," "that supreme and supremely eloquent Demosthenes," and "the greatest orator, Demosthenes" become decidedly unstable in the context of the oration, and readers are left wondering whether these epithets are to be read literally as praise or rhetorically as insult.

There are further contradictions in the argument of the *Oratio contra Rhetoricam*. Jewel questions whether speaking well is an art, arguing that "the faculty of speaking and language are innate and implanted in the minds of all." He maintains that to speak intelligibly, clearly, and simply, there is no need of art, and he states his preference for the "lasting silence" of the Pythagoreans and the "brevity and plainness" of the Spartans. However, Jewel begins this specific argument by stating, "All that is to be said about rhetoric I do not promise here to say; nor do I judge that anyone, in any place, unless a prater and rhetor indeed, could in so brief a time tell all." Here, paradoxically, he claims that brevity is the product of art, an art whose existence he later denies.

Jewel's style itself is often at odds with the apparent substance of the oration. It is difficult not to be suspicious when the speaker extols the simplicity of an ordinary mode of speaking but repeatedly ornaments the oration with figures and schemes. Jewel condemns oratorical *actio*, the art of delivery; yet, he does so using rhetorical questions:

> What do they want of such faces? Why that thrashing about of the body? Why that sudden contraction? that waving of the arms? that slapping of the thigh? that stamp of the foot? Why is it they speak not with the mouth, not with the tongue, not with the jaws, but the hand, fingers, joints, arm, face, and the whole body?

Arguing that whoever introduced eloquence was ill-advised, he uses repeated paralepsis—the trope in which the orator claims not to talk about a subject and then proceeds to talk about it—to enumerate the faults of rhetoric: "I shall not speak of the oaths called into doubt. . . . I shall not mention seditions, factions, conspiracies, treasons, wars, burnings."

Jewel then proceeds to enumerate in detail how Demosthenes, Marcus Cato, Brutus, Cassius, Critias, and Cicero injured their states. He criticizes orators who call the gods down from heaven; yet, elsewhere in the oration he exclaims "Ye Gods!" and swears "by the immortal Gods." He condemns ornamental rhetorical art that "for free and untrammeled discourse contrive[s] feet, rhythm, and like fetters"; yet, when he argues that Cicero brought about the destruction of Rome "not by sagacity but by loquacity, not by reason but by eloquence" (or in the original Latin: "non prudentia sed eloquentia, non ratione sed oratione"), his use of rhyme and isocolon (syntactical balancing) are fully, and paradoxically, apparent. Surely when he questions rhetoricians' need "of these tropes, figures of speech, *schemata,* and what they call 'colors' (to me they seem *shades*),—epanorthosis, antimetaboles, suspensions . . . ," his learned audience of rhetoricians would likely note that his substituting "shades" for "colors" is an epanorthosis. Here, as elsewhere, his language fails to square with what it says.

The instability of the teaching on rhetoric in *Oratio contra Rhetoricam* is compounded by its echoes of mock epideictic forms that precede it, specifically Agrippa's *De incertitudine & vanitate scientiarum & artium,* Pico's letter to Barabaro, and Erasmus's *Praise of Folly.* When Jewel asserts that it is "shameful, beyond question, that one who has a soul, who has a mind, who has a heart, should cultivate only a tongue," he is rehearsing Agrippa's argument that "the seat of truth is not in the tongue but in the heart" and Pico's claim that rhetoricians "had the god of eloquence not on the tongue but in the heart." Similarly, Jewel's argument that speech proceeds for nature, obviating the need for art, also echoes Agrippa's claim "that eloquence could not be comprehended within the bounds of any art, but that it proceeds from Nature, which is the common school mistriss of mankind, and as the occasion serves, teaches everyone to soothe, to relate pleasant stories, and to use arguments." Jewel comes close to paraphrasing Agrippa when he recounts the familiar charges that Protagoras made the worse appear the better cause, that Carneades used eloquence to speak at Rome against justice, and that Pericles, when outdone by his adversary, used smooth words to make defeat look like victory. He also follows Agrippa closely when he cites the example of "Ctesiphon, whom when he professed him-

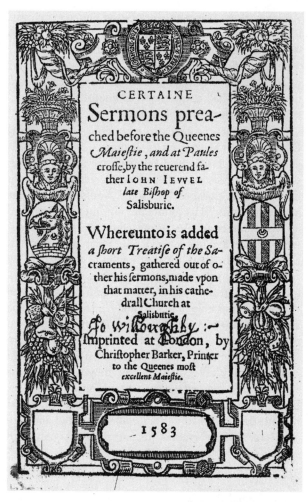

Title page for a posthumously published collection of Jewel's sermons

self 'able to speak for a day at a time, the Spartans ordered to be expelled and banished.'"

Similarly, Jewel's critique of *actio* (oratorical delivery), his argument that rhetoric caters to "the rabble and the mob," is drawn directly from Erasmus. His list of rhetoricians whose eloquence has destroyed states—"why should I mention the Graachi, Brutus, Cassius, Critias, and Alcibiades, when I have mentioned the leaders and the prince Demosthenes"—is paraphrased from *The Praise of Folly*. Jewel also borrows Erasmus's examples of the rhetorician whose "conscience and the thought of his crimes do not let him send wholly at ease," in particular Plato: "For why did reason and speech suddenly desert Plato when about to speak before the judges on behalf of his teacher, Socrates . . . ?" This question is the only mention of Plato in the oration, and the context is negative. It is puzzling that Jewel makes no use of Plato's attack on rhetoric: the *Gorgias* is neither cited, nor is its argument rehearsed. More puzzling still is the absence

of any reference to the Church's critique of ornamented speech. Agrippa concludes his argument by condemning rhetoric for its role in promoting heresy and its blasphemous claim that scripture lacks eloquence "because it abounds not in Ciceronian phrases." Jewel avoids any reference to religion, and apart from an amusing digression that includes an anecdote about a woman from Kent who fears for her country because of a proliferation of lawyers, the *Oratio contra Rhetoricam* stays resolutely classical in its range of reference. If Jewel had wanted to dissuade his audience from the study of rhetoric, it is surprising that he did not bring the two major sources of arguments against rhetoric—Plato and the Church—into play. Their omission, however, and in particular the omission of the religious critique, serves to maintain the playfulness of the oration.

There is little doubt that much of Jewel's *Oratio contra Rhetoricam* is to be read ironically. The question, however, is how much. The danger in Jewel's choosing to speak in *serio ludere* (to play in earnest) is that his audiences, both then and now, are left wondering which portions are offered in jest, which in earnest. Rosalie Colie was correct when she asserted in her *Paradoxica Epidemica: The Renaissance Tradition of Paradox* (1966) that paradox works "at the limits of discourse"; it "plays back and forth across terminal and categorical boundaries . . . the effect, of course, is to remove all standards by which the discourse may be measured, to keep the reference wholly internal, so that readers are constantly off balance. . . ." What then were Jewel's intentions in delivering the *Oratio contra Rhetoricam?* Hudson suggests one "might grant him such serious purposes as the exposure and denunciation of rhetorical excesses and the promotion of sound literary studies," but the "might" is sure indicator of his uncertainty. Wilbur S. Howell suggests that "perhaps he [Jewel] means by this only that his subsequent lectures will concern the humanities as his past ones have concerned rhetoric." His "perhaps," however, suggests he is also uncertain about Jewel's intentions.

One thing is certain. The goal of the paradoxist is to surprise and dazzle his audience with the incongruities of his discourse. The writer of paradoxes seeks to reduce his audience to a state of wonder. George Puttenham, in *The Arte of English Poesie* (1589), gives the figure of paradox the English name "wonderer." The speaker who sets out with the intention of being paradoxical assumes that his audience possesses sufficient linguistic sophistication to discern and enjoy the paradoxes included in his language. Jewel could assume that he spoke to such a coterie. His audience, as he says in the *Oratio contra Rhetoricam,* consisted of "most learned youths"—"young men of excellent parts, of highest hopes,—young men you have been born for the special mastery of letters, and in these continuously trained." The *Oratio contra Rhetoricam* is an attempt to surprise those "trained to expect the unexpected" by turning language against itself.

Jewel's conception of rhetoric in the *Oratio contra Rhetoricam* is highly aesthetic. As paradoxist, he is more interested in delighting his audience than teaching or moving them. In the *Oratio contra Rhetoricam* Jewel realizes the goals of the epideictic orator, but he does so at the expense of the deliberative role of oratory in composing pragmatic discourse turned out to the world. The picture of rhetoric that emerges in the *Oratio contra Rhetoricam*—charmingly skeptical, more literary than agonistic, ironic, playfully aloof from practical affairs—is finally a product of the historical circumstances of its composition. The *Oratio contra Rhetoricam* is a university rhetoric that marks the debut of a talented reform-minded rhetorician, whose rhetoric is nonetheless comfortably insulated from the emerging controversies of the day.

The conditions in which an academic and aesthetic rhetoric could flourish came to an abrupt end with the death of Edward VI in 1553. From an early age Jewel had been identified with the protestant cause. Having enjoyed the support of Parkhurst at the outset of his university studies, he later found patrons in James Curthorpe and Richard Chambers, both of whom provided funds for reform-minded scholars. In the late 1540s Jewel was also befriended by Peter Martyr, the leading reform theologian, who had assumed the regius chair of theology at Oxford. In fact, Jewel may have delivered his *Oration contra Rhetoricam* when he was serving as a substitute lecturer for Martyr. Jewel acted as his secretary in his 1549 disputation over the eucharist with William Tresham and William Chedsey, assuming a role he would later perform for both Thomas Cranmer and Nicholas Ridley. Sometime in 1550, Jewel was awarded his B.D. degree and took up a benefice at Sunningwell near Oxford. A license for preaching was issued to him in December 1551. Once the Catholic Mary assumed the throne Jewel initially found it impossible to act in accordance with his reform principles. In his role as the public orator of the university, he composed a measured and carefully prudent address congratulating the new queen. Also in 1554 he publicly complied when asked to subscribe to the essential doctrines of Roman Catholic faith. His recantation of Protestantism, however, did not free him from suspicion, and, fearing arrest, he fled to Frankfort in 1555. During this period of Marian exile, he reunited with Martyr and such leading English protestants as Alexander Nowell, William Cole, John Ponet, Edmund Grindal, Edwin Sandys, Sir Anthony Cooke, Thomas Lever,

and James Pilkington. Together this group established the program of religious reform that was implemented after Mary's death.

Jewel returned to England in March 1559, three months after the ascension of Elizabeth I. Jewel's rhetorical talents were called on once again. His contributions to the art of rhetoric during this period, and for the remainder of his life, were more practical than theoretical. The disengaged, literary rhetoric of the *Oratio contra Rhetoricam* was displaced by the engaged rhetoric of sermons and religious controversies. As a preacher and as a disputant with both Catholic recusants and English Puritans, Jewel established himself as the pre-eminent agonistic rhetorician of his day. The importance of these contributions to an English imitative tradition of rhetoric, the emerging body of rhetorical practice as distinct from rhetorical theory, is attested to by Daniel Featley, the author of the biography prefixed to *The Works Of The Very Learned And Reuerend Father in God Iohn Ievvell* (1609): "what more quick, pithy, material & fraight with all variety of choice both new and ancient learning can any require, than was his controuersies with M. Harding, his Apologie, his Sermons."

Jewel's sermons and controversial writings are significant to the study of rhetoric because they provide a window into Elizabethan rhetorical culture during a period of transformation. During Elizabeth's reign, and increasingly during the seventeenth century, the rhetorical culture that renaissance humanists inherited underwent a series of shocks from which it has never recovered. The classical notion of the rhetorician as an individual speaking, not writing, to an audience, not to a group of readers, on a subject of some immediate urgency was rapidly fading. By the mid-seventeenth century, orations—as John Milton's *Areopagitica* (1644) attests—were something to be read, not heard. Also during this time the rhetorical reforms of theorists such as Pierre de La Ramée (known as Petrus Ramus), specifically his reduction of rhetoric to the art of style, made rhetoric more literary and less concerned with the effects of discourse in a particular context. In Jewel's orations during this period, the scholar finds a rhetoric still tied to antiquity.

The best known of Jewel's sermons, *The Challenge Sermon,* was delivered at Paul's Cross in London on 26 November 1559, and, according to Le Bas, "such was, at that time, the attraction of his name, that a more crowded congregation was never witnessed in the same place." This challenge to the doctrines of the Roman Catholic Church was delivered a second time, at court on 17 March 1560, and a third time, somewhat revised, at Paul's Cross on 30 March 1560, after which it was published as *The copie of a Sermon pronounced by the Byshop of Salisbury at Paules Crosse the second Sondaye before Ester in the yere of our Lord. 1560.* Jewel's sermons exemplify the Christian humanist adaptation of classical rhetoric to serve the needs of reformation preachers, putting into practice the precepts that Andreas Gerardus (Hyperius) presented in *The Practise of Preaching* (translated by John Ludham, 1577). As a Christian orator, Jewel modified the traditional duties of the orator (to teach, delight, and move) so that they were consistent with the obligations of the preacher. These new duties were derived from 2 Timothy 16, where Paul argues that all scripture can be used to instruct, to correct, to exhort, and to rebuke. Following the reformed art of invention, Jewel composed his sermons as expositions of a scriptural citation, in which all points of doctrine are proven by scripture, by the authority of early Church Fathers, and, in some instances, by works from pagan antiquity. The reformed art of disposition directed Jewel to arrange his sermons as orations, and the sermons maintain with slight modifications the six-part structure of the classical oration. Elocution, a vexed topic for Jewel because of the parallel between ornamented sermon styles and ornamental religion, recommended a plain style. Jewel used tropes and schemes, but did so sparingly. Regarding Jewel's style, Laurence Humphrey wrote "he ever loved eloquence, but *non effaeminatem sed virilem,* that is, that which sheweth it life [sic] not so much in the fresh and lively colour of the blood, in the rhetoricall figures and cadencies, as in the sprightlie and sinewish motions of arguments."

Jewel prepared his sermons painstakingly. Throughout his career, he railed against extemporaneous preaching, and he advocated several humanist educational reforms and ecclesiastical regulations designed to provide the Elizabethan church with a cadre of preachers with sufficient learning for their pastoral tasks. Jewel also spent considerable time rehearsing his delivery. Le Bas wrote that, when Jewel was a young man, "the practice of Demosthenes suggested to him the discipline by which he might prepare himself for public speaking; only that the woods of Shotover, instead of the Ocean beach, were the scenes of his solitary exercises in declamation." No doubt, Jewel's pulpit delivery benefited from his prodigious powers of memory, and the extent to which Jewel employed mnemonic techniques associated with the various arts of memory is significant. Many stories have circulated about his power of recall. According to Le Bas, "he seems, also, to have been in possession of some artificial method, by which the native capacity [of his memory] was prodigiously strengthened and improved. . . . He was once put to the test by John Hoper . . . who presented him with a list of forty Welch and Irish words. Jewel went

aside; and, after a short recollection, repeated them backward and forward."

Jewel's sermonic defense of the Elizabethan religious position was just one among many delivered within the parishes throughout England shortly after Mary's death. When he first delivered his *Challenge Sermon* he had been nominated bishop of Salisbury, and he was consecrated bishop at Lambeth on 21 January 1560. Thus, he spoke as one of Elizabeth's ecclesiastical luminaries, and, as such, it is not surprising that the sermon occasioned spirited responses from a variety of recusant writers, including figures such as Henry Cole, Nicholas Sanders, Thomas Stapleton, John Rastell, and Thomas Heskyns. Thomas Harding, however, proved to be Jewel's greatest and most tenacious antagonist. Their extended exchanges are not without significance to the history of English rhetoric; indeed the controversy is, in many ways, the best example of the rhetoric of disputation during the Elizabethan era. According to Harvey, "Harding and Iewel were our Eschines and Demosthenes; and scarcely any language in the Christian world hath affoorded a payre of aduersaries equiualent to Harding and Iewell, two thundring and lighting Orators in diuinity. . . ." Harding, who had assumed the Hebrew professorship at New College, Oxford, in 1542, had, like Jewel, shifted his declared religious loyalties with the pressure of the times. He had appeared congenial with protestant reform under Edward, but had returned to Roman Catholicism under Mary. On Elizabeth's ascension to the throne, he and many other recusants had retired to Louvain in Flanders. His controversy with Jewel began with *An Answere to Maister Juelles Chalenge* (1564), a reply to Jewel's *Challenge Sermon.* Jewel responded with *A Replie Vnto M. Hardinges Ansvveare* (1565). After Jewel published his *Apologia Ecclesiæ Anglicanæ* (1562), Harding responded with *A Confutation of a Booke intituled An Apologie of the Church of England* (1565), which occasioned Jewel's *A Defence of the Apologie of the Churche of Englande, Conteininge an Answeare to a certaine Booke lately set foorthe by M. Hardinge, and Entituled, A Confutation of &c.* (1567). This pamphlet was answered by Harding's *A detection of sundrie foule errours, vttered by M. Jewel* (1568), to which Jewel responded in an enlarged edition of *A Defence of the Apologie of the Churche of Englande* in 1570.

The styles of the controversialists are rather different. In a letter to Martyr, Jewel complained of his "adversaries . . . seeking to recommend themselves to the ignorant multitude, by the attractions of their style, and the craftiness of their sophistry." In *A Defence of the Apologie of the Churche of Englande* Jewel advocated what became the standard reformist line on the art of elocution: "Good reader, Truth is plaine and homely, and hath no need of these habilments." Jewel's controversial writing rarely achieves the dignified eloquence of the sermons. Following the customary practice of disputation, Jewel responded to his antagonists point by point, and as one would expect there is little formal artistry at work. Moreover, as the rhetorical goals of the controversialist are largely didactic, the prose tends to reflect the plainer style associated with logical appeals and avoids the more vivid and artistic language associated with ethical and emotional appeals.

At the same time as Jewel was defending the Elizabethan position from attacks by recusants from abroad, he was also drawn into controversy with the Puritan opposition at home. Between 1565 and 1571 Jewel participated in the disputations concerning the propriety of ecclesiastical vestments within the Elizabethan church. Jewel argued the establishment position that ecclesiastical vestments were a "thing indifferent," that is, of no theological significance, and thus found himself in opposition to reformers such as Thomas Sampson and Laurence Humphrey who regarded cope, tippet, and surplice as vestiges of popery. This controversy is of rhetorical significance only insofar as its terms anticipate an emerging quarrel about sermonic style. This dispute over how "plain" a plain style must be became increasingly heated toward the end of the Elizabethan era and culminated in the opposition to rhetorical ornamentation in the sermons of Thomas Cartwright and in William Perkins's Puritan preaching manual, *Prophetica* (1592), translated as *The Arte of Prophecying into Englande* (1607).

In 1570 Jewel wrote *A Viewe Of A Seditiovs Bul* opposing the excommunication of Elizabeth I by Pope Pius V, and in the following year he preached his last sermon at Paul's Cross. In the remaining two years of his life he was preoccupied primarily with pastoral duties in Salisbury and the building of the library at Salisbury Cathedral. During this time he also supported the studies of Richard Hooker, a promising student, whose *Of the Lawes of Ecclesiaticall Politie* (1593) later consolidated and extended the apology of the English church that Jewel had initiated. Jewel, who had been prone to illness throughout his life, delivered his last sermon in Laycock in Wiltshire. He then rode to Monkton Farleigh, where he was consigned to bed and died 23 September 1571. His remains were deposited in the middle of the choir of Salisbury Cathedral.

Jewel's presence in the Anglican Church eventually extended well beyond Salisbury. Shortly after Jewel's death, Matthew Parker, Archbishop of Canterbury, ordered that *A Defence of the Apologie of the Churche of Englande* should be chained to reading desks in every parish in the country, thus preserving the legacy of the greatest ecclesiastical rhetorician of the Elizabethan era for future Christian orators.

Letters:

Hastings Robinson, ed., *The Zurich Letters Comprising the Correspondence of Several English Bishops and Others, with Some of the Helvetian Reformers, During the Early Part of the Reign of Queen Elizabeth* (Cambridge: Cambridge University Press, 1842).

Biographies:

Laurence Humphrey, *Ioannis Ivelli angli, Episcopi Sarisburiensis, vita & mors, eiusq; veræ doctrinæ defensio, cum refutatione quorundam obiectorum, T. Hardingi, N. Sanderi, A. Copi, H. Osorij Lusitani, Pontaci Burdegalensis* (London: Printed for J. Dayum, 1573);

Daniel Featley, "The Life Of The Worthie Prelate And Faithfvll Servant Of God Iohn Ievvel sometimes Bishop of Sarisbvrie," in *The Works Of The Very Learned And Reuerend Father in God Iohn Ievvell, not long since Bishop of Salisbury. Newly set forth with some amendment of diuers quotations: And a briefe discourse of his life* (London: Printed by John Norton, 1609);

Antony à Wood, "John Jewell," in *Athenae Oxonienses. An Exact History of All the Writers and Bishops Who Have Had Their Education in the University of Oxford. To Which Are Added the Fasti, or Annals of the Said University*, third edition, 4 volumes, edited by Philip Bliss (London: Printed for F. C. and J. Rivington, 1813–1820), I: cols. 389–396;

Charles Webb Le Bas, *The Life of Bishop Jewel* (London: J. G. & F. Rivington, 1835);

"The Life and Death of John Jewel," in *Abel Redevivus; Or, The Dead Yet Speaking. The Lives And Deaths Of The Modern Divines*, 2 volumes, by Thomas Fuller and others (London: William Tegg, 1867), I: 354–370.

References:

J. W. H. Atkins, "The Rhetoric Tradition: Jewel, Wilson, and Ascham," in *English Literary Criticism: The Renascence* (London: Methuen, 1947), pp. 66–101;

J. W. Binns, *Intellectual Culture in Elizabethan and Jacobean England: The Latin Writings of the Age*, ARCA Classical and Medieval Texts, Papers and Monographs, edited by Francis Cairns and others, no. 24 (Leeds, U.K.: Francis Cairns, 1990);

John Booty, "The Bishop Confronts the Queen: John Jewel and the Failure of the English Reformation," in *Continuity and Discontinuity in Church History: Essays Presented to George Huntston Williams on the Occasion of His 65th Birthday*, edited by F. Forrester Church and Timothy George (Leiden: E. J. Brill, 1979), pp. 215–231;

Booty, *John Jewel As Apologist of the Church of England* (London: Clowes & Dons, 1963);

Booty, *Three Anglican Divines on Prayer: Jewel, Andrewes, and Hooker: Lectures Given for the Society of St. John the Evangelist, Cambridge, Massachusetts, November 1977* (Cambridge, Mass.: The Society, 1978), pp. 1–13;

Ruth Chavasse, "The Reception of Humanist Historiography in Northern Europe: M. A. Sabellico and John Jewel," *Renaissance Studies,* 2 (1988): 327–338;

Thomas Dorman, *A request to M. Jewell,* English Recusant Literature, 1558–1640, no. 148 (Menston, U.K.: Scolar Press, 1973);

Arundell James Kennedy Esdaile, "An Apology of Private Mass, 1562," *Library,* 1 (21 December 1921): 161–164;

Thomas Harding, *A detection of sundrie foule errours,* English Recusant Literature, 1558–1640, no. 202 (Menston, U.K.: Scolar Press, 1974);

Wilbur S. Howell, *Logic and Rhetoric in England: 1500–1700* (Princeton: Princeton University Press, 1956);

Charles Edward Mallet, *A History of the University of Oxford,* 2 volumes (London: Methuen, 1924);

James McConica, ed., *The History of the University of Oxford: Volume III: The Collegiate University* (Oxford: Clarendon Press, 1986);

John Rastell, *A confutation of a sermon pronounced by M. Iuell. 1564.,* English Recusant Literature, 1558–1640, no. 13 (Menston, U.K.: Scolar Press, 1970);

G. Gregory Smith, ed., *Elizabethan Critical Essays,* 2 volumes (Oxford: Clarendon Press, 1904), pp. 239–282;

Wyndham Mason Southgate, *John Jewel and the Problem of Doctrinal Authority,* Historical Monographs, no. 49 (Cambridge, Mass.: Harvard University Press, 1962);

John Strype, *Strype's Works,* 27 volumes (Oxford: Clarendon Press, 1822);

David K. Weiser, *The Prose Style of John Jewel* (Salzburg: Institut für Englische Sprache und Literatur, Universität Salzburg, 1973).

Papers:

There are three extant manuscripts for John Jewel's *Oratio contra Rhetoricam.* Two are at Corpus Christi College, Oxford (MSS.clvii and ccciv), and the third is at the British Library ("Oratio in Vituperium Rhetoricae per D. Juellium ex Corp. Christi collegio hapita coram omnibus ejusdem colegii alumnis," Harkian MS. 129.72), which has other manuscripts and letters as well.

Ralph Lever

(circa 1527 – 15 March 1585)

Jon D. Orten
Ostfold College

BOOKS: *The most ancient and learned playe, called the philosophers game. Set forth by W. F.,* anonymous (London: Printed by R. Hall for J. Rowbotham, 1563); republished as *The most noble auncient, and learned playe, called the Philosophers game, inuented for the honest recreation of students, and other sober persons, in passing the tediousnes of tyme, to the release of their labours, and the exercise of their wittes. Set forth with such playne precepts, rules, and tables, that all men with ease may understande it, and most men with pleasure practise it. By Rafe Leuer and augmented by W. F.* (London: Printed by R. Hall for J. Rowbotham, 1563);

The Arte of Reason, rightly termed, Witcraft, teaching a perfect way to Argue and Dispute (London: Printed by Henrie Bynneman, 1573).

Edition: *The Art of Reason, 1573,* English Linguistics, 1500–1800, no. 323 (Menston, U.K.: Scolar, 1972).

OTHER: "The Assertion of Raphe Lever touching the Canon Law, the English Papists, and the Ecclesiastical Offices of this Realm, with his most humble Petition to Her Majesty for Redress," in *Annals of the Reformation and Establishment of Religion, and Other Various Occurrences in the Church of England, during the first twelve years of Queen Elizabeth's happy reign . . . ,* by John Strype, second edition, 4 volumes (London: Thomas Edlin, 1725–1731), pp. 357–361.

Ralph Lever, D.D., canon of Durham Cathedral and master of Sherburn Hospital, was a gifted Cambridge graduate with Puritan leanings who took on important ecclesiastical positions in the bishopric of Durham. During much of his life he was involved in controversies of different kinds. Today Lever is chiefly remembered as the author of *The Arte of Reason, rightly termed, Witcraft, teaching a perfect way to Argue and Dispute* (1573), an early English work on logic within the Aristotelian tradition. His efforts at finding English rather than Latin terms for traditional logical concepts have aroused the interest of many linguists and language historians.

Little is known about Lever's early years, and the year of his birth is not known. Judging from the career of one of his older brothers, Thomas, who was born in 1521 and graduated with a B.A. from St. John's College of the University of Cambridge in 1542, one can reasonably assume that Lever was born around 1527 because he graduated with a B.A. from the same college in 1548. The Lever family came from Little Lever, now a township that is part of Bolton in southern Lancashire. The family had been established as lords of half of the Little Lever manor by the thirteenth century. Ralph's father, John Lever (who died in 1540), was assessed at £4 for lands in the subsidy roll of 1524. He appears to have been a principal trustee of Bolton School and was instrumental in giving the grammar school a new start in 1525. John Lever had seven sons, of whom Thomas, later a Puritan divine, was the second and Ralph third among the younger sons. After Elizabeth's accession to the throne in 1558, another son, John, became the first headmaster of Tonbridge School in Kent. It is reasonable to suppose that John Lever's sons all attended Bolton School, which their father, as a founding trustee, supported strongly.

Like his brother Thomas, Ralph Lever attended St. John's College, Cambridge, which was becoming a Puritan stronghold and where the best education of the day was to be obtained. Cambridge was at that time the center of the "new learning" and the reformed religion. Sir John Cheke, the first regius professor of Greek, "taught Cambridge and King Edward Greek," as John Milton put it. Among Cheke's students was Thomas Wilson, who graduated with an M.A. from King's College in 1549. Roger Ascham, a friend of Wilson's and of Lever's brother Thomas, became a fellow of St. John's in February 1534 and a Greek reader at the same institution in 1538. Interestingly, there was a strong Bolton contingent at St. John's during this period, including James Pilkington, who was to become the first protestant bishop of Durham, his brother Leonard, and

 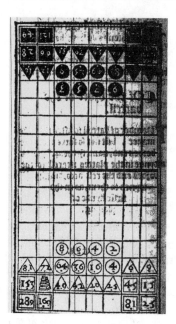

Title-page vignette and illustration of the game board from The most ancient and learned playe, called the philosophers game *(1563),*
Ralph Lever's book about rythmomachy, a board game that may have been invented by Pythagoras

Richard Longworth, both later elected Durham preben-
daries. Thomas Lever, the Pilkington brothers, and
Richard Longworth all became masters of St. John's
College. Some time during Leonard Pilkington's mastership (1561–1564), Ralph Lever took advantage of
his Lancashire connections to lease Bassingbourne
Manor in Fordham, Cambridgeshire.

Lever took his M.A. in 1551 and was admitted as
a fellow of St. John's by the royal visitors on 4 July
1551. In the same year his brother Thomas was made
master of St. John's College by royal mandate. Thomas
was a leader of the extreme party of Protestant reformers in the university. When King Edward VI died in
1553, he supported the cause of Lady Jane Grey to succeed Edward to the throne. Thomas even dined with
the duke of Northumberland, who had persuaded
Edward to name Lady Jane as his successor, when the
duke visited Cambridge to proclaim Lady Jane queen.
Two months after Queen Mary's accession, Thomas
resigned the mastership of St. John's and fled to Zurich.
Mary's government deprived twenty fellows of St.
John's of their positions, and of these, nine followed
their master into exile. Both Ralph and John Lever
accompanied their brother Thomas and during the
Marian exile may have spent time in several Continental towns. Ralph probably resided with Thomas at Zurich and Aarau. Among other places that Thomas is
known to have visited, and to which it is reasonable to
suppose that Ralph might have accompanied him, are
Geneva, Strasbourg, Bern, and Frankfurt. Furthermore,
it is highly probable that Ralph, like Thomas, made the

acquaintance of the Swiss Protestant reformer Heinrich
Bullinger in Zurich and that he attended the lectures
and sermons of John Calvin in Geneva.

Returning from the Continent following the death
of Queen Mary, Lever was elected a senior fellow of St.
John's College on 30 July 1559, and exactly one year
later he was incorporated M.A. at Oxford. According to
Thomas Baker's *History of the College of St. John the Evangelist, Cambridge* (1869), Lever, Thomas Cartwright, William Fulke, and Percival Wiburn, while fellows of St.
John's, "infected the college with an almost incurable
disaffection, and laid the seeds of our succeeding divisions." In other words, Lever was clearly associated
with the Puritan faction.

"The Assertion of Raphe Lever touching the
Canon Law, the English Papists, and the Ecclesiastical
Officers of this Realm, with his most humble Petition to
Her Majesty for Redress" was written in 1562 and first
published in the second edition of John Strype's *Annals
of the Reformation and Establishment of Religion, and Other
Various Occurrences in the Church of England, during the first
twelve years of Queen Elizabeth's happy reign* . . . (1725–1731).
The text consists of twenty-one paragraphs asserting
the authority of the Canon Law, the authority of Queen
Elizabeth in Protestant England, and the responsibility
of Her Majesty's delegates to make just use of the laws.
Lever petitions the queen for redress of all inconveniences and mischiefs that have taken place since the
last Parliament and describes the sad state of the universities, with decreasing numbers of students choosing the
study of divinity. Lever's opposition to papist influence

is quite marked, and his support of the queen as temporal and spiritual leader is exceptionally strong. Such definite declarations of loyalty were both necessary and wise in order to obtain royal favor. But other aspects of the "Assertion" are less cautious politically. For example, Lever points out that "a man may bear Office in a Christian Society, and yet be a Preacher of the Word too. . . ."–an interesting assertion typical of the Puritan preaching ministry but hardly popular among ecclesiastics close to power.

In 1563 Lever became reader or tutor to Walter Devereux, the oldest son of Sir Richard Devereux. Walter was viscount Hereford and later became the first earl of Essex. He received a careful education at home, for part of which Lever must have been responsible. At this early stage Walter was already married and lived in temporary retirement at his house at Chartley, Staffordshire.

Lever's first book, *The most ancient and learned playe, called the philosophers game,* was printed at least twice in 1563 but apparently without Lever's authorization or due respect for his manuscript. He makes this disclaimer in his next book, *The Arte of Reason, rightly termed, Witcraft, teaching a perfect way to Argue and Dispute* (1573): "Surely I thinke my selfe muche discredited, and that great wrong is offred unto me, for that the same is set forth, and suffred to passe under my name, without my knowledge, or assent." The two issues of *The most ancient and learned playe* have slightly different title pages, one claiming that the book was "set forth by W. F.," the other that it was "By Rafe Leuer and augmented by W. F." The *Dictionary of National Biography* takes these initials to stand for William Fulke. However, compared with Fulke's other works, this somewhat strange treatise seems strikingly out of character. Indeed, it seems more apt to attribute the augmentation of *The Philosophers Game* to William Fulwood (or Fullwood), whose literary production was smaller but more versatile than that of Fulke. This assumption is strengthened by the fact that an acrostic reading "WILYAM FVLVOD" appears on the fifteenth page of the book.

The rules of *The Philosophers Game* are quite intricate, as befitting a logician's mind. Also called "the battell of numbers," the game is played with forty-eight pieces, twenty-four on each side; it ends when one of the two kings is taken, as in chess. The board consists of 128 squares in two contrasting colors, the breadth of one chessboard and the length of two. Eleanor Rosenberg has identified the game as rythmomachy, which may have been invented by Pythagoras.

In his dedicatory epistle, written in verse, bookseller James Rowbotham goes to considerable length defending the publication, stating that the game is not a wicked pastime but has been profitably used "in French

and Latin eke" and is still practiced by learned men. The unsigned address to the reader repeats many of the claims of the epistle, but in prose, emphasizing the importance of refreshing oneself, preserving one's honesty, and exercising one's wits. Whether the address is to be attributed to Rowbotham, Fullwood, or Lever is open to conjecture, but the plain statement that it is presented "in Englishe" (much as the same is underscored in *The Arte of Reason*) reminds one of Lever's interest in the English language. "[T]he bookes verdicte" reveals the writer's awareness of his deficiency in the use of the vernacular: "Wanting I haue bene long truly, In english language many a day."

Starting in the mid 1560s, Lever experienced great changes in his career. James Pilkington, the bishop of Durham since 1560, was able to provide his Bolton friends with benefices in his bishopric. He gave Thomas Lever the mastership of Sherburn Hospital, and he remembered Ralph Lever as well. On 5 November 1565 Ralph was made rector of Washington in county Durham. In *The History and Antiquities of the County Palatine of Durham* (1816–1840) Robert Surtees describes Washington as "a scattered village on irregular broken ground" and its parsonage as "an excellent brick house, with good gardens." On 21 August 1566 Ralph became archdeacon of Northumberland, with the rectory of Howick, and in 1567 he was installed a canon of Durham. As such, he was one of several ecclesiastics responsible, under the dean, for the cathedral. Lever is repeatedly referred to as a prebendary–that is, a canon whose income originally came from a prebend, the portion of the revenues of a cathedral granted him as a stipend. Among the canons Ralph was the second person to occupy the fifth stall in the cathedral, and he held it until his death.

The work for which Lever is chiefly remembered today, *The Arte of Reason,* was published in 1573. It is preceded only by Wilson's *Rule of Reason* (1551) as a complete treatise on logic written in English. R. C. Alston maintains that Lever's book was written and almost ready for the press when Wilson published his treatise. The delay in the publication of Lever's work may indicate that it was eclipsed by Wilson's; at any rate, its impact was felt much later than would have been the case if the two books had been published in the same year. If it is true that the greater part of Lever's work on logic was written by 1551, it follows that its composition was to a large extent simultaneous with his preparing for, or taking, the M.A. degree. In "The Epistle dedicatorie" Lever says that "Martine Bucer read ouer this arte, in his old days, and renewed in his age, the rules that he learned thereof in his youth." Wilbur Samuel Howell takes this statement to mean that *The Rule of Reason* was completed in the

THE ARTE
of Reaſon, rightly
termed, *Witcraft*, teaching
a perfect way to argue
and diſpute.

Made by Raphe Leuer.

Seene and allowed according to the order
appointed in the Queenes Maieſties Iniunctions.

¶ *Imprinted at London, by*
H. Bynneman, dwelling in Knight-
rider ſtreate, at the ſigne of the
Mermayde. Anno. 1573.

Theſe Bookes are to be ſolde at his Shop at
the Northwweſt dore of Paules church.

¶ To the right ho-
norable Lorde, Walter,
Earle of Eſſex, Uiſcount Hereford
and Lord Ferris of Chartley, Lord Bourghchier, and Louaine, and Knight of the moſt honorable order of the Garter: Raphe Lener
wiſheth encreaſe of knovvledge,
with the true feare of god.

I pleaſed you,
(righte honorable) aboute
nine yeares ago, to accepte
me into your ſeruice: and
being then deſirous to ſtu-
dye the arte of reaſoning, ye made me your
reader: and vſed at ſundry times to conferre
vvith me in that kinde of learning. There
vvas in you (be it ſpoken to the praiſe of
God, and vvithout all ſuſpition of flaterie)
both a gentle nature, eaſie to be trained to
take pleaſure in ſtudie: and alſo a ſharpnes
of vvit, readie to conceiue at the firſt anye
doctrine that vvas orderlye taught. So that
doubtleſſe, if there had not bene a lacke in
∗.ii.   me

Title page and first page of the dedication for the second complete English-language treatise on logic

period between 1549 and 1551, when both men were at Cambridge. It is debatable, however, whether the reference to Bucer in dating the treatise is relevant in this case. Bucer died in England in 1551, but he could not speak English, and the reference might rather illustrate Lever's wish that Walter Devereux, the subject of the dedication, would do as Bucer had done in renewing the study of logic in his later years. *The Arte of Reason* is Lever's only work on logic, and nowhere does he indicate that he made any other contribution to the field of logic or rhetoric either in his youth or later.

The dedication "To the right honorable Lorde, Walter, Earle of Essex, Viscount Hereford and Lord Ferris of Chartley, Lord Bourghchier, and Louaine, and Knight of the most honorable order of the Garter" is in part an apology. Lever makes it clear that he had nine years earlier been accepted into Devereux's service because his lordship had been "then desirous to studye

the arte of reasoning." Lever was, however, unable to lead his scholar as far as would have been desirable because he, the teacher, "vsed no good trade to cause [his] L[ordship] to take pleasure in studye, and not to faile of [his] appointed houres." He says that for the tutor to men of noble birth it is necessary "that besides knowledge and diligence to teach, they have also a certain sleight, and cunning, to cause their scholers to delight in learning." While he has failed to inspire his own student properly, he feels that *The Arte of Reason* might be of great profit to many other students. In the dedication there is, however, an indication that Lever must have put a great deal of effort into the book prior to its publication: he says that his shortcomings as a teacher to the earl were the chief occasion for his writing the book on logic. In other words, the book may not have been as complete by 1551 as scholars such as Alston and Howell suppose.

In the "Forespeache" Lever argues for the use of English in the art of reasoning. He sees the possibilities of devising new words in place of the traditional Greek and Latin terms. In choosing English he wants to "proue that the arte of Reasoning may be taught in englishe." The choice of the mother tongue also shows that Lever was thinking of those (such as the earl of Essex) who wanted to reason correctly without having to master either of the classical languages. One of the striking aspects of Lever's treatment is the consciousness with which he approaches the English language. He is by no means afraid of employing English as his linguistic medium, because he is well aware of its potentials:

> Nowe whereas a number of men doe suppose, that our language hath no words fitte to expresse the rules of this Arte: and where as some men do agree, that it must needes be so, bycause they that speake or write thereof at large, use termes and wordes, that no mere English man can understande: It is playn, that neyther their supposition is true: not yet their reason good. For as time doth invent a newe forme of building, a straunge fashion of apparell, and a newe kinde of artillerie, and munitions: so doe men by consent of speache, frame and deuise new names, fit to make knowen their strange deuises.

Lever allows the use of foreign terms but shows skepticism for their undue use: "As for straunge and inkhorne terms, (used of many without cause) they argue a misuse to be in the speaker: but they prove not directly, that there is anye lacke in oure language." Such views are in line with those of several Tudor writers concerned about the prestige of the vernacular, the adequacy of its vocabulary, and its suitability for scholarship. In fact, Lever might have done as Wilson chose to do: select an English vocabulary out of the forms of the established Latin vocabulary. But Lever chose the other option, which was the use "of simple vsual wordes, to make compounded termes, whose seuerall partes considered alone, are familiar and knowne to all english men." He believes that the vernacular is specially equipped to meet the challenge of both "deuising of newe termes, and compounding of wordes." The reason for this is "that the moste parte of Englyshe woordes are shorte, and stande on one sillable a péece. So that two or thrée of them are oft times fitly ioyned in one."

Lever's approach to the task of creating an English logic is thus quite radical. Moreover, his arguments in "The Forespeache" reflect an admirable proficiency in the workings of language, no doubt acquired through his classical training. The fact that the "Forespeache" is to a great extent a defense of Lever's choice of linguistic medium is in itself a reminder that the struggle for recognition of English in all fields had not yet been completely won. In actually choosing native terms, Lever ended up with a set of words that posed a challenge to the reader. While Wilson had borrowed the Latin terms and anglicized them to produce words such as "logic," "rhetoric," "definition," and "conclusion," Lever translated the Latin terms directly, producing such neologisms as "witcraft," "spéechcraft," "saywhat," and "endsay" for these same four terms, respectively. To "predicate" Lever preferred "backset," for "category" he used "storehouse." In *The Arte of Reason* "proposition" becomes "saying," "declarative proposition" gives "shewsay," and "affirmation" "yeasay," while "negation" becomes "naysay." Similarly, for "premise" Lever has "foresaye," for "induction" "reason by example," and for "deduction" "reason by rule."

In the mid sixteenth century, at a time when no established vocabulary existed for English logic, such Anglo-Saxon terms might not have appeared any stranger than Latinate ones, but for a modern reader Lever's terminology may sound quite unfamiliar. For example, discussing arguments in "The fourth Booke," Lever advises: "learne how the foreset and backset agree or disagree together, and what respecte the one beareth to the other: whether the sentence containe one or many shewsayes: whether it bee generall or speciall: a yeasay, or a naysay: and so foorth of other necessary pointes appertaining to the discussing of a shewsay. . . ." Fortunately, at the end of *The Arte of Reason* Lever provides "A note to vnderstand the meaning of newe deuised Termes," which makes the deciphering quite manageable. This note is a useful glossary of terms in English with Latin equivalents and page references to the places in the text where the terms are used.

While in his treatment of language Lever is an innovator, in the field of logic he remains faithful to earlier precepts. There is no indication of the influence of Pierre de La Ramée (known as Petrus Ramus) in his logic, though Walter J. Ong calls it "vaguely Agricolan." Lever is chiefly in line with Wilson, John Seton, and Thomas Blundeville, particularly in his ordering of the two parts of dialectic: judgment first, invention second. Ong notes that these writers, in placing judgment first, may owe a greater debt to Boethius than to Aristotle. Nevertheless, Lever credits the ancient Greeks with this arrangement: "Therfore is witcraft wel deuided of the Grecians into two parts: wherof the firste is called . . . the decerning part: the other . . . the finding part." *The Arte of Reason* is divided into four books. In going through the major divisions of logic, Lever progresses through simpler to more complex units of discourse. The first three books deal with judgment, or the "decerning" part, divided into words in the

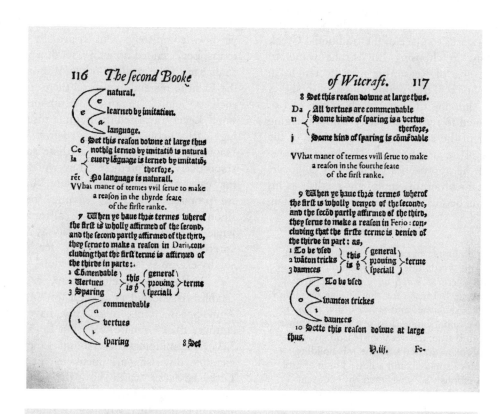

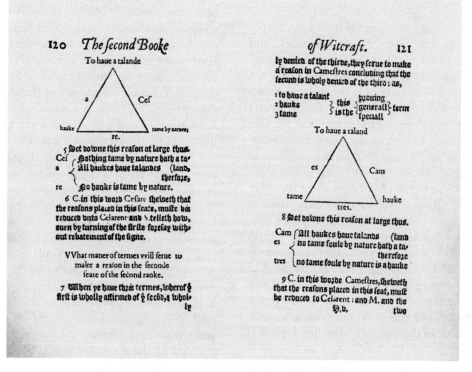

Pages from The Arte of Reason *(1573) with diagrams illustrating types of syllogisms*

first book, sayings (or propositions) in the second book, and reasons (inductive or deductive arguments) in the third book. The fourth book is "Of Inuention or fynding out of argumentes"—that is, of the places or topics. Seton had employed the same order in his *Dialectica* (1545). Wilson in 1551 had adopted the same arrangement without formally dividing it into books, but he added a section on false reasons.

For the fourth book, however, Lever maintains that he will follow his own method. For places he starts with what he terms the ten "storehouses" of words, *storehouse* being in Latin "*praedicamentum, attributum.*" These ten storehouses he lists as the usual ten predicaments: substance, quantity, quality, respect, doing, suffering, where, when, placing, and having. Substance was the first predicable as well as the first predicament: "He that wyll discourse orderly, and search a matter to the bottom, must begin with the substance of the thing he speaketh of." These "storehouses" were accompanied by ten corresponding "demaunders": "1 What? 2 Howe muche, or how many? 3 Whatkynone? 4 To whome, or then what? 5 Dooing what? 6 Suffering what? 7 Where? 8 When? 9 Howe placed? 10 Hauing what?" "The general places . . . gathered out of sundry authors" add up to twenty-two and are later expanded to the final number of forty-four. Lever encourages the reader to "conne by hart, and haue on [his] fingers endes" the fourteen seats (places of arguments) expressed in the third book, as well as the forty-four particular places set forth in the fourth book.

By 20 October 1573 Lever had resigned the archdeaconry of Northumberland, along with the rectory of Howick, to avoid having them taken from him on account of nonresidency. On 17 November 1575 he was instituted to the rich rectory of Stanhope in county Durham; at the same time, or shortly thereafter, he resigned the Washington rectory, which he had held since 1565. The vacancy in the see of Durham, occasioned by the death of Bishop Pilkington in 1575, led to his appointment as commissary to exercise episcopal jurisdiction. On 30 March 1577 Lever and another prebendary, Richard Fawcett, presented a supplication to the Queen "against the Dean and Chapter of Durham, for granting leases of 21 years of the manors, &c., belonging to the prebends." They asked for "redress from Her Majesty by visitation, *sede vacante.*"

Upon the death of his brother Thomas in July 1577, Ralph was given the mastership of Sherburn Hospital, a position Thomas had occupied since January 1563. He immediately resigned the rectory of Stanhope but retained the canonry in the cathedral of Durham. Records also indicate that he was serving as the bishop's chaplain in July 1577.

Sherburn Hospital, situated about one-and-a-half miles to the southeast of Durham, was an old institution, founded by Bishop Hugh de Pudsey (or Puiset) in the twelfth century for the maintenance of sixty-five paupers. The institution had declined considerably by the early 1560s, when Thomas Lever took over. He was charged with the maintenance of only thirteen poor brethren and two lepers. Thomas, and later Ralph, worked hard to revive the institution, and their efforts led to the passing of a new "Act for the Incorporation of the Hospital of Christ in the Town of Sherburne in the Bishoprick of Durham" in the year of Ralph's death.

According to Charles Henry Cooper, Lever was created doctor of divinity at Cambridge in 1578. The doctorate was awarded under a grace stating that he had studied theology for twenty years after receiving his M.A. degree.

From about this time until the end of his life, Lever was engaged in frequent litigation. In April 1578 he was asked to appear repeatedly before the Lords of Her Majesty's Counsel (the Privy Council) on matters related to certain leases and pensions of the Sherburn Hospital. In this same year Lever also became embroiled in a dispute with the widow Margaret Bonne (Bonde or Bowne) of Billingham, a tenant under the Durham Chapter estates. She charged that Lever had expelled her illegally from her tenement. It appears that the same tenement had earlier been granted in lease to Lever's nephew Thomas Lever; then to his son, also named Thomas Lever; and afterward (during the hearing itself) to one John Stubberd, who was paying twenty nobles yearly above ordinary rent to the Dean and Chapter. Apparently the council found Lever's explanation unsatisfactory and authorized the widow to keep the lease until her death, whereupon it was to go to the young Lever.

Writing to Lord William Cecil Burghley in January 1580, Lever stated "some objections to the appointment of Secretary Dr. Wylson as Dean of Durham" but agrees "to act as his Vice-Dean under certain conditions." The man Lever named was Thomas Wilson, author of *The Rule of Reason* and *The Arte of Rhetoric* (1553) and a former secretary of state; he served as the dean of Durham from 1580 until his death the following year. For Wilson this was a preferment for which he had been a candidate in 1563, when William Whittingham was appointed. The reason for Lever's protest against Wilson's election was the fact that Wilson, a doctor of laws, was not ordained. The nomination of a layman to the deanery could be viewed as an assertion of royal supremacy.

After 1580 Lever was at constant odds with Richard Barnes, Bishop of Durham. That relations between Barnes and Lever were strained is revealed in a letter of

27 June 1580 to the lord president of the Council of the North, Henry Hastings, Earl of Huntingdon. The council asks the bishop to abridge the lawsuit and make sure that they avoid the evil report such strife will cause. Two other entries from 1581 in the *Acts of the Privy Council of England, New Series* (1890–1964) show that Lever also had differences with Robert Bellamy, prebendary of the third stall (and master of Sherburn Hospital from 1589), whom Lever accused of withholding money from him.

On 30 September 1583 Lever requested that the council intervene in the matters between him and the bishop of Durham. He cited the denial of justice by the bishop in his private suits and the great injury done by the long vacancy of the deanery between Wilson's death in 1581 and Toby Matthew's appointment to the position in 1583. Lever discussed the ideal qualifications of a dean and stated the wrongs and injuries that he had sustained from the bishop. His comments about the qualifications of a dean were no doubt in response to the previous appointment of the layman Wilson. The fact that Barnes, after having been appointed bishop, had handed over to the Crown a long string of "Manores" belonging to the see might explain some of Lever's frustrations.

Two other references to Lever appear in the *Calendar of State Papers, Domestic Series, of the reigns of Edward VI, Mary, Elizabeth* (1856) for 1585, the year of his death. On 24 February of that year he requested that Lord Burghley forward in Parliament a bill "for assurance of the corporation of the hospital of Sherbourne House." The bill was read the first time in the House of Lords on 24 February 1585. Article 67 notes Lever's suit to increase the number of paupers at Sherburn Hospital from sixteen to thirty brethren. This request must have been made right before his death in March 1585. The *Calendar of State Papers* must be mistaken when it gives "1588?" as the date of a petition by Lever to Lord Burghley, the Earl of Huntingdon, and Sir Francis Walsyngham.

Contemporary allusions or references to Lever are scarce, partly because his *Arte of Reason* appeared right before Ramist theories on logic came to the fore and partly because his treatise was not published in editions subsequent to the first one of 1573. Lever seems to have been overshadowed by Wilson. For example, in *The Arte of English Poesie* (1589) George Puttenham confuses Wilson and Lever, although Puttenham was apparently familiar with Lever's book: "Master Secretary *Wilson* geuing an English name to his arte of Logicke, called it *Witcraft,* me thinke I may be bolde with like liberty to call the figure *Etiologia* [tell cause]." Lever was also commonly confused with his well-known brother Thomas. Thus,

John Bramhall (later the archbishop of Armagh), while bishop of Derry, mentions Lever's book in the preface to his *Castigations of Mr. Hobbes* (1657) but attributes it to Thomas Lever. In an interesting statement Bramhall informs the reader that he desires to retain the proper terms of the schools, while "Mr. Hobs flies to the common conceptions of the vulgar, a way seldom trodden, But by false Prophets, and seditious Oratours." Bramhall refers to Lever as "an odd Phantastick person in our times, one Thomas Leaver, who would needs publish a Logick in our Mother Tongue." Interestingly, Bramhall, a Cambridge graduate of Sidney Sussex College, clearly shows familiarity with Lever's logic:

> And because the received terms of Art seemed to him [Lever] too abstruse, he translated them into English, stiling a Subject an Inholder, an accident an Inbeer, A proposition a Shewsay, an affirmative proposition a Yeasay, a negative proposition a Naysay, the Subject of the proposition the Foreset, the predicate the backset, the conversion the turning of the Foreset, into the Backset, and the Backset into the Foreset.

Not unexpectedly, in view of Bramhall's initial statements, he ends the paragraph: "Let Mr. Hobs himself be judge, whether the common Logical notions, or this new Gibrish were left intelligible." This statement indicates that at the time of Bramhall's student days in Cambridge from 1609 on, Lever's work may still have been studied. Clearly, Lever's Anglo-Saxon terms were not much appreciated by "the Irish Canterbury" (as Oliver Cromwell called Bramhall), but admittedly the bishop merely reflects the prevailing attitude in preferring the very Latin terms that Lever had sought to replace.

In the twentieth century Lever attracted attention precisely because of his linguistic undertaking. Thus, Richard Foster Jones has carefully considered the implications of Lever's efforts toward creating a native terminology. In fact, Jones implies a connection between the linguistic projects of Puttenham and Lever, in that both created new compounds but were at the same time critical of neologisms. Jones indicates a line of writers interested in finding workable native compounds from Cheke and Arthur Golding to Lever and Puttenham. Manfred Görlach makes note of Lever's criticism of stylistic excesses. While viewing Ascham, Wilson, and Cheke as linguistic "purists" in a loose application of the term, Görlach particularly refers to the "purism" (as well as the "historical ineffectiveness," since their new compounds did not catch on) reflected in their translations of Latin terminology: "Golding for medicine, Lever for philosophy and Puttenham for rhetoric." Görlach

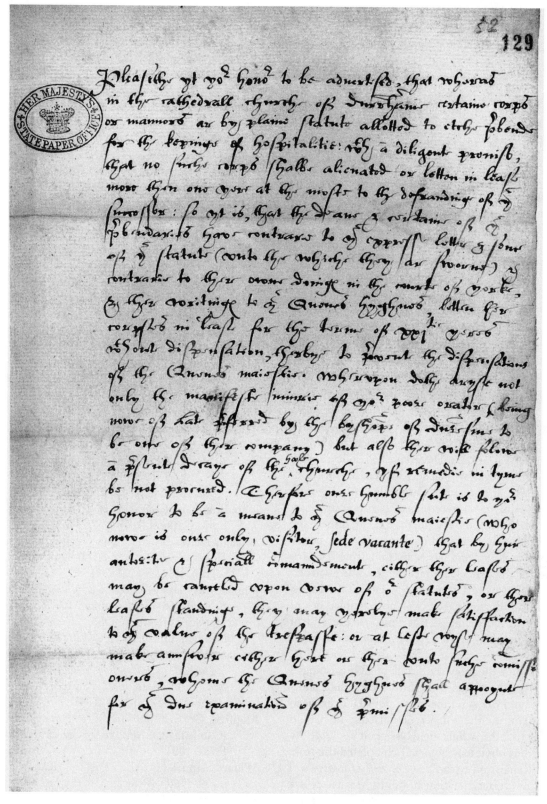

A 1577 letter in which Lever describes his grievances against the dean and chapter of Durham Cathedral for granting leases on lands that belong to the prebends (Public Record Office, London, SP 12/111)

also notes a difference between Cheke's and John Hart's loan translations (compounds formed from the translation of the parts of a term in another language) and Lever's, Golding's, and Puttenham's freer renderings, or loan creations (terms using native forms to convey borrowed meaning). Charles Barber also refers to Lever as a purist. He finds it striking that none of Lever's coinages caught on and that speakers of English today use words derived from Latin expressions that Lever rejected, such as *affirmation* and *conclusion*.

Both Lever and his brother Thomas may have been hampered in their ecclesiastical careers by their association with the zealous Puritans. For Thomas this seems to have been particularly true: "Though a Dissenter from the discipline of the Church of England," writes Surtees, "he was permitted to hold the Mastership of Sherburn, on account of the scarcity of preachers. . . ." Surtees describes Ralph as "a troublesome Non-conformist." The epithet "troublesome" is almost certainly a reference to Lever's many controversies in his later years. Most of the preferments that the Lever brothers received prior to 1575 were owing to Bishop Pilkington's influence.

From a survey of Lever's life it seems that his preoccupation with logic must have been particularly marked in his Cambridge days, and then as a result of his work as a tutor to Devereux. It is not entirely clear whether Lever was closely associated with university circles after leaving Cambridge. At any rate, he appears not to have returned to reside at Cambridge after having moved north. Yet, he must have maintained an interest in the subject of logic, partly by serving as tutor, and partly by preparing *The Arte of Reason* for the press. The fact that he was awarded a D.D. degree from Cambridge as late in his life as 1578 would indicate that he was not completely out of touch with academia at this time. At the end of "The Forespeache" to *The Arte of Reason* Lever states that while he has written much on good reasoning, "of the second [to show the faults of ill reasoning] I mind to write hereafter, if the Lorde God shall make mee able, and occasion me so to do." Had he been able to write on the subject of fallacies, he would have covered the whole field assigned to logic by Aristotle, but obviously he never completed the task. Still, for Renaissance scholars *The Arte of Reason* will continue to attract attention not only because it is a significant treatment of logic and of particular stylistic interest, but also because it occupies a special position in sixteenth-century literature on logic as the second complete treatise on the subject to have been written in English.

Biographies:

Charles Henry Cooper and Thompson Cooper, "Ralph Lever," in their *Athenae Cantabrigienses,* 3 volumes (Cambridge: Deighton, Bell & Macmillan, 1858), I: 507–508;

Wills and Inventories from the Registry of Durham, Part IV, Publications of the Surtees Society, no. 142 (London & Durham: Andrews / Bernard Quaritch, 1929).

Vincent Wayne Leaver, *Thomas and Ralph Leaver: Protestant Reformers During the Edwardian Reformation in Sixteenth Century England* (Miami, Fla.: V. W. Leaver, 1986);

References:

R. C. Alston, note to Lever, *The Art of Reason, 1573,* English Linguistics, 1500–1800, no. 323 (Menston, U.K.: Scolar Press, 1972), p. 4;

Thomas Baker, *History of the College of St. John the Evangelist, Cambridge,* volume 1, edited by John E. B. Mayor (Cambridge: Cambridge University Press, 1869);

T. W. Baldwin, *William Shakspere's Small Latine & Lesse Greeke,* volume 2 (Urbana: University of Illinois Press, 1944);

Charles Laurence Barber, *The English Language: A Historical Introduction* (Cambridge & New York: Cambridge University Press, 1993);

Robert Hood Bowers, Introduction to Thomas Wilson, *The Arte of Rhetorique, 1553* (Gainesville, Fla.: Scholars' Facsimiles & Reprints, 1962);

John Bramhall, *Castigations of Mr. Hobbes, 1658* (New York: Garland, 1977);

William Ernest Brown, "The Old School," in his *The History of Bolton School* (Bolton, U.K.: Bolton School, 1976), pp. 11–38;

John Roche Dasent, ed., *Acts of the Privy Council of England, New Series,* volumes 10–13 (London: Her Majesty's Stationery Office, 1895; reprint edition, Nendeln, Liechtenstein: Kraus Reprint, 1974);

Depositions and Other Ecclesiastical Proceedings from the Courts of Durham, Extending from 1311 to the Reign of Elizabeth, Publications of the Surtees Society, no. 21 (London: J. B. Nichols, 1847);

Manfred Görlach, *Introduction to Early Modern English* (Cambridge & New York: Cambridge University Press, 1991);

Wilbur Samuel Howell, *Logic and Rhetoric in England, 1500–1700* (Princeton: Princeton University Press, 1956);

Richard Foster Jones, *The Triumph of the English Language* (Stanford, Cal.: Stanford University Press, 1953);

Robert Lemon and Mary Anne Everett Green, eds., *Calendar of State Papers, Domestic Series, of the reigns of*

Edward VI, Mary, Elizabeth, 12 volumes (London: Longman, Brown, Green, Longmans & Roberts, 1856–1872);

Patrick Mussett, ed., *Lists of Deans and Major Canons of Durham, 1541–1900* (Durham, U.K.: The Prior's Kitchen, 1974), pp. 42, 62;

Walter J. Ong, *Ramus: Method, and the Decay of Dialogue* (Cambridge, Mass.: Harvard University Press, 1958);

George Puttenham, *The Arte of English Poesie, 1589,* English linguistics, 1500–1800, no. 110 (Menston, U.K.: Scolar Press, 1968);

James Raine, ed., *The Injunctions and Other Ecclesiastical Proceedings of Richard Barnes, Bishop of Durham, from 1575 to 1587,* Publications of the Surtees Society, no. 22 (Durham, U.K.: George Andrews, 1850);

Eleanor Rosenberg, *Leicester: Patron of Letters* (New York: Columbia University Press, 1955), pp. 39–44;

John Strype, *Annals of the Reformation and Establishment of Religion, and Other Various Occurrences in the Church of England, during Queen Elizabeth's Happy Reign, Together with an Appendix of Original Papers of State, Records, and Letters,* third edition, 4 volumes (Oxford: Clarendon Press, 1824);

Strype, *The Life and Acts of Matthew Parker, the First Archbishop of Canterbury, in the Reign of Queen Elizabeth. To Which Is Added, an Appendix, Containing Various Transcripts of Records, Letters, Instruments, and Other Papers, for the Asserting or Illustrating the Foregoing History. In Four Books* (Oxford: Clarendon Press, 1821);

Joseph L. Subbiondo, "Ralph Lever's *Witcraft:* 16th-Century Rhetoric and 17th-Century Philosophical Language," in *History of Linguistics 1993: Papers from the Sixth International Conference on the History of the Language Sciences (ICHoLS VI), Washington D.C., 9–14 August 1993,* edited by Kurt R. Jankowsky (Amsterdam & Philadelphia: John Benjamin, 1993), pp. 179–186;

Robert Surtees, *The History and Antiquities of the County Palatine of Durham,* 4 volumes (London: J. B. Nichols, 1816–1840);

Thomas Wilson, *The Rule of Reason, London (1551),* The English Experience, no. 261 (Amsterdam: Theatrum Orbis Terrarum / New York: Da Capo Press, 1970).

Henry Peacham the Elder

(September 1547 – 23 September 1634)

Shawn Smith
St. Mary's College of Maryland

See also the Peacham entry in *DLB 172: Sixteenth-Century British Nondramatic Writers, Fourth Series.*

BOOKS: *The Garden of Eloquence Conteyning the Figures of Grammer and Rhetorick, from whence maye bee gathered all manner of Flowers, Coulors, Ornaments, Exornations, Formes and Fashions of speech, very profitable for all those that be studious of Eloquence, and that reade most Eloquent Poets and Orators, and also helpeth much for the better vnderstanding of the holy Scriptures. Set foorth in Englishe by Henry Pecham Minister* (London: Printed by Hugh Jackson, 1577); revised and enlarged as *The Garden of Eloquence, Conteining the Most Excellent Ornaments, Exornations, Lightes, flowers, and formes of speech, commonly called the Figures of Rhetorike. By which the singular partes of mans mind, are most aptly expressed, and the sundrie affections of his heart most effectuallie vttered. Manifested, and furnished vvith variety of fit examples, gathered out of the most eloquent Orators, and best approued authors, and chieflie out of the holie Scriptures. Profitable and necessarie, as wel for priuate speech, as for publicke Orations. Corrected and augmented by the first Author. H. P.* (London: Printed by Richard Field for Hugh Jackson, 1593);

A Sermon vpon the three last verses of the first Chapter of Iob: tending to the consideration of Gods prouidence, planting of patience, and applieng of consolation (London: Printed by Richard Jones & Edward Aggas, 1591).

Editions: *The Garden of Eloquence (1593),* edited by William G. Crane (Gainesville, Fla.: Scholars' Facsimiles & Reprints, 1954);

The Garden of Eloquence, 1577, edited by R. C. Alston, English Linguistics 1500–1800, no. 267 (Menston, U.K.: Scolar, 1971);

Henry Peachams "The Garden of Eloquence" (1593): Historisch-kritische Einleitung, Transkription und Kommentar, edited by Beate-Maria Koll, Literarische Studien, volume 4 (Frankfurt: Peter Lang, 1996).

Henry Peacham, who served the Church of England as a clergyman for more than six decades, is known for a single work, *The Garden of Eloquence Conteyning the Figures of Grammer and Rhetorick,* a rhetorical treatise that was first published in 1577 and substantially revised in a 1593 edition. As a commentary on nearly two hundred rhetorical figures, *The Garden of Eloquence* is unrivaled among sixteenth-century studies of *elocutio* (elocution, or style). Although primarily a synthesis of the most important classical and humanistic studies of rhetorical figures that were available to Peacham, the book is more than a translation of Continental studies of elocution—Peacham adds much to his sources, and his analysis of the emotional power of rhetorical figures is an important contribution to the history of Renaissance rhetoric. In many ways, *The Garden of Eloquence* is also more than a textbook, and its contents can be seen to reflect broadly the cultural, social, political, and religious concerns with rhetoric in Elizabethan England.

Henry Peacham, one of nine children born to Richard and Agnes Peacham, was baptized on 11 September 1547 in Burton Latimer, Northamptonshire. There is no record of Peacham's university attendance, but ecclesiastical records indicate that he received both B.A. and M.A. degrees. He married Anne Fairclough, with whom he had five children: Richard, Henry, Thomas, Jane, and Anne. Henry the younger, born in 1578, exceeded his father in fame (of the two, only the younger Peacham merits an entry in the *Dictionary of National Biography*), writing books on graphic arts, epigrams, and emblems, as well as essays and pamphlets on contemporary social, religious and political issues. His most famous work, *The Compleat Gentleman* (1622), is an important contribution to early seventeenth-century courtesy literature, and in both style and content (knowledge of literature and religion is emphasized), the book is a fitting tribute to the ideas of his father. The younger Peacham also produced a 1595 drawing of Tamora appealing to Titus for mercy in William Shakespeare's *Titus Andronicus* (1594)—the first, and only contemporaneous illustration of one of Shakespeare's

Henry Peacham's church at North Mimms, Hertfordshire, where he lived from 1574 until 1595
(Hertfordshire Archives and Local Studies)

plays. The drawing, too, is an apt subject for the younger Peacham, as his father had written so profoundly on the rhetoric of emotion in the 1593 edition of *The Garden of Eloquence.*

Peacham's career in the church began on 14 April 1574 when he was ordained deacon by the Bishop of Peterborough. Then, or shortly thereafter, he was made curate at North Mimms, Hertfordshire, where Thomas More is said to have written part of his *Utopia* (1516). In 1578 he was ordained priest and made rector at North Leverton, Lincolnshire, but with this appointment he also became a pluralist (a holder of two or more ecclesiastical offices at one time), and he appears not to have left North Mimms until after he also received the living of South Leverton in 1595. At North Mimms in the 1580s Peacham witnessed the will of one Thomas Noades, and he ministered to one Audrey Rushley at her deathbed on Christmas Eve 1583: "when he saw there was not tyme enough to wright her will he exhorted her first to prepare her selfe towards god and next he sayd thus vnto her, Mother Rushley to

whom will yo geue your goods, she mode hym aunswer sayinge, to Harrye [her son], hauinge thus sayd she spake no more & so died within two howers after." As one of the clergy of Lincoln, Peacham provided a musket for the 1590 Subsidy of Armor, but the dedications of his 1591 *A Sermon vpon the three last verses of the first Chapter of Iob* and his 1593 edition of *The Garden of Eloquence* place him in North Mimms in the early 1590s, and the 1594 *Liber Cleri* (Book of the Clergy) for the diocese of Lincoln lists Peacham as absent. Peacham had certainly moved to Leverton by 1597, when he signed the Bishop's Transcripts for the first time. In 1601–1602 Peacham is listed as one of "the better sort" of ministers in Lincoln, and was required to contribute 20 s. for the provision of the Light Horse for Ireland. In a February 1602 list of double benefices in Lincoln included in *The State of the Church in the Reigns of Elizabeth and James I,* Peacham is mentioned as being "the parson of Leuerton *borialis* and Leverton *australis* twoe parsonages in one churche and in this deanry wheruppon is resydent servienge bothe the Cures himself," a fact that may help to explain Peacham's continued pluralism after moving to Lincolnshire. Also, the number of communicants in North and South Leverton combined in 1603 was 160—only three of the twenty-one other cures in the district of North Holland had fewer communicants. At the same time, however, nine years after he had settled in Lincolnshire, there is evidence that Peacham continued to maintain financial contacts in Hertfordshire. He remained a trustee of eight acres of parish lands by a 1595 deed of feoffment until June 1604, when the feoffment was conveyed to six residents of North Mimms, though later in the same year the lease was transferred to Peacham for forty years. Because the original deeds have been lost, it is difficult to speculate on the nature of the transactions, but it is possible that the 1604 deeds, which in effect gave Peacham rights to the property without being a legal trustee of it, were prompted by the contempt for pluralism and other clerical abuses that accompanied James's accession to the throne. The canons passed in convocation in July 1604 took a stronger stand against such abuses, and King James I was becoming increasingly vocal in his opposition to pluralism. This political climate, combined with popular appeals for greater ethical responsibility among the clergy in the early Jacobean period, may have caused Peacham to exercise more caution in his affairs, if not to mend his ways entirely.

If Peacham's actions suggest abuse of his position in the church, the relatively sketchy picture of other parts of Peacham's life reveal an even more unseemly zeal for financial gain. Alan R. Young, in his excellent and detailed study of the records of Peacham's life, has gone as far as to say that Peacham was "crafty in his acquisition of material assets, not above the use of violence to ensure a 'good' marriage for a daughter, and not entirely free from the suspicion of fraud." This dim view of Peacham's character is based on a 1618 Chancery case in which Peacham accused his son-in-law John Garner of "great vnthriftines" for having "wasted and spent in idle and vaine expenses all the mooney that was raysed by the sale of those his landes." In 1605 Peacham had abducted the fourteen-year-old Garner when his father died. Peacham subsequently forced Garner to marry his daughter Anne—perhaps because she was pregnant, or perhaps because Garner's property appealed to him. In 1618 Anne and her second husband, William Hawarden, brought the complaint in Chancery against Peacham and his son (Anne's brother) Richard, objecting to Richard's use and profit of the Garner property. Richard claimed rights to the land based on a 1609 agreement in which Garner let the property to him for a period of twenty-one years. Richard and Henry claimed that the original deed of feoffment, which gave the property to Garner and

Anne, had not been properly executed. More significantly, Henry Peacham had "Casually" lost the deed during a trip to nearby Boston in 1617. The Peacham men were cleared, but, as Young speculates, "presumably the acrimony generated within the family over the squabble continued."

Little is known about the social circles in which Peacham traveled, but the dedicatory epistles to his published works indicate a few patrons worth noting. The 1577 edition of *The Garden of Eloquence* is dedicated to John Aylmer, who had become lord bishop of London in March of 1577. In March of the following year Aylmer ordained Peacham priest. Aylmer had also served as archdeacon of Lincoln from 1562 to 1576 and may have played some role in obtaining Peacham's livings in Leverton. Aylmer appears to have aided Peacham in his publication of *A Sermon vpon the three last verses of the first Chapter of Iob,* which was entered in the Stationers' Register to the publisher, Richard Jones, on 4 January 1591 "vnder the handes of the Bishop of LONDON and the wardens." The book is dedicated to Margaret Clifford, Countess of Cumberland, and her sister, Anne Dudley, Countess of Warwick. The records of the diocese of Lincoln indicate that Dudley had also played a role in Peacham's acquisition of the Leverton benefices. Peacham had probably met Dudley in Hertfordshire, where she lived in Northaw (and where Clifford was known to have visited her), the parish adjacent to North Mimms. The 1593 edition of *The Garden of Eloquence* is dedicated to Sir John Puckering, Lord Keeper of the Great Seal, who had been speaker of the House of Commons in the 1584 and 1586 Parliaments. It is unclear why Peacham changed dedicatees when he republished *The Garden of Eloquence,* though Aylmer's intolerant and quarrelsome disposition as lord bishop of London had earned him a great many enemies, and Peacham may have wanted to dedicate his book to a less controversial figure. Puckering had distinguished himself as an orator in Parliament during his tenure as speaker and afterward, delivering in February 1593 the opening speech on the first day of Parliament. In the dedicatory epistle of the second edition of *The Garden of Eloquence* Peacham describes Puckering as sitting "at the sterne of the commonwelth in these daies of danger." Peacham appears to have made good use of his patrons: with the exception of Puckering (who died in 1596), all were involved in furthering his professional goals as a clergyman as well as his publishing endeavors.

Some scholars have found a pecuniary interest even in Peacham's composition of *The Garden of Eloquence*. In the dedicatory epistle to the 1577 edition, Peacham says that his aim is "to profyte this my country, and especially the studious youth of this Realme, and

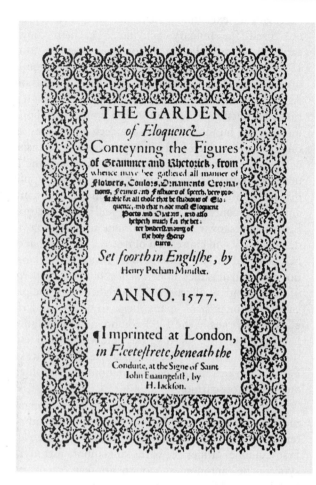

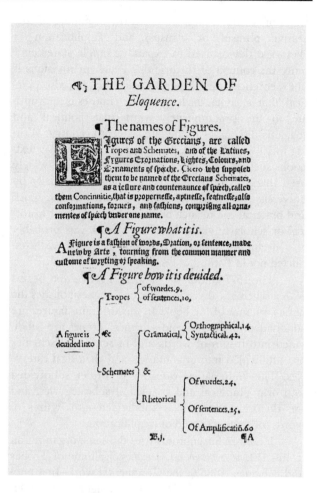

Title page and first page of text in Peacham's elocution book, which begins by dividing rhetorical "figures" into tropes and schemes and subdividing them into other categories

such as haue not the vnderstanding of the Latyne tongue, sure I am, it may profyte many, and I dare be bold to say, it can hurte none." By writing in English, however, Peacham stood to profit as well; T. W. Baldwin refers to the project as a "get-rich-quick scheme." Thomas M. Conley describes an "economic" Peacham, "who never held an academic appointment," and "evidently aimed his book at an audience of young scholars who wished to obtain a rhetorical education without first troubling to learn Latin, an audience that grew during the sixteenth century."

The Garden of Eloquence is, however, more than the trifle of a greedy scholar. Peacham provides his own justification for the project in the dedication to Aylmer in the 1577 edition:

When of late I had consydered the needefull assistaunce that the one of these do requyre of the other, that wisedome doe requyre the lighte of Eloquence, and Eloquence the fertillity of Wysedome, and saw

many good bookes of Philosophy and precepts of wysedome, set forth in english, and very few of Eloquence: I was of a sodaine mooued to take this little Garden in hande, and to set therein such Fyguratyue Flowers, both of Grammer and Rhetorick, as doe yeelde the sweete sauour of Eloquence, & present to the eyes the goodly and bewtiful coulors of Eloqution: such as shyne in our speech like the glorious stars in Firmament: such as bewtify it, as flowers of sundry coullors, a gallant Garland: such as garnish it, as precious pearles, a gorgious Garment: suche as delight the eares, as pleasaunt reports, repetions, and running poyntes in Musick. . . .

The Ciceronian idea of the dual necessity of philosophy and eloquence is an important part of the intellectual tone of *The Garden of Eloquence,* which insists that the function of rhetorical figures is not merely ornamental, but integral to the effective transmission of ideas in civil society. This utility of eloquence is evident in Peacham's own justification of the project, which gains force and momentum through his use of *anaphora* (repetition of words or expressions at the beginning of successive phrases or clauses) and amplification (a rhetorical device used to expand a simple statement). Since the context of rhetoric that Peacham envisions is not theoretical (that is, purely academic), but also practical (that is, civic), the language he chooses is appropriate to the predominately vernacular political and religious discourses of the late sixteenth century. Writing in 1994, Brian Vickers argued that vernacular textbooks such as Peacham's may have been more widely used than has previously been thought, especially by university students who were interested in the quick and practical use of such books rather than their historical or scholarly value. Peacham's work was probably also useful for lawyers, whose daily work was conducted not in Latin, but English and Law French.

The 1577 edition of *The Garden of Eloquence* begins with a schematic division of "figure" that establishes the basic structure of the book. In this diagram, figures are subdivided into tropes and schemes. Tropes are subdivided into tropes of words and of sentences; schemes are subdivided into grammatical and rhetorical categories. The grammatical category is further subdivided into orthographical and syntactical subcategories, and the rhetorical category is subdivided into figures of words, of sentences, and of amplification.

Johannes Susenbrotus uses the same organization in his *Epitome troporum ac schematum* (Epitome of Tropes and Schemes, 1535?), the Continental work–first published in London in 1562–that most significantly influenced Peacham's work. Peacham uses all but 3 of Susenbrotus's 132 figures in the 1577 edition, and all but 2 in the 1593 edition. Richard Sherry uses a structure similar to Susenbrotus's in his *A Treatise of the Figures of Grammer and Rhetorike* (1555), but, as Conley has noted, Peacham's outline is somewhat clearer (especially in the 1593 edition) because he adds to each division further subdivisions and expands certain categories, such as schemes of syntax and rhetoric, to include more precise subcategories. The outline also indicates that Peacham's primary concern is elocution and that he has excluded from his direct attention the other traditional parts of rhetoric: invention, arrangement, memory, and delivery. Thomas Wilson's *The Arte of Rhetorique, for the vse of all suche as are Studious of Eloquence* (1553) had considered all five parts of rhetoric (though some scholars have found Wilson's treatment of elocution to be somewhat weak).

If Peacham's rhetoric appears to be limited to figures of "mere ornament," the content of his book reminds the reader that one should be careful of ascribing to the figurist rhetoricians a superficial approach to rhetoric. Many historians of rhetoric have noted that the Latin *ornatus* means not "decoration," but "gear"

necessary for executing a particular task, such as weapons used for military activities. Peacham himself exploits this metaphor in the dedicatory epistle to the 1593 edition of *The Garden of Eloquence,* calling the figures "martiall instruments both of defence & inuasion." As tools for intellectual debate, the figures have a wide range of function, as Miriam Joseph notes: "the approximately two hundred figures of speech which they distinguish represent an analysis of practically every aspect of grammar, logic, and rhetoric." For Peacham, the figures are central to the rhetorical dimension of public discourse in the most general way, and in addition to amplifying concerns of grammar and logic, rhetorical figures are shown to be important to the successful development and expression of nearly any idea that can be conveyed in speech or writing. Peacham's orator is not only a man skilled in eloquence, but "the emperour of mens minds & affections." The figures are "the principal instruments of mans help in this wonderfull effect," he writes in the 1593 edition, adding to human language not only beauty, but intellectual and emotional clarity. Metaphors, for example, "giue pleasant light to darke things, thereby remouing vnprofitable and odious obscuritie."

Peacham understands a trope to be a change in meaning that can occur in both single words and sentences. In the 1577 edition of *The Garden of Eloquence* he first examines tropes of words (metaphor, metonymy, synecdoche, antonomasia, onomatopoeia, catachresis, metalepsis, antiphrasis, and acyrologia), most of which depend on a metaphorical shift of meaning. As a general term for the entire category, metaphor is treated extensively and is further divided according to the kinds of conditions in which metaphorical relationships emerge. Each of the five senses, for example, contains a readily identifiable vocabulary that can be effectively translated into non-sensory contexts: "because the mind and the sight do much resemble one another, we may wel borrow of the one and beare it to the other." Relationships are found between reasonable and unreasonable things ("when mens manners be such as cannot be expressed with those wordes, which doe properly belong to men, wee borrow wordes of these brute beastes, and other creatures wanting reason") and between living and lifeless things ("the frost doth bite"). Peacham's tropes of sentences (allegory, enigma, paroemia, irony, sarcasm, mystery, asteismus, diasyrmus, charientismus, and hyperbole) likewise depend on a change in meaning, as in irony, "when a sentence is vnderstood by the contrary."

Most of *The Garden of Eloquence* is devoted not to tropes, but to schemes. While a trope is a change in meaning, a *scheme* is a change in form, which Peacham further divides into schemes of grammar and rhetoric.

Grammatical schemes are in turn divided into orthographical and syntactical schemes. Under orthographical schemes Peacham includes fifteen forms of *metaplasmus,* the changing of letters or syllables into unconventional arrangements. Schemes of syntax are divided into four "orders" that are not indicated in Peacham's schematic diagram. The first order includes six figures in which a constituent part of the syntax is missing: *eclipsis* (missing word), *aposiopesis* (part of a sentence missing), *zeugma* (one word governs the construction of other clauses), *syllepsis* (verb incongruent with one of its subjects), *prolepsis* (a general word or idea is later divided into discrete parts), and *anapodoton* (missing consequent clause). The second order consists of six figures of excess (perissologia, macrologia, parelcon, epanalepsis, and tautologia), generally termed *pleonasmus:* "when there be moe wordes heapt vpon a construction, then be necessary." The third order involves figures of *hyperbaton,* the alteration of conventional word order: anastrophe, hysterologia, hysteron proteron, tmesis, parenthesis, hypallage, synchisis, and amphibologia. Peacham says these figures are useful for making "the oration very darke & obscure." The fourth order includes eight figures that lack "aptnesse and dignitie": tapinosis, bomphilogia, cacozelia, cacemphaton, paroemion, periergia, cacosyntheton, and soraismus. According to Peacham, only poets are allowed to use such figures, and they "doe make the oration faultie." The fifth order includes figures that can be used to form compound sentences (asyndeton, polysyndeton, scesis onomaton, hyrmos, epitheton, periphrasis, emphasis, and litotes) and figures of the sixth order depend on a change in case, number, gender, mood, tense, or person (alleotheta, antiptosis, enallage, hendiadys, and anthimeria). Again, Peacham singles out the sixth order as a group of figures that should be used only by poets.

The greatest part of the 1577 edition of *The Garden of Rhetoric* is taken up by schemes of rhetoric, which are also divided into orders. The first order examines twenty-four figures of anaphora, three of which (asyndeton, polysyndeton, and zeugma) were also discussed in the section of schemes of syntax. The second order is a vague classification of twenty-six figures that "make the Oration not onelye pleasante and plausible, but also very sharpe and vehement," such as ecphonesis and interrogatio. The third, and largest order includes sixty-six figures of amplification. The sheer accumulation of material set forth without more detailed division, especially in the second order, makes this section somewhat unwieldy, and it is to this part of the book that Peacham devotes most of his attention in the second edition. In the dedicatory epistle of the first edition of *The Garden of Eloquence,* Peacham promises a future revision, saying that his book, "at the nexte edition I

trust shall come forth more perfect and trimly pullished, which now lacke of leysure hath left vndone."

The 1593 edition of *The Garden of Eloquence* includes significant changes, not only in the addition of more tropes and examples, but in the fundamental character of Peacham's attitude toward rhetoric. The later edition becomes less a vernacular rhetorical textbook and more an "independent English text on the subject," as Baldwin describes it. The revision also succeeds in reflecting the rhetorical values of Elizabethan culture in a way that extends beyond the classroom and into a variety of political, social, religious, and literary contexts. In his dedicatory epistle to Puckering, Peacham refines his comments on the relationship between wisdom and eloquence by describing "these meane and simple frutes of my studies":

> The argument whereof albeit I confesse it subiect to the exceptions of many, and peraduenture to the reprehensions of some, which seeme to make a diuorce betweene nature and art, and a separation betweene pollicie and humanitie.

The distinction is between intellectual discourse and rhetorical convention, but there is also an implicit division between the expression of rational ideas and their latent emotional content. Perhaps Peacham's greatest contribution to the history of rhetoric is his attempt to grapple with the powerful and problematic role of the emotions in rhetoric at a time when political and literary writing was becoming increasingly aware of the intricate power relationships inherent in the use of rhetoric.

The second edition of *The Garden of Eloquence* is customarily referred to as "the 1593 edition," based on the information on its title page. Prior to enactment of the Calender Reform Act of 1751, however, the new year officially began on 25 March (although 1 January was popularly considered New Year's Day). Peacham's dedicatory epistle to Puckering is dated 3 February 1593; if this date is old style, the book should be re-dated to 1594, new style. Neither edition of *The Garden of Eloquence* is entered in the Stationers' Register, but *A Sermon vpon the three last verses of the first Chapter of Iob,* dated 1591 on the title page, was registered on 4 January 1591 (new style), and its dedicatory epistle is dated 1 January 1590. Insofar as Peacham was an official of the church, addressing in his dedication a government official, and because Peacham himself uses the old style dating system in his dedication to *A Sermon vpon the three last verses of the first Chapter of Iob,* a case can be made for dating the book to 1594. Without further corroborative evidence, however, it is impossible to make that change with certainty. It is also possible that the publisher made both references conform to a 1593 new style publication date. The fact that the second edition is dedicated to Puckering, who had just been made Lord keeper of the Great Seal and delivered the opening speech in Parliament at the end of February 1583, strongly suggests that the book was published in that year and may have appeared in early April as the 1583 Parliament came to a close.

The most obvious structural change in the second edition of *The Garden of Eloquence* is the omission of the sections on orthographical and syntactical schemes, though six of the schemes of syntax (aposiopesis, zeugma, epanalepsis, asyndeton, polysyndeton, and periphrasis) are incorporated into other parts of the revised edition. Some scholars have pointed to the omission of the schemes of orthography as an indication of the influence of Pierre de La Ramée (known as Petrus Ramus), who distinguished elocution from grammar, but it is more likely that Peacham was simply refining the scope of his work, which in the 1593 edition is more directly aimed at an audience of orators than poets. The section on orthography in the 1577 edition notes that such schemes are "lawfull only to Poets," but the title page of the 1593 edition specifically describes its contents as being "Profitable and necessarie, as wel for priuate speech, as for publicke Orations." Peacham continues to point out figures that are "copious both to Poets and Orators" (such as metaphor), and many of his examples are derived from poetry, but there is a sense that questions of orthography are far too marginal to be considered among the larger, psychological questions of rhetoric taken up in the second edition. Peacham was not alone in this belief; contemporaries such as George Puttenham, in his *The Arte of English Poesie* (1589), also considered figures of orthography to be "of the smallest importaunce."

As did the earlier edition, the 1593 edition of *The Garden of Eloquence* begins with an examination of eight tropes of words. Only one trope from the first edition, *acyrologia* (using language incorrectly), is omitted, though it is mentioned later in the definition of *taxis* (arrangement). The introductory section on metaphor is also expanded to include metaphorical uses of the four elements and the relationship between man and God. Both editions treat the same ten tropes of sentences, but the 1593 definitions are somewhat expanded.

The most obvious change in the analytical style of the 1593 edition is the addition to the end of each definition of two sections that comment on the "use" and "caution" of a particular figure. Hyperbole, for example, "serueth most fitly for amplification, and that especially when matters require either to be amplified in the greatest degree, or diminished in the least," but one must also be careful "that this figure be not vsed to amplifie trifles, or diminish the estimation of good things." It is not uncommon for rhetoricians to include warnings about particular aspects of rhetoric—the anonymous author of the *Rhetorica ad Herennium* (Rhetoric to Herennius, 86–82 B.C.), Cicero, and Quintilian all repeat a phrase from Apollonius the rhetor that "the appeal to pity must be brief, for nothing dries more quickly than a tear"—but Peacham's systematic commentary on a figure's potential for indecorous or deceptive applications is a unique contribution to the history of rhetoric.

With the elimination of the schemes of orthography and syntax, the rest of the 1593 edition is divided into three orders of rhetorical schemes that are more satisfactorily organized than in the 1577 edition: figures of words, figures of affection, and figures of amplification. Each order is further subdivided into more or less discrete categories. The first order is the least changed, and begins with a section on eleven figures of repetition, all taken from the 1577 figures of anaphora, except for paroemion, which had earlier been classified as a scheme of faulty syntax. The second category includes two figures of omission (zeugma and asyndeton), the third figures of conjunction (polysyndeton, homoiopoton, homoioteleuton, and paregmenon), and the fourth figures of separation (paronomasia, antanaclasis, articulus, membrum, compar, hypozeuxis, and taxis), all of which had earlier been treated as figures of anaphora.

The most radical change in the content of the 1593 *Garden of Eloquence* is the addition of thirty-seven "figures of affection" in the second order, which also includes ten figures from the vague 1577 second order of rhetorical schemes. These figures are divided into four categories: twenty-four figures of exclamation, seventeen figures of moderation, six figures of consultation, and nine figures of permission or concession.

Peacham says the function of these figures is to "attend vppon affections, as ready handmaids at commaundement to express most aptly whatsoeuer the heart doth affect or suffer." To move an audience emotionally is "a principall and singular vertue of eloqution" for Peacham, and this emphasis on the emotive power of rhetorical figures is part of a shift that Vickers, in 1988, describes as taking place in Renaissance rhetoric in the second half of the sixteenth century in which *movere* (to move) was emphasized over the other two traditional goals of rhetoric, *docere* (to teach) and *delectare* (to please). Peacham's contribution to this tradition is important, because, in addition to recognizing the powerfully persuasive emotional effects of the figures, he also describes, in the "use" and "caution," correct methods for using emotion in a rhetorical context. Peacham defines *paramythia* (consolatio) as "a forme of speech which the Orator vseth to take away, or diminish a sorrow conceiued in the minde of his hearer," and his advice for how to focus this emotion is extensive:

> The vse of this figure is great, and most necessarily required in this vale of misery, where mens harts are often fainting, and their mindes falling into despaire, for so great are mens losses in this fraile life, and so little is their fortitude to beare them, that they fall downe in their weaknesse lying still opprest vnder their heauy burthen, neuer able to rise againe, without the strength of comfort and consolation.

Peacham then outlines four conditions in which caution must be exercised: first, consolation should not be extended to those who do not need or deserve it, such as "hypocrites and scorners of Gods iudgements"; second, it should be offered in a timely manner, neither too soon, "when the wound is new made, and the bloud running swiftly in the streame of effusion," nor too late, "as when the sorrow is either forgotten, or wel asswaged"; third, "that it be not vnproper and impertinent to the cause and necessitie to which it is applyed"; and fourth, "that it be not weake by reason of the foundations consisting only in Philosophy and humane wisedome which do many times rather increase sorrow then diminish it."

In general, Peacham's theory of the emotions is Aristotelian, requiring that the passions be moderated so they can be used in the service of virtue. This moderation applies not only to the figures that fall under the category of "figures of moderation," but to any figure that has a potential for arousing emotion in an audience. Peacham's warnings are most often directed against behavior that reflects too much emotion, or an emotional disposition that is improperly or indecorously directed, as in the case of *onedismus* (reproaching a person for ingratitude or impiety):

> Wisedome and charity ought to direct the vse of this figure, lest it be vsed for euery little displeasure as foolish persons are wont to do, making a new account of an old reckoning, which is an absurditie offending against good manners, a folly repugning wisedome, and an effect of mallice opposed against charitie.

Peacham occasionally finds fault with those who do not express enough emotion, or who do not express a proper amount of emotion at the proper times. In the "caution" for *threnos* (lamentation), Peacham warns that "heed ought to be taken that the lamentation be not great when the cause is litle, or litle when the cause is great, the one of these is found in children lamenting for litle losses, the other in stoicall nature or carelesse

Title page for the sermon in which Peacham decried "the absurdity of the Stoics' opinion"

people." Peacham holds particular contempt for the Stoics—in his *A Sermon vpon the three last verses of the first Chapter of Iob* he refers to "the absurdity of the Stoics' opinion."

Peacham is also concerned about the potentially deceptive power of the emotions in rhetoric. Threnos should be "most serious and voyd of fiction & faining," *apocarteresis* (giving up hope and turning to another) is "most abused when the sufferance and despaire is counterfayted," and *martyria* (confirming something by personal experience) should not be "abused by the vntruth of the testimonie." Of *asphalia* (offering oneself as surety for a bond), Peacham cautions: "How much this forme of speech is abused, the examples of deceitfull warrants may dayly teach." In such cases, the sections on "use" and "caution" indicate an early modern shift in attitude about the role of rhetoric in civic duty. While many rhetoricians of antiquity—Aristotle, Cicero, and Quintilian especially—understood rhetoric to be a quality of the *vir bonus dicendi peritus* (a good man skilled in speaking), some Renaissance thinkers distanced themselves from this ideal, and Ramus even discusses an *orator bene dicendi peritus* (orator skilled in speaking well) in his *Brutinae Quaestiones* (Inquiries of the *Brutus*, 1547). Although the rhetoric of Renaissance civic humanism sought to retain a classical conception of civic virtue, the specter of Niccolò Machiavelli had by the end of the sixteenth century forced upon most public figures an awareness of the ambiguous and unstable contexts of power in political oratory. This instability of emotional rhetoric can be seen in Peacham's definition of *philophronesis,* which describes a rhetoric of humble submission "to mitigate the ryger and crueltie of his aduersary." The section on "use" distinguishes it as being "of a singular vertue, both in respect of ciuill pollicie and spirituall wisedome." But the "caution" warns that "the counterfait submission of hypocrites is opposed to the true vse of this figure. . . . such a one vnder colour of humble submission, will execute his malice vpon thee before thou shalt be able to preuent him." The "caution" for the figure *syngnome* (fellow feeling, forgiveness) that immediately follows likewise warns: "That foolish pitie, vndoeth many a Citie."

The third order of rhetorical schemes in the 1593 edition is comprised of seventy-one figures of amplification, only a few more than were treated in the corresponding section in 1577. Like the other categories of rhetorical schemes, amplification is divided into four orders–distribution, description, comparison, and collection:

> the fower mighty and plentifull streams of copious eloquence which are continually fed and filled with the perpetuall and pleasant springs of mans wit: I meane those figures and formes of speech which the reason of man, the principall part and power of his minde, hath by long and diligent search found out, to the admirable vtterance of his knowledge, and glory of his wisedome.

In his *Institutio Oratoria* (Institutes of Oratory), book 8, Quintilian also identified four kinds of amplification (augmentation, comparison, reasoning, and accumulation) that can be used either to elevate or diminish a subject. Peacham's categories differ somewhat from Quintilian's, but he is essentially in agreement with the classical view that amplification is used to intensify a particular part of the oration: "*Amplification* is a certaine affirmation very great and weighty, which by large and plentifull speech moueth the mindes of the hearers, and causeth them to beleeue that which is said." Peacham's use of the phrase "large and plentifull speech" might be seen to indicate that aspect of Renaissance rhetoric in which amplification is less a means of intensifying dialogue and more an academic search for abundant and copious means of expressing the same thing. Desiderius Erasmus's *De duplici copia rerum et verborum* (On the

Abundance of both Topics and Words, 1512; first London edition, 1556), in which Erasmus at one point gives 150 ways of saying "your letter pleased me very much," is the most important Renaissance text on the subject. As an educational principle that urges the accumulation of historical and literary examples that can be drawn on "as from a most plentifull fountaine," Peacham (as his own collections of examples reveal) values the Erasmian concept of *copia* (expansive richness of utterance) but with regard to the practical uses of such exercises he remains a student of Quintilian, as the "caution" to incrementum indicates: "In this figure order must be diligently obserued . . . otherwse the signification shal not encrease . . . but become a *Congeries* which respecteth not the increase of matter but multitude or wordes." In using *symphoresis* ("word heaps") one is likewise warned against making "too great an heape."

According to Peacham, amplification is useful because it intensifies the emotional conditions of rhetoric that he had discussed in the previous section on figures of affection. In his general discussion of amplification he notes:

> Matters which fall into this kind of exornation, ought to be great, excellent good, or notorious euill, cruel, horrible, maruellous, pleasant, or pittifull: after which may follow and that worthily, desire, hatred, feare, admiration, hope, gladnesse, mirth, pittie, weeping, and such like affections.

The emotional power of amplification is evident generally in figures such as *pathopeia* (excitement of the passions) which "pertaineth properly to moue affections," but Peacham also attributes to some forms of amplification specific emotional components. Of all the figures, Peacham says, there is "none more forcible to moue pittie" than *pragmatographia* (concrete description); "to represse boldnesse in the rude, pride in the arrogant, security in the hipocrite, and unconstancie in the vnwise" *inter se pugnantia* (reproaching an adversary) can be used; and *auxesis* (amplification, words or clauses placed in a climactic order) is useful for "signifying the greatnesse and excesse of suffering." The emphasis is always on controlling the emotions in rhetorical situations, or in directing them towards a specific end, as in the case of *medela* (healing with good words and pleasing speech), which "pertaineth properly to extenuate offences, to excuse infirmities, to appease displeasure, and reconcile friends offended."

As are most Renaissance studies of rhetoric, Peacham's work is an eclectic synthesis of preceding classical and humanistic rhetorical treatises, and as such it is often difficult to determine when and how Peacham is drawing on a particular source. The anonymous *Rhetorica ad Herennium* (ascribed to Cornificius by Peacham), Cicero, and Quintilian are the most important classical sources for Peacham, though he also makes reference to Julius Rufinanus, and may have had some exposure to the thought of Hermogenes, if only through intermediate works. Peacham's definitions and examples are drawn mostly from sixteenth-century sources such as Susenbrotus's *Epitome troporum ac schematum* and Sherry's *A Treatise of the Figures of Grammer and Rhetorike,* which were the most important studies of elocution in England at the time. Peacham mentions Philip Melanchthon in the 1593 definition of expolitio, though it is difficult to tell whether he has firsthand knowledge of Melanchthon's rhetorical works or if he is working from Leonard Cox's *The Arte or Crafte of Rhetoryke* (1530), the first English rhetorical treatise, which is heavily based on Melanchthon's *Institutiones Rhetoricae* (Institutes of Rhetoric, 1521). To make questions of transmission even more complicated, Susenbrotus and Sherry rely on Erasmus's *De duplici copia rerum et verborum* and Melanchthon's rhetorical works, and Sherry refers to Petrus Mosellanus's *Tabulæ de Schematibus et Tropis* (1529), which is also an important source for Melanchthon. Even Susenbrotus's schematic division of *figura* (figure), upon which Peacham's organizational scheme is based, is derived from the structure of Melanchthon's treatment of elocution in *Elementa Rhetorices* (The Basics of Rhetoric, 1531). Peacham mentions Thomas Wilson ("Mayster Wylson") in the 1577 definition of *cacozelon* (studied affectation of style), and given the great popularity of Wilson's *The Arte of Rhetorique* (1553), which went into seven editions before 1600, it is likely that this treatise too was close at hand. In formulating his terminology, Peacham appears to have consulted the Latin-English dictionaries of Sir Thomas Elyot (1538, 1548) and Thomas Cooper (1565, 1578), Robert Estienne's *Thesaurus Linguae Latinae* (Thesaurus of the Latin Tongue, 1531), and Henri Estienne's *Thesaurus Graecae Linguae* (Thesaurus of the Greek Tongue, 1572–1573). Scholars have suggested several other rhetorical works that Peacham may have consulted, including: Bede's *Liber de Schematibus et Tropis* (Book on Schemes and Tropes, written circa 691–703 A.D., published 1527), George of Trebizond's *Rhetoricorum Libri Quinque* (Five Books of Rhetoric, circa 1440), Martinus Capella's *Liber de Arte Rhetorica* (Book on Rhetorical Art, 1499), Dudley Fenner's *The Arte of Logike and Rhetorike* (1584), Angel Day's *The English Secretorie* (1586), Abraham Fraunce's *The Arcadian Rhetorike: Or The Præcepts of Rhetorike made plaine by examples* (1588), Puttenham's *The Arte of English Poesie,* and virtually all of the minor authors included in anthologies of rhetorical works, such as the one published by the Aldine Press in 1523.

A cursory examination of Peacham's relationship to his sources reveals that, in the 1593 edition especially, he contributes as much if not more information and analysis than his predecessors in the consideration of each figure. Peacham's entry for *compar* (isocolon), begins with language that can be traced back as far as the *Rhetorica ad Herennium,* but which also comes to him through Susenbrotus, and perhaps obliquely through Sherry:

> Compar, of the Grecians called *Isocolon* and *Parison,* is a figure or forme of speech which maketh the members of an oration to be almost of a iust number of sillables, yet the equalitie of those members or parts, are not to be measured vpon our fingers, as if they were verses, but to bee tried by a secret sence of the eare: vse & exercise may do much in this behalfe, which maketh it an easie matter to make the parts accord in a fit proportion. First, when the former parts of a sentence, or of an oration be answered by the later, and that by proper words respecting the former.

The author of the *Rhetorica ad Herennium* says that isocolon is comprised of phrases "quæ constent ex pari fere numero syllabarum" (which consist of a nearly equal number of syllables); Susenbrotus uses the same language: "quæ expari fere numero syllabarum constant"; and Sherry simply says the clauses must "be made of euen number of sillables." The author of the *Rhetorica ad Herennium* says the syllables should not be counted, "nam id quidem puerile est" (for that is indeed childish) but "usus et exercitatio" (practice and exercise) will help one to develop a facility, "ut animi quodam sensu par membrum superiori referre possimus" (that by a sort of instinct we can produce again a clause of equal length to the prior one). Susenbrotus says of the symmetry: "non digitis, sed aurium sensu quodam dijudicanda est. Puerile siquidem est numerare syllabas" (not by fingers but by the sense of the ears such a thing should be decided. It is indeed childish to count syllables). Sherry writes: "thys equalitie must not stand by numbryng of them, but by perceyuyng of it in the mynd." Peacham's reference to "use and exercise" is from the *Rhetorica ad Herennium,* the description of counting on fingers from Susenbrotus, and although Sherry offers him little useful information, a comparison shows that Peacham, in this case, has more thoroughly digested the source material. Wilbur S. Howell has shown that in the case of some figures, such as *partitio* (dividing the whole into parts), Peacham depends on Sherry to a greater extent. Peacham also adds much more here than he takes; for example, by expanding the concept of compar to include the correspondence of words and sentences that do not occur close to each other in the oration: "effects may be made to answer their efficients, consequents their antecedents, habite priuation: also contrariwise." In his examples, Peacham notes that the figure can function as a counterpart to antithesis because it "coopleth contraries." In the section on "use" Peacham discusses *compar* as being "most harmonicall," and says that it is "more agreable for pleasant matters than graue causes, and more fit for Commedies then Tragedies." In the "caution" he considers the problems of inequality inherent in the figure and argues that in its "most artificaill forme" it should not be used in "graue and serious causes."

Although Peacham takes many of his examples from the usual classical sources (Cicero, Julius Caesar, Virgil, Ovid, Horace, Terence, Livy)—and these often by way of previous rhetorical treatises—one of the distinguishing characteristics of Peacham's treatise is its extensive use of the Bible as a source for most of the examples. Biblical examples were used by earlier rhetoricians, such as Sherry and Wilson, but for Peacham, the Bible is integral to the mission of *The Garden of Eloquence*. The title page of the 1577 edition proclaims that the book "helpeth much for the better vnderstanding of the Bible," and the 1593 title page notes that its examples are taken "chieflie out of the holie Scriptures." As a clergyman, Peacham would have found the Bible to be the most readily available source of material for his rhetorical writings, and his primary interest in rhetoric was probably related to how it could serve his professional interest in spiritual affairs. If vernacular rhetorical treatises such as those by Cox, Sherry, and Wilson ran contrary to the prevailing pedagogical interests of the English schools, as Conley has noted, such treatises were entirely consistent with the interests of the English Church, which favored a vernacular education, especially one that centered on the scriptures. Copies of Erasmus's paraphrases of books of the Bible had been placed in English churches alongside the vernacular Bible, the Book of Homilies, and the Book of Common Prayer since the Reformation—except, of course, during the reign of the Catholic queen Mary I (1553–1558). With Peacham's treatise the tools that humanistic learning provided for reading and understanding the scriptures, especially in the reformed churches, became more widely available.

An even deeper reflection of Peacham's interest in the rhetoric of the Bible can be found in his only other publication, *A Sermon vpon the three last verses of the first Chapter of Iob,* which was published in 1591. Although rarely mentioned in commentaries on Peacham's work, the sermon does much to illustrate the fundamental concerns of Peacham's rhetoric by displaying what rhe-

torical forms Peacham himself chose in addressing an audience. In the dedicatory epistle Peacham says that his aim is to persuade those who have forgotten their duty to God to return to a spiritual life:

> . . . they neuer regard what the Creator commaundeth or forbiddeth . . . neither doo they turne their eiesight inward, I meane their mindes to looke into themselues, and to consider what their affections are, and to examine well whither their intentes leade them.

The point is made in a highly amplified form with a succession of metaphors for the wayward Christian:

> Therefore no marueile though hastie climers suddainely fall, and rash Diuers are often drowned: and no woonder that their guidelesse shippes suffer wracke, considering that they striue against so mightie a winde and forcible streame, as is the high and moste mightie prouidence of God.

The specific focus of the sermon is on the words and actions of Job in the last three verses of the first chapter of the biblical account of his ordeal. By examining Job's behavior in the face of extreme suffering, Peacham seeks to provide an example of spiritual virtue and steadfastness in times of adversity. But the rhetorical context of the sermon is somewhat more complicated. On the one hand, Peacham is engaged in an analysis of Job's own rhetorical situation with God—what he says and does when confronted with pain, loss, and emotional distress. On the other hand, Peacham must also amplify the emotive elements of the text in order to move his audience to an emotional response in which the value of the spiritual life Job represents will be recognized and embraced.

In the first, internal rhetorical context, Peacham's analysis of Job's actions reveals the same sort of moderate character discussed as a rhetorical ideal in *The Garden of Eloquence*. Peacham observes that the rapid succession of misfortunes sends Job into an excessive and potentially uncontrollable lament, where a longer interval between incidents might have allowed for a time of emotional and psychological healing:

> men are not so deeply drown'd in the excesse of mourning, when they once see the flood of their sorrowes so far past experience proueth daily that time it selfe by litle and litle abateth the high tide and vehemencie of mens passions. . . . But *Sathan* knowing mans nature in this behalfe, doth speedily represent to *Iob* the whole fact, as yet not fully finished, but now a doing, to the intent that the sorrowfull man might (as it were) stand and look on, beholding the whole Tragedie to his greater griefe.

In the sermon, Satan appears to take on the role of the deceptive rhetor who knows the emotional power of rhetoric but uses it to evil ends, a character Peacham warned the reader about in his rhetorical treatise. Job's response, in turn, represents the emotionally informed, but moderate response of religious modesty:

> hee argued . . . that hee was a man almost swallowed vp in the gulfe of his woful passion, yet held himselfe (through the supporting hand of God) so vpright in the meane, that as he armed not himslefe with a stonie hardnesse of heart, to resist all sorrowfull affection, which had bene an unnaturall part of a parent, and an open breach of godly modestie: So he kept himselfe vnstained of excesse, into which many fall through lacke of faith and want of patience: this meane is alwaies that cycle & compasse wherein vertue consisteth.

Peacham is careful to distinguish Job's disposition from that of the Stoics, who equate wisdom with "flinty hardnes," and he warns against "certaine newe Stoickes . . . amongst the Christians," who mock Christian morality by "smyling at the funerals of their deare Parents." Peacham then points to Jacob, Joseph, David, and Jesus as examples of how the holiest of men "were not void of affections." The message is exactly that which is unfolded in Peacham's discussion of the figures of affection in *The Garden of Eloquence:* there is a correct and moderate emotional response to which one should aspire because it is noble, virtuous, and wise.

The external rhetorical context of Peacham's sermon attempts to engage the audience emotionally so that the message of Job's piety can be embraced. Here the reader finds Peacham employing the tropes and schemes defined in *The Garden of Eloquence.* When Peacham refers to Job as "this wofull man, this wofull and good man," he is using *diacope* (cutting in two): "a figure which repeateth a word putting but one word betweene, or at least verie few," and when he says that human hearts are "made of flesh and not of flints," he is using *paronomasia* (punning, playing on words that sound alike). Peacham's description of human grief is an excellent example of *asyndeton* (connecting without conjunctions) and amplification:

> The sea swolloweth down the Merchants ship: Murraine killeth cattel, tempestes destroy haruest, fire consumeth Princes pallaces, robbers spoile rich men of their wealth, thunder & lightening suddainly strike man and beasts dead. . . .

Peacham's sermon is, however, far from an exercise in rhetorical display. He uses rhetorical figures sparingly, subtly, and effectively, especially in passages of descrip-

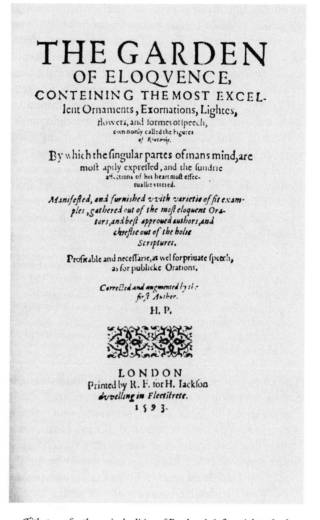

Title page for the revised edition of Peacham's influential textbook

tive amplification that are designed to elicit an emotional response in the audience:

> his cattel hurried away before the theeuish drouers: his seruants vnder the sword of their cruell Murtherers, his deare Children vnder the importable burthen of the huge building, yet laboring for life, & often gasping for their last breath.

Although Peacham's prose may lack some of the stylistic richness of writers such as Lancelot Andrewes or John Donne, it fully represents the sort of application Peacham himself has in mind in *The Garden of Eloquence.*

As Peacham uses the principles of rhetoric to probe the spiritual depth of a character such as Job, the reader begins to see that Peacham's aim is to give much more than a theory of rhetoric. However much Peacham wants to confine his audience to one of "orators," in magnifying the Elizabethan exuberance for rhetoric as an emotionally and psychologically rich process he inevitably codifies certain trends in the rapidly changing literary culture of England in the 1580s and 1590s. In the sections on "use" and "caution," his work simultaneously invokes and suppresses the rhetorical excess of John Lyly's school of Euphuism, which both exemplifies and abuses the figures of rhetoric. Euphuism took rhetoric to an extreme that was brought under control by Shakespeare, whose writing in many ways mirrors Peacham's attitudes toward the emotional and moral function of rhetoric. For example, Shakespeare's character Falstaff, in *1 Henry IV* (1598, quotations from 1623 edition), amplifies in manner that is readily explained according to the terms of elocution that Peacham helped to define for the Elizabethan world:

> No, my good Lord, banish Peto, banish Bardolph, banish Poines: but for sweete Iacke Falstaffe, kinde Iacke Falstaffe, true Iacke Falstaffe, valiant Iacke Falstaffe, and therefore more valiant, being as hee is olde Iack Falstaffe, banish not him thy Harryes companie, banish not him thy Harryes companie; banish plumpe Iacke, and banish all the World.

The passage is rich with figures of repetition and amplification common to all studies of elocution, ancient and Renaissance, English and Continental—but Shakespeare, as is Peacham, is dedicated to a use of rhetorical figures that is so finely intertwined with a speech's emotional and intellectual fabric that it is wholly in the service of the forms and ideas of human relationships, and it can only be identified peripherally as artifice or convention. Falstaff speaks the language of amplification because he is amplification, and without that congruence the speech would seem artificial.

Peacham's examples also provide a collection of rhetorical commonplaces the reader can use as a point of departure for critical examinations of the development of rhetorical applications in Elizabethan literature. From one of Susenbrotus's examples for hyperbole, "niue candidior" (whiter than snow), Peacham gives us "whiter then snow," a commonplace that Shakespeare combines with hyperbaton in *The Tragedie of Othello, the Moor of Venice* (performed circa 1604; published 1622), when Othello says of Desdemona that he will not "scarre that whiter skin of hers, then snow." Peacham's work probably did not significantly influence the flourishing of rhetorical drama in England toward the end of the sixteenth century (though Joseph argues that Shakespeare was aware of Peacham's work) so much as it reflects issues of style and taste as the literary culture shifted from Lyly to Shakespeare. In this regard it is an extremely important work—especially in conjunction with Puttenham's *The Arte of English Poesie*—for understanding the poetic values of the period. Salomon Heg-

nauer's essay on Peacham's definition of systrophe and Herbert David Rix's *Rhetoric in Spenser's poetry* demonstrate how sometimes Peacham is the only guide for certain aspects of rhetoric in Elizabethan poetry because in some instances Peacham's treatment of rhetorical figures is more extensive than that of other classical and Renaissance rhetoricians, and in the case of *systrophe*, Peacham's is the only definition available.

Henry Peacham died on 23 September 1634 at the age of eighty-seven. He was presumably buried in the chancel of his church at Leverton, as his will requests. Both of Peacham's churches, St. Mary's in North Mimms and St. Helena's in Leverton, still exist and contain evidence of his presence. At St. Mary's a stone sundial bearing the name "Henricvs Pecham" and the date 1584, that once stood in the porch, is now set in one of the porch's buttresses, and, at St. Helena's, Henry Peacham the Younger's name is carved into the vestry window ledge with the date 1597. Peacham's bequest in his will to Anne Hawarden and her children may indicate that the wounds inflicted in the Chancery case years before had been healed.

Although Peacham's disreputable qualities (insofar as scholars such as Young have discovered) date to a much later period, in examining his life in light of his rhetorical writing, which is so keen to recognize the potentially deceptive side of the power of rhetoric, the reader may wonder how Peacham's experiences and relationships contributed to the development of his ideas on this subject. Indeed, Peacham's insistence on the careful use of tropes of compassion and charity is so at odds with the events of his later life that one is at a loss to explain his actions based on the available evidence. Whatever Peacham's personal shortcomings may have been, his service to the Church for sixty-three years, combined with his writings' dedication to spiritual enlightenment, distinguish him as a man of civic and spiritual piety. It is for these qualities that Henry Peacham the Younger remembered his father when he dedicated the epigram "Zeleus in Deum" (Zeal for God) to him in *Minerva Britanna* (British Minerva, 1612). Even in death Peacham's thoughts were with his parish; his will provides forty shillings to be distributed among "the most poore people of Leverton."

But Peacham's most important legacy is as a man of letters. In an inventory of Peacham's "goodes and Chattells" drawn up at the time of his death (now in the Lincolnshire Archives), Peacham's "librarie" is the second item listed, and is given the same value as the first item, "his purse and his apparell," £10. Providing a glimpse into the rhetorical sensibilities of England in the 1590s, *The Garden of Eloquence* is, especially in conjunction with Puttenham's *The Arte of English Poesie*, an important guide to the literary, religious, and political writing of the period. It is likely, too, that Puttenham's book was to some degree influenced by Peacham's 1577 edition, especially in Puttenham's treatment of the figures *tapinosis* (lowering), when something is desccribed in inappropriate language (for example: saying a town has been "harmed" when it has been "razed"); and *bomphiologia* (pompous speech), using elaborate language to describe insignificant things. Peacham's work certainly influenced later studies of rhetoric and oratory, and he is often credited for his contributions to John Hoskins's *Direccōns for Speech and Style* (1599?) and John Smith's *The Mysterie of Rhetorique Vnvail'd* (1657). The continued relevance of Peacham's study of the figures can be seen even four centuries after his work first appeared, in Willard R. Espy's homage to Peacham, *The Garden of Eloquence: A Rhetorical Bestiary* (1983), which includes modernized excerpts from Peacham's 1577 text.

Biography:

Alan R. Young, "Henry Peacham, Author of *The Garden of Eloquence* (1577): A Biographical Note," *Notes and Queries,* 24 (1977): 503–507.

References:

T. W. Baldwin, *William Shakspere's Small Latine & Lesse Greeke,* volume 2 (Urbana: University of Illinois Press, 1944);

Joseph X. Brennan, "The *Epitome Troporum ac Schematum:* The Genesis of a Renaissance Rhetorical Text," *Quarterly Journal of Speech,* 46 (1960): 59–71;

Thomas M. Conley, *Rhetoric in the European Tradition* (Chicago: University of Chicago Press, 1990), pp. 136–138;

William G. Crane, *Wit and Rhetoric in the Renaissance: The Formal Basis of Elizabethan Prose Style* (New York: Columbia University Press, 1937);

Willard R. Espy, *The Garden of Eloquence: A Rhetorical Bestiary* (New York: E. P. Dutton, 1983);

Charles W. Foster, ed., *The State of the Church in the Reigns of Elizabeth and James I: As Illustrated by Documents Relating to the Diocese of Lincoln,* Publications of the Lincoln Record Society, volume 23 (Lincoln: Printed for the Lincoln Record Society, 1926);

Salomon Hegnauer, "The Rhetorical Figure of Systrophe," in *Rhetoric Revalued: Papers from the International Society for the History of Rhetoric,* edited by Brian Vickers (Binghamton, N.Y.: Center for Medieval & Early Renaissance Studies, 1982), pp. 179–186;

Wilbur S. Howell, *Logic and Rhetoric in England 1500–1700* (Princeton: Princeton University Press, 1956);

Sister Miriam Joseph, *Rhetoric in Shakespeare's Time* (New York: Harcourt, Brace & World, 1962);

Wayne A. Rebhorn, *The Emperor of Men's Minds: Literature and the Renaissance Discourse of Rhetoric* (Ithaca, N.Y. & London: Cornell University Press, 1995);

Herbert David Rix, *Rhetoric in Spenser's Poetry,* Pennsylvania State College Studies, no. 7 (State College: Pennsylvania State College, 1940);

Brian Vickers, *In Defence of Rhetoric* (Oxford: Clarendon Press, 1988);

Vickers, "The Power of Persuasion": Images of the Orator, Elyot to Shakespeare," in *Renaissance Eloquence: Studies in the Theory and Practice of Renaissance Rhetoric,* edited by James J. Murphy (Berkeley: University of California Press, 1993), pp. 411–435;

Vickers, "Some Reflections on the Rhetoric Textbook," in *Renaissance Rhetoric,* edited by Peter Mack (Basingstoke, U.K.: Macmillan, 1994; New York: St. Martin's Press, 1994), pp. 81–102.

Henry Perri or Perry

(1561 – 1617)

Andrew Breeze
University of Navarre

BOOK: *Eglvryn Phraethineb. sebh, Dosparth ar Retoreg, vn o'r saith gelbhydhyd, Yn dyscu lhuniaith ymadrodh, a'i pherthynassau* (London: Printed by John Danter, 1595).

Editions: *Rhetoreg neu Rheitheg, a ddechreuwyd gan y Mr. Wiliam Salisbury, a anghwanegwyd ac a orphenwyd gan Mr. Henri Perri, trwy draul Sir Sion Salisbury o Leweni yn Sir Ddinbych, 1580. Egluryn Fraethineb, sev Dosparth ar Retoreg, un o'r saith gelvyddyd, yn dysgu lluniaith ymadrawdd a'i pherthynasau,* edited by Owain Myfyr and William Owen Pughe (London: S. Rousseau, 1807);

Rhetoreg, neu rheitheg, a ddechreuwyd gan Mr. William Salisbury; a anghwanegwyd ac a orphenwyd gan Mr. Henri Perri; trwy draul Sir Sion Salisbury o Leweni, yn sir ddinbych, 1580; Egluryn ffraethineb, sef, Dosparth ar Retoreg; un o'r saith gelfyddyd, yn dysgu lluniaith ymadrawdd a'i pherthynasau (Gwyndod-Wryf, Llanrwst: Printed by John Jones, 1829);

Egluryn Ffraethineb sef dosbarth ar retoreg: un o'r saith gelfyddyd, edited by Griffith John Williams (Cardiff: University of Wales Press, 1930).

Henry Perri is well known among Welsh scholars as the author of *Eglvryn Phraethineb. sebh, Dosparth ar Retoreg, vn o'r saith gelbhydhyd, Yn dyscu lhuniaith ymadrodh, a'i pherthynassau* (The Pattern of Eloquence, that is, an Account of Rhetoric, one of the seven arts, teaching figurative language and its relationships, 1595). This book is of interest for the way it uses the resources of medieval and sixteenth-century bardic poetry to impart educational ideals deriving from English intellectual life. Although resembling works by English writers in its view of the moral, social, and religious values inculcated by the study of rhetoric, it contrasts with them in its attitude toward earlier vernacular literature. Perri was able to use earlier Welsh poetry for his purposes in a way English writers could not use medieval English poetry for theirs. While his treatise thus shows the appearance in Welsh of attitudes toward discourse that derived from England and beyond, it also provides striking evidence for the continuity of Celtic bardic tradition.

Born at Maes-glas, or Greenfield, near Holywell in Flintness (northeast Wales in 1561), Henry Perri was a descendant of the Tudurs of Penmynydd in Anglesey, the Welsh ancestors of the English Tudor dynasty. Anthony à Wood and others identify him with the Henry Perry, or Parry, who at the age of eighteen matriculated on 20 March 1579 at Balliol College, Oxford; was B.A. from Gloucester Hall on 14 January 1580; M.A. on 23 March 1583; and B. D. from Jesus College on 6 June 1597. Bishop Humphrey Humphreys, in one of his additions to the 1813 edition of Wood's *Athenae Oxonienses* (1691, 1692), provides further information from Perri's son-in-law, Thomas Maurice: "[Perri] travelled much abroad and had bin marryed and setled in another counry. . . . Hither he came first as chaplain to Sir Richard Bulkley, and upon the death of his first wife, he married the daughter of Robert Vaughan, of Beaumares, gent. upon which he was accused, that his first wife was yet living; but he cleared that poynt by certificate and proof of her death, and shewed the accusation to be malitious."

Sir Richard Bulkeley (of Baron Court, near Beaumaris, Anglesey) was a friend of Queen Elizabeth I, an antagonist of Robert Dudley, first Earl of Leicester, and one of the most powerful men in Anglesey. No doubt through his influence, Perri obtained the Anglesey livings of Rhoscolyn "cum capellis de Llanvihagell yn howyn et Llanvairyneubwll" (with the chapels of Llanfihangel yn Nhowyn and Llanfair-yn-Neubwll) in 1601, of Trefdraeth in 1613, and of Llanfachreth "cum capellis de Llankynhenedl et Llanvaigail" (with the chapels of Llanynghenedl and Llanfigael) in 1613. He became canon of Bangor Cathedral in 1612–1613. He must have died before 30 December 1617, when William Hill was appointed to his place.

Perri's grandson was Henry Maurice (1647–1691), Lady Margaret Professor of Divinity at Oxford. Maurice's father was Thomas Maurice, B.D., perpetual

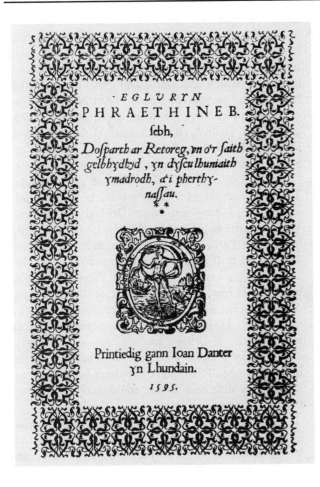

Title page and the coat of arms of the Salisbury family from Perri's Welsh rhetoric. The motto of the Salisburys,
Perri's patrons, may be translated as "to be noble and unwilling."

curate of Llangristiolus, Anglesey; his mother was Perri's daughter, Sidney.

Perri was praised as a Welsh scholar by Thomas Wiliems of Trefriw and John Davies of Mallwyd. In the introduction (written in 1604) to his Welsh dictionary (still unpublished), Wiliems speaks of assistance for his work from Sîon Dafydd Rhys, Henry Salesbury, the historian David Powel, and Henry Perri. In the Latin introduction to his great dictionary of the Welsh language, published in 1632, John Davies speaks of Perri as an authority on this language and others: "vir Linguarum cognitione insignis" (a man distinguished for his knowledge of languages).

Although medieval Welsh bards paid much attention to the study of grammar, Perri's modern editor Griffith John Williams notes that they had little interest in the study of rhetoric. Perri's book was, therefore, a turning point in Welsh literature. However, it had a precedent in a manuscript treatise, written in 1552, by the humanist William Salesbury. (Perri may have read it in what is now Aberystwyth, National Library of Wales,

MS Peniarth 159.) In his prefatory letter to the poet Gruffudd Hiraethog (died 1564), Salesbury declares that he has compiled this work for the benefit of the Welsh bards. Welsh scholar Sir Ifor Williams has argued that Salesbury derived his knowledge of rhetoric from medieval Latin sources, which he translated and adapted, while taking his examples from Welsh bardic poetry. Salesbury's treatise was not published until 1856 but was used in manuscript by Simwnt Fychan, William Cynwal, and Thomas Wiliems.

The publication of Perri's book in 1595, however, put the subject on a new basis. Griffith John Williams emphasizes Perri's debt to English works on rhetoric, especially Thomas Wilson's *The Arte of Rhetorique* (1553), which Perri certainly used, and Richard Sherry's *A Treatise of the Figures of Grammer and Rhetorike* (1555), which may have been one of Perri's schoolbooks. Williams believes that Perri's aim was to do in Welsh what had been done in English by Leonard Cox in his *The arte or crafte of Rhethoryke* (1530?) and George Puttenham in his *The Arte of English Poesie* (1589), as well as by Wilson and Sherry. Williams describes Perri's claim that the sole branches of rhetoric are *elocutio* (the use of figures of speech, *Adhurneg*) and *pronuntiatio* (the art of speaking, *Lhabbaredigeth*) as an English symptom, and his eulogies of rhetoric as being characteristic of writers of that age. Williams also notes that, like other sixteenth-century writers on rhetoric, Perri takes examples of his figures of speech from the Bible, perhaps indirectly from Sherry's *A Treatise of the Figures of Grammer and Rhetorike,* which maintains that the Bible cannot be understood fully unless one has a knowledge of rhetoric, or perhaps from Dudley Fenner's *The Artes of Logike and Rethorike* (1584). William A. Mathias and R. Brinley Jones have confirmed the influence of Fenner. They place Perri's book in the Ramist tradition, following *Rhetorica* (1567) by Omer Talon, known as Audomarus Talaeus (written under the direction of Pierre de La Ramée, known as Petrus Ramus), and two English books based on it, Fenner's *The Artes of Logike and Rethorike* and Abraham Fraunce's *The Arcadian Rhetorike* (1588). Perri's division of rhetoric into the two parts of elocutio and pronuntiatio follows the system set out by them. However, Perri also used *The Garden of Eloquence* (1593) by Henry Peacham the Elder. The "warnings" at the end of some of the chapters against misuse of figures are taken from this book. Mathias also confirms that some of the Bible quotations are taken from Fenner's *The Artes of Logike and Rethorike,* though more are from *The Garden of Eloquence.*

It was often said, especially in the seventeenth and eighteenth centuries, that Perri's book was merely a revision of William Salesbury's account of rhetoric, published under Perri's name without acknowledgment to its real author. John Davies, in his grammar of 1621, thus mentions "De Figuris Syntaxeos consule Wilhelmi Salesburij Rhetoricam MS. ab Henrico Perrio interpolatam & in lucem editam" (A rhetorical manuscript by William Salesbury on the figures of syntax, extended and published by Henri Perri). The 1807 reprint of Perri's book therefore states (in Welsh) on its title page that the book "was begun by Mr. Wiliam Salisbury, and enlarged and completed by Mr. Henri Perri." Although Perri uses the same terms as Salesbury, often follows him word for word, and takes many of his examples from him, Salesbury deals with some fifty figures of speech not mentioned by Perri, and Perri with some thirty not mentioned by Salesbury. Perri's account is also much fuller and more detailed than Salesbury's. He takes seventeen pages to discuss metonymy; Salesbury, on the other hand, takes just half a page. The main author of *Egluryn Ffraethineb* is Perri, not Salesbury.

Perri's only book shows a thorough knowledge of the Welsh poetry of the fifteenth and sixteenth centuries. It is a volume of twenty unnumbered pages, with an introduction, poems in praise of the work, and other matter, followed by the main text on pages numbered 1 to 108. Its title appears above a device showing Opportunity as a naked woman standing on a wheel floating on the sea, with a ship sailing and a ship sinking behind her, and the surrounding motto "Aut Nunc aut Nunquam" (Now or Never). Below this phrase is "Printiedig gann Ioan Danter yn Lhundain" (Printed by John Danter in London) and the date, 1595. On the reverse are the arms of the Salusbury family, with the motto "Posse Nobile et Nolle" (To be noble and unwilling). The next four pages include a letter in Latin to John Salusbury of Llewenni (near Denbigh in northeast Wales), squire of the body to Elizabeth I (who knighted him in 1601) and minor poet in English (whose poems were edited in 1929 by Carleton Brown of the Modern Language Association). In his letter, Perri praises Salusbury's generosity as patron and stresses the importance of the art of rhetoric, quoting Greek authors and Cicero to this effect. He is also slavish in his praise of Elizabeth I as defender of Britain, perhaps because Salusbury's elder brother Thomas was executed in 1586 for his part in the Babington Plot. Perri throughout his book is careful to show deference to the established authorities in Britain.

This Latin letter is followed by a five-page preface in Welsh to the gentlemen, priests, and bards of the Welsh people. On the first page Perri sets out the deficiencies of Welsh literary culture that make his book necessary:

> But, as this is known to the wise, familiar to the learned, and evident to whoever considers it duly, I have set out deliberately and boldly presumed (whether the design be successful or not), with the permission and succour of every learned Welshman, to take up the challenge and set down a classification of one of the seven liberal arts called Rhetoric, which is one of the handmaidens of true wisdom, which is mistress and governess over the works of all the men in the world. Does the reader ask him what this wisdom is, splendid as the dawn? He need not doubt that it is the knowledge of God and man through expressing well every kind of action to its appropriate end. And as we know that this wisdom is the intended aim and cherished thought of every learned and dextrous man in this world, we should none of us neglect one of the means which lead and draw us to it.

As one of the seven liberal arts, then, rhetoric is a means to self-knowledge and the knowledge of God. Human beings attain this wisdom by practicing each art properly and successfully, and rhetoric is no exception.

Perri goes on to distinguish between logic and rhetoric and to explain the important uses of both. Although logic and rhetoric are among the seven liberal

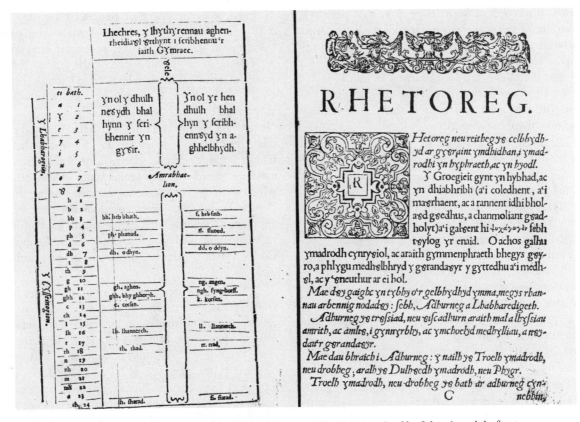

The end of the front matter for Eglvryn Phraethineb, *with Perri's systematic table of rhetoric, and the first page of the text, which begins with Perri's definition of his subject*

arts (with grammar, music, geometry, arithmetic, and astronomy), logic and rhetoric have a special relationship since each was created to serve one of the two parts of human knowledge, which he describes as follows:

> Since human knowledge has only two parts, first, in distinguishing between one thing and another, and, second, in discoursing eloquently and well, then the reader must know that it is from the first that there arose the art which is called logic, and from the second there sprang up and budded rhetoric. The first enables us to teach rightly, to give instruction wisely, to reason without error. The second enables us to give fair colour to discourse, and to vary eloquence pleasingly; to adorn mannerly speech and each kind of acceptable splendour.

Perri then shows his basic view that logic is a method, which is especially relevant to teaching, while rhetoric is a manner of expression that gives pleasure:

> Therefore, from being able to define the nature of all things, from being able to distinguish with discrimination, from being able to analyze with skill, and judge wisely, it will be known that man is a reasonable creature. From being able to converse eloquently, speak wisely, and tell pleasingly of the setting out of the soul's

ideals, and the unfolding of the meditations of the heart in seemly, credible, skilled, and delightful words, it will also be known that a man is a sociable creature. Therefore, so that a man can express his purposes in orderly fashion, and his intent, Nature ordained this art; giving us a powerful talent to be able to set forth, and sense to compare, fluent words and excellent sentences, to shape and build up this art, to practise it cheerfully, and to mark it in necessity for the benefit of those who speak one's own language, and for praise of the living God.

Perri goes on to consider both logic and rhetoric as meta-arts, or arts of arts: "Further, as logic enables one to reason and to distinguish between truth and falsehood, not in one art, but in every kind of knowledge and skill, in the same manner eloquence teaches one to speak eloquently and discourse well in Divinity, medicine, law, the study of war, and every affair amongst men."

Later in his preface, after citing examples of figures of speech in Chaldean, Syriac, Arabic, Spanish, and other languages, Perri makes an impassioned plea for the preservation of the Welsh language and the cultivation of native eloquence by "lords, priests, gentlemen, bards, and others," for the sake of the remembrance of forebears, discretion of knowledge, praise of parents, maintenance of valor, and so on. He bids them to maintain it boldly, adorn it in praiseworthy fashion, and use it to write to each other. It is from neglect of the language that the Welsh are so unlearned in it; and it is, therefore, necessary for them to know his little book, to acquire true eloquence and console them in adversity and become them in prosperity.

The preface is followed by preliminary verses, which are interesting in helping to define Perri's intellectual circle. The poems are by "R. V.," in Latin; John Dee, in Latin; unsigned, in Greek, about John Salusbury; "Da. Rob.," in Latin; Henry Holland, in Latin; William Midleton, poet, soldier, and sailor, in Welsh; Ludovic Lloyd, courtier and compiler, in English; William Mathew, in English; "I. H." of New College, Oxford, in Latin; William Rankins, in English; Hugh Lewys, cleric and translator, in Latin; and Henry Salusbury, both in Latin and Welsh. The first part closes with a systematic table of rhetoric, which analyzes its aspects through up to eight stages of division, and another table of the initial mutations of the Welsh language.

The text itself consists of forty-two short chapters, followed by three pages with indexes of rhetorical terms and authors, and a brief farewell to the reader. In chapter 1 Perri defines rhetoric as "the art of skilful discourse (celbhydhyd ar gywraint ymdhidhan), and expressing oneself eloquently and fluently." He divides the subject into two parts: elocutio and pronuntiatio, which Perri subdivides further. Sixteen chapters are then devoted to elocutio. Chapter 2, the first of five chapters on metonymy, deals with agent—that is, causes or objects that produce effects. Perri quotes from the King James version of Ezek. 7:15: "The sword is without, and the pestilence and the famine within," explaining that "sword" here stands for "slaughter," and the other terms for "death." He goes on to say that the names of Aristotle, Tully (Cicero), Livy, Plato, and Moses can be used for learning, eloquence, the art of warfare, profound thought, and divinity, since by these authors are meant their books. He also quotes from a Welsh poem by Edmund Prys, in which Dwned (Donatus) is used to mean "the grammar book written by Donatus." This uniting of scriptural, classical, and Welsh sources is fundamental to Perri's approach. He closes this part with a warning (one of many in the book), telling readers not to confuse agent and effect, and referring contemptuously to cler y dom (dunghill minstrels), the lowest class of Welsh poet, who are guilty of such confusion when trying to imitate a master poet in his work. Having dealt with the metonymy of agents, Perri in the next four chapters discusses other aspects of metynomy. In chapter 3 he writes of it as concerning material or matter used, as in

"Cursed is every one that hangeth on a tree" (Gal. 3:13), in which "tree" means "cross," the material standing for the object meant; in chapter 4, as concerning effects, as in "Jacob sware by the fear of his father Isaac" (Gen. 31:53), in which "fear" stands for "true God"; in chapter 5, as concerning subject, in which the substantial or fundamental is used for the adjunct, as in "It hath pleased Macedonia and Achaia to make a certain contribution" (Rom. 15:26), in which the place-names stand for dwellers therein, or "I call heaven and earth to record this day against you" (Deut. 30:19), in which these places mean the creatures living there. In chapter 6, he gives an account of the metonymy of adjuncts, as in Jesus Christ "made unto us wisdom, and righteousness, and sanctification, and redemption" (1 Cor. 1:30), in which attributes stand in place of the original.

Chapter 7 deals with satire and closes with a warning that satire must not be used without urgent cause or inopportunely, or by lower-class persons to officeholders, those of higher estate, or social superiors, since what they say "would be unseemly, and ignorant of good in the presence of all and judgement of all." The next five chapters discuss paralipsis, or pretending not to say something that has already been said; sarcasm, or the use of bitter, mocking speech; mycterism, or showing scorn through facial expressions; euphemism, or making something seem better than it is; and metaphor, the use of a word in other than its literal sense. At the end of his account of metaphor, Perri warns against using unlikeness instead of alikeness, as if one were to say, "the bull barks." Perri's warning and example are translated directly from the 1593 edition of Peacham's The Garden of Eloquence. A second chapter 12, probably a printer's or author's error, deals with onomatopoeia, the creation or use of words that imitate sounds. Not until chapter 13 does Perri treat one of the most important tropes in Ramist rhetoric books: synecdoche, or the calling of a thing by the name of one of its parts or by the name of its cause or effect. In the same chapter Perri includes a discussion of antonomasia, the use of an epithet in place of name. Perri's treatment of allegory, or extended metaphor, in chapter 14 leads to short discussions of riddles and proverbs. Perri shows the relation between these by quoting for the first, "Whose fan is in his hand, and he will thorough purge his floor, and gather up his wheat into the garner" (Matt. 3:12). For the second, he refers to Nebuchadnezzar's dream of the tree in the midst of the earth (Dan. 4:10–17). In chapter 15, Perri discusses hyperbole, usually regarded as a form of intentional exaggeration. According to Perri, however, it can involve overstatement ("as when a pretty girl is called an angel" or meiosis or understatement. Chapter 16, the last in the section on elocutio, deals with catachresis, the supplying

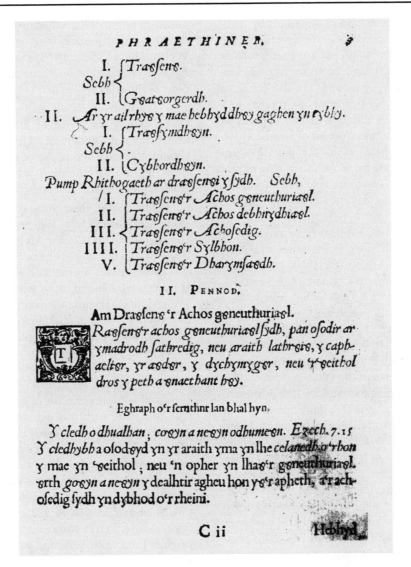

Page from the second chapter of Eglvryn Phraethineb, *the first of five dealing with metonymy, the figure of speech in which the name of one thing is used for something with which it is associated (such as "crown" for "king")*

of a related word for an elusive proper term (often regarded as an abuse or vice of language), such as "blood of the grape" in Deut. 32:14.

The next section, consisting of twenty-six chapters, concerns *pronuntiatio,* or delivery. Chapter 17 describes the comma, the colon, and the question mark, as referring to delivery by an orator. Chapters 18 to 24 deal with the following figures of speech: *epizeuxis,* the repetition of a word in rapid succession; *diacope,* the separation of a compound word by interposing another word; *tmesis,* the repetition of a word in close proximity; *parenthesis,* the separation of parts of a sentence by inserting an aside; *anadiplosis,* the repetition of a word or phrase at the end of one sentence and the beginning of the next, as with "a good land, a land of brooks of water" in Deut. 8:7; climax, a gradual building toward a conclusion; and *anaphora,* the repetition of a word at the beginnings of sentences (for example, "Where is the wise? where is the scribe?" in 1 Cor. 1:20). A second chapter 24 discusses *epiphora,* the repetition of a word at the ends of sentences, including *homoeiteleuton* (words with the same or similar endings) and *homoeoptoton* (words in the same case or with similar inflection). In chapter 25 Perri deals with *epanalepsis* (the repetition of a word at the beginning and end of the same sentence), including *diaphora* (the use of the same expression at the beginning and at the end of a phrase or sentence, as in "physician heal thyself if thou art a physician"), *ploce* (the repetition of a word in altered or pregnant sense, as in "Arthur in that victory showed himself to be Arthur") and *antanaclasis* (the repetition of a word in an altered sense, as in "hope against hope"). Chapter 26 describes *epanodos* (the reiteration of something by naming its parts), including *antimetabole* (the reversal of the same words, as in Molière's "do not live to eat, but eat to live") and *eutrepismus* (where parts are listed before being enlarged on in orderly manner). In chapter 27, as an example of *paranomasia,* or punning, Perri refers to 1 Chron. 2:7, in which the name of Achan appears as "Achar," because he was "the troubler of Israel." Quoting Welsh examples, Perri states that the best use of this figure is to express contrasts, as in the Welsh phrase *"nid meddru: ond methu"* (not to be able, but to fail), in which there is an obvious play on words between *meddru* and *methu.*

Chapter 28 deals with *polyptoton* (repeating a word in different cases or inflections in the same sentence); chapter 29 deals with *ecphonesis* (exclamation), *thaumasmus* (exclamation of wonder), cursing, deprecation, *threnos* (lamentation), *mempsis* (reproach), eulogy, *orcos* (confirmation with an oath), *epiphonema* (an exclamation concluding a discourse), and *parrhesia* (boldness of speech). Chapter 30 discusses *epanorthosis* (recalling a word to substitute it with a more correct term), including *restrictio* (disentanglement); the following chapter discusses *aposiopesis,* or coming to a sudden halt in speech; chapter 32 discusses *symphoresis* (accumulation of similar words), with *asyndeton* or omission of the conjunction; chapter 33 discusses *apostrophe,* or address of a person not present or living; the next chapter discusses *prosopopoeia,* or personification; and chapter 35 discusses *aporia,* or hesitation. To illustrate this last, Perri quotes Psalm 139:6–11, in which the psalmist declares God's knowledge is too wonderful for him, and asks himself whither he shall go from the Lord's spirit or flee from his presence, and notes that the poet addresses himself as if in confusion of mind in considering the greatness of God and his judgments. After quoting another instance from a medieval bard, Perri warns that this figure should not be used too often, lest the user seem ignorant or forgetful.

Chapter 36 deals with *periphrasis;* chapter 37, *congeries* (diverse descriptions of one thing); chapter 38, *communicatio,* or the rhetorical question; chapter 39, *subjectio* and *hypophora,* or the answering of one's own questions; chapter 40, *anachoresis* (retreat in Greek), including *anthypophora* (counter-inference or allegation) and *epitrope* (permission given in earnest or jest to an opponent); and chapter 41 discusses *synoiceosis* (yoking contraries together; this term is broader than oxymoron). The book concludes with remarks on how the orator should use his voice and body. For all these terms Perri gives equivalent terms in Welsh, many his own coinages.

For his examples, Perri quotes more than thirty Welsh bards, among them Dafydd ap Gwilym, Tudur Aled, and Lewys Môn. He shows special care to quote poems in praise of the Salusbury family. His Old Testament scriptural quotations do not always come from the Welsh Bible of 1588, perhaps suggesting that he wrote *Eglvryn Phraethineb* before then, making his own translations of these texts.

Perri's book shows an unusual use of medieval Welsh poetry for forms of literary analysis deriving from classical humanism. His derogatory remarks about the papacy and praise of the Tudor dynasty also show his full identification with the Elizabethan religious settlement and his loyalty to the authorities.

There were three subsequent editions of *Eglvryn Phraethineb*. Griffith John Williams states that the second edition, edited by Owain Myfyr and William Owen Pughe, came out in parts from 1805 to 1807 in *Y Greal,* a Welsh-language journal edited by Pughe and others, and was republished as a whole in 1807, but Huw Walters, a librarian at the National Library of Wales, has checked the journal and can find no evidence that the work came out in parts. He notes that the paper wrapper of issue number 7 (December 1806) states: ". . . Bydd y rhiv nesav o'r *Greal* yn cynnwys y cyvan o'r *Eglvryn Phraethineb*" (The next issue of the *Greal* will comprise the whole of the *Eglvryn Fraethineb*). The complete work was published as a supplement to issue number 9 (21 June 1807) in an unhistorical system of orthography devised by Pughe, now long obsolete; many changes were made in the text itself; the editors also omitted the letter of address in Latin and the prefatory verses in Latin and English. The third edition, published at Llanrwst in 1829, followed that of 1807 fairly closely. Perri's work was thus not accessible in its original form until Williams published a facsimile text in 1930.

Biographies:

Garfield H. Hughes, "Henry Perri," in *The Dictionary of Welsh Biography Down to 1940,* edited by John Edward Lloyd and R. T. Jenkins (London: Honourable Society of Cymmrodorion, 1959), p. 747;

Anthony à Wood, "Henry Perry [or Parry]," in *Athenae Oxonienses. An Exact History of All the Writers and Bishops Who Have Had Their Education in the University of Oxford. To Which Are Added The Fasti, or Annals of the Said University,* 4 volumes, edited by Philip Bliss (London: Printed for F. C. & J. Rivington, and others, 1813–1820; New York & London: Johnson Reprint Corporation, 1967), I: columns 666–667.

References:

Glenda Carr, *William Owen Pughe* (Cardiff: University of Wales Press, 1983);

Ceri Davies, trans., *Rhagymadroddion a Chyflwyniadau Lladin 1551–1632* (Latin Prefaces and Introductions, 1551–1632) (Cardiff: University of Wales Press, 1980);

R. Geraint Gruffydd, ed., *A Guide to Welsh Literature, c. 1530–1700,* volume 3 (Cardiff: University of Wales Press, 1997), pp. 38, 133, 139, 202, 265;

Garfield H. Hughes, ed., *Rhagymadroddion 1547–1659* (Prefaces 1547–1659) (Cardiff: University of Wales Press, 1951), pp. 84–88;

R. T. Jenkins, "Henry Maurice," in *The Dictionary of Welsh Biography Down to 1940* (London: Honourable Society of Cymmrodorion, 1959), p. 623;

R. Brinley Jones, "Geirfa Rhethreg 1552–1632" (The Vocabulary of Rhetoric 1552–1632), *Ysgrifau Beirniadol* (Critical Writings), 9 (1976): 118–146;

Jones, *The Old British Tongue: The Vernacular in Wales, 1540–1640* (Cardiff: Avalon, 1970), pp. 74, 76–78, 115;

Jones, *William Salesbury* (Cardiff: University of Wales Press, 1994), pp. 33–36;

William A. Mathias, "Llyfr Rhetoreg William Salesbury" (William Salesbury's Book of Rhetoric) *Llen Cymru* (The Literature of Wales), 1 (1951): 259–268; 2 (1952): 71–81;

Mathias, "William Salesbury," in *The Dictionary of Welsh Biography Down to 1940* (London: Honourable Society of Cymmrodorion, 1959), p. 898;

Griffith John Williams, "Rhagymadrodd" (Preface), *Egluryn Ffraethineb sef dosbarth ar retoreg: un o'rsaith gelfyddyd* (Cardiff: University of Wales Press, 1930), pp. v–x.

John Prideaux

(17 September 1578 – 29 July 1650)

Diana B. Altegoer

BOOKS: *Tabulæ Ad Grammatica Græca Introdvctoriæ. In Qvibvs Succinctè compingitur, brevissima, sed tamen expedita, singularum partium orationis declinabilium, Variandiratio. Accessit Vestibuli vice, ad eandem linguam παραινέσις, in gratiam tyronum, quibus vt convenit explicatiora evolvere, ita necesse est hæc ipsa ad vnguem tenere* (Oxford: Printed by Joseph Barnes, 1607);

Castigatio Cvivsdam circvlatoris, qvi R. P. Andream Evdæmon-Iohannem Cydonivm E Societate Iesu seipsum nuncupat. Opposita Ipsivs Calumnijs in Epistolam Isaaci Casavboni ad Frontonem Ducæum. Per Iohannem Prideavx SS. Theologiæ Doctorem & Collegij Exoniensis Rectorem (Oxford: Printed by Joseph Barnes, 1614);

Ephesvs Backsliding Considered And Applyed To These times, in a Sermon preached at Oxford, in Sᵗ Maries, the tenth of Iuly, being the Act Sunday. 1614. By Iohn Prideavx, Doctor of Divinity, and Rector of Exceter College (Oxford: Printed by Joseph Barnes, 1614);

Christs Covnsell For Ending Law Cases. As It Hath Beene Delivered in two Sermons vpon the 25ᵗʰ Verse of the 5ᵗʰ of Matthew. By John Prideavx Doctor of Divinity and Rector of Exceter Colledge (Oxford: Printed by Joseph Barnes, 1615);

Eight Sermons, Preached By Iohn Prideavx, Doctor of Diuinity, Regius Professor, Vice-Chancellor of the Vniuersity of Oxford, and Rector of Exceter Colledge. The Severall Texts and Titles of the Sermons, follow in the next leafe (London: Printed by Felix Kyngston for Iohn Budge, 1621)—comprises *Christs Counsell For Ending Law Cases* (in two sermons), *Ephesvs Backsliding: Considered and Applyed to These Times, A Christians Free-Will Offering, The First Frvits of the Resvrrection, Gowries Conspiracie, Higgaion & Selah: For the Discovery of the Powder-Plot,* and *Hezekiahs Sicknesse and Recoverie;*

Alloqvivm serenissimo regi Iacobo Woodstochiæ habitvm 24. Augusti. Anno 1624 (Oxford, 1624);

Perez-Vzzah: Or The Breach of Vzzah: As it was deliuered in a Sermon before His Maiesty at Woodstocke, August the 24. Anno 1624. By Iohn Prideavx, Rector of Exceter Col- ledge, *His Maiestie's Professor in Divinity, and at that time Vice-Chancellor of the Vniversity of Oxford* (Oxford: John Lichfield & William Turner, 1624)—includes *Alloqvivm serenissimo regi Iacobo Woodstochiæ habitvm 24. Augusti. Anno 1624;*

Lectiones Novem De Totidem Religionis Capitibus præcipuè hoc tempore controversis prout publicè habebantur Oxoniae in Vesperijs. Per Iohannem Prideavx Exoniensis Collegii Rectorem, & S. Th. Professorem Regium (Oxford: Printed by John Lichfield & William Turner for Henry Cripps, 1625); revised and enlarged as *Lectiones decem. De Totidem Religionis Capitibus praecipuè hoe tempore controversis prout publicè habebantur oxoniae in Vesperijs. Per Iohanmem Prideavx Exoniensis Collegij Rectoram, & S. Th. Professorem Regium. Editio secunda, priori emaculatior, & auctior* (Oxford: Printed by John Lichfield & William Turner, 1626); revised and enlarged as *Viginti-duæ Lectiones De Totidem Religionis Capitibus, Praecipve Hoc Tempore controversis, prout publicè habebantur Oxoniae in vesperiis. Quibus accesserunt Tredecim Orationes Inavgvrales, De totidem Theologiæ Apicibus Scitu non indignis, prout in promotione Doctorum in Comitiis habebantur. Subnectuntur Sex Conciones Pro More Habitæ, Ad Artium Baccalaurios in die Cinerum. Per Johannem Prideaux Exoniensis Collegii Rectorem, & S. Th. Professorem Regium, Editio tertia, prioribus emaculatior, & duplo fere auctior* (Oxford: Printed by Henry Hall for Henry Cripps, Henry Curteyn & Thomas Robinson, 1648);

A Sermon Preached On The Fifth Of October 1624: At The Consecration Of St Iames Chappel In Exeter Colledge. By Iohn Prideavx, Rector of Exceter Colledge, His Maiesties Professour in Diuinity, and at that time Vice-Chancellour of the Vniuersity of Oxford (Oxford: Printed by John Lichfield & William Turner, 1625);

Orationes Novem Inavgvrales, De Totidem Theologiæ Apicibvs, scitu non indignis, prout in promo.tione Doctorum, Oxoniæ publicè proponebantur in Comitijs. Accedit ad Artium Baccalaureos, de Mosis Iustitutione Concio, pro more habita in die Cinerum, An. 1616. Per Iohannes Prideavx, Exoniensis Collegij Rectorem, & SS. Th. Professorem Regium

(Oxford: Printed by John Lichfield & William
Turner for William Turner, 1626);

*Concio Habita Oxoniæ ad Artium Baccalaureos in Die Cinerum
Feb. 22°. 1626. Per Iohannem Prideavx S.S. Th. Professorem Regium, & P. T. ejusdem Academiæ Vicecancellar-
ium* (Oxford: Printed by John Lichfield & William
Turner, 1626);

*Tyrocinivm Ad Syllogismvm Legitimum contexendum, & captio-
sum dissuendum, expeditissimum. In Qvo Ad formam
expensa Syllogisticam perstringuntur punctim Sophismata,
nec minus solidè, quàm vulgò fit, ratione materiæ; Excerp-
tis ex optimis Authoribus exempli Græcolatinis, vt majori
cum voluptate & fructu, ex vtriusq; linguæ candidatis &
legantur, & intelligantur* (Oxford: Printed by John
Lichfield, 1629);

*The Doctrine Of The Sabbath. Delivered in the Act at Oxon.
Anno, 1622. By Dr. Prideavx his Majesties Professour
for Divinity in that Vniversity. And now translated into
English for the benefit of the common People,* translated
by Peter Heylyn (London: Printed by Elizabeth
Purslowe for Henry Seile, 1634);

*The First Frvits Of The Resvrrection. A Sermon Preached On
Easter Day, At St Peters in the East, in Oxford. By Iohn
Prideavx, Doctor of Divinity, Regius Professor, and Rector
of Exeter Colledge* (Oxford: Printed by Leonard
Lichfield, 1636);

*Heresies Progresse. A Sermon Preached At The Covrt. By Iohn
Prideavx, Rector of Exeter Colledge, His Maiestie's Pro-
fessor in Divinity in the Vniversity of Oxford* (Oxford:
Printed by Leonard Lichfield, 1636);

*Hezekiahs Sicknesse And Recovery. A Sermon Preached Before
The Kings Maiestie at Woodstocke. By Iohn Prideavx,
Doctor of Divinity, Regius Professor, and Rector of Exeter
Colledge* (Oxford: Printed by Leonard Lichfield,
1636);

*A Plot For Preferment. A Sermon Preached At The Covrt. By
Iohn Prideavx, Rector of Exeter Colledge, His Maiestie's
Professor in Divinity in the Vniversity of Oxford* (Oxford:
Printed by Leonard Lichfield, 1636);

*Wisedomes Ivstification. A Sermon Preached at the Covrt. By
Iohn Prideavx, Rector of Exeter Colledge, His Maiestie's
Professor in Divinity in the Vniversity of Oxford* (Oxford:
Printed by Leonard Lichfield, 1636);

*Certaine Sermons Preached By Iohn Prideavx, Rector of Exeter
Colledge, his Maiestie's Professor in Divinity in Oxford,
and Chaplaine in Ordinary* (Oxford: Printed by
Leonard Lichfield, 1637)—comprises *Christs Covn-
sell for Ending Lavv Cases* (in two sermons), *Ephesvs
Backsliding, A Christians Free-Will Offering, The First
Frvits Of The Resvrrection, Gowries Conspiracie, Hig-
gaion & Selah, Hezekiahs Sicknesse And Recovery,
Perez-Vzzah, Alloqvivm Serenissimo Regi Iacobo Wood-
stochiae Habitvm, A Sermon Preached On The Fift* [sic]
Of October 1624, The great Prophets Advent, Reverence

*To Rvlers, The Dravght Of The Brooke, Davids Reioyc-
ing For Christs Resurrection, The Christians Expectation,
Wisdomes Ivstification, Heresies Progresse, A Plot For
Preferment, The Patronage Of Angels,* and *Idolatrovs
Feasting;*

*Heptades Logicae Sive Monita Ad Ampliores Tractatus Introduc-
toria* (Oxford: Printed by Leonard Lichfield for
Thomas Allam & E. Pearse, 1639);

*Conciones Sex. Ad Artivm Baccalavreos Habitæ, In Die
Cinerum pro more in Templo B. Mariæ, ante Publicas in
Scholis Disputationes, per totam insequentem Quadragesi-
mam ab illis continuandas. Per Johannem Prideaux Col-
legii Exoniensis Rectorem, & S. T. Professorem Regium*
(Oxford: Printed by Leonard Lichfield for Henry
Cripps, Henry Curteyne & Thomas Robinson,
1648);

*XIII. Orationes Inavgvrales, De Totidem Theologiæ Apicibus,
Scitu non indignis, prout in promotione Doctorum in
Comitiis habebantur. Per Johannem Prideaux Exoniensis
Collegii Rectorem, & SS. Th. Professorem Regium*
(Oxford: Printed by Henry Hall for Henry
Cripps, Henry Curteyne & Thomas Robinson,
1648);

*Fasciculus, Controversiarvm Theologicarvm Ad Juniorum, Aut
occupatorum Captum sic colligatus, ut in præcipuis Fidei
Apicibus Compendiosè Informentur, aut sparsim aliàs
Lecta vel audita, faciliùs recolant & expendant. Per
Johannem Prideaux, haud ita pridèm apud Oxonienses
S. T. Professorem Regium, & posteà Episcopum Wigorni-
ensem* (Oxford: Printed by Leonard Lichfield,
1649; revised edition, 1664);

*Hypomnemata Logica, Rhetorica, Physica, Metaphysica, Pneu-
matica, Ethica Politica, Œconomica Per Jo: P: Coll: Exon*
(Oxford: Printed by Leonard Lichfield, 1650?);

*Conciliorvm Synopsis, Per Johannem Prideaux, haud ita pridèm
apud Oxonienses S. T. Professorem Regium, & Posteà
Episcopum Wigorniensem* (Oxford: Printed by
Leonard Lichfield, 1651);

*Scholasticæ Theologicae Syntagma Mnemonicum. Per Johannem
Prideaux, haud ita pridèm apud Oxonienses S. T. Profes-
sorem Regium, & Posteà Episcopum Wigorniensem*
(Oxford: Printed by Leonard Lichfield, 1651);

Theologiae scholasticae syntagmati (Oxford: Printed by
Leonard Lichfield, 1651);

*A Synopsis of Councels By John Prideaux late Regius Professour
of Divinity at Oxford and Bishop of Worcester* (Oxford:
Printed by Leonard Lichfield for Thomas Robinson, 1654);

*Evchologia: Or, The Doctrine of Practical Praying. By the Right
Reverend Father in God, John Prideaux, Late Bishop of
Worcester. Being a Legacy left to his Daughters in Private,
directing them to such manifold Uses of our Common
Prayer Book. As may satisfie upon all Occasions, without*

looking after New Lights from Extemporal Flashes (London: Printed for Richard Marriot, 1655);

Συνειδησιλογίαοr, *The doctrine of conscience, framed according to the points of the catechisme, in the Book of Common-Prayer. By the Right Reverend Father in God, John Prideaux, late Lord Bishop of Worcester, for the private use of his wife* (London: Printed for Richard Marriot, 1656);

Manvdvctio Ad Theologiam Polemicam. A R. Patre, Et Dòctissimo præsule Johanne Prideavx, Haud ita pridem Professore Regio Acad. Oxon: posteà Epis. Vigorniensi (Oxford: Printed by Leonard Lichfield for Thomas Robinson, 1657);

Sacred Eloquence: Or, the Art of Rhetorick, As it is layd down in Scripture. By the Right Reverend Father John Prideavx late Lord Bishop of VVorchester (London: Printed by W. Wilson for George Sawbridge, 1659);

Reverendi in Christo Patris, Joannis Prideaux, D. Episcopi Vigorniensis, Ad Nobilissimum Dominum, D. Joannem Roberts, Baronem de Trvro De Episcopatu Epistola, by Wilson and John Roberts, Baron Truro (London: Printed by J. F. for R. Royston, 1660).

Editions: *Nine Sermons Heretofore Preached Upon severall occasions, and printed 1636. And Now Pvblished without any alteration 1641* (Oxford: Printed by Leonard Lichfield for Henry Cripps & Henry Curteyne, 1641)—comprises ten sermons *Christs Covnsell for Ending Lavv Cases* (in two sermons), *Ephesvs Backsliding, A Christians Free-Will Offering, The First Frvits Of The Resvrrection, Govvries Conspiracie, Higgaion & Selah, Hezekiahs Sicknesse And Recovery, Perez-Vzzah, Alloqvivm Serenissimo Regi Iacobo Woodstochiae Habitvm*, and *A Sermon Preached on the Fifth of October 1624;*

The Doctrine of Prayer by John Prideaux. New Ed. To Which Are Added Certain Godly Prayers from Early Editions of the Book of Common Prayer and the Treatise of St. Athanasius on the Use and Virtue of the Psalms, by Sidney W. Cornish (Oxford: John Henry Parker, 1841).

OTHER: Untitled poem, in *Academiæ Oxoniensis Pietas Erga Serenissimvm Et Potentissimvm Iacobvm Angliæ Scotjæ Franciæ & Hiberniæ Regem, fidei defensorem, Beatissimæ Elisabethæ nuper Reginæ legitimè & auspicatissimè succedentem* (Oxford: Printed by Joseph Barnes, 1603), pp. 184–187;

"In insequeus Geographium opus Decastichon," in *A Geographicall And Anthologicall description of all the Empires and Kingdomes, both of Continent and Ilands in the terrestriall Globe. Relating their scituations, Manners, Customes, Provinces, and Gouernements*, by Robert Stafford (London: Printed by Thomas Cotes for Simon Waterson, 1607), sig. A4^r;

"Avgvstissimo Principi Domino Svo Clementissimo," in *Ivsta Oxonjensivm* (London: Printed for John Bill, 1612), sig. B2^v;

Untitled poem, in *Ivsta Fvnebria Ptolemæi Oxoniensis Thomæ Bodleii Equitis Avrati Celebrata in Academiâ Oxoniensi Mensis Martij 29. 1613* (Oxford: Printed by Joseph Barnes, 1613), p. 8;

"Memoria, Illustrissimi Baronis, Domini Iohannis Petrei Mecaenatis mei benignissimi S.," in *Threni Exoniensivm In Obitvm Illvstrissimi Viri D. Iohannis Petrei, Baronis De Writtle, Filij honoratissimi viri D. Gvilielmi Petrei ordinis aure Periscelidis Equitis clarissimi, & quatuor Principibus à consilijs secretioribus. Qui Exoniense Collegium octo Socijs, amplis reditibus, plurimis privilegijs, auxerunt liberaliter & ornârunt, Benefactores, Mecænates, & Patroni munificentissimi. Per ejusdem Collegij Alumnos & ceteros studiosos* (Oxford: Printed by Joseph Barnes, 1613), sig. A3^r;

Untitled poem, in *Epithalamia. Sive Lvsvs Palatini In Nvptias Celsissimi Principis Domini Friderici Comitis Palatini Ad Rhenvm, &c. Et Serenissimæ Elisabethæ Iacobi Potentissimi Britanniæ Regis Filiæ Primogenitæ* (Oxford: Printed by Joseph Barnes, 1613), sig. B2^v;

"In Faelicem Serenissimi Regis nostri Iacobi è Scotia Reditum," in *Iacobi Ara Cev, In Iacobi, Magnæ Britanniæ Franciæ Et Hiberniæ Regis Serenissimi, &c.: Avspicatissimvm Reditvm E Scotia In Angliam, Academiæ Oxoniensis Gratvlatoria* (Oxford: Printed by John Lichfield & William Wrench, 1617), p. 6;

"In obitum Annae Reginae augustissimae, Regis nostri Iacobi coniugis serenissimae" and "Ad Carolum Filium in obitum Matris dilectissimae maestissimum," in *Academiæ Oxoniensis Fvnebria Sacra. Æternæ Memoriæ Serenissimæ Reginæ Annæ Potentissimi Monarchæ Iacobi Magnæ Britanniæ, Franciæ, & Hiberniæ Regis &c. Desideratissimæ Sponsæ, Dicata* (Oxford: Printed by John Lichfield & Jacob Short, 1619), sig. B^{r-v};

Untitled poem, in *Carolvs Redvx* (Oxford: Printed by John Lichfield & Jacob Short, 1623), sig. A2^r;

"Ad Potentissimvm Carolvm Magnae Britanniae, Franciae, & Hiberniae Regem, &c.," in *Epithalamia Oxoniensia. In Avspicatissimvm, Potentissimi Monarchæ Caroli, Magnæ Britanniæ, Franciæ, et Hiberniæ Regis, &c. cum Henretta Maria, æternæ memoriæ Henrici Magni Gallorum Regis Filia, Connubium*, edited by Prideaux? (Oxford: Printed by John Lichfield & William Turner, 1625), sig. §2^{r-v};

"Ad Potentissimvm Carolvm, Magnae Britanniae, Franciae, & Hiberniae Regem, &c.," "In Obitvm Regis Iacobi," and "Conclusio ad Lectorem," in *Oxoniensis Academiae Parentalia Sacratissimæ Memoriæ potentissimi Monarchæ Iacobi, Magnæ Britanniæ, Franciæ & Hiberniæ Regis, Fidei Orthodoxæ defensoris celeberrimi,*

&c. *Dicata,* edited by John Prideaux? (Oxford: Printed by John Lichfield & William Turner, 1625), sig. §3ʳ, §3ᵛ–4ʳ, L2ʳ;

Untitled poem, in *Britanniae Natalis* (Oxford: Printed by John Lichfield, 1630), p. 76;

Untitled poem, in *Solis Britannici Perigæum. Sive Itinerantis Caroli Avspicatissima Periodvs* (Oxford: Printed by John Lichfield & William Turner, 1633), sig. §2ᵛ;

Untitled poem, in *Vitis Carolinæ Gemma Altera Sive Avspicatissima Dvcis Eboracensis Genethliaca Decantata ad Vadaisidis* (Oxford: Printed by John Lichfield & William Turner, 1633), sig. A3ʳ;

Untitled poem, in *Coronae Carolinæ Qvadratvra. Sive Perpetvandi Imperii Carolini Ex Qvarto Pignore Feliciter Svscepto Captatum Augurium* (Oxford: Printed by Leonard Lichfield, 1636), sig. A3ʳ;

"Ad Potentissimvm Carolvm Magnae Britanniae Franciae & Hiberniae Regem, E Scotia Reducem," in *Evcharistica Oxoniensia. In Exoptatissimvm & Avspicatissimvm Caroli Magnæ Britanniæ Franciæ & Hiberniæ &c. Serenissimi & Clementissimi Regis Nostri E. Scotia Reditum Gratulatoria* (Oxford: Printed by Leonard Lichfield, 1641), A2ʳ⁻ᵛ;

Matthias Prideaux, *An Easy and Compendious Introduction For Reading all sorts of Histories: Contrived, In a more facile way than heretofore hath been published, out of the Papers of Mathias Prideaux, Mr of Arts and sometime Fellow of Exeter Colledge in Oxford,* edited by John Prideaux? (Oxford: Printed for Leonard Lichfield, 1648);

Prideaux, *Of the History of Svccessions In States, Countries, Or Families. With A Particular Instance in the Succession of Governments, and Governours, in this our own Country, which may serve for a Directory of Contrivance for other States. According to the Method observed in the two former Tracts,* by Matthias Prideaux, edited by John Prideaux (Oxford: Printed by A. & L. Lichfield, 1648);

Untitled letter to Archbishop Usher, dated 27 August 1628; "Survey of Exeter College"; "Account of John Prideaux, Rector, from the morrow of All Saints 1638 to the same day 1639"; in *Registrum Collegii Exoniensis: Register of the Rectors, Fellows, and Other Members on the Foundation of Exeter College, Oxford, with a History of the College and Illustrative Documents,* by Charles William Boase (Oxford: Clarendon Press for the Oxford Historical Society, 1894), pp. ciii, 311–320, 345–348.

John Prideaux, bishop of Worcester, rector of Exeter College, and vice-chancellor of Oxford University, was the author of several works on rhetoric and logic. He is best known, however, as an educator working within the scholastic tradition of Thomas Aquinas as it was being revitalized in the early to mid seventeenth century. Prideaux can be linked to the theories of the continental logicians Bartholomew Keckermann and Johann-Heinrich Alsted, who charted a course between the ideas of Pierre de La Ramée (known as Petrus Ramus) and scholasticism in an attempt to combat the Ramist tendency towards constructing dichotomies. Prideaux, like Keckermann, attempted to construct a method for reasoning based upon dividing and subdividing a subject into many parts–in Prideaux's case, seven parts–while still remaining distanced from the strict logical boundaries imposed by the Peripatetics (or Aristotelians). Prideaux's motive was, no doubt, to find a compromise between a Puritan logic associated with Ramus and a Catholic one that relied upon the works of Aristotle and Cicero.

Prideaux was a moderate at a time in England's history when Puritans were constantly attacking the theological position of those groups that argued against predestination. He succeeded in protecting the Calvinist, or Puritan, cause in Oxford against the educational reforms of Archbishop William Laud, while still maintaining the favor of the crown. In his lifetime Prideaux published a textbook on grammar and two on logic. His only full-length book on rhetoric, *Sacred Eloquence: Or, the Art of Rhetorick, As it is layd down in Scripture* (1659), was published after his death. During his university and church career, however, Prideaux did arrange to publish twenty sermons, some of which were published as many as four times apiece. In addition, he delivered in 1622 a history of the Sabbath, which later proved to be a contentious document in his 1635–1636 conflict with the theologian and historian Peter Heylyn, also the protégé of Archbishop Laud, on the responsibilities of the church in the spiritual guidance of individuals.

John Prideaux, the fourth of the seven sons of John and Agnes Prideaux, was born at Stowford in the parish of Hartford, near Ivybridge, Devonshire, on 17 September 1578. The family, which also included five daughters, was of modest means. Prideaux first aspired to be parish clerk of the church of Ugborow, having a good hand and a tuneable voice. In competition with another parishioner for the post, however, Prideaux failed to obtain the position. Lady Fowel, the mother of Edmond Fowel, took some compassion on him, told him "not to grieve at the loss, for God might design him for greater things," and subsequently helped to furnish him an Oxford education when he turned eighteen. Later in life Prideaux is reported to have said that "if I could have been clerk of Ugborough, I had never been bishop of Worcester."

On 14 October 1596 Prideaux matriculated at Exeter College, where he studied under the direction of rector and regius professor of divinity at Oxford Thomas

HEPTADES
LOGICAE.
SIVE

MONITA AD AMPLIORES
Tractatus Introductoria.

Pugnus quo compreßior eò ferit fortiùs.

OXONIÆ,
Excudebat LEONARDUS LICHFIELD,
Impenfis Tho. Allam & Eliæ Pearfe.
An. Dom. 1639.

Title page for one of John Prideaux's logic textbooks

Holland and the tutor and subrector William Helme. He was admitted B.A. on 31 January 1600, was elected fellow of Exeter in 1601, and proceeded M.A. on 11 May 1603. He was admitted B.D. on 6 May 1611, and on 4 April 1612 he was elected rector of Exeter College and was permitted to take the degree of doctor of divinity that same year. Prideaux took holy orders in 1603 and became chaplain to Prince Henry, the first son of King James I. After the prince's death in 1612, Prideaux was appointed chaplain to the king; was given the vicarage of Bampton, Oxfordshire, in 1614; and was appointed regius professor of divinity in 1615. He received the canonry of Christ Church in 1616; the vicarage of Chalgrove, Oxfordshire, and a canonry in Salisbury Cathedral in 1620; the rectory of Bladon in 1625; and the rectory of Ewelme, Oxfordshire, in 1629. In 1641 he was consecrated bishop of Worcester.

Prideaux's first wife, Mary, was the granddaughter of Rowland Taylor, a Protestant cleric executed during Queen Mary's reign. With her he had a son, William, later killed in the Battle of Marston Moor. Prideaux's second wife, also named Mary, was the

daughter of Sir Thomas Reynell. By his second wife, he had three children who died young and three who lived to adulthood: Matthias, Sarah, and Elizabeth. Matthias was later the author of *An Easy and Compendious Introduction For Reading all sorts of Histories* (1648), which his father may have cowritten or edited. Matthias's book included his father's *A Synopsis of Councels,* which was published again separately in 1654.

Under the rectorship of Prideaux, Exeter College "flourished more than any house in the university with scholars, as well of great as of mean birth: as also with many foreigners that came purposely to sit at his feet to gain instruction," according to Anthony à Wood. Many distinguished Englishmen and Scotsmen were under Prideaux's care, including the politician and parliamentarian Anthony Ashley Cooper, later the first Earl of Shaftesbury, who described him as just and kindly; Secretary of Scotland Robert Spottiswood; and the politician James Hamilton. Among the Germans, Dutch, Swedes, and Poles under Prideaux's care were the Continental scholastic and metaphysician Johann Combachius, author of a book on metaphysics that was dedicated to Prideaux; the German geographer Philip Cluverius (Philipp Clüver); the Dutch linguist Sixtinus Amama; the philosopher James Casaubon, brother of the French theologian Isaac Casaubon; and the Greek Christoph Angelus, who wrote several treatises on his persecution by the Turks, as well as *An Encomium of the Famous Kingdom of Gr. Britain, and the two flourishing sister-Universities Cambridge and Oxford* (1619). Several of these Continental scholars—especially Combachius, Cluverius, and Amama—came to Exeter for the express purpose of studying with Prideaux. Amama, who taught Hebrew for twelve years in Oxford, speaks well of Prideaux's management in the preface to his edition of *Drusius de Sectis Judaicis* (1619). According to Wood, several Englishmen who were not friends to the Church of England or the state also studied under Prideaux, including John, Lord Robert Earl of Radnor, "a severe predestinarian, and a promoter of the grand rebellion," and Philip, Lord Warton, another promoter of rebellion. Stephen Nettles dedicated his *An Answer to the Jewish Part of Mr. Selden's History of Tithes* (1625) to Prideaux, and the philosopher and geographer Nathaniel Carpenter paid him homage in *Geography delineated forth in two Books; Containing the Spherical and Topical Parts therof* (1625). Isaac Casaubon's letters to Prideaux can be found in *Epistolae Casauboni* (1709).

Prideaux was one of a group of university lecturers and administrators backing the scholastic revival that was part of a broadly European Protestant movement of the early seventeenth century. His first academic textbook, *Tabulæ Ad Grammatica Græca Introductoriæ* (Introductory Tables to Greek Grammar), was published in 1607 and then republished in 1629 with *Tyrocinivm Ad Syllogismvm Legitimum contexendum, & captiosum dissuendum, expeditissimum* (The Easiest Start toward the Constructing of Correct Syllogism and the Unraveling of Sophisms). The 1639 edition adds *Heptades Logicae* (The Sevens of Logic) to *Tabvlæ Ad Grammatica Græca Introdvctoriæ* and *Tyrocinivm Ad Syllogismvm Legitimum contexendum*—three works with separate title pages all bound together. In 1650 Prideaux added to his list of publications on logic *Hypomnemata Logica, Rhetorica, Physica, Metaphysica, Pneumatica, Ethica Politica, Œconomica* (Notes on Logic Rhetoric, Physics, Metaphysics, Pneumatics, Ethics, Politics, and Economics). His texts on logic can be characterized as a compromise between scholasticism and Ramism, with an emphasis on the figure seven as a way of combating the Ramist mode of theorizing in terms of dichotomies. In *Heptades Logicae* Prideaux provides seven terms that denote the processes of intellectualizing, objectifying, stating, reasoning, methodizing, analyzing, and synthesizing. In *Hypomnemata* these concepts are represented by the scholastic-Ramistic terms, respectively, of predicables, predicaments, proposition, syllogism, method, analysis and synthesis, all of which denote not mental operations but the results of such operations.

In his logic, as in his rhetoric, Prideaux showed a preference for the theories of his Continental contemporaries Keckermann and Alsted. In both *Heptades Logicae* and *Hypomnemata* Prideaux devises seven contemporary schools of logic: the Aristotelian, based on the *Organon* of Aristotle and the most secular of the schools; the Lullian, based on the work of the Catalan philosopher Ramon Llull (Raymond Lully) and emphasizing religious mysticism and alchemy; the Ramistic, based on the work of Ramus, who critiqued Aristotle and devised a system of classification based mainly upon dichotomies; the mixt, or systematic, based on the passionate, Continental tradition of Keckermann and Alsted; the forensic, based on the law courts and the writings of Cicero; the Jesuitic, based on the neo-Thomistic beliefs of the Roman Catholic Jesuits; and the Socinian, based on the writings of Italian theologian Faustus Socinus (Fausto Paolo Sozzini), denying the divinity of Christ and the Trinity. Prideaux favored the mixt, or systematic, school. The systematics were said by the English logician Robert Sanderson in his *Logicae Artis Compendium* (Compendium of the Art of Logic, 1631) to chart a middle course between the peripatetics (Aristotelians) and the Ramists. Sanderson criticized the systematics for cutting everything to pieces in their methods of dividing and subdividing subjects. While Prideaux did not position himself as a systematic as described in Sanderson's terms, he showed his intellectual allegiance by dividing his methods into the inventive, synthetic, analytic, topical, dramatic, historical, and cryptic, the first three of which are in keeping with conventional systematic procedures.

Prideaux wrote a handbook for disputations in scholastic metaphysics based on his lectures, *Fasciculus, Controversiarvm Theologicarvm* (A Packet of Theological Disputations, 1649), and was a major influence on the Continental scholastic metaphysician Combachius, who dedicated the Oxford Press edition of his *Metaphysicorum Lib. singularis* (Single Book of Metaphysics, 1613) to his honored friend Prideaux. This scholasticism had a particularly Protestant and Calvinist bent and should not be linked, as it has been by several scholars, with Laudianism (named after Archbishop William Laud), a revival of Roman Catholic ceremony and procedure in the Church of England. While generally Calvinist, this generation of scholastics was socially and politically conservative, creating a social alliance of episcopacy, aristocracy, and scholasticism. While they, like their Puritan allies, had no strong belief in the divine origin of episcopacy, "their political outlook," according to Hugh Kearney, "was different from that of more radical colleagues. Scholasticism provided them with a social and political prop as well as a theological crutch."

Still, in his *Oxford and Cambridge in Transition, 1558–1642* (1959), Mark H. Curtis refers to Prideaux as a Puritan, along with John Rainolds, William Perkins, Samuel Ward, and John Preston. In 1625, when settling a theological disputation between John Davenport, the Puritan founder of the colony of New Haven in Connecticut, and an Arminian of Lincoln College at Oxford, Prideaux consistently maintained the Calvinist position. Despite being the champion of the Puritans, in 1619, during his first year as vice-chancellor of Oxford, Prideaux installed Francis Mansell, the nominee of Lord Pembroke, as principal, against the objections of the college dissidents, a group of Puritans who had previously persecuted Mansell. Earlier, in 1617, Prideaux had a dispute about the supremacy of the Church with Daniel Fairclough, alias Featley, a controversialist and a godson of Rainolds, who had attacked Roman Catholic doctrines and the Jesuits.

In the years 1633 to 1636 Prideaux had the most serious controversy of his career, involving Peter Heylyn. In 1627 Heylyn had chosen to dispute the two questions of the visibility and infallibility of the church: *An ecclesia unquam fuerit invisibilis* (whether the Church is invisible) and *An ecclesia possit errare* (whether the Church is fallible). Heylyn answered both questions negatively and argued, against the thinking of Prideaux, that the visible Church of England came from the Church of Rome and not from the Waldenses, twelfth-century Puritan dissenters from the Roman Catholic Church; the Wycliffites, followers of religious reformer John

Decorated title page for the work in which Prideaux wrote that rhetoric is "The art of speaking ornamentally, or, as Aristotle holds, it is the faculty of seeing whatever aims to be suitable to the creating of belief in any thing"

Wycliffe; and the Hussites, followers of the Bohemian religious reformer and martyr John Huss. Prideaux proceeded to call Heylyn a papist and a Bellarminian—that is, a follower of Robert Bellarmine, a prominent scholastic philosopher. While Heylyn was denounced in Oxford, this situation brought him to the attention of Archbishop Laud and King Charles I, who appointed Heylyn a prebend of Westminster Cathedral in 1631. In 1633, in his disputation for the degree of doctor of divinity, Heylyn again had a controversy with Prideaux about the authority of the church, answering affirmatively the three questions: *An ecclesia habeat authoritatem in determinandis fidei controversiis* (Whether the Church has the authority to determine the matters of faith); *An eccles. habeat authoritatem decernendi ritus & ceremonias* (Whether the Church has the authority to determine matters of ritual and ceremony); and *An eccles. habeat authoritatem interpretandi Scripturas sacras* (Whether the Church has the authority to interpret Scriptures). These

answers conformed verbatim with the twentieth of the Thirty-nine Articles of the Church of England and, according to Wood, "were so displeasing to Prideaux the professor, that he fell into very great heats and passion, in which he let fall certain matters very unworthy of the place where utter'd, as also distastful to many of the auditory . . . which after drew some censure on him." The particulars of Prideaux's statements were these: 1) That the Church is *mera chimera.* 2) That it teacheth and determines nothing. 3) That controversies might better be referred to the universities than to the Church. 4) That learned men in the universities might determine controversies without the Bishops or acquainting them with them.

These arguments were laid before the king by Laud, and Prideaux was forced to make a defense of himself. William Sanderson in his *Peter Pursued* (1658) accused Heylyn of being the informer. In August 1633 Prideaux made another defense of himself before the king and at the same time, according to Wood, caused "a paper to be spread about the court touching the business of the vespers in the last act, very much tending to Heylyn's disgrace." Heylyn, to retaliate against the king and Laud for siding with Prideaux, wrote a treatise concerning lawful sports. Heylyn, for the appeasing of it, was ordered in 1636 by the king to write a "history of the Sabbath" as an answer to the objections raised by the Puritans. At the same time Heylyn translated from the Latin Prideaux's discourse on the subject of the Sabbath, which had been read at Oxford in 1622. Heylyn enjoyed a malicious victory over Prideaux by taking a broader view of the matter than was agreeable to the Puritans, who regarded Prideaux as one of their protectors. Wood writes that the translation "conduced much to his majesty's proceedings in what he had done, and also took off much of that opinion which Prideaux had among the puritans."

The controversy with Heylyn not only demonstrates Prideaux's role as a reconciler of opposing factions but also illuminates the rhetorical strategies that he used in his published writings during his lifetime. Most of his publications in English were sermons he had preached in Oxford or at court. One can assume that his textbook on sacred rhetoric, *Sacred Eloquence: Or, the Art of Rhetorick, As it is layd down in Scripture,* was, like *Hypomnemata,* based on lectures that he might have given to undergraduates and divinity students while at Exeter. In the short treatise on rhetoric that forms part of *Hypomnemata* Prideaux notes that "*Rhetorica* est *Ars ornatè* dicendi. vel ut habet *Arist. Facultas* in *quaq re vivendi,* quid contingit esse *Idoneum* ad faciendam fidem" (Rhetoric is the art of speaking ornamentally, or, as Aristotle holds, it is the faculty of seeing whatever aims to be suitable to the creating of belief in any thing). According to Wilbur Samuel Howell, when writing of tropes, figures, and schemes, Prideaux uses style as a pretext for claiming that language creates belief and trust in truth. As in his sermons, he makes use of biblical writers, early church fathers such as St. Jerome and St. Augustine, and the works of Aristotle and Aquinas. There is no real indication that Prideaux's rhetoric is particularly scholastic in nature–that is, concerned with dialectical argumentation rather than with stylistic ornamentation–beyond the introductory statement in *Sacred eloquence* that "sacred Eloquence is a logicall kind of Rhetorick, to be used in Prayer, Preaching, or Conference, to the glory of God, and the convincing, instructing, and strengthning our brethren." Unlike Aristotle or Cicero, Prideaux does not give an explanation of what rhetoric does in relation to dialectic or demonstration; instead, he simplifies the issue by quoting from scripture that meditation on rhetoric "proved a Hammer to Jeremy, that breaketh the rocks in pieces, chap. 23–29;

was St. Pauls Engine, for the pulling down of strong holds, and casting down imaginations, and every high thing that exalteth it self against the knowledge of God, bringing into captivity every thought to the obedience of Christ, 2 Cor. 10. 4,5." Prideaux seems to follow Ramus and Omer Talon (known as Audemarus Talaeus) in limiting rhetoric primarily to *elocutio* (style), negating the importance of *inventio* (invention) and *dispositio* (judgment or arrangement), as well as *memoria* (memory) and *actio* (delivery).

Prideaux divides the text of *Sacred eloquence* into chapters with the following headings: chapter 2, "Of Tropes"; chapter 3, "Of Figures"; chapter 4, "Of Schemes"; chapter 5, "Of Pateticks"; chapter 6, "Of Characters, Descriptions, or Ideas"; chapter 7, "Of Antithesis"; chapter 8, "Of Parables and Similitudes." In the manner of Ramus, Prideaux breaks these divisions into further subsets. Tropes are divided into hyperbole, catachresis, emphasis, metonymia, ironia, metaphora, synecdoche, types, mysteries, apologies, parables, apothegms, and reproofs. Figures are divided into epizeuxis, anaphora, epistrophe, epanalepsis, epanados, paronomasi, and polyptoton. Schemes are divided into ecphonesis, epanorthosis, apostrophe, prosopopoeia, aporia, anacoinosis, and synchoresis. Pathetics are divided into the motives for love, hatred, hope, fear, joy, sorrow, and zeal. Characters are not divided into subgroups (nor are antitheses and parables) but are added to descriptions, or ideas. The chapter on parables also deals with similitudes, or similes.

In *Sacred Rhetoric: The Christian Grand Style in the English Renaissance* (1988) Debora K. Shuger argues that Prideaux's rhetoric was influenced by the German ecclesiastical rhetorics, beginning with Keckermann's *Rhetoricae ecclesiasticae* (1606) and continuing with Alsted's *Orator, sex libris informatus* (1612), Christian Chemnitz's *Brevis instructio futuri ministri ecclesiae in Academia Jenensi antehac publice praelecta* (1660), Johann Hulsemannus's *Methodus concionandi, auctio edita* (1657), and Georgius Sohnius's *Tractatus de interpretatione ecclesiastica* (1616). While Prideaux does not mention any contemporary sources, Shuger points out that in his preference for passionate eloquence and his desire to rejoin sacred discourse and *elocutio,* he followed the examples set, fittingly, by Catholic and Continental Protestant rhetorics. Certainly, his links with Continental thinkers such as Isaac Casaubon and Combachius, and Wood's contention that he consistently attracted the notice of Protestant scholars from the Continent, demonstrate his sympathy with the traditions of Keckermann, who refused to follow the more rationalistic, plain style endorsed by such contemporaries as the philosopher and latitudinarian John Wilkins. Prideaux was interested in studying the spiritual emotions, including the theological virtues, and in analyzing and imitating, according to Shuger, a "sense of the drama, grandeur, and rhetorical exuberance of Holy Scripture." While *Sacred eloquence* was published in the last years of the Interregnum, Prideaux's language reflects the elaborate, sensual, and passionate baroque sensibility of the first decades of the seventeenth century. For example, he defines *prosopopoeia* as "when the person is not there, but brought in upon the stage speaking as if he were present. So a thing that is mute oft-times, is dressed up in a person, and words put in his mouth," and "sometimes, instead of personating one, divers are represented on the theater."

Prideaux follows Cicero in praising rhetoric's ability to turn or change a word from its genuine signification into another, as happens in the case of tropes. He does not denigrate hyperbole or catachresis, arguing instead that these figures demonstrate the abundance of God on the one hand and the abusive ways of mankind on the other. As Shuger claims, "analogy is rhetorical because rhetorical figures reflect the structures of existence. When Prideaux calls the contrast between Christ and Adam an antithesis, he does not mean that it is only a figurative expression but that rhetorical terminology can be mapped onto spiritual reality." Writing on metonymy, the substitution of one thing for another, as in *"Christ our passeover is sacrificed for us,"* he observes that the thing signified—Passover—"is put for the commemorative and sacrifice, by which it was to be presented. In which metonymicall sense, the words of institution of the Lords Supper must be understood." Such a transfiguration, verbally expressed through metonymy, matches the kind of spiritual transformation that happened historically with the coming of Christ and happens (within the structures of spiritual reality or existence) in the life of any Christian believer. Rhetorical figures of embellishment, substitution, or displacement are not snares of deceit and illusion for the unwary Christian. Rather, these tropes, figures, schemes, and characters organize spiritual space and presence. Prideaux does not use rhetorical analysis, as did the Ramists, to strip the figurative language off the plain, naked meaning of Scripture. Instead, he claims that the terms of rhetorical *elocutio,* such as displacement and the "abuse" of linguistic norms, are constitutive of the Christian landscape, both spiritual and political.

This ability to use biblical tropes as a way of organizing political and social space is amply displayed in Prideaux's sermons. Several of his sermons were published, starting with *Ephesus Backsliding Considered And Applyed To These times* (1614) and two sermons published as *Christs Covnsell For Ending Law Cases* (1615). *Ephesus Backsliding Considered And Applyed To These times* was preached in St. Mary's at Oxford on 10 July 1614. The published text is prefaced by the biblical verse "Will yee also goe away?" (John 6:67) and is dedicated to a Dr. Bodley, canon of Exeter and parson of Showbrook in Devon. It was Prideaux's first work published in English, prepared for printing in August 1614, one month after he delivered the sermon. In the preface he tells his patron that he was overruled by some friends in the decision to print this sermon, which was never intended for such a purpose. Throughout the preface he expresses some modesty about the sermon, claiming that it must speak for itself and hoping only that it, like the lark, flies without danger of the net. Prideaux convinces himself not to look at the spectators but at the mark, which is surely a reference to his intentions and motivations for this sermon, a kind of chastisement to all those who have fallen astray from the Church. He calls upon St. Augustine to explain the relationship of this text to his own life in particular, and historical and social situations in general.

Through a rhetorical use of the qualifier *somewhat,* Prideaux conflates biblical history with contemporary events:

> And is not this a just cause, why as here hee taxeth Ephesus so our Savior in like manner should *bine somewhat against us?* And because wee may presume to expostulate with the Jewes in Malachi, wherein and wherein doe we so much transgresse? Let me thrust into this great harvest a little farther my sickle to remember our naturell dulnesse with a therein and therein. Atheisme and flatterie are eminent in the Court; therein our Savior hath *somewhat against us:* sacrilege grates the Church, symony is forced upon the ministry, therein and therein our Saviour hath *somewhat against us.*

Biblical backsliding is related to the contemporary sort by a kind of linguistic mapping of rhetorical and poetical opposites that link simony with ministry and sacrilege with Church, creating a situation in which God is "somewhat" against the Christians of Prideaux's time. At the end of the sermon Prideaux advises his listeners to use biblical metaphors of the book rather than natural metaphors of the world:

> For the motion of a Christian must not be like that of the planets in their epicylces; now ascending, then descending, sometimes stationary, anone retrograde; but rather as the beasts mentioned by Ezechiel, who passing forward returned not againe, his charity is as the fire upon the Lords altar, alwaies kindled, and never extinguished, his grace not as a standing puddle, that quickly putrifieth, but as the fountaine of living water, John the fourth, that bubleth, and springeth up to everlasting life.

Frontispiece and title page for a posthumously published work by Prideaux

Christs Covnsell For Ending Law Cases is similarly designed. The epigraph is taken from Matthew 5:9–"Blessed are the Peace-makers"–and the two sermons that make up the work are likewise tied to Matthew 5:25: "Agree with thine adversarie quickly, whilst thou art in the way with him: least thine adversarie deliver thee to the Judge, and the Judge deliver thee to the Seargant, and thou be cast into Prison." The argument is founded on the disagreements between St. John Chrysostom on the one hand, who extended the injunction only to civil matters; and St. Cyprian, St. Ambrose, St. Jerome, St. Augustine, and the Schoolmen (medieval scholastic philosophers) on the other, who interpreted the matter parabolically, as a moral lesson about spiritual existence. While both

interpretations are true, Prideaux inclines to the latter and leaves to the schools the debate why both interpretations may stand as valid. Appealing as a final resort to the logic of rhetoric rather than a demonstrative syllogism in the manner of the Schoolmen, he reports that he "take[s] the words to be uttered by a way of a similitude, whose substance, or latter part . . . is here omitted, as easie to be gathered, by the shadow . . . or former part expressed; it being usuall in Scripture, and common talke." The rhetorical logic is interrupted with lyrical quotations from both the Old and New Testaments, from Plutarch, and even from Aquinas, warning readers what will befall them with the neglect of reconciliation, in matters both spiritual and civil.

In these early sermons, as opposed to later ones devoted to moralizing about the theological virtues, Prideaux is interested in a citizen's relationship with civil society and with the edicts of the monarch. In *Gowries Conspiracie* (1621) and *Higgaion & Selah: For the Discovery of the Powder-Plot* (1621) he demonstrates the barbarousness of treason and how, in the case of King David's attempts to deal with enemies, God had a purpose, to make a trial of David's faith and patience. Undoubtedly, these sermons demonstrate Prideaux's emphasis on the individual's faith in God, a product of his Calvinism, but also his conservative bias toward retaining the status quo in matters of civil obligation to the monarch. These traits are even more evident in *Higgaion & Selah,* in which he addresses more overtly the matter of Catholic interference with the rule of a Protestant king. Prideaux does not defend James I from the charge of heresy; he goes only so far as to claim that a monarch suspected of heresy must be left to God's judgment and not be unseated by the injunction of the people.

Prideaux uses biblical metaphors to defend James I from the attacks of his enemies in the sermon on *Hezekiahs Sicknesse and Recoverie* (1621). While the sermon mentions no specific date, or any illness attached to the king, the subtext alludes to such a circumstance and allows Prideaux to reiterate his belief in a rational and orderly theology that links biblical metaphors with natural and physical phenomena. He ends the sermon with a reference to the biblical narrative relating the miracle of the sun standing still for Joshua, an obvious reference to divine intervention in the power of the monarchy. Prideaux criticizes views suggesting that God can, at will, disorder the orbs and "leave the starres to flye like birds in the ayre" and instead argues that the sun kept its course (even for Joshua) and the heavens their order; "but the shadow, contrary to his nature, was miraculously brought backe." He objects to the view that if God did yield the shadow independently of the sun, then "God should be put to create a new light, which should have a motion without a subject, and be brighter than the Sunne, to obscure his shadow, and make his owne apparent." To this argument some had answered that there is no such independence of sun and shadow since sunbeams (cast out from the sun) cast the shadow from any gross body.

The political implications of this debate were not lost on Prideaux. One side argues for the independence of the king's subjects, while the other claims that the king (sun) can keep in his course, and still affect the motions of the subjects (the shadows). Prideaux writes that it is not his place to settle the dispute but nevertheless wants to make use of both

interpretations. The good king, resembling the sun, gives life and influence. His course cannot be stayed except by God's hand, which would thereby leave darkness and horror if he departed. In the second interpretation, "our life is a shadow, every minute moving forward, in the Diall of our time, which none can stop, or set backe, but he that gave Hezekiah a sign." This compromise does not answer the fundamental opposition between the two views regarding the subjects' obligation to and dependence on the sun. In his typical tone of reconciliation, Prideaux advises individuals to use their own manner of "reckoning signes." For him, the signs point to God's favor in providing England with "a most gracious Soveraigne, a flourishing Church, a peaceable Common-Wealth, reward for viertue, punishment for vice. Infinite such signes may be reckoned: but what reformation they worke in us, our own conscience can best informe us."

Except for the controversy with Heylyn and Archibishop Laud, Prideaux in the later years of his career continued to appease the monarch, in this case King Charles I, and move away from his alliance with the Puritans. In 1636 Laud asked Prideaux to correct and amend the manuscript for William Chillingworth's *The Religion of Protestants a Safe Way to Salvation,* which was published in 1638. According to Wood, afterward Prideaux "among his friends, would liken it to an unwholsome lamprey, by having a poysonous sting of Socinianism throughout it, and tending in some places to plain infidelity and atheism." He remained the royal chaplain, no doubt on the basis of his later sermons, such as *The great Prophets Advent, Reverence To Rvlers, The Dravght Of The Brooke, Davids Reioycing For Christs Resurrection, The Christians Expectation, Wisdomes Ivstification, Heresies Progresse, A Plot For Preferment, The Patronage Of Angels,* and *Idolatrovs Feasting,* all published in 1637. For his loyalty to the Crown, Prideaux was elected bishop of Worcester on 22 November 1641 and consecrated on 19 December 1641. He was selected in March 1641 as a miscellaneous theologian to discuss plans for church reform and, in April 1642, was nominated by the commons in Parliament as one of the assembly of 102 divines.

In the late 1640s, when the Stuarts were increasingly attacked by members of Parliament, Prideaux's allegiance to the king and the royalists deprived him of his episcopal estates and forced him into poverty. He sought refuge with his son-in-law, Dr. Henry Sutton, rector of Bredon in Worcestershire. According to Wood, Prideaux "became at length 'verus librorum helluo' [real gormandizer of books] for having first by indefatigable studies

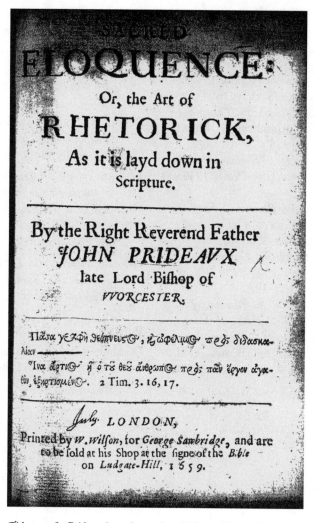

Title page for Prideaux's posthumously published work on pulpit oratory

digested his excellent library into his mind, was after forced again to devour all his books with his teeth; turning them by a miraculous faith and patience into bread for himself and his children, to whom he left no legacy, but pious poverty, God's blessing, and a father's prayers, as it appears in his last will and testament." He died of fever at Sutton's house in Bredon on 29 July 1650 and was buried in the chancel of the church on 15 August; a "great concourse" attended his funeral.

Posthumous publications of Prideaux's works include *Euchologia: Or, The Doctrine of Practical Praying* (1655) and Συνειδησιλογίαοr, *The doctrine of conscience, framed according to the points of the catechisme, in the Book of Common-Prayer* (1656). Perhaps the final and lasting tribute to Prideaux came with a short treatise published in Germany in 1704, *Der gewissenhaffte advocat und procurator* (The Conscientious Advocate and Procurator), which was dedicated to "dem gelehrten Englander Prideaux . . . einen liebhaber der Einigkeit und Friedens" (the learned Englishman Prideaux, a lover of concord and freedom).

Bibliography:

Falconer Madan, *Oxford Books: A Bibliography of Printed Works Relating to the University and City of Oxford, or Printed and Published There,* 3 volumes (Oxford: Clarendon Press, 1895–1931).

Biography:

Anthony à Wood, "John Prideaux," in *Athenae Oxonienses. An Exact History of All the Writers and Bishops Who Have Had Their Education in the University of Oxford. To Which Are Added The Fasti, or Annals of the Said University,* third edition, edited by Philip Bliss, 4 volumes (London: Printed for F. C. & J. Rivington, 1813–1820; reprint edition, New York: Johnson Reprint, 1967), III: cols. 265–273.

References:

Charles William Boase, *Registrum Collegii Exoniensis: Register of the Rectors, Fellows, and Other Members of the Foundation of Exeter College, Oxford, with a History of the College and illustrative Documents* (Oxford: Clarendon Press/Oxford Historical Society, 1894);

William T. Costello, *The Scholastic Curriculum at Early Seventeenth-Century Cambridge* (Cambridge, Mass.: Harvard University Press, 1958);

Mark H. Curtis, *Oxford and Cambridge in Transition, 1558–1642* (Oxford: Oxford University Press, 1959), pp. 174, 189, 208, 225;

Wilbur Samuel Howell, *Logic and Rhetoric in England, 1500–1700* (Princeton: Princeton University Press, 1956), pp. 311–316, 333–335, 376;

Hugh Kearney, *Scholars and Gentlemen: Universities and Society in Pre-Industrial Britain 1500–1700* (Ithaca, N.Y.: Cornell University Press, 1970);

William Laud, *The Second Volume of the Remains of the Most Reverend Father in God, and Blessed Martyr, William Laud, Lord Arch-Bishop of Canterbury* (London: Printed for Sam. Keble, Dan. Brown, Will. Hensman, Matt. Wotton & R. Knaplock, 1700), pp. 63–66;

Mark Pattison, *Isaac Casaubon, 1559–1614,* second edition (Oxford: Clarendon Press, 1892), pp. 22, 56, 295, 365–366, 368, 393–394;

William Sanderson, *Peter Pursued, or Dr. Heylin Overtaken, Arrested, and Arraigned* (London: Tho. Leach, 1658);

Debora K. Shuger, *Sacred Rhetoric: The Christian Grand Style in the English Renaissance* (Princeton: Princeton University Press, 1988), pp. 89, 96–98, 213;

William Twisse, *Of the Morality of the fourth commandement, as still in force to binde Christians, Delivered by way of Answer to the translator of Doctor Prideaux his Lecture, concerning the doctrine of the sabbath* (London: E. G. for John Rothwell, 1641);

Nicholas Tyacke, ed., *The History of the University of Oxford, Volume IV: Seventeenth-Century Oxford* (Oxford: Clarendon Press, 1997).

Papers:

Documents by or relating to John Prideaux can be found in the Bodleian Library, Oxford, and the British Library.

Richard Rainolde

(circa 1530 – December 1606)

Grant Williams
Nipissing University

See also the Rainolde entry in *DLB 136: Sixteenth-Century British Nondramatic Writers, Second Series*.

BOOKS: *A booke called the Foundacion of Rhetorike, because all other partes of Rhetorike are grounded thereupon, euery parte sette forthe in an Oracion vpon questions, verie profitable to bee knowen and redde; Made by Richard Rainolde Maister of Arte, of the Uniuersitie of Cambridge* (London: Printed by John Kingston, 1563);

A Chronicle of all the noble Emperours of the Romaines, from Iulius Caesar, orderly to this moste victorious Emperour Maximilian, that now Gouerneth, with the great warres of Iulius Caesar, & Pompeius Magnus: Setting forth the great power, and deuine prouidence of almighty God, in preseruing the godly Princes and common wealthes (London: Printed by Thomas Marshe, 1571).

Editions: *The Foundacion of Rhetorike,* edited, with an introduction, by Francis R. Johnson (New York: Scholars' Facsimiles & Reprints, 1945);

The Foundacion of Rhetorike, The English Experience, no. 91 (Amsterdam: Theatrum Orbis Terrarum / New York: Da Capo, 1969);

The Foundation of Rhetoric, 1563, English Linguistics 1500–1800, no. 347 (Menston, U.K.: Scolar, 1972).

Richard Rainolde's recognized contribution to rhetoric is his treatise *A booke called the Foundacion of Rhetorike, because all other partes of Rhetorike are grounded thereupon* (1563), the first English handbook to teach composition through formulaic speech genres. The treatise, whose explanations basically conform to a contemporaneous Latin translation of Aphthonius's Greek *Progymnasmata,* provides valuable insight into the ways in which Tudor writers adapted the richness of classical oratory to the exigencies of English culture. It especially provides insight into the role rhetoric played in fashioning the English courtier, in guiding the English poet, and in constructing the English commonwealth.

Little biographical information on Richard Rainolde (also known as Reynolds in the Short Title Catalogue and the Library of Congress catalogue) is extant. He was born in Essex County, probably around 1530, but his exact birth date and birthplace are not known. Records from his days at Cambridge University are relatively more helpful. On 10 November 1546 he was admitted sizar of St. John's College for William Bill, who later became dean of Westminister. Rainolde's entrance status gives a good indication of his lower social station, for an undergraduate member of Cambridge admitted under the designation *sizar* performed duties later held by college servants and, in turn, received from the college an allowance to help finance his studies. A year later Rainolde progressed to a scholar on the Lady Mary foundation and in 1548 transferred to the recently formed (in 1546) Trinity College.

Rainolde's praise in the preface to *The Foundacion of Rhetorike* for Thomas Wilson's *The Art of Rhetoric* (1553) may have arisen from esprit de corps, since both rhetoricians attended Cambridge at the same time. Wilson obtained from King's College his B.A. in 1546 and his M.A. in 1549, while Rainolde obtained from Trinity his B.A. in 1550 and his M.A. in 1553. Both rhetoricians studied during a transitional phase in the history of Cambridge, when the humanist curriculum was weakening the dominance of scholasticism in education. The Royal Injunctions of 1535 prescribed works by reformers of logic and rhetoric, such as Roelof Huysman (known as Rodolphus Agricola) and Philipp Melanchthon, to replace the convoluted glosses and pedantic quibblings of John Duns Scotus and other schoolmen. In 1549 Rainolde saw the institution of new statutes, which, altering the government of the university and the program of learning, further entrenched humanism. For example, the new second-year arts course was to cover dialectic and rhetoric, not traditional logic, and drew upon the texts of Aristotle, Cicero, Quintilian, and Hermogenes. During his studies Rainolde would have been exposed to strong currents of religious reform as well, in particular zealous and inspiring advocates for Continental Protestantism;

so influential was Martin Bucer, an eminent Protestant from Strasbourg—who taught at Cambridge from 1549 until his death in 1551—that three thousand people attended his funeral. The lack of records on Rainolde's activity during the reign of Queen Mary I (1553–1558) may attest to a prudent withdrawal from public life, since several Cambridge-educated Protestants were executed by the Catholic monarchy and many others went into exile.

Rainolde's most critically significant work is *The Foundacion of Rhetorike,* which is an adaptation of Reinhard Lorich's 1542 Latin edition of the fourth-century *Progymnasmata* by Aphthonius of Antioch. The progymnasmata constitute a consequential branch of classical rhetoric not as well known as the five canons (invention, arrangement, style, memory, and delivery) or the three modes of persuasion (ethos, pathos, and logos) and, as such, require explanation in order to impart a sense of Rainolde's contribution to English rhetoric.

Meaning "preliminary exercises," the progymnasmata comprise a type of schoolbook, which prepared young students for the composition and performance of complete practice orations, called gymnasmata or declamations. Even though earlier, more prominent classical rhetoricians, such as Cicero and the author of *Rhetorica ad Alexandrum* (Rhetoric for Alexander), refer to these exercises, the four earliest surviving textbooks of progymnasmata come from the first four centuries A.D.: those of Theon (first century), Hermogenes (second century), Aphthonius, and Nicolaus (fourth century). Out of the four, Aphthonius's textbook of composition exerted the greatest influence in Byzantine education.

During the fifteenth century Agricola translated Aphthonius's textbook into Latin, and it soon became widely used throughout Western European schools. Aphthonius's popularity in antiquity and in the Renaissance—which produced many versions and translations of his text—stems no doubt from the full examples he includes with the exercises. He also lays out the exercises in a straightforward fashion, making the textbook accessible to young schoolboys. Each exercise in the *Progymnasmata* observes the same standard format. First, Aphthonius provides a definition of the exercise; for example, narrative is an exposition of a real or an imagined action. Second, he divides the exercise into its component parts; for example, there are three types of narrative: dramatic or fictitious, historical, and political. And third, he gives a complete example of the exercise; for a fictitious narrative, he relates the story of how the rose got its red color. While explaining an exercise, he may also raise issues of style; for example, narrative should exhibit the four virtues: clarity, brevity, persuasiveness, and purity of language.

His textbook runs through fourteen compositional exercises, which Rainolde follows closely. The first two are exercises based on composing stories: *fable* instructs the student to paraphrase or produce a parable-like story after the model of Aesop, and *narrative* instructs the student to retell an action taken from poetry or history. The second two exercises are expository in nature: *chreia* (memorable advice) and *gnome* (proverb or maxim) teach the student to expand a saying by praise, paraphrase, statement of cause, contrast, comparison, example, testimony, and conclusion. The chief difference between chreia and gnome is that the latter does not have a known author. *Refutation* and *confirmation,* the fifth and sixth exercises, develop argumentative ability through examining a myth. For both examples, Aphthonius uses the myth of Apollo and Daphne and demonstrates whether or not the story is credible according to six criteria: clarity, probability, possibility, logic, suitability, and expedience. The seventh exercise is *commonplace,* a composition that amplifies either inherent evils or inherent virtues, usually devoting itself to the former. Commonplace prepares the student for the next two exercises and differs from them by dealing with a general virtue or vice, such as tyranny. Thus, the eighth and ninth exercises, *encomium* and *vituperation,* teach how to praise a particular person or thing for inherent virtues and to dispraise a particular person or thing for inherent evils. Both exercises are closer to a complete speech than to commonplace, which does not have an introduction. *Comparison,* the tenth exercise, builds on the previous pair, setting its subject beside something that is greater or equal to it. For the most part, comparison is either a double encomium or an encomium combined with a vituperation. The eleventh exercise is *impersonation* (personification), which teaches the student how to imitate through monologue the character of a person, who might be real or imagined, dead or living. As an example, Aphthonius refers to the words Hercules might have said to his enemy Eurystheus, who charged him with twelve labors. If the eleventh exercise invents the speech of a person, the twelfth, *ekphrasis* (description), brings a subject to vivid pictorial life. Aphthonius illustrates this exercise with a description of the Acropolis at Alexandria.

The last two exercises involve more challenging compositions that move into the realm of complete speeches. *Thesis* is an exercise preparatory for deliberative oratory—speechmaking to the legislative assembly—and is the first exercise in the handbook to expect the student to consider both sides of a question. As an example, Aphthonius argues whether one should marry or not. The last exercise, *law,* trains the student in taking a pro or con position against a specific legislation, typically from ancient times. Halfway between thesis and declamation, between progymnasmata and gymnasmata, law prepares the student for further studies in rhetoric, coming closest to an authentic deliberative speech.

These fourteen exercises function as a pedagogical sequence, proceeding from the simple to the complex. Beginning with narrative, the progymnasmata move through expository, argumentative, encomiastic, and descriptive techniques toward the sophistication of a practice oration. Each exercise builds on the skills that the student learned in the previous one and thus gives him a sense of development and accomplishment. The exercises also fall into convenient clusters reinforcing the sense of deliberate development; just as narrative and fable make a logical couple, the other progymnasmata come in pairs, with the possible exception of the commonplace and comparison, which seem to be derivatives of encomium and vituperation.

Although Aphthonius avoids explaining the theoretical rationale behind his *Progymnasmata,* other contemporaneous writers firmly situate the preliminary exercises within a comprehensive view of rhetoric. In the preface to his *Progymnasmata,* Nicolaus elucidates the relations between the exercises and higher rhetorical forms. The exercises serve the more complicated activity of making a speech. In a political oration, for instance, one of the five parts—proemium, narration, antithesis, rebuttal, and epilogue—may easily incorporate a fable, an ekphrasis, or a comparison, because each of the exercises shares goals with at least one of the five parts. Nicolaus also claims that each exercise may fit under one or more of the three main types of rhetorical discourse—forensic, deliberative, and panegyric. Byzantine commentators specifically divided the progymnasmata thusly: fable, chreia, and gnome belonged to deliberative rhetoric; refutation, confirmation, law, and commonplace belonged to forensic; and encomium, vituperation, comparison, and impersonation belonged to panegyric. Narrative, thesis, and ekphrasis were the three exercises that could be included under more than one type.

As an adaptation of Lorich's edition of Aphthonius, *The Foundacion of Rhetorike* maintains the definition and division of each exercise and their overall sequence. Rainolde translates the fourteen exercises as *fable, narration, chreia, sentence, confutation or destruction, confirmation, commonplace, praise, dispraise, comparison, ethopoeia, description, thesis,* and *legislatio.* However, whereas Lorich's work provides a close Latin translation of each exercise with detailed commentary, Rainolde does not follow the Latin translation of Aphthonius rigorously but interweaves explanatory material from Lorich with his own observations. Furthermore, even though he employs for many of the exercises models mentioned

Title page for Richard Rainolde's most important work, an adaptation of Reinhard Lorich's 1542 Latin edition of the fourth-century Progymnasmata *by Aphthonius*

by Aphthonius and Lorich, he composes his own examples for fable, sentence, confutation, confirmation, commonplace, praise, dispraise, and description, as well as examples for narration historical and narration judicial. Through these illustrative orations he reveals his own application of the progymnasmata.

The manner in which Rainolde amplifies each exercise into an oration, generally fuller than any of those in Aphthonius's text, suggests that he fuses the progymnasmata with a Renaissance development in classical rhetoric, the principle of *copia* (discursive amplication). Popularized by Desiderius Erasmus's treatise *De duplici copia rerum ac verborum commentarii duo* (Two Commentaries on the Abundance of Both Things and Words, 1512), copia covers an entire program of compositional techniques for showing students how to produce abundant discourse. This term, etymologically linked to the horn of plenty, emphasizes the principle that effective discourse includes a generative feature continuously appetizing and nourishing to the reader. Erasmus's revision of classical rhetoric in terms of copia was not only a force behind sixteenth-century literature, but also a major influence in humanist education. Rain-olde would have experienced such an influence through Lorich's commentary and would have also been exposed to Erasmus's legacy at Cambridge, where Erasmus had been the first teacher of Greek. More sig-nificantly, throughout the sixteenth century, two of the most widely used textbooks in English grammar curric-ula were Lorich's Latin translation of Aphthonius's *Pro-gymnasmata* and *De duplici copia rerum et verborum,* which Erasmus originally wrote for John Colet's newly founded St. Paul's School in England.

In addition to his pervasive fondness for using "copiousness" and its analogues–"dilation," "abun-dance," and "plenty"–Rainolde's first extended defi-nition of rhetoric registers his dependence on Erasmian copia:

> Rhetorick in most ample and large maner, dilateth and setteth out small thynges or woordes, in soche sorte, with soche aboundaunce and plentuousnes, bothe of woordes and wittie inuencion, with soche goodlie dis-posicion, in soche a infinite sorte, with soche pleasaunt-nes of Oracion, that the moste estonie and hard hartes, can not but bee incensed, inflamed, and moued thereto.

Similarly, Erasmus underscores the importance of variety in speaking and writing. Because the mind, like nature, delights in discovering new things, the bland repetition of form or content will produce bore-dom and ruin the speech. In practice, then, Rainolde appears to regard these fourteen exercises as means of amplifying one's discourse. For instance, Rainolde uses an eight-part formula for dilating the exercise of fable into an exercise for composing a full-fledged speech, whereas Aphthonius only provides an exam-ple of a fable. In other words, Rainolde composes an oration by fable, using it as a moral or theme for amplification. Unlike Erasmus, who remains at the level of figure and argument, Rainolde raises copia to the level of the complete speech.

By transforming "preliminary" exercises into exercises for composing full-fledged speeches, Rainolde departs from the pedagogy underlying the progymnas-mata tradition. Despite acknowledging the introductory nature of the exercises, Rainolde repeatedly refers to them as "orations": "Of every one of these [exercises], a goodlie oration maie be made." In contrast, classical progymnasmata preceded the writing of sample speeches or gymnasmata. Nicolaus's *Progymnasmata* is clear about the place that the exercises occupy in the curriculum: they encourage the student to practice the parts and types of rhetoric singly, not all at once. Since, according to Theon, they are the foundation of every idea of speech, the student needs time to strengthen these basic compositional skills before graduating to more complex rhetorical forms. As with the five-part process for composing the classical speech, progymnas-mata take an incremental approach to teaching compo-sition. Tudor, as well as Byzantine, education observes this design, for statutes from several Elizabethan gram-mar schools stipulate Aphthonius as an authority. Thus, Rainolde's desire to portray the exercises as pro-ducing actual orations indicates a new educational pur-pose for the progymnasmata, one less concerned with elementary pedagogy.

In fact, there is no reason to believe that Rain-olde's text was either used in grammar schools or even intended for grammar schools. It appears to have been written for the fashioning of the courtier, not the train-ing of the schoolboy. Rainolde dedicated his book to Robert Dudley, first Earl of Leicester, favorite of Eliza-beth and the most prominent literary patron of the age. Notwithstanding the attempt to reap material gains for his labors, Rainolde's dedication to Leicester orients the progymnasmata toward the competitive, unpredictable world of the court. Rainolde regards eloquence as enabling a courtier

> to drawe unto theim the hartes of a multitude, to plucke doune and extirpate affeccions and perturba-cions of people, to moue pitee and compassion, to speake before Princes and rulers, and to perswade theim in good causes and enterprises, to animate and incense them, to godlie affaires and busines, to alter the counsaill of kynges, by their wisdome and eloquence, to a better state. . . .

In its capacity to prepare the noble for situations that demand courtly eloquence, *The Foundacion of Rhetorike* may be associated with the Renaissance discourse of self-fashioning, whose most celebrated representative is Baldasarre Castiglione's *Il Cortegiano* (The Courtier, 1528). The progymnasmata equip a counselor like Leicester–who had earned a place in the Privy Council in 1559–with strategies necessary for copiously dilating material into a ready, winsome oration. Whether or not Rainolde received any patronage from Leicester is not known, but Rainolde's second publication is dedicated to William Cecil, first Baron Burghley, Elizabeth's chief minister, sober adviser, and one of Leicester's rivals.

The Foundacion of Rhetorike may have influenced the Tudor practice of everyday rhetoric in another, no less significant, way. Rainolde's translation furnished writers with rhetorical strategies for amplification, since English literature shows signs of having woven progymnasmata into the warp and woof of their nar-ratives. This textual phenomenon is consistent with ancient theory and practice. Theon argues in the pref-ace of his textbook that training in exercises is "a necessity not only for those who are likely to speak in public but also if someone wishes to pursue the craft of poets or writers of history or any other discourse." In addition to their immediate influence on the teaching of rhetoric, the classical progymnasmata had long-term effects on literate culture. Not only did Greek sophistry under the Roman Empire employ progymnasmata, but also the composition of Latin literature bears the mark of these exercises. Ovid's *Heroides* are personifications written in verse, while his *Metamorphoses* depends on several progymnasmatic forms as structural units, including fable, narrative, and ekphrasis. When comparing Greeks and Romans in his *Lives of the Noble Grecians and Romans,* Plutarch exploits another common exercise, the comparison. Tudor poetry is no less informed by progymnasmata. In William Shakespeare's *The Rape of Lucrece* (1594), the detailed description of the painting that depicts the fall of Troy superbly illustrates ekphrasis; the lengthy monologues of Tarquin and Lucrece exemplify impersonation; and Lucrece's exposition of Tarquin's evil resembles vituperation. In Christopher Marlowe's *Hero and Leander* (1598), Venus's glass—that is, the graphic floor of her temple—receives ekphrastic treatment; Leander's attack on virginity resembles the exercise of thesis; and the long digression, which explains why the Destinies no longer love Cupid, is clearly a narrative. The debt Tudor poetry owes to Rainolde and the progymnasmata tradition may be also gleaned from Herbert David Rix's analysis of the February eclogue in Edmund Spenser's *The Shepheardes Calender Conteyning tvvelve Æglogues proportionable to the twelve monethes* (1579). Drawing upon *The Foundacion of Rhetorike* as his model, Rix demonstrates how Spenser closely follows several of the parts comprising an oration based on a fable. Rix further exclaims that in the eclogues "nearly all of the devices treated by Rainolde are to be found." Rainolde's translation unquestionably enables modern readers to appreciate the extent to which progymnasmata perform prominent roles in structuring English poetry, especially narrative verse and longer declamatory lyrics.

Contemporary critical reception of *The Foundacion of Rhetorike* was limited, probably in part because the book was not reprinted. It did not enjoy the popularity of Wilson's *The Art of Rhetoric,* which in 1563 was reprinted for the fourth time by John Kingston, the publisher of Rainolde's text. The most complimentary response to *The Foundacion of Rhetorike* occurs in William Fullwood's manual on the forms and conventions of letter writing. In *The Enimie of Idlenesse: Teaching the maner and stile how to endite, compose and write all sorts of Epistles and Letters: as well by answer, as otherwise* (1568). Fullwood mentions Rainolde alongside Wilson, when considering the kinds of "matter" one can write about—whether the

matter be just, doubtful, slanderous, or obscure. Not going into any detail on this topic, Fullwood directs readers to two authorities: "Who will more circumspectly & narrowly intreat of such matters, let them reade Maister Wilsons Rhetorike, or Maisters Raynoldes." The gesture seems to imply that both books are on a level playing field. A second mention occurs in John Jones's *Art and Science Preserving Body and Soul in Health, Wisdom, and Catholic Religion* (1579), which approvingly acknowledges Rainolde's argument on the parts of the body being "the pattern of all laws, regiment, and unity."

Another, more meaningful, reference to Rainolde's text may occur in John Brinsley's *Ludus Literarius; or The Grammar Schoole* (1612), an educational treatise cast in the form of a dialogue. In chapter 13, called "Of making Theames full of good matter, in a pure stile and with judgement," Philoponus, one of two schoolmasters in this dialogue, states, "I have heard of some good ensamples in English, viz. Thirteen Declamations; but I have not been able to finde them out," admitting that such declamations are less appropriate for grammar school than for university. If Philoponus indeed refers to Rainolde's text—as William Phillips Sandford contends—then a contemporary account corroborates the notion that Rainolde made the progymnasmata available not to elementary pedagogy, but to advanced studies in preparation for the court.

Twentieth-century responses to *The Foundacion of Rhetorike* were more sustained and more involved than were Elizabethan responses. Scholars of rhetoric have long recognized Rainolde's contribution to Tudor education. Warren Taylor situates *The Foundacion of Rhetorike* in the Roman school of *declamatio* and regards it as both a sign of the influence of Hermogenes in the universities and a companion to Alexandre van den Busche's book of model orations, *Epitomes de cent histoires tragiques* (Epitomes of A Hundred Tragic Histories, 1581), translated by Anthony Munday (alias L.P.) as *The orator: handling a hundred seuerall discourses, in forme of declamations: some of the arguments being drawne from Titus Liuius and other ancient vvriters, the rest of the authors owne inuentions: part of which are of matters happened in our age* (1596). William G. Crane discusses Rainolde in his chapter on rhetoric in sixteenth-century schools, significantly noting that Rainolde's prefatory remarks on natural gifts is a common practice in Renaissance rhetorical treatises. Thomas O. Sloane, in his *On the Contrary: The Protocol of Traditional Rhetoric* (1997), regards *The Foundacion of Rhetorike* as an "important textbook," relating it to elementary training in arguing on both sides of a question.

Generally speaking, literary critics have been slower to give *The Foundacion of Rhetorike* its due. Literary criticism steeped in romantic beliefs about creativ-

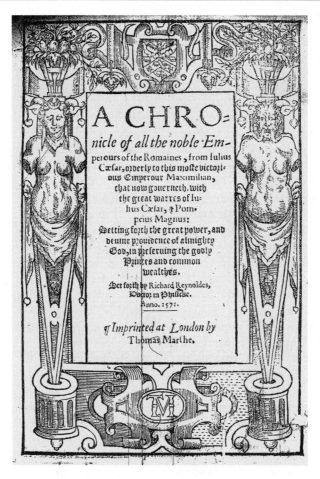

Title page for Rainolde's history of Roman emperors, in which he draws parallels between Roman and English history

ity is dismissive of formulaic rhetoric and appears to be equally dismissive of *The Foundacion of Rhetorike;* for instance, C. S. Lewis grudgingly concedes that one can learn something about Elizabethan methods of composition from this "foolish book" of "specimen orations." However, the turn to rhetoric in English studies since the early 1980s has facilitated a scholarly climate that is not dismissive of the seemingly prescriptive nature of composition manuals. Critics appreciate *The Foundacion of Rhetorike* for the valuable insights it affords into English literature and culture. Insights into the relationship between literature and rhetoric may be as basic as that of Annabel Patterson and Ann Coiro in *The Spenser Encyclopedia* (1997), who acknowledge Spenser's debt to Rainolde for the eight-point amplification of the fable in the February eclogue—an acknowledgment no doubt derived from Rix's earlier work; or insights into the relationship between literature and rhetoric may be as theoretically rich as that of Marion Trousdale in *Shakespeare and the Rhetoricians* (1982). Trousdale's introductory chapter focuses on

Rainolde's text to illustrate the concept of transformational language. Arguing for and against the veracity of the Trojan War, Rainolde's exercises of confirmation and destruction constitute an ideal illustration of the way in which verbal models act as a grammar for generating further literary texts; in other words, any verbal structure has the capacity to be reordered by another verbal structure, such as one of the progymnasmata. In Trousdale's text *The Foundacion of Rhetorike* thus becomes a powerful instrument for understanding the rhetorical mode of Shakespeare's works. Finally, supplying a cultural context quite different from those articulated by Rainolde's other commentators, Wayne A. Rebhorn may be said to implement a New Historical approach to Rainolde's text. Rebhorn weaves passages from *The Foundacion of Rhetorike* into many discussions on the discourse of Renaissance rhetoric and develops persuasive arguments on Rainolde's resistance to tyranny and ambiguity toward social mobility. Undoubtedly, Trousdale and Rebhorn take Rainolde's text to an innovative critical plane.

There have been two noteworthy critiques of Rainolde's text. First, Sandford, in his *English Theories of Public Address, 1530–1828* (1931), accuses Rainolde of allowing the "degenerate rhetoric of the Second Sophistic" to pass into English. According to Sandford, the Second Sophistic, that is, the renaissance of Greek writing in the second century A.D., emphasizes an invention that is overly reliant upon stock models and far inferior to Aristotle's invention. Sandford argues that by unnecessarily resurrecting progymnasmata Rainolde's text corrupts the English tongue. This critique, however, seems to be directed more against Aphthonius than against Rainolde. The second critique comes from Francis R. Johnson, editor of the 1945 facsimile reprint of *The Foundacion of Rhetorike*. Despite recognizing Rainolde's value for shedding light on contemporary literary composition, Johnson disputes his ability to amplify meaningful discourse, accusing him of the vice of padding: "an unhappy profusion of words and matter lacking in real weight and relevance."

However, what Johnson regards as an unhappy profusion of words and matter is perhaps the most fascinating element of Rainolde's modest achievement. Whereas the theoretical explication of the exercises predictably conforms to Aphthonius, Rainolde's orations betray a more individual stamp on his subject. His examples should not be dismissed as failing to put into practice a copious style; they, rather significantly, provide a commentary on the social and political function of rhetoric. In his prefatory remarks Rainolde makes this point clear. He tells the reader that he has employed his diligence to profit many, not with "Eloquence beutified and adorned" but "as the matter requireth." Rainolde may have inherited his reluctance to embrace style from Cambridge, where John Cheke and Roger Ascham were outspoken and influential opponents against florid writing. Instead, Rainolde's orations are more concerned with presenting virtuous precepts and famous histories, because, as he says in his dedication, his end is to "plante a worke profitable to all tymes, my countrie and common wealthe"; and so his orations are less models of style than arguments for the civil importance of eloquence, "by the which the florishyng state of commonweales doe consiste: kyngdomes uniuersally are gouerned, the state of euery one priuatlie is maintained." Hence, the building metaphor in his title may refer to the establishment of a firm civil infrastructure, despite also meaning the preliminary nature of the exercises.

Adapting progymnasmata to politics, *The Foundacion of Rhetorike* belongs to an era when England, instituting its own church and declaring itself an empire, developed into a modern sovereign state. During this time, writers of all kinds were actively exploring representations of nationhood. As a vernacular project, then, Rainolde's text does not merely perform the literary service of making a classical work accessible to English readers; it more significantly can be said to win new linguistic and intellectual ground for England. Along with Henry Howard, Earl of Surrey's 1557 translation of books 2 and 4 of Virgil's *Aeneid,* Thomas Hoby's 1563 translation of Castiglione's *The Courtier,* and Arthur Golding's 1565 translation of Ovid's *Metamorphoses,* Rainolde's text colonizes the past on behalf of present-day England. Indeed, the formation of national identity is an activity that also characterizes Rainolde's second major book, uniting these two seemingly different texts under a common purpose.

A Chronicle of all the noble Emperours of the Romaines (1571) traces in chronological order the reigns of the Roman emperors, starting with Julius Caesar. This chronicle, which, according to G. K. Hunter, is partly a translation of Pedro Mexia's *Historia Imperial y Caesarea* (History of the Emperors and Caesars, 1545), does not confine itself to the classical world but continues all the way through the reign of Ferdinand I, Holy Roman Emperor (1556–1564). Rainolde voices his esteem for the genre of the chronicle as early as *The Foundacion of Rhetorike,* where, under confirmation, he praises such histories and monuments for providing readers with edifying witnesses of kingdoms and commonwealths: they are schoolmasters, teaching readers to emulate virtuous princes and governors and to avoid the vices that lead commonwealths toward destruction. In *A Chronicle of all the noble Emperours of the Romaines* Rainolde redoubles his praise for the profitability a courtier will receive from reading history. He expounds on example after example of great princes who learned from history. Scipio Africanus, Octavius Augustus, Alexander the Great, and others made history in part because they were readers of history. They were great princes because they were great readers of chronicles. Rainolde's rhetorical self-consciousness recalls *The Foundacion of Rhetorike,* in which his orations often comment upon the power of oratory while serving as illustrations for the exercises.

Rainolde fulfills the larger designs of his genre chiefly through the rhetoric of exemplarity. "The Chronicle," writes Richard Helgerson, "was the Ur-genre of national self-representation. More than any other discursive form, the chronicle gave Tudor Englishmen a sense of their national identity." Although Rainolde records the succession of Roman emperors, he expects his contemporary reader to use the history as a glass, or mirror, for fashioning English images. Rainolde makes this goal clear when he periodically draws explicit comparisons between Rome and England; for instance, the military prowess of Henry V,

King of England, becomes a parallel for that of Galba Servius Sulpicius (Roman emperor, 68–69), and later on his rectitude becomes a parallel for that of Alexander Severus (Roman emperor, 222–235). Through its various reflections of Rome, England acquires the status of empire.

Rainolde's commitment to the body politic—as manifested in *The Foundacion of Rhetorike* by medical tropes such as amputating body parts and purging humors—anticipates his own curious, at times perplexing, involvement in medicine. Some confusion exists as to whether or not he studied medicine. Edmund Carter, in his *The History of the University of Cambridge* (1753), and Thomas Warton, in his *History of English Poetry* (1774–1781), both of whom consulted university records, attribute a medical degree to Rainolde. And Rainolde seems to have in fact embarked upon such a field of study: in 1567 he went so far as to receive from Cambridge *grace,* that is, a dispensation from some of the statuatory conditions required for the M.D., and, in expectation of possessing the degree, even identified himself as "Doctor in Physic" in *A Chronicle of all the noble Emperours of the Romaines,* which was entered in the Stationers' Register between June 1566 and July 1567. However, the *Dictionary of National Biography,* in addition to other sources, claims he never finished his medical studies. In 1571 the Royal College of Physicians of London forbade him to practice. The biographical confusion over Rainolde's degree results from a special provision granted him by Cambridge. The university seems to have accelerated his admission to the medical faculty in order to facilitate his acceptance at the court of Muscovy (Moscow). As soon as he received admission in 1567, he did not proceed with his education but traveled to Russia, where he entered the service of Tsar Ivan IV. Thus, by admitting him to the medical program, the university was able to supply him with testimonial letters vouching for his credentials.

But a greater biographical question remains: why would Rainolde travel to Russia to perform the duties of a physician in the first place? Rainolde was definitely following in the footsteps of another Trinity fellow, Ralph Standish, whom he most likely knew during his earlier studies. In 1557 Standish became the first English physician to serve a Russian tsar, Ivan III, and a decade later he may have requested a trusted English assistant. Before traveling to Russia, Standish had received a special license from the college of physicians to practice medicine for one year only, so he too was not a fully qualified doctor.

Another explanation for Rainolde's medical mission to Russia may have some connection to his lesser-known publication, whose title remains lost. In 1566 Henry Denham printed an almanac and prog-

nostication, a definite departure from Rainolde's two other scholarly ventures. Such almanacs were chiefly written for students and physicians, providing celestial data important for humoral diagnosis. Perhaps the time spent on the almanac fostered in Rainolde a passion for medicine or captured the confidence of the faculty who gave him *grace.* Whatever the case, no copy of this book is extant. Besides the personal motivations, there may have been a political incentive for Rainolde's trip. By traveling to Russia, Rainolde may have performed a service for Queen Elizabeth I. Since the formation of the Muscovy Company in 1555, trade relations with Russian had been an ongoing concern for the Tudor monarchy. In 1581 Elizabeth even gave Ivan IV her own physician, Robert Jacob—another Trinity fellow—when the tsar requested an expert doctor. So when on 7 August 1568 Elizabeth presented Rainolde with the rectory of Stapleford-Abbots, Essex, she may have been rewarding him for services rendered in what most Englishman regarded as a "rude and barbarous kingdom."

On 24 May 1569 Rainolde received the rectory of Lambourne, also in his home county. This time Catherine Barfoot, the widow and executrix of a London mercer who held Lambourne Manor, presented Rainolde with the rectory. She did so by means of a grant of the advowson, which she had obtained for one turn from Waltham Abbey (an advowson is a right of presentation to a benefice). Despite possessing two ecclesiastical livings, however, Rainolde continued to practice medicine without a license. In 1571 the college of physicians caught up with him, and, after he voluntarily confessed that he had been practicing for two years, the college declared him ignorant and unlearned, ordering his imprisonment until he paid a fine of £20. This incident might have created a temporary scandal, for F. G. Emmison's *Elizabethan Life: Morals & the Church Courts* (1973) states that in 1571—the same year as his impeachment—"Richard Reynolds," parson of Lambourne, was called "a very knave and very villain," ostensibly by parishioners.

Although historical accounts, especially those of Essex County, appear relatively taciturn about Rainolde, *The Foundacion of Rhetorike* offers a possible motivation for his few known exploits. Rebhorn perceptively questions Rainolde's recourse to a fable that celebrates the wit and skill of John Fisher, a cleric whom Henry VIII had executed. Rainolde explains how Fisher used a fable by Aesop to protest Henry's seizure of the religious houses. Rebhorn infers from his use of this dangerous illustration—one that included an unflattering portrait of Elizabeth's father—Rainolde's belief that orators, acting on behalf of the commonwealth, may stand up to rulers. The topos of the orator as a scourge of

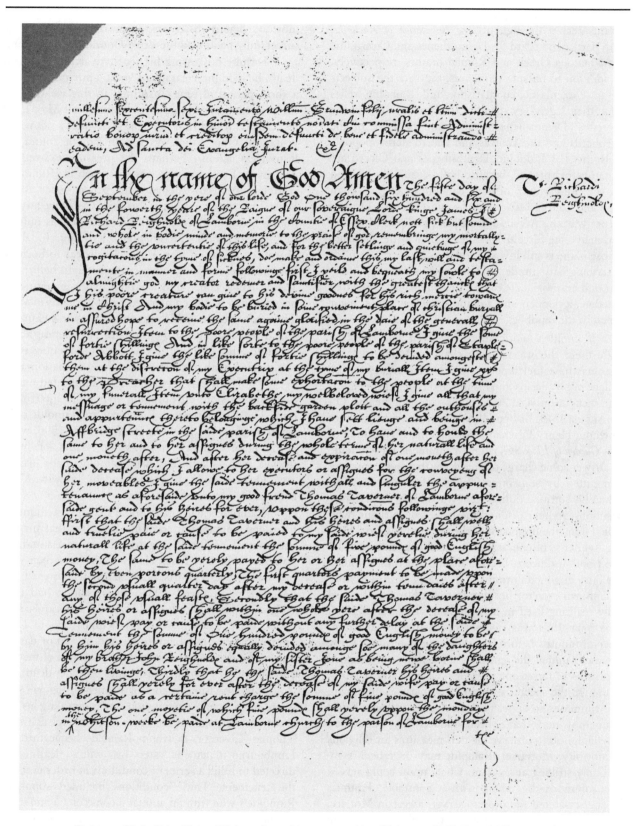

First page of Rainolde's will, in which he made provisions to protect his wife's interests (Public Record Office, London)

tyrants recurs throughout *The Foundacion of Rhetorike,* with particular regard for Demosthenes and Cicero, the most famous Greek and Roman orators, respectively. In addition to passing references, they are the subjects of an encomiastic comparison, and Rainolde relies upon their legendary speeches to illustrate a few of the exercises: Demosthenes' oration on the fable of the Shepherds and the Wolves and Cicero's prosopopoeia of Rome. For Rainolde, Demosthenes and Cicero are paragons of rhetoric, because both steadfastly labored for the preservation of their commonwealths through wise and courageous orations against tyrants: Demosthenes warning Athens against King Philip of Macedon and delivering forceful speeches known as the *Philippics,* whose name is still invoked today as a general term for describing any tirade or bitter denunciation; Cicero through his passionate eloquence convincing Rome that Cataline, a popular and ambitious soldier, was a major threat to the republic.

Rainolde's admiration for–even identification with–these rhetoricians who challenged authority figures may have fueled not only his bold disregard for the college of physicians and his intrepidity in serving a foreign dictator but also his second brush with the law. On 25 August 1579, Bishop John Aylmer, the same Aylmer to whom Henry Peacham dedicated the 1577 edition of *The Garden of Eloquence,* issued a summons for Rainolde to answer some charge of *irregularity,* that is, an apostasy committed by someone of holy orders who has forsaken his spiritual duties. Renowned for his severe persecutions, Aylmer inspired the hatred of Puritans, who called him "the oppressor of the children of God." During Aylmer's episcopate, Essex, which was embraced by the London diocese, became distinguished as a hotbed for Puritan nonconformity, and as early as 1575 Alymer had shown extreme hostility to Essex Puritans, his zeal fully realizing itself in his searching visitation of 1584. The year 1579 was notably oppressive for Puritans. Several months before Rainolde's summons, the Privy Council, under the guidance of Aylmer, proclaimed measures to ferret out vagrant preachers and parsons. Although the specific nature of the charge is unknown, the summons to appear before Aylmer at Saint Paul's Cathedral may have been induced by Rainolde's unwillingness to observe the new measures for religious conformity. Moreover, Rainolde may have been symbolically striking at a tyrant, when, upon being served the summons, he, along with a constable, Frauncis Bushe, assaulted the process server, a certain Morrice, choosing to settle the problem with fists rather than rhetoric. Along with his wife and Bushe, Rainolde was committed to the Marshalsea, a Southwark prison, which in 1583 Aylmer called "the blackest spot" of the London prisons, since it housed during this period mostly religious dissenters. Later that year Rainolde successfully petitioned the Privy Council for a pardon.

Despite possessing his first two livings until his death, he held the vicarage of West Thurrock only for a short period of time. Instituted to this vicarage on the presentation of Humphrey Hayes on 2 May 1578, he resigned it in 1584, the year of Aylmer's notorious visitation. Once more, no reason can be found for Rainolde's actions. Perhaps the pressure exerted by Aylmer on Essex parsons was too much for Rainolde, who had been threatened with prison twice, since West Thurrock vicarage at this time was more a curse than a blessing. Because West Thurrock was outside the archdeacon's jurisdiction, its church drew unwanted suspicion from the ecclesiastical authorities. For example, in 1579 a couple was brought before the archdeacon's court and charged with incontinence because they had been married without banns in West Thurrock church, "which is termed a lawless church." The 1579 marriage also stimulates speculation about the summons. Although Rainolde is not mentioned in conjunction with the ceremony, his association with West Thurrock may have indirectly implicated him in the transgression, encouraging Aylmer to interrogate him. The last noteworthy incident in Rainolde's life again involves the law. On 18 November 1596, while at Stapleford-Abbots, he was the victim of horse thieves, who stole his bay nag. Rainolde made his will on 5 October 1606. It was proved by his wife, Elizabeth, in December of that year.

Rainolde's will offers some details not found in his other biographical accounts. The fact that his will was proved by the Prerogative Court of Canterbury points to affluence. Essex clergy could have their wills proved by several courts, but testators who owned rich benefices or occupied a high social station had their wills proved by Canterbury. His wealth also can be seen in the three tenements he left behind: two in Lambourne and one in Chigwell. He had no son or natural heir, so he designated Elizabeth as executrix of the will and inheritor of the three properties until her death.

The provisions made for women in his will safeguard them against exploitation, again revealing his sensitivity to the potential for abuse in power relationships. Thomas Tavernor, to whom Rainolde bequeathed his Lambourne tenement after his wife's death, was directed to fulfill a series of conditions in order to attain the tenement. These conditions included supplying Rainolde's wife with an annual income of £6 and upon her death raising £100 to distribute to the daughters of his brother John and his sister Jane. Even more significantly, Rainolde left £40 to Jane, stipulating that if her "unthriftie" husband, Ambrose Gray of Cambridge, was not content with his wife receiving such a sum, then the money should go to her daughter Anne. Jane received the same amount as each of Rainolde's brothers, James and John—the second and third tenements going to John's two sons after Elizabeth's death.

The will rather appropriately memorializes Rainolde's devotion to rhetoric: to each parson of Lambourne and Stapleford-Abbots, he annually bequeathed 10s. for "some godly exhortation to be then and there made for the edification and comfort of the people of his charge." However, in his will Rainolde did not bequeath any books, as Essex clergy frequently did. This notable absence may testify to the diminished value that Rainolde placed on scholarly activity later in his life. After receiving his two rectories in Essex, Rainolde appears to have abandoned writing altogether, since his only other extant work is a manuscript, written in Latin and probably composed in the 1560s: "De statu Nobilium Virorum et Principum" (The Condition of Noblemen and Rulers) celebrates the monarchy and Elizabeth I, while attacking Roman Catholicism.

The Foundacion of Rhetorike offers students insight into the practice and application of Tudor composition, most notably poetry. Yet, unlike later English rhetoricians who are preoccupied with style, Rainolde raises copia to the level of the speech and orients the progymnasmata to the court, maximizing the capacity of rhetoric to profit the commonwealth. In effect, he turns a textbook for schoolchildren into a handbook for courtiers, bearing witness to the deeply political nature of Tudor writing. His chronicle equally participates in what appears to be a larger project of representing national identity with models primarily taken from the classical past. His commitment to the political nature of rhetoric prominently manifests itself in his conviction that orators can stand up to tyrants, a conviction that may help to contextualize his apparent sensitivity and even opposition to authority figures throughout his own life.

Biography:

Charles Henry Cooper and Thompson Cooper, "Richard Reynolds," in *Athenæ Cantabrigienses,* volume 2, *1586–1609* (Cambridge: Deighton, Bell & Macmillan, 1861), p. 444.

References:

Eustace F. Bosanquet, *English Printed Almanacks and Prognostications: A Bibliographical History to the Year 1600* (London: Printed for the Bibliographical Society at the Chiswick Press, 1917), p. 196;

John Brinsley, *Ludus Literarius, or The Grammar Schoole,* edited by E. T. Campagnac (Liverpool: University Press, 1917), p. 185;

Edmund Carter, *The History of the University of Cambridge, from its original, to the year 1753* (London: Printed for the Author, 1753), p. 325;

Donald Lemen Clark, "The Rise and Fall of Progymnasmata in Sixteenth and Seventeenth Century Grammar Schools," *Speech Monographs,* 19, no. 4 (1952): 259–263;

J. S. Cockburn, ed., *Calendar of Assize Records: Essex Indictments, Elizabeth I* (London: Her Majesty's Stationery Office, 1978);

William G. Crane, *Wit and Rhetoric in the Renaissance: The Formal Basis of Elizabethan Prose Style* (New York: Columbia University Press, 1937), pp. 62–69, 108, 137–138;

Anthony Glenn Cross, *Cambridge: Some Russian Connections* (Cambridge & New York: Cambridge University Press, 1987), pp. 5–6;

T. W. Davids, *Annals of Evangelical Nonconformity in the County of Essex, from the Time of Wycliffe to the Restoration* (London: Jackson, Walford & Hodder, 1863), p. 102;

Paul Dean, "Contemporary English History in Elizabethan Roman Histories," *Notes and Queries,* new series 33 (1986): 312–316;

H. Arthur Doubleday and William Page, eds., *The Victoria History of the County of Essex,* volume 4: *Ongar Hundred* (London: Constable / Oxford University Press for the Institute of Historical Research, 1903), pp. 77, 81; volume 8: *Chafford Hundred–Harlow Hundred* (London: Constable / Oxford University Press for the Institute of Historical Research, 1903), p. 71;

F. G. Emmison, *Elizabethan Life: Morals & the Church Courts, Mainly from Archdiaconal Records,* Essex Record Office Publications, no. 63 (Chelmsford, U.K.: Essex Record Office, 1973), p. 206;

Emmison, "Wills of Elizabethan Essex Clergy," in *Essex Heritage: Essays Presented to Sir William Addison as a Tribute to His Life and Work for Essex History and Literature,* edited by Kenneth Neale (Oxford: Leopard's Head Press, 1992), pp. 175–192;

Richard Helgerson, *Forms of Nationhood: The Elizabethan Writing of England* (Chicago: University of Chicago Press, 1992), p. 11;

Wilbur S. Howell, *Logic and Rhetoric in England, 1500–1700* (Princeton: Princeton University Press, 1956);

Francis R. Johnson, Introduction to *The Foundation of Rhetorike,* edited by Johnson (New York: Scholars' Facsimiles & Reprints, 1945), pp. iii–xxii;

George A. Kennedy, *Classical Rhetoric and Its Christian and Secular Tradition from Ancient to Modern Times* (Chapel Hill: University of North Carolina Press, 1980), pp. 163–164;

Kennedy, *A New History of Classical Rhetoric* (Princeton: Princeton University Press, 1994), pp. 202–208;

C. S. Lewis, *English Literature in the Sixteenth Century, Excluding Drama,* volume 3 of *Oxford History of English Literature* (Oxford: Clarendon Press, 1954), p. 294;

E. D. Pendry, *Elizabethan Prisons and Prison Scenes,* 2 volumes (Salzburg: Institut für Englische Sprache und Literatur, Universität Salzburg, 1974), pp. 245–250;

Wayne A. Rebhorn, *The Emperor of Men's Minds: Literature and the Discourse of Rhetoric* (Ithaca, N.Y.: Cornell University Press, 1995), pp. 108–109;

Herbert David Rix, *Rhetoric in Spenser's Poetry,* Pennsylvania State College Studies, no. 7 (State College: Pennsylvania State College, 1940), pp. 9–10, 80–81;

Eleanor Rosenberg, *Leicester: Patron of Letters* (New York: Columbia University Press, 1955), pp. 44–46;

William Phillips Sandford, *English Theories of Public Address, 1530–1828* (Columbus, Ohio: H. L. Hedrick, 1931), pp. 45–50, 69;

Joan Simon, *Education and Society in Tudor England* (Cambridge: Cambridge University Press, 1966), pp. 245–267;

Thomas O. Sloane, *On the Contrary: The Protocol of Traditional Rhetoric* (Washington, D.C.: Catholic University of America Press, 1997), pp. 115–116;

Warren Taylor, *Tudor Figures of Rhetoric* (Whitewater, Wis.: Language Press, 1972), p. 23;

Theon, *Progymnasmata;* Nicolaus, *Progymnasmata;* and Apthonius, *Progymnasmata,* in *Readings from Classical Rhetoric,* edited by Patricia P. Matsen, Philip Rollinson, and Marion Sousa (Carbondale & Edwardsville: Southern Illinois University Press, 1990), pp. 253–262, 263–265, 266–288;

Marion Trousdale, *Shakespeare and the Rhetoricians* (Chapel Hill: University of North Carolina Press, 1982), pp. 3–15;

Karl R. Wallace, "Rhetorical Exercises in Tudor Education," *Quarterly Journal of Speech,* 22, no. 1 (1936): 28–51;

Thomas Warton, *History of English Poetry from the Twelfth to the Close of the Sixteenth Century,* volume 4, edited by William Carew Hazlitt (London: Reeves & Turner, 1871), p. 249.

Papers:
Richard Rainolde's manuscript for "De statu Nobilium Virorum et Principum" is in the British Library, London (Harleian Ms. 973). Rainolde's will is located in the Public Record Office, London (PROB 11/108 quire 92 folio 323–324).

Richard Sherry
(1506 – 1551 or 1555)

Shirley Sharon-Zisser
Tel-Aviv University

BOOKS: *A treatise of Schemes & Tropes very profytable for the better vnderstanding of good authors, gathered out of the best Grammarians & Oratours by Rychard Sherry Londoner. Whervnto is added a declamacion, That chyldren euen strayt frō their infancie should be well and gently broughte vp in learnynge. Written fyrst in Latin by the most excellent and famous Clearke, Erasmus of Roterodame* (London: Printed by John Day, 1550)–includes Sherry's translation of Erasmus's *De pueris statim acliberaliter instituendis* (1529);

A Treatise of the Figures of Grammer and Rhetorike, profitable for al that be studious of Eloquence, and in especiall for suche as in Grammer scholes doe reade moste eloquente Poetes and Oratours: Whereunto is ioygned the oration which Cicero made to Cesar, geuing thankes vnto him for pardonyng, and restoring again of that noble mā Marcus Marcellus, sette foorth by Richarde Sherrye Londonar (London: Printed by Richard Tottel, 1555).

Editions: Herbert W. Hildebrandt, "A Critical Edition of Richard Sherry's A Treatise of Scheme and Tropes," 2 volumes, dissertation, University of Wisconsin, 1958;

A treatise of Schemes and Tropes (1550): And His Translation of The Education of Children by Desiderius Erasmus, introduction by Hildebrandt (Gainesville, Fla.: Scholars' Facsimiles and Reprints, 1961).

OTHER: Johannes Brenz, *A verye fruitful Exposizion vpon the syxte Chapter of Saynte Iohn, diuided into X. Homelies or Sermons: Written in Latin by the ryghte excellente clarke Master Iohn Brencious and Translated into English by Richard Shirrye, Londoner,* translated by Sherry (London: Printed by John Day & William Seres, 1550).

In the dedication to his first important work on rhetoric, *A treatise of Schemes & Tropes very profytable for the better vnderstanding of good authors, gathered out of the best Grammarians & Oratours by Rychard Sherry Londoner* (1550), Richard Sherry compares the rewards of the study of the forms of language to the "corporall . . . pleasures" afforded by "a goodlye garden." All of his surviving works—a translation of a religious text and two rhetorical treatises on elocution—evince a strong fascination with and love of language. Language was for him a domain of pleasure and lifelong passion. The fascination, reverence, and care with which he treated language both as a translator and as a theorizing rhetorician won him respect and fame among his contemporaries, and he remains known as one of the foremost rhetoricians of the English Renaissance and the first among the "figurists"—rhetoricians who took elocution, or style, as their focus. What makes Sherry distinct among the figurists, as well as among Renaissance rhetoricians at large, however, is the intriguing split that his work reveals between the conventional attitude to rhetoric as a set of rules and precepts designed to bring language under control and his personal attitude to language as a realm of pleasure, dream, and play that exceeds the law. This split was reflected in his alliance with literary and court circles on the one hand and with Reformist theologians on the other.

Richard Sherry, whose last name appears in various records and publications as *Shirrye, Shyrye, Sherrie, Sherrey, Schyrre, Shere, Sherey,* and *Sherye,* was born in 1506 in the vicinity of London. Both the Oxford University register and Joseph Foster's more detailed *Alumni Oxonienses* (1891–1892), as well as Anthony à Wood's unofficial *Athenae Oxonienses* (1675), indicate that Sherry became a "demy" (scholar of Magdalen College) or a "semicommoner" (one who receives half a fellow's allowance) in 1522. His bachelor of arts degree, for which he supplicated on 9 June 1522, was conferred five years later, on 21 June 1527. His master's degree, for which he had supplicated on 17 January 1530, was conferred on 10 March 1531, a year before the date given by Wood. His occupations in the three following years of his life are unknown. The reference of Sherry's last academic record, "of Magdalen Fasti," dated 1532, is obscure. Yet, although there is no record of Sherry's ever having become a fellow of Magdalen College, he clearly maintained a close affiliation with his alma mater and commanded esteem within it, because in 1534 he was appointed headmaster of the school adjoining this prestigious college (in which, according to Wood, he may have previously served as an "usher"—an underteacher or assistant schoolmaster).

That Sherry's experience as a headmaster at Oxford had a formative intellectual effect on him is clearly indicated by the pedagogic bent of the two rhetorical treatises he published as a "Londoner" in later years. Appended to the first is a translation of Desiderius Erasmus's meditation on the philosophy of education. It urges that "chyldren oughte to be taughte and brought up getly [sic] in vertue and learnage," commending a pedagogy based on affection between tutor and pupil and vehemently denouncing the use of physical violence in the classroom. Sherry's second treatise on rhetoric is advertised by its title as having "especiall" appropriateness for use "in grammar scholes." There is clear evidence that this treatise was indeed used in the grammar school at Saffron Walden shortly after its publication. T. W. Baldwin, in *William Shakspere's Small Latine & Lesse Greeke* (1944), presents evidence that in the year 1557–1558 a boy named Francis Willoughby at Saffron Walden received from his uncle "a booke of Sherez fygueres in Englyshe."

Sherry served in the capacity of headmaster of the Magdalen College School for six years, until 1540, when he was succeeded by a man named Goodall. Subsequently, he settled in London or its environs. He was never part of court circles, but his London acquaintances may have included the poet Thomas Wyatt, to whom he refers with much admiration in the dedicatory epistle of *A treatise of Schemes & Tropes.* Sherry may have met Wyatt before the poet's death in 1542, which he refers to as an event that "hastely deriued us of thys iewel," although his praise of Wyatt may have been occasioned by the appearance of Wyatt's *Certayne Psalmes* in 1549. Sherry's circle seems to have included other contemporary men of letters, such as Arthur Broke (or Brooke), whom he praises in terms that suggest a personal acquaintance. Brooke was, like Sherry, a translator, and his achievements include *The Tragicall Historye of Romeus and Juliet* (1562), an English verse translation from Matteo Bandello's *Novelle* (1554–1573) and the major source for William Shakespeare's 1597 play *Romeo and Juliet.* The publisher of Brooke's translation was Richard Tottel, who seven years earlier, in 1555, had published Sherry's *A Treatise of the Figures of Grammer and Rhetorike, profitable for al that be studious of Eloquence, and in especiall for suche as in Grammer scholes doe reade moste eloquente Poetes and Oratours.* Two years after the publication of Sherry's second treatise, Tottel published the first poetic miscellany of English verse, *Songes and Sonnettes* (1557), also known as Tottel's Miscellany, which includes poems by Wyatt. It is possible, then, that Sherry was allied with an intellectual circle of poets and translators that included Wyatt and Brooke, whose works were promoted into print by Tottel. Further evidence of Sherry's contacts with court circles is the fact that he dedicates his translation of a text by Marcus Tullius Cicero, appended to his second treatise, to William Paget, the first Lord Paget and a minister in the Tudor court.

Sherry, however, had Reformist as well as court and literary leanings. The early editions of Wood's *Athenae Oxonienses* refer to Sherry in their index as "John" rather than "Richard," and it has been conjectured that he may have been the same person who was in 1541 archdeacon of Lewes and rector of Chailey in Sussex and was appointed prebendary and precentor at St. Paul's Cathedral on 27 November 1543. Sherry's intellectual concerns after he left Oxford were also theologically inflected, as is made eminently clear by the fact that his first rhetorical treatise is dedicated to Thomas Brooke, a Reformist theologian, the author of religious books and the preface to the English translation of the Geneva Bible. Sherry's religious leanings are also indicated by his two other publications: *A verye fruitful Exposition vpon the syxte Chapter of Saynte Iohn, divided into X Homelies or Sermons* (1550), a translation of a commentary in Latin by German theologian Johannes Brenz (also known as Brentius); and an undated translation from Greek, *St. Basil the Great his letter to Gregory Nazaanzen, shewing that many hundred years ago, certain godly men used the life commonly called monastical,* no copies of which have survived.

The fact that these two tracts are translations, as are the pedagogical text by Erasmus appended to *A treatise of Schemes & Tropes* and Cicero's "Thankes Geving to Caesar for the restitution of Marcus Marcelus," appended to *A Treatise of the Figures of Grammer and Rhetorike,* indicates that Sherry was seriously and intensely engaged in translation work. Wood states that he was "a person elegantly learned" and that his translations gained him considerable esteem among the "learn'd men" of his time. If Sherry was indeed the person who served as prebendary and precentor at St. Paul's from 1543, he must have died shortly before 24 August 1551, the date when he was replaced in those capacities by Edmond Grindall. According to the *Dictionary of National Biography,* however, Sherry died in 1555, a date that seems plausible in view of the fact that it coincides with the publication date of his last major work, *A Treatise of the Figures of Grammer and Rhetorike.* His four known works, all of them apparently published between 1550 and 1555 in a fruitful half decade preceding his death, seem to manifest a symmetrical division of interest between religious and rhetorical affairs: two are theological tracts, and two are handbooks of elocution.

A verye fruitful Exposition vpon the syxte Chapter of Saynte Iohn appears to be the first of the few sixteenth-century translations into English of the work of Brenz, an influential Reformist exegete whose commentaries on Scripture translated into German went into six printings during the 1550s. Sherry's being one of the few and probably the first of the English translators of Brenz's commentaries grants him a significant role in the transmission of Reformation theology to England in the vernacular. Brenz was esteemed for the clarity of his style, as well as for his exegetical skills, which depended upon his proficiency in the scriptural languages, Hebrew and Greek, and in the Latin in which he wrote most of his commentaries—on his being, like Sherry, a polyglot. Sherry may, therefore, have been drawn to Brenz not only as a Reformist theologian but also as a fellow scholar of the classical languages, one who in his commentaries exercised the same attentiveness to language that Sherry exercised in his translations.

Sherry's predominant concern with language is evidenced not only by his treatises on rhetoric but also by the subjects of the two religious texts he chose to translate. Both the Gospel of St. John and St. Basil's letter to Gregory of Nyssa evince at least as much, if not more, preoccupation with language as with theology. In John 6, Jesus urges that while "the flesh profiteth nothing," it is his "words" that are "spirit" and "life." Sherry's choice to translate a Reformist homiletic exegesis of this Gospel chapter celebrating the linguistic over the fleshly bespeaks the emotional as well as intellectual concerns of a celibate Renaissance scholar whose strongest passion was reflecting upon language and articulating his meditations concerning its categories. Sherry never married, and he apparently lived an ascetic life. His translation of Erasmus's pedagogical tract that is appended to *A treatise of Schemes & Tropes* suggests that his closest bonds were with his pupils. They seem to have functioned psychologically as his "very son[s]," resembling him not only in "fashion of . . . face" and "liniametes of . . . bodye" but also in "giftes of wyt."

Sherry's translation of St. Basil's epistle to Gregory of Nyassa confirms that his choice of texts to translate was in no small measure dictated by a philosophy that privileges the linguistic over the carnal, the imaginary and symbolic over the real. Like John 6, this epistle bespeaks a contempt for physicality as that which engenders dangerous passions and attachments and advocates a strict partitioning of soul and body. When the physical dimension of existence is reduced to a bare minimum, St. Basil claims, the mind is forced to turn inward upon itself in prayerful meditation. The life of St. Basil, as well as his philosophical privileging of the

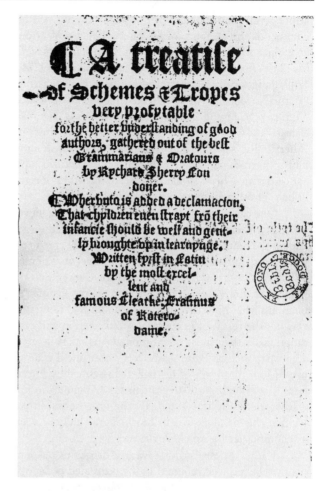

Title page for Richard Sherry's first important work on rhetoric, published in 1550 (Bodleian Library, Oxford University)

word over the flesh, must have appealed as a model for identification to Sherry, who devoted his life to the theorization and craftsmanship of language. St. Basil, however, was not only an advocate of monasticism. Like Sherry, he was well advanced in grammar and rhetoric and aimed at a career as a rhetorician. Like Sherry, he was esteemed as a pedagogue, having been desired by the people of Caesarea to undertake the education of their children. The argumentative tone of the subtitle of Sherry's translation—*shewing that many hundred years ago, certain godly men used the life commonly called monastical*—indexes Sherry's need to find a role model for himself and suggests his adoption of St. Basil for that purpose.

While the dominance of the theoretical and practical preoccupation with language in Sherry's life is manifest even in those of his works whose contents seem to be, at first sight, preeminently theological, it is in his two rhetorical treatises, *A treatise of Schemes & Tropes* and the later but lesser-known *A Treatise of the Figures of Grammer and Rhetorike,* that his love of language and expertise in its study and theorization are most impressively and extensively displayed. While Wood commends the elegance of his mind, Thomas Warton, an eighteenth-century chronicler of English literature, in his *The History of English Poetry* (four volumes, 1774–1789) judges Sherry's performance as a rhetorician as "jejune," according to S. Austin Allibone in *A Critical Dictionary of English Literature and British and American Authors* (1870). Herbert W. Hildebrandt claims in "Sherry: Renaissance Rhetorician" (1960) that Sherry had a "narrow and limited conception of rhetoric" and concludes that his writings are "relatively unimportant in light of other Renaissance rhetorical works."

One cause for the devaluation of Sherry's achievement as a rhetorician is the fact that his declared target audience comprises schoolboys rather than courtiers, merchants, and diplomats, as in the case of Thomas Wilson's *The Arte of Rhetorique* (1553) or George Puttenham's *The Arte of English Poesie* (1589). Sherry's choice to pitch his rhetorical treatises to schoolboys, however, was not the result of intellectual sophistication and erudition lesser than those of a diplomat such as Wilson or a courtier such as Puttenham. Nor was it the dictate of profession, the result of his belief "in schoolboy excercises," as Hildebrandt suggests in his "Amplification in a Rhetoric on Style" (1965). By the time he published his first rhetorical treatise in 1550, Sherry had not been a schoolmaster for an entire decade.

Rather, Sherry's choice was the conscious result of his firm belief, well reflected in the translated pedagogical tract appended to *A treatise of Schemes & Tropes,* that instruction in rhetoric was most necessary and most effective in the early, formative stages of life, when a person is an "infante and yonge babe" whose mind is still "voyde from cares and vices" and susceptible to impression. Ridiculing those who believe they have "done the office of a father when they haue only begotte chyldren," the Erasmian declamation urges the transfer from father to son of the symbolic codes of logic, rhetoric, and philosophy that underpin human interaction. The absence of such pedagogical transferral, the declamation warns, would produce a "man not instructed wyth Phylosophye nor other good sciences," a "creature somewhat worse then brute beastes," subject to the unregulated "dryue[s]" of "ambicion . . . desyre, anger, enuye, tyst and luste," whose curbing is the price of civilization. Sherry's choice to address his rhetorical treatises to an implied audience of schoolboys, then, is based on a philosophy of education that values the earliest learning as most crucial.

This philosophy of education is rooted in a particular epistemology and philosophy of mind that is explicitly articulated in the Erasmian declamation. In the declamation the human mind is conceived as a tabula rasa, as fundamentally "nothyng else the [*sic*] a rude lumpe of fleshe," or, figuratively speaking, of soft "waxe" or moist "claie," that receives formative imprints from the outside from the beginning, "strayght waye assone as [an] infate is borne." Invoking this epistemology in his translation of the Erasmian declamation on pedagogy, Sherry implicitly offers his own avowedly pedagogical manual that precedes the translation as such a formative imprint that "fashions" the students' malleable minds in ways that are "good," or acceptable, to civilization.

The fact that Sherry's rhetorical treatises were designed for the use of students in grammar schools, then, does not make them, as some readers have argued, jejune and inferior in comparison with texts such as Wilson's and Puttenham's. These two works, which purport to provide their readers with skills for the attainment of social and political advantage, seem to have been produced by scholars affiliated with the nobility in response to perceived demand within a cultural context in which mobility had become both more possible and more dependent on mastery of arts, not the least of which was rhetoric. Sherry's treatises, on the other hand, were written by a scholar who was never directly affiliated with the court, who had Reformist and ascetic leanings, and whose most significant professional attachment was to a prestigious academic institution, out of genuine commitment to an epistemology and a philosophy of education in which rhetoric was perceived to be a means not for the promotion of an individual within an increasingly flexible social order but for the preservation of the social order at large.

Twentieth-century readers of Sherry's rhetorical treatises, such as Patricia Parker and Wayne Rebhorn, have noted the way in which such a concern with the preservation of social order informs his definitions of particular forms of elocution. Thus, Sherry's denunciation of barbarism in *A treatise of Schemes & Tropes* as that which "turneth the speche from his purenes, and maketh it foule and rude" has been read as a mystification of a worry about social degradation, and his emphasis in the same treatise on "naturall order" in discourse "as to saye: men & women, daye and night, easte and weste, rather than backwards," as reflecting a social anxiety over the dissolution of hierarchies of gender and of rule, in which "Mistress" might be placed before "Master" and "Counsell" before "King." That Sherry was indeed conscious of the connection between order in discourse and the social order is suggested by his argument, in *A treatise of Schemes & Tropes,* that rhetoricians are useful to the state because they manage "the rude people" who "have commonly a preposterous judgment, and take the worst thynges for the beste, and the beste for the worste." This conscious belief in the importance of rhetoric to the preservation of social

Page from A treatise of Schemes & Tropes, *with a catalogue of rhetorical figures*

order is also clearly articulated in Sherry's translation of the Erasmian declamation on education, which foregrounds the necessity of instruction in the art of rhetoric to a "captayne or officer of the common wealth" who would be a "profytable" one. Without such instruction in rhetoric, Sherry states in this translation through the voice of Erasmus, whose philosophy of education was a major influence on the curriculum of sixteenth-century English grammar schools, a "pricipalitie can not wel be ordered."

Sherry's two rhetorical treatises were written by a philosophically minded pedagogue for an educational system that had the fundamental aim of providing a thorough training in the arts of language and thus performing the ideological function of inculcating legal and patriarchal authority; in this system, rhetoric was counted as the greatest human acquirement and gained a more privileged status than it ever had before. In England, particularly at Oxford, where Sherry received his own academic schooling and imparted schooling to others, the emphasis on rhetoric in the college curricula was most marked—when Bishop Foxe founded Corpus Christi College in 1517, for example, he specified that lectures be given on Cicero's *De Oratore* (On the Orator, 55 B.C.) and Quintilian's *Institutio Oratoria* (Institutes of Oratory, 92–94 A.D.), and this curriculum was adopted and expanded in Trinity and St. John's Colleges in 1555. Magdalen College School, in which Sherry was probably usher and then headmaster, is judged by Foster Watson, in his study *The English Grammar Schools to 1660* (1908), to have been "the school which showed the greatest interest in promulgating new views of grammar" from the late fifteenth to the mid sixteenth century. Sherry's predecessors in the position of headmaster of Magdalen College School included scholars who, like him, were theorists of language, such as John Anwykyll, author of *Compendium totius grammaticae* (A Compendium of the Whole Grammar, 1483); John Stanbridge, author of a series of treatises on accidence (grammatical inflection) between 1520 and 1531; and

Thomas Robertson, author of commentaries on William Lily's Latin grammar.

Another cause for the devaluation of Sherry's treatises by Warton and Allibone and twentieth-century readers such as Hildebrandt is their restrictiveness: in comparison with Wilson's *The Arte of Rhetorique,* which is celebrated for its "venerable mastery" and critical knowledge of all five parts of rhetoric, Sherry's treatises, in their choice to focus on *elocutio* alone, appear sparse and limited, though not as "technical" and "elementary" as Leonard Cox's *The arte or crafte of Rhethoryke* (1530?), only one of two other English rhetorical treatises written in the vernacular to precede them. In this case too, the judgment is misguided because of lack of attention to context. Wilson's treatise indeed remains faithful to the classical five-part division of rhetoric into *inventio* (invention), *dispositio* (disposition or arrangement), *elocutio* (elocution or style), *memoria* (memory), and *pronuntiato* (oratorical delivery), and unlike Cox's earlier treatise, it amply illustrates its precepts with examples in the vernacular. Other rhetorical treatises of the English Renaissance, however, are restricted in comparison with the classical format in one of two ways. Some treatises, such as Dudley Fenner's *The Artes of Logike And Rethorike* (1584) and Abraham Fraunce's *The Arcadian Rhetorike* (1588), follow the example of *Dialecticae institutiones* (1543), by Pierre de La Ramée (Petrus Ramus), in their systematic and logocentric delimitation of rhetoric, which, stripped of the technical arts of invention, disposition, and memory (which were incorporated into logic), was confined to delivery and elocution. Other rhetorical treatises of the English Renaissance follow the example of Johan Susenbrotus's *Epitome troporum ac schematum et grammaticorum et rhetoricorum* (Epitome of Tropes and Schemes Both of Grammarians and Rhetoricians, 1535?) and omit delivery as well as invention, disposition, and memory from their accounts, limiting their texts to the painstakingly fine definition and analysis of approximately two hundred figures of speech. Sherry's two treatises belong to this latter category of "figurist" rhetorics, which later included two of the most famous treatises of the English Renaissance, Henry Peacham's *The Garden of Eloquence* (1577) and George Puttenham's *The Arte of English Poesie* (1589). As William Phillips Sandford puts it in his study *English Theories of Public Address, 1530–1828* (1931), "Sherry recognized that rhetoric has other elements than *elocutio,* but to *elocutio* he gives the place of first importance." In Sherry's mind, "rhetoric is style, and style is a garnishment of speech."

Sherry's figurist focus on elocution has two implications. First, in the absence of sections devoted to the other traditional parts of rhetoric, the discourse on style, comprising the catalogue of tropes and figures, comes to carry the entire burden of the rhetorician's philosophy. When a rhetorical text is occupied exclusively by discussions of the names and structures of figures of speech, the ideological function of such figures of speech is all the more manifest. The figurist format thus has an indoctrinating function, precisely in line with the Erasmian pedagogical doctrine of education as the fashioning of consciousness, which Sherry translated and assimilated into *A treatise of Schemes & Tropes.*

Yet, Sherry's figurist focus, or what Hildebrandt, in his "Sherry: Renaissance Rhetorician," calls "a sympathy devoted exclusively towards style," also has another important implication that is held in dialectical tension with the first. This focus is also a manifestation of an aesthetic sensibility, of a sensitivity to the structures and sounds of linguistic forms. As Puttenham was to be after him, Sherry was acutely aware of the acoustics of speech, commending, in *A treatise of Schemes & Tropes,* the musicality of *tasis* or *extensio* ("wereby a swete and pleasant modulacion or tuna blenes of wordes is kepte")–a form that Puttenham also mentions and defines as "a swete and pleasaunte modulacion or tunableness . . . of the voyce in pleasaunte pronunciation"– and condemning the vice of barbarism not only on nationalistic grounds of its importing foreign speech into the English language but also on the aesthetic-acoustic grounds of its involving "euil pronouncing certein letters." In the later *A Treatise of the Figures of Grammer and Rhetorike* the same sensitivity to the acoustics of speech is manifest in the condemnation of "cacemphaton," the "roughnes or stammering" that occurs when "letters & syllables hang euil fauredly together."

Sherry's sensitivity to the acoustics of speech is apparent from the first sentence of the dedication of *A treatise of Schemes & Tropes* to the Reformist translator Thomas Brooke, who, according to W. S. Howell in his *Logic and Rhetoric in England* (1961), requested that Sherry "put into his mother tongue the stylistic lore that he had formerly taught to his pupils in Latin." In this dedication Sherry declares his concern that "the title of this treatise" will be found "straunge vnto our Englyshe eares," thus anticipating by two centuries a rhetorical treatise fully devoted to these acoustics: Joshua Steele's *An Essay Towards Establishing the Melody and Measure of Speech* (1775), which purports to "blend . . . the study of music and language together, so as to treat the modulation of speech as a genus of music under the rules of Melopoeia."

Yet, contrary to Steele's assertion that before his treatise music and letters had not "been joined together so as to afford mutual support to each other," Sherry shared the concern with the melodiousness of language not only with the figurists Peacham and Puttenham.

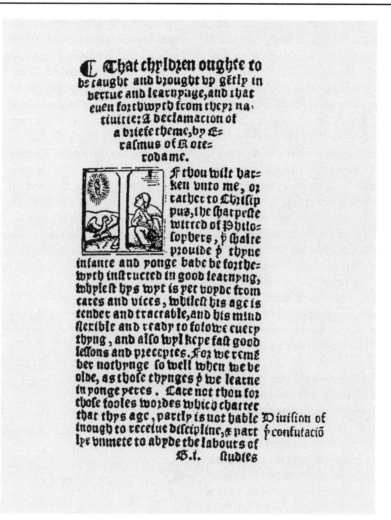

*First page of Sherry's translation of Desiderius Erasmus's meditation on the philosophy of education, published as an appendix
to* A treatise of Schemes & Tropes

The acoustics of style are also a dominant concern of another circle of English men of letters of the mid to late sixteenth century: the Euphuists, many of whom were, like Sherry, Oxonians. The Euphuistic style, which owes its name to John Lyly's influential *Euphues: The Anatomy of Wit* (1578), is "made and measured by the ear" and emphasizes the euphony and harmony achieved by assonance, alliteration, symmetry, and formal balance. Sherry's concern with the euphonic and the acoustic anticipates the formal concerns of Lyly and other Euphuistic rhetoricians and poets such as Francis Meres, Nicholas Ling, Thomas Watson, Thomas Lodge, William Smith, John Dickenson, and Robert Greene. Literary manifestations of Euphuism are often concerned with sleep and dreaming: Greene's *Menaphon* (1589) is subtitled *Camillas Alarum to slumbering Euphues, in his melancholie Cell;* Dickenson's *Arisbas* (1594) is similarly subtitled *Euphues amidst his slumbers;* the one longer poem in Smith's sonnet sequence *Chloris* (1594), which

is also in many senses the thematic core of the sequence, is titled "A dreame." Sherry anticipated this concern, as well. At the end of *A treatise of Schemes & Tropes* he admits that he is not "ignoraunt" of the fact that he has left out "much [that] helpeth bothe to persuasions and copye," including "the proper handlyng of tales taken oute of the nature of . . . dreames," which, he adds, "requyre a longer treatie." Sherry never wrote that "longer treatie" on the rhetoric of dreams, but his insight concerning the connection between the oneiric and the linguistic may have informed the philosophical concerns embodied in the literary, rhetorical, and philosophical texts of the Euphuistic authors.

To be concerned with the oneiric, with the language of slumber, as Sherry is at the end of *A treatise of Schemes & Tropes,* is to disengage from the concerns of waking life such as religion or pedagogy. To the Euphuists, declaring this disengagement from the precepts of waking life was a matter of course. Unlike the

Euphuists were to be, however, Sherry was uneasy and anxious about this fascination, as is strongly suggested by the conjecture that he voices in the dedication that people encountering the focus on the forms, the "schemes and tropes" of language that its title flaunts, "wyl count it but a tryfle, a tale of Robynhoode."

As the reference to Robin Hood suggests, Sherry also shares with the later English figurists a sense of the link between rhetoric and the conventions of the pastoral—an association implied in the title of Peacham's *The Garden of Eloquence* and made explicit by Fraunce in *The Arcadian Rhetorike*. In the dedicatory epistle to *A treatise of Schemes & Tropes,* Sherry finds an "apt similitude" between the experience of reading the treatise and that of a person going into "a goodlye garden garnyshed wyth dyuers kindes of herbes and flowers," who, "besyde the corporall . . . pleasure, knoweth of eueri one the name & propertye." For Sherry, then, becoming acquainted with the names and properties of figures of speech is an experience that is never divorced from "corporall . . . pleasure," the loss of which is one of the features of the pastoral genre.

That Sherry was familiar with the elements of the pastoral is evident in his translation of Erasmus's pedagogical declamation, in which the commendation of "the verses called Bucolicall" as most "mery" and "conceited" is accompanied by Sherry's marginal notation: "Bucolicall, where y herdmen do speke of nete and shepe." He had a comprehension not only of its conventions but also of its philosophical concern with a foreclosed time and a lost archaic domain of bliss: in *A Treatise of the Figures of Grammer and Rhetorike,* one example furnished for the form of "Chronographia, the discription of tyme," is "the peace worlde in the fourth Eglogue of Virgill." Further, Sherry commends the poetry of Wyatt, whose lovers' complaints are drawn from the pastoral conventions. In the links that he draws between rhetoric and the pastoral, as in his concern with the euphonic and oneiric dimensions of language, Sherry may be said to be a precursor of and a possible influence on the Euphuists.

Wyatt's poetry comprises not only quasi-pastoral "complaints" but also celebrations of consummated desire (such as "The lover reioiceth the enioying of his loue"). It is a poetry that thematizes and performs the connection between "enjoyment" and "joy" and the "corporall . . . pleasure," to use Sherry's term, of amatory joining. For Sherry, as for other men of letters of the English Renaissance, corporeal joining and its attendant enjoyments could not be thought of save in connection with linguistic joining, as Parker noted in her *Literary Fat Ladies: Rhetoric, Gender, Property* (1987) and *Shakespeare from the Margins: Language, Culture, Context* (1996). As the lexicographer John Florio put it in his

aptly titled *Worlde of Wordes* (1598), the denotation of the noun *copula* was both a linguistic "couple" and a "copulation" that involves a "ioyn[ing] together." *A treatise of Schemes & Tropes,* Parker observed, is preoccupied with forms of verbal copulations or copulas, with rhetorical joinings that gesture toward the forms of corporeal joining and enjoyment or pleasure, an association Sherry makes explicit in the beginning of his treatise: the entire "myghte and power of eloquucion," he states, rests on apt words being "founde oute, and after . . . conueniently coupled" or "ioyned together." Indeed, this dialectic of being apart and coming together, analogous to the fluctuations of romantic love, dictates his division of elocution "into two partes, that is, wordes symple, or considered by themselues, and compound or ioyned together in speache." In terms of this dialectic, the "wordes symple," or the figures of word and diction, with which the treatise's elocutionary catalogue begins have an important role to play: so that they may be "founde oute" to be "ioyned," they must be able to perform a seduction; they must be, in terms of the Erasmian declamation, "sweete flattering wordes" that anticipate a "pleasure . . . in tyme to come." In Sherry's catalogue of figures of diction, this seductive anticipation usually takes one of two dialectically related forms. In the cases of *prosthesis, epenthesis, proparalepsis,* and *ectasis,* it takes the form of the addition of a character or syllable to a word that adumbrates its being joined to another, or, in the case of *synolephe,* that already enacts the process of "vowels comyng together." In the cases of *apheresis, syncope, apocope,* or *systole,* anticipation takes the form of a castrative "cuttynge" or "takynge awaye" that exacerbates the desire for "ioyning" all the more.

The greater part of *A treatise of Schemes & Tropes* is taken up with a catalogue of the figures and tropes of elocution similar to that found in Quintilian, the *Rhetorica ad Herennium* (Rhetoric to Herennius, circa 85 B.C.) and Susenbrotus as well as in Mosellanus's *Tabulae de schematibus et tropis* (Tables of Schemes and Tropes, 1529) and later in the figurist treatises of Peacham and Puttenham, in Wilson's traditionalist *The Arte of Rhetorique,* and in the Ramist treatises of Fenner and Fraunce. As William G. Crane notes in *Wit and Rhetoric in the Renaissance* (1937), Sherry's treatise is characterized also by its emphasis upon the principles of *copia,* adapted from Erasmus's *De duplici copia verborum ac rerum* (On Abundance of Things and Words, 1512) principles whose effect is to foreground the ornamental and affective dimension of speech, as well as, according to Terence Cave and Patricia Parker, its symbolic fecundity and maternality. Sherry's choice to emphasize *copia* makes him an important disseminator of Erasmian rhetorical as well as pedagogical theory, theory that in both these dimensions is attentive to language as a medium of affect and seduction as well as of regulation and law.

The larger number of figures of speech that Sherry's treatise conceptualizes distinguishes it both from its precursors and from subsequently published rhetorical treatises of the English Renaissance, setting Sherry out from his contemporaries as the most aesthetically minded of rhetoricians, the one most sensitive to the formal and conceptual nuance of linguistic forms. What makes Sherry's treatise most distinctive is its idiosyncratic principle of organization, which may, at first glance, seem more like a principle of disorganization. The title of *A treatise of Schemes & Tropes* announces its engagement with both categories of elocution; yet, it begins with a discussion of figures of word (divided into figures of diction and figures of construction) and continues with a discussion of "Faute[s] Of Scheme[s]" (errors, or abuses, of schemes) and their "Vertue[s]." It then briefly discusses tropes, after which it returns to a discussion of "figures Rethoricall," followed by a discussion of "figures of sentence." The treatise ends with a discussion of "Proues," which traditionally would have been considered an aspect of invention but includes the category of "similitude," traditionally listed as one of the figures and also mentioned in the course of Sherry's discussion of them.

This seemingly confused organization of subject matter can hardly be thought to be an inadvertent failing on the part of a rhetorician who declares, in his dedicatory epistle, his familiarity with Quintilian's carefully ordered discussion of figures and tropes. Sherry insists in the opening of his treatise that one must "take hede of placinge, and setting in order" of words, and the section on figures of diction that begins his elocutionary catalogue displays symmetrical organization, regularly alternating between figures of addition and of omission. In the context of his familiarity with, commendation of, and undeniable aptitude at compositional organization, Sherry's seemingly erratic and eccentric organization of his treatise must be considered a philosophical statement on the categories of elocution.

In the discourse on elocution that looks back to Quintilian's discussion of figures and tropes in the *Institutio oratoria,* "trope" is the privileged category while "figure" is its devalued binary opposite. The splitting of elocution into binary opposites is born of an identification of language with the oceanic chaos of the primal maternal body, an identification manifest in Sherry's reference to the "great fludde of eloquence" and "great streame of eloqucion" in the beginning of *A treatise of Schemes & Tropes* and even more explicit at the end of *A Treatise of the Figures of Grammer and Rhetorike,* which anxiously speaks of a kind of oration that is "called dissolute, because it waueth hyther & thyther, as it wer

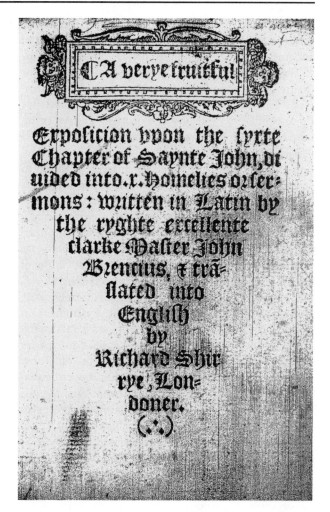

Title page for Sherry's 1550 translation of works by Johannes Brenz, an influential German theologian

without synewe and iointes, stading surely in no point." In response to this anxiety, rhetoricians from Quintilian onwards have partitioned elocution into tropes and figures, assigning the latter the characteristics of a prostituted female body while the former were seen as masculine and conquering. The production of the category of "trope" as a power that is able to conquer and subdue the "dissolute" and "ioint[less]" substance of language that Sherry speaks of depends on the postulation of its binary opposite, the category of "figure." This category retains the symbolic association of language with the feminine, but expressed in a more legitimate form within the purportedly logocentric discourse of rhetoric. In this legitimized, palatable deployment of femininity, "figure" is characterized by ubiquitous references to ornamentation; the feminine is made to be not the oceanic maternal but a seductive female body that awaits and invites penetration and control.

But although Sherry is so explicit in both his treatises in invoking the image of the oceanic chaos of primal signification, and although the title of *A treatise of Schemes & Tropes* declares its implication in the project of bringing that chaos or "fludde" under control by means of its partitioning into seductive feminine "schemes" or "figures" and conquering masculine "tropes," his treatise is distinctive in the relatively restricted importance it grants this latter category of elocution. The overvaluation of tropes in the treatises of Peacham and Wilson is signaled by the choice to position them first in the catalogue of elocutionary forms. This ordering is meant to suggest the importance of hierarchical superiority, as is made clear by the two authors' theorization of "order," in which, Wilson says, "the worthier is preferred and set Before. As a man is set before a woman," a formulation underscoring the associations of masculinity, as well. In Ramist rhetorical treatises such as those of Ramus himself or Audemarus Talaeus's *Rhetorica e P. Rami praelectionibus observata* (Rhetoric Conformed to P. Ramus's Explanations, 1544), both the masculinization of tropes and their valuation over figures is made eminently clear by their categorization as the "master tropes" of metaphor, metonymy, synecdoche, and irony. Sherry avoids both of these approaches, instead flanking his discussion of tropes with discussions of figures: it is preceded by a detailed discussion of many figures of word and of diction and of the faults and virtues of style and followed by a lengthy section on figures of sentence. The trope is also associated with "exornation," a category that Wilson, for example, reserves for the discussion of figure. Sherry's shying away from the overvaluation of tropes is yet further evidence of his uneasy attraction to the conceptually feminine aspects of language, which his peers anxiously seek to control and foreclose.

Perhaps the most telling instance of Sherry's fascination with the seductive, nonlogocentric dimensions of language is the definition of scheme that he provides in *A treatise of Schemes & Tropes*. He writes of scheme as a form of signification that is not "after the vulgar and comen usage," utilizing a formulation that had been the standard way of describing figures since Quintilian's *Institutio oratoria*. This formulation, however, is preceded by a description of scheme that is distinctive in the history of rhetoric. Scheme, Sherry writes in the first theorization of a category of elocution in his treatise, "is a Greke worde, and signifyeth properlye the maner of gesture that dauncers use to make, whe [*sic*] they haue won the best game." This striking formulation underscores Sherry's erudition and proficiency in the classical languages, as does his consistent provision of both the Greek and Latin names of the various schemes and tropes (for example, *prosthesis* and *appositio, aphresis* and *ablatio, zeugma* and *iunctio*). It also powerfully bespeaks Sherry's reverent attitude to classical Greece as an archaic domain of bliss, an attitude that was common among Renaissance men of letters, particularly the Euphuists and other writers of pastoral. Sherry's exceptional theorization of figure explicitly associates it with play and celebratory, ecstatic "daunce," thus underscoring his description in the dedication of rhetorical proficiency as a form of pleasure.

A Treatise of the Figures of Grammer and Rhetorike, published half a decade after *A treatise of Schemes & Tropes* in the year of Sherry's death—if not posthumously—also expresses the association of elocutionary language with pleasure that is so marked in the earlier treatise. For example, repetition is commended as "a pleasaunt figure" and later linked, using terms that have explicit erotic overtones, with the figure of "copulatio" defined as its (possibly incestuous) "cosin." That Sherry should have mentioned pleasure in connection with repetition is remarkable, as other Renaissance men of letters speak of it as an intolerable vice. Sherry's commendation of repetition confirms his attraction to the pleasurable excesses of language that surfaces so often in *A treatise of Schemes & Tropes*. Similarly, his condemnation of "cacemphaton," the "roughnes or stammering" that occurs when "letters & syllables hang euil fauredly together," is yet another manifestation (albeit cast in negative, inverted form) of his sensitivity to the acoustic and oral, which is conceptually linked to his attitude to elocution as a domain of euphony and pleasure.

Yet, despite the continued manifestation of Sherry's attraction to realms of pleasure that exceed the law of language that the rhetorical treatise ostensibly articulates, *A Treatise of the Figures of Grammer and Rhetorike* is much more sober and austere, much less ludic and pleasure oriented than the earlier treatise. Its title invokes grammar, the discipline that provides the structural basis of the symbolic order, of the law and "name of the father" to which Sherry had alluded in *A treatise of Schemes & Tropes* but which he never, in that treatise, quite upheld. In the earlier treatise the "Grammaticall order" is described, through the translated words of Erasmus, as a collection of "preceptes" that are "sowre" rather than pleasurable; in the later treatise it is explicitly identified as a stabilizing grid for the "great floud of eloquence." Sherry stresses the rhetorician's duty to guarantee that figures never "trouble" this symbolic order. Indeed, he intends his treatise specifically for institutions whose express purpose is to inculcate and reproduce the symbolic and social order reflected in the discipline of grammar—"Grammer schooles."

It is in conjunction with the pedagogical and ideological program of grammar schools that Sherry mentions and defines the masculinized category of trope. This elocutionary category involves a change in signification, he writes, occurring at the place where "the grammarian semeth to end his art, and Rhetorician to begin." At the seam between grammar and rhetoric the control that grammar exercises over the chaotic matter of a primal language is suspended and rhetoric becomes most necessary as a disciplinary economy. The regaining of regulation over language is offered in terms of the elocutionary category of trope, whose definition in terms of a narrative of coercive displacement, a "bowing of a worde or speache from his owne signification into another." In his later treatise Sherry wishes to make this category, the definition of which bespeaks control, coercion, and power, into one symbolic of rhetoric as a mechanism that disciplines language. He thus puts forth the category of trope as the display case, the "entraunce to Rhetorike," whose knowledge is "very necessary for chyldren," whose language rhetoric would discipline. Rhetoric thus becomes a "diuine power"—an art by means of which one may excercise utmost, absolute rule.

Sherry's association of rhetoric with disciplinary power in *A Treatise of the Figures of Grammer and Rhetorike* is reflected also in the translated text that he appended to this treatise. The translated text appended to the earlier treatise too is a pedagogical tract explicitly concerned with "discipline." One must bear in mind, however, that the Erasmian tract advocates the pleasures of the learning process, stating that a great "parte of philosophye is lerned by playe," commending the study of the "Bucolicall" poets, and portraying pedagogy in general as a process of seduction, which depends to a large extent on "the handsomnes of the teacher." It is, in other words, a tract very much in line with the sense of the study of language as a "corporall . . . pleasure" that marks the treatise from its inception.

The translated text appended to *A Treatise of the Figures of Grammer and Rhetorike,* on the other hand, bespeaks no such playfulness. It is Cicero's *Pro Marcello,* an oration of "thanksgiving to Caesar for the restitution of Marcus Marcellus," accompanied by Sherry's marginal notations of instances of rhetorical forms that occur in it and of important thematic moments. Its subject matter is political, concerning a dispute on the place in the state of a "singuler wise man" who had dared voice criticism of Caesar while that ruler "warred in Galia." Given the political and martial context of the translated oration, it can hardly be thought incidental that one of Sherry's emphases of thematic moments in the text is the "definition of glory" as a political virtue, "a common reporte of many and great benefites done either to the Citizens, or to the countrey." Nor is it incidental that the first rhetorical form that Sherry points out in the translated text is "A Metaphore." "Metaphore" is defined by Sherry in *A Treatise of the Figures of*

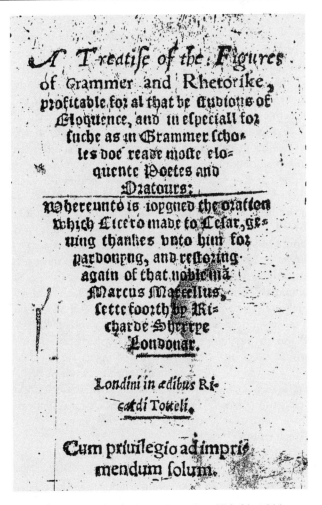

Title page for Sherry's last major work, published in 1555

Grammer and Rhetorike as "a word translated out of his proper place ito [*sic*] another," coinciding with tropes in their associations of conquest and control, and is celebrated as the foremost among rhetorical forms, the rhetorical equivalent of a ruler. "Among all vertues of speche," Sherry states in *A treatise of Schemes & Tropes* when discussing metaphor, "this is the cheyfe." The first metaphor pointed out by Sherry in this oration is described as "taken [out] of the maner of warre," further underscoring the political bent of Sherry's presentation of the text. In this later treatise, language is conceived of not also as a form of "corporall . . . pleasure" but exclusively as a political tool, an instrument of discipline and control.

The shift in Sherry's view of language between the ludic *A treatise of Schemes & Tropes* and the more somber and politically oriented *A Treatise of the Figures of Grammer and Rhetorike* is manifest in other ways as well. Although the impassioned commendation in the earlier treatise of the poetry of Sir Thomas Wyatt indicates the author's familiarity with the vernacular love poetry of his time, in the later treatise Sherry strangely disavows any such familiarity, stating that as he is "not well seen in Englishe Meters," he cannot "exemplifye in Englishe all these forsayde figures in Latin." The use of Latin indeed becomes one of the means through which the affective dimension of language that is foregrounded in the earlier treatise is foreclosed. In both treatises, Sherry flaunts his proficiency in the classical tongues, although this proficiency takes different forms. In *A treatise of Schemes & Tropes* Sherry gives the two names for each rhetorical form, first in Greek and then in Latin, an ordering in line with the author's nostalgia for ancient Greek culture. Greek names of various figures and tropes appear in *A Treatise of the Figures of Grammer and Rhetorike* as well; but in this later treatise they are embedded within a Latin text. The treatise as a whole is bilingual, alternating between Latin, which Sherry makes clear is the language in which he composed the treatise, and an English translation, for which Sherry claims to be unable to supply examples from poetry whose excellence he had celebrated in his earlier treatise. Latin in the later treatise thus becomes not only the mark of a man known even in his own times as one "elegantly learned," but also of that man's turning away from his earlier fascination with Greek language and Greek culture.

It is only natural, therefore, that the attitude to the pastoral reflected in *A Treatise of the Figures of Grammer and Rhetorike* should be different from that in the earlier treatise. Sherry continues to allude to pastoral works by citing the "peace worlde in the forth Egloge of Virgill" and the "foure ages in the fyrste of Metamorphoseos"—the first of which is the golden, pastoral age—when discussing the figure of "Chronographia, the description of time," but he neglects to mention the genre in his discussion of the figure that immediately precedes "Chronographia": "Topothesia." As "the faynyng of a place, when a place is descrybed, as paraduenture suche none is," topothesia has clear correspondences to the foreclosed, unattainable domain that is represented in the ancient form. Yet, Sherry prefers to exemplify topothesia with "the Utopia of Syr Thomas Moore," a text that also represents an idealized, nonexistent domain; but its content and context are more political than amatory and erotic, and it is projected toward the future rather than, like pastoral, the past.

In his last work, Sherry's concept of language is more politically than erotically oriented, and his implicit view of the rhetorician is no longer that of a poet-seducer offering language, upon its sonorous modulations, as "corporall . . . pleasure," but of a learned man involved in the affairs of state, as were two people to whom he alludes in this treatise, the Roman Marcus Marcellus and Sir Thomas More, and as was William Paget, the Tudor minister to whom Sherry dedicated his translation of the Ciceronian oration for Marcus Marcellus. Yet, Sherry's choice to allude to a learned Roman who had dared criticize Caesar and to a near contemporary who had refused to put his king above his conscience is revealing. It suggests that even when he represents rhetoric as an instrument of discipline, as he does in *A Treatise of the Figures of Grammer and Rhetorike,* Sherry is acutely aware of language as the domain not of law but of possibility.

Wood suggests that Richard Sherry was respected and known in his own time for his erudition and elegance, and he is routinely mentioned in surveys of English letters and studies of the history of rhetoric. At times, however, these references are diminutive, as in the case of historians of English literature Thomas Warton and Austin Allibone and even in the case of Herbert W. Hildebrandt, one of the modern editors of Sherry's first treatise. Other scholars refer to his work in passing, as they do to the work of the other English Renaissance rhetoricians. Yet, despite his singularity among English rhetoricians of the Renaissance, which is most manifest in his foregrounding of the affective, euphonic, seductive dimension of language in *A treatise of Schemes & Tropes* and his intriguing comment at the end of that treatise about the connection between rhetoric and dreams; despite the complexity of his personality, which is manifest in his conflicting interests in poetry, Reformist theology, education, politics, music, asceticism, and physical pleasure, and which is united only by a lifelong fascination with language, Richard Sherry's work has to date not been the subject of any extended study, apart from Hildebrandt's 1958 dissertation. His contribution to literature, to philosophy, and to psychology as an early modern theorist of language, as one fascinated by the many forms and implications of figures of linguistic joining and their relation to "corporall . . . pleasures," invites exploration and serious consideration.

Biography:

Anthony à Wood, "Richard Sherrey or Shirrie," in *Athenae Oxonienses. An Exact History of All the Writers and Bishops Who Have Had Their Education in the University of Oxford. To Which Are Added The Fasti, or Annals of the Said University,* edited by Philip Bliss, 4 volumes (New York & London: Johnson Reprint Corporation, 1967), I: column 189.

References:

S. Austin Allibone, *A Critical Dictionary of English Literature and British and American Authors: Living and Deceased from the Earliest Accounts to the Latter Half of the Nine-*

teenth Century, 3 volumes (Philadelphia: Lippincott, 1870–1871), II: 2083;

T. W. Baldwin, *William Shakspere's Small Latine & Lesse Greeke,* 2 volumes (Urbana: University of Illinois Press, 1944);

Terence Cave, *The Cornucopian Text: Problems of Writing in the French Renaissance* (Oxford: Clarendon Press / New York: Oxford University Press, 1979);

Eric Cheyfitz, *The Poetics of Imperialism: Translation and Colonization from The Tempest to Tarzan* (Oxford & New York: Oxford University Press, 1991; revised and enlarged edition, Philadelphia: University of Pennsylvania Press, 1997);

Clarence Griffin Child, *John Lyly and Euphuism* (Leipzig: Deichert, 1894);

William G. Crane, *Wit and Rhetoric in the Renaissance: The Formal Basis of Elizabethan Prose Style* (New York: Columbia University Press, 1937);

A. S. G. Edwards, "An Early Allusion to Wyatt," *Notes and Queries,* 227, no. 5 (1982): 402;

George J. Engelhardt, "The Relation of Sherry's *Treatise of Schemes and Tropes* to Wilson's *Arte of Rhetorique,*" *PMLA,* 62, no. 1 (1947): 76–82;

Joseph Foster, *Alumni Oxonienses: The Members of the University of Oxford, 1500–1714* (London: Parker, 1891–1892);

Richard Halpern, "A Mint of Phrases: Ideology and Style Production in Tudor England," in his *The Poetics of Primitive Accumulation: English Renaissance Culture and the Genealogy of Capital* (Ithaca: Cornell University Press, 1991), pp. 19–60;

Herbert W. Hildebrandt, "Amplification in a Rhetoric on Style," *Southern Speech Journal,* 30, no. 4 (1965): 294–307;

Hildebrandt, "Sherry: Renaissance Rhetorician," *Central States Speech Journal,* 11, no. 3 (1960): 204–209;

Wilbur S. Howell, *Logic and Rhetoric in England, 1500–1700* (Princeton: Princeton University Press, 1956);

Sister Miriam Joseph, *Rhetoric in Shakespeare's Time: Literary Theory of Renaissance Europe* (New York: Harcourt, Brace & World, 1962);

Jacqueline Lichtenstein, *The Eloquence of Color: Rhetoric and Painting in the French Classical Age,* translated by Emily McVarish (Berkeley: University of California Press, 1993);

Patricia Parker, *Literary Fat Ladies: Rhetoric, Gender, Property* (London & New York: Methuen, 1987);

Parker, *Shakespeare from the Margins: Language, Culture, Context* (Chicago & London: University of Chicago Press, 1996);

Wayne A. Rebhorn, *The Emperor of Men's Minds: Literature and the Renaissance Discourse of Rhetoric* (Ithaca & London: Cornell University Press, 1995);

William Phillips Sandford, *English Theories of Public Address, 1530–1828* (Columbus, Ohio: H. L. Hedrick, 1931);

Shirley Sharon-Zisser, "From 'Guest' to Occupier? Unstable Hospitality and the Ahistoricity of Tropology," in *Philosophy and Rhetoric,* 32, no. 4 (1999): 309–333;

Sharon-Zisser, "'Illustrer nôtre langue maternelle': Illustrative Similes and Failed Phallic Economy in Early Modern Rhetoric," *Exemplaria,* 9 (October 1997): 393–419;

Sharon-Zisser, "Tropes and Topazes: The Colonialist Tropology of the Tropics," *Textual Practice,* 11, no. 2 (1997): 285–303;

Brian Vickers, *In Defense of Rhetoric* (Oxford: Clarendon Press, 1988);

Thomas Warton, *The History of English Poetry, from the Close of the Eleventh to the Commencement of the Eighteenth Century,* 4 volumes (London: J. Dodsley, 1774–1789) IV: 248;

Foster Watson, *The English Grammar Schools to 1660: Their Curriculum and Practice* (Cambridge: Cambridge University Press, 1908);

Stephen Whitworth, "Far from Being: Rhetoric and Dream-Work in John Dickenson's *Arisbas,*" *Exemplaria,* 11 (Spring 1999): 167–194.

Richard Taverner

(circa 1505 – 14 July 1575)

Dakota L. Hamilton
Humboldt State University

BOOKS: *A Catechisme or institution of the Christen Religion, Newely setforthe by Richard Tauerner* (London: Printed by Richard Bankes, 1539);

The garden of wysdom wherin ye maye gather moste pleasaunt flowres, that is to say, proper wytty and quycke sayenges of princes, philosophers, and dyuers other sortes of men. Drawen forth of good authours, as well Grekes as Latyns, by Rycharde Tauerner (London: Printed by Richard Bankes for John Harvey, 1539; revised and enlarged edition, London: Edward Whitechurch for William Telotson, 1540?);

The secōd booke of the Garden of wysdome, wherin are conteyned wytty, pleasaunt, and nette sayenges of renowmed personages collected by Rycharde Tauerner (London: Printed by Richard Bankes, 1539)—includes *Of the garden of wysdome thyrde boke* in *The second booke of the Garden of wysdome.*

OTHER: *A ryght frutefull Epystle deuysed by the moste excellent clerke Erasmus in laude and prayse of matrymony translated in to Englyshe by Rychard Tauernour which translation he hathe dedicate to the ryght honorable Mayster Thomas Cromwel most worthy Counseloure to our souerayne lorde kyng Henry the eyght,* translated by Taverner (London: Printed by Robert Redman, 1531?);

The confessyon of the fayth of the Germaynes exhibited to the moste victorious Emperour Charles the .v. in the Councell or assemble holden at Augusta the yere of our Lorde. 1530. To which is added the apologie of Melancthon, translated by Taverner (London: Printed by Robert Redman, 1536);

Cōmon places of scripture ordrely and after a cōpendious forme of teachyng, set forth with no litle labour, to the gret profit and help of all such studentes in gods worde as haue not had long exercyse in the same, by the ryghte excellent clerke Erasmus Sarcerius. Translated in to Englysh by Rychard Tauerner, translated by Taverner (London: Printed by John Byddell, 1538);

The Nevv Testament Of Ovr sauiour Jesu Chryst, translated in to English: and newly recognised with great diligence after

moost faythfull exemplars, by Rycharde Taverner, translated by Taverner(London: Printed by Thomas Petyt for Thomas Berthelet, 1539);

The Most Sacred Bible, which is the holy scripture, conteyning the old and new testament, translated in to English, and newly recognised with great diligence after most faythful exemplars, by Rychard Taverner, translated by Taverner (London: Printed by John Byddell for Thomas Berthelet, 1539);

The summe or pith of the 150 psalms of David, reduced in to a forme of meditations (London: Printed by John Byddell, 1539); revised as *An Epitome of the Psalmes, or briefe meditacions vpon the same, with diuerse other moste christian prayers,* translated by Richard Taverner, translated by Taverner (London: Printed by Richard Bankes? for Anthony Clarke?, 1539);

Prouerbes Or adagies with newe addicions gathered out of the Chiliades of Erasmus by Richard Tauerner. Hereunto be also added Mimi Publiani, edited by Taverner (London: Printed by Richard Bankes, 1539);

Flores Aliqvot Sententiarvm Ex Variis collecti scriptoribus. The Flovvers Of Sencies gathered out of sundry wryters by Erasmus in Latine, and Englished by Richard Tauerner, edited and translated by Taverner (London: Printed by Richard Bankes, 1540);

The Epistles and Gospelles with a brief Postill vpon the same from Aduent tyll Lowe sondaye whiche is the (Wynter parte) drawen forth by diuerse learned men for the singuler cōmoditie of all good christen persons and namely of Prestes and Curates newly recognized, edited by Taverner (London: Printed by Richard Bankes, 1540);

The Epistles and Gospelles with a brief Postil vpon the same from after Easter tyll Aduent, which is the Somer parte, setforth for the singuler cōmoditie of all good christen men and namely of Prestes and Curates, 2 parts, edited by Taverner (London: Printed by Richard Bankes, 1540);

Catonis Disticha Moralia Ex Castigatione D. Erasmi Roterodami una cum annotationibus & scholijs Richardi Tauerneri anglico idiomate conscriptis in usum Anglicæ iuuentutis, edited and translated by Taverner (London: Printed by Richard Bankes, 1540);

The Principal lawes customes and estatutes of England which be at this present day in ure, compendiously gathered togither for ye weale and benefit of the kinges Maiesties most louing subiects, newely recognised and augmented, edited by Taverner (London: Printed by Richard Bankes, 1540);

The gospels with brief sermōs vpon them for al the holy dayes in ye yere, translated by Taverner (London: Printed by Richard Bankes, 1542?);

"The poesie of Richard Tauerner Gent.," in *A registre of Hystories, conteining Martiall exploites of worthy warriours, Politique praaises of Ciuil Magistrates, wise Sentences of famous Philosophers, And other matters manifolde and memorable* (London: Humphrey Middleton for Thomas Woodcocke, 1576).

Editions: *Postils on the Epistles and Gospels compiled and published by Richard Taverner in the year 1540,* edited by Edward Cardwell (Oxford: Oxford University Press, 1841);

Proverbes; or Adagies gathered out of the Chiliades of Erasmus (New York: Agathynian Club, 1867);

The Augsburg Confession. Translated from the Latin, in 1536. By Richard Taverner, edited by Henry E. Jacobs (Philadelphia: Lutheran Publication Society, 1888);

Proverbs or Adages by Desiderius Erasmus Gathered out of the Chilliades and Englished by Richard Taverner, 1569, introduction by DeWitt T. Starnes (Gainesville, Fla.: Scholars' Facsimiles and Reprints, 1956);

"Richard Taverner: Postils on Epistles and Gospels," in *English Reformers,* edited by T. H. L. Parker, Library of Christian Classics, volume 26 (Philadelphia: Westminster, 1966), pp. 221–252;

Desiderius Erasmus, Proverbes or Adagies, London 1539 reprint of *Proverbes or adagies with newe addicions gathered out of the Chiliades by Richard Tauerner. Hereunto be also added Mimi Publiani,* The English Experience, no. 124 (Amsterdam: Theatrum Orbis Terrarum / New York: Da Capo, 1969);

Confessyon of the fayth of the Germaynes; The apologie by Melancthon, The English Experience, no. 771 (Amsterdam: Theatrum Orbis Terrarum / Norwood, N.J.: W. J. Johnson, 1976);

"*In Laud and Praise of Matrimony,* trans. Richard Taverner," in *Daughters, Wives, and Widows: Writings by Men about Women and Marriage in England, 1500–1640,* edited by Joan Larsen Klein (Urbana: University of Illinois Press, 1992), pp. 65–89.

Richard Taverner earned his reputation mainly, though not exclusively, as a translator of work by the renowned European humanist scholar Desiderius Erasmus of Rotterdam. While Erasmus generally distanced himself from the Lutheran-inspired Reformation, his work nevertheless was turned into moderate Protestant tracts by men such as Taverner. The translation of work written by decidedly Protestant Continental reformers, however, often went in the opposite direction: the work of men such as Wolfgang Capito, Erasmus Sarcerius, and John Calvin, all three translated by Taverner, was moderated for Henry VIII, who, though enjoying freedom from papal authority after the English Reformation of the 1530s, was still relatively conservative in matters of religion. The selection of at least some of these translation projects directly involved Taverner's patron and the king's chief minister, Thomas Cromwell, who was interested in producing treatises that supported the burgeoning Henrician church of the 1530s. Even those works that were translated at Taverner's own initiative nevertheless were produced with contemporary religious and political aims in mind, however. Taverner, then, was in large measure an apologist for the Crown, and in his work he was most concerned about teaching right thinking about the new Anglican Church and the politics that underpinned it.

Three of his translations, however, have a secondary dimension: the education of young readers in rhetoric. *The garden of wysdom wherin ye maye gather moste pleasaunt flowres, that is to say, proper wytty and quycke sayenges of princes, philosophers, and dyuers other sortes of men* (1539), *Prouerbes Or adagies with newe addicions gathered out of the Chiliades of Erasmus* (1539), and *Flores Aliqvot Sententiarvm Ex Variis collecti scriptoribus* (1540) are taken primarily from the writings of Erasmus and generally consist of the wise sayings of famous figures from history. Taverner, though, makes his own distinctive contribution through his careful selection and translation of these sayings and his accompanying commentary on them. For Taverner, these wise old saws serve a dual purpose: they help develop and refine certain rhetorical skills while at the same time promoting correct thinking about religion and politics. The fact that the latter was more important to Taverner does not diminish the pedagogical importance of his works.

Richard Taverner is commonly said to have been born about 1505 in Brisley, county Norfolk. He was the eldest son and heir of John Taverner and his wife, Alice Silvester, who was an heiress in her own right. Taverner had at least three younger brothers, two of whom sat for Parliament, Robert in 1545 and Roger in 1554. Information on Taverner's early years is scant, but he received enough of an education to be admitted to Corpus Christi College, Cambridge, in 1520. While at Cambridge, Taverner was counted a member of "Little Germany," a group consisting of fifty to sixty students who eagerly–and illegally–seized upon and debated the

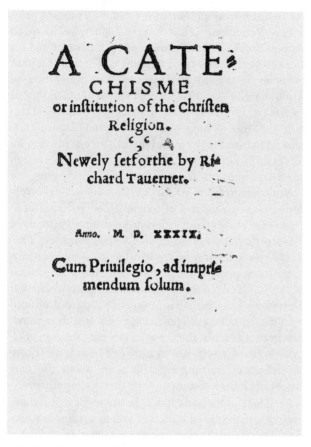

A CATE-
CHISME
or inſtitution of the Chriſten
Religion.

Newely ſetforthe by Ri-
chard Tauerner.

Anno. M. D. XXXIX.

Cum Priuilegio, ad impri-
mendum ſolum.

Title page for Richard Taverner's translation of John Calvin's 1537 catechism, the first work by Calvin to be published in English

Lutheran literature then coming out of Europe. Taverner kept company with men who later were leading figures in the English Reformation: Thomas Cranmer, Hugh Latimer, Nicholas Ridley, John Bale, Matthew Parker, and John Foxe. The religious and civil authorities did not look favorably on this group, and in 1525 many members were forced either to recant their heretical beliefs or flee to the safety of the Continent. Taverner, like most in the group, submitted himself to the authorities. Some scholars have attributed Taverner's transfer by 1527 to Cardinal College (later Christ Church), Oxford, to Cardinal Thomas Wolsey, then chief minister to Henry VIII. Wolsey was anxious to attract scholars to his recent foundation, although Taverner may himself have decided on the change owing to his recent troubles in Cambridge.

Taverner may also have been influenced in this decision because his kinsman, John Taverner, was headmaster of the choristers at Cardinal College. He graduated with a B.A. on 21 June 1527 and supported his continuing studies at Oxford through a petty canonry he obtained. In 1528 certain college members were found to be in possession of heretical books and

were taken into custody. Historians frequently have confused Taverner with John Taverner and indicated that he was implicated with this group. There seems to be no question, however, that it was indeed John who was arrested, although Taverner might well have counted himself lucky to have escaped notice, given his Protestant inclinations and his connection to the choirmaster. There is no firm date for his return to Cambridge, although this incident may have prompted the move. Taverner's bachelor of arts degree was incorporated at Gonville Hall in 1529–1530, and he gained his M.A. degree at about the same time.

At some point Taverner traveled to the Continent to study, although it is impossible to pinpoint exactly when. He wrote two letters to Cromwell probably, as Sir Geoffrey Elton suggested in *Reform and Renewal: Thomas Cromwell and the Common Weal* (1973), in late 1530. In the first letter he related the information that he had left a teaching position at Cambridge in order to study abroad but that his unnamed patron had died and he was now destitute. Cromwell's response was favorable to Taverner's request for help, and in the second letter Taverner thanked the minister for his willingness to speak to the king on his behalf and also for persuading the duke of Norfolk to grant him an annuity. In gratitude Taverner almost immediately set to work translating Erasmus's *Encomium Matrimonii* (In Praise of Marriage). Elton argued convincingly that Taverner's translation, *A ryght frutefull Epystle deuysed by the moste excellent clerke Erasmus in laude and prayse of matrymony,* was published in 1531, not some five years later, as stated in the *Dictionary of National Biography* and the *Short-Title Catalogue,* and was in response to Cromwell's kindness toward Taverner in his predicament and not a direct commission. The work, which addresses the contentious issue of clerical celibacy, is dedicated to Cromwell, who by then had some indication of Taverner's literary skills.

Taverner continued at Cambridge for another year, if not under Cromwell's direct patronage, then at least through his good offices. In 1533 he took up residence at Staire or Strand Inn, an inn of Chancery, where he probably remained until 1537, when he was admitted to the Inner Temple, another of the London law courts. He was an active member of the Inner Temple until at least 1561 and possibly even longer. Though ostensibly studying the law, Taverner apparently entered more directly into Cromwell's service when he went up to London. Martin Tyndall seems to have assumed as much in a letter to the minister dated 2 July 1533, in which he sent Cromwell a translation of his from Erasmus and asked him to have Taverner evaluate its merits. While philosophy and theology reputedly were two of Taverner's key subject areas while at Cambridge, he was especially noted for his command of Greek. Taverner's great-grandson, the noted antiquary Anthony à Wood, writing in the middle of the next century, reported that Taverner's language skills were so exceptional that while at the Strand Inn and Inner Temple he translated, at will, English law into Greek. Cromwell was most in need of exactly these sorts of language skills during the middle and late 1530s.

Taverner may have transferred into the king's service in 1536 and been appointed a clerk of the signet in 1537, but he actually continued to answer to Cromwell, who employed him first and foremost as a translator of texts—Erasmian texts especially—that could be used to support and defend the reforms of the Church of England and the politics that underpinned it. Taverner was joined in this task by other leading English humanists such as Richard Moryson and Thomas Starkey, who were also in Cromwell's service. The part that Taverner and his fellow humanists played in the English Reformation, however, was of greater literary significance than even Cromwell himself might have imagined, though in a quite unexpected way.

Taverner was very much in step with the Continental reformers both in their theology and their method of dissemination. He might have taken a slightly stronger theological line (or rather, might have rendered more precisely the doctrine of the German Protestants) in his translations had the conservative Henry VIII been more sympathetic to the Protestant movement, but in general, Taverner was a religious moderate, as were many of the early English reformers. Taverner, like the Continental reformers, also believed firmly in the use of persuasion rather than force in effecting reform. With force consciously eschewed by Protestants such as Taverner, rhetoric took on a particular importance within the whole of the Reformation itself. The application of classical rhetoric to biblical texts as a method to understanding and interpreting them was a relatively new and also somewhat controversial practice, but humanists such as Erasmus and German Protestants such as Martin Luther and Philipp Melanchthon gave legitimacy to this *theologia rhetorica*, this rhetorical approach to scripture. Rhetoric became more than a means of understanding and interpreting, however; it became a method of dissemination as well. Taverner himself preferred action, right reason, and truth to stand on their own, but he recognized the necessity of rhetoric or eloquence in the face of "flowle and detestable raylynges" (as he called them in *The garden of wysdom*) surrounding debate about Christian doctrine. Taverner and his contemporaries knew that converts would be made through reason and persuasion and responded accordingly.

Taverner's translations, then, served various purposes, some of them explicit, some of them more subtle. First and most importantly, they promoted right thinking about the evolving doctrine of the English church. Secondly, they provided models on which both children and adults might pattern themselves and their behavior. Thirdly, some of them also served as handbooks in the art of rhetoric and persuasion in speech and writing. Lastly, Taverner's translations introduced an increasingly literate English public to men whose work had previously been available only to a well-educated elite. Indeed, some of the work of Erasmus was translated into English for the first time by Taverner, who is also credited with being the first English translator of John Calvin.

The first recorded official duty Taverner performed for Cromwell was translating the Augsburg Confession and Melanchthon's defense of it, which appeared in 1536 as *The confessyon of the fayth of the Germaynes exhibited to the moste victorious Emperour Charles the .v. in the Councell or assemble holden at Augusta the yere of our Lorde. 1530. To which is added the apologie of Melanchthon.* The doctrine of these documents supports the kinds of religious changes Cromwell was then trying to effect, although the political elements behind his decision to have these particular tracts translated were also certainly there. The Germans insisted on England accepting the confession as a condition of their entry into the Schmalkaldic League (a defensive alliance against France and the Holy Roman Empire), and Cromwell ordered Taverner to translate both works. The confession promotes the doctrine of justification by faith alone, a concept central to Protestantism, but one that Henry VIII never endorsed. Taverner later had reason to be concerned about the decidedly Protestant content of this work and others. The Augsburg Confession was burned at Paul's Cross in 1546, as was Taverner's next major work, *Cõmon places of scripture ordrely and after a cõpendious forme of teachyng, set forth with no litle labour, to the gret profit and help of all such studentes in gods worde as haue not had long exercyse in the same, by the ryghte excellent clerke Erasmus Sarcerius*, produced in 1538.

Cõmon places of scripture was taken from *Loci communes* (Common places) of Erasmus Sarcerius, who was closely associated with Melanchthon. Taverner was particularly interested in this work because it was intended for young students and those who did not know Scripture well. Commonplace books were popular among young and old alike from the late Middle Ages throughout the sixteenth century, forming a basic part of a boy's education. Students read widely, taking careful notes of wise sayings, choice phrases, and pithy sentences, and then arranged them under various headings, or *loci communes*. The commonplace book, then,

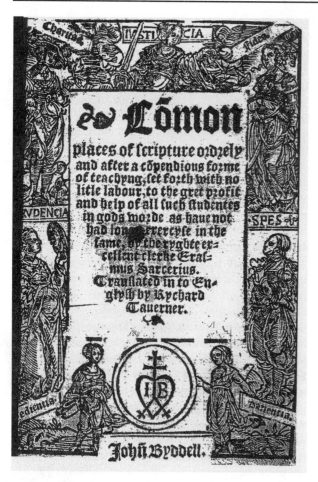

Title page for Taverner's adaptation of Erasmus Sarcerius's Loci communes, *a collection of wise sayings, choice phrases, and pithy sentences drawn from the Bible*

served as a ready rhetorical aid to argument and style both in oration and writing. Such books began to be produced commercially in the first part of the sixteenth century; they often featured classical material prominently, although their content broadened considerably over time, as Taverner's own *Cōmon places of scripture* suggests.

Cōmon places of scripture is an early example of rhetorical deconstruction, but with the Protestant perspective that was typical of the Reformation. It served as a rhetorical aid, but it also provided a method of understanding and interpreting selected passages of Scripture. In keeping with the principles of Protestant humanism, Taverner subtly guides the reader in the doctrine of this deconstruction. He occasionally uses the figure of a hand, drawn in the margin and pointing to particular passages, to highlight what he considered to be important points. The section on auricular confession was one such passage, and while penitents were advised to seek counsel of their curate, neither Sarcerius nor Taverner meant formal confession as understood in the

Catholic Church. There was no mention of a priest, and the curate's role was more like that of a friend and counselor. Further, justification by faith alone was also promoted, although expressed in somewhat abstract and unobtrusive language. So while Sarcerius's piece, and Taverner's translation of it, was moderate (at least in comparison with other contemporary Lutheran works), it was still Protestant in outlook and thus earned condemnation in 1546.

Taverner's appointment as a clerk of the signet in 1537, along with some assurance of extra income generated from Cromwell's literary assignments, probably gave him the financial security he needed in order to marry. In August of that year he married Margaret Lambert, whose father was a goldsmith in London. They had a large family, four sons and three daughters; unusually for the period, all of them survived their father. Soon after the marriage, and about the time that *Cōmon places of scripture* was published, Taverner took a forty-year lease on a London property described as "le Sarsons Hed," which probably referred in some way to the Saracen's Head, a well-known local inn. Taverner's house was situated in Fletestrete (Fleet Street), near St. Paul's Cathedral, in the part of London in which most of the book trade was centered. He was thus literally in an excellent position to oversee the publication of his work.

The year 1539 was exceptionally productive for Taverner, with a total of seven publications. It is difficult to date these works firmly much beyond the year of publication. It seems likely, however, that Taverner's *The Nevv Testament Of Ovr sauiour Jesu Chryst, translated in to English: and newly recognised with great diligence after moost faythfull exemplars,* appeared early in the year, before his *The Most Sacred Bible, which is the holy scripture, conteyning the old and new testament, translated in to English, and newly recognised with great diligence after most faythful exemplars.* Taverner was an excellent Greek scholar, and biblical scholars generally credit his version of the New Testament with being one of the finest translations made in the sixteenth century, which makes it all the more curious that its impact was negligible on the official English versions of the Bible of the period, including the 1611 King James Version. What made Taverner's edition so original was his word choice. Instead of using the Latinate version of a word, he instead chose the Anglo-Saxon, and in both the New Testament and the Old Testament he generally worked toward brevity and clarity in his translation. Consequently, his New Testament is in the vernacular of the day and relatively accessible to the common people. Despite Taverner's Protestant perspective, his work had significant influence on the 1582 Rheims edition of the New Testament and the Douai Old Testament of 1609–1610, both Counter-Reformation English translations.

Taverner's Bible, which probably followed closely upon his New Testament, was really a slight reworking of the so-called Matthew Bible of 1537. Taverner knew no Hebrew and relied on the Latin translations exclusively, especially William Tyndale's outlawed 1534 edition of the Bible. He dropped most of Tyndale's offending marginalia and also his highly controversial prologue to the book of Romans. Taverner's edition still has a decidedly Protestant gloss, though not so much in the commentary, which is scant, but in the actual translation itself, in his phrasing and his word choice. Again he uses a drawing of a hand in the margin to point to particular passages that merit special attention, such as Rom. 5:1, which reads "Justified by faith."

The impetus for Taverner's translation is somewhat curious. Some scholars maintain that Cromwell, his patron, had put him to work on it; yet, the minister had arranged for others to produce an official version of the Bible based on Miles Coverdale's edition of 1535, the result being the Great Bible of 1539. In his dedication to Henry VIII, Taverner writes that the printer, Thomas Berthelet, had asked him to make the translation and that he had done so in great haste. The reason for his haste is not known, but it may have had to do with resentment on the part of Berthelet, who was the king's printer, that he was not given the commission to publish the official Great Bible and with his desire to hurry a competing version into print. This haste would account for the modest physical appearance of Taverner's Bible, which lacks standard ornamentation such as illustrations and decorative borders. Although Taverner's Bible was soon superseded by an official edition, his work was not entirely in vain: some of it reappeared in a Bible produced under the direction of Bishop Edmund Becke in 1551. Becke chose the least original of Taverner's work to reprint, using his Old Testament instead of his New Testament. For the latter, Becke relied on the earlier Tyndale edition.

Five more publications, mainly translations of the works of others, appeared before the end of 1539. There were two versions of *An Epitome of the Psalmes,* published in 1539. The earlier of the two seems to be *The summe or pith of the 150 psalms of David, reduced in to a forme of meditations,* published by John Bydell, which was immediately followed by a revised version, *An Epitome of the Psalmes, or briefe meditacions vpon the same, with diuerse other moste christian prayers,* published by Richard Banks later that year. The mention of Anne of Cleves, who became the king's fourth wife early in 1540, in the dedication places the publication of *An epitome of the Psalmes* probably late in 1539. In the prologue of the former,

addressed to the Christian reader, Taverner fully credits Wolfgang Capito, a German reformer, with the original work and states that Cromwell had ordered him to make the translation. The preface of the second edition, addressed directly to the king, is long and full of lavish praise. Reference to Capito is dropped in the second edition, and a section of scriptural prayers is added.

The words *summe, pith,* and *epitome* in the two titles refer to succinct statements that carry great weight. For Taverner, nothing could carry more weight than biblical texts and no treatment better suited that kind of material than brevity and simplicity. This approach was especially appropriate, since *An Epitome of the Psalmes* was concerned with the religious instruction of laypersons, not the learned clergy, and may have been aimed at young adults in particular. Parts of the work, in fact, found their way into the official 1545 "King's Primer," which gave a child's first lessons in the alphabet and catechism. Based on this evidence, as well as stylistic similarities between passages in the primer and Taverner's other work, Charles C. Butterworth argued convincingly in his 1953 book that Taverner was responsible, under Cranmer's close guidance, for editing the "King's Primer." Taverner was also linked to another, slightly earlier primer produced by the Protestant printer Edward Whitchurch in 1541, which, Butterworth suggested, lends further credence to Taverner's association with the official primer four years later. Certainly Taverner was interested in instructing and catechizing the young, and the primer projects were in keeping with those concerns. Dairmaid MacCulloch, in *Thomas Cranmer* (1996), and Eamon Duffy in his *The Stripping of the Altars: Traditional Religion in England c. 1400 – c. 1580* (1992) both observed that Cranmer was greatly influenced by Taverner's work on these primers in the preparation of the 1549 *Book of Common Prayer.*

Taverner's *A Catechisme or institution of the Christen Religion, Newely setforthe* (1539) is similar in nature to *An Epitome of the Psalmes,* and the two volumes may have been stimulated by Taverner's work on revising the Bible and rendering a new translation of the New Testament. The catechism may also have had the nominal approval of the king, who, in the preface, is likened to King Hezekiah of Judah, a religious reformer (though a poor military commander) in the Old Testament. In content the catechism is a loose translation of John Calvin's *An Instruction in Faith,* published in French in 1537 and Latin in 1538, and is notable for being the first work of Calvin's to be published in English. At the time, however, Taverner was unable to acknowledge this connection to Calvin, whose works were forbidden in England.

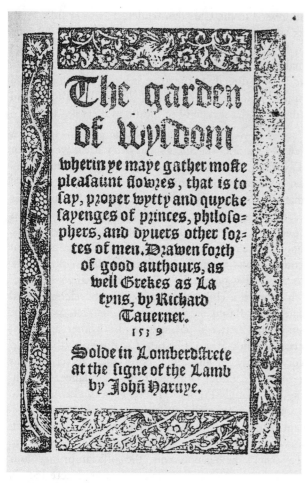

*Title page for the book Taverner wrote to instruct
young readers in rhetoric*

Taverner states in the preface to *A Catechisme or
institution of the Christen Religion* that the general lack of
knowledge of Christian faith prompted him to produce the work, but he aims it especially at godparents
regarding their religious responsibilities toward godchildren. He makes some changes in Calvin's text in
order to conform with the mildly conservative "Bishops Book" of 1537, which outlined official English doctrine. Still, Taverner's translation manages a
discussion of justification by faith alone ("In Christ we
be made righteous by faith") discreet enough not to
have incurred the wrath of the authorities. His discourse on the Lord's Supper is handled with equal del-
icacy. Where Calvin denied the real presence of Jesus
in the Eucharist outright, Taverner avoids the issue
and writes only that Christ "keepeth His residence in
heaven and no longer in earth."

The last three of Taverner's works for 1539 are
directly connected to each other and have decidedly
pedagogical elements. *The garden of wysdom* initially
appeared as three texts, with the second and third parts

published together in one volume. The material for the
first and second books of *The garden of wysdom* comes
mainly from Erasmus's *Apophthegmata* (1531), a word that
Taverner notes in his second book comes from the
Greek and means "shorte and quycke speakynges." In
essence, then, the two books consist of anecdotes about
great men from history, and Taverner included roughly
fifty of the nearly six hundred passages from the original
work. In the first book Taverner acknowledges his debt
to Erasmus and follows his order of the names closely.
He does not credit Erasmus in the second book and
writes that he kept no particular order but rather wrote
the "prouerbe that fyrst commeth to the hand that I
write"; about one-third of that work still derives from
Apophthegmata, however. Charles R. Baskervill, in "Taverner's *Garden of Wisdom* and the *Apophthegmata* of Erasmus" (1939), noted that additional material for the
second book came from other sources, one of them
undoubtedly being Herodotus, though not firsthand.
DeWitt T. Starnes, in "Richard Taverner's *The garden of
wisdom,* Carion's *Chronicles,* and the Cambyses Legend"
(1956), identified the intermediary source of Herodotus
as coming from the 1532 publication *Chronica durch Magis-
tru,* produced by Johann Carion, a professor of mathematics at Frankfort, Germany. Carion's work was
translated from German into Latin by Hermann Bonnus
in 1537, and from this text Taverner made his own translation. Starnes also linked Thomas Preston's play, *A
Lamentable Tragedy mixed full of Mirth conteyning the Life of
Cambises, King of Percia,* written in about 1569, directly to
Taverner's translation of the King Cambyses story, as
told by Carion from Herodotus. Taverner added some
of his own material to both books as well, passages, for
example, that praise Henry VIII and deal with contemporary problems and issues. Through the deliberate
selection of these anecdotes and the carefully written
comments on them, Taverner tailors the material to support the religious policies of the day.

It was customary of translators to be rhetorically
self-deprecating about their skills, and Taverner was no
exception. In the address to the reader in the second
book of *The garden of wysdom* Taverner asks pardon for
his "incondite and grosse phrase." But however self-effac-
ing, Taverner employs his humanistic training to good
effect. Taverner notes in his second book the importance
of rhetoric or eloquence, especially in terms of producing
a respect for law and order. He also professes that he
would rather employ arts of persuasion than threats of
force in emphasizing a point. Both of these books served
as a kind of handbook in the gentle art of persuasion,
and Taverner uses a traditional humanistic technique to
demonstrate his methods. *The garden of wysdom* is distinctive among Taverner's works in combining the
humanistic concept of providing a "precept" and an

"example" from which the reader might learn not only wise conduct but also rhetorical skills.

The first two books of *The garden of wysdom* differ markedly, both in terms of style and content, from the third book, which initially was published with the second book but was almost immediately enlarged and published separately under the title *Desiderius Erasmus, Proverbes or Adagies, London 1539 reprint of Proverbes or adagies with newe addicions gathered out of the Chiliades of Erasmus by Richard Tauerner. Proverbes or adagies,* which also includes Taverner's translation of Erasmus's *Mimi Publiani,* comprises some 187 passages (about 50 more than were originally published) from Erasmus's *Adagiorum chiliades* (1508). A second edition, published in 1545, was enlarged to include 235 proverbs and went into three more editions by 1569. Erasmus did much to popularize proverbs in the sixteenth century, and he expounded on their educational and rhetorical nature: they taught philosophy, argument, and gracefulness in speech and writing while also giving added meaning to classical texts. In form, Erasmus gave the adage in a brief Latin phrase or sentence and provided a commentary running anywhere from a few lines to more than fifty. In some cases he included information on sources, meaning, and application in his discourse. Taverner also gives the adage in Latin, but he then translates it into English. Generally speaking, Taverner excludes the material on sources and concentrates on commentary, some of which was of his own composition and was clearly intended to support Henry VIII and his new church. Some of the proverbs included in Taverner's translation entered into English for the first time.

Taverner's fifth translation of Erasmus is *Flores Aliqvot Sententiarvm Ex Variis collecti scriptoribus. The Flovvers of Sencies gathered out of sundry wryters,* published in 1540. The title alludes to the rhetorical nature of the work, the "flovvers" being the best sayings of wise and learned men, from which readers were to learn and pattern not only their behavior but also their writing and speech. The educational nature of the work is further revealed in Taverner's dedication to the "florentissima pubes Britannica" (the flower of Britain's youth). In Erasmus's version of the work, a Latin translation of a Greek precept was provided, but without scholarly apparatus. Taverner includes the Latin but translates or paraphrases it in English. Like the rest of Taverner's translations, *Flores Aliqvot* was an extremely popular work, and three more editions were forthcoming over the next twenty years. Although there is no direct evidence that this particular text was specifically designed for or used in schools, it did fit in well with the kind of texts that schoolchildren used, especially from the reign of Edward VI forward. It seems likely that William

Shakespeare owned or at least had seen texts such as these during his lifetime, and it is tempting to speculate that the playwright, who frequently incorporated proverbs into his plays, may even have owned something by Taverner, whose works were still in circulation at the end of the century.

The Epistles and Gospelles wyth a brief Postil, Taverner's next major work, appeared in two volumes in 1540—the first, or winter, volume covering Advent to Easter, and the second, or summer, volume spanning Easter to Advent—with a third, *The gospels with brief sermõs vpon them for al the holy dayes in ye yere,* added around 1542. These volumes are credited with being the first biblical commentary in English. They were almost certainly produced to help the clergy comply with the Injunctions of 1538, which, among other things, admonished them to deliver a sermon each week on the Epistles and Gospels. Taverner wrote that he produced the winter part "wyth the help of other sobre men which be better learned" than he was, perhaps including Miles Coverdale. Taverner's work was derivative, with material coming from men such as Latimer and Cuthbert Tunstall, bishop of Durham.

The dedicatory page of the winter volume seems to indicate that it was published before Cromwell's fall in June 1540; as Duffy observed, "the preface has the confident tone of a man favoured by authority and speaking for it, even threatening clergy who did not make good use of the book with royal wrath and the ending of all hope of preferment." Conversely, the dedication of the second volume, Duffy continued, has "a positively panic-stricken air about it and contains a strident defense of Taverner's own orthodoxy and rectitude." In the summer volume Taverner admonishes "obedience to God and to hys commaundements, obedience to the kynges maiestie and to his lawes, obedience to the holsome tradicions of the churche." Although he may err in his writings, "an heretique I can be none," and he castigates Anabaptists, Sacramentaries, and other like heretics.

His earlier published position on various issues clearly made him nervous: "The sacrament of the aultar, the sacrament of penaunce with the other sacraments of the church be here not heretically contemned, but catholikely [universally] auaunced." He also demonstrates a new caution on the issue of justification by faith and the role of good works: "Fayth is here not so nakedly extolled, but that good workes also be necessarily requered to be in a christen man. Neyther yet be good workes here in suche sorte magnified, that fayth whiche ought to be the foundacion of the christen religion is defrauded of her due place." Significantly, he made clear his willingness to submit to correction: if he had erred or offended, he "wol not obstinately defend

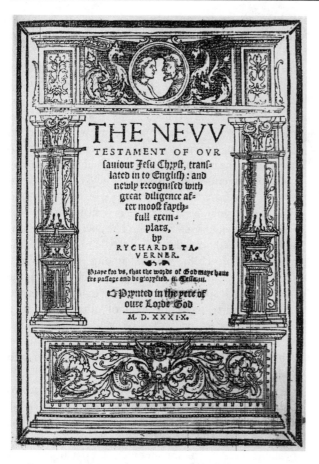

THE NEVU

TESTAMENT OF OVR
sauiour Jesu Chryst, trans=
lated in to English: and
newly recognised with
great diligence af=
ter moost fayth=
full exem=
plars,
by
RYCHARDE TA=
VERNER.

Praye for vs, that the worde of God maye haue
fre passage and be glospred. ii. Cessa.iii.

Prynted in the yere of
oure Lorde God

M. D. XXXI.X.

*Title page for Taverner's vernacular translation of the Bible, which
influenced the translators of the 1582 Rheims edition of
the New Testament*

the same, but submyt my selfe to the iudgement of the
church." After having protected himself somewhat by
expressing a willingness to recant anything that the
authorities might object to, Taverner nevertheless bases
his commentary on the premise of justification by faith
alone. In this choice he still follows the doctrine set out
by the Bishops Book and the Ten Articles, although justification by faith alone was soon to be rejected in the
King's Book of 1543, which superseded the Bishops
Book. Taverner avoided altogether the controversial
points covered in the 1539 Act of Six Articles, which
confirmed belief in transubstantiation, communion in
one kind for the laity, clerical celibacy, observation of
vows of chastity, private masses, and auricular confession. However nervous Taverner may have been at the
possible reception of this work in 1540, it was looked
upon favorably two reigns later: some of Taverner's
material was included verbatim in the Elizabethan *Book
of Homilies* (1563).

Taverner's next publication was considerably
less contentious. As with *Flores Aliqvot, Catonis Disticha
Moralia Ex Castigatione D. Erasmi Roterodami una cum*

*annotationibus & scholijs Richardi Tauerneri anglico idiomate
conscriptis in usum Anglicæ iuuentutis* (1540) was taken
from Erasmus's *Opuscula aliquot* (1514) and was
intended for the youth of England ("en usum Anglicae
iuuentutis"). Cato's verse proverbs were the original
source, and in keeping with his earlier translations of
Erasmus, Taverner cites the Latim epigram and then
provides an English, and sometimes edited, translation
of Erasmus's commentary. Like *Flores Aliqvot, Catonis
Disticha Moralia* went through several reprintings—six
by 1569–1570—and was the sort of text that schoolmasters employed in their curriculum.

Cromwell's fall in the middle of 1540 was a crip-
pling blow to the reformers and caused panic not only
in Taverner but also in many others besides. Aside
from the fact that progressive reform seemed at an
end, there was also the troubling matter of religious
positions taken, asserted, and promulgated during the
1530s. In the preface to the second part of *The Epistles
and Gospelles wyth a brief Postil* Taverner is clearly nervous about his earlier positions and his new relationship with Henry VIII.

Taverner did indeed find himself in trouble with
the authorities, but it had nothing to do with Cromwell
or even his own beliefs, as has often been asserted. In
December 1541, in the middle of the investigations into
the infidelities of Catherine Howard, the fifth wife of
Henry VIII, rumors circulated among Taverner, his
family, and some of their acquaintances that Henry's
fourth wife, Lady Anne of Cleves, was still actually
married to the king and had recently been delivered of
his child. Some of them went further, suggesting that
the whole sordid business about Catherine Howard
was God's judgment upon the king. The story was
traced back through a series of sources to Taverner's
wife; although Taverner had reported the matter to the
authorities, he was imprisoned in the Tower of London
for not coming forward in a timely fashion. His wife
was also detained. Taverner was soon released, and
remarkably there was no lasting damage done to his
career by the incident.

Although the years immediately following Cromwell's death were fragile ones for the English Reformation, Taverner may have had renewed hope in the
progress of reform in 1545. In that year the king authorized the first official English Primer, a project with
which Taverner probably was intimately involved. He
may also have continued to exercise his considerable
language skills, now under the king's own direction, in
promoting at least religious moderation. Anthony á
Wood credits Taverner with having translated Erasmus's *De Sarcienda Ecclesiae Concordia* (On Repairing the
Unity of the Church, 1533), calling it "An introduction
to Christian Concord and Unitie in Matters of Reli-

gion." It does not appear to have made it into print, although Wood said that it had been produced specifically to correspond with Henry VIII's last appearance in Parliament in 1545, when the king called for an end to religious discord.

Taverner's position in the signet office meant that he moved on the periphery of the main events of the last half of Henry VIII's reign, including the Pilgrimage of Grace in 1536–1537 and the war with France in 1544. He may also have had a part in the moves by other leading humanists at court to save Cambridge University in 1545–1546 from the kind of dissolution that had taken place with the monasteries in the previous decade. Taverner was elected to Parliament in 1547, and perhaps also in 1545 and 1553 (the returns for those parliaments are incomplete). The religious changes that came almost immediately upon the accession of Edward VI in 1547 brought the Church of England well within the Protestant fold. Within the first year of the new reign, the government, finding that many clerics from Henry VIII's reign were unwilling to follow the now decidedly Protestant agenda, licensed Taverner and many other Protestant laymen to preach. Taverner was reputed to have preached even before Edward VI himself.

Although remembered mainly for his translations of Erasmus and Continental reformers, Taverner's interest in the law remained with him throughout his life. In 1540 he wrote a prologue to, and probably edited, *The Principal lawes customes and estatutes of England*. Another expanded edition appeared in March 1547, just two months into Edward's reign. Despite the rather general title of the work, Taverner concentrated especially on those laws concerning property rights. His study of the subject apparently prepared him well for the flurry of land transactions he engaged in from the mid 1540s and forward. Taverner and two of his brothers were actively engaged in land speculation well into Elizabeth's reign. In 1552, though, Taverner's acquisitiveness touched a nerve. In a letter he wrote to Sir William Cecil, then the duke of Northumberland's secretary, Taverner expressed his willingness to give up his government position and take up preaching exclusively, provided that he was compensated with a grant of £100 per annum. No reply survives, but the fact that Taverner did not leave office until after Mary's accession in 1553 suggests that he received a negative response.

When Mary came to the throne in 1553, Taverner addressed "An Oration gratulory" to her, but the new Catholic queen still removed him from the signet office and the Surrey judicial bench. Taverner went into retirement, although to what extent he conformed himself to the new Catholic regime is unknown. Five

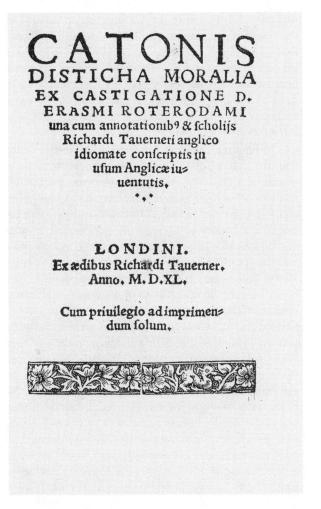

Title page for Taverner's adaptation and translation of Cato's verse proverbs and Desiderius Erasmus's commentaries on them

years later, when Elizabeth ascended the throne, he sent the queen a Latin congratulatory epistle, no doubt more heartfelt than the one he had sent to her sister some years before. In September 1553 Elizabeth appointed Matthew Parker as archbishop of Canterbury, and, while none of the exiting conservative bishops would agree to consecrate him (three former bishops from her father's reign were recalled from retirement to preside), Taverner was there to bear official witness to his old Cambridge friend's acceptance of the appointment.

The queen, needing loyal and, importantly, Protestant men to manage the shires, offered to knight Taverner early in the reign. Although Taverner declined the honor, supposedly because he could not at the same time make the queen a loan of one hundred pounds, he was still active in the management of local affairs: in 1562 and 1564 he was appointed a member of the Commission of the Peace for Oxfordshire, and in 1569–1570 he was named high-sheriff for the same county. In 1573 he was named to a special Commission of Oyer and Terminer for Oxfordshire to investigate the county's compliance with laws concerning religious uniformity and practice. He apparently kept well informed about other important matters as well, because in 1570 he sent Cecil, then Elizabeth's chief minister, a long letter about the need for a royal exchange in order to stop the usurious speculation in foreign currencies.

Margaret Taverner was buried 21 January 1562, and the following month Taverner was actively in search of a new wife, as he told Matthew Parker. He soon found another partner in the person of Mary Harcourt, daughter of Sir John Harcourt, an important figure in the county of Oxford. By her he had another family, one son and a daughter named Penelope, who was the grandmother of Anthony à Wood. It is through Wood that some sense of Taverner's personality has come to light. In his *Historia et antiquitates Universitatis Oxoniensis* (History and Antiquities of the University of Oxford, 1674), Wood records that his great-grandfather was in the habit of catechizing children on the streets of Oxford. He also told the tale of Taverner preaching in the pulpit of the church at Oxford University, which he did "out of pure charity, with a golden chain about his neck, and a sword as 'tis said by his side (but false without doubt, for he always preached in a damask gown) and gave the Academicians, destitute of evangelical advice, a Sermon beginning with these words: Arriving at the Mount of St. Mary's in the Stony stage where I now stond, I have brought you some fyne Bisketts baked in the oven of Charitie, carefully conserved for the chickens of the Church, the sparrows of the Spirit, and the sweet swallowes of salvation, etc."

What role Taverner may have had in overseeing reprints of his work is unknown. His direct literary activities seem to have virtually ceased after 1547. He did send an undated note to John Foxe, another old Cambridge friend, and a copy of the last will and testament of Cardinal Reginald Pole, Parker's predecessor as archbishop of Canterbury, to be included in Foxe's *Acts and Monuments* (1563), an exceedingly popular narrative record of the martyrs to Protestantism. Taverner wanted Foxe to note in his history the "superstition" behind Pole's leaving money for the creation of two chantries to pray for his and his parents' souls. At some point, perhaps in the last year of his life, he seems to have written a poem in English for Abraham Fleming's translation of Claudius Aelianus' *A registre of Hystories, conteining Martiall exploites of worthy warriours, Politique praaises of Ciuil Magistrates, wise Sentences of famous Philosophers, And other matters manifolde and memorable* (1576). Fleming's translation of a work by Claudius Aelianus is similar in content to several of Taverner's earlier works. Although his poem was actually included in *A registre of Hystories*, he did not live to see it in print.

Taverner may have had some early indication that his health was failing. His will, which is preserved at Somerset House, (P.C.C., 32 Pyckering), was dated 15 June 1575, and he died a month later, on 14 July. He was buried next to his first wife, immediately in front of the altar in the chancel of the parish church of Wood Eaton, Oxford, where he had spent the last years of his life. Wood described the memorial that was erected to Taverner "on the north wall of the said chancel, an helmet, standard, pennon and other cognisances belonging to esquires"—all of which was taken down late in the seventeenth century by the Nourse family, who had become lords of Taverner's old manor of Wood Eaton. Taverner's house, on which he had spent a great deal of both time and money, was still standing in 1676, although only the church still exists. Wood estimated that his great-grandfather's estate was worth £1,500 at his death, a substantial figure in Elizabethan England. The Wood Eaton church also has in its possession a chalice and patten cover that are dated 1575. They may have been given by Taverner when his son, Richard, became rector in June of that year, a month before the elder Taverner's death. Richard, who like his father had studied at Oxford and the Inner Temple, did not long enjoy the position, dying in 1577.

Taverner earned his reputation primarily as a translator, which is perhaps why he does not stand out as one of the great literary figures of the English Renaissance. Even in his own time, his work was seen largely in religious and political terms, at least by those who employed him. His job was to produce translations of Erasmus and Continental Protestant reformers that could be used to support the doctrine of the burgeoning Anglican Church. That they sometimes also illuminated and taught concepts of rhetoric was largely owing to the thoroughly humanist and classical education that Taverner himself had received. Taverner's name undoubtedly will become better known as the popularity of Erasmian studies continues to increase in colleges and universities around the world.

Bibliography:

E. J. Devereux, *Renaissance English Translations of Erasmus: A Bibliography to 1700* (Toronto: University of Toronto Press, 1983), pp. 24–31, 38–47, 117–119, 188–199.

References:

W. A. Armstrong, "The Background and Sources of Preston's *Conbises*," *English Studies,* 31 (1949?): 129–135;

T. W. Baldwin, *William Shakspere's Small Latine & Lesse Greeke,* 2 volumes (Urbana: University of Illinois Press, 1944), pp. 596–598, 602–604;

Charles R. Baskervill, "Taverner's *Garden of Wisdom* and the *Apophthegmata* of Erasmus," *Studies in Philology,* 29 (1939): 149–159;

R. H. Brodie and others, eds., *Calendar of Patent Rolls, Edward VI,* 6 volumes (London: HMSO, 1924–1929);

Charles C. Butterworth, *The English Primers (1529–1545), Their Publication and Connection with the English Bible and the Reformation in England* (Philadelphia: University of Pennsylvania Press, 1953), pp. 144–145, 181–182, 194–199, 215, 227–238, 262, 268, 270, 272;

Butterworth, *Lineage of the King James Bible 1340–1611* (Philadelphia: University of Pennsylvania Press, 1941), pp. 125–128, 151, 236;

Margaret Christian, "'I knowe not howe to preache': The Role of the Preacher in Taverner's Postils," *Sixteenth Century Journal,* 29, no. 2 (1998): 377–397;

J. H. Collingridge and R. B. Wernham, eds., *Calendar of Patent Rolls, Elizabeth* (London: HMSO, 1948–1964), vols. 2–4;

E. J. Devereux, "Richard Taverner's Translations of Erasmus," *Library,* fifth series, 19 (1964): 212–215;

Eamon Duffy, *The Stripping of the Altars: Traditional Religion in England c. 1400 – c. 1580* (New Haven & London: Yale University Press, 1992), pp. 425–427, 446–447;

Geoffrey Elton, *Reform and Renewal: Thomas Cromwell and the Common Weal* (Cambridge: Cambridge University Press, 1973), pp. 17–18, 24–25, 35, 61;

Elton, *The Tudor Revolution in Government* (Cambridge: Cambridge University Press, 1962), pp. 305–306;

Willard Farnham, *The Medieval Heritage of Elizabethan Tragedy* (Berkeley: University of California Press), pp. 263–269;

M. S. Giuseppi, ed., *Calendar of Patent Rolls, Phillip and Mary,* 4 volumes (London: HMSO, 1937–1939);

John Holmes, "Taverner's Postels," *British Magazine and Monthly Register of Religious and Ecclesiastical Information,* 29 (1 April 1846): 361–368;

Harold H. Hutson and Harold R. Willoughby, "The Ignored Taverner Bible of 1539," *Crozer Quarterly,* 16 (July 1939): 161–176;

C. S. Knighton, ed., *Calendar of State Papers, Domestic Series, of the Reign of Edward VI 1547–1553* (London: HMSO, 1992);

David B. Knox, *The Doctrine of Faith in the Reign of Henry VIII* (London: James Clarke, 1961), pp. 151, 180–184, 205, 212–215;

Robert Lemon, ed., *Calendar of State Papers, Domestic Series, of the Reigns of Edward VI, Mary, Elizabeth 1547–1580* (London: HMSO, 1856);

James K. McConica, *English Humanists and Reformation Politics under Henry VIII and Edward VI,* revised edition (Oxford: Clarendon Press, 1968), pp. 347–348;

J. F. Mozley, *Coverdale and His Bibles* (London: Lutterworth, 1953);

Hugh Pope, *English Versions of the Bible,* revised and amplified by Sebastian Bullough (St. Louis & London: Herder, 1952), pp. 205–215;

James H. Pragman, "Richard Taverner (1505?–1575) and the English Reformation," unpublished D.Th. thesis, Concordia Seminary, St. Louis, 1971;

DeWitt T. Starnes, "Richard Taverner's *The garden of wisdom,* Carion's *Chronicles,* and the Cambyses Legend," *University of Texas Studies in English,* 35 (1956): 22–31;

S. M. Thorpe, entry on Richard Taverner in *The History of Parliament: The House of Commons 1509–1558,* edited by S. T. Bindoff (London: Secker & Warburg, 1982), III: 424–425;

Brooke F. Westcott, *A General View of the History of the English Bible,* revised by William A. Wright, third edition (New York: Macmillan, 1922), pp. 102, 106, 207–211;

Olive B. White, "Richard Taverner's Interpretation of Erasmus in Proverbs or Adagies," *Publications of the Modern Language Association of America,* 59 (1944): 928–943;

Anthony à Wood, *Athenæ Oxonienses,* edited by Philip Bliss (London: F. C. & J. Rivington, 1813);

Wood, *The Life and Times of Anthony Wood, antiquary, of Oxford, 1632–1695, described by Himself,* volume 1: *1632–1663,* edited by Andrew Clarke (Oxford: Printed for the Oxford Historical Society at the Clarendon Press, 1891);

John K. Yost, "German Protestant Humanism and the Early English Reformation: Richard Taverner and Official Translation," *Bibliothèque d'humanisme et Renaissance. Travaux et documents,* 32 (1970): 613–625;

Yost, "Protestant Reformers and the Humanist *Via Media* in the Early English Reformation," *Journal of Medieval and Renaissance Studies,* 5, no. 1 (1975): 187–202;

Yost, "Taverner's Use of Erasmus and the Protestantization of English Humanism," *Renaissance Quarterly,* 23 (1970): 266–276.

Papers:

The British Library holds various letters by Richard Taverner, including a 1546 letter to Matthew Parker (Additional MS 19,400, fols. 23–23v), a 1552 letter to William Cecil (Lansdowne II, fols. 193–194), and an undated letter to John Foxe (Harley 416, f. 125).

Thomas Vicars
(1591 – August 1638)

Douglas Bruster
University of Texas at Austin

BOOKS: Χειραγωγία: *Manvdvctio Ad Artem Rhetoricam, Ante paucos annos in priuatum quorundam Scholarium usum concinnata, nunc verò in studiosæ juuentutis uniuersæ gratiam publici juris facta. Opera & studio Thomæ Vicarsi in Artibus Magistri & Coll: Regin: Oxon: Socij.* (London: Printed by Augustine Mathewes, 1621; enlarged edition, N.p.: George Eld & Miles Flesher, 1624; enlarged edition, London: Printed by John Haviland for Robert Milbourne, 1628);

Pvsillvs Grex. Ελεγχος. Refvtatio Cvivsdam Libelli De Amplitvdine Regni Coelestis Svb Ementito Caelii Secvndi Cvrionis Nomine In Lvcem Emissi. Qua docetur ex Scripturis beatorum numerum majorem non esse numero damnatorum, sed potius minorem. Ad excutiendum securitatis veternum nostris hominibus potissimùm conscripta. Authore Thoma de Vicariis S. T. Bac. Postore Cockfieldiensi in agro quondam Australium Saxonum (Oxford: Printed by William Turner, 1627);

Ρομφαιοφερος The Sword-Bearer: Or, The Byshop of Chichester's Armes emblazoned in a Sermon preached at a Synod By T. V. B. of D. sometimes Fellow of Queenes Colledge in Oxford, and now Pastor of the Church at Cockfield in Southsex (London: Printed by Bernard Alsop & Thomas Fawcet for Robert Milbourne, 1627);

The Grovnds Of That Doctrine which is according to Godlinesse. Or A briefe and easie Catechisme, (gathered out of many other) with Graces and Prayers for them that want better helps. By T. V. B. of D. Vicar of Cockfield in Southsex. The second Edition (London: Printed by Thomas Cotes & Richard Cotes for Michael Sparke, 1630);

Edom And Babylon Against Jervsalem, Or, Meditations on Psal. 137.7. Occasioned by the most happy Deliverance of our Church and State (on November 5. 1605.) from the most bloody Designe of the Papists-Gunpowder-Treason. Being the summe of divers Sermons, delivered by Thomas Vicars B. D. Pastor of Cockfield in South-Sex. This our Deliverance was such a marvellous worke of God, that it ought to be had in an everlasting remembrance; and the rather for that the Papists in blinde corners, most shamelesly give out, and goe about to perswade simple people, that there was never any such thing intended by them, as the Gunpowder-treason, but that it is a thing meerly put upon them to make their religion more odious* (London: Printed by Elizabeth Purslowe for Henry Seyle, 1633).

OTHER: Untitled poem, in *Ivsta Fvnebria Ptolemæi Oxoniensis Thomæ Bodleii Eqvitis Avrati Celbrata in Academiâ Oxoniensis Mensis Martij 29. 1613* (Oxford: Printed by Joseph Barnes, 1613), p. 99;

Robert Mandevill, *Timothies Taske: Or A Christian Sea-Card, guiding through the coastes of a peaceable conscience to a peace constant, and a Crowne immortall. Wherein I. Pastors are put in minde of their double dutie, and how to discharge it. 1. Personall, as watchfull men. 2. Pastorall, as faithfull watchmen. II. True doctrine is advanced. III. Traditions discountenanced, & their rancour discovered. In two Synodoll assemblies at Carliell, out of two seuerall, but sutable Scriptures. This of 1 Timoth. 4.16. and that of Actes 20.28. Since concorporate, and couched with augmentation vnder their prime Head: By Robert Mandevill, sometimes of Queenes Colledge in Oxford, and Prencher of Gods word at Abbey-holme in Cumberland,* edited, with a dedicatory epistle, by Vicars (Oxford: Printed by John Lichfield & James Short, 1619);

Bartholomew Keckermann, *Ουρανογνωσια. Heauenly Knowledg. A Manuduction To Theologie. Written in Latin by Barthol. Keckerm. done into English by T. V. Mr of Arts,* translated by Vicars; bound with *A Briefe Direction how to examine our selues before we go to the Lords Table, how to behaue our selues there, and hovv to try our selues aftervvards. By T. V.,* by Vicars (London: Printed by Augustine Mathewes, 1622); republished as *Heauenly knowledg directing a Christian to ye assurance of his salvation in this life. Written in Latin by Barthol. Keckerm.; done into English by T. V.,* with *A Treatise Written to the Glory of Gods Grace, against Freewill,* by Vicars (London: Printed for Thomas Jones, 1625);

Untitled poem, in *Vltima Linea Savilii Sive In Obitvm Clarissimi Domini Henrici Savilii Equitis Aurati, Mathematicorum facilè Principis, nuperrimè Collegij Mertonensis Custodis Vigilantissimi, Etonensis iuxta Vniversitate Oxoniensis optimè meriti. Iusta Academica* (Oxford: Printed by John Lichfield & Jacob Short, 1622), sig. B3ʳ;

George Carleton, *Αστρολογομανια: The Madnesse of Astrologers. Or An Examination of Sir Christopher Heydons Booke, Jntituled A Defence of Iudiciarie Astrologie. Written neere vpon twenty yeares ago, by G. C. And by permission of the Author set forth for the Vse of such as might happily be misled by the Knights Booke. Published by T. V. B. of D.*, published, with a dedicatory epistle, by Vicars (London: Printed by William Jaggard for William Turner, 1624);

Charles Robson, *Nevves From Aleppo A Letter written to T[homas] V[icars] B. of D. Vicar of Cockfield in Southsex. By Charles Robson Master of Artes, Fellow of Qu: Col: in Oxford, and Preacher to the Company of our English merchants at Aleppo. Containing many remarkeable occurrences obserued by him in his iourney thither* (London: Printed by John Dawson for Michael Sparke, 1628);

"To His Singvlar good Cousen Mʳ. John Vicars. The most Praiseworthie Authour of Englands Hallelu-jah," in *Englands Hallelu-jah, Or, Great Brittaines Gratefull Retribution, for Gods Gratious Benediction. In our many and most famous Deliuerances, since the Halcyon-Dayes of euer-blessed Queene Elizabeth, to these present Times. Together, with diuers of Dauids Psalmes, according to the French Metre and Measures,* by John Vicars (London: Printed by Thomas Purfoot for Henry Seile, 1631).

Thomas Vicars's place in the history of rhetoric depends on his *Χειραγωγία: Manvductio Ad Artem Rhetoricam* (1621), a Latin rhetoric for students. The Greek word at the beginning of the title may be transliterated as *cheiragogia;* it means "a leading by the hand," which is also the meaning of the Latin *manuductio* immediately following. Vicars's handbook remains noteworthy for its catechistical structure; its emphasis on genre; its Ciceronian material; its presentation of instruction in both the composition and analysis of orations; and its use of the diagrammatic methodology of the followers of Pierre de La Ramée (known as Petrus Ramus) in this analysis.

Vicars was born at Carlisle in 1591, where he attended grammar school. He was a cousin of John Vicars, the Puritan polemicist, and later contributed prefatory verses to one of his cousin's publications. On 19 June 1607 Thomas Vicars matriculated as plebeian at Queen's College of Oxford University; he was graduated B.A. on 16 December 1611 and M.A. on 17 June

1615. Vicars's industriousness there helped his steady advancement. He was first elected tabarder (name for a sizar at Queen's College); then, on 7 July 1615, chaplain; and, on 20 April 1616, fellow of the college. Six years later, on 10 May 1622, Vicars was licensed to preach and received at that time the degree of B.D. On 11 August 1622 Vicars married Anne Carleton, daughter of George Carleton, Bishop of Chichester; at the end of the year he was preferred by his new father-in-law to the first in a series of livings, or benefices. In 1619 Vicars edited a book of sermons by Robert Mandevill titled *Timothies Taske: Or A Christian Sea-Card.*

Vicars was appointed to Cuckfield on 19 December 1622; the following year, on 8 June 1623, to Cowfold; and, on 12 July 1624, to the prebend of Eartham. He and Anne had four daughters: Joanna, Mary, Abigail, and Elizabeth. Two other children died young: a daughter, Anne, and a son, George. During the 1620s and 1630s Vicars kept a scrupulous record of church improvements and possessions, providing valuable insight into the maintenance of a rural church of the era. On a personal level, the details of his administration at Cuckfield suggest a superintendent deeply concerned with both the spiritual and physical well-being of his charges. This care appears to have extended to the Cuckfield grammar school as well. *The Victoria History of the County of Sussex* (1907) relates that Vicars, along with two other men, signed an order to dismiss a schoolmaster named Edward Francis "for his savage behaviour to the boys and errors in governing the school." His replacement, James Sicklemore, contributed a dedicatory acrostic poem to the 1631 edition of Vicars's *The Grovnds Of That Doctrine which is according to Godlinesse,* first published in 1630.

In 1624 Vicars edited and introduced *Αστρολογομανια: The Madnesse of Astrologers,* a work by his father-in-law, Carleton, that responded to Sir Christopher Heydon's defense of judicial astrology (which had been published more than two decades earlier, in 1603). A story that Vicars relates in his dedicatory epistle to Carleton's book tells something about his childhood and character. Once, when a mute "cunning man" visited the Vicars family residence in Carlisle, he was asked to tell the fortunes of young Thomas and a schoolmate. The cunning man predicted, in pantomime, that Vicars would become a scrivener and his friend, a preacher. Vicars proudly relates that things have turned out precisely the opposite and asks readers to see in this anecdote the danger of superstition. Like St. Augustine calling astrology into question through the example of twins who, born under the same alignment of stars, went on to have various levels of success in life, Vicars employs reason to discredit a worldly

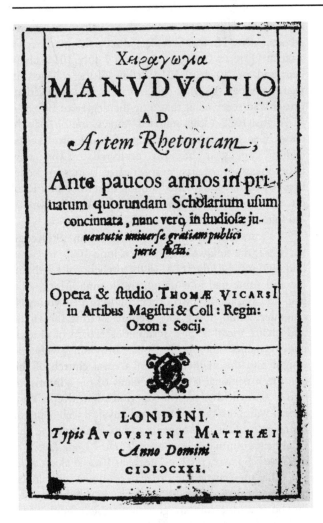

Χειραγωγια

MANVDVCTIO

A D

Artem Rhetoricam;

Ante paucos annos in pri-
uatum quorundam Scholarium ufum
concinnata, nunc verò, in ftudiofæ ju-
uentutie uniuerfe gratiam publici
juris facta.

Opera & ftudio Thomæ Vicarsi
in Artibus Magiftri & Coll: Regin:
Oxon: Socij.

LONDINI
Typis Avgvstini Matthæi
Anno Domini
CICIOCXXI.

Title page for Thomas Vicars's Latin rhetoric textbook

form of magic. As Keith Thomas notes, while it is tempting to see such antipathy for astrology as a mark of the links between Puritanism and the rise of science, it is more likely that this animus sprang from a bedrock belief in the impenetrable nature of an omnipotent God's mysteries. In any case, Vicars's anecdote, no less than the fact that he contributed to Carleton's volume, indicates an orientation toward what has come to be called Puritanism.

Indeed, Vicars seems at first glance almost a caricature of a Puritan divine. Throughout his writings he displays a profound dislike for popular superstition, a devotion to Old Testament strictures and to the truth of the Book of Revelation, and a related belief that preachers were justified in using the sharpest possible rhetoric—even biblical curses—to reform the wickedly "obstinate." He moved in Protestant circles that included Michael Drayton, Anne Neville, and Mabel Blenerhasset. Vicars's historical vision reflected his religious beliefs: to him, the most important events in post-

biblical history were the many martyrdoms of individual Protestants, the St. Bartholomew's Day Massacre, and the Gunpowder Plot. Yet, if Vicars was a Puritan divine, he departed from the stereotype in important ways. He saw Presbyterianism as an error and was neither anti-Catholic nor anti–Roman Catholic but opposed what he called the church "court" of Rome. It is a mark of Vicars's eclecticism that in *Χειραγωγία: Manvductio Ad Artem Rhetoricam* he approves of the works of Peter of Spain (formerly thought to be Pope John XXI) and those of the Jesuit scholar Cypriano Soares. One might call Vicars an uncontroversial controversialist, for he had a habit of responding to works long after their publication. This trait corresponds with the unctuous, careful character evident in his dedications and preface epistles, which are even more sycophantic than was usual for that time. It is worth noting, too, that Vicars had a lifelong attraction to the ornate, something apparent not only in the many anagrams and puns found in his works but also in his beautifying of the church at Cuckfield. Among his expenses were funds for "painted glass" and "A little greene cushion with TV on the one side and Cockfield on the other."

Part of Vicars's will was reprinted in volume 45 of *Sussex Archæological Collections, Relating to the History and Antiquities of the County* (1902), from which many of the factual details about Vicars's life in Sussex are drawn. The bulk of his estate was left to his wife, Anne. Vicars made provisions to have part of the remainder go to ten "ancient poor women" and to ten "young poore maides of the most religious of the parrishe." Friends and relatives were also remembered. For example, Vicars left instructions that his godchildren were to be given octavo editions of the Bible; he specified that they be inscribed in a particular manner: "on the inner side of the cover whereof on white paper I would have their names written, and under it this—Lett not this booke of God's law depart out of thy mouth, but meditate therein that thou maist observe to do all that is written therein for so shalt thou have good success in all thy business." That Vicars felt such success had eluded him may have been the reason for a peculiar request in his will. He asked to be buried in the night "without any manner of solemnity," explaining this request with some self-criticism: "because I have not gained that honour to God in my life that I ought, therefore I will have no honour done unto mee at my death."

The Greek-Latin conjunction in the title of Vicars's *Χειραγωγία: Manvductio Ad Artem Rhetoricam* is echoed on the title pages of two other texts with which he was associated. From these titles one might sense, besides the author's inveterate pedantry, an intent to meld Greek and Latin traditions. The full title of

Χειραγωγία: Manvductio Ad Artem Rhetoricam may be translated as follows: "A handbook to the art of rhetoric, in which the genesis and analysis—that is, the system of artfully composing and skillfully untangling orations—is taught clearly and methodically." This page also announces that the work is intended for use in schools. With four editions published from 1621 to 1650, it was obviously an influential text.

The augmented third edition of Χειραγωγία: Manvductio Ad Artem Rhetoricam, published in 1628, acknowledges the major differences among the various editions. It opens with a dedicatory epistle to Vicars's father-in-law, Carleton, Bishop of Chichester, announcing the rationale for the text. Having examined the teaching of rhetoric and grammar in Chichester, Vicars observes, he found existing texts insufficient as introductions to the composition and analysis of orations. The book is his solution to that problem. A descriptive preface is dated 18 December 1620 and addressed to his friend Thomas Wilson, Rector of St. George the Martyr at Canterbury, Provost of Queen's College (of which, like Vicars, he was a graduate), and Bishop of Carlisle. In the preface Vicars describes the relation of his book to works by such authorities as Bartholomew Keckermann, Lorenzo Valla, Justus Lipsius, and Charles Butler.

Following the preface is a diagrammatic chart displaying the topics and chapters of the volume, which is divided into two books or sections: the first explores the "genesis" or composition of orations, the second their "analysis" or untangling. Following the chart are two pages of commendatory poems and a section providing bibliographical aid to readers. Here Vicars gives the precise editions of the authorities he cites in the text and in his marginal notes. These authorities include Quintilian, St. Augustine, Cicero, Aristotle, Soares, Ramus, Keckermann, Johann Alsted, Gerardus Vossius, and the Englishman William Thorne. Vicars closes this section by confessing that his debts to Petrus Hispanus (Peter of Spain) are too great to be confined to mention of a text, and that he hopes to avoid charges of plagiarizing him.

One of the most remarkable things about Χειραγωγία: Manvductio Ad Artem Rhetoricam is that the majority of the text is written in the form of a catechism. Vicars in this way extended the Reformation's emphasis on cultivating responsible subjects through question and answer (he compiled a spiritual catechism of his own later in the 1620s). It is not clear that all of the contents of the book lend themselves readily to this format, even given the prevalence of this mode of education and the capacious memories of early modern students, because some answers are quite lengthy and involve many citations and quotations. Yet, Vicars sus-

tains the question-and-answer form throughout most of the text. In this respect one might compare it to William Dugard's Rhetorices Elementa (The Rudiments of Rhetoric, 1648), which was also cast in question-and-answer form. In contrast to Vicars's book, however, Dugard's has little amplification in its answers, making it more like a brief dictionary. Dugard's ability to resist complexity—never one of Vicars's talents—may have contributed to the great popularity and endurance of his text.

The first book of Χειραγωγία: Manvductio Ad Artem Rhetoricam begins with the question "Quid est Rhetorica?" (What is rhetoric?) and is devoted to explaining the five-part division of rhetoric: inventio (invention), dispositio (disposition), elocutio (elocution or style), memoria (memory), and pronuntiato (oratorical delivery). About invention Vicars has little to say. He paraphrases Cicero's De Inventione (On Invention) in defining invention as devising true things or probable arguments that—when treated in a formal speech—render the case (causa) acceptable. Other than relating that one ought carefully to consider the case, question, theme, or matter about which one is occupied, Vicars does not dwell on invention. Instead, he assumes the ready availability of causae to be argued, and devotes the next three chapters of the section on invention (chapters 2, 3, and 4) to the three main genres of these causae: demonstrative, deliberative, and judicial.

One may derive some sense of the texture of these chapters from Vicars's methodology in his remarks on the demonstrative genre. He poses the question, "What kinds of things may be praised?" and answers: persons, deeds, and things. Later, Vicars relates that in praising persons, seventeen discrete factors may be considered—including nationality, sex, body type (for example, whether nimble, graceful, or beautiful), and occupation. He seeks to elicit these categories individually through question and answer. Likewise, in relating that cities may be praised and rehearsing the aspects that one might touch upon, Vicars punctuates his account by calling for an example (cedo exemplum). The example turns out to be the description of Syracuse in Cicero's sixth speech against Verres. In relation to the praise of buildings, Vicars cites the example of the Temple of Carthage in Virgil's Aeneid; for praise of mountains he cites various descriptions of Aetna; and for a laudatory description of a river, Pliny's description of the Nile.

In these chapters Vicars instructs students first to set out a status, or plan, for their oration, and next to adorn the various parts: exordium (introduction), narratio (narration), partitio (division), confirmatio (confirmation), confutatio (confutation or refutation), and peroratio (conclusion). These parts are described at length in chapter

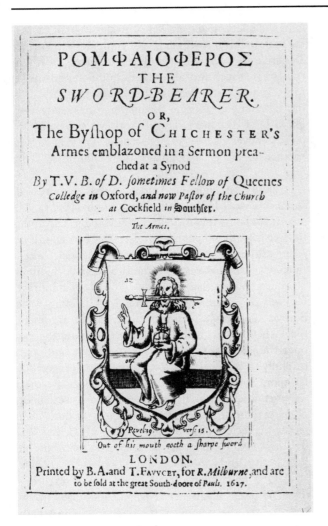

ΡΟΜΦΑΙΟΦΕΡΟΣ
THE
SWORD-BEARER.
OR,
The Byſhop of CHICHESTER's
Armes emblazoned in a Sermon prea-
ched at a Synod
By T.V. B. of D. ſometimes Fellow of Queenes
Colledge in Oxford, and now Paſtor of the Church
at Cockfield in Southſex.

The Armes.

Out of his mouth goeth a ſharpe ſword

LONDON.
Printed by B.A. and T.FAVVCET, for R.Milburne, and are
to be ſold at the great South-doore of Pauls. 1627.

Title page for a sermon by Vicars, which features the coat of arms of his father-in-law, George Carleton

5, which concerns disposition. Chapter 6 takes up style, setting out the three registers of style and the genres to which they are appropriate, and then provides an annotated list of tropes and figures. In a passage first found in the 1624 edition, Vicars interrupts this list with mention of four English writers remarkable for their use of language–Geoffrey Chaucer, Edmund Spenser, Michael Drayton, and George Wither–and includes three English poems, two praising Drayton and one concerning Wither. Vicars resumes his discussion to deal with such figures as epizeuxis, anadiplosis, and anaphora. Chapter 7 addresses memory, providing a list of authorities on the topic and also a mnemonic alphabet by John Shaw. Vicars closes this section with a chapter on oratorical delivery, annotating various techniques for voice and gesture.

With the exception of the additional passage dealing with English authors, the summary of *Χειραγωγία: Manvductio Ad Artem Rhetoricam* so far describes material

that appeared in the first and subsequent editions. The second book, however, is composed of material included only with the editions of 1624 and after. It opens with a brief chapter on analysis, including a definition of what it is and how it is to be done. This is followed by individual chapters that–still in the form of a catechism–analyze four of Cicero's speeches: *Pro Sexto Roscio Amerino* (On Roscius), *Pro Archia Poeta* (On Archius the Poet), *Pro Lege Manilia* (On the Manilian Law), and *Pro Milone* (On Milo). Each chapter begins by asking, "What is the question of this whole oration?" and then goes on to inquire, "What are the parts of this whole oration?" The second chapter of the book, concerning *Pro Roscio,* is the longest and most intensive. In it, Vicars carefully leads his catechumens through the various parts of Cicero's speech and the parts of those parts. Asking what the orator does in the narration, for instance, the text answers that the limbs of the narration extend in two directions: externally, which is divided into preparation for the narration and the digression after it; and internally, which is divided into the exposition of events and the manifest conclusion of the narration. Similar division and subdivision of parts mark Vicars's analysis of the remainder of *Pro Roscio,* and of the three classical speeches (of various rhetorical genres) that follow. *Χειραγωγία: Manvductio Ad Artem Rhetoricam* closes with a speech by Vicars–an academic address on the Gospel of Luke delivered at Queen's College at the beginning of Michaelmas term in 1619. It may have been offered, somewhat immodestly, as a further oration for analysis, since Vicars labels the various parts and sections.

Vicars's work was better known in the seventeenth century than in the present time. On at least two occasions, *Χειραγωγία: Manvductio Ad Artem Rhetoricam* was singled out by his contemporaries as a particularly valuable book, especially as an introduction to various traditions and texts. In *A Consolation for Our Grammar Schools* (1622), John Brinsley the Elder recommends Vicars's work in relation to Aphthonius and Ramus: "For helpes for Theames both for matter and maner, besides the understanding of *Aphthonius* common Places, and the chiefe heads of Invention by *Ramus* and others, see Maister *Vicars* his *cepagwgia,* or *Manuductio,* leading the scholar (as by the hand) to the use of Rhetoricke; especially for making Theames, Declamations, or Orations." Richard Holdsworth's "Directions for a Student in the Universitie"–probably composed between 1615 and 1637 but not published until 1961–recommends Vicars's text as a stepping-stone to Nicolas Caussin's *De Eloquentia Sacra et Humana* (On Sacred and Human Eloquence, 1630).

What remains noteworthy about these contemporary responses to Vicars is that each aligns him with authors and traditions that differ significantly from one another. Whereas Brinsley recognizes Vicars in relation to his helpfulness with Ramus's "chief heads of Invention," Holdsworth connects Vicars to the encyclopedic fullness of Caussin's *De Eloquentia Sacra et Humana,* a work in which the interest in emotion, affect, and eloquence are, though not alien to Ramus's philosophy, divergent enough in emphasis to constitute a distinct orientation. What makes these responses particularly interesting, however, is not merely that they interpret Vicars differently, but that in so doing they anticipate the reception of his handbook during the twentieth century.

It may be useful to consider two related issues. The first concerns a pattern in histories that have included mention of Χειραγωγία: *Manvductio Ad Artem Rhetoricam.* The modern understanding of Vicars's handbook has been shaped by the tendency, in histories of rhetorical theory, to replicate the habits of their subject matter. Just as rhetorical theory often categorizes parts and kinds of speech, many historians of rhetoric have likewise devoted their energies to categorizing rhetorical theorists, aligning this figure with one tradition and that figure with another. While such histories are invariably useful to those making sense of the shape of rhetorical theory over time, they can serve to limit knowledge of particular authors when such authors are folded into a larger tradition. The treatment of Vicars in histories of rhetoric provides a good example of the limitations of this process, for, ever since the seventeenth century, and particularly in the twentieth century, he has rarely been studied for his own sake. More often than not, he has served as a placeholder in groupings of rhetorical theorists.

The second issue involves the primary categories with which historians of rhetorical theory have described Vicars, especially in relation to Χειραγωγία: *Manvductio Ad Artem Rhetoricam.* Such commentators have largely been content to identify Vicars and his handbook with either Ciceronian or Ramist energies. Among the works by Cicero influential in Vicars's time were not only legal and political orations, but also such tomes of rhetorical theory as *De Oratore, Brutus, Orator,* and *Topica;* to these can be added as well the *Rhetorica ad Herennium,* which, though not by Cicero, was long thought to have been written by him. Shaped in part by humanism and the theories of Quintilian, Ciceronian rhetorical theory focused on the production of the citizen orator—a man engaged in the active life who, dutifully and for the good of the polity, used an ethical eloquence.

In significant contrast to such Ciceronian themes were the theories of Ramus. Ramus's sixteenth-century works, which include the *Dialecticae Libri Dvo* (Two

Books of Dialectic, 1572) and, with his colleague Omer Talon (known as Audemarus Talaeus), the *Rhetoricae libri duo* (Two Books of Rhetoric, 1569), stress reason (*ratio*) over speaking (*oratio*). Indeed, Ramist thought emphasizes the determination of truth through the dialectical process, often involving a spatialized series of dichotomies. Instead of a civic figure speaking persuasively for the public good—the "perfect" orator, in Cicero's view—Ramus imagines a truth-seeker arriving at certainty through an essentially private sequence of divisions and syllogisms. These, then, are the categories in relation to which many historians of rhetorical theory have explained Vicars and his work: Vicars the Ciceronian and Vicars the Ramist.

William P. Sandford suggests that, while Vicars's definition of rhetoric "smacks of the stylistic tradition," his discussion of the five parts of rhetoric is "quite in accordance with the classical practice." Similarly, Wilbur S. Howell describes Vicars's handbook as "Neo-Ciceronian"—that is, Ramist only in certain minor aspects. Other "Neo-Ciceronian" rhetorics, according to Howell, are Thomas Farnaby's *Index Rhetoricus* (Rhetorical Index, 1625), William Pemble's *Enchiridion Oratorium* (Oratorical Manual, 1633), and Obadiah Walker's *Some Instructions Concerning the Art of Oratory* (1659).

Since the publication of Howell's book in 1956, Vicars has received only passing mention in the literature. Thomas O. Sloane cites the works of "Neo-Ciceronians" such as Vicars as evidence that "the English Ciceronians never managed to produce a coherent rhetorical theory." A more casual disappointment marks Thomas M. Conley's description of Χειραγωγία: *Manvductio Ad Artem Rhetoricam* as "little more than a school text, serving up a stew of Cicero and Ramus with a dash of Keckermann as seasoning." Two bibliographers have tried to pin Vicars down, with predictably various results. On the one hand, in *Ramus and Talon Inventory* (1958) Walter J. Ong classifies Vicars as both a "Ramist, at least in general tendency" and a "Semi-Ramist or syncretist of some sort." On the other hand, in *English Renaissance Rhetoric and Poetics: A Systematic Bibliography* (1995) Heinrich F. Plett groups Vicars's book with classical and humanist rhetorics.

More recently, Elizabeth Skerpan has classified Vicars's handbook with Farnaby's *Index Rhetoricus,* Butler's *Oratoriæ Libri Dvo* (Two Books of Oratory, 1629), and John Clarke's *Formulae Oratoriae* (The Formulas of Oratory, 1630) as works constituting a new genre: that of neo-Ramist rhetoric. According to Skerpan, the neo-Ramists revived the classical oratorical genres and emphasized the centrality of situation to rhetorical composition and analysis. To be sure, Vicars, like Ramus, sees orations as spaces; his students are asked to remember the spatial form of various rhetorical genres

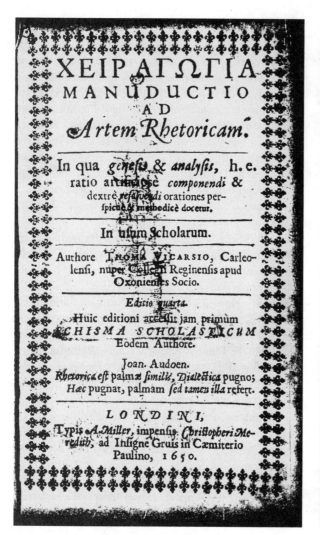

Title page for the revised fourth edition of Vicars's rhetoric book and a page showing the outline of book 1

and instances. But one might qualify an enthusiasm for Vicars's Ramist influences with an understanding of the influence of Keckermann on his rhetorical system. Keckermann's works are cited more frequently in *Χειραγωγία: Manvductio Ad Artem Rhetoricam* than those of Ramus, and Vicars appears to take from Keckermann and others a conviction that rhetoric must be affective in order to persuade. In 1622, the year after the first edition of his handbook, Vicars translated Keckermann's *Systema Theologiae* (System of Theology, 1602) as *Ουρανογνωσια. Heauenly Knowledg. A Manuduction To Theologie.*

Vicars's achievement is perhaps best understood not by enlisting him and his handbook in the various camps of Renaissance rhetorical theory but by analyzing *Χειραγωγία: Manvductio Ad Artem Rhetoricam* in rela-

tion to the diverse influences that shaped its various editions. It is not clear that Vicars was more Ramist than he was Ciceronian, or that Cicero had a greater influence on his thinking than Keckermann—or even that evaluating his handbook in relation to any of these figures is especially helpful. What is clear is that categorizing Vicars's work in this way has ensured that few have read it. There is much research yet to be done on his life and works. His handbook, in particular, merits extensive study. It may well be found that Vicars's rhetoric is best thought of as an eclectic text, a bricolage of various rhetorical traditions. Hindsight suggests that some of these traditions are logically incompatible with one another, yet all of them seemed important enough to Vicars to warrant inclusion in his seventeenth-century school text. Further study of *Χειραγωγία: Manv-*

ductio Ad Artem Rhetoricam is likely to show that our current taxonomies of Renaissance rhetoric are not supple enough to account for the text's embrace of variety.

In 1627 Vicars published *Pvsillvs Grex. Ελεγχος,* a work of "controversy" that rebutted Celio Secondo Curione's *De Amplitudine Beati Regni Dei, Dialogi sive libri duo* (1554; republished in 1610), long out of print. A more notable publication that year was his *Ρομφαιοφερος The Sword-Bearer,* the text of a sermon. At the conclusion of the text is a blazon of his father-in-law's coat of arms. Carleton's coat of arms features Christ with a bloody, two-edged sword between his teeth, under which is written, from the Book of Revelation, 19:15: "out of his mouth goeth a sharpe sword." The image appears in at least three other passages in Revelation: 1:16 ("out of his mouth went a sharp two-edged sword"), 2:16 ("I . . . will fight against them with the sword of my mouth"), and 19:21 ("And the remnant were slain with the sword of him that sat upon the horse, which sword proceded out of his mouth"). It was obviously a favorite of Vicars's. Indeed, he was so impressed with the appropriateness of this image that one might take it for something like a personal symbol for the agency of the Word in his imagination. He appears, for instance, to have been drawn to the oral, as is suggested by the instruction in his will for the inscription in his godchildren's Bibles: "Lett not this booke of God's law depart out of thy mouth. . . ." What also seems to have appealed to Vicars about the image of the coat-of-arms was the efficacy of rhetoric it implies. The notes to the Geneva Bible (1557, 1560) describe Christ's "strength inuincible and with a mightie word. By his operations, that he ruleth the ministery of his seruants in the Church . . . by the sword of his word." Such passages gave Vicars a genealogy for impassioned rhetoric and, by extension, a justification: because the word of God is described as a sword, as an instrument of punishing truth, a speaker is justified in employing the strongest possible speech in the service of righteousness.

In 1628 Vicars must have assisted in the publication of Charles Robson's *Nevves From Aleppo,* a travel letter addressed to him. In 1630 the second edition of Vicars's *The Grovnds Of That Doctrine which is according to Godlinesse* was published; this text is a catechism that draws heavily on those of Thomas Cranmer, Alexander Nowell, and William Perkins. It serves as a reminder of how central the catechistical form was to Vicars. The date of the putative first edition is unknown; no copies seem to be extant.

In 1631 Vicars contributed verses to his cousin John Vicars's *Englands Hallelu-jah.* This book is a poetic record of God's "many and most famous Deliuerances" of Great Britain, from Elizabeth's time to the present, including several biblical precedents and parallels. Vicars's poem, which he could not resist annotating with marginal remarks, runs as follows:

> These Lines and Layes, once, twice, *againe, o're- read,
>   Deo repetita placebunt
> Refresht my Soule, and rauisht haue, my Heart;
> So great Content and Comfort, in Mee, bred,
> I could not choose, but to your-selfe, impart:
> They haue Mee chang'd, for once, & made mee Poet,
> Your Muse, Nought-els, that I do know, could doe it.
>
> I'll Say in Prose, what you doe Sing in Verse
> Most Christianly; The Lord is to be praised;
> And in a home-spunne Speach, I'll still reherse,
> What you most sweetly, soundly, heere, haue phrased.
> In this Angellike Song, a part I Loue;
> And though I say't but Here, I'll Sing't Aboue.
> *Reuel. cap, 19 verse 13

The awkwardness of the poem leaves the reader little choice but to acknowledge that Vicars truly knew his limitations. The "home-spunne Speach" recalls George Herbert's poems, which champion a plain style of devotion in more memorable ways. If Vicars's poem lacks interest from an aesthetic standpoint, it does bear relevance for understanding themes that run throughout his work. Two things in particular stand out; each is glossed by Vicars with a marginal, supporting note. First is his justification for reading *Englands Hallelu-jah* over and over again: "Deo repetita placebunt" (Repeated things will be pleasing unto God). This marginal note casts God as a kind of listener, one pleased by that which is repeated, and can be said to analogize the religious life to the life rhetorical. Second is Vicars's distinction between the representational modes of his work and that of his cousin in *Englands Hallelu-jah.* That is, Vicars sees the prose mode of his writing and performance as saying, whereas verse is singing. For this distinction he offers, in part, Revelation 19:13 as support. Chapter 19 opens with a description of the angels in Heaven praising God (here taken from the Geneva Bible): "And after these things I heard a great voyce of a great multitude in heauen, saying, Hallelu-iah, saluation, and glory, and honour, and power *be* to the Lord our God." Verse 13, which precedes one of Vicars's favorite biblical passages, describes a martial Christ: "And hee was cloathed with a garment dipt in blood, and his name was called, THE WORD OF GOD." The point of this citation seems to be that, while the two Vicars cousins have chosen different modes—verse and prose—to express their message, it is, at base, one and the same message, one and the same "word."

Vicars died in late August 1638 and was buried on 29 August. He was survived by his wife, Anne; his mother, Eve; a brother, William; and a sister, Elizabeth.

Vicars's final work, published in 1633, was one of his most impressive and speaks to his skill as an orator. *Edom And Babylon Against Jerusalem, Or, Meditations on Psal. 137.7* consolidates various sermons that he had delivered on the Gunpowder Plot. Vicars analogizes the "jesuited Papists" responsible for this treason to the wicked of Edom and Babylon (Psalms 137:7–8). He defends the practice of commemorating 5 November, the date the plot was discovered, especially in light of what he sees as the fading memories of the incident. To resurrect the horror of the Gunpowder Plot, he constructs an imaginative "Sciagraphie," or sketch, in which King Charles I and Queen Henrietta Maria, along with "all the Nobles, Bishops and Judges," are assembled in Parliament. Vicars's imaginative scenario pictures these worthies blown apart by "thirty Barrels and foure Hogsheads of Gunpowder with Faggots and iron Barres upon them." In a horrific passage, the most intense in all his works, he asks his readers to

> imagine the traine to be laid, the powder fired, the terrible blow given, and on a sudden . . . the whole building to cracke asunder, the plankes all on a flame, the beams and stones flying in the ayre, the joynts and members of all the worthies of our Land, rent and torne and scattered one from another, the walls of the streete bedawbed with mens braines, the waies bedewed with mens blood, scarcely so much as one bone left of a great many for buriall.

This passage hints at greater powers of imaginative writing than Vicars shows elsewhere. It recalls the Elizabethan grotesque style, reminiscent of the energy behind such authors as Thomas Nashe and John Webster, while demonstrating a force of vision not unlike that in the sermons of John Donne or Thomas Adams. The passion behind the writing is, to be sure, apocalyptic in nature, and not out of keeping with Vicars's interest in the Book of Revelation. Perhaps Vicars wrote like this so seldom because he could bring himself to imagine the end-time only with great pain. Because he did not live to see the realization of what he describes in this work as "the whole Kingdome turn'd topsy turvy," one can only wonder what Vicars would have thought of the English Civil Wars.

Bibliography:

Falconer Madan, *Oxford Books: A Bibliography of Printed Works Relating to the University and City of Oxford or Printed and Published There with Appendixes and Illus-* *trations,* volume 1: *The Early Oxford Press, 1468–1640* (Oxford: Clarendon Press, 1895).

Biographies:

J. H. Cooper, "The Vicars and Parish of Cuckfield in the Seventeenth Century," in *Sussex Archæological Collections, Relating to the History and Antiquities of the County,* volume 45 (Lewes, U.K.: Farncombe, 1902), pp. 1–33;

Anthony à Wood, "Thomas Vicars," in *Athenae Oxonienses. An Exact History of All the Writers and Bishops Who Have Had Their Education in the University of Oxford. To Which Are Added The Fasti, or Annals of the Said University,* 4 volumes, edited by Philip Bliss (London: Printed for F. C. & J. Rivington, 1813–1820; reprint edition, New York & London: Johnson Reprint, 1967), II: col. 443.

References:

John Brinsley the Elder, *A Consolation for Our Grammar Schooles* (London: Printed by Richard Field for Thomas Man, 1622);

Thomas M. Conley, *Rhetoric in the European Tradition* (Chicago: University of Chicago Press, 1990);

Richard Holdsworth, *Holdsworth's "Directions for a Student in the Universitie,"* in Harris Francis Fletcher, *The Intellectual Development of John Milton,* 2 volumes (Urbana: University of Illinois Press, 1961), II: 623–664;

Wilbur Samuel Howell, *Logic and Rhetoric in England, 1500–1700* (Princeton: Princeton University Press, 1956);

Walter J. Ong, *Ramus and Talon Inventory* (Cambridge, Mass.: Harvard University Press, 1958);

William Page, ed., *The Victoria History of the County of Sussex,* volume 2 (London: Constable, 1907);

Heinrich F. Plett, *English Renaissance Rhetoric and Poetics: A Systematic Bibliography of Primary and Secondary Sources* (Leiden & New York: E. J. Brill, 1995);

William P. Sandford, *English Theories of Public Address, 1530–1828* (Columbus: Ohio State University Press, 1929);

Elizabeth Skerpan, *The Rhetoric of Politics in the English Revolution, 1642–1660* (Columbia: University of Missouri Press, 1992);

Thomas O. Sloane, *Donne, Milton, and the End of Humanist Rhetoric* (Berkeley: University of California Press, 1985);

Keith Thomas, *Religion and the Decline of Magic* (New York: Scribners, 1971).

John Wilkins

(1614 – 19 November 1672)

Scott Manning Stevens
Arizona State University

BOOKS: *The Discovery Of A World In The Moone. Or, A Discourse Tending, To Prove, that 'tis probable there may be another Habitable World in that planet,* anonymous (London: Printed by E. Griffin for Michael Sparke and Edward Forrest, 1638); republished with *A Discourse Concerning a New Planet, The Second Book,* as *A Discourse Concerning a New World & Another Planet. In 2 bookes* (London: Printed by John Maynard for Samuel Gellibrand, 1640);

Mercvry, Or The Secret and Svvift Messenger: Shewing, How a Man may with Privacy and Speed communicate his Thoughts to a Friend at any distance, anonymous (London: Printed by John Norton & John Maynard for Timothy Wilkins, 1641);

Ecclesiastes, Or, A Discourse concerning the Gift Of Preaching as it fals under the rules of Art. Shewing The most proper Rules and Directions, for Method, Invention, Books, Expression, whereby a Minister may be furnished with such abilities as may make him a Workman that needs not to be ashamed. Very seasonable for these Times, wherein the Harvest is great, and the skilfull Labourers but few (London: Printed by Miles Flesher for Samuel Gellibrand, 1646);

Mathematical Magick: Or, The Wonders that May Be Performed by Mechanicall Geometry. In Two Books. Concerning Mechanicall Powers [and] Motions. Being One of the Most Easie, Pleasant, Usefull (and Yet Most Neglected) Part of Mathematicks. Not Before Treated of in This Language. By I.W., M.A. (London: Printed by Miles Flesher for Samuel Gellibrand, 1648);

A Discourse concerning the Beauty of Providence In all the rugged passages of it. Very seasonable to quiet and support the heart in these times of publick confusion. By John Wilkins. B.D. (London: Printed for Samuel Gellibrand, 1649);

Discourse Concerning the Gift of Prayer, Shewing what it is, wherein it consists, and how far it is attainable by industry, with divers useful and proper directions to that purpose, both in respect of matter, method, expression. By John Wilkins. D.D. (London: Printed by Thomas

John Wilkins (portrait by Mary Beale; Wadham College, Oxford)

Ratcliffe & Edward Mottershead for Samuel Gellibrand, 1651);

An Essay Towards a Real Character, And a Philosophical Language. By John Wilkins D.D. Dean of Ripon, And Fellow of the Royal Society (London: Printed by J. M. for Samuel Gellibrand and John Martyn, 1668)– includes *An Alphabetical Dictionary Wherein all English Words According to their Various Significations, Are either referred to their Places in the Philosophical Tables, Or explained by such Words as are in those Tables;*

A Sermon Preached before the King, upon the Seventh of March, 1668/9 by John, Lord Bishop of Chester (London: Printed by Thomas Newcomb, 1669);

A Sermon Preached before the King, upon the Twenty seventh of February, 1669/70. By John, Lord Bishop of Chester (London: Printed by Anne Maxwell for S. Gellibrand, 1670);

A Sermon Preached before the King, upon the Nineteenth of March, 1670/1 1669/70. By John, Lord Bishop of Chester (London: Printed by Anne Maxwell for S. Gellibrand, 1671);

Of the Principles and Duties of Natural Religion: Two Books. By the Right Reverend Father in God, John late Lord Bishop of Chester. To which is added, A Sermon Preached at his Funerals, by William Lloyd, D. D. Dean of Bangor, and Chaplain in Ordinary to His Majesty (London: Printed by Anne Maxwell for Thomas Basset, Henry Brome & Richard Chiswell, 1675);

Sermons Preached Upon several Occasions Before the King at White-Hall. By the Right Reverend Father in God, John Wilkins, late Lord Bishop of Chester. To which is added, A Discourse Concerning the Beauty of Providence By the same Author (London: Printed by Henry Cruttenden for Robert Sollers, 1677);

Sermons Preached upon Several Occasions: By the Right Reverend Father in God, John Wilkins, D.D. And late Lord Bishop of Chester, Never before published (London: Printed for Thomas Basset, Richard Chiswell & William Rogers, 1682);

A Scheme and Abstract of the Christian Religion. Comprized in fifty two heads, with the texts of Scripture, on which they are grounded. And some short indications, how they were more largely handled. By a Lover of Truth and Peace, sometimes attributed to Wilkins, edited by Archbishop John Tillotson (London, 1682);

The Mathematical and Philosophical Works of the Right Reverend John Wilkins, late lord bishop of Chester, to which is prefixed the author's life, and an account of his works (London: Printed by John Nicholson, 1708).

Editions: *The mathematical and philosophical works of the Right Rev. John Wilkins, late lord bishop of Chester to which is prefix'd the author's life, and an account of his works,* 2 volumes (London: Printed by C. Whittingham for Vernor and Hood, 1802);

An Essay Towards a Real Character, and a Philosophical Language, 1668 (Menston, U.K.: Scolar Press, 1968);

Of the principles and duties of natural religion, introduction by Henry G. Van Leeuwen (New York: Johnson Reprint, 1969);

The Discovery of a World in the Moone (1638), The English Experience, no. 494 (Amsterdam: Theatrum Orbis Terrarum / New York: Da Capo Press, 1972);

The Discovery of a World in the Moone (1638) (Delmar, N.Y.: Scholars' Facsimiles and Reprints, 1973);

The Discovery of a World in the Moone, Anglistica and Americana, no. 95 (New York: Olms, 1981);

Mercury: Or, the Secret and Swift Messenger (1707), Foundations of Semiotics, no. 6 (Amsterdam & Philadelphia: John Benjamins, 1984).

OTHER: Seth Ward, *Vindiciæ Academiarum Containing, Some briefe Animadversions upon Mr Websters Book, Stiled, The Examination of Academies. Together with an Appendix concerning what M. Hobbs, and M. Dell have published on this Argument,* introduction by Wilkins (Oxford: Printed by Leonard Lichfield for Thomas Robinson, 1654).

Edition: *VindiciæAcademiarum* (1654), in *Science and Education in the Seventeenth Century: The Webster-Ward Debate,* by Allen G. Debus (London: Macdonald / New York: American Elsevier, 1970), pp. 193–259.

John Wilkins was a man of often contested qualities and allegiances whose life illustrates the profoundly complex and turbulent culture of seventeenth-century England. Both the brother-in-law of Oliver Cromwell and the father-in-law of John Tillotson, who became archbishop of Canterbury after the restoration of the monarchy, Wilkins witnessed the religious controversies and political struggles leading to the English Revolution, partook in the scientific debates of the period, and wrote several works popularizing the "new science." During the Interregnum he oversaw Wadham College, Oxford, and at the beginning of the Restoration he played a key role in the founding of the Royal Society. Establishing himself as one of the leading latitudinarian preachers of his day, he served as dean of the Collegiate Church of Ripon and bishop of Chester under Charles II. Though he is primarily remembered for his defining influence on English rhetoric and literary styles, Wilkins's other major early publications—*The Discovery Of A World In The Moone* (1638), a defense of the new astronomy; *Ecclesiastes, Or, A Discourse concerning the Gift Of Preaching as it fals under the rules of Art* (1646), a handbook on preaching; and *Mathematical Magick: Or, The Wonders that May Be Performed by Mechanicall Geometry* (1648), a primer on mechanics—prove Wilkins a polymath typical of those men with whom he later helped to found the Royal Society. Each of these works was widely read and went through several printings throughout the century. The subject of Wilkins's last important work, *An Essay Towards a Real Character, And a Philosophical Language* (1668), a proposal for an artificial and universal language, suggests why scholarship on Wilkins's life and works has crossed disciplines to include rhetorical, literary, and linguistic studies, as well as histories of science and religion.

Scholars of both religious and secular rhetoric continue to debate Wilkins's impact on the English rhetorical style. An examination of the evolution of Wilkins's notions concerning style is an excellent means of illustrating the two major movements in early modern England that exerted influence on seventeenth-century rhetoric. The first of these movements follows the general interest in rhetorical reform associated with Pierre de La Ramée (known as Petrus Ramus) and later with the proponents of Senecan rhetoric over the traditional Ciceronian model. The second major influence derived from the rise of experimental science and the need for a more accurate style for describing the nature of things. Wilkins's interest in this field of study is evident not only in his works popularizing the "new science," but in his highly influential work on preaching, *Ecclesiastes*. According to Wilkins, both the natural sciences and preaching sought to disseminate knowledge, and therefore they had similar rhetorical goals. While some scholars have seen Wilkins's reforms as having led to the devaluing of eloquence and grandeur in sacred rhetoric, others have pointed to his advocating of the plain style as paving the way for the prose style for which the Royal Society became celebrated and a preaching style accessible to a popular audience. In any case, Wilkins's contribution to seventeenth-century rhetoric remains central.

John Wilkins was born at the Northamptonshire house of his maternal grandfather, the Puritan divine John Dod (1549–1645), who was well known for his exposition on the Ten Commandments. Walter Wilkins, an Oxford goldsmith, had married Jane Dod in 1611, and the couple lived in Northamptonshire until shortly after the birth of their son. In 1615 the elder Wilkins took his family to Oxford, where he was active in city government until ill health forced him to retire in 1623. Walter Wilkins died two years later, leaving behind his wife and five children. Shortly thereafter, Jane Wilkins married Francis Pope and had two more children, a daughter who did not survive, and a son, Walter Pope (circa 1630–1714), who remained close to John Wilkins throughout his life.

John Wilkins's schooling may have originally been undertaken by his grandfather John Dod, but by nine years of age Wilkins was a member of All Saints parish in Oxford and attending Edward Sylvester's grammar school. Sylvester was a noted Greek and Latin scholar connected with the university and its primary church, St. Mary-the-Virgin. In May of 1627 Wilkins matriculated at New Inn Hall (later united with Balliol College), but he transferred to Magdalen Hall that same year. He received his B.A. from Magdalen in 1631 and his M.A. degree in 1634. While a student, Wilkins studied under the tutor John Tombes, who later became known for his opposition to infant baptism. There is some debate over Tombes's

influence on Wilkins's theological and scientific views. Aside from his religious dissent, Tombes was mostly known as an able scholar of Greek and Hebrew and probably contributed primarily to the traditional aspects of Wilkins's education.

Wilkins's scientific and mechanical interests may have begun in his childhood through the influence of his father. While none of the Wilkins children followed their father's profession as goldsmiths, he seems to have influenced them in other ways. According to seventeenth-century biographer John Aubrey, Walter Wilkins was "a very ingenious man [who] had a very mechanical head. He was very much for trying experiments, and his head ran much upon the perpetual motion." This early exposure to the practical application of scientific principles and amateur experimentation may have influenced the young John Wilkins. At university he encountered lively debate concerning the "New Science." The newly endowed Savilian lectures in astronomy and geometry brought the Copernican hypothesis to the university community throughout the 1620s and early 1630s. Such figures as Henry Briggs and John Bainbridge were both lecturing on Nicolaus Copernicus during Wilkins's student days at Oxford.

By 1634 Wilkins was a tutor at Magdalen Hall and counted among his own tutees Walter Charleton, Thomas Sydenham, and Jonathan Goddard, all future men of science. Oxford University during this period was in the midst of the theological and political controversies that came to a head in the Caroline period. While the Puritans remained a strong presence at Cambridge, they had been in retreat at Oxford since the election of William Laud to the position of chancellor of the university in 1630. There is no evidence that Wilkins entered into the Arminian controversy there with any zeal. What is known is that he remained at Magdalen Hall for another three years after receiving his M.A.

Early in 1637 Wilkins obtained his first clerical position and was soon thereafter ordained in Christ Church Cathedral at Oxford in 1638. He then succeeded his grandfather John Dod as vicar of Fawsley in Northamptonshire. Dod, though allied with the Puritans, was no extremist. As William Lloyd reported, Dod had "no delight in contradiction" and could not find it "in his heart to disturb the Peace of the Church in these matters." Dod may have given up his position in order that Wilkins could be ordained. Laudian policy limited ordination to those about to receive positions, thus restricting the ordination of Puritans in the church. Wilkins did not stay long at Fawsley, and at some point in 1638 Dod resumed the post, remaining until his death in 1645. Wilkins became chaplain to William Fiennes, first Viscount of Saye and Seale.

OR,
A DISCOVRSE
Tending,
TO PROVE,
that 'tis probable there
may be another habitable
World in that Planet.

*Quid tibi inquis ista prodérunt?
Si nihil aliud, hoc certe, sciam
omnia angusta esse.* SENECA.
Præf. ad 1.Lib. N. 2.

THE
DISCOVERY
OF A
WORLD
IN THE
MOONE.

LONDON,
Printed by *E.G.* for *Michael Sparke*
and *Edward Forrest*, 1638.

Two-page title page for John Wilkins's first book, in which he defended the Copernican hypothesis that the Earth revolves around the Sun

As Fiennes's chaplain, Wilkins traveled in more-urbane circles than those of Northamptonshire. During this period of transition away from the university and into the service of more-active political figures, he published his first book, *Discovery Of A World In The Moone. Or, A Discourse Tending, To Prove, that 'tis probable there may be another Habitable World in that planet,* in 1638. A defense of the new astronomy, this work was clearly the result of those scientific interests piqued at Oxford. Though students of the history of science recognize the importance of this early popularization of the Copernican hypothesis in England, one should also attend to the so-called Ross-Wilkins Controversy that was the result of this publication and its effects on religious and literary culture.

Alexander Ross, the headmaster of the Free School at Southampton, published *Commentum de Terræ Motu circulari* (A Commentary on the Circular Movement of the Earth), his first attack on the Copernican hypothesis, in 1634. Ross held that acceptance of the new astronomy would prove detrimental to the Christian religion, basing his charge on a narrow and literal interpretation of scripture that he believed to uphold the old geocentric model of the cosmos. Wilkins, who was familiar with the Copernican and Galilean positions—not only from the Savilian lectures at Oxford but also from his wide reading on the subject—clearly felt the need to respond to Ross's reactionary position. Two years after the publication of *The Discovery of a World,* Wilkins published an enlarged edition, to which he added *A Discourse Concerning a New Planet, The Second Book,* in which he developed and expanded themes from the earlier piece and countered Ross's argument point for point. In *The Discovery of a World* Wilkins expressed a desire to "rise up some more active Spirit to a Search after other hidden and unknown Truths," while simultaneously convincing the layman that such inquiry was not contrary to religious belief. Expanding on these themes in 1640, Wilkins cited the works of Copernicus and Johannes Kepler to describe the new astronomy, and he drew on Galileo's *Siderius nuncius* (The Starry Messenger, 1610) and Tommaso Campanella's *Apologia pro Galileo* (The Defense of Galileo, 1622) to defend the new hypothesis.

Wilkins's primary strategy was to divide the truth into two categories, theological and physical. One may seek the first in scripture but the second is to be found through the scientific observation of nature:

> In the search of Theological Truths, it is the safest method, first of all to looke unto Divine Authority; because that carries with it clear evidence to our Faith, as any thing else can to our reason. But on the contrary, in the examination of Philosophical points, it were a preposterous course to begin at the testimony and opinion of others, and then afterwards to descend unto reasons that may bee drawne from the Nature and Essence of the things themselves.

Here Wilkins took the Baconian position concerning the separate realms of theology and nature that became standard in the Restoration concept of natural philosophy. Ross's argument depended on the authority of Aristotelian physics, the judgments of the Church Fathers, and the literal statements of scripture. Wilkins most disputed the last position. For him the revelation in scripture of the mysteries of natural science had been "accommodated" to the limited capacities of the unlearned so as not to contradict the apparent evidence of their senses. As the faults of human senses were compensated by improved investigative methods and technologies, the understanding of natural phenomena could become more perfect. Wilkins concluded his 1640 observations with a position that anticipated the later Enlightenment "argument from design": "Astronomy proves a God and a Providence," and "a more accurate and diligent enquiry into their Natures, will raise our Understandings unto a nearer Knowledge, and greater Admiration of the Deitie. . . . Likewise may it serve to confirme unto us the Truth of the Holy Scriptures."

Though Ross continued the controversy with his 1646 rebuttal, *The New Planet No Planet, Or, the Earth No Wandring Star: Except in the Wandring Heads of Galileans,* the tide of learned opinion was already turning toward Wilkins's position. The popularity of Wilkins's text in England is confirmed by the fact that it was reprinted several times within the first five years of its initial publication. By 1656 it had been translated into French,

extending Wilkins's influence to the Continent. The wide currency of the debate over the Copernican hypothesis and the notion that the moon might be another world can be seen not only in the circulation of the works of Wilkins and Francis Godwin but also in Savinien Cyrano de Bergerac's *Histoire comique des états et empires de la Lune* (The Comical History of the States and Empires of the Moon, 1656) and the passage in book 8 of John Milton's *Paradise Lost* (1667) in which Adam speculates on the nature of the cosmos. Both these works almost certainly drew directly on Wilkins. As late as 1713, Wilkins's astronomical treatises were being translated into German with a commendatory foreword by professor of mathematics Johan Dopplemayer, who called the works the best explanation of Copernicus then available.

By the time *Mercvry, Or The Secret and Svvift Messenger: Shewing, How a Man may with Privacy and Speed communicate his Thoughts to a Friend at any distance* was published in 1641, Wilkins was chaplain for a new patron, George Lord Berkeley. This work, which Wilkins dedicated to Berkeley—himself an accomplished linguist—represents another type of amateur foray into a then-popular subject, cryptology. With increased literacy came a desire to develop systems for delivering secret communications. *Mercvry* deals not only with the standard practices of communicating through metaphor, allegory, neologisms, and the like but also with signs and gestures. This field, known to Wilkins as "semeology," was a forerunner of the contemporary field of semiotics. Beyond Wilkins's interests in ciphers and signs are the serious beginnings of his lifelong desire to develop a universal language. The works of Francis Bacon and Johann Amos Comenius (Jan Ámos Komenský) in England had given rise to the desire to find a means of creating such a language and thus undoing the curse of Babel. After examining the multiplicity of languages and the written symbols for expressing them, Wilkins suggested the creation of a "Universal Character to express things and notions as might be legible to all People and Centuries, so that Men of Several Nations might with the same ease both write and read it." This project had to wait until after the Restoration, when Wilkins put forward perhaps his most important work, *An Essay Towards a Real Character, And a Philosophical Language,* in 1668.

During the intervening years Wilkins published works in still more varied fields while becoming increasingly influential in preaching and the new science. Wilkins remained in the service of Berkeley for roughly three years after the publication of *Mercvry*. Considering that Berkeley was a moderate Anglican who exhibited Royalist sympathies during the latter period of the struggle between the king and Parliament, it is unlikely that Wilkins could be considered a Puritan in any extreme sense. Because of Wilkins's early exposure to Puritanism through Dod and his education at Magdalen Hall, Wilkins's critics often assumed that he was not true to his religious convictions, and some, as reported by seventeenth-century biographer Anthony à Wood, considered him an opportunist. The bulk of this criticism stems from presumptions about what kind of Puritan Wilkins was and from the fact that he accepted a bishopric after the passage of the Act of Uniformity in 1662. Yet, Wilkins was consistently moderate in his religious opinions and demonstrated the same dislike of factionalism that his grandfather did. He is rightly understood as a latitudinarian—even if an ambitious one. At some point in 1644 Wilkins became chaplain to Charles Louis, Prince Elector Palatine, who had come to London in hopes of receiving parliamentary support for the restitution of his lost territories. The Parliament was inclined to support the elector because of his status as a Continental Protestant leader; some members of Parliament even considered offering Charles Louis the English throne. They later voted him a generous pension and apartments in Whitehall. Charles Louis was an energetic and scholarly figure, who turned his attention increasingly toward amateur scientific experiments as it became evident that he was not a serious contender for the throne. During his service to the elector, Wilkins was able to accompany him abroad. Wood observed that Wilkins seemed "bred in the court, and was a piece of a traveller, having twice seen the prince of Orange's court at the Hague, in his journey to, and return from, Heydelburg, whither he went to wait upon the prince elector palatine, whose chaplain he was in England."

Wilkins's association with the elector also brought him into contact with influential figures at home. Primarily because he was the elector's chaplain, Wilkins was officially engaged as a preacher at Gray's Inn sometime late in 1645. The Inns of Court had long been the preferred venues for influential theologians and preachers residing in London. As a result of his twelve years of pastoral experience, Wilkins made another important contribution, this time to English religious life and literary style, with the publication of *Ecclesiastes, Or, A Discourse concerning the Gift Of Preaching as it fals under the rules of Art* in 1646. As the subtitle indicates, Wilkins was primarily concerned with reforming the method and style of preaching. *Ecclesiastes* provided clergymen with a handbook of references to other divines that they could use in the construction of more-effective sermons.

Though Wilkins's goal was to foster the plain style in preaching, such general stylistic reforms were not novel and had been advocated since the latter half of the sixteenth century by such influential figures as Ramus in his teachings on logic and rhetoric and Francis Bacon in his *Advancement of Learning* (1605). Though not published until four years after Wilkins's *Ecclesiastes* appeared, *A Priest to the Temple* (1652), a manual on the pastoral life written by poet George Herbert in the early 1630s, had argued for similar reforms. Wilkins was clearly influenced by such intellectual movements and had a distaste for the Ciceronian and arcane "metaphysical" preaching style associated with Lancelot Andrewes and John Donne. That tradition of highly complex and allusive sermons had become increasingly associated with court preaching and the followers of Archbishop Laud during the Caroline period. Contrary to such elaborate rhetoric, Wilkins held that sermons

> must be plain and natural, not being darkened with the affection of Scholasticall harshnesse, or Rhetorical flourishes. Obscurity in the discourse is an argument of ignorance of the minde. The greatest learning is to be seen in the greatest plainnesse. The more nearly we understand any thing our selves, the more easily we expound it to others.

Plainness for Wilkins did not mean simplicity. Even though he advocated the plain style, Wilkins demanded that a preacher be both learned and rigorous. The primary requirements of a preacher were: "A right understanding of sound doctrine, an ability to propound, confirm, and apply it to the edification of others." One preparing for pastoral office should study and consult many authors; Wilkins warned that this vocation demanded "vast industry and time, scarce consistent with the frequent returns of public service required of a constant Preacher, unless he be beforehand qualified for this by education and leisure at the University." Among the authors Wilkins recommended in the generous lists of exempla were a large number of classical or "Heathen" authorities on morality whose works, in his view, confirmed Christian doctrine. Principle among these writers were Seneca and Plutarch, but Wilkins also commended Plato, Aristotle, Cicero, Epictetus, Theophrastus, Plotinus, Xenophon, and other less well-known ancients. Unlike the Cambridge Platonists, who relied on long quotations or elaborate allusions to such authors in their oratory styles, Wilkins recommended simply reminding an audience of the substance of these classical sources: "To stuff a Sermon with citations of Authors, and the witty sayings of others, is to make a feast of vinegar and pepper; which are healthful and delightful being used moderately as sauces, but needs be very improper and offensive to be fed upon as a diet."

Wilkins relied on planning and method over ex tempore inspiration. In order to encourage this approach he put forward a concise tripartite model consisting of "Explication, Confirmation, Application." By adopting a more uniformly natural diction Wilkins sought to explicate a given passage of scripture so that it might become accessible to the majority of his auditors. Only then did he bring secondary examples as a means of "confirming" the truthfulness of his explication through comparison to other Christian and pagan authorities. *Ecclesiastes* lists dozens of pastoral and scholarly examples, ranging from Peter Lombard and Thomas Aquinas to the staunchest of the reformers, but Wilkins listed no living authorities so as to avoid factionalism. As with his classical sources the works of these other divines were intended to aid the preacher more than the parishioner. A well-constructed sermon was situated between the arcane artfulness of a preacher such as Lancelot Andrewes and the lengthy Puritan style of the Cambridge Platonists, who often dissected the text into minute parts and enlarged on each. Wilkins's sermons were known for their clarity of exposition and simplicity of organization. At his funeral service Wilkins's fellow latitudinarian divine, William Lloyd, described Wilkins's sermon delivery in the following terms: "He spoke solid truth, with as little show of Art as possible. He exprest all things in their true and Natural colours; with that aptness and plainness of Speech, that grave and Natural way of Elocution, that showed he had not design upon his hearers. His plainness was best for instruction of the simple. . . . He applied himself more to the understanding than Affections."

From its original publication until well into the Restoration, Wilkins's *Ecclesiastes* was the best-known book on preaching. Between 1646 and 1718 it was reprinted twelve times. The 1653 edition also includes Wilkins's extremely popular sermon *A Discourse concerning the Beauty of Providence In all the rugged passages of it* (1649). With each subsequent reprinting and addition to his original contribution on preaching, Wilkins's influence grew, extending to High Church conservatives such as Robert South, on the one hand, and Puritan divines such as Cotton Mather, on the other. Wilkins's greatest influence, of course, was on other moderate Anglicans who came to prominence in the Restoration church. Important figures such as Joseph Glanvill, Archbishop John Tillotson, William Lloyd, and Gilbert Burnet all adopted the style advocated by Wilkins. By the end of the seventeenth century it is safe to say that Wilkins's plain style had become general to the Church of England. For this reason literary scholars since the early twentieth century have had a tendency to concentrate on Wilkins's *Ecclesiastes* and

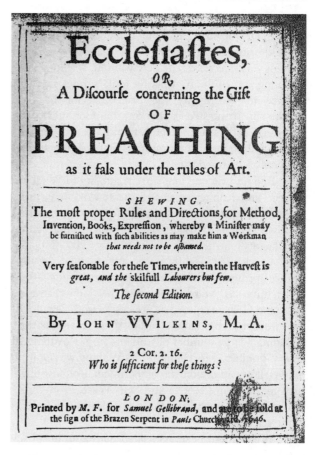

Title page for the manual that had a major influence on simplifying preaching style in the Church of England

his other religious writings in connection with the development of Restoration prose styles. Connections between Wilkins's supposed Puritanism and his scientific interests have also been proposed, though much of the existing biographical data on Wilkins throws into question his status as a Puritan. It is safe to say that because of the popularity of Wilkins's work on preaching scholars have tended to focus on this aspect of his writings, somewhat to the exclusion of his other works, when seeking to describe Wilkins's contribution to English literature.

Yet, by the mid seventeenth century Wilkins's sphere of influence extended well beyond his obvious role in the popularization of the new science and his impact on preaching styles. During the Interregnum his presence at Oxford University as warden of Wadham College had a lasting effect on the development of the natural and experimental sciences in England. He was appointed to this position in 1648, while he was still in the service of the prince elector. In May 1647 Parliament had passed an ordinance that empowered a committee to oversee the "regulation and reformation" of Oxford after the Royalist forces had been driven out.

The next year parliamentary visitors ejected the former warden, Dr. John Pitt, for "high contempt and denial of the authority of Parliament." The thirty-four-year-old Wilkins was selected as the new warden. Not long after accepting the position, Wilkins took a brief leave of absence to accompany the prince elector back to reclaim his contested lands on the Continent. On returning to Oxford several months later, Wilkins immediately became an important figure in the administration of the university.

Besides bringing long-absent stability to Wadham College and helping to ensure the return of the hundreds of students who had quit the university during the Civil War, Wilkins also oversaw the appointment of new faculty and fellows to his college. His moderate religious views and enthusiastic advocacy of the new sciences proved to be Wilkins's greatest virtues during his tenure as warden. Under his administration Wadham College entered its greatest period. Because of the warden's reputation, admissions rose sharply, including a large number of students from Royalist and gentry families. Most important, Wilkins was able to draw fellows interested in "experimental philosophy," such as Lawrence Rooke and Seth Ward, from Cambridge, greatly enhancing the reputation of the college in the sciences.

Wilkins had been associated with a group of scientifically progressive men since 1645, when a group of amateur and scholarly scientists had begun to meet in London at Gresham College. There Wilkins had made valuable contacts with several of the men he later brought to Oxford. Wilkins had a laboratory set up at the college, and soon a nucleus of the men that later made up the Royal Society was to be found at Wadham. This group included John Wallis, Jonathan Goddard, William Petty, Ralph Bathurst, Thomas Willis, and Robert Boyle. The addition of such esteemed men to the faculty eventually drew some of the most talented students in England to enroll as undergraduates at Wadham.

The same year Wilkins accepted his wardenship he also published a primer on mechanics, *Mathematical Magick: Or, The Wonders that May Be Performed by Mechanicall Geometry*. Though the title may suggest that this work takes up the theoretical concerns of the previous decades, the book is actually focused on the practical application of a variety of recent technological innovations and efforts to better understand the more ancient ones. The part of his book subtitled "Archimedes or Mechanical Powers" deals with the balance, lever, wheel, pulley, wedge, and screw and attempts to explain the mechanical principles behind them as labor-saving devices. The utility of these devices had long been known, but a mathematical understanding of how they

functioned was only recently being worked out by such figures as Guidobaldo del Monte in his *Liber mechanicorum* (Book of Mechanics, 1577) and Marin Mersenne in his *Cogitata physico-mathematica* (Considerations on Physical Mathematics, 1644). Wilkins drew heavily on both these works.

The second part of *Mathematical Magick,* "Daedalus or Mechanical Motions," treats the application of those basic mechanical functions described in the first section to a variety of possible inventions, some practical and some bizarre; including flying machines, submarines, wind-driven land vehicles, Archimedes' screw, automata, and perpetual-motion machines. Even the strangest of these would have been considered the subject of legitimate scientific investigation. What is more important to note here is that as with Wilkins's previous ventures into the realm of science, *Mathematical Magick* represents an attempt to bring into plainly rendered English debates and research previously reserved for university men who read Latin, thus making them available to all who had interest in these subjects. In his address "To the Reader" Wilkins made it clear that he wanted to effect a "real benefit" for the gentlemen and "common artificers" who read the work whether it be in the draining of mines and coalpits or a "right understanding of the grounds and theory" of the arts they practiced. The broader implications of such a work were in keeping with Wilkins's notions about "natural religion," which he first indicated in his earlier astronomical writings, in that he hoped to show how "a divine power and wisdom might be discerned, even in those arts which are so much despised."

Besides the practical issues discussed in *Mathematical Magick,* Wilkins also put forward his belief in the necessity for freedom of inquiry. According to Wilkins it was the responsibility of those "in search of Truth" to "preserve a Philosophical Liberty." A true scientist was one who approached a task with "an equal Mind, not swayed by Prejudice, but indifferently resolved to assent into that Truth which upon deliberation shall seem most probable unto thy Reason." This desire for unbiased investigation made Wadham College, under the wardenship of Wilkins, a haven for men of science regardless of their religious or political affiliations. As the reputation of Wadham grew, so did its ability to attract some of the most gifted students of the period. Among them were Christopher Wren, who had known Wilkins since adolescence, Wilkins's half brother Walter Pope, Thomas Sprat, William Lloyd, William Neile, and Samuel Parker. Other students who attended Oxford were also drawn to the scientific meetings at Wadham, and among these scholars was the young Robert Hooke, who later in his famous *Micrographia* (1665), paid tribute to Wilkins, saying: "There is scarce

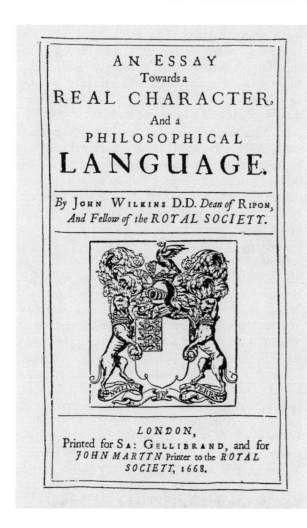

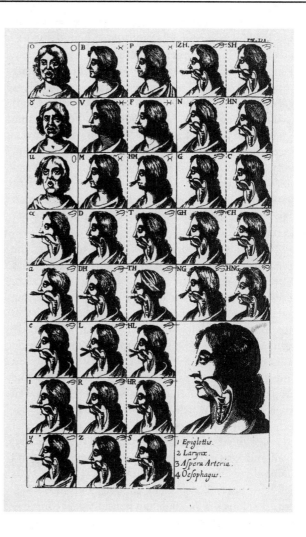

Title page for Wilkins's attempt to create a universal language and an illustration from that work showing how sounds are formed

any one invention, which this nation has produced in our age, but it has some way or other been set forward by his assistance. . . . He is indeed a man born for the good of mankind, and for the honor of his country. In the sweetness of whose behavior, in the calmness of his mind, in the unbounded goodness of his heart, we have an evident instance, what the true and the primative unpassionate religion was, before it was soured by particular factions."

Beyond his support for the sciences and greater intellectual freedom, Wilkins also had the important task of serving on the governing delegation of the university under its parliamentary chancellor, Oliver Cromwell. With both the universities increasingly under attack by radical factions within Parliament, and Oxford in particular because of its associations with Laud and the Caroline court, Wilkins struggled to regain some of the autonomy Oxford had lost. In 1653

the political and religious radicals of the "Barebones Parliament" were the closest they had yet been to dominating the political system. During this period Parliament entertained a motion that called for "suppressing the Universities and all Schools of Learning, as heathenish and unnecessary." Only with the collapse of the Parliament and institution of the Protectorate did this threat end.

In the following year another attack came from the radicals, this time in the form of a pamphlet written by the former Army Chaplain John Webster. In his *Academiarum examen* (The Examination of the Academies, 1654) Webster attacked the universities and their curricula as being overly dependent on Aristotle, presuming to teach what can only proceed from the spirit of God and excluding the works of mystics such as Jakob Böhme. In reply Seth Ward wrote *Vindiciae academiarum* (A Vindication of the Academies, 1654), a pamphlet in which he responded to Webster's charges point by point. Wilkins contributed an introduction to the work, which challenged Webster on both religious and scientific grounds, asserting that the universities were willing to oppose Aristotle "as any contrary evidence does engage them, being ready to follow the banner of Truth by whomsoever it should be lifted up"; at the same time the pamphlet flatly refuted the contention that university education presumed to displace divine inspiration. Finally, on the recommendation that the university adopt the mystical works of Böhme and others, Wilkins asserted that Böhme or any of the "highly illuminated fraternity of Rosicrucians" were unacceptable for the university curriculum.

Wilkins's main intent was always to protect the universities from the likes of Webster, whom he saw as a "credulous fanatick reformer." Because of his dual interest in maintaining a learned clergy and fostering the sciences, Wilkins was a champion of both Christian humanism and the new science, but it was mostly through his moderate temperament and insistence on greater autonomy for the colleges that Wilkins achieved so much for the entire institution. Tillotson later wrote of Wilkins's contribution to the university: "It is so well known to many worthy persons yet living, and has been so often acknowledged even by his enemies, that in the late times of confusion, almost all that was preserved and kept up of ingenuity and learning, of good order and government in the University of Oxford, was chiefly owing to his prudent conduct and encouragement." Wilkins's reputation as a judicious and conscientious administrator led to his next major academic appointment, master of Trinity College, Cambridge.

After the death of Oliver Cromwell, Wilkins—who in 1656 had married Cromwell's sister, Robina, the widow of Peter French, Canon of Christ Church—became a close adviser to Richard Cromwell and was appointed to the position at Cambridge in 1658. Richard was familiar with Wilkins's work at Oxford and hoped for the same results at Trinity. Wilkins's tenure, though, lasted only one academic year. Taking the post in September of 1659, he was forced to relinquish it some eight months later, in May of 1660. The Restoration of the monarchy had revived the claim of Henry Ferne, who had been promised the post at Trinity by Charles I. In July of 1660 the fellows, after considerable dissent and a failed petition on Wilkins's behalf, accepted Ferne as master. Even in the brief time that Wilkins was at Cambridge his interaction with the Cambridge Platonists was noteworthy. Like them, Wilkins was a latitudinarian, and he used contact with this group to further refine his positions on sectarian tolerance and natural religion. He reentered his active clerical life in the Restoration with a strong sense that

religion, rightly understood, both revealed and natural, was essentially governed by reason. Just two months after his ejection from Trinity, Wilkins received a royal appointment as dean of the collegiate church of Ripon and a prebendary at York Cathedral. Like most other clerical authorities in the period, Wilkins administered these duties from his home in London.

After returning to London at the beginning of 1661, Wilkins was soon elected preacher at Gray's Inn. He held this prestigious post, along with a rural benefice in Cranford, for a year until he was made vicar of the prominent city parish of St. Lawrence Jewry. The congregation was made up of many influential figures in city government, and the Guildhall was within the boundaries of the parish. Wilkins shared preaching responsibilities at St. Lawrence with his immensely popular son-in-law John Tillotson, husband of Wilkins's stepdaughter, Elizabeth French, and the future archbishop of Canterbury. One of the main benefits of Wilkins's position there was that it allowed him to remain in the city and continue his participation in the scientific meetings at Gresham College. As early as November 1660 this group came together to plan the founding of an academy dedicated to the promotion of "physico-mathematical experimental learning"—this gathering was the beginning of the Royal Society, and Wilkins was elected its president. Two years later this same group was incorporated officially as the Royal Society. At this point Wilkins's young friend Sir Robert Moray had become the president, no doubt owing to his close associations with the king and the desire of the society to secure royal patronage.

Wilkins was among the most active members of this body from its inception until his death. He was not only involved in a great variety of experiments but was an important factor in the recruiting of new members and in the administration of the society. Members of the old Gresham College group and others from Oxford made up the majority of the Royal Society in its first years; these men included Hooke, Wren, Sprat, Boyle, Charleton, Walter Pope, Goddard, Petty, Wallis, Bathurst, and Willis. Among those who had not been part of the original Gresham set at Oxford were the diarists John Evelyn and Samuel Pepys, who formed friendships with Wilkins and mentioned him frequently in their diaries. Promoting the Royal Society and its work occupied a large amount of Wilkins's time in the early days of that organization, and in the fourth year of the society Wilkins proposed that Bishop Sprat undertake a history of its founding and its accomplishments thus far. Sprat's well-known volume, which had been overseen by Wilkins throughout its composition, appeared in 1667 on the fifth anniversary of the Royal Society.

Though Wilkins, like many others, suffered hardships and temporary displacement as a result of the Great Fire of London in 1666, he returned to his work in London near the end of 1667. All Wilkins's personal papers were destroyed in the fire, including those of his ongoing project on a universal language. This project, which had long interested Wilkins, had seeds in his early work *Mercury*. Unlike the linguistic mysticism of Böhme and Webster, Wilkins's desire for a universal language was practical and reform-minded. The fantasy of recuperating the original or "Adamic" language had preoccupied a variety of European thinkers since the Middle Ages. Figures such as Robert Fludd held that careful study of Hebrew would reveal the roots of the language purportedly spoken by Adam before the Fall and that in knowing this language humanity could escape the "curse of Babel." Beyond representing the dream of a common language, proponents of the Adamic tongue also believed that a truer understanding of the nature of things would mystically be revealed were such a language to be recovered. The logic behind this notion lay in the belief that Adam had named the objects in nature and all living things before his understanding had been corrupted by the original sin; therefore, if these original words could be reconstructed linguistically, humankind's understanding of nature would be repaired.

Wilkins and Ward had ridiculed just such a mystical notion in *Vindiciæ Academiarum*, but Wilkins had also seen the appeal of a universal language. Language had been the object of serious attention by scholars on many fronts since the advent of humanist philology. Added to the study of classical rhetoric was the seemingly endless variety of languages encountered with the continuing exploration of the non-European world. The Americas and Africa presented European linguists with an entire array of languages that appeared unrelated to any they had known. With a better understanding of Asian writing systems also, came the notion that whole words or ideas could be expressed in a single character. Wilkins therefore set out to develop an artificial language and a new system of written characters through which it could be communicated. He worked on this project for several years in the early 1660s, but the original manuscript was destroyed in the Great Fire. Sometime after his return to London in 1667 Wilkins began to rewrite what became arguably one of his most important works, *An Essay Towards a Real Character, And a Philosophical Language* (1668).

Wilkins's essay stands out as one of the largest and most complete systems for an artificial language developed in the seventeenth century. Though Wilkins did not consider the 1668 edition to be a finished product, it was highly praised and widely read from its first

Engraved portrait of Wilkins published as the frontispiece to the 1680 edition of his Mathematical Magik, *first published in 1648 (courtesy of The Lilly Library, Indiana University)*

appearance. Members of the Royal Society saw to the wide distribution of *An Essay Towards a Real Character, And a Philosophical Language* throughout England and the Continent. Within a short time Wilkins's efforts were being praised by some of the leading minds of the day. In England it found an appreciative audience in the likes of Christopher Wren, John Locke, and Isaac Newton—all of whom both referred to it in their early works and recommended it to friends. The king learned to write in the character and started a brief vogue for the work in courtly circles, while abroad Wilkins was commended by such figures as Gottfried Wilhelm Leibniz and Comenius. Several such artificial language systems had been proposed before, including those by Leibniz and Comenius, but none was as complete or systematic as Wilkins's "real character." After initial interest in Wilkins's essay abated, however, no new edition was printed until an abstract of the work appeared in the 1708 edition of Wilkins's *Mathematical and Philosophical Works.*

Though greatly admired at its publication, *An Essay Towards a Real Character, And a Philosophical Language* had little actual effect on the writings of the scientific or philosophic members of the Royal Society. No one in the end adopted the system, and after a flurry of interest, it simply faded away. The greatest actual influence of the work was incidental and developed only in reaction to Wilkins's work in the field of taxonomy. At this point taxonomy was still seen as a valid method for better knowing the nature of things. Wilkins sought the aid of John Ray as he prepared the botanical tables to be used as examples in the essay, but because Wilkins organized his tables based on his own arbitrarily prescribed system, Ray found the classification divisions unworkable. Ray wished to "follow the lead of nature" in classification and saw the dangers in relying on taxonomy itself as an epistemological tool. This desire led to Ray's own pioneering work in plant classification and, on a larger scale, to a general critique of taxonomy. Locke later emphasized the limits of taxonomy in comparison with the complexities of nature, and Newton's physics later proved physical phenomena to be better comprehended in mathematical and not linguistic terms.

Wilkins's essay remains an important work in the history of linguistics and has been perhaps the most widely studied of his works in the late twentieth century. When placed in context with Wilkins's other projects, whether they be in astronomy or preaching, the essay reveals Wilkins's primary concern with the reform of language and the desire for greater precision of expression. Wilkins continued to work on the essay intermittently after its publication, but this task took a secondary place to his clerical duties after he was named bishop of Chester in 1668. From that point on, Wilkins was actively engaged in working out a compromise between nonconformists and the established church, while simultaneously combating the reactionary policies of other High Church bishops during the last years of his life. He remained active in the Royal Society but was less frequently in London, where he died on 19 November 1672 at the house of John Tillotson.

Wilkins's works continued to be republished throughout the seventeenth century and into the beginning of the eighteenth. Among his posthumously published works are *Of the Principles and Duties of Natural Religion* (1675), a work that anticipated some of the arguments of Enlightenment deists; *Sermons Preached Upon several Occasions Before the King at White-Hall* (1677) and *Sermons Preached upon Several Occasions* (1682), Tillotson's collections of Wilkins's most popular sermons;

and *The Mathematical and Philosophical Works of the Right Reverend John Wilkins* (1708), the only collection of his major secular works. Scholars in the areas of the history of science, linguistics, and literary studies continue to study Wilkins's work and his position in the intellectual developments and politics of seventeenth-century England. It is a telling fact about seventeenth-century culture that reference to Wilkins's achievements may be found in studies across the contemporary academic divisions of the physical and social sciences, as well as the humanities.

Bibliography:
H. M. Lord, "A Bibliography of John Wilkins," thesis, Library School, University of London, 1957.

Biographies:
Anthony à Wood, "John Wilkins," *Athenae Oxonienses. An Exact History of All the Writers and Bishops Who Have Had Their Education in the University of Oxford. To Which Are Added The Fasti, or Annals of the Said University,* 4 volumes, edited by Philip Bliss (London: Printed for F. C. and J. Rivington, 1813–1820), III: cols. 967–971;

P. A. Wright Henderson, *The Life and Times of John Wilkins* (Edinburgh: Blackwood, 1910);

John Aubrey, "John Wilkins," in *Brief Lives,* edited by O. L. Dick (Ann Arbor: University of Michigan Press, 1957);

Barbara Shapiro, *John Wilkins 1614–1672: An Intellectual Biography* (Berkeley: University of California Press, 1969);

Hans Aarsleff, "John Wilkins (1614–1672): A Sketch of His Life and Work," in the *Dictionary of Scientific Biography,* 18 volumes, edited by Charles Coulston Gillispie (New York: Scribners, 1970–1990), XV: 361–381.

References:
Douglas Bush, *English Literature in the Earlier Seventeenth Century* (Oxford: Oxford University Press, 1942);

Francis Christensen, "John Wilkins and the Royal Society's Reform of Prose Style," *Modern Language Quarterly,* 7 (1946): 179–187;

Francesca Chiusaroli, *Categorie di pensiero e categorie di ligua: l'idioma filosofico di John Wilkins* (Rome : Il Calamo, 1998);

I. Bernard Cohen, *Revolution in Science* (Cambridge, Mass.: Harvard University Press, 1985);

Frederic Dolezal, *Forgotten but Important Lexicographers, John Wilkins and William Lloyd: A Modern Approach to Lexicography before Johnson* (Tübingen: M. Niemeyer, 1985);

Lia Formigari, *Language and Experience in 17th-Century British Philosophy* (Amsterdam: John Benjamin, 1988);

Wilbur Samuel Howell, "The New Rhetoric (1646–1800)," in his *Eighteenth-Century Logic and Rhetoric* (Princeton: Princeton University Press, 1971), pp. 441–691;

Richard F. Jones and others, *The Seventeenth Century: Studies in the History of English Thought and Literature from Bacon to Pope* (Stanford: Stanford University Press, 1951; London: Oxford University Press, 1951);

James Knowlson, *Universal Language Schemes in England and France 1600–1800* (Toronto: University of Toronto Press, 1975);

J. Andrew Large, *The Artificial Language Movement* (Oxford: Blackwell, 1985);

William Lloyd, *A sermon preached at the funeral of the Right Reverend Father in God John, late Lord Bishop of Chester, at the Guildhall Chappel London, on Thursday the 12. of December, 1672* (London: Printed by Henry Brome, 1675);

Lawrence Manley, *Convention 1500–1750* (Cambridge, Mass.: Harvard University Press, 1980);

Frank E. Manuel and Fritzie Manuel, *Utopian Thought in the Western World* (Cambridge, Mass.: Harvard University Press, 1979);

Ian Michael, *English Grammatical Categories and the Tradition to 1800* (Cambridge: Cambridge University Press, 1970);

William F. Mitchell, *English Pulpit Oratory from Andrewes to Tillotson: A Study of Its Literary Aspects* (New York: Macmillan, 1932);

G. A. Padley, *Grammatical Theory in Western Europe, 1500–1700: Trends in Vernacular Grammar,* 2 volumes (Cambridge: Cambridge University Press, 1985);

Walter Pope, *The life of the Right Reverend father in God Seth, Lord Bishop of Salisbury . . . : With a brief account of Bishop Wilkins, Mr. Lawrence Rooke, Dr. Isaac Barrow, Dr. Turbervile, and others* (London: W. Keblewhite, 1697);

Margery Purver, *Royal Society: Concept and Creation* (Cambridge, Mass.: MIT Press, 1967);

Gerard Reedy, *Robert South (1634–1716): An Introduction to His Life and Sermons* (Cambridge: Cambridge University Press, 1992);

Vivian Salmon, *The Studiy of Language in 17th-Century England* (Amsterdam: John Benjamin, 1979);

Deborah K. Shuger, *Sacred Rhetoric: The Christian Grand Style in the English Renaissance* (Princeton: Princeton University Press, 1988);

Mary M. Slaughter, *Universal Languages and Scientific Taxonomy in the Seventeenth Century* (Cambridge: Cambridge University Press, 1982);

W. M. Spellman, *The Latitudinarians and the Church of England, 1660–1700* (Athens: University of Georgia Press, 1993);

Thomas Sprat, *History of the Royal Society* (1667), edited by Jackson I. Cope and Harold Whitmore Jones (St. Louis: Washington University Press, 1958);

Robert E. Stillman, *The New Philosophy and Universal Languages in Seventeenth-Century England: Bacon, Hobbes, and Wilkins* (Lewisburg, Pa. & London: Bucknell University Press / Cranbury, N.J.: Associated University Presses, 1995);

Joseph L. Subbiondo, "From Pragmatics to Semiotics: The Influence of John Wilkins' Pulpit Oratory on His Philosophical Language," *Historiographia Linguistica,* 23 (1996): 111–122;

Subbiondo, ed., *John Wilkins and 17th-Century British Linguistics* (Amsterdam: John Benjamins, 1992);

Nicholas Tyacke, ed., *The History of the University of Oxford, Volume IV: Seventeenth-Century Oxford* (Oxford: Clarendon Press, 1997);

Brian Vickers, "The Royal Society and English Prose Style: A Reassessment," in *Rhetoric and the Pursuit of Truth: Language Change in the Seventeenth and Eighteenth Centuries,* by Vickers and Nancy Struever (Los Angeles: William Andrews Clark Memorial Library, University of California, 1985), pp. 1–76;

George Williamson, *The Senecan Amble: Prose Form from Bacon to Collier* (Chicago: University of Chicago Press, 1951).

Thomas Wilson

(1523 or 1524 – 16 June 1581)

Tita French Baumlin
Southwest Missouri State University

See also the Thomas Wilson entry in *DLB 132: Sixteenth-Century British Nondramatic Writers, First Series.*

BOOKS: *The rule of Reason, conteinyng the Arte of Logique set forth in Englishe, by Thomas Vuilson* (London: Printed by Richard Grafton, 1551; revised and enlarged, 1552; revised again, 1553);

The Arte of Rhetorique, for the vse of all suche as are studious of Eloquence, sette forth in English (London: Printed by Richard Grafton, 1553); enlarged edition (London: Printed by John Kingston, 1560);

De Maria Scotorum Regina, totáque eius contra Regem coniuratione, fœdo cum Bothuelio adulterio, nefaria in maritum crudelitate & rabie, horrendo insuper & deterrimo eiusdem parricidio: plena, & tragica planè Historia, anonymous, by Wilson and George Buchanan (London: Printed by John Day?, 1571); enlarged, and translated by Wilson, as *Ane Detectiovn of the duinges of Marie Quene of Scottes, touchand the murder of hir husband, and hir conspiracie, adulterie, and pretensed mariage with the Erle Bothwell. And ane defence of the trew Lordis, mainteineris of the Kingis graces actioun and authoritie* (London: Printed by John Day, 1571);

A Discourse vppon usurye, by vvaye of Dialogue and oracions, for the better varietye, and more delite of all those, that shall reade thys treatise. By Thomas Wilson, doctor of the ciuil lawes, one of the maisters of hir maiesties honourable courte of requests. Seene & allowed according to the Queenes Maiesties iniunctions (London: Printed for Richard Tottel, 1572).

OTHER: *Vita Et Obitvs Dvorvm Fratrvm Suffolciensium, Henrici et Caroli Brandoni, prestanti virtute, et splendore nobilitatis ducum illustrissimorum, duabus epistolis explicata. Adduntur Epitahia et acroamata in eosdem graece et latine conscripta, cum Cantabrigiensiu tum Oxoniensiu iugi cōmentatione et industria. Affiguntur præterea ad calcem libri quædam Epigrammata in alios præclaros, cum viros tum etiam mulieres, quibus nomen memorabile fuit, et vita summis ornamentis illustrata,* edited, with contributions

Thomas Wilson in 1575 (portrait by an unknown artist; National Portrait Gallery, London)

in prose and poetry, by Wilson (London: Printed by Richard Grafton, 1551);

De obitu doctissimi et sanctissimi theologi doctoris Martini Buceri, Regii celeberrima Cantabrigiensi Academia apud Anglos publice sacrarum literarum prælectōris epistolæ du æ. Item, epigrammata varia cvm Græcæ tum Latiné conscripta in eundem fidelissimu[m] diuini uerbi ministrum, edited by Sir John Cheke, includes a Latin epigram by Wilson (London: Reginald Wolf, 1551);

Walter Haddon, *D. Gualteri Haddoni, regii professoris in ivre ciuili, Cantabrigienses: siue Exhortatio ad literas,* edited, with dedication and poem, by Wilson (London: Printed by Richard Grafton, 1552);

Haddon, *G. Haddoni Legvm Doctoris, S. Reginæ Elisabethæ a supplicum libellis, lucubrationes passim collectæ, & editæ. Studio & labore Thomæ Hatcheri Cantabrigiensis. Ad lectorem. Ne quaeras lector, cur quae iuueniliter olim Scripserat Haddonus, publica facta legas. Omnia coniunxi, quia mel, quia succus in illis, Et condita suo quaeq[ue] lepore iuuant,* edited by Thomas Hatcher, includes commendatory letter by Wilson (London: Printed by William Seres, 1567);

The Three Orations of Demosthenes chiefe Orator among the Grecians, in fauour of the Olynthians, a people in Thracia, novv called Romania: vvith those his fovver Orations titled expressely & by name against king Philip of Macedonie: most nedefull to be redde in these daungerous dayes, of all them that loue their Countries libertie, and desire to take vvarning for their better auayle, by example of others. Englished out of the Greeke by Thomas Wylson doctor of the ciull lawes. After these orataions ended, Demosthenes lyfe is set foorth, and gathered out of Plutarch, Lucian, Suidas, and others, with a large table, declaring all the princcipall matters conteyned in euerye part of this booke. Seene and allowed according to the Queenes Maiesties iniunctions, translated by Wilson (London: Printed by Henry Denham, 1570);

Speech against usury before Parliament, in *Journals of All the Parliaments During the Reign of Queen Elizabeth Both of the House of Lords and the House of Commons,* by Sir Symonds D'Ewes (London, 1682), pp. 172–173;

Oration delivered at the funeral of Edward Courtenay, in *Ecclesiastical Memorials, relating chiefly to religion, and the reformation of it: and the emergencies of the Church of England, under King Henry VIII. King Edward VI. and Queen Mary I. with large appendixes, containing original papers, records &c,* by John Strype, 3 volumes (Oxford: Clarendon Press, 1822), III, part 2: 420–427;

"A discourse touching this kingdoms perils with their remedies," in "A Treatise on England's Perils," by Albert J. Schmidt, *Archiv für Reformationsgeschichte,* 46 (1955): 243–249.

Editions: *Wilson's Arte of Rhetorique, 1560,* edited by G. H. Mair (Oxford: Clarendon Press, 1909);

A Discourse upon Usury by Way of Dialogue and Orations: For the Better Variety and More Delight of All Those That Shall Read This Treatise [1572], edited by R. H. Tawney (London: G. Bell, 1925);

The Arte of Rhetorique, 1553, edited by Robert Hood Bowers (Gainesville, Fla.: Scholars' Facsimiles & Reprints, 1962);

Demosthenes, *The Three Orations in Favour of the Olynthians (London 1570),* translated by Wilson, The English Experience, no. 54 (Amsterdam: Theatrum Orbis Terrarum / New York: Da Capo Press, 1968);

The Rule of Reason (London 1551), The English Experience, no. 261 (Amsterdam: Theatrum Orbis Terrarum / New York: Da Capo Press, 1970);

The Rule of Reason, Conteinyng the Arte of Logique, edited by Richard S. Sprague (Northridge, Cal.: San Fernando Valley State College, 1972);

Arte of Rhetorique, edited by Thomas J. Derrick, The Renaissance Imagination, no. 1 (New York and London: Garland, 1982);

A Critical Old-Spelling Edition of Thomas Wilson's "The Arte of Rhetorique" (1553), edited by John Michael Crafton, dissertation, University of Tennessee, 1985;

The Art of Rhetoric (1560), edited by Peter E. Medine (University Park: Pennsylvania State University Press, 1994).

The most widely circulated English rhetorician in the sixteenth century, Thomas Wilson is remembered primarily for his logic, *The rule of Reason, conteinyng the Arte of Logique* (1551), and his comprehensive Ciceronian rhetoric, *The Arte of Rhetorique, for the vse of all suche as are studious of Eloquence* (1553), each the first of its kind in the English language and the most reprinted of its kind at the time: three editions and four reprints of *The rule of Reason* and two editions and six reprints of *The Arte of Rhetorique* appeared during the sixteenth century alone. The impact of these two works upon the literary and political milieu of sixteenth-century England, and indeed upon the writers and orators of subsequent ages, should not be underestimated. Two works of midcareer, a translation of *The Three Orations of Demosthenes chiefe Orator among the Grecians, in fauour of the Olynthians* (1570) and *A Discourse vppon usurye, by vvaye of Dialogue and oracions, for the better varietye, and more delite of all those, that shall reade thys treatise* (1572), not only reflect Wilson's continued interests in classicism and rhetorical disputation, but also point to his continued personal attempts to direct Elizabethan public policy. He was esteemed so highly by his contemporary scholars that many dedications to him exist. A study of his remarkable career reveals the life of this Cambridge scholar and Protestant extremist to be that of a most distinguished, if occasionally distressed, civil servant whose high and low points include elevation to the post of principal secretary of the Privy Council under Elizabeth I from 1577 to 1581 and imprisonment and torture during the Inquisition under Pope Paul IV in 1558–1559. The most recent and perhaps most thorough criticism of Wilson's works, Thomas O. Sloane's *On the Contrary: The Protocol of Traditional Rhetoric* (1997), has argued that Wilson's life shows not only a strong interest in ruling-class power and frank self-aggrandizement but also a "very deep interest in humanism and its protocol." Perhaps like that of any person living in an age of such tumultuous reversals in ideologies and political regimes, a detailed study of Thomas Wilson's life and works reveals a man of substantial complexity if not paradox.

Born probably as early as August 1523 or as late as January 1524 in either Lincoln or Strobie (present-day Strubby) in the marshlands of Lincolnshire, Wilson (named Thomas after at least three previous Thomas Wilsons in that county) was the eldest of five sons of Thomas and Anne Wilson. Although not a gentleman, the elder Thomas Wilson had established himself in Lincolnshire as an unusually wealthy member of the yeoman class, allowing him to marry Anne Cumberworth, heiress to her family's estate in Lincolnshire, and to buy or otherwise receive monastic lands at the dissolution of the monasteries. Wilson himself later made disparaging reference to his native shire, writing in *The Arte of Rhetorique* that it were better to be born "in London than in Lincoln," where "the air is better, the people more civil, and the wealth much greater, and the men for the most part more wise." Indeed, it was a commonplace belief that humidity was injurious to the humors, and so the discussion in *The Arte of Rhetorique* of the ill effects of moisture upon the faculty of memory—"who hath seen a print made in water of any earthly thing?"—and references to fens and marshes may well owe much to his boyhood experiences in Lincolnshire, where he returned to live at various points in his adult life and which he even represented in Parliament in 1571. Thomas J. Derrick, in his introduction to a 1982 edition of *The Arte of Rhetorique,* argued that Wilson spices his work with Lincolnshire references for rhetorical effect, discreetly distancing himself so as to imply his having risen above his provincial origins. After his inheritance of properties following his father's death in 1551, he identified himself in a deposition as "Thomas Wilson of Wasshyngboroughe in the Countie of Lyncoln. Gent[leman] of the age of XXIX years."

Though nothing is known of Wilson's boyhood until his matriculation as a king's scholar at Eton in 1537, it is worth noting that if he were at home until that date he would have witnessed the Lincolnshire rebellion of 1536, a Catholic uprising against Protestant reform that earned its participants charges of treason. That event and his parents' associations with local Protestant royalists may have contributed to Wilson's lifelong hatred of treason and zeal for Protestantism, though more practically the circumstances may well have resulted in Wilson's selection to Eton. Although no particular information is extant regarding Wilson's training at Eton, it was among the first grammar schools to incorporate into its curriculum Desiderius Erasmus's *Adagia* (1500, 1508), *De duplici copia rerum ac verborum* (1512), and *Colloquia* (1518, 1526); no doubt these works had a formative impact on Wilson's education, since Erasmus taught that early learning should consist not merely of grammar lessons in Latin but of reading and imitating great authors of antiquity. Such reading and imitation furnished the schoolboy Wilson not only with fundamental Latin instruction in the five parts of rhetoric but also with copious schemes, tropes, anecdotes, fables, topics, and model *sententia,* all of which figure prominently in his English works years later. At Eton, Wilson probably developed his friendship with Nicholas Udall, who was master of Eton during this time and whom Wilson later represented in a court of law, and, still later, testified on behalf of in a court proceeding. Although some scholars believe that Wilson did not adopt Protestantism until his years at Cambridge, others have suggested that his staunch Protestantism may have been influenced by his proximity at Eton to Udall and Robert Aldrich, provost at the school and a former student of Erasmus; both Udall and Aldrich were more-zealous Protestants than most of their peers. In these men the young Wilson may have found models of the scholar he eventually became, one who combined commitments to humanism, Protestantism, and royal service.

In 1542 Wilson was selected to attend King's College, Cambridge, where he earned the bachelor of arts degree in 1547 and the master of arts degree in 1549. There he met two individuals who became highly influential in his career: Sir Thomas Smith, chairman of civil law, and Sir John Cheke, chairman of Greek studies, both of whom maintained friendships with Wilson long after the three men had left the university. Peter E. Medine, in his *Thomas Wilson* (1986), argues that, in addition to the content of Wilson's studies, there are at least three other major Cambridge influences on Wilson's life and letters. First, religious reform and academic reform were there seen to be inextricably linked; among its scholars and fellows during this time, Cambridge numbered such Protestant reformers as Miles Coverdale, Thomas Bilney, Hugh Latimer (possibly the most famous preacher in early-sixteenth-century England), and Matthew Parker (archbishop of Canterbury under Elizabeth I). Indeed, Cambridge furnished the royal tutors to Henry's children, Edward and Elizabeth, insuring further church reform in the years to come. Several key elements of Protestant academic reform were officially ensconced at Cambridge, notably the removal of canon law from study and the encouragement of all scholars to private Bible study.

A second influence on Wilson was curricular, specifically Scholasticism, since the form of study still emphasized disputation as the major form of academic exercise. Here the university required of its students a thorough knowledge of Aristotle and strong skills in dialectic, both of which figure prominently in Wilson's works. Third, although the use of the vernacular in religious tracts was

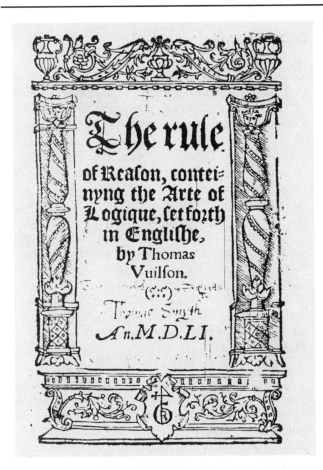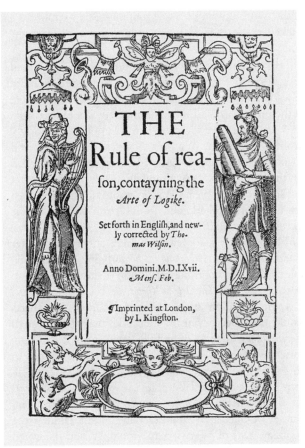

Title pages for the first edition and the revised third edition of Wilson's popular and influential book on logic

among the general propositions of the Protestant cause, Cambridge scholars in particular were among the strongest advocates for the use of English in scholarly writings, as well. This shift to vernacular was part of the English nationalism–pride in the language symbolizing English power. More generally, the Tudor monarchies had instituted a new governmental system that initiated major social change: rather than clergy and nobility, laymen and commoners became the primary servants to the monarch; hence the university system began to flourish with the influx of wealthy commoners seeking a foundation in humanist education, which seemed requisite to receiving royal preferment. This development was not without controversy, however: Erasmus himself seemed ambivalent as to the propriety of making available to all classes every element of education, and, even as late as 1531, Thomas Elyot in *The Booke Called the Governour* urged that only the sons of the noble class should be allowed a complete education in the deepest humanist sense. Among many others, Wilson was a "middle class opportunist," Sloane argues, who recognized the mobility afforded by a humanist education and who used this new insight to "expand his connections and reach for the top."

Wilson began his formal writings at Cambridge, contributing Latin verses to *De obitu doctissimi et sanctissimi theologi doctoris Martini Buceri, Regii celeberrima Cantabrigiensi Academia apud Anglos publice facrarum literarum prelectoris. Epistolæ duæ* (1551), Cheke's collection of tributes for the funeral of Martin Bucer, the great German reformer who had been appointed Regius Professor of Divinity at Cambridge, only months before his death. Later in 1551 Wilson and Walter Haddon edited *Vita Et Obitus Dvorvm Fratrum Suffolciensium, Henrici et Caroli Brandoni, prestanti virtute, et splendore nobilitatis ducum illustrissimorum, duabus epistolis explicata,* a collection of Latin and Greek eulogies for two young sons of Katharine Willoughby Brandon (dowager duchess of Suffolk, also from Lincolnshire and a Protestant extremist), to which Wilson contributed a prose biography and several poems in Latin. Wilson had tutored Henry and Charles Brandon since 1548 and had even housed them during the epidemic of "sweating sickness" that took their lives. Wilson's effectiveness as a tutor is evident in that verses written by the adolescent Brandons themselves had been given place in Cheke's Bucer memorial, *De obitu doctissimi.* Some twelve years later, in *The Arte of Rhetorique,* Wilson describes the deaths of the two Brandon boys as proof that God's wrath for a wicked realm is visited on the innocent as well as the guilty.

The later years of his Cambridge study opened several doors for patronage, a most important financial development for a Renaissance scholar, for, as he wrote in the preface to the 1560 edition of *The Arte of Rhetorique,* "it were better be a carter than a scholar for worldly profit." Whatever Wilson's sources of income and encouragement, this portion of his life was distinguished by the young scholar's abundant productivity. Within the space of three years Wilson wrote or edited at least six full works in addition to his contributions to the Bucer memorial: *Vita et Obitus* (1551), *The rule of Reason* (1551), with revised editions in 1552 and 1553; Walter Haddon's oration *Exhortatio ad literas* (1552), which Wilson edited, also contributing a Latin dedicatory poem to Edward VI; and *The Arte of Rhetorique.* It is assumed that, had the Brandon boys survived, Wilson's prospects would have been even brighter; still, probably through the dowager duchess of Suffolk, Wilson met such luminaries as Henry Grey, Duke of Suffolk (and father to Jane Grey), to whom he dedicated *Vita et Obitus;* Sir William Cecil, later Lord Burghley, to whom he dedicated the Demosthenes orations; Sir Edward Dymoke; John Dudley, Duke of Northumberland; John Dudley the younger, Earl of Warwick, to whom Wilson dedicated both the *Exhortatio* and *The Arte of Rhetorique;* and Robert Dudley, Earl of Leicester, to whom he dedicated *A Discourse vppon usurye.* Wilson also managed to secure support from the king's printer, Richard Grafton. According to Wilson's preface to *The rule of Reason,* it was Grafton, himself a loyal Protestant and printer of several Bibles of the English Reformation as well as the first Book of Homilies and the first two Books of Common Prayer, who encouraged him to write it.

All that is known of Wilson's life during his composition of *The rule of Reason* comes from his preface for the second edition, in which he calls the work "suche fruictes, as haue growen in a poore Studentes Garden"; in the "Admonition to the Reader for Faults Escaped in the Printing" he states that he wrote the book during a time when he had "not so convenient leisure for the good placing and true examining thereof" and wished he could have "remedied" it before its publication. Scholars have surmised that this wording suggests that *The rule of Reason* was written during the period surrounding the deaths of the Brandon boys or of his father, or both, or perhaps during Wilson's final passage of study at Cambridge. Whatever the reasons for Wilson's hasty preparation of the first edition of the work, it is apparent that Wilson's second edition owed much to the suggestions and marginal notes (still extant) of Sir Thomas Smith, who was by now quite a prominent scholar.

The rule of Reason begins with the English "Epistle Dedicatory to King Edward VI," followed by Latin poems composed by Haddon and Wilson himself, and Wilson's introduction in English. The three major sections of the book then offer sections on judgment, invention, and logical fallacies and dilemmas. *The rule of Reason* was not intended as an original work, since it was a condensation of Aristotle's seven logical treatises collectively known as the *Organon,* the "tool" or "instrument of knowledge." C. S. Lewis, in *English Literature in the Sixteenth Century Excluding Drama* (1954), calls it "a mere work of popularization" that is "dark and crabbed" for the modern reader. No doubt in Wilson's mind its innovation lay in its making accessible to the "vulgare people," as Wilson's dedicatory epistle proposes, those elements of Aristotle's logic that had never before been available in English, his "countrey men" having been by virtue of their "tongues . . . vnacquaynted" with the *Organon.* He states that logic is "as apt for the English wittes, and as profitable for their knowlege, as any thother sciences are, [and] might with asmuche grace be sette furthe in the Englishe, as the other artes, heretofore haue been."

Though he emphasizes with apparent pride that "no Englishman vntill now, hath goen through with this enterprise" and that this "fruicte" is "of a straunge kynde (suche as no Englishe grounde hath before this tyme, and in this sorte by any Tillage brought furthe)," he also states his humble hope that the book be a "spurre or a whetstone" to "sharpe the pennes of some other, that thei maie polishe, and perfect that I haue rudely and grosly entred." Indeed, the successful innovation of this work may be gauged by the fact that by the end of the century five other English logic manuals had appeared. Medine argues that the strongest indicator of Wilson's continuing authority in the field of logic is the fact that, nearly fifty years later, Thomas Blundeville's *Art of Logic* (1599) incorporated verbatim whole passages from *The rule of Reason* without mentioning the source. Wilson displays throughout the book a keen awareness that he is breaking new ground, as, for example, in the first page of the text he explains patiently to his English reader, "For there is none other difference betwixt the one and thother, but that Logique is a Greke woorde, and Reason is an Englishe woorde."

Yet, the title itself represents a play on words, as Sloane notes, since "rule" can denote a method of measurement or a reign of a monarch; hence, "the rule of reason" implies a work that will both measure the rational faculty and demonstrate its supremacy. Since, early in the work, Wilson writes that reason itself is aligned with the human faculty of speech—man is "a liuing creature endued with reason, hauing aptnesse by nature to speake"—his view of rationality is discursive and language-bound, placing this work clearly prior to the anti-Aristotelian movement spurred by the works of Pierre de La Ramée (known as Peter Ramus) in the latter half of the sixteenth century. While, traditionally, dialectic (the science of argumentation) was separated from rhetoric (the science of persuasion), for Wilson, logic and rhetoric both belong to the province of dialectic, their major difference being the rhetorical use of ornamentation and amplification: "Bothe these Artes are much like, sauyng that Logique is occupied about al matters, and dooeth plainly and nakedly setfoorth with apt woordes, the summe of thinges, by the waie of argumentation. Again of thother side, Rethorique useth gaie painted sentences, and setteth foorth those matters with freshe colours and goodly ornamentes, and that at large. In so muche, that Zeno beeyng asked the difference, betwene Logique and Rethorique, made aunswere by demonstration of his hande, declaryng that when his hande was closed, it resembled Logique, when it was open and stretched out, it was like Rethorique." Wilson would have equated logic with *logos*, or demonstration, rhetoric adding the two other Aristotelian *pisteis* or proofs, *pathos* and *ethos*, but all would belong to the general province of dialectic.

Though comparatively much condensed, *The rule of Reason* follows the general Aristotelian approach in its ordering of concepts from simple to complex. Wilson's structure, however, is more distinct, and he predicts the organization of the book in an early statement in the introduction: "Logique, otherwise called Dialect (for thei are bothe one) is an Art to trie the corne from the chaffe, the trueth from euery falshod, by definyng the nature of any thing, by diuidyng the same, and also by knittyng together true argumentes, and untwinyng all knottie subtleties that are bothe false, and wrongfully framed together." This fundamental division of logic into judgment (analysis, or "defining" and "dividing") and invention ("knitting together" arguments) is attributed to the early Renaissance professor of philosophy, Rodolphus Agricola, whose *De Inventione Dialectica* (1515), following Aristotle's *Topics* and Cicero's Romanized version of Aristotle, emphasizes topical invention over other aspects of the *Organon*.

Modern scholars have therefore debated whether *The rule of Reason* leans more toward medieval Scholasticism or the newer humanism. G. H. Mair, in the introduction to his edition of *Wilson's Arte of Rhetorique* (1909), argues that the work is simply "one long Protestant tract in which the doctrines of Geneva are enforced by the apparatus of mediaeval logic." Since the Aristotelian differentiation between logic and dialectic was already collapsed in Scholasticism, Wilbur Samuel Howell argues, in *Logic and Rhetoric in England, 1500–1700* (1956), the book is most closely aligned with medieval Scholastic logic in its equation of logic and dialectic. Conversely, Walter J. Ong, in *Ramus, Method and the Decay of Dialogue* (1958), contends that Wilson's dependence on Agricola

marks the book as "antischolastic humanist" in orientation. Medine, too, finds the work to be "manifestly humanist" in that it offers logic as essentially dialectical in nature, and its theory of invention is closely aligned with principles of rhetoric, such a "hybrid text" being thoroughly in keeping with earlier humanist Latin logics, such as George of Trebizond's *Isagoge* (1430), Philipp Melanchthon's *Erotemata Dialectica* (1520), and John Seton's *Dialectica* (1545). Sloane maintains that Wilson's book "places a humanist twist on Scholastic logic," since Wilson's use of the medieval divisions of logic are "hardly orderly or methodical in the Scholastic sense." Moreover, as Sloane argues, the true humanist bent of *The rule of Reason* is its "self-reflexive view of Scholastic logic" as seen from the standpoint of rhetoric itself; that is, Wilson sees logic, like rhetoric, to be a servant of causes, and, for Wilson, the causes in question were "Protestantism, patriotism, rhetoric, and Wilson himself." More than a digest of medieval Scholasticism, Wilson's *The rule of Reason* offers, as Sloane suggests, an argument cleverly directed at two different audiences—the unlearned and the learned—with two distinctly different intended effects: the unlearned would find a summary of Aristotle's teachings that had hitherto been unavailable to them, while the learned would see before them a lively example of a debate, cleverly demonstrating the rules of dialectic that are the thesis of the book.

After discussing the differences between logic and rhetoric and explaining the twofold division of logic into invention and judgment (a division traditionally ordered with invention placed first), Wilson next explains his unusual placement of judgment first: "The first parte standeth in framyng of thinges aptly together and knittyng woordes for the purpose accordyngly, and in Latine is called *Iudicium*. The seconde parte consisteth, in findyng out matter, and searchyng stuffe, agreable to the cause, and in Latine is called *Inventio*." The ordering is appropriate, he says, because "A reason is easilier founde, then fashioned," since anyone can know a reason that a thing is as it is but may not be "hable to sette thesame in ordre scholerlike, either to proue, or to confute." Further, Wilson's introduction asserts a distinction between logic and sophistry or fallacious reasoning: he proposes that logic is a means for finding arguments on all sides of a question "so ferre as the nature of euery thing can beare," while those who practice sophistry argue without conviction, attempting to pervert the art of logic in order to make the truth appear false and the false appear true. Here the *argumentum ad utramque partem*, the technique of arguing on both sides of a question, is important, with a caveat that sophistry is not seeing the argument from all sides but fabricating an illusion.

While he will later demonstrate that invention is an analytic function, Wilson characterizes judgment as synthetic: it "standeth in framyng of thinges aptly together, and knittyng woordes for the purpose accordyngly"; that is, judgment deals with the "framing" or building of logical discourse. The first element of judgment is the fundamental examination of "questions," which Wilson divides into four points—predicables, predicaments, definition, and division. The predicables, or the five types of logical statements, Wilson calls the "fiue common woordes," or statements that prove a true relationship between a subject and its predicate—statements of genus, of species, of difference, of property, or of accident. As Howell points out, any Latin scholar of the sixteenth century would have recognized here a variation on four of Aristotle's topics (accident, genus, property, and definition, with both species and difference being collapsed into what Aristotle called definition), though Englishmen who knew no Latin would hardly be familiar with them. The second means for determining the truth of a question involves application of predicaments (which were originally presented in Aristotle's *Categories* and which have given rise to disagreements among Aristotle's various interpreters). Wilson calls these predicaments the "moste general woordes," which are differentiated from the "fiue common woordes" or predicables by virtue of the fact that "the Predicables, set foorth the largenesse of woordes" while "the Predicamentes dooe name the verey nature of thinges, declaryng (and that Substauntially) what thei are in very dede." Here, offering examples in context, Wilson outlines ten categories for logically proper statements; these include "Substaunce" (what a subject is, in its essence) and nine "Accidentes" (quantity, quality, relative, action, passion, when, where, placement, and clothing). "Definition" and "Division" form the third and fourth parts of the discussion of questions, since "there is nothing in all this whole arte of Logique, more necessarie for manne to knowe, then to learne diligently the difinicion, and diuision of euery matier, that by reason maie bee comprehended."

Wilson's discussion of judgment next treats the "Proposicion" taken from Aristotle's *On Interpretation* (the second treatise in the *Organon*). Wilson says that it seems only fitting that after discussing "seuerall woordes" (predicables and predicaments) he should discuss how to "ioigne sentences together, and frame Proposicions by knittyng seueral woordes in ordre." He defines the proposition as "a perfeicte sentence spoken by the *Indicatiue mode*, signifying either a true thyng, or a false without al ambiguitie, or doubtefulnesse," and then offers the various kinds of propositions—general, particular, indefinite, singular, opposing, categorical, hypothetical, and conversion (reversal) of subjects and predicates. The treatment of judgment ends with a discussion of argument, the four kinds being *syllogismus* (or reasoning by syllogism), *enthymema* (enthymemic or rhetorical argument), *inductio*

(inductive reasoning), and *exemplum* (argument by example), all based on Aristotle's *Prior Analytics* (fourth century B.C.). These passages bear witness to the fact that there had been no previous English discussions of such matters; Wilson introduces the Latin terms but then offers his own English equivalents, such as his idiosyncratic names for the parts of the syllogism: the middle term he calls "the double Repeate," with the major term being "the terme at large" and the minor term being "the lesse, or seuerall" term. The awkwardness of Wilson's coinage reveals the difficulty of translating technical Latin and Greek into the English vernacular, though Wilson's are hardly as quaint as the Anglicisms of classical rhetoric in *The Arte of English Poesie* (1589), attributed to George Puttenham, and of logic in *The Arte of Reason, rightly termed, Witcraft* (1573), by Ralph Lever. Wilson's *The rule of Reason* faces the same problems that Cicero faced when he sought to translate Greek philosophy into his own vernacular. The originality of Wilson's work cannot be overstated.

The second section of *The rule of Reason* deals with "the second part of Logique, called *Inuentio,* that is to saie, the fynding out of an argumente," or the process of "findyng out matter, and searchyng stuffe, agreable to the cause," an analytic process of selecting specific "stuffe" appropriate to the argument. The length of the discussion on invention reveals Wilson's indebtedness to the Scholastic tradition. The notion that "A reason is easlier founde, then fashioned" implies an assumption that organizing or composing the argument is more difficult than discovering the thesis and subject matter. In fact, Howell argues that "a society which takes such an attitude must be by implication a society that is satisfied with its traditional wisdom and knows where to find it . . . a society that does not stress the virtues of an exhaustive examination of nature so much as the virtues of clarity in form."

Invention involves the topics or "places," as Wilson calls them: "A Place, is the restyng corner of an argumente, or els a marke whiche geueth warning to our memorie what wee maie speake probably, either in the one parte, or the other, vpon al causes that fal in question." He likens the "places" to the "foxe borough" or hiding holes that a good huntsman must "learne by labour to knowe," so that if "perhappes one place faile him, yet shal he finde a dousen other places, to accomplishe his purpose." Wilson follows Cicero's identification of extrinsic and intrinsic places, calling them "outward places" and "inwarde places," though Cicero limits the places to sixteen and Wilson offers twenty-four (many of which he has already introduced under the heading of predicaments—an overlapping of judgment and invention that the later Ramists sought to correct). The goal, Wilson says, is to find agreement among the applications of the places, for "wheras the places agree (that is to saie, all thinges are referred to thone that are referred to thother) there the Proposicion is good. . . . But where the places dooe not agree (that is to saie, some thinges are referred to the one woorde, that are not referred to the other) there the thinges theimselues cannot agree." He acknowledges that some of the places are more "vsed of the Rhetoriciens, then emong the Logiciens," since, as he says, "some argumentes are necessarie [certain], some probable." Wilson demonstrates the usage of the places by examining the question of "whether it bee lawfull for a Prieste to marie a wife or no," to which he applies nineteen of the places, showing the agreement between the conclusions for priesthood and those for wifehood; not surprisingly, given Wilson's Protestant convictions, he concludes that it is lawful for a priest to marry, but he demonstrates this argument from several different angles so as to illustrate various uses of the places.

The third section of *The rule of Reason* deals with the fallacies and insolubles discussed in Aristotle's *On Sophistical Refutations,* proposing two divisions: "deceiptfull argumentes" (or fallacies, such as the false syllogism) and what Wilson calls "trappyng argumentes" or witty fallacies. Since wicked men use "these places of crafte," Wilson maintains that he must identify them clearly in his treatise, so that they may be "auoided, and better knowen" by honest men. Each section of this final division of the book is laid out like a funnel or inverted pyramid at the bottom of the page on which it appears, visually distinguishing the material as distinctive and significant. Sloane argues that the typography of this section, often overlooked by modern editors of *The rule of Reason,* indicates Wilson's view of its importance, which Sloane says Wilson saw "as on a par with the first on judgment and the second on invention." The deceitful arguments are six types that depend on ambiguous diction and/or syntax, that is, "subtilties in the worde or maner of speakyng," and seven types that are independent of word choice. The "trappyng argumentes" Wilson says he offers to "delighte the reader," calling them such "straunge" names as *"Crocodilites," "Antistrephon," "Ceratinae," "Cacosistata," "Asistata," "Vtis,"* and *"Pseudomenos."* The book ends with a visual flourish to emphasize the ideological message, according to Sloane. An appropriate ending to a work filled with strikingly obvious Protestant-oriented examples, the last sentences march in funnel-like fashion down to the final, terse, and pointed sentence: "God bee praised."

The rule of Reason was so popular that three editions emerged during the first two years; during the sixteenth century it was republished by Grafton in 1552 (revised edition) and 1553 (revised edition), and by John Kingston, a former collaborator with Grafton, in 1563, twice in 1567, and in 1580. There is no evidence of authorial

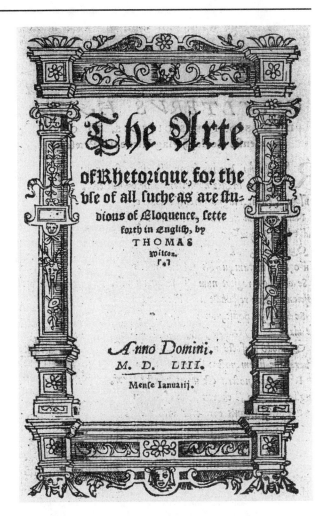

Title page for Wilson's widely read work on rhetoric, which he based largely on the works of Cicero

revision after 1553. The 1552 "newly corrected" edition provides a "table for the ease of the reader" and the conventional list of "Faults Escaped in the Printing," plus added material amounting to approximately twenty octavo pages, while the 1553 revision disburses new material totaling about eight quarto pages of text. Except for one four-page section of entirely new material, "On Disputation," the added content consists of elaborations and further examples, as is the case with one memorable addition to the 1553 edition: Wilson offers an example of fallacious argument depending on diction, identifying it as "an entrelude made by Nicolas Udal." In 1818 a newly discovered, anonymous play, *Ralph Roister Doister* (1566), was attributed to Nicholas Udall on the basis of this excerpt in Wilson's book.

For many modern scholars *The rule of Reason* provides the groundwork for Wilson's next work, *The Arte of Rhetorique,* which Sloane calls "the best and most complete humanist theory of rhetoric ever written in English"; it is a text with "little Scholasticism within it," although it "presupposes a thorough grounding in logic." Indeed, Sloane shows that an astute late-sixteenth-century scholar had bound a copy of *The rule of Reason* and *The Arte of Rhetorique* together, in this order, into one personal volume, revealing perhaps the age's recognition of a relationship between the two works. *The Arte of Rhetorique* was written in late 1551 or 1552. Since Wilson is known to have spent the summer of 1552 at the home of Sir Edward Dymoke in Scrivelsby, Lincolnshire, historians surmise that he probably finished his first draft there, urged on by John Dudley, Earl of Warwick, the eldest son of the duke of Northumberland, who was beheaded in 1553 for his part in the Jane Grey plot; the younger John Dudley fell ill, imprisoned in the Tower on charges of treason for assisting Northumberland, and lived only ten days past his release. Wilson dedicated the book to the younger Dudley, who had told Wilson that he wished that he "might one day see the precepts of rhetoric set forth by me in English, as I had erst done the rules of logic," as Wilson states in the dedication.

The Arte of Rhetorique, for the vse of all suche as are studious of Eloquence was first published in 1553 by Grafton; thereafter, it was published by Kingston in 1560 (revised edition), 1562, 1563, 1567, 1580, and 1584, and by G. Robinson in 1585. As with *The rule of Reason* before it, the chief contribution of *The Arte of Rhetorique* lies in its Englishing of classical material. Unlike *The rule of Reason*, however, *The Arte of Rhetorique* appeared after two previous English rhetorics, Leonard Cox's *Art or Craft of Rhetoric* (1530?), and Richard Sherry's *A treatise of Schemes & Tropes* (1550), both of which provided Wilson with some material, though the overall scope and the audience of Wilson's work differ greatly. Cox presented for grammar-school students only two of the five parts of Roman rhetoric, invention and arrangement, while Sherry treated only style in his *A treatise of Schemes & Tropes* to help readers comprehend literature. *The Arte of Rhetorique* attempts to instruct practitioners of rhetoric—those who would influence the powerful and manipulate public opinion—by covering the entire spectrum of what his age had come to think of as Ciceronian rhetoric. His principal classical sources were the anonymous *Rhetorica ad Herennium*, the works of Cicero (especially the *De oratore*, 55 B.C.), and Quintilian's *Institutio Oratoria* (92–94 A.D.). Derrick maintains that in a variety of ways (for example, Wilson's combining of deliberative rhetoric with the epistolary form, or his use of specific classical allusions and biblical quotations) the breadth of knowledge displayed in *The Arte of Rhetorique* owes more to the corpus of Erasmus's works (including Nicholas Udall's 1542 translation of *Apophthegmata*, 1531) than to any other author. Mark E. Wildermuth, in "The Rhetoric of Wilson's *Arte*" (1989), similarly argues that Wilson's Protestant cause, fitting preachers with classical rhetorical strategies,

was thoroughly Erasmian in intent. Janel M. Mueller, in *The Native Tongue and the Word* (1984), shows that Wilson maintains a Protestant perspective on the unresolvable duality of human nature, while Wayne A. Rebhorn, in his "Baldesar Castiglione, Thomas Wilson, and the Courtly Body of Renaissance Rhetoric" (1993), finds *The Arte of Rhetorique* to reveal an opposition between the courtly social body and the grotesque, anti-authoritarian social body (as theorized by Mikhail Bakhtin), this duality remaining unresolved because of Wilson's own conflicted class position.

Contemporary remarks show the strong impact and influence that *The Arte of Rhetorique* had on English letters: Gabriel Harvey's marginalia in his copy of Quintilian states that Wilson's book had become "daily bread" in the courts of law for "our common pleaders and discoursers"; in *A booke called the Foundacion of Rhetorike* (1563) Richard Rainolde calls *The Arte of Rhetorique* "a learned work of rhetoric . . . compiled and made in the English tongue, of one who floweth in all excellency of art, who in judgment is profound, in wisdom and eloquence most famous." Modern appraisals include Mair's view of it as a "landmark in the history of the English Renaissance" that is "indispensable to the historian of English literature"; for J. W. H. Atkins, writing in *English Literary Criticism: The Renascence* (1947), it "occupies the central position" in sixteenth-century English rhetoric; Russell H. Wagner, in "Thomas Wilson's *Arte of Rhetorique*" (1929), says that it "restored the body and, to some extent, reformed the concepts of rhetorical theory. In recalling rhetoric from the museum to the marketplace, he not only re-established the ancient conception of rhetoric as the art of the speaker, but, because of his own self-imposed purpose of adapting old doctrines to new times and new needs, he effected far reaching changes which have greatly influenced the theories of public address we hold today." Modern critics such as Hardin Craig, Winifred Nowottny, Thomas J. Derrick, Marie Cornelia, and Beverley Sherry have explored the influence of *The Arte of Rhetorique* on such subsequent literary artists as William Shakespeare, John Donne, and John Milton.

The 1553 edition of *The Arte of Rhetorique* begins with four Latin dedicatory poems by Haddon, Udall, Robert Hilermy, and Wilson himself. The English dedicatory epistle to the earl of Warwick is followed by prefatory remarks called "Eloquence First Given by God, After Lost by Man, and Last Repaired by God Again." The 1560 edition is revised to place the dedicatory epistle first, followed by an added "Prologue to the Reader," the "Eloquence" preface, and the Latin poems by Haddon and Wilson. The 1560 edition also offers an interesting revision of the earlier title page: while the 1553 edition frames the title with reusable, generic woodcut designs, the framing woodcut for the later edition is remarkably distinctive, adding to the top a conventional emblem for Renaissance humanists, the debate between Mars and Venus. Figures of the two deities are shown face to face in tense juxtaposition, neither yielding (contrary to the traditional myth of Venus's triumph). The emblem effectively functions as a symbol of *The Arte of Rhetorique* itself, illustrating the Ciceronian humanist emphasis on *controversia,* or debate, where *pro* and *contra* are given equal time; the figures' representation within one circle placed at the top of the page also portrays iconographically the premier concept in humanist teaching, the *argumentum ad utramque partem.*

In both editions, the major text that follows is divided into three books that, together, fully cover all five of the traditional parts of rhetoric, the first dealing with invention, the second with invention and disposition, and the third with "elocution" (style), delivery, and memory. Yet, *The Arte of Rhetorique* is much more than a mere translation of sources. Sloane believes that Wilson's own disposition in this book, his overlapping and "apparently unorderly distribution of the five offices of this art into three books," actually "serves a major part of his stated intention, to show that all these offices 'go together.'" In fact, Wilson's frequent use of Protestant *exempla* and his display of English ruling-class values make his work valuable as a cultural artifact of his time. In addition, many historians agree that *The Arte of Rhetorique* is the first work to offer an extensive examination of English prose.

The preface on "Eloquence" is based loosely on a passage in Cicero's *De inventione* (91–89 B.C.), in which he asserts the importance of oratory by narrating the myth of the transformation of early humankind through the arts of eloquence from a brutish existence into a civilized and humane culture. Wilson layers over it certain Judeo-Christian elements, such as God being the source of the gift of Adamic language, and the Fall in Eden being redeemed through eloquence: "But after the fall of our first father, . . . all things waxed savage. . . . Therefore even now when man was past all hope of amendment, God still tendering his own workmanship, stirred up his faithful and elect to pursuade with reason all men to society. . . . Such force hath the tongue and such is the power of eloquence and reason, that most men are forced even to yield in that which most standeth against their will." Wilson's myth of eloquence is not only Protestant ("faithful" invoking Luther's doctrine of justification by faith) but specifically Calvinist in its reference to God's "elect."

This prologue also includes a passage that implicitly valorizes the class structure: who would not try to live like a lord, he writes, rather than an underling, "if by reason he were not persuaded that it behooveth every man to live in his own vocation and not to seek any higher room than whereunto he was at the first appointed?" Sloane argues that here as well as in his consistent use of examples addressed or appealing to the wealthy and the powerful, Wilson displays a thoroughly non-Erasmian bent by revealing rhetoric to be not only a power for social control but also a means of self-aggrandizement for the skilled middle-class person. The prologue ends with an encomium to persuasive language: "For he that is among the reasonable of all most reasonable, and among the witty of all most witty, and among the eloquent of all most eloquent—him think I among all men not only to be taken for a singular man, but rather to be counted for half a god. For in seeking the excellency hereof, the sooner he draweth to perfection, the nigher he cometh to God, who is the chief wisdom, and therefore called God because he is most wise, or rather wisdom itself." As Tita French Baumlin argues, Wilson's notion that rhetorical proficiency brings one closer to God is a surprising reversal of the classical *bonus vir* tenet, which specifies that virtue facilitates persuasiveness; thus, *The Arte of Rhetorique* comfortably discusses *logos* and *pathos* but effectively renders the concept of *ethos* ambiguous.

The first book of *The Arte of Rhetorique,* which is as long as the other two combined, opens with Wilson's definition of rhetoric, "an art to set forth by utterance of words matter at large, or as Cicero doth say, it is a learned, or rather an artificial, declaration of the mind in the handling of any cause called in contention, that may through reason largely be discussed." He outlines the two "sorts" of questions possible: "an infinite question and without end" (usually called a thesis), that is, those general questions "without the comprehension of time, place, and person, or any such like, that is to say, when no certain thing is named"; and a question "definite and comprehended within some end" (usually termed a hypothesis) that thereby "set[s] forth a matter with the appointment and naming of place, time, and person." The three offices or duties required of a rhetorician are to teach, to delight, and to persuade, and there is a style appropriate to each "end" of rhetoric, though Wilson argues that to delight is the most "needful" of them all, since "even these ancient preachers must now and then play the fools in the pulpit to serve the tickle ears of their fleeting audience, or else they are like sometimes to preach to the bare walls, for though the spirit be apt and our will prone, yet our flesh is so heavy, and humors so overwhelm us, that we cannot without refreshing long abide to hear any one thing." This reference is the first of many to the preacher's need of rhetoric to convince his hearers of the truth of his message; Mueller argues that Wilson's focus throughout *The Arte of Rhetorique* on preachers' and lawyers' need for rhetoric is a function of

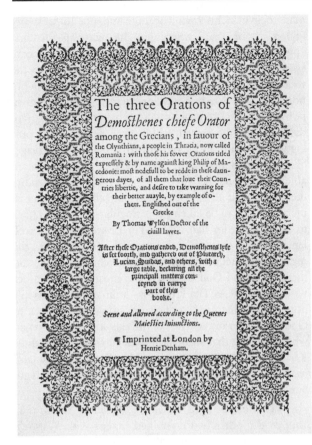

Title page for Wilson's translation of Demosthenes, in which he explicitly parallels the Greek orator's statements against Philip of Macedonia with contemporary warnings about Philip II of Spain

his Protestant belief in the divided nature of humanity, as well as his emphasis on preaching over the Catholic Mass and the dispensing of sacraments.

Next, Wilson addresses "By What Means Eloquence Is Attained" and "To What Purpose This Art Is Set Forth," offering three means—nature, art, and practice—principles espoused by Isocrates that Wilson developed from Cicero's *De oratore*. Nature is the least dependable of the three, since art facilitates the rhetorician's self-reflexivity and practice (the imitation of learned men) perfects one's art. Sloane points out, however, that Wilson's treatment of these means differs from Cicero's and from Quintilian's in that the Roman sources treat writing as a means of achieving eloquence but not necessarily as the medium of eloquence it becomes in Wilson's treatment. Mueller argues that *The Arte of Rhetorique* is so significant, in part, because it overtly makes such connections between written prose and the spoken oration, a connection that is a hallmark of the developing literacy of the sixteenth century.

The "Five Things to Be Considered in an Orator" reasserts the five traditional parts of rhetoric—invention, disposition, style or "elocution," memory, and delivery or "utterance." A thorough discussion of invention follows, with Wilson briefly outlining the "Seven Parts in Every Oration"—the "entrance or beginning," the narration, the proposition, the "division or several parting of things," the confirmation, the confutation, and the conclusion. He asserts that there are four "causes" for orations (taken from the *Rhetorica ad Herennium*): honest, "filthy" ("when either we speak against our own conscience in an evil matter, or else withstand an upright truth"), doubtful (when the matter is "half-honest and half-unhonest"), and "trifling" ("when there is no weight in them," such as, he says, Homer's description of the battle of frogs or Virgil's praise of the gnat). Fashioning an argument must always depend upon the nature of the "judges" (that is, the intended audience), in order to find those "reasons that best serve to further our cause" and practice "always to use whatsoever can be said to win the chief hearers' good wills and persuade them to our purpose."

Wilson next discusses the three basic kinds of orations—demonstrative (the praise or blame of men or things), deliberative ("whereby we do persuade or dissuade, entreat or rebuke, exhort or dehort, commend or comfort"), and judicial (the forensic rhetoric of accusation and defense). Each of these three sections includes several subdivisions and often lengthy examples. The discussion of demonstrative orations outlines inventive strategies for praising or blaming a person, using rhetorical places concerning events before, during, and after the person's life; each of these places is further subdivided into *topoi,* guiding the reader through the invention of such an oration. An example of such a speech is Wilson's own commendation of the two boys Wilson had tutored, "two brethren that lately departed, the one Henry, duke of Suffolk, and the other Lord Charles, his brother, whom God, thinking meeter for heaven than to live here upon earth, took from us in his anger, for the bettering of our doings and amendment of our evil living."

A similar discussion for demonstrative orations regarding "Some Deed Done" follows, regarding which the *topoi* include whether the deed is honest, possible, or impossible, and easy or difficult; the relevant circumstances may be discerned by questions regarding who, what, when, which Wilson offers in handy poetic form for memory's sake: "Who, what, and where, by what help, and by whose; / Why, how, and when, do many things disclose." The example is a commendation of "King David for Killing Great Goliath," where the description of David's courage to risk himself "for the love of his Country, for the maintenance of justice, for the advancement of God's true glory, and for the quietness of all Israel" reveals Wilson's Protestant patriotism, according to some commentators. The praise or blame of some thing (such as "virtue, vice, towns, cities, castles, woods, waters, hills, and mountains") requires confirming whether the thing is "honest," "profitable," "easy," or difficult. He says that the learned among his readers will understand how to use the places of logic in constructing such an oration, for "these [places] of logic must first be minded ere the others can well be had. For what is he that can call a thing honest and by reason prove it, except he first know what the thing is, the which he cannot better do than by defining the nature of the thing?" Thus, a certain overlap of, or "confound[ing] with," rhetoric and logic seems to him unavoidable but also useful. Sloane maintains that the example given, the "Commendation of Justice, or True Dealing," follows the more abstract form of discourse outlined in *The rule of Reason* and seems to be fashioned for only a general audience and for no observable occasion, but it well displays Wilson's ruling-class values and sets up the next section, the deliberative oration, in which the example involves advising a young man to pursue the study of law. Sloane argues that this deliberative oration is a prime example of the "pro-con thinking which pervades humanist rhetoric."

Wilson offers further lengthy examples of deliberative orations, including his own translation of Erasmus's letter to Mountjoy, *Encomium Matrimonii* ("An Epistle to Persuade a Young Gentleman to Marry")—which Derrick has shown to owe nothing to Richard Taverner's earlier translation, *A Ryght Frutefull Epystle* (1531)—and an oration that Wilson says he himself used in comforting the mother of the Brandon boys (and is imitative of, Derrick argues, Erasmus's *Declamatio de morte,* 1518). Wilson's use of such real-life examples throughout *The Arte of Rhetorique* not only offers his reader effective and practical suggestions but also demonstrates himself to be a practicing rhetorician. Sloane notices the peculiar stances that Wilson's circle, if not the Elizabethan Age more broadly, apparently found persuasive: for example, in the "comforting" oration when Wilson argues that it is actually best to die young, since travailing longer in this "wretched world, where vice beareth rule and virtue is subdued" might have led the youths to fall into sin later in life; to the rejoinder that the boys had been brought up to remain virtuous, Wilson argues, "Commodus was a virtuous child and had good bringing-up, and yet he died a most wicked man." Sloane admits, however, that reading the piece biographically and not rhetorically is "to use it in a way that Wilson at the conclusion of the example urges that rhetorical matters *not* be used."

The first book concludes with the definition of judicial rhetoric, "when matters concerning land, goods, or life, or any such thing of like weight are called in question," calling for "an earnest debating in open assembly of some weighty matter before a judge." Central to forensic argument is the classical doctrine of *stasis* (or the Latin *status,* which Wilson translates literally as "state"): "A state . . . generally is the chief ground of a matter and the principal point, whereunto both he that speaketh should refer his whole wit, and they that hear should chiefly mark." The *stasis* arguments possible in judicial oration are "Conjectural" ("Whether the thing be or no"), "Legal" ("What it is"), and "Juridical" ("What manner of thing it is"), and he offers definitions, short examples, and lists of *topoi* or places of confirmation for each state. Included is a fairly short conjectural oration to prove a wealthy and "worthy" farmer's murder by a "beastly" soldier.

The second book includes discussion of disposition or arrangement, focusing on the parts common to most kinds of orations, though Wilson says at the onset that he intends to keep judicial oratory as his main emphasis. The "Entrance" or exordium may be approached either directly (a "plain beginning") or indirectly (a "privy twining, or close creeping-in . . . otherwise called insinuation"), depending upon the subject at hand, one's character and interests, and the desires of one's audience. He discusses the pros and cons of the lengthy opening and the humorous opening or the "merry toy" (telling an unrelated joke) to gain audience approval. Though he does not specifically mention the classical precepts that stress the importance of establishing one's *ethos* in the exordium, he offers advice as to how to "get the good wills of our hearers" by speaking positively (though "modestly") of one's self, negatively of one's adversaries, flatteringly of the audience, and finally of the matter itself.

In "Narration" the basic case must be set forth and "lively told . . . in a gross sum," emphasizing what the classical rhetorics called the doctrine of *enargeia,* suited to narrative, which seeks to present the case as an engaging, imaginative story and to raise *pathos* in the audience. "Division" covers "such principal points whereof we purpose fully to debate and lay them out to be known." The "Proposition" then follows, which is to be a "pithy and sentitious proposition" that will enable the audience to remember the essence of the argument at hand. Discussion of "Confirmation" ensues, where the emphasis is on what the classical texts call *logos;* he offers that the places of logic can assist the rhetorician in "making first the strongest reasons that we can, and next after gathering all probable causes together, that being in one heap they may seem strong and of great weight." The "Conclusion" is "the handsome lapping-up together and brief heaping of all that which was said before, stirring the hearers by large utterance and plentiful gathering of good matter," *pathos* having been the aim of the *peroratio* in the classical sources.

Next, Wilson gives emphasis to "the Figure Amplification": "Among all the figures of rhetoric, there is no one that so much helpeth forward an oration and beauti-fieth the same with such delightful ornaments as doth amplification." The heart of amplification is "copy," or copiousness, wherein one is "well stored ever with such good sentences as are often used in this our life," and Wilson offers many examples of "good sentences" appropriate to a variety of circumstances. Scholars have shown that this section (and parts of the third book) owes much to Erasmus's *De copia* and *Ecclesiastae sive de ratione concionandi* (1535), Cicero's works, the *Rhetorica ad Herennium,* and Sherry's *A treatise of Schemes & Tropes.* Throughout, Wilson emphasizes the primacy of the appeal to *pathos,* which he calls the "apt moving of affec-tions," and he outlines with detail the arts of "moving pity and stirring men to mercy" and of "Delighting the Hearers and Stirring Them to Laughter." He defines var-ious kinds of jokes, such as "a jest in a word and a jest uttered in a long tale," offering copious examples of each. These sections on pleasantness and laughter are the lengthiest of this book, inducing some scholars to specu-late on the possibility that Wilson himself had a fine sense of humor, though others object that his humor is often at the expense of Catholics and priests. The second book ends with a brief discussion of "Disposition and Apt Ordering of Things," a section on reasons for adher-ing to and for departing from the traditional ordering of the parts of an oration.

The third book features Wilson's discussion of style, or "elocution," a word which in his time was equated with eloquence and which, following Ciceronian precepts, cannot be separated from all the other offices of rhetoric: "Therefore Tully [Cicero] saith well: 'To find out reason and aptly to frame it is the part of a wise man, but to commend it by words and with gorgeous talk to tell our conceit [meaning], that is only proper to an ora-tor.' Many are wise, but few have the gift to set forth their wisdom. . . . Whom do we most reverence and compt half a god among men? Even such a one, assur-edly, that can plainly, distinctly, plentifully, and aptly utter both words and matter, and in his talk can use such composition that he may appear to keep a uniformity and (as I might say) a number in the uttering of his sen-tence." As Baumlin has argued, Wilson's repeated use of "appear," particularly in conjunction with his lofty claims for the power of rhetoric to make audiences view the skilled orator as "half a god," raises unanswered ques-tions about the ethics of self-fashioning in this age of unstable social and political conditions. Wilson writes that eloquence can help a "smally learned" man to per-suade more effectively than a "great learned clerk" who lacks the copiousness of words to embellish his matter; he disparages such academicians by likening them to "some rich snudges that having great wealth go with

their hose out at heels, their shoes out at toes, and their coats out at both elbows."

The four parts of eloquence (elsewhere often called "virtues of style") are plainness, aptness, composition, and exornation. The first three require appropriate word choice and syntax so that "neither the ear shall espy any jar, not yet any man shall be dulled with overlong draw-ing out of a sentence, nor yet much confounded with mingling of clauses, such as are needless, being heaped together without reason and used without number." Sub-sequent scholars have therefore often equated Wilson's rhetoric with the defense of the plain style, though such an equation distorts Wilson's actual examinations of high, middle, and low styles. He has been credited with either inventing or at least popularizing the disparaging term *inkhorn* for pretentious diction, possibly Wilson's most famous contribution to literary rhetoric, since it points out the euphuistic trend in Elizabethan "learned" discourse.

"Exornation" involves "boldly commend[ing] and beautify[ing] our talk with divers goodly colors and delightful translations, that our speech may seem as bright and precious as a rich stone is fair and orient"; it is "a gorgeous beautifying of the tongue with borrowed words and change of sentence or speech with much vari-ety," or what he says Cicero called the "juice of speech." The discussion of figures offers three kinds—tropes, "when the nature of words is changed from one significa-tion to another"; schemes (*schemata verborum* in the Latin sources), "when [words] are not changed by nature but only altered by speaking"; and exornation or colors (*sche-mata sententiae*), "when by diversity of invention a sen-tence is many ways spoken, and also matters are amplified by heaping examples, by dilating arguments, by comparing of things together, by similitudes, by con-traries, and by divers other like." Wilson discusses such tropes as metaphors, "word-making" (onomatopoeia), "intellection" (synecdoche), "abusion" (catachresis), "transmutation" (metonymy), "transumption" (metalep-sis), "change of name" (antonomasia), "circumlocution" (periphrasis), "mounting" (hyperbole), and allegory. He lists six possible word schemes, giving brief examples of each, in which syllables are added to or subtracted from words at the beginning, in the middle, or at the end; later in the book he discusses sentence schemes, such as repe-tition, parallelisms, and gradation. The discussion of "colors" and the many examples make up the largest portion of this third book, wherein Wilson examines such ornamentations as "A Stop, or Half Telling of a Tale," "Witty Jesting," "Digression," "Iterating and Repeating Things Said Before," "Stomach Grief," and "Asking Others and Answering Ourself." The most detailed ornamentations, he says, involve the learned use of copious examples taken from history, fables, mythology, and Scripture; Wilson borrows heavily from Erasmus throughout. The third book ends with brief discussions of memory (for those not endowed with a natural gift for memorization, Wilson details the traditional "places" as mnemonic devices for memorizing orations) and delivery (pronunciation and gesture).

Typically ignored by modern editors, the typography at the ending of the book offers a penultimate paragraph in the shape of an hourglass, possibly evoking a Protestant emblem on the perfect end of time. Utilizing the "funnel-like" shape of the endings of all the major sections, Wilson concludes with the statement that "as my will hath been earnest to do my best, so I wish that my pains may be taken thereafter. And yet what needs wishing, seeing the good will not speak evil and the wicked cannot speak well. Therefore, being stayed upon the good and assured of their gentle bearing with me, I fear none because I stand upon a safe ground." Six months after the publication of *The Arte of Rhetorique,* however, with its pointedly Protestant *exempla* and forthright dedication to Edward VI, the young reforming king was dead and succeeded by the Catholic Mary I. Within another half year, many of Wilson's major patrons and supporters were arrested for treason (indeed, two of the families to whom Wilson had attached himself, the Greys and the Dudleys, were enmeshed in the plot to prevent Mary's succession) or excluded from court, and it likely became clear to Wilson that he could not prosper by remaining in England. Further, his own Protestantism was perhaps not as flexible as that of his friends Haddon and Roger Ascham, who both managed to stay in England during Mary's reign.

While most of the eight hundred Marian exiles immigrated to the relative safety of Protestant Germany and Switzerland, Wilson chose Padua, probably for several reasons. Cheke, his mentor, had taken up residence at the prestigious University of Padua, which was renowned for its civil-law faculty and second only to Bologna in scholarly prestige throughout Europe; and Wilson's former professor of civil law at Cambridge, Sir Thomas Smith, had taken his degree from Padua. These inducements, combined with the traditional antipapism and independence of the Republic of Venice, probably enticed Wilson to Padua by early 1554. While this choice ultimately proved painful for him, this passage of his life furnished him not only with a doctoral degree in civil law in 1559, but also with an introduction to foreign governments and politics and with an even stronger allegiance to the Protestant position—all of which served him richly under Elizabeth I.

In Padua, Wilson apparently lived on income from his inheritance (which the Crown had not confiscated, as it had in many other cases) and from tutoring, but scholars believe it unlikely that he received anything like the support that other exiled Englishmen enjoyed from wealthy sympathizers at home. During his study, he was in the company of other such prominent English scholars as Sir William Temple, Sir Thomas Hoby, and Sir Philip Hoby; in addition, he apparently befriended and possibly tutored Edward Courtenay, a young man of Plantagenet birth who had been accused of plotting to marry Elizabeth and to dethrone Mary. Courtenay survived in Italy only a matter of months (rumor had it that his death was aided by Peter Vannes, Mary's ambassador, who was his only visitor besides his physicians). Wilson composed and delivered a Latin funeral oration, later published by the historian John Strype, which he delivered in the Church of St. Anthony in Padua in 1556. Critics have pointed to this oration as evidence of Wilson's abilities as a rhetorician as well as his development as a politician: not only does his oration deal skillfully and tactfully with the young man's implication in the conspiracies (Wilson characterizes him as a man who saw himself not as the world saw him but as deserving to be a king and husband of a queen), but it also, curiously enough, offers an encomium of admiration for an avowed Catholic. Further, Wilson delivered it in one of the most ornate bastions in all of Europe, a church of "Copes, . . . Candlestickes, . . . Belles, . . . Tapers, . . . Censers, . . . Crosses . . . Banners," as he himself had earlier disparaged the Catholic Mass in *The Arte of Rhetorique.* His strategies are fraught with complexities, however: as Medine argues, Wilson was possibly attempting to ingratiate himself with the English court by showing deference to a Catholic, speaking in a Catholic church, and making respectful references to the queen and her court, since his own situation had not improved much after his arrival in Italy; on the other hand, Courtenay himself had been regarded as a threat to the Crown (and may have been murdered by one of its emissaries), which suggests that Wilson was possibly sincere in praising him, since he could hope to gain nothing from England for this particular encomium.

The Marian exiles' situation in Europe became more desperate as the Crown began to confiscate their property and to send agents to seize certain Englishmen, Wilson's friend and mentor Cheke among them, for extradition. Cheke even formally recanted his Protestantism before court under such pressure and died a year later. Perhaps because of desperate financial circumstance as well as these other frightening developments, Wilson accepted employment in an English divorce suit being appealed in Rome before the papal court; the queen had taken a particular interest in the suit, and Wilson may have hoped that some kind of preferment might ensue. Some scholars have questioned whether Wilson publicly conformed to Catholicism while in Italy, but there is no evidence of such behavior in his letters. Wil-

A Difcourfe

vppon vfurye, by vvaye of
Dialogue and oracions, for the
better varietye, and more delite of all thofe, that fhall
reade thys treatife.
(∴)

By Thomas Wilfon, doctor
of the Ciuill lawes, one of the
Mafters of her maiefties honorable courte of requeftes.

¶ Seene & allowed, according to the Queenes Maiefties iniunctions.
1572.

Title page for the work C. S. Lewis called Wilson's masterpiece

son's skill as rhetorician gained him access to Pope Paul IV, which Mary's own ambassador, Sir Edward Carne, could not obtain. While Wilson may have used his own and the Pope's shared antipathy toward Mary and Philip to ingratiate himself, Derrick argues that Wilson probably misrepresented his credentials in order to observe firsthand Paul's political vulnerabilities.

Rather than earning him a reward from his queen, Wilson's work evoked bitter complaints from Carne and earned him a royal summons to return to England and answer charges that he had participated in an assassination plot against Cardinal Reginald Pole. Wilson ignored two such summons. Someone, probably Carne (though some have suggested it may have been Pole) and possibly at the queen's command, then had Wilson seized by the Inquisition, who tried him for heresy on the basis of his anti-Catholic content in *The rule of Reason* and *The Arte of Rhetorique*. As he later writes in his 1560 preface to *The Arte of Rhetorique*, he felt he was not guilty of heresy, having been already pardoned through the absolution granted to the English by Pope Julius III "for all former offenses or practices devised against the Holy Mother Church, as they call it." If he argued such a position at his trial, his argument failed; he was convicted and imprisoned, most probably in

the Castel del Sant' Angelo. Within the same month, in November 1558, Mary was dead and the Protestant Elizabeth had succeeded her in England.

Wilson's account of these events appears in his preface to his 1560 edition of *The Arte of Rhetorique,* in which he maintains his refusal to recant, even under torture, his Protestant faith—"I took such courage, and was so bold, that the judges then did much marvel at my stoutness," he writes. He also implies a good bit about his interrogators' and his own uses of rhetoric: his judges "sought . . . to take advantage of my words and to bring me in danger by all means possible," through "long debating with me," but Wilson states that he was "ware as I could be not to utter anything for mine own harm" at the hands, he says, of either his worldly interrogators or his heavenly judge. Wilson endured some nine months of prison until the Pope's death on 18 August 1559; in the four days of rioting that followed, mobs stormed the buildings of the Inquisition and Wilson escaped. It is unknown where he traveled immediately thereafter. He took his doctor of civil laws degree at the University of Ferrara on 29 November 1559 (this degree was later incorporated at Oxford in 1566 and at Cambridge in 1571) and may have spent further time in Italy before returning to England the following September, when he was appointed master of the College of Stoke-by-Clare. Indeed, scholars conjecture that not only Wilson's study of civil law in Italy but also some observations of business practices in Venice gave him much of his material for his later work, *A Discourse vppon usurye* (1572).

Wilson reports in his preface to the 1560 edition that, upon his return, someone requested that he "amend" *The Arte of Rhetorique.* This person was most probably Kingston, printer of that edition, though Wilson does not record whether the requested amendments regarded its religious content or some other aspect. The preface (dated 7 December 1560) reports that he refused. "'Amend it?', quod I. 'Nay, let the book first amend itself and make me amends.' . . . Now, therefore, I will none of this book from henceforth. . . . I do wash my hands if any harm should come to [anyone] hereafter, and let them not say but that they are warned." Although Albert J. Schmidt takes this preface at face value as evidence that Wilson returned to England "disillusioned and penniless," this refusal may be a rhetorical strategy designed to cover the fact that he added nearly two full quarto pages of material, mostly additional anti-Catholic jokes spliced into the section on humor. Aside from a later correction in the "Faults Escaped" list that may have been Wilson's (but was more likely the printer's), there is no evidence of authorial revision after the edition of 1560. This abandonment may have been due to his stated sentiments— that is, that he wanted no more involvement with the book that had caused him such distress—or perhaps simply to the heavy political responsibilities that dominate the second half of his life. Sloane argues it may also have been due to the increased interest in Ramism in England, particularly among radical Protestants, during the later decades of the sixteenth century.

If in the second half of his life Wilson did not produce the same level of scholarly work that characterizes the first half, he did achieve an unarguably greater level of worldly success. Little is known of his marriage to Agnes Brooke except that she was widow to William Brooke and sister to the prestigious naval admiral Sir William Winter, that Wilson married her some time after his return to England in 1560, and that they produced three children (Nicholas, Mary, and Lucrece) by 1565. Sometime in the 1560s, Wilson became an advocate in the Court of Arches and a master of the Court of Requests. Late in 1560 he delivered his Latin *Oratio de Clementia* to Queen Elizabeth as a New Year's gift, at which time he also renewed his ties to the Dudley family, in December becoming secretary to Robert Dudley, the Earl of Leicester, a favorite of the queen. In addition to this alliance with Leicester, Wilson also wrote many letters in the 1560s to Cecil and to Sir Nicholas Throckmorton, both of whom were powerful at court and bitter enemies to Leicester. Wilson's attempts to secure their patronage while enjoying Leicester's has been interpreted variously: it may have been an attempt to display himself as impartial and thus worthy of Elizabeth's notice, or perhaps he desired only advancement at court by any means possible. His correspondence earned him the disdainful remarks that have been attributed to Samuel Johnson, characterizing Wilson as one who "persecuted [Cecil] with letters . . . in the most abject strain, that venality could dictate."

In the autumn of 1561 the queen appointed Wilson master of the Royal Hospital of St. Katharine, a thirteen-acre church and precinct (which no longer exists in modern London) that was located near the East Gate of the Tower and had been maintained since the thirteenth century as lodgings for the poor. Wilson and his family lived in the master's house until 1578, when he bought a twenty-room country estate in Middlesex. While also tending to his other governmental activities, Wilson held this mastership until his death in 1581. The post did not bring a fixed salary, but, with the exemption of the hospital from the jurisdiction of the city and bishop and with its possession of a strategic dock just east of the Tower of London, the mastership of St. Katharine's brought potential political influence and assured revenues.

Wilson's management improved its charitable and tax-exempt status, but it also earned him occasional accusations of profiteering, of wasting revenues, and even in 1563 of fleecing the coffers through excessive overpayment of his brother Godfrey for a loan that had provided building materials for housing improvements (although

in later, unrelated correspondence Wilson expressed suspicions of Godfrey's dishonesty, which could imply his innocence in this particular matter). In 1564 it was said that he attempted to blackmail the London city authorities over resumption of ancient fair rights for the hospital, since its twenty-one-day fair would presumably bring in revenue but would strategically compete with the London fair held nearby on the same dates. Officials threatened litigation, and Wilson negotiated in 1567 a cash settlement of £300 in return for forfeiting the fair rights. Later, he accepted a partial payment from London aldermen (with the balance to be due upon completion of the deal) to sell St. Katharine's into city tax control; ultimately, it was prevented by his tenants' bitter petitioning to the queen, charging Wilson with the "subversion" of the haven for "his pryvate lucre and benefite." In at least one instance, however, Wilson was probably unjustly accused of profiteering: modern scholars have shown that a charge of "selling the choir" likely meant not that he took down the choir loft and sold it for personal profit (as was believed even by A. W. Pollard, writing an entry about Wilson for the *Dicionary of National Biography*), but rather that he discontinued the singing choir in the chapel, an act entirely in keeping with a Protestant distaste for liturgical music. Still, it has seemed unusual to some scholars that the wealthy Wilson left no provisions in his will for any alms to St. Katharine's or its tenants.

In 1570 Wilson's English translation of seven orations of Demosthenes was published by Henry Denham under the title *The Three Orations of Demosthenes chiefe Orator among the Grecians, in fauour of the Olynthians, a people in Thracia, novv called Romania: vvith those his fovver Orations titled expressely & by name against king Philip of Macedonie: most nedefull to be redde in these daungerous dayes, of all them that loue their Countries libertie, and desire to take vvarning for their better auayle, by example of others.* No Englishman had yet published translations of Demosthenes in English or Latin prior to Wilson's. His dedicatory epistle reports that, while he was "musinge" on his books, he remembered Cheke's lectures on Demosthenes more than ten years earlier at the University of Padua and "did then seeke out amongst my other writings for the translation of them, and happily finding some, although not all, I was carried streightways . . . to make certaine of them to be acquainted so nigh as I coulde with our Englishe tongue." This wording, that he sought "for the translation[s]" among his papers, led the eighteenth-century historian John Strype, in *Historical Memorials, Ecclesiastical and Civil* (1721), to believe that Wilson had merely translated into English Cheke's Latin translations of the orations. In his preface, however, Wilson claims that Cambridge and Oxford scholars advised him variously in this project, and he says he makes this acknowledgment "bicause I woulde not defraude any of their prayse." Medine argues the unlikelihood that Wilson would have tried to pass off anyone else's work as his own.

The collection begins with Latin dedicatory poems by Haddon; Giles Lawrence, professor of Greek at Oxford; Thomas Byng, professor of Oratory at Cambridge; one John Cox at St. Paul's School; and one "I.M., a Londoner." Wilson's dedicatory epistle to William Cecil follows, dated 10 June 1570; Wilson appeals to Cecil's good will by recalling the background and family connections common to Cecil and Cheke, Wilson's mentor in these Greek studies—Cheke had tutored Cecil, and Cecil had married Cheke's sister—as well as the more flattering comparison between Cecil and Demosthenes, both great statesmen: "he is your glasse, I am well assured, whereupon you do often joke, and compare his time, with this time." In this way Wilson implicitly identifies Cecil as the originator of the contemporary political application of the book. "A Preface to the Reader, conteyning the commendation of Demosthenes" offers reasons for reading the orator who "passed greatly all others, that euer weare."

Wilson prefaces the orations with various prose historical materials, such as "The testimones and reports made of Demosthenes" by various great men such as Aristotle and Cicero, "The Description of Athens," and short summaries ("Arguments") of each oration. He follows the translated orations with a biography of the orator, "The Life and Doings of Demosthenes, Gathered Out of Plutarch, Suidas, Libanius, Lucian, and Others," which principally praises Demosthenes' courage and patriotism in struggling for the benefit of his beloved city against Philip of Macedonia. The orations themselves feature political themes defining the properties of a true statesman: the wisdom of being vigilant to recognize a foreign enemy's hostility, of aiding allies against foreign enemies, of seizing the timeliest moment for action. Throughout is illustrated the crucial need for politicians who are courageous enough to protect their countries at all times from foreign threats.

While other translators of the period often added moral or Christian interpretations to classical texts, Wilson is unusual among such translators in that he overtly politicizes his prose prefaces so that English readers may read in Demosthenes' statements against the Macedonian Philip various contemporary warnings against the Spanish Philip II. At this time England was debating whether or not to send military aid to Protestant rebels in the Netherlands against Spain; Cecil favored military intervention, but Elizabeth and other Privy Council members took generally a more moderate position. Hence many commentators have suggested that Wilson published these orations in order to attempt to influence the council toward military intervention, for Wilson writes that "euery good subject according to the leuell of his witte, should compare the time past with the time present, and ever when he heareth Athens, or the Athenians, to remember Englande and Englisshmen, and so all other thyngs in like manner incident thereunto, that we may learne by the doings of our elders howe we may deale in our owne affayres." Indeed, an anonymous eighteenth-century article attributed to Johnson states that Elizabeth asked Cecil to appoint a scholar to translate Demosthenes precisely to stir up the English against Spain; but while Sir Henry Ellis, in his *Original Letters of Eminent Literary Men of the Sixteenth, Seventeenth, and Eighteenth Centuries* (1843), prints the Latin letter from Wilson to Cecil in 1569 thanking him for permission to dedicate the book to him, there is no other evidence of such a claim. Medine argues that, since the queen appeared to be annoyed with those who favored an aggressive approach to foreign policy in the Netherlands at this juncture, and since the letter makes no mention of such a request or of the political climate of the day, it is not likely that Wilson wrote the book at the request of the Crown. Clearly, Wilson thought his authority at court strong enough to warrant such an overt discussion of foreign policy, especially if his position opposed the queen's.

Even as he translated Demosthenes, Wilson likely worked on the draft material for *A Discourse vppon usurye*, since his dedicatory epistle to the orations mentions "other studies." *A Discourse vppon usurye* was published by Richard Tottel in 1572 (reprinted in 1584 by Roger Warde), but Wilson's dedication to the earl of Leicester is dated 1569—a discrepancy that scholars have sought to explain. The book essentially urges a legal definition of usury (discussed but undefined in Scripture) as the taking of any interest whatsoever on a loan, a definition that had been rigidly maintained under Edward VI by the Act Against Usury of 1552. R. H. Tawney, Wagner, and Sloane provide discussions of the complex history of usury in England, contrasting the medieval practices of lending at interest (where both lender and borrower stood to profit or lose from the venture) with the early modern practices of protecting only the lender, where abuses were naturally more pervasive. By the late 1560s, the 1552 act was under reconsideration in Parliament, and Elizabeth tended to favor a repeal of it, not only because her Protestantism was more moderate than Edward's but also because the rampant inflation of the midcentury had produced a perceived greater need for borrowing under controlled circumstances at home, rather than borrowing abroad at abusive rates.

Scholars have conjectured that the Crown possibly prevented the publication of Wilson's book in 1569 because there remained before Parliament a pending act of legislation to repeal the Act of 1552, effectively reinstating the Act of 1545, which had defined usury punishable by law as interest over the rate of 10 percent. Such a conjecture, if true, would support the notion that the queen believed Wilson to have strong political influence within the houses of Parliament; however, Wilson delivered a speech before the Parliament of 1571, arguing many of the same points covered in the book, but nevertheless the Act Against Usury of 1571 was instituted, permitting interest rates at 10 percent. Others have conjectured that the manuscript was written solely to influence Leicester and others during the debate and that the act of 1571 caused such subsequent abuse in the economic system that Wilson published his book in 1572 as an implicit call for the repeal of the act. Regardless of his inability to influence lawmaking at this time, the book remained influential and often-quoted by other writers on the subject well into the next century. In the twentieth century, C. S. Lewis praised *A Discourse vppon usurye* above *The Arte of Rhetorique* as Wilson's masterpiece because it "handles with more intelligence and more imagination a theme of more permanent interest" and because, "unlike most literary dialogues, it gives fair play to both sides." Sloane calls it Wilson's most mature work and notes that *A Discourse vppon usurye,* like all others of Wilson's works, displays a characteristic "perversity of outlook and an irrepressible mirth" that mark Wilson as a "humanist *par excellence*," pointing to Wilson's Erasmian irony and affirmation of the *via diversa.*

An odd feature of *A Discourse vppon usurye* is that the dedicatory preface addressed to the earl of Leicester noticeably lacks many of the common humility *topoi* of contemporary dedications, such as the appeals for patronage and for protection against detractors. Although Wilson begins the preface with a flattering statement that, as God created all, then Leicester is "goddes lively image upon earth," the remainder of the lengthy dedication speaks forthrightly about "Adame's falle," the evil of this world, and Wilson's admonition that "your honor and others of youre callinge shoulde never at any tyme lette slippe any good occasion offerd for the welfare of Englande, muche lesse to bee carelesse in that greate trust which is committed unto you." Wilson states that he dares to speak so boldly because "I have knowne you, and that noble race of youre brethren, even from their younge yeares." In addition to his familiarity with Leicester, Wilson's tone in the preface indicates a comfortable sense of his own authority and of his influence with the Privy Council.

Wilson casts *A Discourse vppon usurye* in the highly popular form of dialogue, initiated by Plato and popularized by Cicero; to this end, "A Christian Prologue to the Christian Reader" sets up the four major characters who will speak, giving the major characters' Greek names (which never appear thereafter) and their English equivalents. The preacher is named *Misotókos* ("interest hater") or Ockerfoe (since *ocker* was the Middle English form for

usury) whom Wilson calls the "enemy to usurie." The merchant's name is *Kakémporos* ("evil merchant"), referred to throughout as Gromelgayner (a popular term in the sixteenth century for a miser), whom Wilson calls "the wrong Merchant or evil occupier." The Lawyer is simply referred to as such, his Greek name being *Kerdaléos* ("shrewd one"), while the fourth speaker, *Politikós* ("for the citizens"), is referred to as the "Advocate" or "Civilian." The prologue also offers a clever self-defense, saying that the author does not actually condemn all forms of usury, for he advocates what he terms "a spiritual usury," lending money without monetary interest in the hope of gaining heavenly reward. Thereafter follow Latin commendatory poems by William Wickham, John Garbrand, and John Cox, along with a posthumously published English letter from John Jewel, Bishop of Salisbury, commending Wilson for the draft he had seen in 1569 and its ability to present each speaker in such a way that he "speake[s] naturally like hym selfe, as if you had beene in eche of them, or they in you."

Rather than the shorter, more conversational exchanges of Platonic dialogue, Wilson's dialogue utilizes a Ciceronian form, giving lengthy, formal speeches to each speaker but crafting the lengthiest speech as the centerpiece of the book. The action takes place in the wealthy merchant's house, to which the others have been invited for dinner, after which they agree to debate the issue of usury. Two rounds of speeches constitute the debate. Ockerfoe offers an oration, replied to in succession by the Lawyer and Gromelgayner, and, after another speech by Ockerfoe, the Civilian offers the central oration; Ockerfoe's final oration ensues, and the other three respond briefly to conclude the dialogue. Medine notices that the structural pattern of the dialogue follows the form of the classical oration as a whole: Ockerfoe's first oration functions as the exordium; the successive speeches of the Lawyer, Gromelgayner, and Ockerfoe form the refutation; the Civilian's speech is the confirmation; Ockerfoe's final speech functions as the peroration.

Ockerfoe's first speech bears the tone of a sermon, quoting extensively from Scripture and the church fathers. In traditional Scholastic form, he argues that "the worlde is almoste at an ende" because of avarice (a sentiment that Wilson himself earlier had stated in the dedicatory preface). Humanity must instead embrace the love commanded by God that "is the perfection of the lawe," for "without love neither god nor man is either honoured or used as eyther of them ought to bee." Usury is evil because one is lending not out of love but out of desire of profit, and "whosoever lendeth his mony for gayne, doth steale, and desirethe hys neighboures goodes unlawfullye."

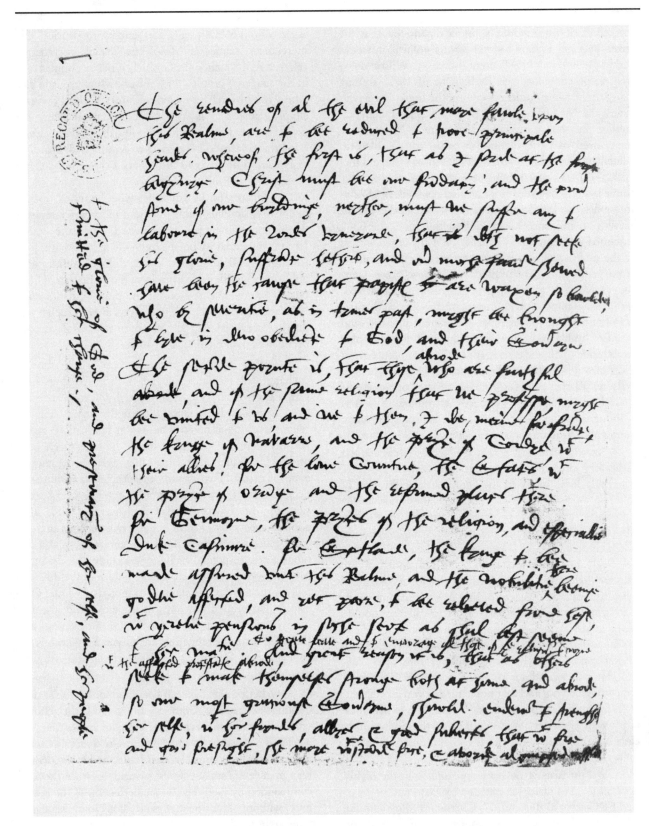

Concluding page from the manuscript for Wilson's "A discourse touching this kingdoms perils with their remedies," written in 1578 and first published in 1955 (Public Record Office, London, SP 12/123/17)

The Lawyer's oration answers Ockerfoe by redefining love: "charity beginneth first at it selfe," he says, and thus to lend at reasonable interest rates is good business, since "there is no man that lendith but susteineth losse for the want of it, because he might better benefit him self by employing it in divers wais, . . . besides the danger that maye happen when a mans money is out of his own handes." The Lawyer maintains that all interpret the words of the Scriptures as they wish, so he attempts to redefine usury through the Old Testament discussions of usury and the etymology of the Hebrew term *neshech,* "whiche is nothinge else but a kind of bitinge." Therefore, he argues, if one does not "bite" one's neighbor—that is, if one charges reasonable interest rates—then the act is not usury. Further, in Greek and in Latin, the term for usury is "a birth or born creature (as I am enformed)," that is, a "prety babe" that has come forth from lending; here, as in several places in *The Arte of Rhetorique,* Wilson may be indulging in a barb directed at common lawyers, since this lawyer artlessly confesses that "I knowe neither hebrue nor greke, nor latine neither very wel, but onlye do smatter of broken latine, as the most of us lawiers doe, seeking not for anye deepe skill or sounde knowledge therein." Gaining a loan, he says, even if one must pay interest, profits the borrower, since without the money he cannot do business at all; further, it can be shown that even royalty and nobles need to borrow in these times. If a man does not make as much lawful profit as he can while he lives, what happens to his widow and children upon his death, who might have been saved had he increased his wealth by charging reasonable interest?

Gromelgayner's short oration that follows makes the point that merchants cannot survive in an economy that does not allow them to profit through investment, and, if merchants fail, the entire economy collapses: "if you forbid gaine, you destroy entercourse of marchendize, you overthrowe bargaininge, and you bring all tradinge betwixte man and man to suche confusion, as either man wil not deale, or els they will say they cannot tell howe to deale one with an other." These arguments have a ring of authenticity to them; journals of parliamentary sessions show that many of them were the same arguments that Wilson heard during the debates over the Act of 1552.

"The Preachers Replicacion" now answers each of the former contentions, arguing always that love and God's law must be at the center of all human interactions and that taking more than a thing's simple worth is theft, which is contrary to God's law. He also contends that usury, "next after their horrible lothinge of holesome religion," was the cause of the downfall of Queen Mary's reign, since usury caused a desperate economic condition that incited rebellion. At his conclusion, he calls upon the

Civilian to "saye your minde, whom we long al to here, that god may be praysed, and we all edified according to your good learning and doctrine."

After opening with customary humility—"You looke for more at my hande, than I am able to perfourme"—the "Civilians or Doctours Oracion" actually covers more than three times the length of any other speech, forming the centerpiece of the dialogue by amplifying Ockerfoe's condemnation of interest through copious details and arguments drawn from holy and classical authors and, most importantly for the modern reader, from contemporary English life. Scholars have suggested that the Civilian is the voice of the author, since, like Wilson, he is a civil lawyer and referred to as "Doctor." The introduction to the oration forecasts its six major sections: an examination of "what usurye is"; an argument that usury "is evill, and by what lawes forbidden, and for what causes"; a description of "divers kyndes of contracts, and trades in bargayning commonlye used"; an argument regarding "what ys not usurye"; a historical catalogue of the "punyshmentes for usurye"; and "lastlye" a statement of "myne opynion, what is expedient to bee donne at this time." The third section of his oration offers the strongest innovative aspect of the dialogue, for other reform documents of the age do not offer such depth of detail on contracts, interest rates, contemporary economic practices in such centers as London and Antwerp (where Elizabeth herself was paying exorbitant interest rates), and even the controversial enclosures of the countryside. The speech evokes *pathos* by portraying usury metaphorically as a poison that will waste the body of the commonwealth and a caterpillar that will devour the fruit of England.

After the Civilian closes, Ockerfoe offers "The Preachers Reioynder, and Laste Oracion," which rebukes each participant in turn, including the Civilian (whom the Preacher says trusts too much in his intellect), and effectively brings the Lawyer and Gromelgayner to a miraculous conversion of their economic and religious views. The Lawyer confesses, "I doe see it [the truth] is clene contrary, and I confesse myselfe to have erred, for whyche I am sorie. . . . For I doe nowe plainlie finde that even the verye sufferance of usurie, although it were for a meane rate." Gromelgayner says that through the "heavenly doctrine" he has heard, he has become "a new man, praysed be god and you therefore. And nowe I do asmuche abhorre to lend money for gaine hereafter, as I doe abhorre to steale by the hyghe waye, or to murder any man violentlye for his goods, which god forbyd that ever I shoulde thinke or minde to doe." An aspect curious to the modern reader, perhaps, exists in the Merchant's mention of the plague, which all fear "merveillously here in London," and the implicit equation of it with the effects of usury; similarly, the Lawyer states that usury is the "cause of much dearthe and scarcitie" in the land. The Civilian undergoes his own kind of conversion, promising henceforth "to renounce mans reason, and to followe his most holy will, . . . and preferre the truethe of hys woorde before all other learninge whatsoever."

The 1569 draft of *A Discourse vppon usurye* ends: "With that, they all tooke theire leaves, and departed in charitye one with an other, like ioyful and spirituall brethren in Christ. God graunte all others to doe the like. Amen. Finis." For publication, however, Wilson added a "Conclusion to the Loving Reader," wherein he expresses doubt as to whether such conversions will last and offers a "mery tale" that is "somewhat to the purpose of thys last speech." The Pope requires a priest in Rome to enjoin his people to pray for peace in the war against the Holy Roman Emperor, Charles V, but since the Pope himself has created the war, the priest tells his flock that he recognizes that "your prayers wilbe in vayne; and yet pray, sirs, for maner [manner's] sake." The epilogue ends with Wilson's own observation that "betwixt doyng and saiynge there is greate oddes" and with a prayer for the swift coming of the "perfite ending of all thynges." Sloane finds a rhetorical double strategy operating in this conclusion, in that it concedes the reasonableness of law (since it is uncertain whether humanity will ever abide by the scriptural law) while it also refuses to abandon Wilson's personal truth that, even if allowed by the Act of 1571, the taking of interest is still usury. The ambiguity of this epilogue, along with the general presentation of the *agrumentum ad utramque partem* throughout, leads Sloane to conclude that if Wilson was less than optimistic about the nature of humanity, he was at least optimistic about the interpretive powers of his readers.

In this last half of his life, Wilson found increasing employment in the service of the Crown. He served in Parliament in 1562(?), 1563, 1571, and 1572. The queen dispatched him for crucial foreign embassies to Portugal (1567–1568) and the Netherlands (1574–1575, 1576–1577) during two periods of critical foreign relations. He was said to have participated in at least one raid on English Catholics attending Mass on the Continent. In the 1560s and early 1570s Wilson served on several committees appointed by the queen's Privy Council, often performing for the Crown interrogations of various political prisoners held in the Tower. He examined many suspects and resorted to torture when necessary. Perhaps his most notable case involved the long interrogations (conducted with Sir Thomas Smith in 1571–1572) of conspirators and informants in the so-called Ridolfi plot to replace Elizabeth with Mary Stuart of Scotland, which resulted, eventually, in the first treason trial of Elizabeth's reign and the execution of Thomas Howard, Duke of Norfolk. Upon completion of the examinations, Wilson was among the parliamentary delegates to urge Elizabeth to order executions for both Norfolk and Mary Stuart; Wilson later told Parliament he warned her that, "If further proceeding were not [to result in execution], no safety could follow, the Protestants [being] in great danger." Although Elizabeth refused to sign the order, telling Wilson that the Protestants would find that as their queen "hath found them true, so will she be their defence," she relented within two weeks and signed the warrant for Norfolk's execution in 1572. (Mary Stuart's did not follow until 1587.) Evidence in Wilson's correspondence suggests that he contributed nearly a hundred pages of material (the "Actio" section and the translation of the "Literæ" section) to George Buchanan's *De Maria Scotorum Regina* (1571), a pamphlet designed to discredit Mary Stuart, and that Wilson translated the book into the Scottish dialect ("handsome Scotch," he tells Cecil in a letter in 1571) to appear as *Ane detectioun of the duinges of Marie Quene of Scottes* (1571) for circulation among Protestants in Scotland. Again, Wilson's translation indicates his sensitivity to the fact that reaching the largest possible audience demanded use of the vernacular rather than Latin.

Some scholars have found it paradoxical that Wilson, who describes in print the horrors of his own imprisonment and torture, should himself become an interrogator and "a remorseless torturer or an officious priest-catcher," as Schmidt characterized him in his "Thomas Wilson, Tudor Scholar-Statesman" (1957). As he writes in the preface to the 1560 edition of *The Arte of Rhetorique,* "indeed the prison was on fire when I came out of it, and whereas I feared fire most (as who is he that doth not fear it?), I was delivered by fire and sword together. And yet now thus fearful am I that having been thus swinged and restrained of liberty, I would first rather hazard my life presently hereafter to die upon a turk [scimitar] than to abide again without hope of liberty such painful imprisonment forever. . . . I think the troubles before death, being long suffered and without hope continued, are worse a great deal than present death itself can be." Thus modern scholars have questioned Wilson's *ethos* in *The Arte of Rhetorique,* conjecturing whether he was a zealous or diffident interrogator in his civil service. Pollard says that Wilson's correspondence during these examinations shows him to have been "so engross[ed] [in] this occupation that he took up his residence, and wrote letters 'from prison in the Bloody Tower.'" Schmidt conjectures that his experiences in Rome "left him embittered and little inclined to pity those who opposed him." Derrick, however, argues that Wilson was reluctant to perform these duties—probably, he says, because they "evoked frightening memories" of his own pains in Rome—and cites Wilson's and Smith's written complaint to Cecil that their "unpleasant and painful" task of threatening or applying the rack to Norfolk's three secretaries had surely yielded all the information they could hope for, likening their jobs to those of the Homeric judges of Hades. Medine maintains that Wilson and Smith only delivered to the Ridolfi suspects questions written by Cecil and that eventually they "were ordered by an impatient and perhaps vindictive queen to resort to torture."

In sum, Wilson's involvement in Tower interrogations and his religious intolerance remain fundamental problems in Wilson's *ethos* from the modern perspective, since, as Schmidt points out, scholars throughout the ages have felt that "his character was a vital force in his writings and actions." Medine devotes the entire final chapter of his biography of Wilson to commentators' views of his character, pointing out that his "rackmastering" seems of more concern to moderns than to many before the nineteenth century. Indeed, Strype praises Wilson for his "sentences of great importance and practical wisdom," though he cites as an example Wilson's statement, "Sweet is that sacrifice to God when the lives of lewd men are offered up to suffer pains of death for wicked doings." Not surprisingly, the Catholic historian Robert Lechat equated Wilson with the notorious Borgias for his ambassadorial work. In *Thomas Wilson* Medine calls him "a man of some complexity," detailing Wilson's vociferous anti-Catholicism but also pointing, as an example of the paradox in Wilson's nature, to his inexplicable generosity and kindness toward the exiled Catholics Edward Courtenay and Sir Thomas Copley, for whom Wilson attempted to help regain confiscated lands.

Still, his function as an official crown interrogator of prisoners at least attests to Wilson's interest and skill in, and successful execution of, the sort of rhetoric that forces "most . . . men even to yield in that which most standeth against their will," as he wrote in *The Arte of Rhetorique*. Similarly, his ambassadorial work reveals his grasp of decorum when, for example, even given his own personal distaste for Catholic Spain, he created strong political liaisons with several notable Spaniards whose correspondence shows deep esteem for him. In his service in the Privy Council, Wilson managed to sustain good relationships with both Cecil and Leicester, who were themselves bitter enemies. Thus it may be argued that Wilson's civic duties attest to his superb practice of the arts of discourse, as well as to Elizabeth's shrewd judgment, as some have noted, in elevating the author of *The Arte of Rhetorique* to a level of governmental service inferior perhaps only to Cecil and Sir Francis Walsingham.

Historians suggest that, as a rule, diplomatic work rarely led to membership in the Privy Council; neverthe-less, it is probably Wilson's work as ambassador that earned him the appointment of principal secretary to the council (as distinguished from the Latin and French secretaries, who merely composed diplomatic documents) upon Principal Secretary Thomas Smith's death in 1577; intermittently sharing this office with Walsingham, Wilson held the post until his death in 1581. His formal duties required attending the queen daily, joining the rest of the council to advise her in all matters, sitting in Parliament, and obtaining the queen's signature on official documents. Hence, informally, he no doubt heard many personal petitions of suitors hoping through him to gain access to the queen. Though there is no record of his actual salary, it is likely that a great deal of wealth came to him through this office. In 1601 it was estimated that the secretaryship was worth nearly £3,000 per year; both Walsingham and Wilson received full salaries, though they split any proceeds for individual signet fees and warrants. Still, suitors often paid lump sums or granted annuities to those who presented their concerns at court, so many avenues existed for obtaining unofficial income. How scrupulous Wilson was in regard to this aspect of his office is unknown. He held the appointment during several historic passages in Elizabeth's reign, notably during Elizabeth's controversial attempts to marry Anjou and her various conflicts with Puritan nonconformists in England. His service on appointed committees and in the Privy Council also likely involved him in several other literary figures' legal troubles, notably Richard Puttenham's rape case in 1561; George Puttenham's alleged implication in a plot against Cecil's life in 1570, and enmity with his brother-in-law, Sir Nicholas Throckmorton, that led to Puttenham's imprisonment and a series of appeals to the Privy Council from 1578 to 1585; and the case of Richard Rainolde's assault against a process-server in 1579. Yet, it is curious that while all the men who made up the Privy Council during the 1570s (including Wilson) became exceedingly wealthy, Wilson was the only one among them who did not receive a knighthood or a title.

A portrait of Wilson by an anonymous Flemish artist (said to be in the tradition of Antonio Moro) hangs in the National Portrait Gallery in London. It was probably painted during Wilson's first ambassadorial assignment to the Low Countries, in 1574–1575. The inscription in the upper left corner reads *"FIAT VOLUNTAS DEI / AETATIS LII / 1575"* (God's will be done. / Fifty-two years of age / 1575) and has been used to conjecture Wilson's birthdate. The coat of arms combines Wilson's paternal and maternal families. The lower left corner bears an erroneous inscription, "Nicholas Bacon Lord / Chancellor of England," which led to a misidentification of the portrait—in spite of the fact that it differs greatly from an extant portrait of Bacon and that Bacon was sixty-five years of age at this date—from the seventeenth through the nineteenth century, when the coat of arms was at last identified. The image itself shows Wilson to have had grey eyes, brown hair and moustache, and greying beard. Sloane argues that the image "confronts the viewer" but with "little of the arrogance or awesomeness of the politically powerful of the time"; that it also lacks notably any sign of the irony, wit, or humor evident in Wilson's books leads Sloane to conclude that "Wilson's most significant likeness . . . is to be found in his writings." However, the portrait actually is thoroughly in keeping with the conventions of humanist portraiture in the High Renaissance style, which attempted to render physically the interior qualities of the individual. The portrait is principally that not of the Cambridge scholar and author but rather of the Crown servant destined soon to be principal secretary: Wilson grasps not a book in the foregrounded hand but a letter, implying that he has received a missive of royal instructions or that he has composed a reply to the royal directives. His right index finger bears a signet ring with the reverse-image of the royal arms for sealing diplomatic documents. Whether at Wilson's request or because this perspective truly represents his contemporaries' view of him, this sober image clearly portrays Wilson as the dependable public servant and diplomat. Dressed not as a middle-class scholar but as a wealthy, though not ostentatious, aristocrat, he is clothed in a fine, black robe with broadly applied, brown fur edging, white ruff and cuffs, and the fashionable flat-crown cap. The most memorable aspect of the portrait is Wilson's face, which scrutinizes the spectator with piercing eyes and a serious, remarkably furrowed brow that imply depth of thinking and an ability for intense concentration. His body offers a comfortable, though formidable, stance that portrays a capable, practicing rhetorician who is able to put his audience (and adversaries) at ease without giving ground. If, indeed, the portrait does not convey the nuances of personality evident in his writing, it does offer a valuable view of the public image either that Wilson wished to promulgate or that his contemporaries saw.

Plausibly, his long, meticulous correspondence during his embassies and his reputation for intelligent discourse led the queen in 1578 to create for Wilson an office "for keeping papers and records concerning matters of state and council" which she termed the clerk of the papers. Thus Wilson is credited with being the first keeper of the Public Record Office. In that same year, he wrote an unpublished treatise in English, the endorsement of which calls it "A discourse touching this kingdoms perils with their remedies," in which he outlines his own analysis of international and domestic problems facing England. Schmidt includes the full treatise in his article "A Treatise on England's Perils, 1578" (1955),

maintaining that it not only gives a sense of Wilson's own prescriptions for foreign policy but also provides a useful view of the factions within Elizabeth's own government at this critical passage in English history. Not surprisingly, Wilson argues that England should strengthen the Protestant foundation at home, particularly with regard to Scotland, and that foreign policy should be adjusted according to the respective religions of the countries on the Continent: "papists . . . myghte bee brought to lyve in due obedie'ce to God, and their Sov'ayne[,] . . . [and] those abrode who are faithful, and of the same religion that we professe, myght be united to us, and we to them."

His appointment as dean of Durham Cathedral was obviously a political reward by the queen, intended only for its economic value to Wilson rather than for any value Wilson might have been to the operations of Durham. Wilson never paid a visit to the place—even his installation was carried out by proxy—and he openly conferred all cathedral dealings to the subdeans. There were oppositions to his appointment from the start: Ralph Lever, prebendary of Durham and a Puritan nonconformist (also apparently a longtime rival to Wilson, a graduate of Cambridge who had written his English logic in 1573 and had intended to write a rhetoric), complained that the office of dean should belong only to a clergyman. In an apparent attempt to placate him, Cecil appointed Lever to be Wilson's proxy, an office that Lever refused to carry out, saying that he would later have "to yeld an accounte to God." Wilson thereafter carried out his duties purely through correspondence. Lever then complained of Wilson's absenteeism and received court censure in response, after which he wrote submissively to Cecil that he understood that Wilson could not be present at Durham because of his attending to "more weighty affairs in the commonwealth." Wilson received two other such Crown managerial appointments, the rectory at Mansfield Skegby and the manor at Saltfleetsby, from which he was allowed to keep all profits.

Little is known of his domestic life. The records of the 1570s show an apparently wealthy Wilson investing in Sir Martin Frobisher's explorations to find the northwest passage to China and buying up many acres of land principally in Lincolnshire, such that by the time of his death he owned, in addition to his estate known as Pymmes at Edmonton in Middlesex, lands in Washingborough, Strubby, Sheepwash, and Woodthorpe. His first wife, Agnes, died in 1574; two years later, he married Jane Pinchon, who was the granddaughter of Henry VII's infamous minister, Sir Richard Empson (not his daughter, as is sometimes erroneously reported). She lived only three years more, and Wilson survived her by only two years.

Based on Wilson's various references in correspondence to his "reins," Schmidt conjectures that Wilson died of kidney disease, owing to his love of wine; he cites correspondence as early as 1574 that reports that Wilson "hardly ever left their banquets sober" during his ambassadorships on the Continent. He wrote to Leicester in 1580 that he had missed two weeks of council duties due to the "great heat in my reins." Wilson was advised by his physician, a Dr. Hector, to "drink morning and evening a full pint of Tower Hill water which doth me great good and hath taken away the thirst wherewith heretofore I have been troubled," as he stated in a letter to Cecil in 1580. Although he may be speaking literally of the thirst associated with a fever, "the thirst wherewith heretofore I have been troubled" may be a veiled reference to his well-known weakness for Rhenish wine. His last appearance in the Privy Council was 3 May 1581; he died at St. Katharine's on 16 June 1581, and the following day, according to his request, he was buried "without pomp or charge" in its churchyard. His overseers appointed by his will—Walsingham, his brother-in-law Winter, and his cousin Matthew Smith—created a household inventory of Pymmes that provides a glimpse of his wealth and taste for luxuries, though his style of living could not be considered extravagant. Curiously enough, among the several apparently inexpensive artworks detailed in the inventory, Wilson owned at his death three portraits worthy of note: Bishop John Jewel of Salisbury, his friend and great divine who had died ten years earlier; "the Duke of Suffolk his youngest Son," his brilliant student dead thirty years earlier; and the "Castle of St. Angelly," the site of his imprisonment twenty-three years earlier.

Assessments of Thomas Wilson's life and work may be categorized roughly into two viewpoints. One perspective affirms the view of David Lloyd, the seventeenth-century biographer, who believed that Wilson "had the breeding of courtiers so long until he was one himself. . . . It was his interest as well as his gift to be more learned than witty, more reverend than plausible, more considerate than active. His thoughts were as his inclination, grave; his discourse as his reading, subtle; his actions as his education, well weighed, regular as his temper." G. H. Mair's often-quoted 1909 characterization of Wilson concurs, portraying him not as an Elizabethan but as a Henrician, belonging to an "elder and graver age" of medieval sensibilities and moral stability, "one of a band of grave and dignified scholars" who railed against the revolutionary individualism that was destroying the old order. On the other hand, recent scholars have tended to note Wilson's self-interest and flexibility, characterizing him as a creature of that new order who shrewdly advanced himself through every political and social development. In Sloane's words, he was "a self-made man in a great age of self-fashioning," who "found his chief instruments—in more ways than one—through logic and rhetoric." Medine concurs but adds the speculation that, because he was ultimately not as successful in his political work as Walsingham or Cecil, "one suspects that at several points in his career, Wilson may have reflected longingly on the scholar's life that he had abandoned." Sloane also finds that earlier critics' overriding emphasis on the gravity of the Protestant moralist overlooks Wilson's propensity for humor, irony, and brilliant wit, and that, as Tawney suggests, perhaps it was that self-made versatility—what Sloane calls "lawyerliness" of mind—that finally caused him to be ranked as inferior to the depth and range of Sir Thomas More, Erasmus, or even Cheke. Yet, his written and public works influenced his own age greatly and provide crucial knowledge about his sixteenth-century culture and the life of that now-extinct breed, the humanist scholar-statesman.

Letters:

Sir Henry Ellis, *Original Letters of Eminent Literary Men of the Sixteenth, Seventeenth, and Eighteenth Centuries,* volume 23 (London: Camden Society, 1843).

References:

J. W. H. Atkins, "The Rhetoric of Tradition: Jewel, Wilson, Ascham," in his *English Literary Criticism: The Renascence* (London: Methuen, 1947), pp. 66–101;

E. J. Baskerville, "Thomas Wilson and Sir Thomas Smith at Cambridge," *Notes & Queries,* 27 (April 1980): 113–116;

Tita French Baumlin, "'A good (w)oman skilled in speaking': *Ethos,* Self-Fashioning, and Gender in Renaissance England," in *Ethos: New Essays in Rhetorical and Critical Theory,* edited by Baumlin and James S. Baumlin (Dallas: Southern Methodist University Press, 1994), pp. 229–264;

Carey H. Conley, *The First English Translators of the Classics* (New Haven: Yale University Press, 1927);

Marie Cornelia, "Donne's Humour and Wilson's 'Arte of Rhetorique,'" *Ariel,* 15 (January 1984): 31–43;

Hardin Craig, "Shakespeare and Wilson's *Arte of Rhetorique:* An Inquiry into the Criteria for Determining Sources," *Studies in Philology,* 28 (October 1931): 618–630;

David Cram and Ruth Campbell, *A 16th-Century Case of Acquired Dysgraphia* (Netherlands: Historiagraphia Linguistica, 1992), pp. 57–64;

Thomas J. Derrick, Introduction to *Arte of Rhetorique by Thomas Wilson,* The Renaissance Imagination, no. 1 (New York: Garland, 1982), pp. vii–cxl;

Derrick, "Merry Tales in *Much Ado About Nothing,*" *Thalia,* 8 (Fall/Winter 1985): 21–26;

George J. Engelhardt, "The Relation of Sherry's *Treatise of Schemes and Tropes* to Wilson's *Arte of Rhetorique*," *PMLA,* 62 (March 1947): 76–82;

P. W. Hasler, ed., *The History of Parliament: The House of Commons, 1558–1603* (London: Her Majesty's Stationery Office for the History of Parliament Trust, 1981), I: 102–110; III: 629–631;

Patsy Ann Hollander, "Thomas Wilson, Study of a Tudor Bureaucrat," dissertation, University of Washington, 1976;

Wilbur S. Howell, *Logic and Rhetoric in England, 1500–1700* (Princeton: Princeton University Press, 1956);

Catherine Jamison, *The History of the Royal Hospital of St. Katharine by the Tower of London* (London & New York: Oxford University Press, 1952), pp. 69–79;

Samuel Johnson?, "The History of Our Own Language," *Literary Magazine,* 3 (January–August 1758): 149–153;

Donald Edward Kennedy, "An Appreciation of Thomas Wilson's 1570 Translation of Demosthenes' Olynthiacs and Philippics," dissertation, University of Melbourne, 1982;

Robert Lechat, *Les réfugiés anglais dans les Pays-Bas espagnols durant le règne d'Elisabeth, 1558–1603* (Louvain, Belgium: Bureau du Recuiel, 1914);

C. S. Lewis, *English Literature in the Sixteenth Century Excluding Drama* (Oxford: Clarendon Press, 1954), pp. 290–292;

David Lloyd, *Statesmen and Favorites of England Since the Reformation* (London, 1665);

James Richard McNally, "'Prima pars dialecticae': The Influence of Agricolan Dialectic upon English Accounts of Invention," *Renaissance Quarterly,* 21 (1968): 166–177;

Peter E. Medine, Introduction to *The Art of Rhetoric (1560),* by Thomas Wilson (University Park: Penn State University Press, 1994), pp. 1–31;

Medine, *Thomas Wilson* (Boston: Twayne, 1986);

Janel M. Mueller, *The Native Tongue and the Word: Developments in English Prose Style, 1380–1580* (Chicago: University of Chicago Press, 1984);

J. E. Neale, *Elizabeth I and Her Parliaments,* 2 volumes (London: Cape, 1953, 1957);

Winifred Nowottny, "Some Features of Shakespeare's Poetic Language Considered in the Light of Quintilian and Thomas Wilson," *University of Hartford Studies in Literature,* 4 (1976): 125–138;

Walter J. Ong, *Ramus, Method and the Decay of Dialogue* (Cambridge, Mass.: Harvard University Press, 1958);

Wayne A. Rebhorn, "Baldesar Castiglione, Thomas Wilson, and the Courtly Body of Renaissance Rhetoric," *Rhetorica,* 11 (Summer 1993): 241–274;

A. W. Reed, "Nicholas Udall and Thomas Wilson," *Review of English Studies,* 1 (July 1925): 275–283;

"Retrospective Review: Wilson's *Discourse of Usury* (1572)," *Gentleman's Magazine* (February 1906): 53–62;

Albert J. Schmidt, "A Household Inventory, 1581," *Proceedings of the American Philosophical Society,* 101 (1957): 459–480;

Schmidt, "A Humanist Prescribes and Describes: Thomas Wilson and Medicine," *Bulletin of the History of Medicine,* 34, no. 5 (1960): 414–418;

Schmidt, "Some Notes on Dr. Thomas Wilson and His Lincolnshire Connections," *Lincolnshire Historian,* 2, no. 4 (1957): 14–24;

Schmidt, "Thomas Wilson and the Tudor Commonwealth: An Essay in Civic Humanism," *Huntington Library Quarterly,* 23 (November 1959): 49–60;

Schmidt, "Thomas Wilson, Tudor Scholar-Statesman," *Huntington Library Quarterly,* 20 (1957): 205–218;

Schmidt, "A Treatise on England's Perils," *Archiv für Reformationsgeschichte,* 46 (1955): 243–249;

Beverley Sherry, "Speech in *Paradise Lost*," *Milton Studies,* 8 (1976): 247–266;

Thomas O. Sloane, *Donne, Milton, and the End of Humanist Rhetoric* (Berkeley: University of California Press, 1985), pp. 130–137;

Sloane, *On the Contrary: The Protocol of Traditional Rhetoric* (Washington, D.C.: Catholic University of America Press, 1997), pp. 193–274;

R. H. Tawney, Introduction to *A Discourse uppon usurye,* by Thomas Wilson (New York: Harcourt, Brace, 1925), pp. 1–172;

Russell H. Wagner, "Thomas Wilson's *Arte of Rhetorique*," *Quarterly Journal of Speech,* 15 (November 1929): 525–537;

Wagner, "Thomas Wilson's Contributions to Rhetoric," in *Papers in Rhetoric and Poetic,* edited by Donald C. Bryant (Iowa City: University of Iowa Press, 1965), pp. 1–7;

Wagner, "Thomas Wilson's Speech against Usury," *Quarterly Journal of Speech,* 38 (February 1952): 13–22;

Wagner, "Wilson and His Sources," *Quarterly Journal of Speech,* 15 (November 1929): 525–537;

Mark E. Wildermuth, "The Rhetoric of Wilson's *Arte:* Reclaiming the Classical Heritage for English Protestants," *Philosophy and Rhetoric,* 22 (1989): 43–58.

Papers:

The unpublished letters and papers of Thomas Wilson may be found in the Public Record Office (London), the British Library, the Cambridge University Library, the Pierpont Morgan Library, Bradford Central Library, and Trinity College, Dublin.

Appendix

Continental European Rhetoricians, 1400–1600, and
Their Influence in Renaissance England

Glossary of Terms and Definitions of Rhetoric and Logic

A Finding Guide to Key Works on Microfilm

Continental European Rhetoricians, 1400–1600, and Their Influence in Renaissance England

Matthew DeCoursey
Koç University

I. The Development of Rhetorical Thought

Rhetoric was central to the European Renaissance. Hundreds of works on the topic were published between 1400 and 1600, including an appreciable number in England. The English treatises were local productions, significant only to their home country and eventually to overseas colonies, but the same is not true of the more important Continental writings. Renaissance rhetoric came to England from the Continent, and the most important interpreters of classical authors and the principal innovators in the field were from the Continent, especially Italy and the Netherlands. This appendix will focus on those Continental rhetoricians most significant to early modern England. Four threads run through the history of European rhetoric. Two are strictly rhetorical: the questions of invention and style. The third might be called philosophical, since rhetoric was associated with new views of the individual in society and of the nature of social life. Finally, the ambitions of rhetorical thinkers deeply affected the development of scholarship: it was in search of ancient eloquence that the humanists created modern techniques of text-editing and linguistic research. Throughout this appendix there will be some biographical accounts of the major figures, as their personal contacts, literary influences, and religious obsessions are vital to the story–they honed their skills and developed their notions in real polemical conflicts, often with each other. Further, rhetoricians, like artists, had patrons and religious commitments, which can only become clear in a general account of their lives.

Rhetoric is the art of expressing oneself well, the goal of which is eloquence in speech and writing. Originally, rhetoric was concerned with formal oral communication, or oratory. The art of rhetoric is said to have arisen first in ancient Sicily, where litigious colonists developed the art to help them in lawsuits. The legendary Corax of Syracuse (fifth century B.C.) carried rhetoric to Athens, where it became established as a central aspect of the duties of a citizen: a man should be able to defend himself and his family in court, just as he should be able to defend himself and them with weapons. Accordingly, Greek and, later, Roman rhetoric tended to focus especially on *forensic oratory,* the oral technique of the courtroom. It proved possible to apply rhetoric equally to legislative assemblies, resulting in a form of expression now called *deliberative oratory.* In both of these genres, a speaker marshaled his resources to procure an immediate result: a decision by the court or the legislature in the speaker's favor. A less immediate goal was the encouragement of virtue, often through the praise or blame of famous men. This last form of oratory was called *epideictic* or *demonstrative.* It was the least important of the three in classical rhetorical theory, but perhaps the most important in the Renaissance. Rhetoric retained an oral emphasis throughout the classical period, but many of the same ideas applied to writing, and some famous teachers of rhetoric, such as Isocrates (436–338 B.C.), were primarily writers.

Marcus Tullius Cicero (106–43 B.C.), the most famous of Roman orators, divided the process of oratory into five parts, but only two of them are broadly significant to the history of rhetoric during the Renaissance. His five were: *inventio,* invention, the finding of arguments; *dispositio,* arrangement, the decision as to their ordering; *elocutio,* style, the choice of words, figures of speech, and sentence structure; *memoria,* memorization; and *actio* or *pronuntiatio,* the act of speaking, including voice and gestures. Although a few treatises on memory and delivery were published, Renaissance theorists were most interested in invention and style, the aspects most applicable to writing. Arrangement tended to be treated as an aspect of invention.

Under the heading of invention, there was much discussion of the best technique for finding good arguments. Broadly, there were two currents of thought on the matter, scholastic logic and place–logic, both of which derive from classical treatises by different routes. Aristotle (384–322 B.C.) had called the application of logic to a specific issue *dialectic*. He had built up a subtle discussion of logical propositions, their formation and their consequences, and, especially, the formation of syllogisms, so as to reach conclusions with absolute validity. Medieval Aristotelians from the twelfth century onward had further developed the philosopher's points, coining an elaborate Latin terminology with technical meanings especially associated with dialectic. This "scholastic" Latin achieved many of its goals in that it became a precise tool for philosophical speculation, but scholastic Latin was difficult to learn and to use and bore only a problematic relation to the Latin known in surviving classical texts. The rhetoricians needed dialectic in order to write and speak persuasively, but this form of it often did not suit their purposes. Classical rhetorical treatises took a somewhat different approach to the invention of arguments, derived from works such as Cicero's *Topica* (The Topics, 44 B.C.). It used "commonplaces," "places," or "topics," which were meant to suggest ways of arguing. For example, Roland MacIlmaine (otherwise called M'Kilwein or Makylmaneus, flourished 1565–1581) writes that a preacher must divide his subject matter by logical rules, then "entreat of every head in his own place with the ten places of invention, showing them the causes, the effects, the adjoints and circumstances."

From each of these "places," it was possible not only to build up logical arguments, but also to show the greatness of the topic, and thereby to affect the feelings of the audience. This place-logic was not so much a strict way of reasoning as a way of finding arguments by running through certain standard categories. (To translate the matter into more familiar terms, a place-logic of murder investigation would include such topics as "motive" and "opportunity.") Many rhetorics included topics, but in time there was a move to situate this place-logic in dialectic.

With style, there were many disputed issues, large and small. Cicero had set out three classes of style: high, middle, and low. These were distinguished by diction, use of figures of speech, and sentence structure. The three styles were felt to be appropriate to different circumstances: the highest was like the speech of tragedy, while the lowest was like comedy. There was, and still is, dispute over the definitions of these styles. Hermogenes of Tarsus (second century A.D.) set out a much more complex taxonomy that sometimes coexisted with the Ciceronian scheme in Renaissance texts. He divided style into twenty categories and subcategories, designed to deal more subtly with the variety of emotional impacts possible in oratory, from a vague pleasantness to sublimity, and from clarity to wrenching emotional force. There was also some discussion of rhythm in prose, to which Cicero had obscurely

Desiderius Erasmus in 1517 (portrait by Quentin Metsys; Galleria Nazionale d'Arte Antica, Rome)

alluded in the *Orator* (The Orator, 46 B.C.). Cicero insisted that rhythm was highly important, being the chief distinction between excellent and ordinary prose, but what he meant by prose rhythm and the nature of prose rhythm in vernacular languages were matters of debate during the Renaissance. Rhetoricians further took positions on the number, definition, and use of figures of speech. By and large they agreed that there were two kinds: tropes, or figures of words like metaphor, where the word changed meaning somehow; and schemes like antithesis, which had to do with the arrangement of words but did not affect their meaning. There are Renaissance rhetorical works that list figures in isolation from rhetorical impact, only defining and naming them. Others take great pains to discuss the potential force of each figure on the emotions of the reader or audience.

Besides these strictly rhetorical issues, rhetoric had an effect on general views of the individual in society. The early Italian humanists believed in *vita activa*, an active and political life, as opposed to *vita contemplativa*, the contemplative life of monasticism. Cicero, the greatest hero of the humanists, had been a legislator, and rhetoricians in general viewed his contribution as greater than that of a monk, who only prayed. In Christian humanism, the contemplative life was often devalued in favor of an active religious life, not a retreat from the world but an engagement with it through preaching and pastoral work. In rhetorical thought, language–as in legislative speeches or in preaching–often came to be what is central to social life and to one vision or another of the good society. In the sixteenth century, a rhetorical conception of society became the foundation of a new view of theology. While medieval theologians had, in a humanist view, spent their time in quibbles using a technical language that no one understood, Christian humanists valued effectiveness: using eloquence to move the emotions of the listener toward virtue and toward God.

Finally, the enthusiasm for rhetoric brought an ambition toward scholarship in some Renaissance humanists. In part, this ambition arose from the desire to recapture the genuine rhetorical principles of the ancient authorities, since the surviving manuscripts were often corrupt and words had often been misunderstood. Even more, the humanists looked to the example of eloquent men in the past and sought to recover their texts exactly as they were written. From this ambition arose the tremendous enterprise of editing and translating that marked the Renaissance. Several scholars, such as Hanna H. Gray in "Renaissance Humanism: The Pursuit of Eloquence" (1968), have suggested that Renaissance humanism itself derives from rhetoric.

So important was this scholarly activity that classical works on rhetoric may be divided according to the time and manner of their reception. Some works had been known throughout the Middle Ages, notably including Cicero's *De inventione* (On Invention, circa 85 B.C.), the *De doctrina christiana* (On Christian Doctrine, 426 A.D.) of Augustine of Hippo (354–430 A.D.), and especially the anonymous *Rhetorica ad Herennium* (Rhetoric to Herennius, circa 85 B.C.), often wrongly attributed to Cicero. Aristotle's *Rhetoric* (circa 360 B.C.) was also known but was read as a treatise on ethics and psychology. These works were not forgotten during the Renaissance but were reinterpreted in the light of later discoveries. Other Roman works had long been out of circulation and survived in one or two manuscripts in monastic libraries. These included Cicero's *Orator, De oratore* (On the Orator, circa 55 B.C.) and *Brutus* (circa 46 B.C.), as well as Quintilian's *Institutio oratoriae* (Institutes of Oratory, before 96 A.D.). Most of these were rediscovered in the early years of the fifteenth century. Finally, certain Greek works came into prominence in Italy, some about the same time and some later, through the efforts of Greek émigrés such as George Trebizond (1395–circa 1472). These included Dionysius of Halicarnassus's *Peri syntheseos onomaton* (On Literary Composition, 1st century B.C.), Longinus's *Peri hypsous* (On the Sublime, 1st century A.D.), and especially Hermogenes' *Peri ideon* (On Types of Style) and *Peri stasis* (On Status, 2nd century A.D.).

Medieval views of rhetoric tended to emphasize the invention aspect over style or emotional persuasiveness, in part due to the survival of texts on invention, as above, and in part due to the influence of Boethius (circa 480–circa 525 A.D.). Boethius held in book 4 of *De differentiis topicis* (On Differences in Topics, circa 520 A.D.) that the difference between rhetoric and dialectic lay chiefly in the nature of the subject matter: dialectic was concerned with general questions–philosophical propositions held to be universally true or untrue–whereas rhetoric, consistently with its origins in the law courts, dealt with specific questions. If one must deal with the multiplicity of details and circumstances in everyday life, plainly the nature of one's reasoning is one step removed from the satisfying cleanliness of theoretical logic. Part of the distinction lay in differences of audience: where a university audience might be expected to follow involved structures of argumentation, rhetorical works were addressed to a broader public, and reasoning may be simplified to accommodate the nonspecialist. Consequently, medieval rhetoric typically involves incomplete syllogisms, or enthymemes, rather than complete and rigorous reasoning through syllogisms. Medieval theory of the verbal arts (to generalize broadly) distinguishes, then, between appropriate styles of logic, with no great discussion of the social engagement of a political speaker, nor of the impact of a speech on the audience's character and emotions. Medieval and later writers used an image derived from Zeno the Stoic (335–263 B.C.) of a closed fist and an open hand: the closed fist represented the tight style of argumentation to be found in dialectic, while the open hand represented the necessarily looser style to be used when specific questions are at issue.

From the twelfth century onward, rhetorical works dealing with style were written and were quite popular, but were divided into three separate fields: versification, preaching, and letter writing. The treatises on versification dealt minutely with different kinds of figures and variants on the complex metrical systems used in Latin and described the order to be used when telling a story, but there was little discussion of the emotional impact of technique on the reader. For example, Geoffrey of Vinsauf (flourished 1210), in *Poetria nova* (New Poetics, circa 1210), sets out the technique of beginning a story in the middle and returning to the beginning later–but in medieval style, he credits a logical function to the technique, in that the reader may grasp the principal features of the story in a short space. Renaissance rhetoricians read these treatises, and the

Poetria nova may have influenced Desiderius Erasmus, also known as Erasmus of Rotterdam (circa 1466–1536). Preaching was certainly concerned with impact, as the point was to save souls, but the structure advocated in the treatises remained extremely logic-oriented: frequently, a preacher was to take a quotation from the Bible and identify three logical problems in it, treating each in order. The general idea was Plato's notion that if the reason is persuaded that something is good, the soul must necessarily follow. The last category, letter writing, was known as *dictamen* or *ars dictaminis*. It arose from the need to write official letters in late medieval Italy. This art required a careful consideration of the relative ranks of writer and addressee, and conformity to a rhythmic prose style known as *cursus,* which had developed in the court of the Popes. *Dictamen,* especially as practiced in Italy, is often thought to be the ancestor of Renaissance humanism. Paul Oskar Kristeller has emphasized in *Renaissance Thought: The Classic, Scholastic, and Humanist Strains* (1961) that the humanists were the professional successors of these men and that the idea of "humanist" itself can best be thought of as a professional category: that is, a humanist is one who engages in practical rhetoric for a living.

The writings of Francesco Petrarca, or Francis Petrarch (1304–1374), introduced a new view of rhetoric, now called "humanist." He was an enthusiast for classical antiquity, but not the philosophical antiquity of the Aristotelians: rather, he wished for contact with the personalities of the great writers. He idealized Cicero, as the Renaissance always would, and even wrote letters to him. He possessed and treasured a manuscript of Homer (circa eighth century B.C.), though his Greek was limited and he was unable to read it. He believed that speech was the "index of the soul" and that written texts could communicate the man as well as could speech. Where medieval rhetoric had sought to appeal to the reason, Petrarch's notion was to address the whole person and use the passions and desires of the body to move the will toward virtue. As Eugenio Garin has shown in *Italian Humanism: Philosophy and Civic Life in the Renaissance* (1965), he also contributed to a redefinition of virtue itself, based on classical models: the stress on rhetoric goes together with a view of the ideal man not primarily as contemplative, but as active in the world. The role of oratory and of writing was to stress the necessity of civic virtue, so that the state will run well and favor the development of a genuinely civil society. This goal creates a natural stress on epideictic oratory, the persuasion to the distant goal of genuine virtue. Petrarch thought of rhetoric as central to a vision of human society as based on communication. The influence of Petrarch's Italian verse on English poetry is well known, but in fact his Latin prose works,

such as *De sui ipsius et multorum ignorantia* (On His Own Ignorance and That of Many Others, 1367) also continued to be read during the sixteenth century, and there may have been some direct influence of Petrarch on English rhetorical thought. He did not, however, produce any works directly on rhetoric, and therefore he should be seen as a precursor rather than as a directly influential figure.

After Petrarch, humanists gained a remarkable ascendency in Florence and then elsewhere in Italy. The period of civic humanism saw a series of chancellors of Florence who were both important writers and decision-makers in the state: Lino Coluccio di Piero Salutati (1331–1406), Leonardo Bruni (1369–1444), and Gian Francesco Poggio Bracciolini (1380–1459). They embodied the ideal of *vita activa* even as they expressed it in their writings. They praised marriage as part of a full life in the world, contributing to, in Garin's words from *Italian Humanism,* "an ideal republic in the soil of which our spiritual life strikes roots and finds its nourishment." Poggio Bracciolini even wrote a dialogue in praise of money. As a consequence of their interest in social life, they stressed the details of concrete existence in their written work over the abstractions of philosophy or theology. They wrote on history, making up speeches for historical figures as their classical models Livy (59 B.C.–17 A.D.) and Sallust (86–34 B.C.) had done, and stressed the political and physical situation of each speech as determining the meaning of what was said. Nancy Struever has argued in *The Language of History in the Renaissance: Rhetoric and Historical Consciousness in Florentine Humanism* (1970) that the practical and political nature of their histories derives from the humanist concern with rhetoric and is deeply involved with the origins of modern historiography. Where medieval chronicles had stressed the hand of God in all things, the humanist histories emphasized the ebb and flow of politics and alliances and the biographies of individual men and women. Later in the century Bartolomeo Sacchi (known as Platina, 1421–1481) wrote *Liber de vita Christi ac omnium pontificum* (Book of the Life of Christ and All of the Popes, circa 1472) on these principles, stressing alliances over the grace of God in the preservation of the papacy. These ideas were significant to such writers of the English Reformation as William Tyndale (circa 1491–1536) and John Bale (1495–1563).

At the same time, the humanist effect on scholarly pursuits was already beginning. The great example and advocate of civic virtue was Cicero, and the new understanding of his works led to a desire for more of Cicero and of other ancient writers. Petrarch had discovered two previously unknown orations of Cicero in a monastic library. Poggio Bracciolini made a career of seeking out new manuscripts before he became chancellor: his discovery of Quintilian's complete *Institutiones oratoriæ* (Institutes of Oratory) in 1416 had deep implications for the history of rhetoric.

LORENZO VALLA

Lorenzo Valla, also known as Laurentius Vallensis (circa 1407–1457), was significant for the theoretical turn of his writings on invention, for his impact on Latin style, and for his development of philology as a means of studying language. Valla was born and raised a Roman, and his uncle was papal secretary. He was to a great extent self-taught. The first of his major works was *De voluptate* (On Pleasure, 1431), which in later editions was called *De vero bono* (On the True Good). He obtained a teaching position on rhetoric in Pavia, south of Milan, which he was forced to leave because of a pamphlet he had written attacking an established legal authority for ignorance of the classics. In 1435 he entered the service of Alfonso V of Aragon (1396–1458), who was then engaged in an ultimately successful struggle to become king of Naples. During his thirteen years there he wrote his most significant works. Within an extremely short period, he first circulated the *Repastinatio dialecticæ et philosophiæ* (Revision of Dialectic and Philosophy, 1440), in subsequent editions called the *Dialecticæ disputationes* (Dialectical Disputations, 1440), and *De professione religiosorum* (On the Profession of the Religious, 1442), and the *Elegantiæ* (Elegances, 1441). About the same time, he published the *De falso credita et ementita Constantini donatione declamatio* (Declamation on the Falsely Believed and Forged Donation of Constantine), which demonstrated that the documentary basis for the Pope's claim to be a secular prince was a forgery. This piece of writing used the techniques of rhetoric and philology to argue a point not only valid in scholarly and philosophical terms, but also useful to his master, Alfonso, since Pope Eugene IV was then supporting the claim of his rival, René of Anjou (1409–1480). In 1443 Valla produced a volume of notes on the New Testament, the *Collatio Novi Testamenti* (Collation of the New Testament). This work criticized the established Latin translation of the Bible, the Vulgate, for infidelity to Greek originals. The following year, he appeared before the Inquisition on charges of heresy. King Alfonso intervened to save him from conviction, and Valla asserted his orthodoxy in an *Apologia* addressed to the Pope. After a change of popes from Eugene IV to Nicholas V, he became a *scriptor* in the papal curia in 1448, and became papal secretary, as his uncle had been, in 1455. It appears that Poggio Bracciolini caused the delay in his promotion: the two exchanged polemical works in 1452–1453. One of the issues here was the authority of the classical writers: Valla claimed the right to call them liars if he thought

he had evidence, and Poggio Bracciolini insisted on more reverence. At the date of his death in 1457, he was still papal secretary despite Poggio Bracciolini's enmity.

In Valla's *Repastinatio dialecticæ* he sought to use rhetoric to develop a clearer understanding of dialectic and of the workings of language. The scholastics, or university Aristotelians, had tried to fashion words into self-consistent structures, analytical trees that divided and subdivided ideas, so as to suit language to concepts considered to match the real world. From the desire for logical consistency had come, for instance, Aristotle's classification of causes as final, material, efficient and formal. For the Aristotelians, each of these terms had a fully self-consistent definition that did not overlap with any of the others. Taken together, they were meant to offer a full explanation of the notion of causality, leaving nothing out. Valla's notion was that as language exists only in practice, in use, the usage of the best authors should govern the meanings of words, even for philosophical speculation. Thus, if the poet Virgil (70–19 B.C.) or the orator Cicero used one word in three senses, none of which is analytically pure in the sense of the scholastics, it was important to study and define those usages, no matter how philosophically incoherent they may appear. Valla mocked the distinctions of Aristotle, and mocked the scholastic philosophers who followed him. Aristotle had stated at one point that "one" is not a number; Valla held that this assertion was absurd, and that real usage should bind philosophical usage. This critique of medieval dialectic had wide implications for the practice of rhetoric, since dialectical invention, as it was then practiced, rested upon principles that Valla denied. Richard Waswo claims in *Language and Meaning in the Renaissance* (1987) that Valla's view of language was so radical as to dwarf the Copernican revolution and, being transmitted through intermediaries, affected the European understanding of language permanently.

One result of his position on language as dependent upon custom was his great work, the *Elegantiæ*. It defined a wide variety of Latin words and morphemes based on a painstaking observation of real usage in classical texts. This work had a great impact on Latin style by holding the classical writers as ideal examples of precise and strong expression. Valla encouraged his readers to study the exact sense of each Latin word as it appears in the "best" authors, and to use that sense in their own writing, shunning the usage of the Middle Ages. In later generations, humanists would mock their contemporaries for using "barbarisms" in their writing, for sticking with medieval usages rather than returning to the shining example of classical style as seen in Cicero, Seneca (50 B.C. – 40 A.D.) or Tacitus (56–circa 118 A.D.). Beyond holding up this ideal in the *Elegantiæ*,

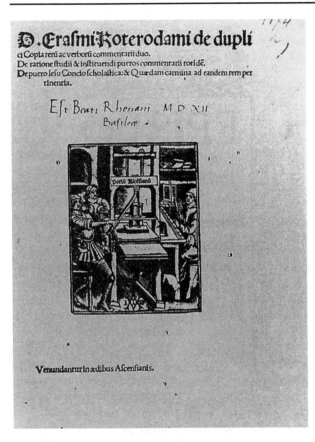

Title page for Erasmus's book on "the abundant style"
(rhetorical embellishments), which became
a standard textbook in England

Valla did the practical work required, listing hundreds of pairs of words and drawing distinctions between them, based on usage. The rigorous method required for the scholarship behind the *Elegantiæ* is now called "philology," and Valla is considered to be the founder of this kind of language study. He most famously exercised his skills in *De falso credita donatione Constanini declamatio*. His refutation of the papacy's claim to legitimate temporal power worked partly by showing that the document that gave the Western Empire to the Pope could not have been written in Constantine's time, as words appeared in senses that they acquired only later. Philology had a second branch in Angelo Poliziano, still sometimes called Politian (1454–1494), who stressed the importance of tracing textual traditions and investigating the details of ancient life so as to have a context for interpretation. Not coincidentally, Poliziano was also famed for his excellent epistolary style, and his letters were widely used as models. Poliziano was important in England above all for his style, but his philological method influenced such scholarly figures as William Camden (1551–1623).

Valla was also significant for his combination of Epicureanism with Christianity. In his dialogue *De voluptate,* he argued that the desire for pleasure made a better spur to virtue than a life of asceticism, whether Stoic or monastic. The pleasure involved may well be the expectation of beatitude in heaven, but this vision of pleasure was also the foundation of his rhetorical ideas. Rhetoric may use pleasure in language and in life to encourage virtue: the pleasure in language may derive from the artistic skills of the speaker or writer, while a speaker may also appeal to experience of pleasure in listeners to encourage a commitment to virtue. For Valla, the acceptance of pleasure meant the acceptance of life and an identification of virtue–as Maristella da Panizza Lorch has it in *A Defense of Life: Lorenzo Valla's Theory of Pleasure* (1985)–with "evidence of a strong will" and "energy." In short, Valla's positive view of pleasure involved a view of the human subject as ideally active in the world. According to Valla the ultimate purpose of rhetoric was Christian: one must use pleasure in language and in life to persuade one's fellow creatures to turn to the love of God.

Valla's ideas later had wide influence in England, primarily, but not exclusively, through the mediation of Erasmus. His treatise on the Donation of Constantine was available, and read, and his ideas on dialectic were known. Thomas Elyot cited the *Elegantiæ* in the introduction to his dictionary of 1538.

GEORGE TREBIZOND

The early humanism from Petrarch to Bruni had followed its Roman models in admiring Greek literature and rhetoric, but there was little true involvement with Greek rhetorical thought before the arrival of certain rhetoricians from the east, particularly from the Venetian colony of Crete. The most important of these was Trebizond, who introduced the ideas of Hermogenes on invention and style. He came to Venice from Crete in 1416 at the invitation of the Venetian humanist Francesco Barbaro (1390–1454). He was then twenty years old. He learned Latin so well after his arrival that his style came to be among the most admired of the century. By 1420 he had become a Venetian citizen, and Barbaro was trying to obtain a post for him as a teacher of Latin eloquence. He converted to the Roman Catholic Church and defended Western ways of thinking to his former compatriots. He worked as a tutor and in 1426 succeeded in obtaining the public chair of Latin in Vicenza, near Venice. The following year, 1427, he lost his position in Vicenza and was even expelled from the city, for reasons unknown. He opened a private school in Venice and during these years wrote his *Rhetoricorum libri quinque* (Five Books of Rhetorics), published in 1433 or 1434. Among much brilliant technical discussion, Trebizond used this book to attack his enemy, Guarino Veronese (circa 1370–1460), whom he blamed for his expulsion from Vicenza. He pointedly used Guarino's short sentences as examples to show how long, rolling periods may be built up. Such quarrelsome tendencies would cause him a great deal of trouble in his life.

In 1437 Trebizond managed to establish himself with the court of Pope Eugenius IV (1383–1447), then at Bologna. Apparently, Barbaro had been able to persuade the Pope that Trebizond would be useful in disputations with the Greek church. Trebizond wrote Greek letters for the Pope and delivered Latin orations. In 1440 he settled in Florence, where he had a glittering reputation. In the same year, he circulated the *Isagoge dialectica* (Introduction to Dialect), a handbook for those interested in rhetoric. About the same time, he bought the office of *scriptor* in the Papal curia. He also wrote some rather curious letters on his own account, urging, for instance, King Alfonso of Aragon and Naples to lead a crusade against the Mamluks in Egypt. In 1444 he became apostolic secretary. During his time with the papal court, Trebizond began a program of translations from Greek into Latin, which make up the bulk of his published work. Besides his translations of Aristotle and of patristic texts, he produced a version of the *Almagest* of Ptolemy (circa 100–circa 165 A.D.), an astrological work, with commentary. The commentary met with severe criticism, which the Pope supported. The Pope ordered him to alter it. He refused and almost immediately became embroiled in a controversy with Poggio Bracciolini. These conflicts became so bitter that in 1452 Trebizond left Rome for the court of Naples. Later he accused Poggio Bracciolini of sending assassins to kill him.

After the fall of Constantinople in 1453 Trebizond's most unusual millenarian tendencies showed themselves. He was convinced that the Turkish conqueror, Mehmet II (1432–1481), was destined to overcome Christian Europe as a whole. He wrote a long letter in Greek to Mehmet, praising him as the king of kings, and urging him to become a Christian. He was not alone in seeking Mehmet's conversion, but his extravagant praise of the Turkish sultan drew suspicion upon him. In 1465 he went so far as to travel to Constantinople in an effort to see the sultan personally and convert him to Christianity. On both counts he failed. As John Monfasani writes in *George of Trebizond: A Biography and a Study of his Rhetoric and Logic* (1976), the remarkable thing is not that he saw things in millenarian terms, but rather that he took upon himself the task of seeing that the evil conqueror became a good conqueror. He must have had great faith in his own eloquence. After his return, letters he had written to the sultan caused such suspicions that the Pope jailed him for four months, though he was by then seventy-one

years old. As Trebizond approached the end of his life, the new art of printing brought his works unprecedented diffusion, and his widest influence occurred after he died, about 1472 or 1473.

Trebizond's early works included orations in praise of eloquence and of Cicero. He is best known for his integration of the Latin and Greek rhetorical traditions, especially in his *Rhetoricorum libri V* and the complementary *Isagoge dialectica*. The *Rhetoricorum libri V* was the first full-fledged rhetorical treatise of the Renaissance in that it covered the entire subject, as Quintilian had done: invention, arrangement, style, memory and delivery.

Trebizond's innovations to the Latin tradition apply both to invention and to style. Trebizond followed Hermogenes in basing rhetorical invention upon the notion of *status,* or in Greek, *stasis.* This practice means that in a given case, the first and most important step was to understand precisely the nature of the point at issue, and place-logic could do its work from there. Cicero had classified *status* relatively simply and from the point of view of forensic rhetoric: in a murder case, for instance, a conjectural *status* would deal with a dispute over events ("Did Gaius in fact kill Claudius?") while a definitive *status* would ask whether a given killing qualifies as murder or not ("We agree that Gaius killed Claudius, but was it a legal killing?"). Plainly the "places" involved in reasoning from these *status* would differ: a conjectural *status* would involve topics of place, circumstances, and motive, while a definitive *status* would involve topics drawn from jurisprudence and arguments over the meanings of words found in the law. Trebizond drew a ten-part taxonomy of *status* from Hermogenes and characteristically related the Greek elements to Cicero's discussion of the same topic in *De inventione.* The long discussion of invention in *Rhetoricorum libri V* both begins and ends with *status.*

Trebizond's understanding of style was based on a taxonomy of styles, also derived from Hermogenes, that was far more subtle than Cicero's basic three-part division of high, middle and low. Hermogenes divided the "forms" of style into twenty categories and subcategories, distinguishing, for example, "clarity" from "beauty" and "vehemence" from "dignity." Hermogenes had illustrated his ideas with examples from Demosthenes; Trebizond adapted them to Latin, finding the same qualities in passages of Cicero and Virgil. Given the popularity of Trebizond's treatise, whenever readers encounter a Renaissance writer criticizing the excessive simplicity of Cicero's system in favor of a more complex one, they should suspect the influence of Hermogenes by way of Trebizond. For Trebizond, sound played a significant role in style: his treatment of sound, under the heading of *compositio,* was influential on later writers. Remigio Sabbadini, in *Il metodo degli umanisti* (The method of the humanists, 1920), credits Trebizond with the first Renaissance analysis of alliteration.

Trebizond was the only modern rhetorician mentioned in the same breath with the ancient well into the sixteenth century. His name often appears in English rhetorical books up to about 1570, and even after. He was also the only source for the ideas of Hermogenes available in Latin until Hermogenes' own works began to be available in Latin translation in the 1540s. His *Isagoge dialectica* had a new lease on life in the sixteenth century.

As humanist views of language grew, the older views often grouped as "scholastic" did not diminish, as professional philosophers and theologians largely retained control of the universities. The difference is sometimes framed in terms of the relation between the intellect and the will. The philosophers of the universities generally accepted Plato's argument that the will must follow the intellect in making a choice, because no one would choose the worse knowing it was worse. A defective choice, then, must follow from defective reason. The humanists, in spite of manifold variations, globally believed that the will was at best only partially under the sway of the reason. One may know the better and choose the worse because of rebellious feelings and temptations. The study of rhetoric, for them, may be justified from the need to have an effect on the reader or listener's feelings as well as on his or her reason. Scholastic argumentation, governed by logic, seemed to humanists terribly ineffective: it might move the reason, but not the will. The form of this argument best known in England was that set out in book 4 of the dialogue *Il Cortegiano* (The Courtier, 1528) by Baldessare Castiglione (1478–1529).

The previous existence of medieval dialectic was partly what created a problem for the place of invention in Renaissance rhetoric. The medieval writings were too technical to use for the more general purposes of the humanists, but the medieval writers had occupied the entire ground, defining for the humanists what logic was. Trebizond was fundamentally respectful of the Aristotelian tradition represented in the universities. His own work on dialectic, *Isagoge dialectica,* was merely an introduction to the subject for students of rhetoric, simplifying the issues for a field less demanding of logical rigour: he recognized the validity of dialectic as a discipline beside rhetoric. Valla, much more radically, wished to absorb dialectic into rhetoric, on the grounds that language in use took priority over language used in mere theoretical terms.

Valla wrote against Trebizond's point of view in the matter in a letter of 1450.

RODOLPHUS AGRICOLA

The only significant northern European of the fifteenth century for the history of rhetoric was a Dutchman, Roelef Huysman, more usually known as Rodolphus Agricola (1444–1485). His father was not only a monk, but also the abbot of the Benedictine monastery at Selwert. After studying at various universities in Germany and the Low Countries, he traveled to Italy in 1469, making his home in Pavia and Ferrara. In Ferrara he became organist in the court of Duke Ercole d'Este. He gained a reputation for his translations from Greek into Latin, and after his return to Germany in 1479, he completed the work that constitutes his importance to the history of rhetoric: *De inventione dialectica* (On Dialectical Invention). After a period in Gröningen he moved to Heidelberg in 1484, where he participated in university disputations and learned Hebrew. He traveled with the bishop of Worms to Rome, where he delivered an oration before Pope Innocent VIII (1432–1492). He became ill on the return journey and died. He was buried in a Franciscan habit.

Where Valla had subordinated dialectic to rhetoric, Agricola reversed the process, subordinating rhetoric to dialectic. Nevertheless, the two are not exactly opposed, as Agricola reformulated dialectic in a way quite different from the medieval tradition, bringing it closer to rhetoric. While Boethius had considered dialectic to be concerned with universals, Agricola incorporated into it the specific concerns of Boethius's rhetoric. In this practice he was in agreement with Valla: there was no legitimacy for either of the two writers in excluding the particular from the realm of dialectical enquiry. It is even claimed that Valla was influential on Agricola in eliminating the Boethian distinction between rhetoric and dialectic, a question examined by Peter Mack in *Renaissance Argument: Valla and Agricola in the Traditions of Rhetoric and Dialectic* (1993). Where medieval logic was chiefly concerned with establishing standards for the validity of propositions and syllogisms, Agricola used place-logic to develop a way of inventing arguments by finding something in common between the subject and predicate of a proposition. Once invented, there still needed to be standards to judge the validity of arguments. Agricola's treatise did not deal with this problem, and in the early decades of the sixteenth century it would often be used together with Trebizond's *Isagoge dialectica,* which was seen as concerned with *iudicium,* or the testing of propositions. Walter J. Ong makes the claim in *Ramus, Method, and the Decay of Dialogue: From the Art of Discourse to the Art of Reason* (1958) that medieval logic had been more precise, but that Agricola's dialectic was successful because of the need for a simpler dialectic for use in the schools.

This description of Agricola tends to make him appear to have much in common with the scholastics, who also subordinated questions of emotion and character to impersonal logic. The difference, by Renaissance accounts, lay in his effort to use dialectic to analyze entire texts, rather than treating it as a way of dealing with individual propositions. Thus, he was indeed a humanist insofar as he refused to fragment texts, but dealt with them in context. Further, Agricola was unlike the university Aristotelians in that he laid a certain stress on inspiring pleasure. He wished that the reader or listener should find gladness in "all that is great, wonderful, unfamiliar, unexpected, unheard of," and thereby come to love the sacred. Agricola did not believe that stress on dialectic required a lack of attention to emotion: he insisted, indeed, that the topics of strong emotion, or *pathos,* were the same as those of dialectic.

The Italian rhetorical tradition touched England only once in the fifteenth century, when the humanist monk Lorenzo Guglielmo Traversagni (1422–1503) published his *Nova Rhetorica* (New Rhetoric) there in 1478. It is mentioned by Wilbur S. Howell in his *Logic and Rhetoric in England, 1500–1700* (1956) as conventionally Ciceronian, being notable only for its use of examples from the Bible and from the writings of St. Jerome (circa 347–419 or 420 A.D.) and St. Augustine rather than from classical sources. The editor of Traversagni's epitome of this work, Ronald H. Martin, agrees, saying that it is "in the broadest terms, a transcription of the *Ad Herennium* with additions and modifications." The derivative nature of the work creates some difficulty in knowing whether it had subsequent influence in England.

During the fifteenth century, humanist views of rhetoric were but vaguely known in England. Italian ideas, however, began to be known about 1500. A small number of Englishmen who had studied in Italy taught in England, and some were coming to prominence at this time. William Grocyn (born 1449) had returned from his studies in 1490 and lectured on Greek at Oxford. John Colet (circa 1467–1519), the dean of Saint Paul's Cathedral, had also traveled and apparently studied in Italy. Neither of these men was thoroughly a humanist, but they did bring a certain contact with classical ideas to England. They had a circle around them that notably included Thomas Linacre (1460–1524), the grammarian and translator of Galen (129–circa 200); Thomas More (1478–1535), an English law student; and Erasmus, a brilliant young Dutchman.

DESIDERIUS ERASMUS

Erasmus is the key figure for any understanding of rhetoric in the sixteenth century. This is true for Europe as a whole, but especially for England. Throughout Western Europe his thought formed the schools. In England it formed the church as well. He was the first best-selling writer of the age of print, although he wrote entirely in Latin and spent most of his life speaking Latin.

Erasmus was born in Rotterdam, Holland, between 1466 and 1469, the second illegitimate son of a priest. That city was not the massive industrial port of today, but a backwater, hardly more than a village. From the age of nine he was a pupil of the Brothers of the Common Life at Deventer, where he learned Latin and perhaps the basic elements of Greek. The director of the school was Alexander Hegius (died 1498), a friend and student of Agricola, and Erasmus later recalled seeing the great man once during his teenage years.

Erasmus's mother died when he was about seventeen, and he came into the care of guardians. They encouraged him, apparently, to enter a monastery, and he did so with some reluctance in about 1485. He chose a convent of Augustinian Canons at Steyn, near Gouda. The young monk became impassioned for eloquence and poetry. His earliest surviving letters are addressed to other young monks and include quotations from Virgil. He also urged his friends to read Valla's *Elegantiæ,* so as to write and speak better Latin.

In 1493 he had the opportunity to escape the convent when he was made the secretary of Hendrik of Bergen, Bishop of Cambrai, whom he accompanied to Paris. Two years later he became a student at the Collège de Montaigu of the University of Paris. Academic Aristotelianism did not agree with him, however, any more than did the living conditions at the college, and he never completed a degree. He stayed on in Paris, and tutored students in Latin. One pupil was the young William Blount, Lord Mountjoy (born 1480), who invited Erasmus to return with him to England. This he did in the summer of 1499. While staying at Mountjoy's estate in Greenwich (now London) he met the young law student More, who introduced him to the future Henry VIII (1491–1547), as well as to Colet and Grocyn.

Erasmus left England for France in January of 1500. The time in England had been formative for him. On his return to Paris he completed and published the first edition of his *Adagia* (Adages, 1500), dedicating it to Mountjoy. This collection of classical quotations with commentary was the most successful of his books published during his lifetime. It lent to relatively ordinary writers the ability to tap the elegance and erudition hitherto available only to the most expert. For example, there is a reference in Aristotle's *Nicomachean Ethics* to "the Lydian rule," a ruler

Frontispiece portrait of Pope Sixtus IV and title page for a scribal copy of Bartolomeo Platina's Lives of Jesus and the Popes, *written circa 1474 (Vatican Library; Vat. Lat. 2044 fols. 2 verso 3 recto)*

for measuring made of soft lead so that it could be bent to the shape of the object being measured. Erasmus explained in his commentary that an allusion to the Lydian rule is appropriate whenever someone twists the principles of ethics and religion to his or her own advantage. They are using a "Lydian rule" where there should be a rigid standard. More, in his "Letter to Dorp" (1515), used his knowledge of Erasmus's work to score points off his adversary, Maarten van Dorp (1485–1525), by showing that Dorp had used the phrase incorrectly. The first edition included only Latin quotations, but subsequent, enlarged editions would incorporate a good deal of Greek.

At the same time, Erasmus felt the need to serve and promote the Christian religion. He never returned to his cloister, but from this date he repeatedly expressed his determination to help renew the faith. In humanist fashion, he thought he could best do this by using rhetorical techniques to promote the sincere emotion of Christian life. In 1504 he published the *Enchiridion militis christiani* (The Handbook of the Christian Soldier). This work offers the first concise statement of a program that Erasmus called *philosophia christi* (philoso-

phy of Christ), developed later in his prefaces, in *Ratio seu compendium theologiæ* (The Method or Summary of True Theology, 1519), and in *Ecclesiastes, siue de ratione concionandi* (Ecclesiastes, or On The Method of Preaching, 1535). In brief, the *philosophia christi* involved a rejection of the theological distinctions of the scholastics and a reformulation of the theologian's role as encouraging the holy emotion of a true Christian soul. A preacher truly devoted to the good of his flock would use all the techniques of eloquence to move their souls to a true love of virtue and of God. His program of editing had similar goals: he wished to reveal the full eloquence of the best writers so that their holy souls might continue the work they began in their lifetimes on earth.

In the following years he lived an itinerant life. He stayed in Louvain (Leuven), in what is now Belgium, returned to Paris, and went to England again in 1505. Finally, in 1506 he had an opportunity to fulfill a longtime dream by traveling to Italy. He received a doctorate in theology from the University of Turin without ever studying there. He arrived in Bologna in wartime and witnessed the triumphal entry of the warlike Pope Julius II (1443–1513), against whom he later wrote a satirical dialogue, *Julius exclusus* (Julius Excluded, 1517–1518), about the dead Pope's being kept out of Heaven. He came in contact with the well-known Venetian printer Aldo Manuzio, or Aldus Manutius (1449–1515), and succeeded in having a greatly expanded edition of his *Adagia* printed at the Aldine press, which was appropriate, since Erasmus had added a great many Greek adages to his text and Aldus was the foremost printer of Greek texts in Latin Europe.

In 1509 Henry VII died in England, and Erasmus's English friends persuaded him to return there, to take advantage of the putative generosity and interest in learning of the new king, Henry VIII. The promised royal patronage never materialized, but in the course of the journey there Erasmus conceived his most durable work, the *Encomium moriæ* (1511; translated as *The Praise of Folie*, 1549). He did much of the writing while staying in the house of Sir Thomas More, to whom the book is dedicated. Erasmus lectured on Greek and theology at Cambridge, and during this period he participated in the founding of Saint Paul's School in London. Besides discussing the program of the school with its founder, Colet, and suggesting a master, Erasmus contributed his best-known textbook, *De duplici copia ac verborum rerum* (On Abundance of Things and Words, 1512).

In 1514 Erasmus left England and traveled to Basel, Switzerland, where he began a long and fruitful professional relationship with the printer Johann Froben (1460–1527). In the years following, Erasmus put out two of his greatest scholarly works: his edition of the New Testament and his edition of St. Jerome's writings, both published in 1516.

These were Erasmus's glory years. He was the best-known writer in Europe. At the same time, there was much criticism of him from conservative theologians. The Louvain theologian Dorp had written a letter in 1514 attacking the *Encomium moriæ* for its disrespect to theologians, and through them, to the church. He also condemned Erasmus for proposing to correct the Vulgate Latin Bible, which, it was then believed, had been translated by St. Jerome under the inspiration of the Holy Spirit. Both Erasmus and More wrote to Dorp in defense of humanist revision of the Bible and use of philology and rhetoric. Despite these difficulties, Erasmus had the support of Pope Leo X (1475–1521) and was in a strong position. He was so confident that he established himself in Louvain, in close proximity to Dorp and other opponents, in 1517.

That same year, Martin Luther nailed his ninety-five theses to the church door in Wittenberg, Saxony. This event had serious repercussions for Erasmus. As Luther became more influential and more radical, Erasmus's Catholic critics claimed victory over him, asserting that "Erasmus had laid an egg, and Luther had hatched it." Erasmus had suggested that certain words were mistranslated in the Latin New Testament, and Luther had used these doubts to raise questions about the foundations of the church. Further, Erasmus's vision of religion had opposed what he saw as superstition and corruption in the church: although Erasmus and Luther did not hold the same theology, they often criticized the same flaws. Indeed, Erasmus's works sometimes appeared in vernacular translation with highly Lutheran commentary, and Protestant writers recommended some of Erasmus's writings to their own readers. The English Protestant William Tyndale, for instance, referred the readers of *The Obedience of a Christen Man* (1528) to Erasmus's "Paraclesis" (1516) and the preface to *Paraphrasis in Evangelium Matthaei* (Paraphrase of the Gospel of Matthew, 1524) for testimony on the corruption of the church and on the need for vernacular Bibles. He translated Erasmus's *Enchiridion militis Christiani*. Later, Richard Taverner dressed his translations of Erasmus into English in Anglican garb.

Despite his need to defend himself in print, Erasmus was tremendously productive between 1517 and his death in 1536. He produced new editions of the *Adagia* and *De copia* as well as multiple editions of *Vera ratio sey compedium theologiæ,* and he edited the works of many classical and patristic authors. His last major work was his only full-scale work on rhetoric, *Ecclesiastes, siue de ratione concionandi* (Ecclesiastes, or On The Method of Preaching, 1535). In 1536 he died in bed, which was a true accomplishment for so prominent a figure in those days of summary executions.

Erasmus's *philosophia christi,* the key to an understanding of his rhetoric, is at once highly theological and highly rhetorical. In Erasmus's view, the bad condition of Europe arose from a lack of emotional commitment to genuine virtue. In his own life he found that inspiration to virtue arose from reading three kinds of writings: classical literature, the Bible, and the writings of the Church Fathers. The inspiration, for Erasmus, came largely from style. He was relatively uninterested in invention, or rather, he subordinated invention to style, seeing the invention in a text primarily as an aspect of the author's personality. He believed that contact with the personality of authors through style would transmit good judgment, and that this judgment was largely beyond the capacity of explicit reason. For example, Erasmus wrote about Cicero that when he reads the great man's work, he feels the influence of Cicero's virtue in his own soul, even more than one would feel from the great man's physical presence.

Erasmus's program of education derives from this vision: it was the task of a teacher to use classical literature to promote secular virtue in his students and lead them to the higher virtues of religion. Thus, a student would learn justice, fortitude, temperance, and discernment from classical works, and later, having learned to be good in human terms, learn to be Godlike through the theological virtues of faith, hope, and charity. Classical education is thus a preparation for a Christian life. The teacher, being more knowledgeable and (presumably) more advanced in virtue than the pupils, must accommodate their weakness, setting out the material in a way that is accessible to them. Erasmus laid great stress on this accommodation, seeing it not only as a practical way of putting the message across, but also as an expression of two virtues: the secular virtue of *prudentia,* or discernment, and the theological virtue of *caritas,* Christian charity. Indeed, the act of accommodation reflects in human beings the act of God in becoming a man, lowering himself to a human level in order that human beings may be raised. Hence, the rhetorical principle of adapting discourse to audience becomes a moral and religious principle for Erasmus.

When Erasmus wrote on preaching in *Ecclesiastes,* he used a similar model. The preacher was the knowledgeable, religious, and virtuous man who communicated his good character at once by real example and by the exercise of rhetorical technique. Erasmus's great examples of accommodation in preaching were Jesus Christ and St. Paul. Jesus had accommodated his audience by using parables, little stories derived from everyday life, so that the most ordinary people could understand the nature of the Kingdom of Heaven. St. Paul had demonstrated his *prudentia* and *caritas* in Athens, where he had used the inscription on an idol to begin his sermon on the notion of monotheism. Erasmus points out that St. Paul did not immediately preach the Incarnation, as this concept was alien to the pagan Greeks, but rather used what was familiar to the Greeks, keeping the less familiar, though most important, aspects for later. Hence, a consideration of the audience's needs affects the matter of what is presented, therefore invention, and also the style of presentation.

Erasmus exercised his own notion of accommodation in the *Encomium moriae.* This little work is fictionally a speech made by the goddess Folly herself in her own praise. There is a great deal of satire in it in portraits of different kinds of foolishness, and sometimes simple comedy in its defense of foolishness as constituting a better way of life than wisdom. Yet, in the last section of the book, Erasmus turned toward St. Paul's notion of foolishness as a good thing, in that a good Christian must be a fool for Christ. That is, a Christian must sacrifice the respect of the world in order to be true to God. Erasmus used the pleasure of amusement to advance the cause of religion. In his letter to Dorp, Erasmus emphasized that the *Encomium moriæ* is on the same subject as his earlier, and more overtly religious, treatise, the *Enchiridion militis christiani.*

The *Encomium moriae* made trouble for Erasmus because of its satire of conventional theology. He presented scholastic theologians as ineffective in their true work of advancing the Christian religion, because their books were weighty and incomprehensible to the ordinary Christian. Even moral theology involved excessively detailed consideration of questions that rarely presented themselves. In Erasmus's 1518 preface to the *Enchiridion militis christiani,* the "Letter to Paul Volz," he mocked the unwieldiness of these large books, saying that one might as well ask a sick person to read weighty medical books in the hope of recovering from an illness. His own treatise was meant to be a short and convenient guide to the Christian life. Later in the same letter he compared theologians to the Philistines who blocked up the wells of Abraham, refusing the goodness of spiritual truth to those who needed it. Part of their wrongness lay in their unwillingness to use their God-given capacity for expression to affect the souls, as well as the minds, of listeners and readers. Erasmus saw them as inarticulate and often compared them to animals.

For Erasmus anything that served to transform the mind of the reader or listener already partook of the spiritual. This view meant that he saw the works of the most eloquent pagan writers, including Plato and Cicero, as manifestations of the Holy Spirit. The aid of the Holy Spirit did not obliterate the need for technique in speaking and writing, since, as Erasmus explained in *Ecclesiastes,* the Holy Spirit could work best with well-prepared material. In part, this belief explains his subordination of invention to style: if one can feel spiritual effect with certainty, it is unnecessary to know whether the reasoning involved is philosophically valid. An understanding of style was necessary because it carried the good or bad character of an author, mirroring his virtues and failings. A mind was like a source, producing language as a source produces water. Others "swallowed" the discourse of any given mind and were themselves moved toward evil or toward good, according to the quality of the water.

With the best authors it is possible to attain something like true contact with the author himself, and for Erasmus, this contact is the spiritual moment, the time of sacramental ecstasy in reading. In *Rhetoric and Theology: The Hermeneutic of Erasmus* (1994), Manfred Hoffmann has spoken of "the inverbation of Christ in scripture," but in fact, the same effect may be had with Cicero. This moment of ecstasy in reading is particularly promoted by vehemence in writing styles. Erasmus sometimes spoke of *vehementia* with a false etymology: *vehere mentem,* to carry away the mind. Indeed, Michael Screech has shown in *Erasmus: Ecstasy and the Praise of Folly* (1980) that Erasmus's ideal holy state was one of transport from the everyday world to a state of mystic grace.

As was Trebizond, Erasmus was dissatisfied with Cicero's division of styles into high, middle, and low. Where Trebizond used Hermogenes' twenty categories, Erasmus had six or seven, which partly overlap with Hermogenes' seven principal categories: Erasmus's were seriousness, clarity, copiousness, vividness, pleasure, vehemence, and splendor or sublimity. Erasmus saw two of the seven as master groupings: pleasantness and vehemence, corresponding to Quintilian's *ethos* and *pathos*. Four of the other five serve one of these two, but vividness, an especially important one, could serve either of them. The nature of the style was determined largely by the figures used, and Erasmus set out his overall understanding of figures in style in his last work, *Ecclesiastes*.

First published in 1535, the *Ecclesiastes* constitutes Erasmus's most complete statement of his rhetorical ideas. It consists of four books. The first praises preaching as the highest function of a priest, sets out the attitude and approach appropriate to this function, and describes the character necessary for a preacher. The second is about the right education for a preacher and describes the invention of a sermon. The third, after a brief passage on delivery and a short passage on arrangement, sets out the stylistic qualities necessary for a good sermon. Much of the space here is taken up with *amplificatio,* an exposition of techniques used to make things of themselves good feel powerfully good to the congregation, and conversely to make sin appear loathsome to them. Erasmus also catalogues figures of speech, setting out the virtues of style promoted by each. He notes, for example, that brief phrases repeated rhythmically are often useful for making a style more vehement. He ends with some examples of good *amplificatio.* The fourth book is a catalogue of topics for use in preaching.

Erasmus's devotion to the best authors made him an editor, and his texts of classical and patristic writers continued to be used for decades, sometimes for centuries. He was keenly aware that medieval manuscripts were frequently corrupt, and much of his energy went into the effort to recover the original texts of the best authors, using the philological techniques of Valla. Erasmus searched for old manuscripts of the works he meant to edit and compared them, seeking to combine various texts into a single, edited text as close as possible to the intentions of the author. Erasmus is credited with "the principle of the harder reading." This means that where two manuscripts give different words in the same place, the reading most likely to be authorial is the one more difficult to interpret. That is, an earlier scribe is more likely to have made a mistaken correction than to have introduced an interpretive problem into the text. Another kind of philology lies in the investigation of words. After the fashion of Valla, he sought out multiple examples of particular words in context, and he developed an argument as to the way they should be understood in general. In philology there was a scientific side to Erasmus, which contrasts with the mystical passion of his rhetoric.

Through the categories of style and through the presence of the author in style, rhetoric came to be not only a way of speaking and writing, but also a way of reading. In the *Enchiridion militis christiani,* Erasmus explained that one should read the Bible, watching for characteristic metaphors, like the use of light to represent the truth of the Holy Spirit. Thereafter, says Erasmus, one should think of the Holy Spirit when looking at a sunrise, and conversely use the sweet memory of the sunrise to create emotion in oneself when reading the Bible. That is to say that the orator or author is not solely responsible for the emotion of the audience, as had been the case in Cicero's rhetorical theory, but shares this responsibility with the audience or reader. "So read," wrote Erasmus, "as to be transformed." Erasmus's works for preachers emphasized the need for rhetorical training for them, not only so that they might speak eloquently from the pulpit, but also so that they could read the Bible privately to good effect. Their good private reading would have a positive effect on their preaching, and the entire community would move closer to God.

Erasmus's influences are difficult to state firmly, since he was as shy of acknowledging influence as any other humanist. Nevertheless, it is clear that he agreed with Valla on most issues. In his few remarks on invention, he recognized, as other humanists did, the need for a brief work on dialectic for students. The work he advocated was Agricola's *De inventione dialectica,* though it is not clear that he used it much himself. Lisa Jardine has argued in *Erasmus, Man of Letters: The Construction of Charisma in Print* (1993) that his promotion of Agricola was fundamentally an act of self-promotion, in that he needed to provide himself with a scholarly genealogy. Two French critics, Charles Béné (*Érasme et Saint Augustin ou Influence de saint Augustin sur l'humanisme d'Érasme,* Erasmus and Saint Augustine, or, The Influence of Saint Augustine on the Humanism of Erasmus, 1969) and André Godin ("The *Enchiridion militis christiani:* The Modes of an Origenian Appropriation," 1982), have forcefully argued that Erasmus's rhetoric derived from patristic sources.

Indeed, for Erasmus the possibility of reaching the truth entirely through reason seemed remote, and that is why he is sometimes called a skeptic, one who

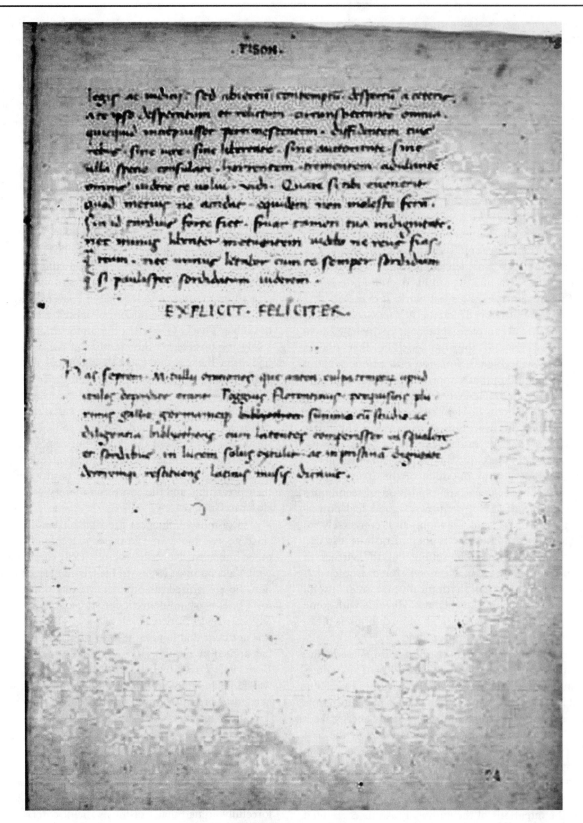

Page from a transcription of Cicero's Orationes, *copied by Papal secretary Gian Francesco Poggio Bracciolini while on leave from the Council of Constance in 1417 (Vatican Library; Vat. Lat. 11458 fol. 94 recto human25 JH.50)*

doubts the possibility of knowledge. In philological matters he tended to the inductive methods of Valla, seeking multiple examples of any particular word and arguing from them that it probably carried one meaning and not another. In spiritual matters he depended on a mystical sense of certainty, the intuition that there was wholeness and harmony in a certain conviction gained from reading. Here again, the reading of God's word in the Bible overlapped with the reading of the best human writers: it was from this conviction of harmony, for instance, that Erasmus distinguished the works of St. Jerome from the many forgeries of the time. He used his intuitive sense of St. Jerome's style, and the harmony he believed he could feel in St. Jerome's true works, to weed out the false works. His study of rhetoric served, then, to sharpen his intuitive sense of a writer's style.

To recapitulate, Erasmus offered a grand model linking the details of communication with the transformation of the spirit and the renewal of the entire society. He envisaged an education for boys that would allow the virtues of classical writers to pass into schoolboys, raising them to a point where the holier theological virtues were accessible to them. The best of them would then become preachers, communicating their love of God and of virtue not only through their sermons, but through every movement of their bodies and the holiness of their lives. Through preaching, the virtues of the clergy would become the virtues of the populace. All of these projects depend upon a strong belief in the power of language, and the infallible property of language to reflect the soul of the speaker or writer. Conversely, Erasmus excoriated the "sins of the tongue," claiming that to pollute another person's soul through filthy language was the worst of crimes.

In England, Erasmus's writings became central both to the educational system and to the Church of England. Partly through the influence of Saint Paul's School, Erasmus's textbooks became standard in most parts of the grammar-school curriculum. The Erasmian vision of education, first defended in England in More's "Letter to Oxford University" (1516), found many advocates in England. For the Church, Taverner and others produced translations of Erasmus's works to promote the piety of the laity. Erasmus's paraphrases of the New Testament were placed in every church in England. As James K. McConica has demonstrated in *English Humanists and Reformation Politics under Henry VIII and Edward VI* (1965), all sides of Tudor political and religious debates were thoroughly Erasmian. For rhetoricians, Erasmus's works were fundamental sources.

PHILIP MELANCHTHON

Among Erasmus's fellow humanists was Philip Melanchthon (1497–1560), who was a young profes-

sor of Greek at the University of Wittenberg when he first fell under the influence of Luther's ideas. He was much more of a humanist than was Luther, and he carried on an intermittent correspondence with Erasmus for many years.

Melanchthon was born Philip Schwartzerdt or Schwarzerd, the son of an armorer, and a relation by marriage of the humanist Hebrew scholar Johann Reuchlin (circa 1454–1522). Reuchlin gave him the name Melanchthon (a Greek rendering of his German name) when the boy was fifteen in order to recognize the boy's already great achievements in the classical languages. In 1514 at the age of seventeen, he obtained his M.A. degree from the University of Tübingen in southwestern Germany. Along with the standard dialectical program, Melanchthon read classical and humanist authors, especially Angelo Poliziano. The Swiss scholar and future reformer Joannes Oecolampadius (1482–1531) gave him a copy of Agricola's *De inventione dialectica,* which influenced his ideas considerably. By the time of his arrival in Wittenberg in 1518, he had already published an oration on education titled *De artibus liberalibus* (On the Liberal Arts, 1517).

With the increasing storm over what would become Protestant religion, Melanchthon became the most important German defender of reformed religion after Luther. When Luther was in hiding in Wartburg Castle after his condemnation at the Diet of Worms in 1521, Melanchthon carried on the advancement of the new program in Wittenberg. His religious positions differed from those of Luther in some ways, and his relation to Erasmus's theology is a matter of debate. Melanchthon remained on reasonably good terms with both men up to Erasmus's death in 1536. Ten years later, Melanchthon wrote of Erasmus in complimentary terms.

The young Melanchthon was predisposed toward dialectic. In his 1517 treatise he criticized the Scholastic refusal to accommodate an audience, but he was still convinced that dialectic was the guarantee of truthfulness. In this conviction he differed from Erasmus. Where Erasmus had put his faith in the true formation of the preacher's character and believed that this character would appear in style, Melanchthon sought precision on theological points, and the guarantee of precision, for him, was dialectic. He therefore distrusted any style that made great use of external ornament, seeing stylistic artifice not as revealing the speaker's character, but as obscuring the logic of a preacher's positions. The Reformation lent a greater urgency to the problem of truthfulness in oratory, since it was the task of the preacher to transmit the word of God accurately, and one had to be sure that the movement of doctrine from the Bible to the preacher's words was free from error. Accordingly, and like Agricola, he stressed not so much rhetoric per se as "true" dialectic, free of the lying and excessive subtlety of the Scholastics.

For Melanchthon, dialectic and rhetoric were not fundamentally distinct arts but a single activity of teaching. In his early years Melanchthon wrote on rhetoric without discussing two points traditionally seen as fundamental to it: consideration for the opinions of the audience and the technique to be used to move their feelings. As had the Scholastics, he recognized that one must expand on the dialectical process in addressing the unlearned. Melanchthon also recognized the need to move the audience but insisted that this be done through clarity of illustration. By the time of his *Encomium eloquentiae* (Praise of Eloquence, 1523), Melanchthon's opinion had begun to shift. Similarly to Erasmus, he began to stress putting an image, in Cicero's words, "before the eyes" of the listeners through vivid description. The vivid and accurate presentation of physical things stands as the most important of various techniques of "amplification." These are techniques to make the qualities of things stand out in relief: for example, the tininess of something extremely small might be emphasized by comparison and contrast with something extremely large: the *amplificatio a contraria*, "amplification from a contrary thing." For the morally serious Melanchthon, amplification is most often aimed at making the good feel excellent to the audience and the bad feel contemptible. Thereby a preacher may encourage virtue and discourage sin.

Melanchthon's mature position on rhetoric appeared in his *Elementa rhetorices* (Elements of Rhetoric, 1531). The first book addresses the distinction between rhetoric and logic, the three classical genres of oratory and the arrangement of material, while the second book discusses style, specifically figures of speech and the characteristics of the high, middle, and low styles. Melanchthon's catalogue of figures includes lengthy expositions of figures of amplification: the figures of amplification occupy twelve columns of exposition, compared to four and a half for the other two classes combined. Melanchthon stressed, then, those aspects of style closest to dialectical invention.

Melanchthon had not abandoned the fear that such use of poetic technique would obscure the movement from the true word of the Bible to preaching or teaching. He therefore set out what he had already called the *genus didaskalion* (teaching genre). This genus is a fourth genre of speaking, along with the classical three: forensic, deliberative, and epideictic. While for Ciceronians, the "low" style was appropriate to unemotional teaching (as well as to comedy), and the "high" style used ornament to move the audience's feelings, Melanchthon described a style that would be at once rigorously

dialectical and moving. For Melanchthon the best example of a successful style of this kind was to be found in Cicero, and therefore Melanchthon was an advocate for the imitation of Cicero in writing practice.

Melanchthon frequently cited Erasmus, but his interpretation of Erasmus's rhetoric tended to recall Agricola. He demonstrated his rhetorical ideas through the analysis of texts, particularly biblical texts. He sought in them not so much tropes as figures of thought, and he characterized these in terms of place-logic. For example, as Kees Meerhoff shows in "The Significance of Philip Melanchthon's Rhetoric in the Renaissance" (1994), in discussing the first Psalm, Melanchthon states what he takes to be the base proposition of the poem: "Those who govern themselves according to God's word are blessed." He then goes on to talk about the kinds of amplification involved in terms of the places: "the proposition is amplified first from its contraries, then from its effects," as Meerhoff renders the Latin in his article. Melanchthon draws a link between this proceeding and the short second book of Erasmus's *De copia*, which discusses "copiousness of matter"—and it is true that Erasmus partly uses the dialectical places to organize his material. Where Erasmus regarded these techniques primarily as an aspect of style, Melanchthon derives them from Agricolan dialectic. That is not to say that Melanchthon favored a dry, logical approach to religious questions. One can work from the dialectical topics to affect the passions of the reader or listener.

Melanchthon's influence was enormous throughout Protestant Europe, and even at times in Catholic Europe. As did Erasmus, he wrote textbooks which were used in many Protestant schools, on rhetoric, dialectic, and other subjects. The first rhetoric in English, Leonard Cox's *Arte or Crafte of Rhetoryke* (1531), is primarily a translation of Melanchthon, and texts of Melanchthon continued to appear in England to the end of the sixteenth century. His influence was especially strong on preaching manuals.

The rhetorical ideas of Melanchthon and Erasmus interacted in subsequent textbooks. The standard edition of Erasmus's *De copia* included a commentary by Joannes Weltkirch or Veltkirchius, which classifies Erasmus's figures after the fashion of Melanchthon, while Johan Susenbrotus (died 1543), in his *Epitome troporum ac schematum* (Epitome of Tropes and Schemes, 1541) divided primarily Erasmian examples by the same method.

PETRUS RAMUS

Pierre de la Ramée, known as Petrus Ramus (1515–1572), was, after Erasmus, the most influential figure in the verbal arts of the sixteenth century. Unlike Erasmus, he was closely associated with the universities, and specifically the University of Paris. This fact would affect his way of thought.

Ramus was born in Cuts, in Picardy. His father was a farm laborer. He attended the village school and went on to study in Paris in spite of his family's poverty, supporting himself as a servant to a rich student. At the Collège de Navarre, University of Paris, he studied dialectic: he became attached to the subject and disenchanted with the way it was taught. By his account, scholastic disputation was little more than "loud and vigorous cries" and the categories of Aristotle like "a ball that we give children to play with." Taking inspiration from Plato, Ramus began to question the authority of Aristotle, and the result was his master's examination in 1536, disputed on the topic, "All that Aristotle has said is false." He succeeded and received his degree with honors. He began to teach at the Collège du Mans of the University of Paris, and began his long association with Omer Talon, known as Audomorus Talaeus (circa 1510–1562), a professor of rhetoric. In 1543, being apparently influenced by Agricola, Melanchthon, and perhaps Juan Luis Vives (1492–1540), Ramus published *Dialecticæ partitiones* (Divisions of Dialectic) and *Aristotelicæ animaduersiones* (Remarks on Aristotle). The latter continued and expanded his attack on Aristotle. Ramus knew this would create trouble, and he prudently sent a presentation copy to the king. Two professors defended Aristotle and correspondingly attacked Ramus. The next year, Ramus was charged with being an enemy of religion before the Parlement of Paris. The king appointed a five-man commission to look into the matter. The commission persuaded the king to suppress the books, and Ramus was forbidden to teach philosophy. He therefore took up the teaching of rhetoric. Talaeus, the professor of rhetoric, took Ramus's place in teaching philosophy. The king, in time, cancelled the commission's sanctions. Ramus soon had himself in even worse trouble over his newly published criticisms of Cicero and Quintilian. A professor from another college, Jacques Charpentier, succeeded in having the college of Ramus and Talaeus banned from the university and their students denied degrees. Ramus used his influence with the cardinal of Lorraine to have the decision reversed. To prevent any future persecution, the king appointed him to the Collège Royal in 1551, the forerunner of the Collège de France, in the newly minted position of "Professor of Philosophy and Rhetoric."

There were suspicions fairly early that Ramus had Protestant sympathies. After the Colloquy of Poissy of 1561 failed to attain agreement between Catholics and Protestants, he apparently decided to no longer be prudent about his beliefs, and he publicly affirmed his Calvinism. Along with hundreds of his fellow Protestants, Ramus was murdered in the St. Bartholomew's Day Massacre in August 1572.

Ramus's simplest innovation lay in his reformulation of the relation between dialectic and rhetoric. He argued that there existed no distinctive invention, arrangement or art of memory for rhetoric, and that school and university curricula should keep these elements under the heading of dialectic. Rhetoric was thus reduced to style and delivery. Talaeus published a rhetoric according to these principles, *Rhetorica* (Rhetoric, 1548). These works appeared in several English translations and adaptations, the first being Roland MacIlmaine's *Logike* (1574), followed by *The Lawiers Logike* (1581) of Abraham Fraunce (circa 1561–1633). Dudley Fenner (circa 1558–1587) produced an epitome of Ramistic doctrine in his *The Artes of Logike and Rhethorike* (1584). Talaeus's rhetoric appeared in English in a version by Fraunce, *Arcadian Rhetorike* (1588).

The Ramist way of thought involved a sort of rage for order, simplicity, and consistency. Every subject must have its own matter to deal with, and the number of categories involved must be reduced to the strict minimum, usually two, and the two must as much as possible be mutually exclusive. Ramus wrote two long treatises criticizing Cicero and Quintilian largely for lacking method, and particularly for using confused terminology. While Valla and Erasmus had most exactly defined the common usage of Latin terms and based all on *consuetudo*, or usage, Ramus and his collaborators sought to reform terminology so that it would become a precise tool of analysis. That is, Valla and Erasmus had idealized the usage of the best authors, whether or not it was simple or analytically sound, whereas Ramus sought to clarify distinctions, reformulating ancient distinctions freely for the needs of the modern world.

Within dialectic Ramus sought to simplify terminology by the use of dichotomies. Editions of his works sometimes contain large charts by which some concept is broken down by successive dichotomies into a large number of parts. This visual schema is consistent with another Ramist principle: that the "natural order" of presentation for any subject lies in the movement from general to particular. This tendency to schematization has led Ong, in *Ramus: Method, and the Decay of Dialogue*, to propose that Ramism was distinctively visual, and was dependent on the increasing currency of print. Ong asserts that the Ramist scheme of dialectic could not be taken seriously by modern logicians, but is governed, rather, by "pedagogical exigency": that is, it is not reasoned from philosophical first principles, as was the case with scholastic dialectic, but was set out with simplicity of presentation and practical utility in mind. As with Agricola, Ramus's dialectic does not derive from medieval logic, nor from Aristotle's *Analytics,* but rather from the topics, as set out by Aristotle and Cicero.

For Ramus and Talaeus, the reform of dialectic was a necessary first step in an overall reform of subject matter. Clarity was to replace obscurity and simplicity was to replace unnecessary difficulty. The same logical reforms were to affect every discipline.

In rhetoric, Ramus and Talaeus sought to simplify terminology, reducing the number of figures and tropes recognized, and dividing them more consistently into categories. To illustrate, Ramus and Talaeus divided rhetoric into two parts, style and delivery. Style has two parts, tropes and figures. There are two kinds of tropes: those that relate parts to wholes, such as synecdoche, and those that relate parts to parts, such as metaphor. Figures divide into figures of diction and figures of thought, and so on.

Undoubtedly, this reformulation of the verbal arts reduces the field of rhetoric to something seen as relatively trivial: the ornamentation of a logical structure built up by more serious means. While Valla and Agricola had both sought to create excellent expression by unifying the arts, Ramus separated them, potentially reducing the power of discourse. Yet, the contemporary reception of Ramus's ideas in England indicates nearly the opposite. Gabriel Harvey, in *Rhetor* and *Ciceronianus,* two books of Cambridge lectures published in 1577, praised Ramus, Talaeus, and their school for returning a concern with content to the craft of writers and orators. Harvey accused himself and his contemporaries of being overly preoccupied with smooth and beautiful style, and he credits Ramus and Talaeus with showing that one must not only speak well, but also about excellent things. This putative improvement would be the result of having a separate art concerned with content, which obliges attention to matter as well as to art. Indeed, as Meerhoff writes in "Agricola et Ramus–Dialectique et rhétorique" (Agricola and Ramus–Dialectic and Rhetoric, 1988), for Ramus it was essential to separate the arts in theory but to use them together in practice.

MacIlmaine, who translated Ramus into English, explained that Ramus had accomplished three things in his reform of rhetoric. He had excluded everything that pertained to another art. He had omitted false reasons or sophistries. Finally, he had organized the information with no vain repetitions. Fraunce explained in his *Lawiers Logike* why Ramistic logic and rhetoric won such favor:

Where he [Aristotle] hath too much, Ramus cutteth off, where too little, addeth, where any thing is inuerted, hee bringeth it to his owne proper place, and that according to the direction of Aristotle his rules. Then, whereas there can bee no Art both inuented and perfected by the same man, if Aristotle did inuent logike, as hee perswadeth you, hee did not perfect it.

In the preface to his book, Fraunce reports the complaints of an angry Aristotelian: "Herbey it comes to passe that euery Cobler can cogge a Syllogisme, euery Carter crake of Propositions." To which Fraunce, the Ramist, responds: "Coblers bee men, why therfore not Logicians? and Carters haue reason, why therefore not Logike?" There is, of course, exaggeration here: cobblers did not, in general, care much about dialectic. Yet, this satiric exchange underscores one of the advantages and attractions of Ramus's work: the simplification of difficult things.

Ramism had many and varied consequences for England, affecting education and patterns of thought. Its greatest influence seems to have been among Ramus's fellow Calvinists in England, the Puritans. Among the most interesting effects for a literary reference work such as this one is the effect Rosemond Tuve claims for Ramism, in her *Elizabethan and Metaphysical Imagery: Renaissance Poetic and Twentieth-Century Critics* (1947), on the form of seventeenth–century poetry. She attributes the clear syllogistic form of much seventeenth–century poetry to a Ramist education.

Ramism also bred a reaction in some rhetoricians of the early seventeenth century. The German Bartholomaeus Keckermann (1571–1609) and the Dutchman Gerhard Johann Vossius (1577–1649) both wrote lengthy general rhetorics that incorporated aspects of Ramist thought but also used Aristotle's *Rhetoric* to lay a greater emphasis on emotion than had Ramus and Talaeus. Whereas Ramus and Talaeus had given primacy to system, method, and rational organization, Keckermann and Vossius stressed the need to move the will of the listener or reader through emotion. Over hundreds of pages of his *Systema rhetoricæ* (System of Rhetoric, 1614), Keckermann demonstrated the centrality of emotion to rhetoric, and he differentiated between kinds of rhetoric according to the emotional goal of speaking. The central aspect of rhetoric, then, for Keckermann, as for the late Erasmus, was amplification, the use of verbal technique to make the good feel excellent to the audience, and the bad feel terrible. Keckermann recognized that some kinds of speech were more involved in emotion than others, and so he distinguished between *dogmatica oratio,* or "teaching speech," and *oratio affectuosa,* or "impassioned speech." Nevertheless, he insisted that emotion was always present as a goal for the orator. Vossius, as Thomas M. Conley writes in *Rhetoric in the European Tradition* (1990), describes himself as an Aristotelian, and he is, but his

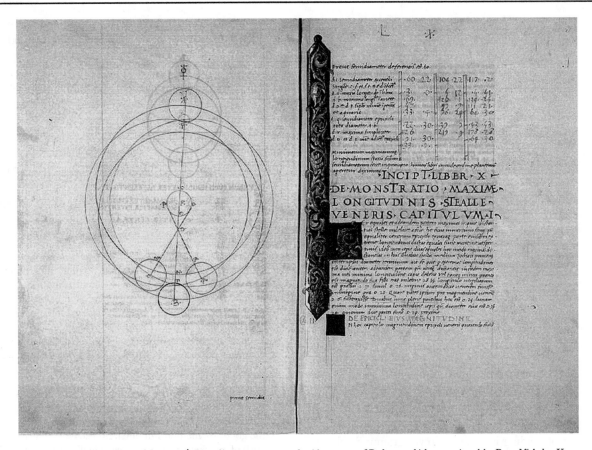

Page from a scribal copy of George Trebizond's commentary on the Almagest *of Ptolemy, which was rejected by Pope Nicholas V. This copy was prepared by Trebizond's son Andreas and presented to Pope Sixtus IV in about 1482 (Vatican Library; Vat.Lat. 2058 fols. 170 verso).*

Aristotle is an *Aristoteles keckermannianus.* In his *Rhetorices contractæ* (1621), Vossius discusses and develops Aristotle's writings on the emotions of the audience, dividing kinds of people as Aristotle does, by age and fortune. The works of Keckermann and Vossius appeared in classrooms in England, and they had an impact, especially on "the grand style" in preaching.

For sixteenth- and seventeenth-century England, the most important Continental theorists were Erasmus and Ramus. Erasmus consciously modeled his own thought on a tradition going back to Valla, stressing at once excellent style and the rigorous study of language in use. Ramus's work bears much more resemblance to the works of Agricola and Melanchthon in that he stressed dialectic as the master discipline, giving form to all others. In some ways, Ramus returned humanist dialectic to its university roots, as in his interest in methodological rigor, but he was much more practical in his interests. He sought to give the schools and universities a clear path forward. Melanchthon's contribution is distinctive in that he stressed the figures of amplification as the meeting place of dialectic and style.

II. Practical Rhetoric

Valla, Trebizond, Agricola, Erasmus, Melanchthon, Ramus, and Talaeus are the principal Continental thinkers who had a major impact on general thought about rhetoric in England. The remainder of this appendix will be devoted to a consideration of various specific areas of rhetoric and the works that shaped them. The categories are formed from the topics of extant treatises: education, letter writing, preaching, prose style, and, finally, vernacular poetics.

EDUCATION

The place where Englishmen first met with rhetoric was generally grammar school. The influence of Continental rhetorical thought shaped both the general form of schooling and special instruction in rhetoric in the final years. The boys learned grammar, reading, and writing, and they practiced declaiming, which is formal speechmaking on set topics. Education in reading was concerned primarily with grammar and style, while practice in writing and declaiming appeared together with instruction in invention.

The founding articles of Saint Paul's School of 1510 required that boys entering be able to read and write both English and Latin. On entry, boys would concentrate on Latin, being forbidden to speak any other language while at school. The lower levels of schooling were devoted to reading specified Latin texts, including Latin versions of Aesop (circa sixth century B.C.), the *Disticha* (Distichs, moral precepts in verse), attributed to Cato (234–149 B.C.), and some of Cicero's simpler letters. Later, they moved on to plays of Terence (circa 195–circa 159 B.C.) and Plautus (circa 254–184 B.C.), poetry by Virgil and Ovid (43 B.C.-17 A.D.), and speeches of Cicero. In the last two or three years of grammar school the boys studied rhetoric and practiced declamation, always in Latin.

Erasmus's influence on English education in this period is incalculable. He was an active participant in the founding of the influential Saint Paul's School, writing a grammar and a poem for memorization specially for the school, besides his dedication of the *De copia* to the founder of the school, Colet. His more general writings affected English education as much as they affected education elsewhere in Europe. Erasmian influence takes three forms: first, in general philosophy Erasmus affected both schoolmasters and published writers on education; second, his rhetorical emphasis affected the teaching of reading in Latin in lower grammar school; third, he instituted and formed the teaching of eloquence in style and invention in upper grammar school.

The teacher, in Erasmus's view, should form the moral character of schoolboys, and thus the teacher was an orator, using the eloquence of ancient writers to move the boys' souls. The pupil began as a small child, learning the basics of language. As the best that had been thought and written was in Latin and Greek, the child needed to learn these languages. After mastering the fundamentals of grammar, he (or perhaps she, though Erasmus had his doubts) began to study the texts of secular literature, learning moral precepts and using the rhetorical qualities of the text to transform himself. The pupil was required to study humbly, practicing, for example, the tenacity of Virgil's Aeneas in life, and learning to distinguish virtue from vice. In the process of reading, the pupil also learned to distinguish the rhetorical figures one from another and gained a feel for their impact on the thoughts and feelings of a reader or listener. In time he began to use them in speech and in writing. The study of the Bible, using this rhetorical awareness, resulted in a transformation of the spirit, such that rhetorical skill would inevitably be used for good. The acquisition of virtue, for Erasmus as for Plutarch (circa 46 – circa 120 A.D.) among the ancients, was parallel to the learning of skills: in each case, one had to learn in principle, then practice, and finally the skill or the virtue became second nature. Ideally, the pupil would become a preacher, speaking of God and salvation to the less learned, with the skills of eloquence gained in the process of education. Thus, even the unlearned will gain from the classical and spiritual education of the elite. It may be seen then, that on an Erasmian model the school system as a whole is rhetorical, meant to form the students' moral character and subjectivity. As we have seen, the essential element to read in a text is the personality of the author, and this personality is seen in style, so initial emphasis is on style.

On the means of gaining education, Erasmus wrote in *De pueris instituendis* (On Education for Children, 1529):

> Tota vera ratio felicitatis humanæ tribus potissimum rebus constat, natura, ratione et exercitatione. Naturam appello docilitatem ac propensionem penitus insitam ad res honestas. Rationem voco doctrinam, quae monitis constat et praeceptis. Exercitationem dico usum ejus habitus quem natura insevit, ratio provexit. Natura rationem desiderat, exercitatio nisi ratione gubernetur, multis periculis atque erroribus est obnoxia.

> (As a general principle, human happiness depends on three prerequisites: nature, method and practice. By nature I mean man's innate capacity and inclination for the good. By method I understand learning, which consists of precepts and warnings. Finally, by practice I mean the exercise of a disposition that has been implanted by nature and molded by method. Nature is realized only through method and practice, unless it is guided by the principles of method, is open to numerous errors and pitfalls).

Jean-Claude Margolin has shown in his 1966 edition of *De pueris instituendis* that what unites the pupil and the master for Erasmus is *ratio,* which means both method and reason. What essentially makes education is practice governed by *ratio*. Especially by imitating an author's style, the students will begin to imbibe his virtues, and the process of education will make good men.

Erasmus's Epicureanism—which he learned from Valla—shows itself in the *De pueris* by his advocacy of pleasure as a means of encouraging children. Hence, he advocates the use of humorous stories from Aesop and Homer (fifth century B.C.) to retain students' attention long enough to teach valuable moral precepts. In another place he describes teachers ,of antiquity who baked letters of the alphabet into cakes, so that the pleasure of eating would encourage children to remember them. Nor did he believe that pain could be educational: he was a strong opponent of corporal punishment in the schools, holding that it actually interfered with education. These notions affected England both directly and by the mediation of Roger Ascham.

Erasmus's rhetorical ideas affected not only instruction in rhetoric as such, but also the approach to reading from an early stage of grammar-school instruction. From a basis in his rhetorical ideas, he chose or wrote the texts. The only classical work that had been used in medieval schools and survived to the Renaissance curriculum was the *Disticha* of Cato, a book of moral precepts in Latin verse. Erasmus edited it for use in the schools. Erasmus's own *Colloquia* (Colloquies, 1518) were fictional dialogues meant to teach pupils pure spoken Latin and moral lessons in the process. The first edition was in 1518, and he revised the texts periodically for the rest of his life, often adding new colloquies and substantially revising others. Both the *Disticha* and the *Colloquia* taught both Latin language and good morals, and the excellence of their expression was seen as contributing to the moral formation of the student.

Erasmus's *De ratione studii* (On the Method of Study, 1511), which was also written for Saint Paul's School, not only sets out which Latin and Greek texts are to be studied, but also discusses how they should be read:

> inter legendum auctores non oscitanter obseruabis, si quod incidat insigne verbum, si quid antique aut noue dictum, si quod argumentum aut inuentum acute aut tortum apte, si quod egregium orationis decus, si quod adagium, si quod exemplum, si qua sententia digna quae memoriae commendetur. Isque locus erit apta notula quapiam insigniendus. Notis autem non solum variis erit vtendum, verum etiam accommodatis, quo protinus quid rei sit admoneant.

> (you will carefully observe when reading writers whether any striking word occurs, if diction is archaic or novel, if some argument shows brilliant invention or has been skillfully adapted from elsewhere, if there is any brilliance in the style, if there is any adage, historical parallel or maxim worth committing to memory. For not only must a variety of marks be employed but appropriate ones at that, so that they will immediately indicate their purpose).

These elements of reading must have found their place in masters' lectures from an early stage. They relate to rhetoric in their stress on the impact of style upon the reader. The point of noticing the style is to be more affected by it, to learn to be as virtuous as the writer.

In his *De conscribendis epistolis* (On the Writing of Letters, 1522), Erasmus is more specific, and he pushes the technique of reading to activities possible only after a certain amount of rhetorical instruction:

> Lectionem quidem auditam continuo relege, ita vt vniuersam sententiam paulo altius infigas. Deinde a calce rursus ad caput redibis, et singula verba excutere incip-

ies, ea duntaxat inquirens, quae ad grammaticam curam attinent. . . . Hoc vbi egeris, rursum de integro percurrito, ea iam potissimum inquirens quae ad artificium rhetoricum spectant. Si quid venustius, si quid elegantius, si quid concinnius dictum videbitur, annotabis indice, aut asterisco apposito. Verborum compositionem inspicies, orationis decora scrutabere. Autoris consilium indagabis, qua quidque ratione dixerit. . . . Releges . . . quarto, ac quæ ad philosophiam, maxime vero ethicen referri posse videantur, circunspicies, si quod exemplum, quod moribus accommodari possit.

> (Review immediately a reading you have heard in such a way that you fix the general meaning a little more deeply in your mind. Then, go back over it, starting at the end and working back to the beginning, examining individual words and observing only points of grammar in the process. . . . After doing this, run through the passage completely again with particular attention to points of rhetorical technique. If any phrasing seems to have special charm, elegance, or neatness, mark it with a sign or an asterisk. Examine the arrangements of words, and the fine turns of expression. Analyze the author's purpose, why he phrased things in a certain way. . . . Read it again . . . for the fourth time, seeking out what relates to philosophy, especially ethics, to discover any example that may be applicable to morals).

By such analysis, Erasmus hoped, the student might persuade himself to become ever more virtuous. English schoolboys—and men in later life, as well—followed Erasmus's advice, as there are surviving copies of books with just such labels in the margin, indicating what figure of speech is being used where. For moral improvement, many educated Englishmen kept commonplace books, recording what seemed both most pleasurable and most improving in their reading.

When it came to instruction in writing, schools using Erasmian principles worked systematically. In the early stages, students would write easy sentences and would work toward weaving them together into a "theme." They would learn principles of rhetoric and logic by way of providing coherence for their writing. They wrote in verse some of the time, to fix the Latin meters in their minds. A large part of learning was in imitation, and the source for imitation was in the early stages the *Progymnasmata* (Preparatory exercises) of Aphthonius of Antioch (flourished circa 400 A.D.), who had given examples for exercise of all the minor prose forms. Having gained practice in the written theme, the students would begin to write longer declamations and to deliver them orally.

In the process of learning to write, students would need some notion of invention. This aspect appeared in Erasmian schools, but Erasmus's own works were not significant for it. T. W. Baldwin demonstrates in *William Shakspere's Small Latine & Lesse Greeke* (1944) that

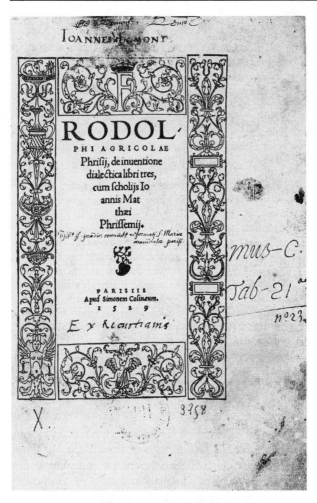

*Title page for Rodolphus Agricola's influential rhetoric book
(Bibliothèque Nationale, Paris)*

William Shakespeare (1564–1616) knew Cicero's *Topica,* and he believes that it was widely used, although this work does not seem to be specified in the statutes of any school. Where it was used, it was likely in an edition with a commentary by Melanchthon. Thomas Elyot (circa 1490–1546) recommended Agricola's *De inventione dialectica,* as did Melanchthon, and Richard Sherry knew the same work, so it may well have been used as a schoolbook in England, especially early in the century. Even as late as 1579, Harvey recommended the use of Agricola's book. Some schools may have used Melanchthon's *Erotemata dialectices* (Dialectical Enquiries, 1548). Elyot also thought that if the student were not ambitious, the second book of Erasmus's *De copia* might do. This recommendation shows that he, like Melanchthon, thought of this book as dialectical in nature, though it certainly does not go very far in the matter. The statutes of many schools recommend the pseudo-Ciceronian *Rhetorica ad Herennium,* which does have a section on invention, involving dialectic. Late in

the century, the works of Ramus gained some significance, though it is not clear that they had much effect on English schooling before 1600.

Erasmus's main contribution to the rhetorical curriculum was *De copia. Copia* is two things: the first sense of the word is "storehouse," and this work is principally a compendium of examples, illustrating the schemes and tropes, and ways of developing a composition; in its second sense, *copia* is a quality of style, translated into English as "abundance" or "copiousness." In his introduction Erasmus distinguishes between a laconic style and an abundant one, and he praises the educational usefulness of striving for variation in writing, using synonyms, tropes, figures, vivid description, arguments of various kinds, and many other resources to please and impress the listener or reader. Late in the century, the habit of expanding with synonyms sometimes deteriorated into a mere verbal tic, and it came to be seen as a plague. The comic schoolmasters of Shakespeare, who habitually throw redundant synonyms into their speech just to be abundant, are much impoverished heirs of Erasmus.

The full title of the work was *De duplici copia verborum ac rerum,* but the effective topic of the book was style. The first book, on *copia* of words, is four times the length of the second, and Baldwin says sixteenth-century copies of the *De copia* show much more wear on the first book than on the second. *De copia* was generally used, however, in English schools in an edition with a commentary by Veltkirchius, which takes Melanchthon's line that the first book is about style and the second is about invention. Erasmus does not discuss the distinction between style and invention within the *De copia,* but "abundance of matter" appears in *Ecclesiastes* in the section on style, book 3.

In English schools, the *De copia* was standard for teaching the use of figures of speech, but it did not constitute an introductory textbook, since it tended to presuppose that the student already knew what the figures were and only needed exercise in their use. To fill this gap, the German writer Peter Schade, usually called Mosellanus (circa 1493–1524), produced a short work giving the rhetorical figures in a form that could be posted on the wall, *Tabulæ de Schematibus et Tropis, Tables of Schemes and Tropes* (1516). Mosellanus recommended this proceeding, pointing out that Erasmus had suggested something similar. The *De copia* was linked with Mosellanus in the curriculum of Eton specified in 1528–1530. About midcentury, Mosellanus's *Tabulæ* came to be superseded by Susenbrotus's *Epitome troporum ac schematum.* This work consists of an extensive list of more than 130 figures and stylistic defects with their subtypes, with definitions and examples. The treatise is based largely on the *Ecclesiastes,* the *De copia* (and

Veltkirchius's commentary on it), and the *Rhetorica ad Herennium,* with significant contributions from Quintilian and the English grammarian and translator Thomas Linacre. There are scattered passages from other authors, including even the Venerable Bede (circa 672–735 A.D.). Mnemonic verses are drawn from the *Carmen de floribus* (Song about Flowers, 1489) of Antonio Mancinelli (1452 – circa 1505).

A treatise on schemes and tropes would seem to be self-evidently about style, but in Susenbrotus the reader encounters the same ambiguity as in Melanchthon, so that elements of invention were taught under the heading of style. That is, there is extensive discussion of "figures of amplification," which derive from dialectic: figures that serve to "amplify" the characteristics of something being described, whether its goodness, badness, or just size. They occupy a curious middle position between invention and style. Their logical form is dialectical, as "causes," "results," and "circumstances" are certainly matters of logical form, but their use to move the passions is one traditionally associated with style. Further, they often come close to figures of style as such. For instance (to draw an example from Erasmus), one may emphasize the tremendous size and strength of Achilles by describing the size of his sword. This description is, in dialectical terms, an argument *ab instrumento,* but it is also an expanded trope, a metonymy, creating a verbal effect by putting an instrument in place of the one who uses it.

Susenbrotus's treatise went through at least twelve editions in England before 1635, and this was at a time when a high proportion of Latin books were imported. The textbook was so well known that a satirical Latin play called *Susenbrotus* was performed before King James I in 1615 or 1616. The character Susenbrotus is, not unnaturally, a pedant.

Erasmus's method of teaching centrally involved precepts to aid the development of skill, but there are few such precepts in the *De copia;* these precepts came from classical rhetorics, most notably the pseudo-Ciceronian *Rhetorica ad Herennium.* The statutes of more ambitious schools prescribed works by Quintilian in the last year as well.

In England, Erasmus was directly influential primarily through his Latin writings. The original English thinker most deeply influenced by Erasmus was Elyot, whose treatise *The Boke Named the Governour* (1531) shows signs of Erasmus's thorough influence throughout. Elyot, like Erasmus, places great stress on the need to accommodate children by beginning from the concrete things they understand and attracting them to a more-abstract way of thought through legitimate pleasure. Erasmus's educational theory frequently reached through Elyot those who did not read Latin.

Late in the century, the works of Ramus and Talaeus gained some significance in English schooling, altering the teaching both of invention and of style. This significance is most obvious in *The Education of Children in Learning* (1588) by William Kempe (circa 1563–1601). Kempe's treatise divides dialectic from rhetoric after the Ramist fashion. Schoolboys are asked to learn the rules of each separately (formulated in dichotomies after the fashion of Ramus), observe the applicability of rules in canonical literary works, and finally produce their own writings in themes. It seems likely that Kempe put this Ramistic method into practice at his own school in Plymouth, and the same method may have been used at other schools. In 1597 the educator and clergyman Charles Butler produced a version of Talaeus's *Rhetorica* for schoolboys, titled *Rameæ rhetoricae libri duo* (Two Books of Ramistic Rhetoric). In a second, expanded edition of 1598, it was frequently reprinted during the seventeenth century.

The influence of these two great figures was not exclusive. The most influential Continental writers on education in England after Erasmus and Ramus were Vives and Johann Sturm (1507–1589).

JUAN LUIS VIVES AND JOHANN STURM

Vives was the son of converted Spanish Jews, and his parents were executed by the Inquisition for alleged apostasy. He left Spain for Paris in 1509, at the age of sixteen, where he studied at the Collège de Montaigu. He was no more satisfied with his experience there than Erasmus had been: he later wrote a polemical work against university philosophers called *Adversus Pseudodialecticos* (Against the Pseudo-Dialecticians, 1519). In 1512 he traveled on to Bruges (Brugge), in what is now Belgium, which became his home. Four years later, he spent some time in Louvain, attending Erasmus's lectures and making himself known as a scholar. Erasmus was much impressed and predicted that the young man would eclipse him. The two began to collaborate soon after on an edition of Augustine's *De civitate dei* (*The City of God,* 1522). As was Melanchthon, Vives was most devoted to Erasmus and Agricola among all modern writers. Between 1523 and 1528 he lived chiefly in England, where he tutored the young Princess Mary and lectured at Corpus Christi College, Oxford. Appropriately, he published a treatise on the education of Christian women, *De institutione foeminæ christianæ* (On the Education of a Christian Woman, 1524). This book is one of many educational treatises and textbooks that gained some currency in England and elsewhere, of which the most compendious was *De disciplinis* (On the Disciplines, 1531). The second book of this work, a program for education throughout life, was also pub-

Last page of a scribal copy of Lorenzo Valla's translation of Thucydides's Histories
(Vatican Library; Vat. Lat. 1801 fol. 184)

lished separately under the title *De tradendis disciplinis* (On the Transmission of the Disciplines).

As did Erasmus, Vives had a great belief in the power of eloquence to move the soul either to virtue or to vice. Erasmus thought mainly of the potential of good writing to encourage virtue. Vives laid greater stress than Erasmus on the dangers of bad writing. In his educational treatises he condemned all novels and had only reserved praise for poetry. An early treatise of his on poetry is titled *Veritas fucata* (Painted Truth, 1514). He recognized that King David had written poetry in the Psalms, and for that reason he believed that poetry had originally been a good thing. Yet, he saw a degeneration in the art that is already apparent in Homer and Hesiod, and the great majority of verse, he thought, served sensual appetites and not virtue at all. He would allow popular songs that passed appropriate religious truths to the common people, without any inappropriate disrespect. While Erasmus had cheerfully recommended the plays of Plautus and Terence, saying only that one should interpret carefully, Vives tended to prefer the moralistic plays of his own time. Vives, like Colet, also promoted early Christian writers thought to be inferior by Erasmus and other influential educators.

Vives's greatest originality lay in his empirical approach to pedagogy and psychology. In *De anima et vita* (On the Soul and Life, 1538), he began from Galen's well-known theory of the humors that served to relate psychology to physiology. (A person's character would be explained from the balance of fluids in his or her body: the fluids blood, phlegm, yellow bile, and black bile would make a person respectively sanguine, phlegmatic, choleric, or melancholic.) He observed how these temperaments are affected by external circumstances, and he asserted the need to base one's decisions on a sound knowledge of the student or the person addressed.

Perhaps his close attention to individual students was what led Vives to a certain pragmatism in his pedagogical program. He advocated the use of the vernacular in early stages of education and suggested that modern history might be studied in vernacular books. He wrote that the objective of education should be not only moral and religious, as with Erasmus, but also practical. That is why, for example, he laid far more stress on physical education than did Erasmus.

Vives's textbooks were used in England, and as an educational theorist he considerably influenced the works of Richard Mulcaster (circa 1531–1611), notably including *Positions vvherin those primitiue circumstances be examined, which are necessarie for the training vp of children, either for skill in their booke, or health in their bodie* (1581) and *The first part of the Elementarie: vvhich entreateth chefelie of the right writing of our English tung* (1582). Mulcaster appreciated Vives's emphasis on individual students and the practical cast of his pedagogy. Both Vives and Mulcaster might be said to be rhetorical in their approach to education, in that they felt the presentation of material should be adapted to students. As had Vives, Mulcaster rejected the ideal of private tutoring presupposed in many educational treatises of his time in favor of public schools like Saint Paul's.

Sturm came from the Rhineland in western Germany, and like Erasmus, studied at a school of the Brothers of the Common Life. He went on to the famous Trilingual College at Louvain. He became involved in a printing business after his master's degree, and soon went to Paris to sell books. After he began to take a medical degree there, he came to the attention of influential people, in part because of his 1531 translation of Galen. He became one of the earliest lecturers of the Collège Royal (later Collège de France), where he taught the works of Cicero and the dialectic of Agricola. Ramus was his student. Sturm became involved in efforts to reconcile the French crown with the Lutherans: he wrote to Melanchthon to encourage him to continue his efforts at establishing peace. In 1537 he accepted a teaching position in Strasbourg, and the following year he became the first rector of the original Gymnasium, one of the most influential schools of Protestant Germany. Throughout the following years Sturm combined his educational activities with exercise of rhetoric in diplomacy, not only mediating between France and Protestant Germany, but also between Lutherans and Calvinists. When the French religious wars broke out, Sturm reduced himself to poverty providing loans for the relief of Protestants, which were never repaid. Toward the end of his life, Lutheran theology hardened into the Formula of Concord of 1577, and ultra-Lutherans accused Sturm, like so many rhetoricians before him, of heresy. In 1581 he was removed from his position as rector. For the last eight years of his life he gardened, kept bees, and wrote a treatise on the Turkish war. Among his visitors in his old age was Sir Philip Sidney (1554–1586).

Sturm's educational program was ambitious and thoroughly based in rhetoric. It was well known throughout Europe, since he published an exact description of it in *De literarum ludis recte aperiendis* (The Correct Opening of Elementary Schools of Letters, 1538) and other works. As Erasmus had done, he combined the ambition of good speech with a highly serious program of promoting piety. His approach to religion was naturally rather different, as Lutheran theology emphasizes faith over the development of virtue. His approach to rhetoric was much influenced by Hermogenes, whom he translated into Latin. Besides the precepts of Hermogenes and other rhetoricians, he required a close imitation of Cicero, more than Erasmus would have approved. He was extremely demanding. Boys only seven years old were required to read eclogues of Virgil. Knowledge of the New Testament was based on readings in Greek beginning when the boys were only ten. Unlike Erasmus, he used corporal punishment, although he did favor teaching through pleasure as much as possible. He introduced dialectic earlier in the program than did Erasmus, and in the first year of the Gymnasium he published Melanchthon's dialectic with an introduction of his own. Sturm, with Trebizond, was responsible for bringing the rhetorical ideas of Hermogenes into the mainstream of Western European rhetoric and education.

Ascham carried on a long–term correspondence with Sturm, but he was also much affected by Erasmus. He carried prestige as an educator, in part because he had been the tutor of the future Queen Elizabeth. In his *The Scholemaster* (1570), Ascham stressed the importance of close parental attention to the raising of children, and the superior efficacy of praise over punishment. Owing to Sturm, Ascham recommended Hermogenes as a basis for a rhetorical education, and perhaps he also took from Sturm his emphasis on Cicero as an exclusive model of style. From both, Ascham drew a particularly Christian perspective on humanist education.

Several treatises in English are closely associated with these fundamentally educational Continental works. Sherry's *Treatise of Schemes and Tropes* (1550) includes sections translated from Mosellanus, the *Rhetorica ad Herennium,* and Erasmus's *De copia.* The classification of tropes is Melanchthon's. Thomas Wilson's *The Arte of Rhetorique* (1553) draws to a great extent on school textbooks in rhetoric. Henry Peacham the Elder's *The Garden of Eloquence* (1577), its editor William G. Crane remarks, was modeled on Susenbrotus and drew from Sherry. His acknowledged sources included Cicero, Quintilian, Erasmus, Mosellanus, Melanchthon, and Wilson. Peacham continued Melanchthon's tendency, communicated especially through Susenbrotus, to incorporating elements of invention under the headings of figures.

A formulary of classical examples for imitation in English, consisting mainly of translated excerpts from Aphthonius's *Progymnasmata,* appeared as *A booke called the Foundacion of Rhetorike* (1563) by Richard Rainolde. These English treatises were fairly popular either with those who had not been to grammar school or for those whose work did not involve Latin from day to day, so that they could no longer read Latin easily. Perhaps Fraunce indicated a large part of the readership of such books in his title, *The Lawiers Logyke.*

LETTER WRITING

Letter writing was a separate topic in sixteenth-century England, and it is especially interesting as Renaissance disputes over style become obvious in epistolary textbooks. Epistolary style began as a grammar-school subject, but it overflowed the boundaries of the curriculum in vernacular letter-writing manuals. These were aimed at merchants and other people who did not have the advantage of a grammar-school education, but who did have occasion to write letters in the vernacular.

Erasmus's Latin textbook on letters, *De conscribendis epistolis,* is a major source for much writing both in Latin and in the vernacular. It sought to reform the remaining elements of the medieval *ars dictaminis,* and later the excesses of Ciceronianism. *Dictamen* had treated letter-writing as if it were oratory, dividing the letter normally into five parts: salutation, exordium, narration, petition, and conclusion. The salutation received the most attention, with fine distinctions of relative rank decreeing its form. Letters were written in a rhythmic prose style called *cursus,* which had originated in the papal court. Petrarch had begun to criticize *dictamen* on Ciceronian grounds as early as 1345, but Salutati had used elements of the medieval style, and it persisted up to the sixteenth century.

Erasmus's early unpublished versions of the *De conscribendis epistolis,* written in the last years of the fifteenth century, opposed the elaborate formality of *dictamen,* insisting for example that the oratorical divisions were absurd for a letter. Erasmus criticized the Italian humanist Francesco Negro (born 1452) for insisting that every letter should have an exordium. Nothing should interfere with the classical view of letters as a conversation between absent friends. There should be no uncommon words, far-fetched metaphors, or grandiloquent expressions, such as would be acceptable in an oration. Furthermore, for Erasmus letter writing must be adapted to the personality as well as the social standing of the addressee.

As Judith Rice Henderson has shown in "Erasmus on the Art of Letter-Writing" (1983), Erasmus began in the 1520s to satirize the classical purism of the Ciceronians in letter writing. He held that the insistence on imitation of Cicero conflicted with the need to adapt one's approach to subject matter and circumstances. The Ciceronians insisted, as Erasmus had done earlier, that a letter must be simple and brief, but their dogmatism in the matter conflicts with the need for expression: if one is writing about something grave and majestic, one needed to use a grave and majestic style.

Accordingly, Erasmus's *De conscribendis epistolis* classifies letters according to their subject and purpose, frequently using what would now be called speech acts.

Hence, there are chapters on "the letter of request," "a reply to a consolation," and "the letter of congratulation." For each, Erasmus offers some precepts and an example or two. In this work Erasmus's concern with adaptation to audience shows its relation to ethics, as he discusses how to write to a bereaved person, "lest like unskilled doctors we aggravate rather than alleviate a wound that is still raw and fresh." The examples are frequently from his own correspondence, and some of the fictional letters are pure flight of fancy. For example, under the heading of "accusatory letter," Erasmus invents a houseguest who had been saved from a shipwreck and responded by robbing his host. Not content with that, he had seduced both the maidservant and daughter of the Good Samaritan, whose rhetorical task it is to reproach the evildoer. He also includes several letters of Cicero, Pliny (23–79 A.D.), and Poliziano.

Also used in the grammar schools were the *De conscribendis epistolis* (1534), a treatise by Vives, *Methodus conscribendi epistolas* (Method of Writing Letters, 1526), by Christoph Hegendorff (Christophorus Hegendorphinus, 1500–1540), and *Epistolica* (Epistolary Matters, 1543), by Georgius Macropedius (Joris van Lanckvelt, 1486–1558). Vives's treatise is shorter than that of Erasmus, and it deals with Greek as well as Latin letter writing. He developed Erasmus's interest in the relation between psychology and writing, and he roundly condemned insincerity. Hegendorff was a thorough Erasmian, but his distinctive contribution involves a stress on dialectic that may be derived from Melanchthon. Macropedius is conservative in that he reverts to the requirement of medieval *dictamen* that a letter have the parts of an oration, though otherwise he follows Erasmus. He also includes a catalogue of figures and tropes. In London in 1573 there appeared a work on letter writing by Aurelio ("Lippo") Brandolini (died circa 1497), *De scribendo libri tres* (Three Books on Writing, first published in 1549) with the treatises on letter writing by Erasmus, Vives, Conrad Celtis (1459–1508), and Hegendorff. It seems to have been popular in England, as there were copies in several private collections and university libraries.

The tradition of English letter-writing manuals begins with William Fullwood's *The Enimie of Idlenesse* (1568). It is translated from an anonymous French work and consists mostly of examples. Many of the letters are twice-translated versions of Cicero or Poliziano, both of whom had been prominent in Erasmus's work. This book, however, includes a wider variety of Renaissance letter writers, including Marsilio Ficino (1433–1499), Georgius Merula (1431–1494), Giovanni Pico della Mirandola (1463–1497), and Pope Innocent VIII. It was popular, with at least seven editions appearing before the end of the sixteenth century. The English letters in this work were probably used in schools for translations into

Philip Melanchthon in 1532 (portrait by Lukas Cranach; Gemaldegalerie, Dresden)

Latin, which could then be compared to the Latin originals.

Abraham Fleming entered the field next with *A Panoplie of Epistles* (1576), a manual containing many model letters, as well as a dialogue and a section of precepts translated or adapted from Hegendorff's *Methodus conscribendi epistolas*. The letters are gathered and translated from various Latin sources, both classical and contemporary, including the letters of Walter Haddon (1516–1572) and Ascham. Cicero and Isocrates are especially well represented.

The *English Secretorie* (1586) by Angel Day is the best-known of the letter-writing manuals of the period, and the most original. He lists his sources as Erasmus, Vives, Hegendorff, and Macropedius. The principles he sets out are mostly those of Erasmus, though like Macropedius he returns to the older tradition by insisting that a letter should have five parts similar to those of an oration. He enthusiastically advocates an extensive use of figures, which any Ciceronian would have shunned. From Hegendorff, Day draws the German emphasis on dialectic. For example, there is a letter in praise of the Black Prince, which, as Katherine Gee Hornbeak points out in *The Complete Letter Writer in English 1568–1800* (1934), follows a list of places by Hegendorff, recommending praise of "birth, childhood, adolescence, youth, age and death." In a second edition Day added a catalogue of schemes and tropes. This work also was popular. There were at least four editions before the end of the century.

PREACHING

In preaching, there were two formative influences, Erasmus and Melanchthon, and one major issue: the appropriateness of art in religious discourse. There is a long tradition in Christian writing that opposes all that is artificial, believing, after the fashion of Plato, that art is a form of hypocrisy. A true preacher, this tradition says, would set out the truth of religion simply, and the commitment of the preacher, together with the grace of God, will be enough.

The most famous exposition of this problem is to be found in Erasmus's dialogue *Ciceronianus* (The Ciceronian, 1528). One of the interlocutors relates that he had once gone to hear a famous Latin preacher in Rome, who was supposed to deliver what promised to be a tour de force in praise of Christ. The preacher, however, was of the rhetorical school that insisted upon the imitation of Cicero. Christian vocabulary, of course, was foreign to Cicero, who died before Christ was born, and so the preacher ridiculously used circumlocutions that recalled pagan Rome and not the church at all. Even more seriously, the preacher imitated the balanced artfulness of Cicero without capturing any of his moral seriousness or expressing any true religious conviction. Erasmus's story may well be fictional, but it captures something of sixteenth-century anxieties about oratory on matters of religion.

In his writings connected with preaching, Erasmus was always careful to emphasize the need for prayer and for a pure mind. Georges Chantraine points out in "Théologie et vie spirituelle: Un aspect de la méthode théologique selon Érasme" (Theology and Spiritual Life: An Aspect of the Theological Method of Erasmus, 1968) that Erasmus required that the task of preaching, as the reading of the Bible, be approached "with clean feet": in *Methodus* (Method, 1516), one of Erasmus's introductions to the New Testament, he used the figure of the Temple of Jerusalem, where one approaches the Holy of Holies by a series of stages, with purifications on the way. Book 1 of the *Ecclesiastes* was primarily concerned with the character and religious commitment of the preacher: the English clerics William Warham (circa 1450–1532) and John Fisher (circa 1469–1535) were prime examples. Erasmus also recognized that God might, although rarely, give the ability to preach to one who had never studied the art. Nevertheless, Erasmus's view of preaching involved much that could be seen in other circles as artificial and deceptive. The *Ecclesiastes* offered long discussions of figures and the effect that they might have on an audience. The key, for Erasmus, lay in the development of good moral character and discernment in the preacher. For Erasmus, it is safe for the preacher to use any device, if only he is properly prepared.

The role and mission of the preacher, for Erasmus, was in line with other elements of Erasmian doctrine. Good preaching would lead the souls of the faithful to greater perfection and would form and transfigure them. The preacher would use rhetorical technique to make sin horrible and blessedness attractive. He advocated the conscious use of figures but discouraged excessive theatricality. He recounted that an Italian preacher once wore armor into church under his habit, and at a dramatic moment tore off his robe to reveal his determination to be a Christian soldier. This act, thought Erasmus, was excessively contrived. His presentation of style as a result of artistic endeavor was matched with an insistence on sincerity. He insisted that no preacher can expect to move a congregation who was not moved himself.

The nature of the ideal preacher's discourse had much to do, according to Erasmus, with the virtue of vividness. In the *Ecclesiastes,* Erasmus described how a preacher should deal with the story of Jesus' healing of a paralytic, expanding on elements of the story to make vivid the desperate plight of the sick man, the charity of Jesus, and finally to preach how the congregation should bring the same virtues into their own lives. This emphasis on the personality of Christ was central both to Erasmus's theology and to his view of rhetoric: he saw the attainment of salvation as a true reception of discourse that flowed from the divine personality of Christ, and he viewed rhetoric as a contact between personalities resulting in transfiguration.

Melanchthon's scattered writings on preaching, particularly his *De officiis concionatoris* (On the Duties of the Preacher, 1529), carry his customary emphasis on dialectic and figures of amplification at the expense of tropes and stylistic effect. Although Melanchthon did not consistently condemn the use of stylistic artifice, his approach turned out to be congenial to those who did. Philosophically, one might ask why the artifice of invention is less artificial than that of style. The answer to this seems to be that intelligent invention merely allows the excellence of the subject matter to be shown to full advantage, while stylistic manipulation adds external persuasive devices to what is sufficient in itself.

Erasmus and Melanchthon offer a contrast in the oratorical genre assigned to preaching, and both contrast with a wide Catholic consensus. Erasmus defined preaching as belonging to the *genus suasorium,* the persuasive genre, an adapted form of Cicero's *genus deliberativum,* the deliberative genre. That is to say that the emphasis in preaching is on persuading the congregation to a point of view, to a decision. For Melanchthon and his Lutheran contemporaries, this genre smacked of rhetorical trickery, and that is why Melanchthon coined the *genus didaskalion* (teaching genre) based in dialectic, but open to emotional appeal. Some Catholic theorists preceding both (including Traversagni), and many afterward, saw preaching as belonging to the *genus demonstrativum,* the demonstrative or epideictic genre, the genre of praise and blame. The difficulty with this last genre for many others was that it was associated for Cicero with a gentle, pleasant way of speaking that was not felt to be appropriate in the pulpit.

The change in theology of the Reformation had its effect on preaching. For Luther, Melanchthon, and English converts such as Tyndale, there was a separation in religious experience between the terrible condemnation of God's law and the mercy of the promise. Protestant writers presented a model narrative of religious conversion that moved from the misery of knowing oneself condemned to the bliss of faith in God's grace. This theological structure can affect preaching in two ways: it may appear as the central movement within a sermon, or, as in Melanchthon's commentary on Timothy (1550 or 1551), may provide a taxonomy of sermons: the preacher may teach the principles of religion, may warn of damnation, or may comfort his parishioners with the hope of salvation. As he had rejected an emphasis on works, Melanchthon desired that preaching should focus on these matters of faith and not on the deeds of Christ, as the Italian tradition had done, and as Erasmus had advocated.

The debate over style in preaching reflects the terms of that over style in letter writing, but as if in reverse. With letters, the purist Ciceronian view insisted upon simplicity and brevity, while Erasmus held that a wider range of styles was required for different letters. With preaching, Erasmus came to be identified with a loosely Ciceronian view that justified the use of artifice in preaching, while the opposite tendency insisted upon abstention from all that is elaborate and a dependence on the preacher's emotion to produce emotion in the congregation.

In general, it appears that Erasmus's influence was strongest in England in the first half of the sixteenth century, and Melanchthon came to be more significant as the century wore on. In the first half of the century Erasmus's *Ecclesiastes* was widely read. Wilson used Erasmus's treatise as the main source for his many comments on preaching in his *The Arte of Rhetorique.* Even writers not particularly involved with preaching, such as Cox and Sherry, acknowledged their use of the *Ecclesiastes.* In the latter case, the relevant passage would be an extended discussion of figures in book 3. Erasmus's influence waned in the last half of the century in England but never disappeared. In the second half of the century, the Puritan notion of preaching as allowing the word to speak

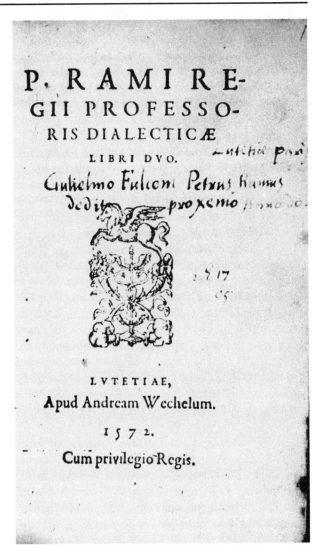

Title page for an edition of Petrus Ramus's writing on dialectic, published the year he was killed in the St. Bartholomew's Day Massacre

through the preacher encouraged distrust of artificiality. William Perkins (1558–1602) wished that the preacher should make people believe "that it is not he that speaketh, as the Spirit of God in him and by him." Even so orthodox an Anglican as Richard Hooker (1553–1600) stressed the "spirit" over technique. While Erasmus had accepted the need for inspiration, the greater the emphasis on inspiration, the more an obviously skillful preacher might be seen as a deceptive hypocrite. The anxiety about skillful deception is plain in *The Faerie Queene* (1590–1609) of Edmund Spenser (circa 1552–1599), in which deceptive characters such as Duessa repeatedly take in the virtuous and ignorant, leading them into sin.

Ramus's point of view on discourse, stressing firm logic and regarding ornament as external, is naturally consistent with the "plain style" view of preaching.

Ramist styles of writing tend toward a plainly evident logical line. Owing to this feature, and perhaps also to Ramus's own Calvinist convictions, Ramistic works were popular in English Puritan milieu. There are no extant Puritan manuals of preaching, which may well be because any such manual would have raised the suspicion of artificiality and deception. The logical method of Ramus might have been enough.

A Melanchthonian model of preaching first appeared in English in *The Preacher* (1574), a translation of Niels Hemmingsen's *Pastor siue Pastoris optimus vivendi agendique modus* (The Pastor, or the best way of life and action of a pastor, before 1574). Three years later Andreas Hyperius's *De formandis concionibus sacris* (On Forming Sacred Sermons, first published in 1553) appeared under the title *The Practis of Preaching* (1577). These treatises, as Debora Shuger shows in *Sacred Rhetoric: The Christian Grand Style in the English Renaissance* (1988), follow Melanchthon in emphasizing figures of amplification. Already with Hyperius, however, other figures have begun to reappear. In Hyperius as in Erasmus and in the later works of Melanchthon, vividness of presentation is very important as a means of moving the emotions of the parishioners. Hyperius rejected the notion of fitting preaching into the classical genres, claiming that genres for preaching should be drawn from the Bible.

The *Clavis scripturæ sacræ* (Key to the Sacred Scripture, 1562) by Matthias Flacius Illyricus (Matija Vlacik; circa 1520–1575) appears to Shuger a key text in the development of preaching rhetoric, even though it is not of itself a rhetoric, but an analysis of biblical language. Flacius used Hermogenes and Demetrius extensively, discussing the condensed poetic style of the Bible and the impact of biblical style on religious readers: it can "move, form and reform their hearts . . . until finally Christ is formed in them." Flacius's link between stylistic features and emotion contrasted with the insistence on plainness that characterized most Protestant writing on preaching in his time. Like Erasmus and then Hyperius, Flacius stressed vividness as calling forth a strong emotional response.

Keckermann published a treatise on preaching titled *De rhetorica ecclesiastica* (On Ecclesiastical Rhetoric, 1600), and in his general rhetoric, *Systema rhetoricae,* he exercised some influence over the development of an emotional "Christian grand style" in England. In the overall tension between the Melancthonian and Erasmian traditions, Keckermann represents a development of the Erasmian view of preaching, with close attention being given to the audience's emotional response to the preacher's words. In reaction to the Ramist division of dialectic from rhetoric, Keckermann treated both together. Vossius, a Dutch Protestant, published a series of works beginning with *Institutiones oratoriæ* (Oratorical

Institutes, 1609). More radically than any of the rhetoricians seen, Vossius based his ideas on Aristotle, but, Conley points out, he follows Keckermann in stressing emotional impact over dialectic. He presented his work as a response to Ramus's railing against Aristotle and Cicero.

PROSE STYLE

There were also shifts in the style of published artistic prose. Toward the end of the sixteenth century, a strong anti-Ciceronian movement in prose style arose under the leadership of Joest Lips or Justus Lipsius (1547–1606). Lipsius came from a Catholic family in what is now Belgium. He initially attended a Jesuit school, but his parents withdrew him from it for fear of excessive Jesuit influence over him. As he began his career his main influences were Melanchthon, Sturm, and the Venetian humanist Pietro Bembo (1470–1547), all Ciceronians. He became a professor at the Calvinist university of Leiden. While there, he wrote a treatise justifying the execution of Protestants by burning, *Politicorum, sive Civilis Doctrinæ Libri Sex* (Six Books of Politics, or of Civil Doctrine, 1589). Remarkably enough, he remained at the same university for another two years before leaving, apparently of his own will. He joined a Jesuit community in Leuven and devoted himself to the cause of the Catholic Reformation until he died in 1606.

By the account of Morris Croll in "Juste Lipse et le Mouvement Anticicéronien à la fin du XVIe et au Début du XVIIe Siècle" (Joest Lips and the Anti–Ciceronian Movement at the end of the 16th and the beginning of the 17th Century, 1966), Lipsius received his education in a world of rigid Ciceronianism. Lipsius's teachers and influences encouraged oratorical writing in long, rolling periods. Lipsius wrote in this style for some time before beginning to admire the styles of Seneca and Tacitus. Neither has the beautiful balance of Cicero, but they rather tend to offer short, pithy *sententiæ,* lacking harmony, but carrying expressiveness. In 1569 Lipsius published an anthology of classical Latin writings that featured Seneca and Tacitus, *Variae lectiones* (Various Readings). In 1577 he set out some of his principles in *Quæstiones Epistolicæ* (Epistolary Questions). He produced an edition of the works of Tacitus in 1575 and immediately began to work on one of Seneca, which appeared only in 1605, the year before his death.

Both the significance of this movement and its impact on England have been the subject of some discussion by modern scholars. For most of the twentieth century the view of Croll prevailed: Senecanism constituted a positive movement from Renaissance obscurantism toward the clarity of modern science. The greater simplicity of expression in Lipsius's Senecan movement enabled the kind of limpid thought necessary for scientific investigation. The truth of this observation may be seen in the subsequent work and reputations of major Senecan figures: Michel de Montaigne (1533–1592) and especially Francis Bacon (1561–1626). Croll's presentation of Senecan prose as near to science has come under attack from Shuger in her *Sacred Rhetoric,* while Brian Vickers, in "Bacon and Rhetoric" (1996), denies that Bacon was Senecan at all.

This issue has not yet been settled. Meanwhile, it does seem clear that Lipsius's work was known in England, and even if Bacon was not a Senecan, it seems likely that Lipsius's approach to rhetoric influenced other writers.

VERNACULAR POETICS

The last area of potential influence of Continental rhetoricians on English writings lies in vernacular poetics. Here, the problem divides in two: there was a need to defend poetry itself in England against Puritans, and a need to defend the vernacular as an appropriate medium for writing poetry.

The arguments in defense of poetry, and the general philosophical view of what poetry is, derive partly from Julius Caesar Scaliger (1484–1558). Scaliger was an Italian soldier and physician who settled in Agen, southwestern France, in 1524 or 1525. Apparently his motive was love: he married a young woman from Agen. He knew the writer François Rabelais (circa 1490–1553) there, and he began a life of letters. In 1531 he took the attention of the humanist world by opposing Erasmus's *Ciceronianus* in print in *Pro Cicerone, contra Desiderium Erasmum* (For Cicero, against Desiderius Erasmus). In 1535, like so many other rhetoricians, he was obliged to defend himself against a charge of heresy. His last years were devoted to the massive and posthumous *Poetices libri septem* (Seven Books of Poetics, 1561). Like Erasmus and Sidney he regarded poetry largely in the light of incitement to virtue. In this work he defended the legitimacy of poetry against the critique of Plato, holding that Virgil had succeeded in resolving the danger of poetry to the state, and that he was therefore superior to Homer. He is sometimes credited with originating the detailed *explication de texte* tradition of literary criticism.

In the sixteenth century considerable attention came to be paid to Aristotle's *Poetics,* and particularly to the commentary of Ludovico Castelvetro (1505–71; translation and commentary of the *Poetics,* 1570). The commentator's most famous innovation was the introduction of the three unities in theater: that is, Castelvetro laid down the rule that plays must take place within one day, within the limits of one town, and have a single plot. Sidney supported these restrictions in his *Apologie for Poetrie* (1595), but owing to Shakespeare, they had not much fortune in English vernacular literature. These views of liter-

ature relate to rhetoric, insofar as plays were consciously rhetorical products, written with the categories of the rhetoricians in mind. The consideration of aesthetic categories as such mark the beginnings of a division between poetry and consciously rhetorical discourse.

The other Italian writer on poetics who needs to be mentioned is Antonio Sebastiano Minturno, Bishop of Crotona (circa 1500–74), whose Latin *De poeta* (On the Poet, 1559) and Italian *L'Arte poetica* (The Art of Poetry, 1563) apparently influenced Sidney. Sidney adopted Minturno's notion that "admiration" should be added to Aristotle's "pity and fear" as the emotions involved with tragic catharsis.

The movement to the vernacular was closely associated with the defense of poetry. In the fifteenth century and well into the sixteenth century, humanism had been largely a Latin-speaking and Latin-writing movement. Humanists loved the notion of a *res publica litterarum,* a commonwealth of letters, united by a single international language. That is why More wrote the *Utopia* in Latin and published it on the Continent. Yet, there were movements in favor of the vernacular, and those who spoke different languages influenced each other in writing on these topics. Most relevant to England are the French writings on vernacular poetry, particularly *Deffence et illustration de la langue françoise* (Defense and Illustration of the French Language, 1549) of Joachim Du Bellay (circa 1522–1560). This work offers several arguments for writing in the vernacular, borrowed from the *Dialogo delle Lingue* (Dialogue of Languages, 1542) of Sperone Speroni (1500–1588). Among other arguments, such treatises depend heavily on Cicero as the defender of his own language, Latin, against Greek. Similar points, whether drawn from Du Bellay or not, appear in the *Arte of English Poesie* (1589) of George Puttenham (circa 1529–1591) and the *Apologie for Poetrie* of Sidney. Meerhoff suggests in *Rhétorique et poétique au XVIe siècle en France* (Rhetoric and Poetics in the Sixteenth Century in France, 1986) that Ramism was also significant in promoting the vernacular, since Ramus's *Ciceronianus et Brutinæ quæstiones* (The Ciceronian and Brutus' Problems, 1574), though in Latin, included an argument to this effect.

In France there was also a tradition of rhetorics of poetry in the vernacular, such as the *Art poétique françois* (French Art of Poetry, 1548) of Thomas Sebillet (1512–1589). The art of poetry was often known as "second rhetoric," and vernacular treatises discussed poetic questions in these terms. An important question, as Meerhoff has shown in *Rhétorique et poétique au XVIe siècle en France,* was the nature of poetic rhythm and its relation to classical meters and authorities. In England, as in France, there were factions that favored the importation of classical meters into the vernacular. In both countries modern

Juan Luis Vives (engraving by Jean Jacques Boissard, 1541) and the title page for Vives's polemical work against university philosophers

accentual-syllabic meters won out, partly owing to the prestige of Dante Alighieri (1265–1321) and Petrarch.

In England three works offered defenses at once of poetry and of the vernacular, while presenting some sort of comment on the use of good technique in the writing of verse. It appears that the immediate stimulus was a pamphlet by Stephen Gosson (1554–1624), *Schoole of Abuse* (1579), which is a condemnation of poetry and theater. For defense against such attacks, Bembo and Du Bellay had established that an essential step in defending the legitimacy of vernacular writing was to discuss whether worthy models of imitation existed in the vernacular. The two had differed in their approach to the question: Bembo held that Dante, Petrarch, and Boccaccio were such models, while Du Bellay only expressed a determination that such models should exist in the future. William Webbe (flourished 1568–1591), in *Discourse of English Poetry* (1586), put Spenser forward as such a model. Sidney was more classically oriented. Nevertheless, he praised Geoffrey Chaucer (died 1400) and John Gower (1325–1408) as equivalents of the earliest Roman poets, such as Ennius.

Puttenham appears as an eclectic, discussing a large number of poets in *The Arte of English Poesie*. His treatise is the work on poetry that is most firmly ensconced in the rhetorical tradition. The standard edition, edited by Gladys Doidge Willcock and Alice Walker in 1936, provides sources (Erasmus and Susenbrotus) for examples used in the text, but tends to assert more originality than seems likely. In his introduction to a 1970 facsimile edition, Baxter Hathaway more credibly suggests that the work is thoroughly conventional and derives largely from Italian and French treatises preceding the Aristotelian movement that influenced Sidney.

At the beginning of the sixteenth century, classical rhetoric, as revived in Italy, had been practically unknown in England. The movements that became significant to England were largely Flemish and Dutch, because of Agricola, Erasmus, Vives, and later Lipsius. Where German influences became primary was in preaching, since English loyalty to a general Protestant cause led to a great influence of Melanchthon and other Lutheran writers on sacred eloquence. Early in the century, even Valla's influence was largely mediated through Erasmus. As the century wore on and rhetoric became increasingly involved with literary issues, there came to be more direct influence of Italian ideas. It cannot be overemphasized that within the sixteenth century there is no independent English tradition of rhetorical writings. The main current of rhetorical thought was always elsewhere, and English writings carry originality only as variations on that main theme.

References:
General Histories of Rhetoric

Thomas M. Conley, *Rhetoric in the European Tradition* (New York: Longman, 1990);

Anthony Grafton and Lisa Jardine, *From Humanism to the Humanities: Education and the Liberal Arts in Fifteenth- and Sixteenth-Century Europe* (Cambridge, Mass.: Harvard University Press, 1986);

Hanna H. Gray, "Renaissance Humanism: The Pursuit of Eloquence," in *Renaissance Essays: From the Journal of the History of Ideas,* edited by Paul Oskar Kristeller and Philip P. Wiener (New York: Harper & Row, 1968), pp. 199–216;

Jill Kraye, ed., *The Cambridge Companion to Renaissance Humanism* (Cambridge: Cambridge University Press, 1996);

Paul Oskar Kristeller, *Renaissance Thought: The Classic, Scholastic, and Humanist Strains* (New York: Harper & Row, 1961);

R. P. McKeon, "Rhetoric in the Middle Ages," in his *Rhetoric: Essays in Invention and Discovery,* edited by Mark Backman (Woodbridge, Conn.: Ox Bow Press, 1987), pp. 121–166;

James J. Murphy, ed., *Medieval Eloquence: Studies in the Theory and Practice of Medieval Rhetoric* (Berkeley: University of California Press, 1978);

Murphy, ed., *Renaissance Eloquence: Studies in the Theory and Practice of Renaissance Rhetoric* (Berkeley: University of California Press, 1983);

Heinrich Plett, *English Renaissance Rhetoric and Poetics: A Systematic Bibliography of Primary and Secondary Sources* (Leiden, New York & Cologne: E. J. Brill, 1995);

Charles Edward Trinkaus, *In Our Image and Likeness: Humanity and Divinity in Italian Humanist Thought,* 2 volumes (London: Constable, 1970; Notre Dame, Ind.: University of Notre Dame Press, 1995);

Brian Vickers, *In Defence of Rhetoric* (Oxford: Clarendon Press, 1989).

The Early Renaissance

Hans Baron, *The Crisis of the Early Italian Renaissance,* second edition (Princeton: Princeton University Press, 1966);

Eugenio Garin, *Italian Humanism: Philosophy and Civic Life in the Renaissance,* translated by Peter Munz (New York: Harper & Row, 1965);

Eugene F. Rice, *The Renaissance Idea of Wisdom* (Cambridge, Mass.: Harvard University Press, 1958);

Nancy S. Struever, *The Language of History in the Renaissance: Rhetoric and Historical Consciousness in Florentine Humanism* (Princeton: Princeton University Press, 1970).

Lorenzo Valla

Salvatore I. Camporeale, "Renaissance Humanism and the Origins of Humanist Theology," in *Humanity and Divinity in Renaissance and Reformation: Essays in Honour of Charles Trinkaus,* edited by John W. O' Malley, Thomas M. Izbicki, and Gerald Christianson, Studies in the History of Christian Thought, no. 51 (Leiden & New York: E. J. Brill, 1993), pp. 101–124;

Maristella de Panizza Lorch, *A Defense of Life: Lorenzo Valla's Theory of Pleasure* (Munich: W. Fink Verlag, 1985);

Charles Trinkaus, "Lorenzo Valla," in *Contemporaries of Erasmus: A Biographical Register of the Renaissance and Reformation,* edited by Peter G. Bietenholz, volume 3 (Toronto: University of Toronto Press, 1985), pp. 371–375;

Richard Waswo, *Language and Meaning in the Renaissance* (Princeton: Princeton University Press, 1987).

Angelo Poliziano

Anthony Grafton, *Defenders of the Text: The Traditions of Scholarship in an Age of Science, 1450–1800* (Cambridge, Mass.: Harvard University Press, 1991).

Lorenzo Traversagni

Larry D. Green, "Classical and Medieval Rhetorical Traditions in Traversagni's *Margarita Eloquentiae,*" *Quarterly Journal of Speech,* 72 (1986): 185–196;

Ronald H. Martin, ed., *The Epitome Margarite Castigate Eloquentie of Laurentius Guglielmus Traversagni de Saona* (Leeds: Leeds Philosophical and Literary Society, 1986);

James J. Murphy, "The Double Revolution of the First Rhetorical Textbook Published in England: The *Margarita Eloquentiae* of Gulielmus Traversagnus (1479)," *Texte,* 8/9 (1989): 367–376.

George Trebizond

John Monfasani, *George of Trebizond: A Biography and a Study of his Rhetoric and Logic* (Leiden: E. J. Brill, 1976);

Monfasani, ed., *Collectanea Trapezuntiana: Texts, Documents and Bibliographies of George of Trebizond* (Binghamton, N.Y.: Medieval & Renaissance Texts & Studies / Renaissance Society of America , 1984);

Remigio Sabbadini, *Il metodo degli umanisti* (Florence: F. Le Monnier, 1920).

Rodolphus Agricola

Gerda C. Huisman, *Rudolph Agricola: A Bibliography of Printed Works and Translations* (Nieuwkoop: De Graaf, 1985);

C. G. van Leijenhorst, "Rodolphus Agricola," in *Contemporaries of Erasmus: A Biographical Register of the Renaissance and Reformation,* edited by Peter G. Bietenholz (Toronto: University of Toronto Press, 1985), pp. 15–17;

Peter Mack, *Renaissance Argument: Valla and Agricola in the Traditions of Rhetoric and Dialectic* (Leiden & New York: E. J. Brill, 1993).

Desiderius Erasmus

Charles Béné, *Érasme et saint Augustin ou Influence de saint Augustin sur l'humanisme d'Érasme* (Geneva: Droz, 1969);

Terence Cave, *"'Enargeia':* Erasmus and the Rhetoric of Presence in the Sixteenth Century," *L'Esprit créateur,* 16, no. 4 (1976): 5–19;

Jacques Chomarat, *Grammaire et rhétorique chez Érasme,* 2 volumes (Paris: Belles Lettres, 1981);

André Godin, "The *Enchiridion Militis Christiani:* The Modes of an Origenian Appropriation," *Erasmus of Rotterdam Society Yearbook,* 2 (1982): 48–79;

Godin, "Notes sur Érasme et le sacré," *Miscellanea Moreana* (special *Moreana* issue), 26 (1988): 39–53;

Manfred Hoffmann, *Rhetoric and Theology: The Hermeneutic of Erasmus* (Toronto & Buffalo: University of Toronto Press, 1994);

Johan Huizinga, *Erasmus and the Age of Reformation,* translated by F. Hopman (Princeton: Princeton University Press, 1984);

Lisa Jardine, *Erasmus, Man of Letters: The Construction of Charisma in Print* (Princeton: Princeton University Press, 1993);

James K. McConica, *English Humanists and Reformation Politics under Henry VIII and Edward VI* (Oxford: Clarendon Press, 1965);

Silvana Seidel Menchi, *Erasmus als Ketzer: Reformation und Inquisition im Italien des 16. Jahrhunderts* (Leiden & New York: E. J. Brill, 1993);

John C. Olin, "Introduction: A Biographical Sketch," in *Christian Humanism and the Reformation: Selected Writings of Erasmus, with His Life by Beatus Rhenanus and a Biographical Sketch by the Editor,* edited by Olin, third edition (New York: Fordham University Press, 1987), pp. 1–38;

R. J. Schoeck, *Erasmus of Europe: The Making of a Humanist, 1467–1500* (Edinburgh: Edinburgh University Press, 1990);

Schoeck, *Erasmus of Europe: The Prince of Humanists, 1501–1536* (Edinburgh: Edinburgh University Press, 1993);

M.A. Screech, *Erasmus: Ecstasy and the Praise of Folly* (London & New York: Penguin, 1980).

Philip Melanchthon

Kees Meerhoff, "The Significance of Philip Melanchthon's Rhetoric in the Renaissance," *Renaissance Rhetoric,* edited by Peter Mack (New York: St. Martin's Press, 1994), pp. 46–62;

Christian Mouchel, "Figures et adéquation dans la doctrine oratoire de Philippe Mélanchthon," *Études Littéraires,* 24 (Winter 1991–1992): 49–62;

Heinz Scheible, "Philip Melanchthon," in *Contemporaries of Erasmus: A Biographical Register of the Renaissance and Reformation,* edited by Peter G. Bietenholz, volume 2 (Toronto: University of Toronto Press, 1985), pp. 424–429;

Timothy J. Wengert, *Human Freedom, Christian Righteousness: Philip Melanchthon's Exegetical Dispute with Erasmus of Rotterdam* (New York: Oxford University Press, 1997);

Wengert and M. Patrick Graham, eds., *Philip Melanchthon (1497–1560) and the Commentary* (Sheffield, U.K.: Sheffield Academic Press, 1997).

Petrus Ramus

Wilbur S. Howell, *Logic and Rhetoric in England, 1500–1700* (Princeton: Princeton University Press, 1956);

Kees Meerhoff, "Agricola et Ramus—Dialectique et rhétorique," in *Rodolphus Agricola Phrisus 1444–1485: Proceedings of the International Conference at the University of Groningen, 28–30 October 1985,* edited by F. Akkerman & A. J. Vaderjagt (Leiden: E. J. Brill, 1988), pp. 275;

Guido Oldrini, "Le Particolarita del Ramismo Inglese," *Rinascimento,* 25 (1985): 19–80;

Walter J. Ong, *Ramus: Method, and the Decay of Dialogue; From the Art of Discourse to the Art of Reason* (Cambridge, Mass.: Harvard University Press, 1958);

Rosemond Tuve, *Elizabethan and Metaphysical Imagery: Renaissance Poetic and Twentieth–Century Critics* (Chicago: University of Chicago Press, 1947).

Education

T. W. Baldwin, *William Shakspere's Small Latine & Lesse Greeke,* 2 volumes (Urbana: University of Illinois Press, 1944);

Marcel Bataillon, *Érasme et l'Espagne* (Paris: Droz, 1937);

Joseph Xavier Brennan, trans., "The *Epitome Troporum ac Schematum* of Joannes Susenbrotus: Text, Translation, and Commentary," dissertation, University of Illinois, 1953;

Richard L. DeMolen, *Richard Mulcaster (c. 1531–1611) and Educational Reform in the Renaissance* (Nieuwkoop, The Netherlands: De Graaf, 1991);

Charles Fantazzi, ed., Introduction, *De conscribendis Epistolis: Critical Edition with Introduction, Translation, and Annotation,* by Juan Luis Vives (Leiden & New York: E. J. Brill, 1989), pp. 5–9;

Rita Guerlac, Introduction, *Juan Luis Vives Against the Pseudodialecticians: A Humanist Attack on Medieval Logic* (Dordrecht, Holland: D. Reidel, 1979), pp. 1–46;

Guerlac, "Vives, Juan Luis (1493–1540)," in *Routledge Encyclopedia of Philosophy,* edited by Edward Craig, 10 volumes (London & New York: Routledge, 1998), IX: 645–650;

Jean-Claude Margolin, ed., *Declamatio de pueris statim ac liberaliter instituendis: Étude critique, traduction et commen-*

taire, by Erasmus of Rotterdam (Geneva: Droz, 1966);

Connie McQuillen, ed. and trans., *A Comedy Called Susenbrotus,* anonymous (Ann Arbor: University of Michigan Press, 1997);

Jo Ann Hoeppner Moran, *The Growth of English Schooling 1340–1548: Learning, Literacy, and Laicization in Pre-Reformation York Diocese* (Princeton: Princeton University Press, 1985);

Joan Simon, *Education and Society in Tudor England* (Cambridge: Cambridge University Press, 1966);

Lewis W. Spitz and Barbara Sher Tinsley, introduction to their *Johann Sturm on Education: The Reformation and Humanist Learning* (St. Louis: Concordia, 1997), pp. 19–44;

Brian Vickers, *Classical Rhetoric in English Poetry,* revised edition (Carbondale: Southern Illinois University Press, 1989), pp. 48–54;

Vickers, "Some Reflections on the Rhetoric Textbook," in *Renaissance Rhetoric,* edited by Peter Mack, pp. 81–102.

Letter Writing

Thomas W. Best, *Macropedius* (New York: Twayne, 1972);

Judith Rice Henderson, "Erasmian Ciceronians: Reformation Teachers of Letter–Writing," *Rhetorica,* 10 (Summer 1992): 273–302;

Henderson, "Erasmus on the Art of Letter–Writing," in *Renaissance Eloquence: Studies in the Theory and Practice of Renaissance Rhetoric,* edited by Murphy (Berkeley: University of California Press, 1983), pp. 331–355;

Henderson, "Humanism in the Humanities: Erasmus' *Opus de conscribendis epistolis* in Sixteenth-Century Schools," forthcoming in *Letter-Writing Manuals from Antiquity to the Present,* edited by Carol Poster and Linda Mitchell (Columbia: University of South Carolina Press);

Katherine Gee Hornbeak, *The Complete Letter Writer in English 1568–1800,* Smith College Studies in Modern Languages (Northampton, Mass.: Smith College, 1934).

Preaching

Georges Chantraine, "Théologie et vie spirituelle: Un aspect de la méthode théologique selon Érasme," *Nouvelle revue théologique,* 91 (1968): 809–833;

John R. Knott Jr., *The Sword of the Spirit: Puritan Responses to the Bible* (Chicago: University of Chicago Press, 1980);

John W. O'Malley, "Content and Rhetorical Forms in Sixteenth–Century Treatises on Preaching," in *Renaissance Eloquence: Studies in the Theory and Practice*

of Renaissance Rhetoric, edited by Murphy (Berkeley: University of California Press, 1983), pp. 238–252;

O'Malley, *Praise and Blame in Renaissance Rome: Rhetoric, Doctrine and Reform in the Sacred Orators of the Papal Court, c. 1450–1521* (Durham, N.C.: Duke University Press, 1979);

C. S. M. Rademaker, *Life and Work of Gerardus Joannes Vossius (1577–1649)* (Assen, The Netherlands: Van Gorcum, 1981);

Debora Shuger, *Sacred Rhetoric: The Christian Grand Style in the English Renaissance* (Princeton: Princeton University Press, 1988).

Prose Style and Senecanism

Morris W. Croll, "Attic Prose: Lipsius, Montaigne, Bacon," in his *Style, Rhetoric and Rhythm: Essays,* edited by J. Max Patrick and others (Princeton: Princeton University Press, 1966), pp. 167–202;

Croll, "Juste Lipse et le Mouvement Anticicéronien à la fin du XVIe et au Début du XVIIe Siècle," in his *Style, Rhetoric and Rhythm: Essays,* edited by J. Max Patrick, and others (Princeton: Princeton University Press, 1966), pp. 7–44;

Brian Vickers, "Bacon and Rhetoric," in *The Cambridge Companion to Bacon,* edited by Markku Peltonen (Cambridge: Cambridge University Press, 1996), pp. 200–231.

Vernacular Poetics

Visnavath Chatterjee, introduction to *An Apology for Poetry,* by Philip Sidney (London: Sangam, 1975);

Vernon Hall Jr., *Life of Julius Caesar Scaliger (1484–1558)* (Philadelphia: American Philosophical Society, 1950);

Baxter Hathaway, Introduction, *The Arte of English Poesie: Contrived into Three Bookes: the First of Poets and Poesie, the Second of Proportion, the Third of Ornament* by George Puttenham (Kent, Ohio: Kent State University Press, 1970), pp. v–xxxvii;

Kees Meerhoff, Introduction, *Rhétorique et poétique au XVIe siècle en France: Du Bellay, Ramus et les autres* (Leiden: E. J. Brill, 1986), pp. 1–20;

Geoffrey Shepherd, ed., *An Apology for Poetry, or, The Defence of Poesy,* by Philip Sidney (London: Nelson, 1965);

Brian Vickers, "Rhetoric and Poetics," in *The Cambridge History of Renaissance Philosophy,* edited by Charles B. Schmitt and others (Cambridge & New York: Cambridge University Press, 1988), pp. 715–745;

Gladys Doidge Willcock and Alice Walker, eds., *The Arte of English Poesie,* by George Puttenham (Cambridge: Cambridge University Press, 1936).

Glossary of Terms and Definitions of Rhetoric and Logic

The terms in this glossary often had multiple meanings during the Renaissance. Only the most common definitions have been given here. For additional definitions and terms, see Warren Taylor's *Tudor Figures of Rhetoric* (1937), Lee A. Sonnino's *A Handbook to Sixteenth-Century Rhetoric* (1968), and Richard Lanham's *A Handlist of Rhetoric Terms: A Guide for Students of English Literature* (1968), as well as the *Oxford English Dictionary*. Following the glossary are selected Renaissance definitions of rhetoric and logic, demonstrating how those arts were viewed by the subjects of this volume and their contemporaries.

Glossary of Terms

Actio (Action)—oratorical delivery; same as *pronuntiatio*.

Amplificatio (Amplification)—same as *confirmatio*.

Anadiplosis—the repetition of a word at the end of one sentence and the beginning of the next.

Anaphora—the repetition of a word at the beginnings of successive sentences.

Antanaclasis—the repetition of a word in a different sense.

Anthimeria—the substitution of one part of speech for another (e.g., I salted my fries and *ketchuped* my hamburger).

Anthypophora—same as *hypophora*.

Antimetabole—the grammatical inversion of repeated words (e.g., We're here to stay, but not staying here).

Antithesis—the juxtaposition of contrasting ideas in similar grammatical structures (e.g., Neither the promise of Heaven nor the threat of Hell could convince them).

Antonomasia—the generic use of a proper name or the use of an epithet in place of a proper name.

Aporia—the expression of insincere doubt; feigned indecision.

Aposiopesis—stopping abruptly in the middle of a sentence.

Apostrophe—an address to an absent or deceased person or an inanimate object.

Asyndeton—the omission of an expected coordinating conjunction (e.g., Take my hand, my heart, my hope).

Catachresis—a farfetched comparison, or the use of a word in a strained sense.

Cheria or *chria*—a wise saying from an unknown source; also the name of one of the composition exercises included in the *progymnasmata*.

Climax—a gradual building toward a conclusion.

Commonplace—a general theme or argument suitable for memorization and later use in speaking or writing.

Confirmatio (Confirmation)—the arguments in support of the speaker's position; one of the several parts of an oration.

Confutatio (Confutation)—a speaker's rebuttal to possible objections or counterarguments; one of the several parts of an oration.

Congeries—a form of listing or enumeration; also called "word heaping."

Definitio (Definition)—definition of terms and issues to be discussed; one of the several parts of an oration.

Deliberative—a branch of rhetoric dealing with exhorting and dissuading (see also *judicial* and *epideictic*).

Diacope—same as *tmesis*.

Diaphora—the same as *ploce,* only with common nouns rather than proper ones.

Dispositio (Disposition)—arrangement, organization; one of the five parts, or canons, of rhetoric.

Ecphonesis—an expression of strong emotion, often an extended exclamation.

Ecphrasis—same as *energia*.

Elench—a fallacy; in another sense, a logical refutation.

Ellipsis—the omission of a grammatically understood word or phrase (e.g., Just as a dog at a stranger, an old man barks fearfully at change, a father at his son, a teacher at his students).

Elocutio (Elocution)—style or ornamentation; one of the five parts, or canons, of rhetoric.

Enallage–the substitution of one grammatical form for another (e.g., dative for accusative case, third-person masculine for first-person singular).

Energia–a lively description.

Enthymeme–a rhetorical syllogism in which the first two propositions (i.e., premises) are probable rather than certain.

Epanalepsis–the repetition of a word at the beginning and end of the same sentence.

Epanodos–the reiteration of something by naming and elaborating on its parts.

Epanorthosis–recalling a word to use a more correct one.

Epideictic–a branch of rhetoric dealing with praising and blaming (see also *deliberative* and *judicial*).

Epiphonema–summing up by way of exclamation or a wise saying.

Epiphora–the repetition of a word at the ends of successive sentences.

Epitrope–giving an opponent either serious or mock permission to do as he or she pleases.

Epizeuxis–the repetition of a word in rapid succession (e.g., Hurry, hurry, hurry!).

Ethos–persuasion by appeal to ethical values; one of three types of artificial proofs. See also *logos* and *pathos*.

Eutrepismus–dividing a subject into parts and discussing each part in order.

Exordium–introduction or entrance; one of the several parts of an oration.

Explicatio (Explication)–same as *definitio*.

Forensic–same as *judicial;* one of the three branches of rhetoric.

Formulae–model phrases and sentences for imitation.

Hendyadis–presenting two terms as coordinates, rather than one as a subordinate of the other (e.g., nice and hot for nicely hot).

Homoeiteleuton–the use of indeclinable words with similar endings (such as adverbs ending in –*ly*).

Homoeoptoton–the concentrated use of words with the same or similar inflectional endings (e.g., strong verbs ending in –*en*).

Hortatory–same as *deliberative;* one of three branches of rhetoric.

Hypallage–faulty syntax or arrangement of words to distort meaning (e.g., hours of long, hard work for long hours and hard work).

Hyperbation–a general term for any intentional disruption of the natural order of words; see also *hysteron proteron*.

Hyperbole–a form of intentional exaggeration (e.g., I can't answer a million questions at once).

Hypophora–asking a question and answering it immediately.

Hysteron proteron–deliberately violating temporal order (e.g., putting the later before the earlier).

Inventio (Invention)–discovery of matter or content; one of the five parts, or canons, of rhetoric.

Isocolon–syntactical balancing of several phrases or clauses.

Judicial–a branch of rhetoric dealing with accusing and defending (see also *deliberative* and *epideictic*).

Litotes–the affirmation of something by negation of its opposite (e.g., Not bad at all!).

Loci communes–a collection of *commonplaces* (wise sayings, choice phrases, and pithy sentences) that often consist of passages from the Bible or an author's writings.

Logos–persuasion by appeal to reason; one of three types of artificial proofs. See also *ethos* and *pathos*.

Meiosis–making something seem less than it really is; deliberate understatement.

Memoria (Memory)–memorization, mnemonics; one of the five parts, or canons, of rhetoric.

Mempsis–a complaint and/or emphatic request for help.

Metaphor–the use of a word in other than its literal sense.

Metonymy–referring to something by the name of its cause or effect or its subject or adjunct (e.g., The White House issued a press release).

Narratio (Narration)–the explanation of the facts; one of the several parts of an oration.

Orcos–the swearing of an oath to intensify or give credence to a statement.

Oxymoron–bringing together contradictory terms, usually an adjective and a noun (e.g., thunderous silence).

Panegyric–same as *epideictic;* one of the three branches of rhetoric.

Parenthesis–the insertion of a word or comment between two parts of a sentence.

Paronomasia–punning; playing with the meaning or sound of a word.

Parrhesia–free speech; speaking honestly, openly.

Partitio (Partition)–same as *propositio*.

Pathos–persuasion by appeal to emotions; one of three types of artificial proofs. See also *ethos* and *logos*.

Periphrasis–saying something in a roundabout way; circumlocution.

Peroratio (Peroration)–conclusion; one of the parts of an oration.

Personification–giving human characteristics to an animal or inanimate object.

Ploce–the repetition of a proper name in a different sense.

Polyptoton–the repetition of word in a different form (such as behold and beholden).

Polysyndeton–the use of several coordinating conjunctions where one is sufficient (e.g., They walked and ran and sat and talked).

Predicables–the five basic types of predication or assertions that can be made about a subject.

Predicaments–the ten Aristotelean categories of substance, quantity, quality, relation, place, time, posture, possession, action, and passion.

Progymnasmata–a series of composition exercises, such as retelling a famous story or composing a speech from a fictional point of view.

Pronuntiatio (Pronunciation)–oratorical delivery, including gesture and voice; one of the five parts, or canons, of rhetoric.

Propositio (Proposition)–the statement of the speaker's position; one of the several parts of an oration.

Prosopopoeia–same as personification.

Prosthesis–adding a letter or syllable to the beginning of a word.

Refutatio–same as *confutatio*.

Restrictio (Restriction)–qualifying or modifying what has already been said.

Scheme–a figure of speech that manipulates word arrangement to achieve its effect (see also *trope*).

Subjectio (Subjection)–same as *hypophora*.

Syllepsis–allowing one verb to serve two or more subjects differently; similar to *zeugma* (e.g., Tim hit a single, Mary a double, and Fred a spectator).

Syllogism–an argument with three propositions: a major premise, a minor premise, and a conclusion (e.g., All men are mortal. I am a man. Therefore, I am mortal.)

Symphoresis–same as *congeries*.

Synaeresis–shortening two syllables to one (e.g., ever to e'er).

Synecdoche–referring to something by the name of its whole or part or its genus or species.

Synoeciosis–the uniting of contraries; a term broader than *oxymoron* (e.g., His fever made the hot night cold).

Tapinosis–debasing something by naming it inappropriately (e.g., referring to a fancy restaurant as a joint).

Thaumasmus–expressing intense admiration or awe.

Threnos–an expression of grief at someone's suffering (e.g., a politician might lament the plight of starving refugees from a war).

Tmesis–the separation of the two parts of a compound noun by putting another word between them (e.g., in one famous poem the American poet E. E. Cummings invents the word *manunkind*).

Trope–a figure of speech that manipulates word meaning to achieve its effect (see also *scheme*).

Zeugma–allowing one verb to serve many subjects (e.g., Tim hit a single; Mary, a double; and Fred, a home run.).

Definitions of Rhetoric

Thomas Wilson (1553): "Rhetoric is an art to set forth by utterance of words matter at large, or as Cicero doth say, it is a learned, or rather an artificial, declaration of the mind in the handling of any cause called in contention, that may through reason largely be discussed."

Dudley Fenner (1584): "Rhetorike is an Arte of speaking finely."

Thomas Farnaby (1625): "Rhetorica est facultas de unaquaque re dicendi bene, & ad persuadendum accommodate" (Rhetoric is the faculty of discoursing well on anything whatsoever, and to persuading appropriately).

John Barton (1634): "Rhetorick is the skill of using daintie words, and comely deliverie, whereby to work upon mens affections."

John Prideaux (1650?): "Rhetorica est Ars ornatè dicendi. vel ut habet Arist. Facultas in quaq'. re videndi quid contingit esse Idoneum ad faciendam fidem" (Rhetoric is the art of speaking ornately, or, as Aristotle holds, the faculty of discerning in each case whatever is suitable to producing belief).

John Smith (1657): "Rhetorique is a faculty by which we understand what will serve our turn concerning any subject to win belief in the hearer: hereby likewise the end of the discourse is set forward, to wit, the affecting of the heart with the sense of the matter in hand."

Definitions of Logic

John Seton (1545): "Dialectica est scientia, probabiliter de quovis themate disserendi" (Dialectic is the science of discoursing probably on whatever theme you have).

Thomas Wilson (1551): "Logique is an Arte to reason probably, on bothe partes, of al matiers that be putte foorth, so ferre as the nature of euery thing can beare."

Roland Maclmaine (1574): "Dialecticke otherwise called Logicke, is an arte which teachethe to dispute well."

Thomas Blundeville (1599): "Logike is an Art which teacheth us to dispute probably on both sides of any matter that is propounded."

Robert Sanderson (1618): "Logica, quae & Synecdochicè Dialectica, est ars instrumentalis, dirigens mentem nostram in cognitionem omnium intelligibilium" (Logic, and by synecdoche dialectic, is an instrumental art that directs our minds towards the understanding of all things intelligible).

John Prideaux (1650?): "Logica artificialis, est Doctrina quae dirigit rationem innatam, ad quodvis intelligibile, dexterius librandum & discutiendum" (Artificial logic is an acquired skill that directs innate reason towards whatever you would have intelligible, skillfully balancing and breaking apart).

A Finding Guide to Key Works on Microfilm

Some of the British and Continental works discussed in this volume are available in facsimile editions, as part of either the Scolar Press's English Linguistics series or Da Capo Press's English Experience series; other works are available on microfiche in James J. Murphy's Renaissance Rhetoric: Key Texts (which includes works on rhetoric and logic) or on microfilm in British and Continental Rhetoric and Elocution (which includes works on rhetoric, logic, and grammar). Most of the British works on rhetoric and logic are also available on microfilm as part of Early English Books: 1475–1640 or English Books: 1641–1700. These collections are indexed in A. W. Pollard and G. R. Redgrave's *A Short-Title Catalogue* (second edition, 1976–1991) and Donald Wing's *Short-Title Catalogue* (second enlarged edition, 1982–1998), respectively. The following finder's guide has been provided to aid readers in locating works by the subjects of entries in this volume.

Format:
Author: Title of work, date (Catalogue #, Series Reel #: Postion #), and so forth.

Abbreviations for UMI Microfilm Series:
EE = Early English Books, 1475–1640
EB = Early English Books, 1641–1700
ET = Early English Books, Tract Supplement
TT = Thomason Tracts
EC = The Eighteenth Century
BC = British and Continental Rhetoric and Elocution

Abbreviations for Catalogues:
STC = A. W. Pollard, and others, *A Short-Title Catalogue of Books Printed in England, Scotland, & Ireland and of English Books Printed Abroad 1475–1640,* second edition (London: Bibliographical Society, 1976–1991).

Wing = Donald Wing, *Short-Title Catalogue of Books Printed in England, Scotland, Ireland, Wales, and British America and of English Books Printed in Other Countries 1641–1700,* second edition (New York: Modern Language Association, 1972–1994).

ESTC = English Short-Title Catalogue (on-line database).

Ascham, Roger: *The Scholemaster,* 1570 (STC 832, EE 1019:3), 1571 (STC 834, EE 167:13 or 908:7), 1573 (STC 835, EE 278:4), 1579 (STC 835.5, EE 1676:05), 1589 (STC 836, EE 278:5), 1711 (ESTC T139767, EC 1768:4), 1743 (ESTC T139958, EC 1768:5); *Toxophilvs,* 1545 (STC 837, EE 21:29), 1571 (STC 838, EE 306:8); 1589 (STC 839, 278:6); 1788 (ESTC T139768, EC 6216:4).

Bacon, Francis: *Of The Advancement and Proficience of Learning,* 1639/40 (STC 1167, EE 650:09), 1640 (STC 1167:3, EE 1739:68), 1640 (STC 1167:5, EE 1980:11), 1674 (Wing B312, EB 342:6); *Opera . . . De Dignitate & Augmentis Scientiarum,* 1623 (STC 1108, EE 691:03), 1624 (Paris), 1635 (Strasbourg), 1645 (Leiden), 1652 (Leiden), 1654 (Strasbourg), 1662 (Amsterdam); *Francisci de Verulamio . . . Instauratio Magna,* 1620 (STC 1162, EE 871:06), 1620 (STC 1163, EE 911:5); *The Tvvoo Bookes . . . Of the proficience and aduancement of Learning,* 1605 (STC 1164, EE 650:7), 1629 (STC 1165, EE 619:6), 1633 (STC 1166, EE 650:08).

Barton, John: *The Art of Rhetorick,* 1634 (STC 1540, EE 825:07); *The Latine Grammar,* 1652 (Wing B989aA, EB 2648:14).

Blount, Thomas: *The Academie of Eloquence,* 1654 (Wing B3321, EB 14:20 & TT 194:E.1526[1]), 1656 (Wing B3322, EB 1398:4 & BC 1:5), 1663 (Wing B3323, EB 2452:11), 1664 (Wing B3324, EB1119:14), 1670 (Wing B3325, EB 1544:1), 1683 (Wing B3326, EB 1223:3).

Blundeville, Thomas: *The Art of Logike,* 1599 (STC 3142, EE 197:04 & BC 1:6), 1617 (STC 3143, EE 1624:09), 1619 (STC 3144, EE 1058:07).

Bulwer, John: *Chirologia,* 1644 (Wing B5462, EB 85:2 & BC 2:2), 1644 (Wing B5462A, EB 1735:14 & TT 162:E.1092[1]), 1648 (Wing B5464); *Chironomia,* 1644 (part of Wing B5466, EB 85:2 & BC 2:2), 1644 (part of Wing B5467, EB 1735:14 & TT 162:E.1092[1]).

Butler, Charles: *Rameæ Rhetoricae Libri Dvo,* 1597 (STC 4196.5, EE 1773:12); *Rhetoricæ Libri Dvo,* 1598 (STC 4197, EE 185:7), 1600 (STC 4198), 1618 (STC 4199, EE 453:05 & EE 658:03), 1621 (STC 4199.5, EE 593:06 & ET E3:1.Harl.5963[411]), 1627 (STC 4199.7), 1629 (STC 4200, EE 1341:04 & BC 2:7), 1635 (STC 4200.5, EE 1921:3), 1642 (Wing B6264, EB 1456:29), 1642 (Wing B6265, EB 2328:4), 1642 (Leiden), 1649 (Wing B6266, EB 1588:1), 1655 (Wing B6267), 1667 (Wing B6267aA), 1671 (Wing B6267bA, EB 2423:2), 1684 (Wing B6267A, EB 206:9); *Oratoriæ Libri Dvo,* 1629 (STC 4194.5, EE 1811:4); 1633 (STC 4195, EE 1091:12), 1642 (part of Wing B6264, EB 1456:29), 1642 (part of Wing B6265, EB 2328:4).

Chappel, William: *Methodus concionandi,* 1648 (Wing C1956, EB 652:4); *The Preacher,* 1656 (Wing C1957, TT 212:E.1707[1] & BC 3:1); *The Use Of Holy Scripture,* 1653 (Wing C1958, 784:12).

Day, Angel: *The English Secretorie,* 1586 (STC 6401, EE 494:05 & BC 3:6), 1586 (ESTC S126195), 1592 (STC 6402, EE 1727:8), 1595 (STC 6403, EE 214:01), 1599 (STC 6404, EE 380:07), 1607 (STC 6405, EE 1348:16), 1614 (STC 6406, EE 1376:06), 1621 (STC 6406.5, EE 2076:1), 1625 (STC 6407, EE 1831:01), 1625 (STC 6407b, EE 1303:11), 1635 (STC 6408).

Farnaby, Thomas: *Figuræ, Tropi et Schemata,* 1616 (STC 10701.3); *Index Rhetoricvs,* 1625 (STC 10703), 1629 (STC 10703a, EE 592:03), 1629 (STC 10703.5, EE 834:06), 1633 (STC 10704, EE 790:19); *Index rhetoricus et oratorius,* 1640 (STC 10706, EE 2064:5), 1643 (Lyon), 1646 (Wing F454, EB 738:17 & BC 3:9), 1648 (Amsterdam), 1654 (Wing F455, EB 1615:9), 1659 (Amsterdam), 1659 (Wing F456, EB 1864:29), 1664 (Wing F456A, EB 2401:22), 1667 (Wing F456B, EB 1652:12), 1672 (Wing F453, EB 738:16), 1672 (Amsterdam), 1673 (Wing F457, EB 738:18), 1676 (Wing F457A, EB 1884:15), 1682 (Wing F458, EB 1884:16), 1684 (not listed in Wing), 1689 (Wing F459, EB 210:37), 1696 (Wing F460, EB 1964:10), 1704 (ESTC T123365, EC 2216:10), 1713 (ESTC T210893, EC 8955:06), 1728 (ESTC N47183); *Phrases elegantiores,* circa 1625 (STC 10706.4), circa 1627 (STC 10706.7, EE 644:05), 1631 (STC 10707, EE 1023:09), 1638 (STC 10708, EE 834.07), 1641 (Wing F464, EB 738:20), 1647 (Wing F461, EB 28:28), 1648 (Wing F461A), 1658 (Wing F462, EB 738:19), 1661 (Wing F462A), 1664 (Wing F463, EB 1402:13).

Fenner, Dudley: *The Artes of Logike and Rethorike,* 1584 (STC 10765.5, EE 1851: 20 & BC 3:10), 1584 (STC 10766, EE 224:05), 1584 (STC 10766.3, EE 1795:66); 1588 (STC 10767, EE 224:06 & EE 638:17), 1651 (part of Wing L433), 1681 (part of Wing H2212).

Fleming, Abraham: *A Panoplie of Epistles,* 1576 (STC 11049, EE 508:04).

Fraunce, Abraham: *The Arcadian Rhetorike,* 1588 (STC 11338, EE 1097:18 & BC 4:1); *The Lawiers Logike,* 1588 (STC 11343, EE 887:14 & BC 4:2), 1588 (STC 11344, EE 1137:12), 1588 (STC 11345, EE 1172:05).

Fullwood, William: *The Enimie of Idlenesse,* 1568 (STC 11476, EE 294:02), 1568 (STC 1477, EE 243:06), 1578 (STC 11478), 1571 (STC 11477, EE 243:07), 1582 (STC 11479, EE 567:11), 1586 (STC 11480, EE 343:05), 1593

(STC 11481, 1518:18), 1598 (STC 11482, EE 343:06), 1607 (STC 11482.4), 1612 (STC 11482.7, ET E2:2.Harl.5993[91]), and 1621 (STC 11483, EE 1518:19).

Lever, Ralph: *The Arte of Reason* (STC 15541, EE 994:19 & BC 5:11).

Peacham, Henry: *The Garden of Eloquence,* 1577 (STC 19497, EE 348:04, EE 969:08 & BC 6:2), 1593 (STC 19498, EE 331:6).

Perri, Henry: *Eglvryn Phraethineb,* 1595 (STC 19775, EE 1149:12).

Prideaux, John: *Tyrocinivm . . . expeditissimum,* 1629 (part of STC 20363, EE 1734:1), 1639 (part of STC 20364, EE 1756:4); *Heptades Logicae,* 1639 (part of STC 20364, EE 1756:4); *Hypomnemata,* circa 1650 (Wing P3430A, EB 1428:24); *Sacred Eloquence,* 1659 (Wing P 3433, TT 223:E.1790[2] & BC 6:5).

Rainolde, Richard: *A booke called the Foundacion of Rhetorike* (STC 20925a.5, EE 857:15).

Sherry, Richard: *Treatise of Schemes & Tropes* (STC 22428, EE 1007:11 & BC 7:2); *Treatise of the Figures,* 1555 (STC 22429, EE 353:13 & BC 7:3).

Taverner, Richard: *The garden of wysdom,* 1539 (STC 23711a, EE 147:20), 1543 (STC 23712, EE 154:15); circa 1547 (STC 23714, EE 1118:07), circa 1550 (STC 23715, EE 147:22); *The seco[n]d booke of the Garden of wysdome,* 1539 (STC 23712.5, EE 2086:7), circa 1542 (STC 23713, EE 147:21), circa 1547 (part of STC 23714, EE 1118:07), circa 1550 (part of STC 23715, EE 147:22); *Flores Aliqvot Sententiarvm,* 1540 (STC 10445, EE 39:12 & EE 79:03), 1544 (part of STC 24848, 158:12), 1547 (STC 10446, EE 38:13), 1550 (STC 10447, EE 38:14), 1550 (STC 10447, 51832:42c), 1556 (STC 10448, 506:11), 1563 (STC 24850+, EE 506:1), 1563 (STC 24850.7, EE 1825:9).

Vicars, Thomas: Χειραγωγία: *Manvdvctio,* 1621 (STC 24702, BC 7:8), 1624 (STC 24702.5), 1628 (STC 24703, EE 862:14), 1650 (Wing V333, EB 1558:51).

Wilkins, John: *Ecclesiastes,* 1646 (Wing W2188, TT 57:E.356[15]), 1646 (Wing W2188A, EB 620:10), 1647 (Wing W2189, EB 907:9), 1651 (Wing W2190, EB 907:10), 1653 (Wing W2191, EB 991:21), 1656 (Wing W2192, EB 969:19), 1659 (Wing W2192A, EB 1109:23 & EB 1624:16), 1669 (Wing W2193, EB 907:11), 1675 (Wing W2193A, EB 620:11), 1679 (Wing W2194, EB 589:2), 1693 (Wing W2195, EB 589:1 & EB 589:3), 1718 (ESTC T200330).

Wilson, Thomas: *The Arte of Rhetorique,* 1553 (STC 25799, EE 553:9 & BC 9:1), 1560 (STC 25800, EE 402:12), 1562 (STC 25801, EE 471:9), 1563 (STC 25802, EE 1504:02), 1567 (STC 25803, EE 1401:09), 1580 (STC 25804, EE 1124:02), 1584 (STC 25805, EE 403:1), 1585 (STC 25806, EE 1401:10); *The Rule of Reason,* 1551 (STC 25809, EE 1124:03), 1552 (STC 25810, EE 403:3), 1553 (STC 25811, EE 773:04), 1563 (STC 25812, EE 403:4), 1584? (STC 25813, EE 1053:06), 1584? (STC 2814, EE 403:5), 1580 (STC 25815, EE 1225:08).

Checklist of Further Readings

On the subject of rhetoric in Renaissance Britain and Continental Europe, some of the most important and useful studies in English are James J. Murphy's collection of essays titled *Renaissance Eloquence* (1983); Brian Vickers's *In Defense of Rhetoric* (1988), especially chapters 5–7, and the revised edition of his *Classical Rhetoric in English Poetry* (1989); Debra Shuger's *Sacred Rhetoric* (1988), for ecclesiastical rhetoric; Thomas M. Conley's *Rhetoric in the European Tradition* (1990), especially chapters 5 and 6; and Peter Mack's *Renaissance Rhetoric* (1994), another collection of essays. Howell's *Logic and Rhetoric in England, 1500–1700* (1956) and *Eighteenth-Century British Logic and Rhetoric* (1971) have been combined and republished as *History of Logic and Rhetoric in Britain, 1500–1800* (1999). The standard surveys of English letter-writing manuals are still Katherine Gee Hornbeak's *The Complete Letter Writer in English, 1568–1800* (1934) and Jean Robertson's *The Art of Letter Writing* (1942). Frances Amelia Yates's *The Art of Memory* (1966) is the seminal study of memory as art during the Renaissance. The best dictionaries of Renaissance figures of speech are Lee A. Sonnino's *A Handbook to Sixteenth-Century Rhetoric* (1968) and Richard A. Lanham's *A Handlist of Rhetorical Terms* (1968). Two journals that often publish articles on Renaissance rhetoric are *Rhetorica* and *Rhetoric Society Quarterly*.

Some of the most important secondary literature on Renaissance rhetoric is not available in English: Cesare Vasoli's *La Dialettica e la Retorica dell' Umanesimo* (1968); Heinrich F. Plett's *Rhetorik der Affekte* (1975); Kees Meerhoff's *Rhetorique et Poetique au XVIe siecle en France* (1986); Plett's *Renaissance-Rhetorik = Renaissance Rhetoric* (1993), a collection of essays in English, French, and German; and Thomas O. Sloane and Peter L. Oesterreich's *Rhetorica Movet* (1999), a collection of essays in English and German. The standard bibliographies of primary works are Murphy's *Renaissance Rhetoric: A Short-Title Catalogue* (1984) and Plett's *English Renaissance Rhetoric and Poetics* (1995). Lawrence D. Green's "Rhetoric [1500–1700]," a forthcoming volume in the revised *Cambridge Bibliography of English Literature* (1999–), should also be consulted. Bibliographies of secondary literature include Murphy's *Doctoral Dissertations on Rhetoric and Rhetorical Criticism* (1978), Don Paul Abbott's essay in Winifred Horner's *The Present State of Scholarship in Historical and Contemporary Rhetoric* (1983), Peter Sharrat's essays on Ramus scholarship in the journals *Studi Francesi* (1972) and *Rhetorica* (1987), and Plett's bibliography. Charles Standford's bibliography of primary and secondary sources in *Historical Rhetoric* (1980), edited by Winifred Horner, is still useful for its annotations.

On the subject of logic or dialectic in Renaissance Britain and Continental Europe, some of the most important and useful studies in English are Walter J. Ong's *Ramus, Method, and the Decay of Dialogue* (1958); Ivo Thomas's article on Oxford logicians in *Oxford Studies Presented to Daniel Callus* (1964), edited by R. W. Southern; E. J. Ashworth's *Language and Logic in the Post-Medieval Period* (1974); J. A. Trentman's article on logic in seventeenth-century England in the journal *Historiographia Linguistica* (1976); the first chapter in Charles B. Schmitt's *John Case and Aristotelianism in Renaissance England* (1983); Ashworth's introduction to her 1985 edition of Robert Sanderson's *Logicae Artis Compendium;* Ashworth's "Traditional Logic" and Lisa Jardine's "Humanistic Logic," both in *The Cambridge History of Renaissance Philosophy* (1988), edited by Schmitt and others; Peter Mack's *Renaissance Argument* (1993); and Gabriel Nuchelmans's essay on seventeenth-century logic in *The Cambridge History of Seventeenth-Century Philosophy* (1998), edited by Daniel Garber and Michael Ayers. Mordechai Feingold's essay on the humanities in *Seventeenth-Century Oxford* (1997), edited by Nicholas Tyacke, includes an informative section on the study of logic at Oxford. The *Routledge Encyclopedia of Philosophy* (1998) includes clear, succinct entries on many relevant topics, including Renaissance logic by Ashworth, Ramus by Mack, and Bacon by R. L. Milton.

Some of the most important secondary literature in this area is not available in English: Wilhelm Risse's *Die Logik der Neuzeit* (1964), Nelly Bruyère's *Méthode et dialectique dans l'oeuvre de La Ramée* (1984), and Guido Oldrini's *La Disputa del Metodo nel Rinascimento* (1997). Some of the material on Ramism, however, is summarized in Sharrat's bibliographical essays. Bibliographies devoted in whole or part to Renaissance logic include Risse's *Bibliographia Logica*, volume one (1964) and volume two (1973); Ashworth's *The Tradition of Medieval Logic and Speculative Grammar* (1978); and Ong's *Ramus and Talon Inventory* (1958). The first appendix in Schmitt's book on John Case is a list of logic books printed in England before 1620. During the sixteenth and seventeenth centuries, Oxford University Press printed some of the most important textbooks on logic in England, and these are listed in Falconer Madan's three-volume descriptive bibliography *Oxford Books* (1895–1931).

Ashworth, E. J. Introduction to *Logicae Artis Compendium* by Robert Sanderson, edited by Ashworth. Bologna: Editrice CLUEB, 1985, pp. xi–lv.

Ashworth. *Language and Logic in the Post-Medieval Period.* Dordrecht & Boston: Reidel, 1974.

Ashworth. *The Tradition of Medieval Logic and Speculative Grammar from Anselm to the End of the Seventeenth Century: A Bibliography from 1836 Onward.* Toronto: Pontifical Institute of Medieval Studies, 1978.

Atkins, J. W. H. *English Literary Criticism: The Renascence.* London: Methuen, 1947.

Atwill, Janet. *Rhetoric Reclaimed: Aristotle and the Liberal Arts Tradition.* Ithaca: Cornell University Press, 1998.

Aubrey, John. *Aubrey on Education: A Hitherto Unpublished Manuscript by the Author of Brief Lives,* edited by J. E. Stephens. London & Boston: Routledge & Kegan Paul, 1972.

Baldwin, Thomas Whitfield. *William Shakspere's Small Latine & Lesse Greeke,* 2 volumes. Urbana: University of Illinois Press, 1944.

Binns, J. W. *Intellectual Culture in Elizabethan and Jacobean England: The Latin Writings of the Age.* Leeds: Francis Cairns, 1990.

Bochenski, Joseph M. *A History of Formal Logic,* edited and translated by Ivo Thomas. Notre Dame, Ind.: University of Notre Dame Press, 1961.

Bolgar, Robert Ralph. *The Classical Heritage and Its Beneficiaries: From the Carolingian Age to the End of the Renaissance.* London: Cambridge University Press, 1954; New York: Harper & Row, 1964.

Bolgar, ed. *Classical Influences on European Culture, A.D. 1500–1700: Proceedings of an International Conference Held at King's College, Cambridge, April 1974.* Cambridge & New York: Cambridge University Press, 1976.

Brennan, Joseph Xavier. "The *Epitome Troporum ac Schematum* of Joannes Susenbrotus: Text, Translation, and Commentary," dissertation, University of Illinois, 1953.

Broadie, Alexander. *Introduction to Medieval Logic,* second edition. Oxford: Clarendon Press / New York: Oxford University Press, 1993.

Bruyère, Nelly. *Méthode et Dialectique dans L'oeuvre de La Ramée: Renaissance et Age Classique.* Paris: J. Vrin, 1984.

Chandler, Robert M. "Gabriel Harvey's 'Rhetor': A Translation and Critical Edition," dissertation, University of Missouri, 1978.

Clark, Donald Lemen. *John Milton at St. Paul's School: A Study of Ancient Rhetoric in English Renaissance Education.* New York: Columbia University Press, 1948.

Clark, *Rhetoric and Poetry in the Renaissance: A Study of Rhetorical Terms in English Renaissance Literary Criticism.* New York: Columbia University Press, 1922.

Clark, Martin Lowther. *Classical Education in Britain, 1500–1900.* Cambridge: Cambridge University Press, 1959.

Conley, Thomas M. *Rhetoric in the European Tradition.* New York: Longman, 1990.

Copenhaver, Brian P., and Charles B. Schmitt. *Renaissance Philosophy,* volume 3 of *A History of Western Philosophy.* Oxford: Oxford University Press, 1992.

Corbett, Edward P. J., and Robert J. Connors, *Classical Rhetoric for the Modern Student,* fourth edition. New York & Oxford: Oxford University Press, 1999.

Craig, Edward, ed. *Routledge Encyclopedia of Philosophy,* 10 volumes. London & New York: Routledge, 1998.

Crane, William Garrett. *Wit and Rhetoric in the Renaissance: The Formal Basis of Elizabethan Prose Style.* New York: Columbia University Press, 1937.

Costello, William T. *The Scholastic Curriculum at Early Seventeenth-Century Cambridge.* Cambridge, Mass.: Harvard University Press, 1958.

Curtis, Mark H. *Oxford and Cambridge in Transition, 1558–1642: An Essay on Changing Relations Between the English Universities and English Society.* Oxford: Clarendon Press, 1959.

Doherty, Stanley Joseph Jr. "George Puttenham's *The Arte of English Poesie:* A New Critical Edition," dissertation, Harvard University, 1983.

Dumitriu, Anton. *History of Logic,* revised and enlarged edition, 4 volumes, translated by Duiliu Zamfirescu, Dina Giurcaneanu, and Doina Doneaud. Tunbridge Wells, Kent: Abacus Press, 1977.

Enos, Theresa, ed. *Encyclopedia of Rhetoric: Communication from Ancient Times to the Information Age.* New York & London: Garland, 1996.

Feingold, Mordechai. *The Mathematicians' Apprenticeship: Science, Universities and Society in England, 1560–1640.* Cambridge: Cambridge University Press, 1984.

Forbes, Clarence A., trans. *Gabriel Harvey's Ciceronianus,* edited by Harold S. Wilson. Lincoln: University of Nebraska, 1945.

Freedman, Joseph S. "The Career and Writings of Bartholomew Keckermann (d. 1609)," *Proceedings of the American Philosophical Society,* 141, no. 3 (1997): 305–364.

Freedman, *European Academic Philosophy in the Late Sixteenth and Early Seventeenth Centuries: The Life, Significance, and Philosophy of Clemens Timpler (1563/4–1624),* 2 volumes. Hildesheim, Zürich & New York: Georg Olms, 1988.

Garber, Daniel, and Michael Ayers, eds. *The Cambridge History of Seventeenth-Century Philosophy,* 2 volumes. Cambridge: Cambridge University Press, 1998.

Gilbert, Neal Ward. *Renaissance Concepts of Method.* New York: Columbia University Press, 1960.

Glenn, Cheryl. *Rhetoric Retold: Regendering the Tradition from Antiquity Through the Renaissance.* Carbondale: Southern Illinois University Press, 1997.

Grassi, Ernesto. *Rhetoric as Philosophy: The Humanist Tradition.* University Park & London: Pennsylvania State University Press, 1980.

Gray, Hanna H. "Renaissance Humanism: The Pursuit of Eloquence," *Journal of the History of Ideas,* 24 (1963): 497–514.

Green, Lawrence D. Introduction to *John Rainolds's Oxford Lectures on Aristotle's Rhetoric.* Newark: University of Delaware Press, 1986, pp. 9–90.

Green, "Rhetoric," in *The Cambridge Bibliography of English Literature,* third edition, Volume 2: *1500–1700.* Cambridge: Cambridge University Press, forthcoming.

Gruffydd, R. Geraint, ed. *A Guide to Welsh Literature, c. 1530–1700.* Cardiff: University of Wales Press, 1997.

Guerlac, Rita. Introduction to *Juan Luis Vives Against the Pseudodialecticians: A Humanist Attack on Medieval Logic.* Dordrecht & Boston: Reidel, 1979, pp. 1–43.

Hildebrandt, Herbert W. "A Critical Edition of Richard Sherry's *A Treatise of Schemes and Tropes,*" dissertation, University of Wisconsin, 1958.

Hornbeak, Katherine Gee. *The Complete Letter Writer in English, 1568–1800,* Smith College Studies in Modern Languages, volume 15, no. 3–4 (April–July 1934). Northampton, Mass., 1934.

Horner, Winifred P., ed. *Historical Rhetoric: An Annotated Bibliography of Sources in English.* Boston: G. K. Hall, 1980.

Horner, ed., *The Present State of Scholarship in Historical and Contemporary Rhetoric.* Columbia & London: University of Missouri Press, 1983.

Howard, Leon. *Essays on Puritans and Puritanism,* edited by James Barbour and Thomas Quirk. Albuquerque: University of New Mexico Press, 1986.

Howell, Wilbur Samuel. *Eighteenth-Century British Logic and Rhetoric.* Princeton: Princeton University Press, 1971.

Howell, *Logic and Rhetoric in England, 1500–1700.* Princeton: Princeton University Press, 1956.

Howell, *Poetics, Rhetoric, and Logic: Studies in the Basic Disciplines of Criticism.* Ithaca: Cornell University Press, 1975.

Jardine, Lisa. *Erasmus, Man of Letters: The Construction of Charisma in Print.* Princeton: Princeton University Press, 1993.

Jardine and Anthony Grafton, *From Humanism to the Humanities: Education and the Liberal Arts in Fifteenth- and Sixteenth-Century Europe.* Cambridge, Mass.: Harvard University Press / London: Duckworth, 1986.

Jones, R. Brinley. *The Old British Tongue: The Vernacular in Wales, 1540–1640.* Cardiff: Avalon Books, 1970.

Jones, Richard Foster, and others, *The Seventeenth Century: Studies in the History of English Thought and Literature from Bacon to Pope.* Stanford, Cal.: Stanford University Press, 1951; London: Oxford University Press, 1951.

Jones, *The Triumph of the English Language: A Survey of Opinions Concerning the Vernacular from the Introduction of Printing to the Restoration.* Stanford: Stanford University Press, 1953.

Kahn, Victoria. *Rhetoric, Prudence, and Skepticism in the Renaissance.* Ithaca, N.Y. & London: Cornell University Press, 1985.

Kearney, Hugh F. *Scholars and Gentlemen: Universities and Society in Pre-Industrial Britain, 1500-1700.* London: Faber & Faber, 1970.

Kennedy, William. *Rhetorical Norms in Renaissance Literature.* New Haven: Yale University Press, 1978.

Kimball, Bruce A. *Orators and Philosophers: A History of the Idea of Liberal Education,* expanded edition. New York: College Entrance Examination Board, 1996.

Kneale, William, and Martha Kneale. *The Development of Logic.* Oxford: Clarendon Press, 1962.

Kretzmann, Norman, and others. *The Cambridge History of Later Medieval Philosophy from the Rediscovery of Aristotle to the Disintegration of Scholasticism, 1100–1600.* Cambridge: Cambridge University Press, 1982.

Kristeller, Paul O. *The Classics and Renaissance Thought.* Cambridge, Mass.: Published for Oberlin College by Harvard University Press, 1955; revised and enlarged as *Renaissance Thought: The Classic, Scholastic, and Humanistic Strains.* New York & London: Harper & Row, 1961.

Kristeller, *Medieval Aspects of Renaissance Learning.* Durham, N.C.: Duke University Press, 1974.

Kristeller, *Renaissance Concepts of Man and Other Essays.* New York & London: Harper & Row, 1972.

Kristeller, *Renaissance Philosophy and the Medieval Tradition.* Latrobe, Pa.: Archabbey Press, 1966.

La Fontaine, Mary Joan. "A Critical Translation of Philip Melanchthon's *Elementorum Rhetorices Libri Duo*," dissertation, University of Michigan, 1968.

Lanham, Richard A. *A Handlist of Rhetoric Terms: A Guide for Students of English Literature.* Berkeley: University of California Press, 1968.

Lechner, Joan Marie. *Renaissance Concepts of the Commonplaces: An Historical Investigation of the General and Universal Ideas Used in All Argumentation and Persuasion Wit with Special Emphasis on the Educational and Literary Tradition of the Sixteenth and Seventeenth Centuries.* New York: Pageant Press, 1962.

Levin, Carole, and Patricia A. Sullivan, eds. *Political Rhetoric, Power, and Renaissance Women.* Albany: State University of New York Press, 1995.

Lunsford, Andrea A., ed. *Reclaiming Rhetorica: Women in the Rhetorical Tradition.* Pittsburgh & London: University of Pittsburgh Press, 1995.

McConica, James K. *English Humanists and Reformation Politics under Henry VIII and Edward VI.* Oxford: Clarendon Press/ London: Oxford University Press, 1965.

McConica, ed. *The History of the University of Oxford. Volume III: The Collegiate University.* Oxford: Clarendon Press, 1986.

Mack, Peter. "Humanist Rhetoric and Dialectic," in *The Cambridge Companion to Renaissance Humanism,* edited by Jill Kraye. New York: Cambridge University Press, 1996, pp. 82–99.

Mack. *Renaissance Argument: Valla and Agricola in the Traditions of Rhetoric and Dialectic.* Leiden: E. J. Brill, 1993.

Mack, ed. *Renaissance Rhetoric.* New York: St. Martin's Press, 1994.

Madan, Falconer. *Oxford Books: A Bibliography of Printed Works Relating to the University and City of Oxford, or Printed or Published There,* 3 volumes. Oxford: Clarendon Press, 1895–1931.

Matlon, Ronald J., comp. *Index to Journals in Communication Studies through 1990.* Annandale, Va.: Speech Communication Association, 1992.

Meerhoff, Kees. *Rhetorique et Poetique au XVIe Siecle en France: Du Bellay, Ramus et Les Autres.* Leiden: E. J. Brill, 1986.

Meerhoff and Jean-Claude Moisan, eds., *Autour de Ramus: Texte, Theorie, Commentaire.* Quebec: Nuit Blanche, 1997.

Miller, Perry. *The New England Mind: The Seventeenth Century.* Boston & New York: Macmillan, 1939.

Miriam Joseph, Sister. *Shakespeare's Use of the Arts of Language.* New York: Columbia University Press, 1947; republished, in part, as *Rhetoric in Shakespeare's Time: Literary Theory of Renaissance Europe.* New York: Harcourt, Brace & World, 1962.

Mitchell, William Fraser. *English Pulpit Oratory from Andrewes to Tillotson: A Study of Its Literary Aspects.* New York, London & Toronto: Published by Macmillan for the Society for Promoting Christian Knowledge, 1932.

Monfasani, John Edward. *George of Trebizond: A Biography and a Study of His Rhetoric and Logic.* Leiden: E. J. Brill, 1976.

More, Thomas. *Letter to Martin Dorp: Text and Translation,* edited and translated by Daniel Kinney, in *The Complete Works of St. Thomas More,* volume 15. New Haven: Yale University Press, 1986, pp. 1–127.

Murphy, James Jerome. *Renaissance Eloquence: Studies in the Theory and Practice of Renaissance Rhetoric.* Berkeley: University of California Press, 1983.

Murphy. *Rhetoric in the Middle Ages: A History of Rhetorical Theory from Saint Augustine to the Renaissance.* Berkeley: University of California Press, 1974.

Murphy, comp. *Renaissance Rhetoric: A Microfiche Collection of Key Texts, A.D. 1472–1602 from the Bodleian Library, Oxford.* Oxford & Elmsford, N.Y.: Microforms International, 1983.

Murphy, comp. *Renaissance Rhetoric: A Short-Title Catalogue of Works on Rhetorical Theory from the Beginning of Printing to A. D. 1700, with Special Attention to the Holdings of the Bodleian Library, Oxford, With a Select Basic Bibliography of Secondary Works on Renaissance Rhetoric.* New York: Garland, 1981.

Murphy, comp. *Rhetoric and Rhetorical Criticism.* Ann Arbor, Mich.: University Microfilms International, 1977; republished as *Doctoral Dissertations on Rhetoric and Rhetorical Criticism.* Ann Arbor, Mich.: University Microfilms International, 1979.

Murphy, ed. *Arguments in Rhetoric Against Quintilian: Translation and Text of Peter Ramus's Rhetoricae Distinctiones in Quintilianum (1549),* translated by Carole Newlands. Dekalb: Northern Illinois University Press, 1986.

Murphy, ed. *Peter Ramus's Attack on Cicero: Text and Translation of Ramus's Brutinae Quaestiones,* translated by Newlands. Davis, Cal.: Hermagoras Press, 1992.

Nadeau, Raymond E. "The *Index Rhetoricus* of Thomas Farnaby," dissertation, University of Michigan, 1950.

Nelson, Norman E. "Peter Ramus and the Confusion of Logic, Rhetoric and Poetry," *University of Michigan Contributions in Modern Philology,* no. 2 (April 1947): 1–22.

Nuchelmans, Gabriel. *Late-Scholastic and Humanist Theories of the Proposition.* Amsterdam & New York: North Holland Publishing, 1980.

Oldrini, Guido. *La Disputa del Metodo nel Rinascimento: Indagini su Ramo e sul Ramismo.* Florence: Le Lettere, 1997.

Oldrini. "Le Particolarità del Ramismo Inglese," *Rinascimento,* 36 (1985): 19–80.

O'Malley, J. W. *Praise and Blame in Renaissance Rome: Rhetoric, Doctrine, and Reform in the Sacred Orators of the Papal Court, c. 1450–1521.* Durham: University of North Carolina, 1979.

Ong, Walter J. *A Ramus and Talon Inventory: A Short-Title Inventory of the Published Works of Peter Ramus (1515–1572) and of Omer Talon (ca. 1510–1562) in Their Original and in Their Variously Altered Forms with Related Material.* Cambridge, Mass.: Harvard University Press, 1958.

Ong. *Ramus, Method and the Decay of Dialogue.* Cambridge, Mass.: Harvard University Press, 1958.

Ong. *Rhetoric, Romance, and Technology: Studies in the Interaction of Expression and Culture.* Ithaca: Cornell University Press, 1971.

Padley, G. Arthur. *Grammatical Theory in Western Europe, 1500–1700: The Latin Tradition.* Cambridge & New York: Cambridge University Press, 1976.

Padley. *Grammatical Theory in Western Europe, 1500–1700: Trends in Vernacular Grammar,* 2 volumes. Cambridge & New York: Cambridge University Press, 1988.

Patterson, Annabel. *Hermogenes and the Renaissance: Seven Ideas of Style.* Princeton: Princeton University Press, 1970.

Plett, Heinrich F. *English Renaissance Rhetoric and Poetics: A Systematic Bibliography of Primary and Secondary Sources.* Leiden, New York & Cologne: E. J. Brill, 1995.

Plett. *Rhetorik der Affekte: Englische Wirkungsästhetik im Zeitalter der Renaissance.* Tubingen, Germany: M. Niemeyer, 1975.

Plett, ed. *Renaissance-Poetik = Renaissance Poetics.* Berlin & New York: De Gruyter, 1994.

Plett, ed. *Renaissance-Rhetorik = Renaissance Rhetoric.* Berlin & New York: De Gruyter, 1993.

Rabil, Albert Jr., ed. *Renaissance Humanism: Foundations, Forms, and Legacy,* 3 volumes. Philadelphia: University of Pennsylvania Press, 1988.

Rebhorn, Wayne A. *The Emperor of Men's Minds: Literature and the Renaissance Discourse of Rhetoric.* Ithaca & London: Cornell University Press, 1995.

Rebhorn, ed. and trans., *Renaissance Debates on Rhetoric.* Ithaca & London: Cornell University Press, 2000.

Rice, Eugene F. *The Renaissance Idea of Wisdom.* Cambridge, Mass.: Harvard University Press, 1958.

Risse, Wilhelm. *Bibliographia Logica: Verzeichnis der Druckschriften zur Logik mit Angabe ihrer Fundorte. Band I: 1472–1800.* Hildesheim: Georg Olms, 1965.

Risse. *Bibliographia Logica: Verzeichnis der Druckschriften zur Logik mit Angabe ihrer Fundorte. Band II: 1801–1969.* Hildesheim & New York: Georg Olms, 1973.

Risse. *Die Logik der Neuzeit.* Stuttgart-Bad Cannstatt: F. Frommann, 1964.

Robertson, Jean. *The Art of Letter Writing: An Essay on the Handbooks Published in England during the Sixteenth and Seventeenth Centuries.* Liverpool: University Press, 1942.

Rossi, Paolo. *Clavis Universalis: Arti Mnemoniche e Logica Combinatoria da Lullo a Leibniz.* Milan: R. Ricciardi, 1960.

Rummel, Erika. *The Humanist-Scholastic Debate in the Renaissance & Reformation.* Cambridge, Mass. & London: Harvard University Press, 1995.

Sandford, William Phillips. *English Theories of Public Address, 1530–1828.* Columbus, Ohio: H. L. Hedrick, 1931.

Schmitt, Charles B. *Aristotle and the Renaissance.* Cambridge, Mass. & London: Published for Oberlin College by Harvard University Press, 1983.

Schmitt. *John Case and Aristotelianism in Renaissance England.* Kingston, Canada: McGill-Queen's University Press, 1983.

Schmitt and others, eds. *The Cambridge History of Renaissance Philosophy.* Cambridge: Cambridge University Press, 1988.

Seigel, Jerrold E. *Rhetoric and Philosophy in Renaissance Humanism: The Union of Eloquence and Wisdom, Petrarch to Valla.* Princeton: Princeton University Press, 1968.

Sharrat, Peter. "The Present State of Studies on Ramus," *Studi Francesi,* 47–48 (May–December 1972): 201–213.

Sharratt. "Recent Works on Peter Ramus (1970–1986)," *Rhetorica,* 5, no. 1 (1987): 7–58.

Shuger, Deborah. *Sacred Rhetoric: The Christian Grand Style in the English Renaissance.* Princeton: Princeton University Press, 1988.

Sloane, Thomas O. *On the Contrary: The Protocol of Traditional Rhetoric.* Washington, D.C.: Catholic University of America Press, 1997.

Sloane. *Donne, Milton, and the End of Humanist Rhetoric.* Berkeley & London: University of California Press, 1985.

Sloane and Peter L. Oesterreich, eds. *Rhetorica Movet: Studies in Historical and Modern Rhetoric in Honour of Heinrich F. Plett.* Leiden: E. J. Brill, 1999.

Sonnino, Lee A. *A Handbook to Sixteenth-Century Rhetoric.* London: Routledge & Kegan Paul, 1968.

Spitz, Lewis W., and Barbara Sher Tinsley, trans. *Johann Sturm on Education.* St. Louis, Mo.: Concordia, 1995.

Streuver, Nancy S. *The Language of History in the Renaissance: Rhetoric and Historical Consciousness in Florentine Humanism.* Princeton: Princeton University Press, 1970.

Sutherland, Christine Mason, and Rebecca Sutcliffe, eds., *The Changing Tradition: Women in the History of Rhetoric.* Calgary: University of Calgary Press, 1999.

Taylor, Warren. *Tudor Figures of Rhetoric.* Chicago: University of Chicago Libraries, 1937.

Thomas, Ivo. "Medieval Aftermath: Oxford Logic and Logicians of the Seventeenth Century," in *Oxford Studies Presented to Daniel Callus,* edited by R. W. Southern. Oxford: Clarendon Press, 1964, pp. 297–311.

Trentman, John A. "The Study of Logic and Language in England in the Early 17th Century," *Historiographia Linguistica,* 3 (1976): 179–201.

Tuve, Rosemond. *Elizabethan and Metaphysical Imagery: Renaissance Poetic and Twentieth-Century Critics.* Chicago: University of Chicago Press, 1947.

Tyacke, Nicholas ed. *The History of the University of Oxford. Volume IV: Seventeenth-Century Oxford.* Oxford: Clarendon Press, 1997.

Vasoli, Cesare. *La Dialettica e la Retorica dell' Umanesimo.* Milan: Feltrinelli, 1968.

Vickers, Brian. *Classical Rhetoric in English Poetry,* revised edition. Carbondale: Southern Illinois University Press, 1989.

Vickers. *In Defense of Rhetoric.* Oxford: Clarendon Press / New York: Oxford University Press, 1988.

Vickers, ed. *Rhetoric Revalued: Papers from the International Society for the History of Rhetoric.* Binghamton, N.Y.: Center for Medieval & Early Renaissance Studies, 1982.

Vickers and Nancy Struever, *Rhetoric and the Pursuit of Truth: Language Change in the Seventeenth and Eighteenth Centuries: Papers Read at a Clark Library Seminar, 8 March 1980.* Los Angeles: William Andrews Clark Memorial Library, University of California, 1985.

Walsh, Thomas Mart. "A Sixteenth Century Translation of Ramus and of Talaeus: Dudley Fenner's 'The Artes of Logike and Rethorike': An Edition and Study," dissertation, Saint Louis University, 1978.

Watson, Foster. *The Curriculum and Text-Books of English Schools in the First Half of the Seventeenth Century.* London: Blades, 1902.

Watson. *The English Grammar Schools to 1660: Their Curriculum and Practice.* Cambridge: Cambridge University Press, 1908.

Webster, John. Introduction to *William Temple's Analysis of Sir Philip Sidney's Apology for Poetry: An Edition and Translation.* Binghamton, N.Y.: Center for Medieval & Early Renaissance Studies, 1984, pp. 11–56.

Weinberg, Bernard. *A History of Literary Criticism in the Italian Renaissance,* 2 volumes. Chicago: University of Chicago Press, 1961.

Wertheimer, Molly Meijer, ed. *Listening to Their Voices: The Rhetorical Activities of Historical Women.* Columbia: University of South Carolina Press, 1997.

Williamson, George. *The Senecan Amble: A Study in Prose Form from Bacon to Collier.* Chicago: University of Chicago Press, 1951; London: Faber & Faber, 1951.

Wilson, Fred. *The Logic and Methodology of Science in Early Modern Thought: Seven Studies.* Toronto & London: University of Toronto Press, 1999.

Yates, Frances Amelia. *The Art of Memory.* London: Routledge & Kegan Paul, 1966; Chicago: University of Chicago Press, 1966.

Contributors

Cumulative Index

Dictionary of Literary Biography, Volumes 1-236
Dictionary of Literary Biography Yearbook, 1980-1999
Dictionary of Literary Biography Documentary Series, Volumes 1-19

Cumulative Index

DLB before number: *Dictionary of Literary Biography,* Volumes 1-236
Y before number: *Dictionary of Literary Biography Yearbook,* 1980-1999
DS before number: *Dictionary of Literary Biography Documentary Series,* Volumes 1-19

B

G

Cumulative Index

N

Cumulative Index